Building Secure Firmware

Armoring the Foundation
of the Platform

Jiewen Yao
Vincent Zimmer

Apress®

Building Secure Firmware: Armoring the Foundation of the Platform

Jiewen Yao
Shanghai, China

Vincent Zimmer
Issaquah, WA, USA

ISBN-13 (pbk): 978-1-4842-6105-7
https://doi.org/10.1007/978-1-4842-6106-4

ISBN-13 (electronic): 978-1-4842-6106-4

Managing Director, Apress Media LLC: Welmoed Spahr
Acquisitions Editor: Susan McDermott
Development Editor: Laura Berendson
Coordinating Editor: Jessica Vakili

Distributed to the book trade worldwide by Springer Science+Business Media New York, 233 Spring Street, 6th Floor, New York, NY 10013. Phone 1-800-SPRINGER, fax (201) 348-4505, e-mail orders-ny@springer-sbm.com, or visit www.springeronline.com. Apress Media, LLC is a California LLC and the sole member (owner) is Springer Science + Business Media Finance Inc (SSBM Finance Inc). SSBM Finance Inc is a **Delaware** corporation.

For information on translations, please e-mail booktranslations@springernature.com; for reprint, paperback, or audio rights, please e-mail bookpermissions@springernature.com.

Apress titles may be purchased in bulk for academic, corporate, or promotional use. eBook versions and licenses are also available for most titles. For more information, reference our Print and eBook Bulk Sales web page at http://www.apress.com/bulk-sales.

Any source code or other supplementary material referenced by the author in this book is available to readers on GitHub via the book's product page, located at www.apress.com/978-1-4842-6105-7. For more detailed information, please visit http://www.apress.com/source-code.

Printed on acid-free paper

To my lovely wife, Wenjun Zeng. Thank you for your constant encouragement and unconditional support!
—Jiewen Yao

To my parents; to my wife, Jan; and to my daughters, Ally and Zoe. Your support and love are rays of sunshine that warm my days.
—Vincent Zimmer

Table of Contents

About the Authors...xix

About the Technical Reviewer xxi

Organization and What Is Covered xxiii

Acknowledgments xxv

Preface xxvii

Foreword xxix

Part I: Overview 1

Chapter 1: Introduction to Firmware 3

    Similarity Between Firmware and Software 3

    Distinction Between Firmware and Software 5

    Introduction to Firmware Security 6

        Firmware Resiliency 7

        Firmware Measurement and Attestation 8

        Secure Device Communication.. 8

    Introduction to Variants of Host Firmware 9

    Industry Standards.. 10

    Boot Flow and Phased Handoff... 11

    Introduction to Non-host Firmware... 13

    Introduction to Device Firmware... 14

    Summary.. 14

    References.. 15

Chapter 2: Proactive Firmware Security Development 17

Requirement Phase 17

    Security Requirements 17

Threat Model and Architecture Phase 18

    Threat Model Analysis 18

    Security Architecture and Design 31

    Real Example 36

Development Phase 49

    Secure Coding Practice 49

    Security Unit Test 49

    Security Code Review 49

Test Phase 55

    Fuzzing 55

    Static Code Analysis 56

    Dynamic Code Analysis 56

    Vulnerability Scan 57

Release and Maintenance Phase 57

    Security Incidence Response 57

People Education 58

    Before the Project Starts 58

    After the Project Release 58

Fallacy and Pitfall 58

    Security Technology 58

    Security Process 59

Summary 60

References 61

Part II: Security Architecture 65

Chapter 3: Firmware Resiliency: Protection 67

Resiliency Building Block 67

Immutable ROM 69

Integrity 69

Confidentiality 69

Case Study 70

Attack and Mitigation 72

Updatable Firmware 73

Authenticated Update Mechanism 73

Case Study 74

Integrity Protection 93

Case Study 94

Non-bypassability 94

Attack and Mitigation 94

Configurable Data 108

Case Study 108

Attack and Mitigation 110

Summary 111

References 111

Chapter 4: Firmware Resiliency: Detection 115

Secure Boot 115

Detectability 115

Version 117

Policy Revocation 117

Non-bypassability 117

Additional Capability 118

Case Study 118

Attack and Mitigation 149

Secure Configuration 155

Detectability 156

Attack and Mitigation 157

Summary 158

References 158

Chapter 5: Firmware Resiliency: Recovery..**163**

  Image Recovery 163

    RTRec Selection and Recovery Policy 163

    Recovery Image Selection 165

    Recovery Image Location 165

    Case Study 166

    Attack and Mitigation 177

  Configuration Recovery... 178

    Recovery Configuration Selection 178

    Attack and Mitigation 180

  Watchdog 181

  Summary... 182

  References... 182

Chapter 6: OS Resiliency **185**

  Protection... 186

    Automated Update.. 186

  Detection.. 186

    Image Signing.. 186

    Case Study 186

  Recovery 193

    Automated Recovery 193

    Case Study 193

  Summary... 195

  References... 195

Chapter 7: Trusted Boot **197**

  Static Root-of-Trust for Measurement (SRTM)..................................... 198

    Trusted Platform Module (TPM) 198

    TPM Device Type... 201

    Measurement Report.. 202

    Attestation 203

S3 Resume 206

Device Identifier Composition Engine (DICE) 207

Case Study 210

Attack and Mitigation 224

Dynamic Root-of-Trust for Measurement (DRTM) 226

CPU-Based Dynamic Root-of-Trust 227

S3 Resume 229

DEC's Execution Environment 230

Hot Plug 231

Case Study 232

Attack and Mitigation 237

TCG Memory Overwrite 242

Secure MOR 244

MOR for Storage 244

Attack and Mitigation 245

TCG Physical Presence Configuration 246

TCG Storage 246

Summary 246

References 246

Chapter 8: Device Security **257**

Device Firmware Resiliency 257

Secure Device Communication 258

Authentication and Measurement 258

Secure Communication Channel 259

Device Identifier Composition Engine (DICE) 260

Case Study 260

Attack and Mitigation 267

Device Attack Prevention 268

Device Identifier Data 268

Attack and Mitigation 269

Direct Memory Access (DMA) 270

Case Study 275

Attack and Mitigation 283

Message Signaled Interrupt (MSI) 286

Case Study 291

Attack and Mitigation 297

Server RAS (Reliability, Availability, and Serviceability) 300

Case Study 301

Attack and Mitigation 305

Summary 307

References 307

Chapter 9: S3 Resume 313

Threat Model 315

LockBox 317

Case Study 319

Attack and Mitigation 332

Summary 333

References 333

Chapter 10: Access Control 335

Boot Access Control 337

What a User Knows: Password 337

What a User Has: Token 342

What a User Is: Biometrics 342

Other Considerations 342

Case Study 343

Attack and Mitigation 345

TEE Access Control 347

Feature Configuration Control 347

User Physical Presence 347

UEFI Variable 347

Case Study 348

Attack and Mitigation 349

Device Configuration Control 349

    Physical Presence 350

    Secure Console 350

    Case Study 351

    Attack and Mitigation 355

Storage Access Control 356

    Hard Drive Password 356

    Fast Boot Impact 357

    Unlock in a Warm Reset 357

    Auto Unlock in S3 357

    Runtime D3 impact 358

    Password Update 359

    User Password vs. Master Password 359

    Retry Count 359

    Hard Drive Freeze 359

    Secure Console 359

    Case Study 360

    Attack & Mitigation 371

Network Access Control 372

    Case Study 372

    Attack & Mitigation 374

Device Access Control 375

    Case Study 375

    Attack & Mitigation 377

Summary 378

References 378

Chapter 11: Configuration 383

UEFI Variables 383

    Integrity Protection 384

    Availability Protection 406

    Confidentiality Protection 416

Attack and Mitigation 421

UEFI PI Firmware Volume 427

UEFI PI PCD (Platform Configuration Data)... 427

Summary.. 429

References... 430

Chapter 12: Security Model 433

Confidentiality 433

Bell-LaPadula 434

Integrity.. 436

Biba Model 436

Clark-Wilson Model 438

Others 440

Application 441

Trusted Computing Group Security Model 441

Firmware Resiliency (Protection, Detection, Recovery) 443

Summary.. 456

References... 456

Chapter 13: Virtual Firmware 459

New Threats in the Guest Domain... 460

Case Study.. 461

Attack and Mitigation 473

Device Interface 476

Case Study.. 477

Attack and Mitigation 481

Special Feature 482

Case Study.. 483

Summary.. 487

References... 487

Part III: Security Development 493

Chapter 14: Firmware Secure Coding Practice 495

Basic Security Practice 495

Secure Coding Practice 495

Secure Design Practice 517

Boot Firmware Secure Design Practice 522

Advanced Secure Coding Topic 525

Side Channel Attack 525

Fault Injection 545

High-Risk Area in Firmware 551

External Input 552

Race Condition 553

Hardware Input 554

Secret Handling 555

Register Lock 556

Secure Configuration 556

Replay/Rollback 557

Cryptography 558

Summary 559

References 559

Chapter 15: Compiler Defensive Technology 571

Break the Exploit 573

Stack Check 573

Code Protection 577

Address Space Layout Randomization 579

Control Flow Guard 580

Hardware-Based Control Flow Guard 589

Speculative Load Hardening 594

Eliminate the Vulnerability 598

Static Analyzer 598

Address Sanitizer 598

Hardware-Based Address Sanitizer 605

Uninitialized Data Check 608

Arithmetic Check 613

Summary 618

References 618

Chapter 16: The Kernel 625

Break the Exploitation 628

Code Protection 628

Address Space Layout Randomization 634

Control Flow Guard 642

Address Sanitizer 644

Contain the Damage 654

User Mode/Supervisor Mode 654

Virtual Machine Monitor 659

Trusted Execution Environment 669

System Partitioning 670

Summary 672

References 672

Chapter 17: Trusted Execution Environment 681

CPU-Based TEE 681

X86 SMM 681

ARM TrustZone 707

Intel SGX 716

AMD SEV 718

Intel TDX 719

IBM Z 719

RISC-V Keystone 719

RISC-V/ARM-M MultiZone 720

Standards, Frameworks, and SDKs 721

Summary 722

Coprocessor-Based TEE 723

    Intel Converged Security and Management Engine (CSME) 724

    Apple Secure Enclave Processor (SEP)..727

    Google Titan 727

    Microsoft Azure Sphere: Pluton 728

Summary...729

References 732

Chapter 18: Silicon Secure Configuration...745

Flash Lock 745

    BIOS Write Protection 745

    BIOS Region Selection 747

    SPI Region Lock..749

    SPI Region Access Control 750

    SMM Lock 751

    SMRAM Address Alias Lock 754

    SMRR 759

    SMM Code Access Check 759

    Global SMI Lock 760

IOMMU 761

    IOMMU Protection for DRAM..762

    IOMMU Protection for SRAM 762

    Silicon Support for DMA Prevention 762

Summary...764

References 765

Chapter 19: Cryptography 767

Modern Cryptography 767

    Cryptography Usage in the Firmware...770

    Algorithm Recommendation 772

    Some Concepts..772

    Challenge in the Firmware 787

    Attack and Mitigation 790

Quantum Safe Cryptography 792

    Security Challenge 792

    Quantum Safe Algorithm 794

    Quantum Cryptography 805

    Algorithm Recommendation 809

    Preparation for the Future 811

Summary 813

References 814

Chapter 20: Programming Language 825

Assembly Language 825

C Language 828

Rust 828

    Rust Security Solution 830

    Unsafe Code 847

    Current Project 850

    Limitation 851

Others 852

Summary 852

References 852

Part IV: Security Test 855

Chapter 21: Security Unit Test 857

Security Unit Testing Plan 857

Advanced Security Unit Testing 860

    Fuzzing 861

    Symbolic Execution 866

    Formal Verification 868

Design for Security Test 870

Summary 872

References 872

Chapter 22: Security Validation and Penetration Test **875**

Security Validation Plan 875

Penetration Test Plan 886

Summary.. 888

References 889

Chapter 23: Maintenance **891**

Mitigation Strategy and Tactics.. 891

Supply Chain for the Firmware Components 894

    Firmware Component Certificate and Manifest.. 894

    Firmware Attestation Data... 896

Vulnerable Firmware Detection... 899

Antivirus for Firmware 900

Firmware Update 900

Summary.. 901

References 902

Index.. **907**

About the Authors

Jiewen Yao is a principal engineer in the Intel Architecture, Graphics, and Software Group. He has been engaged as a firmware developer for over 15 years. He is a member of the UEFI Security Sub-Team (USST) and the Trusted Computing Group (TCG) PC Client sub-working group. He has presented at industry events such as the Intel Developer Forum, UEFI Plugfest, and RSA Conference. He worked with coauthor Vincent Zimmer to publish 30 "A Tour Beyond BIOS" technical papers for tianocore.org and firmware.intel. com. He holds 40 US patents.

Vincent Zimmer is a senior principal engineer in the Intel Architecture, Graphics, and Software Group. He has been engaged as a firmware developer for over 25 years and leads the UEFI Security Sub-Team. He has presented at industry events such as the Open Source Firmware Conference, LinuxFest Northwest, Intel Developer Forum, UEFI Plugfest, Open Compute Project Summit, Black Hat Las Vegas, BSides Seattle, ToorCon, and CanSecWest. In addition to collaborating with Jiewen Yao on many whitepapers, he has coauthored several books on firmware, papers, and over 400 issued US patents.

About the Technical Reviewer

Tim Lewis is the CTO and head of the Office of Security and Trust for Insyde Software. With over 30 years of BIOS experience, he has served on the UEFI board of directors and chaired the UEFI Security Sub-Team (USST). He is an active member of his local CS2AI chapter near his home in Folsom, California.

Organization and What Is Covered

Currently, we already have books to separately introduce the topics of firmware and security. The purpose of this book is to link these areas together and provide the best practices in the security development of firmware.

The whole book consists of four parts:

Part I: Overview

Chapter 1 includes a brief overview of the firmware in a system.

Chapter 2 describes a proactive development lifecycle for the firmware. We will introduce a general threat model for the firmware and use a real example to demonstrate how to do threat model analysis.

Part II: Security Architecture

Chapter 3 describes the first aspect of the firmware resiliency – protection.

Chapter 4 describes the second aspect of the firmware resiliency – detection.

Chapter 5 describes the third aspect of the firmware resiliency – recovery.

Chapter 6 extends the resiliency concept from the firmware to the operating system (OS).

Chapter 7 introduces the trusted boot concept, besides the firmware resiliency in Chapters 3, 4, and 5.

Chapter 8 focuses on the security aspects of the device firmware, including secure device communication and device attack prevention.

Chapter 9 discusses S3 resume – a special boot path in the system firmware.

Chapter 10 presents the access control technology in the firmware, including boot access control, device access control, feature configuration control, and so on.

Chapter 11 examines the confidentiality, integrity, and availability of the firmware configuration data.

Chapter 12 provides a brief introduction for the security model and maps the Clark-Wilson model to existing firmware features.

Chapter 13 explains the virtual firmware, which may include a new threat model.

Part III: Security Development

Chapter 14 introduces the general secure coding practices for firmware.

Chapter 15 discusses the compiler defensive technologies which may be used in the firmware.

Chapter 16 describes the possible firmware kernel hardening technologies.

Chapter 17 compares different trusted execution environments (TEEs), including system management mode (SMM) and ARM TrustZone.

Chapter 18 shows the silicon secure configuration, such as flash lock and system configuration lock.

Chapter 19 explains the cryptography usage in the firmware space, including an introduction for post-quantum cryptography.

Chapter 20 introduces the Rust language – a type-safe language choice for firmware development.

Part IV: Security Test

Chapter 21 discusses the security unit test, including fuzzing and symbolic execution.

Chapter 22 describes the security validation and penetration test plan.

Chapter 23 recaps the mitigation strategies – eliminate the vulnerability, break the exploitation, contain the damage, and reduce the attack window – and focuses on how to maintain the firmware in the lifecycle.

Whom Is This Book For?

The target audience of this book includes firmware architects, developers, and validation engineers. We assume the reader has basic knowledge on the following domains:

1) Computer system architecture, such as X86, ARM, PCI bus, and so on

2) Operating systems or embedded systems

3) Programming language – C language

4) Firmware design and development experience, such as EDK II, coreboot, ARM Trusted Firmware, and so on

Acknowledgments

We would like to acknowledge our technical reviewer and Apress editors. We would also like to acknowledge the many engineers and collaborators with whom we have worked in the industry, standards groups, and open source communities.

Preface

In 1988, the Morris worm was released from the lab onto the Internet. It was the first time that a computer virus had gained significant mainstream media attention. People started to realize that a software flaw was vital, which changed the perception of security on the Internet. Ten years later, in 1999, the Chen Ing-hau (CIH) virus brought another big impact because the Basic Input/Output System (BIOS) flash chip was attacked and the impacted system could not boot at all. A technician was required to reprogram the BIOS. This was probably the first wave of firmware security. The firmware developers started to invent the idea of locking the flash region in response to CIH.

The second big wave was around 2009. Invisible Things Lab released a series of BIOS attacks and presented in the Black Hat conference. These attacks included the REMAP base address register (BAR) attack, Bitmap (BMP) file attack, system management mode (SMM) callout, SMM cache poisoning, and Authenticated Code Module (ACM) hijack. The firmware developers realized that locking the flash and system management RAM (SMRAM) was far from enough. Similar to the software development process, the firmware development domain also needs to apply the security development lifecycle (SDL).

The third wave of firmware security commenced in 2014, where more and more firmware attacks appeared in different hacking conferences. This next wave of attacks included exploits against the capsule image, setup variable, SMM communication, memory mapped input/output (MMIO) BAR in SMM, Speed Racer, Direct Memory Access (DMA), S3 boot script, and Unified Extensible Firmware Interface (UEFI) secure boot policy – lots of firmware features became the attack point. It is just like the old saying, "If there is a will, there is a way." The firmware engineers started to invent new technologies and processes to harden the firmware design and development.

The war of defense and attack never ends. Today, firmware security has become more and more important. The National Institute of Standards and Technology (NIST) published the documents SP800-193 – Platform Firmware Resiliency Guidelines and SP800-155 – BIOS Integrity Measurement Guidelines. The Trusted Computing Group (TCG) created the Cyber Resilient (CyRes) workgroup to focus on three principles of resilience (protecting, detecting, and recovering), the Device Identifier Composition Engine (DICE) workgroup to explore the security principles for the Internet of Things (IoT) ecosystem, and the Attestation workgroup to provide a framework for attestation. The Distributed Management Task Force (DMTF) created the Secure Protocol and Data Model (SPDM) for device firmware authentication and measurement, as well as key exchange. The Internet Engineering Task Force (IETF) created the Software Updates for Internet of Things (suit) working group to define a firmware update solution for small IoT devices and Remote Attestation Procedures (rats) working group to standardize the formats and procedures for the assertions about the system components. The cloud companies invented different platform Root-of-Trust (RoT) techniques, such as Microsoft Cerberus, Google Titan, and Amazon Nitro. The device vendor started building the device root-of-trust to report the device certificate. In this fourth wave, every firmware engineer needs to understand the aspects of firmware security – from industry standards, architecture, design, and implementation up to the final stages of test and validation.

Foreword

When Saudi Aramco was attacked in August 2012 by the Shamoon computer virus, it was a wake-up call to the entire industry. Saudi Aramco is one of the largest companies in the world and holds the second largest amount of crude oil reserves. A shutdown of Saudi Aramco for a prolonged amount of time would have had a devastating impact on the oil economy, and this could have plunged the world into an economic recession.

The Shamoon virus was by today's standards a relatively simple virus. It overwrote the master boot record on the hard disk with garbage, rendering the system unbootable. While the infestation was effective – reportedly more than 30,000 systems got impacted – the much-feared secondary effect of the global oil supply chain hiccup didn't materialize. That was in part because the hard disk is an "easy" to service component and Aramco was able to replace the hard disks in time to avoid any serious impact.

However, this attack made folks in the industry and intelligence communities around the world wonder: What would have happened if Shamoon went after a non-serviceable component, like the flash chips where the system firmware is stored? This is much harder to repair on-site, and it would have required the systems to be shipped back to the manufacturer. This would have taken a lot more time, and in that case a global oil supply shortage could not have been avoided, potentially even triggering a global recession.

This incident prompted a cross-industry/cross-government collaboration that eventually resulted in a set of recommendations from the National Institute of Standards and Technology (NIST). The first set of recommendations, BIOS Protect Guidelines (NIST SP800-147), described requirements such as

- BIOS update authentication: The firmware needs to be signed by the proper authority.

- Integrity protection: The firmware cannot be modified, either unintended or maliciously.

- Non-bypassibility: There is no way to bypass the authenticated firmware update mechanism.

This specification was followed up in 2018 by another NIST publication, Platform Firmware Resiliency Guidelines (NIST SP800-193). This specification extended the previous one by focusing on recovery. Its central tenet was simple: providing protection against unauthorized firmware updates is not enough. The firmware is a complex piece of software, and it will, probabilistically, contain bugs that can be exploited by an attacker. How do you quickly and seamlessly recover if this happens?

Before you consider this problem to be a PC-only threat, think again. With the proliferation of IoT devices in homes and factories, and SCADA devices to control the national grid, firmware security has become a key part of the world's critical infrastructure protection. Just imagine the harm a malicious attacker could do by taking over the firmware of pipeline controllers in a gas line in Siberia, Russia, during the winter. You'll be hard-pressed to send someone out there to fix the problem.

The Saudi Aramco attack and its resulting NIST secure firmware recommendations solidified the importance of firmware security in the industry. Those recommendations built on years of academic and industrial research in this area. I was personally involved in some of these efforts, ranging from IBM's physical secure coprocessor (IBM 47xx) projects and TCPA/TCG frameworks to secure hypervisor research and working with other industry partners on the foundations of NIST SP800-147.

The authors Jiewen Yao and Vincent Zimmer have bundled together into this book their combined years of experience in developing secure firmware and building resilient systems. Every computer, big or small, starts with firmware, and if that's compromised, all is lost, so following the authors' guidance is as relevant today as it was in 2012.

—Leendert van Doorn
Redmond, WA, USA

PART I

Overview

Firmware is a special type of software. There is a secure software development lifecycle defined for software. These lifecycle practices can be applied to the firmware world.

CHAPTER 1

Introduction to Firmware

This chapter will provide an overview of system firmware. Although the space of implementations of system firmware is quite broad, details that relate to the secure construction of firmware will be discussed.

Similarity Between Firmware and Software

Firmware vs. Embedded System vs. OS Kernel vs. OS Application

Firmware is the lowest layer of software on the platform. Modern firmware, such as UEFI Platform Initialization–based firmware, like EDK II, U-Boot (Universal Boot Loader), coreboot, Open Power skiboot, and so on, are predominately written in C with a small amount of assembly language code. This code is often stored in a non-volatile storage container bound to the platform. The relationship of firmware to the rest of a platform stack is shown in Figure 1-1.

© Jiewen Yao and Vincent Zimmer 2020
J. Yao and V. Zimmer, *Building Secure Firmware*, https://doi.org/10.1007/978-1-4842-6106-4_1

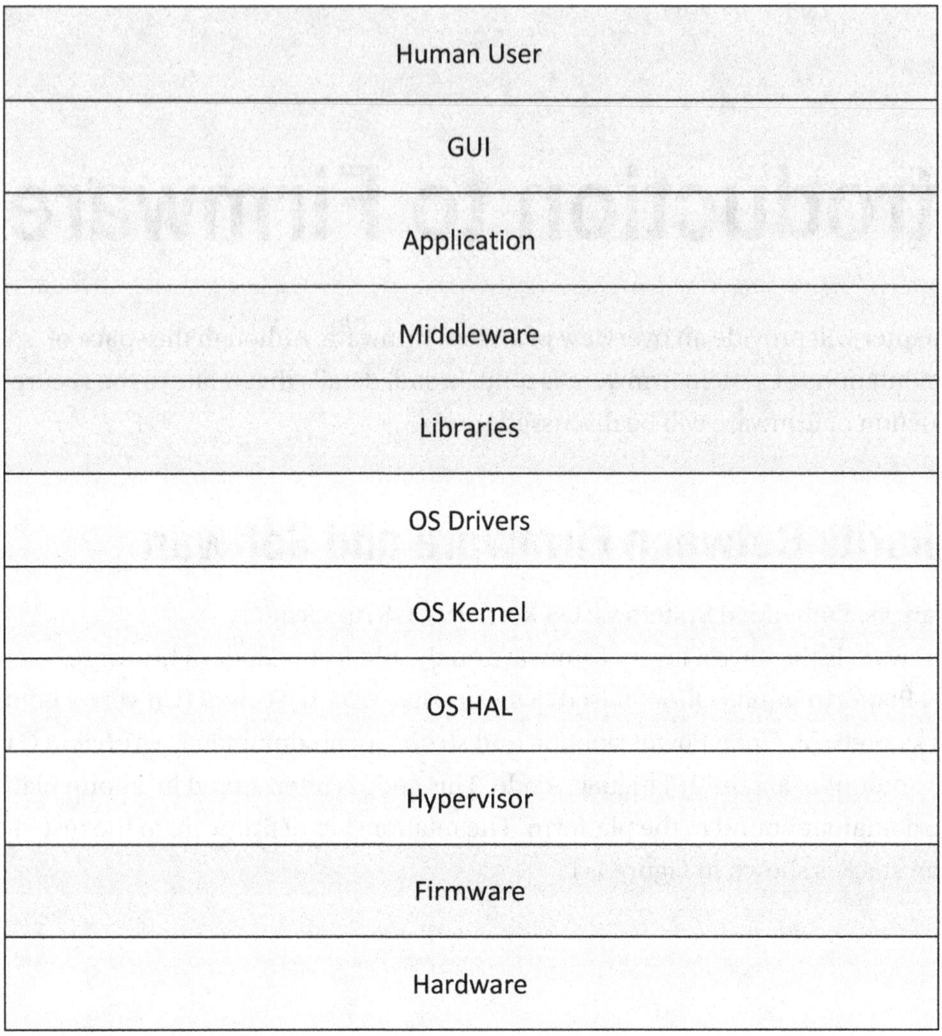

| Human User |
| Hardware |

Human User
GUI
Application
Middleware
Libraries
OS Drivers
OS Kernel
OS HAL
Hypervisor
Firmware
Hardware

Figure 1-1. *Stack from Hardware to User*

Given this C-based provenance, the C code can be susceptible to the class of attacks that afflict higher-level software. These attacks include memory safety issues, involving the variants of buffer overflow, such as stack overflow, heap overflow, and integer overflow. In addition, control flow attacks against C code in the application or OS space can be repurposed against system firmware. Beyond memory issues, other aspects of attack that can occur against the firmware include confidentiality concerns, such as stealing secrets. Beyond that, the firmware often participates in the root-of-trust flow for a system, so integrity considerations are of importance since any unauthorized code flows in the platform can deny the platform promise of that feature. The platform boot can include accessing the network, so considerations of network security can also be applied to the platform firmware. And there are few, if any, platforms that have only a single central processing unit (CPU) core in the system on a chip (SOC), so the firmware must support multiprocessing (MP) and defend against the various classes of attacks, such as race conditions, that inhere in this application domain. Finally, the platform firmware must also defend against other classes of attacks, such as side channels, confused deputy, and time-of-check/time-of-use (TOC/TOU) attacks.

Given these exposure listed, the firmware may have similar platform hardening strategies, albeit with implementations customized for the domain. These include hardening tactics such as stack cookie checks, data execution protection (DEP), address space layout randomization (ASLR), control flow guard/integrity (CFG/CFI), code signing enforcement check, sandbox with interpreter, access control (user authentication and authorization), network security, and cryptography suitable in the firmware execution environment.

Beyond the defenses, the firmware may have similar software security validation strategies, but with different implementations than higher-level software regimes. These validation approaches can include static code analysis, dynamic code analysis (address sanitizer, ASan), fuzzing, symbolic execution, and formal verification when possible.

Distinction Between Firmware and Software

Although firmware is typically written in a higher-level language like C, it often has special requirements. These requirements begin with the environment. Specifically, firmware has a size limitation that is driven by the small ROM size and small RAM size in microcontrollers, only having SRAM or cache that can be used before the DRAM is ready, Management Mode (MM) size leveraging stolen system memory, and limited stack and heap size.

Additional limitations include the execution-in-place (XIP) code of early code. Namely, some code executes in the ROM. One aspect of this is the ROM code, wherein some code has no writable global variable in the data section. And for this early code, such as the UEFI Platform Initialization PI, Slim Bootloader stage 1, and coreboot romstage, there is no memory management, including no virtual memory, although page tables may be used.

Beyond memory management, there are challenges with execution isolation in early code flows. For example, ring separation might or might not be available. As such,

5

some firmware implementations just run all code in supervisor mode. And although the hardware may contain multiple CPU cores, multiprocessing (MP) may or may not be enabling. In fact, most implementations of host firmware execute services on a single processor. Alongside MP, other common capabilities like interrupts may be enabled, but only for usages much simpler than those of operating systems. And unlike the OS, the firmware usually interacts directly with the hardware. Finally, the firmware will have its own executive infrastructure, such as a kernel and loader, distinct from those found in high-level operating systems (HLOSs) like Windows or Linux or hypervisors.

Given these limitations, firmware may have a class of security issues about which we are to be concerned that are not seen in HLOSs. These security concerns can include attack from the hardware, such as registers, device Direct Memory Accesses (DMAs), cache, and so on. Beyond those threat vectors, the host firmware must guard against a permanent denial of service (PDoS) in the ROM which often necessitates complicated and special recovery mechanisms. And if the PDoS concern were not enough, firmware can be susceptible to a permanent root kit in the body of the ROM that is difficult to discover by virus scanning art.

Introduction to Firmware Security

Firmware is the foundation of computer system security. There are more and more hardware/firmware-assisted attacks against the system. In light of the domain-specific aspects of firmware, there may need to be special hardening strategies. We summarized three major directions: firmware resiliency, firmware measurement and attestation, and secure device communication. See Figure 1-2.

Figure 1-2. *Three Pillars of Firmware Security*

Firmware Resiliency

Firmware resiliency includes the triple of protection, detection, and recovery in Figure 1-3. A platform firmware needs to protect itself, detect the tampering, and finally recover to a known good state. Protection ensures that the firmware remains in a state of integrity and is protected from corruption or an attack. Detection happens during system boot to determine if the firmware has been corrupted or attacked. If such corruption or attack is detected, the firmware root-of-trust recovers the firmware to a state of integrity through an authorized mechanism. In addition, there are firmware domain-specific checks including hardware register configuration checks, such as setting of lock bits, to maintain the temporal isolation guarantees of the platform firmware. We will discuss the details in Chapters 3, 4, and 5.

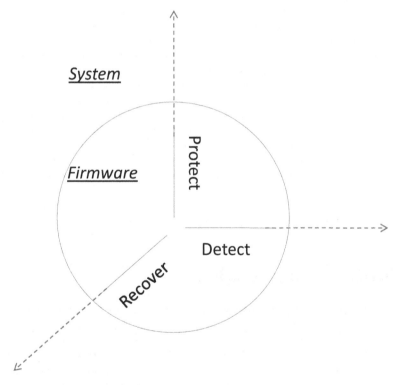

Figure 1-3. *Three Axes of Firmware Resiliency Capabilities*

Firmware Measurement and Attestation

After a platform firmware enables the resiliency to protect itself, the firmware needs
to report its identity and allow a remote agent to verify the integrity state, which is
called attestation. When an Original Equipment Manufacturer (OEM) or Independent
Software Vendor (ISV) deploys a system, they also publish the platform attributes and
golden measurement for the system. When running, the system root-of-trust creates the
measurement log. As such, the remote verifier attests the measurement and verifies it
with the golden measurement to know if the platform is in a trusted state. See Figure 1-4.
We will discuss the details in Chapter 7.

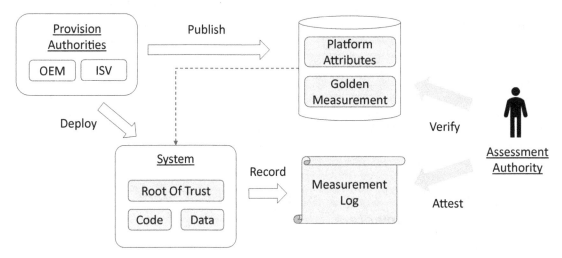

Figure 1-4. *Firmware Measurement and Attestation*

Secure Device Communication

Besides resiliency and attestation, the platform firmware needs to have a secure
way to communicate with other firmware or device components on the board. The
requester endpoint authenticates the responder endpoint, and the responder may
optionally request mutual authentication. Then the two endpoints create a session
for communication to maintain the data integrity and confidentiality in order to resist
hardware bus hijack attack. See Figure 1-5. We will discuss the details in Chapter 8.

Figure 1-5. *Secure Device Communication*

Introduction to Variants of Host Firmware

Host firmware includes firmware running on the main or "host" CPU, as distinct from non-host firmware that runs in the SOC or device firmware that may run in a peripheral. The host firmware has many responsibilities for the platform, including two primary roles: initialize the hardware and launch the next stage of the system. The former task of initializing the hardware spans setting up the state of the central processing units (CPUs), initializing the Dynamic Random Access Memory (DRAM), and enumerating the I/O buses. The latter role of host firmware can include accessing the local block storage or network to download the operating system. Both of these phases have respective threat models and dependencies on the hardware.

A typical platform that includes the host firmware and other device and non-host firmware is shown in Figure 1-6.

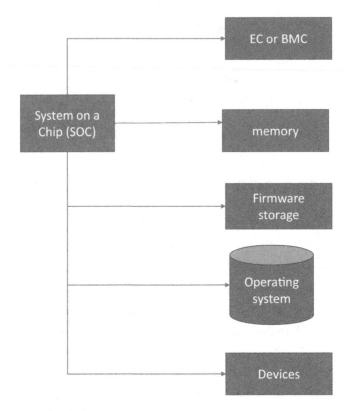

Figure 1-6. *System Block Diagram*

Industry Standards

Of the industry standards, there are several. Some are intended to have interoperability with the I/O devices, such as the Universal Serial Bus (USB) and Peripheral Component Interconnect (PCI). These allow for having more consistent system software that programs against a hardware interface, as distinct from having unique device drivers to abstract the capabilities of every interface. Beyond these device-to-host hardware interfaces, though, there are also standards between the host firmware and the operating system. These include the Advanced Configuration and Power Interface (ACPI) for detailing non-enumerable aspects of the platform and a set of runtime-interpreted tables for both configuring and managing the platform state at runtime. Another important standard is the System Management BIOS (SMBIOS) standard which provides static tables detailing the inventory of the platform. Finally, for purposes of abstracting the platform block, network, and console devices from the operating system loader, there is the Unified Extensible Firmware Interface (UEFI). UEFI complements other standards like ACPI and SMBIOS by providing a well-known mechanism to discover the content, but it goes further. Specifically, UEFI provides a rich set of capabilities and interfaces for discovering executable content, or ".efi" files, in PCI adapter card option ROMs (OROMs) and on storage devices. This allows for decoupling the manufacturer of the platform, such as the Original Equipment Manufacturer (OEM) and the operating system vendor (OSV).

Boot Flow and Phased Handoff

There are various means of restarting the system. These include a cold restart such as an S5, a CPU-only reset such as warm start, a memory-preserving restart such as an S3, or a hibernation-based restart such as ACPI S4.

In general, firmware has at least three phases, including providing a root-of-trust, turning on the SOC and the system's main memory, initializing the platform, and booting the operating system.

There are typically some minimal firmware requirements, such as providing some root-of-trust for measurement, verification, and update. This ensures that the firmware can report the state of the firmware environment while booting and only update itself with some platform manufacturer-approved content.

Typically, the boot of a platform is decomposed into three phases. The first includes turning on the basic system on a chip complex, including system DRAM. This is also where the core root-of-trust for measurement (CRTM) and the static update and verification root-of-trust can commence. This early phase is represented in various firmware architectures, such as the UEFI PI Security (SEC) and Pre-EFI Initialization (PEI), coreboot boot block and romstage, Slim Bootloader stage 1, Open Power self-boot engine (SBE) and hostboot, and U-Boot First Stage Boot Loader (FSBL). Ideally this phase will be predominately SOC-specific code with little vendor code. An example of SOC-only vendor code would be a SOC boot ROM, and a mixed board and SOC code solution can include the Intel Firmware Support Package (FSP).

The next phase of execution can include richer software abstractions since the firmware is guaranteed to have initialized system memory that will maintain its configuration throughout the life of the platform. As such, the UEFI PI Driver Execution Environment (DXE), U-Boot Secondary Program Loader (SPL), Open Power skiboot, Slim Bootloader stage 2, and coreboot RAM stage can have richer algorithmic flows. This stage typically hosts the setup application for a PC class system, creation of ACPI and

SMBIOS tables, and programming of other board-specific capabilities. This phase, unlike the prior one, is less SOC code specific and more system board and product specific. This phase of execution must continue the root-of-trust logic for measurement, update, and verification, though, and the code should be provisioned under the authority of the platform manufacturer. This phase is typically the latest point during which the runtime phase of the platform can be provisioned, including but not limited to allocating memory for management mode, such as X86 system management mode (SMM) RAM (SMRAM), data spaces for the runtime-accessible ACPI and SMBIOS tables, and, finally, data and code spaces for the UEFI runtime services.

Following the board-specific initialization, the persona for operating booting is entered. This persona can include the UEFI-conformant execution environment which allows for third-party extensible executables from disk, PCI host bus adapters, and network. The Boot Device Selection (BDS) is the traditional point at which policy actions around these third-party codes begin and the phase of execution referred to as the Transient System Load (TSL). For the coreboot and Slim Bootloader, this phase of execution is characterized by the launching of a payload. The payload can contain a UEFI-style environment, such as EDK II DXE, or it can contain a Linux-based boot environment such as LinuxBoot. The payloads are typically considered part of the firmware Trusted Computing Base (TCB), in addition to the former two phases.

The predominant role of this last phase of firmware execution is to discover and potentially abstract services for the next phase of execution, or HLOS runtime. As such, upon exiting this phase of execution, the pre-OS phases should quiesce most of the hardware and prepare for the HLOS to take over. In the case of a UEFI system, the end of the TSL is the invocation of ExitBootServices by the OS loader or OS kernel.

Once the HLOS has taken over from the payload and/or UEFI boot service environment, the host firmware plays much less of a role. In fact, the OS kernel or hypervisor will have its own driver stack to manage the state of the processors, SOC, and I/O devices. The host firmware will be largely passive with only limited callbacks into firmware via synchronous invocations from the OS, such as the UEFI runtime services, synchronous traps into management mode via hardware mailbox access from agents outside of the Trusted Execution Environment (TEE), or asynchronous invocation into the TEE via TEE-specific timer sources or side effects of other SOC-specific hardware activations. The integrity of the runtime TEE, such as Management Mode, is still part of the host firmware TCB and should only be services by manufacturer-approved updates.

A typical boot flow with mapping to representative firmware environments is shown in Figure 1-7.

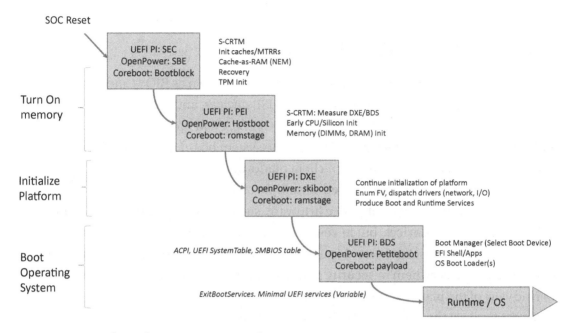

Figure 1-7. *Phased Firmware Initialization*

Introduction to Non-host Firmware

The host firmware, such as EDK II or coreboot, are not the only firmware entities on the platform. Other firmware that are typically under the control of the platform manufacturer include the Baseboard Management Controller (BMC) on servers and Embedded Controllers (ECs) on client platforms. These devices typically interact with the host firmware during the early phases of execution and may in fact run prior to the host firmware since they can provide a root-of-trust for the host firmware or sequence the power capabilities of the platform.

These non-host firmware elements should be recorded by the host firmware root-of-trust for measurement, if possible, and these non-host elements may have their root-of-trust for update (RTU) and verification proxied through the host. In either case, these elements are part of the platform manufacturer's TCB typically and should not be exposed to arbitrary third-party updates.

The OpenBMC project and the Chrome EC are examples of open source non-host platforms available in the market. Given the inclusion in the manufacturer's TCB, following the security practices for firmware development is key for having a robust product.

Introduction to Device Firmware

Beyond the manufacturer's host firmware (sometimes known as BIOS) and non-host platforms (EC, BMC, and so on), the PCI card, USB devices, and other components such as Complex Programmable Logic Device (CPLD), Field Programmable Gate Array (FPGA) or Digital Signal Processing (DSP) on the system board may have their own firmware. In fact, a review of a modern client platform noted sixteen different firmware elements, and a server example quoted a multiple of that figure.

There are some examples of device firmware, such as Open Sound Firmware, for programmable audio devices, but in general the device firmware is opaque to and independent of the host firmware. As such, there are protocols to query these devices for their state and add them to security policy so that the host firmware can provide a holistic view of the platform state to the HLOS.

And given that the device firmware reads in on the platform security posture, construction of this firmware, just like the other non-host firmware devices, is imperative for having a robust platform experience.

Summary

This chapter has described the various aspects of host firmware, including its role in the platform. Given that contemporary firmware is written predominately in C, various classes of security considerations that impact higher-level application software are described. In the next chapter, we will discuss the proactive firmware security development.

References

Book

[B-1] Jiming Sun, Vincent Zimmer, Marc Jones, Stefan Reinauer, *Embedded Firmware Solutions*, 2015, Apress

[B-2] Vincent Zimmer, Michael Rothman, Suresh Marisetty, *Beyond BIOS: Developing with the Unified Extensible Firmware Interface, 3rd edition*, 2017, DeG

[B-3] Vincent Zimmer, Michael Rothman, Robert Hale, *UEFI: From Reset Vector to Operating System*, in Chapter 3 of *Hardware-Dependent Software*, Springer, 2009

[B-4] Sunil Cheruvu, Anil Kumar, Ned Smith, David M. Wheeler, *Demystifying Internet of Things Security*, 2020, Apress

Conference, Journal, and Paper

[P-1] David Weston, "Hardening With Hardware," in BlueHat 2018 https://github.com/microsoft/MSRC-Security-Research/blob/master/presentations/2018_01_BlueHatIL/BlueHatIL18_Weston_Hardening_With_Hardware.pdf

[P-2] David Weston, "Advanced Windows Security," in Platform Security Summit 2019, www.platformsecuritysummit.com/2019/speaker/weston/

[P-3] Eclypsium, "Anatomy of a Firmware Attack," 2019, https://eclypsium.com/2019/12/20/anatomy-of-a-firmware-attack/

[P-4] Eclypsium, "FISMA compliance firmware security best practices," 2019, https://eclypsium.com/2019/05/13/fisma-compliance-firmware-security-best-practices/

[P-5] NIST, "Hardware-Enabled Security for Server Platforms," in NIST whitepaper, 2020, available at https://nvlpubs.nist.gov/nistpubs/CSWP/NIST.CSWP.04282020-draft.pdf

Specification and Guideline

[S-1] UEFI Organization, "UEFI Specification," 2019, available at www.uefi.org/

[S-2] UEFI Organization, "UEFI Platform Initialization Specification," 2019, available at www.uefi.org/

[S-3] UEFI Organization, "ACPI Specification," 2019, available at www.uefi.org/

[S-4] PCI-SIG, "PCI Express Base Specification," 2019, https://pcisig.com/

[S-5] CXL Org, "Compute Express Link Specification," 2019, www.computeexpresslink.org/

Web

[W-1] EDK II, www.tianocore.org/

[W-2] coreboot, www.coreboot.org/

[W-3] Linux Boot, www.linuxboot.org

[W-4] Slim Bootloader, https://slimbootloader.github.io/

[W-5] U-Boot, www.denx.de/wiki/U-Boot

[W-6] Intel Firmware Support Package (FSP), www.intel.com/FSP

[W-7] Sound Open Firmware (SOF), https://github.com/thesofproject

[W-8] Open Baseboard Management Controller (openbmc), https://github.com/openbmc/openbmc

[W-9] Open Power, https://github.com/open-power

CHAPTER 2

Proactive Firmware Security Development

Firmware development is similar to software development. Almost all of the software security development lifecycle (SDL) practices can be applied to firmware development. Figure 2-1 shows the main activities that may be involved in the firmware development.

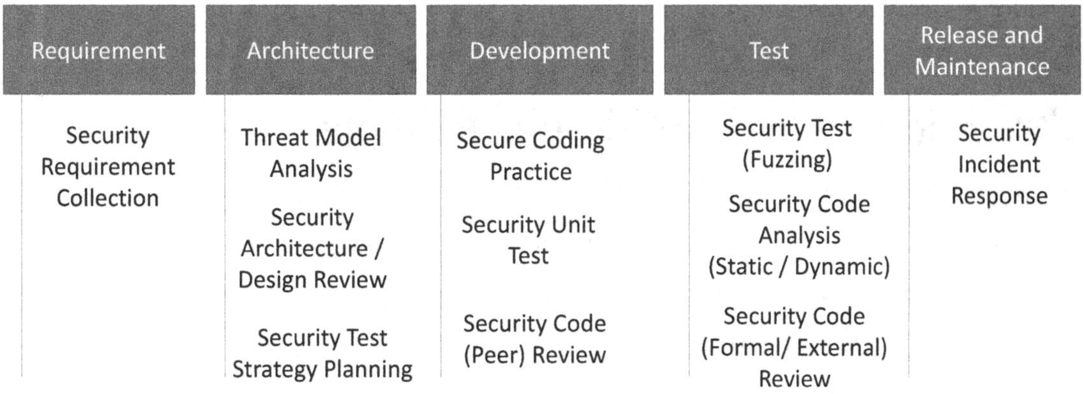

Requirement	Architecture	Development	Test	Release and Maintenance
Security Requirement Collection	Threat Model Analysis Security Architecture / Design Review Security Test Strategy Planning	Secure Coding Practice Security Unit Test Security Code (Peer) Review	Security Test (Fuzzing) Security Code Analysis (Static / Dynamic) Security Code (Formal/ External) Review	Security Incident Response

Figure 2-1. *Security Activities in the Software SDL*

Requirement Phase

Collecting the security requirement is the first step. Without the clear requirement, we don't know what to protect from whom in which condition.

Security Requirements

Any product has a set of requirements. One can view requirements as 'any statement of desire or need.' These can include functional requirements, such as which behaviors the product should perform. There can also be market requirements, such as when

17

J. Yao and V. Zimmer, *Building Secure Firmware*, https://doi.org/10.1007/978-1-4842-6106-4_2

the product should be ready and how much it should cost. Finally, there are security requirements, which can include to what security attributes the product must adhere, including mitigations for various threats.

The security requirements should also include the industry standard requirement. If it is production in the United States, it may need to follow NIST guidelines such as NIST SP800-193 – Platform Firmware Resiliency Guidelines. If it is a production in China, it may need to follow GB (mandatory) or GB/T (recommended) specifications such as GB/T 36639 – Trusted Computing Specification: Trusted Support Platform for Server. If it is an X86 personal computer or server platform, it may need to follow the Universal Extensible Firmware Interface (UEFI) specification and the TCG standard such as the PC Client Platform Firmware Profile (PFP) Specification or Device Identifier Composition Engine (DICE) Architectures. If it is an ARM product, it may need to follow the ARM platform security architecture (PSA) specification or Trusted Base System Architecture (TBSA) for ARMv8M. For the vehicle product, it may need to follow the ISO 26262 functional safety requirement.

Threat Model and Architecture Phase

The threat model and security architecture are derived from the security requirement. They map the customer's language into the developer's language.

Threat Model Analysis

Speaking of threats, threat model analysis is a process to identify a potential threat and prioritize it from a hypothetical attacker's point of view. Threat model analysis should happen in the feature architecture phase. The feature architect should work with the security architect to identify the asset, adversary, and threat (attack surface), then prioritize the threat, and select mitigation. Before those steps, the architect needs to have a clear understanding of how the system works.

There are existing books and tools to teach how to perform threat model analysis. Most of this existing material starts from the control flow analysis (CFA) and the data flow analysis (DFA). CFA focuses on how the code runs from one place to the other place. DFA, on the other hand, focuses on how the data is moved from one place to the other place.

Finally, we need to prioritize the threats. Both the probability of the exploitation and impact of the system should be considered. We may choose to only handle the threat with critical, high priority and define the mitigation. We may choose to not handle the threat with medium or low priority and leave it to future generations of the product. For example, the threat from malicious hardware might not have been considered previously, but now we need to consider it because there are more and more hardware attacks. Some new attacks, such as the glitch attack, might be considered as a medium priority for the commercial platform that is low cost, but they might be a high priority for a high-assurance platform.

To get into specifics, let's take the STRIDE threat model as an example. The threat model discussed here is a general guide and serves as the baseline of the system firmware. For each specific feature, there might be additional feature-based threat models in addition to the general threat model (see Table 2-1).

Table 2-1. *Threat and Desired Property*

Threat	Desired Property
Spoofing	Authentication
Tampering	Integrity
Repudiation	Non-repudiation
Information disclosure	Confidentiality
Denial of service	Availability
Elevation of privilege	Authorization

In system firmware, the denial of service can be temporary in the current boot or permanent, in which case the system never boots again. The latter is more serious, and it is named as a permanent denial of service (PDoS).

For the firmware STRIDE model, we will consider the adversaries shown in Table 2-2.

Table 2-2. *Adversary and Example*

Adversary	Example
Network attacker	The attacker may connect to the system by network in order to eavesdrop, intercept, masquerade, or modify the network packet.
Unprivileged software attacker	The attacker may run ring 3 software in an OS application layer. The attacker may perform a software-based side channel attack (such as using cache timing).
System software attacker	The attacker may run ring 0 software in the OS kernel or hypervisor. Or the attacker may run third-party firmware code in the firmware boot phase. The attacker may perform a software-based side channel attack (such as using cache timing, performance counters, branch information, or power status).
Simple hardware attacker	The attacker may touch the platform hardware (such as the power button or jumper) and attach/remove a simple malicious device (such as a hardware debugger, PCILeech to the external port, PCIe (Peripheral Component Interconnection Express) card to the PCIe slot, memory DIMM, NIC cable, hard drive, keyboard, USB device, Bluetooth device). The attacker may hijack the simple system bus (such as the Serial Peripheral Interface [SPI] bus or I2C bus).
Skilled hardware attacker	The attacker may hijack a complex system bus, such as the memory bus or PCI express bus. The attacker may perform a hardware-based side channel attack, such as power analysis, thermal analysis, or electromagnetic analysis. The attacker may perform a glitch attack.

According to the National Institute of Standards and Technology (NIST) SP800-193, the system firmware design needs to consider protection, detection, and recovery.

To match the requirement to BIOS, the main security objectives of the BIOS include the following:

1) Prevent any unauthorized modification to the BIOS code and critical data (protection).

2) Enable firmware components to be part of the Chain-of-Trust (CoT) and provide the platform attestation (detection).

3) Restore BIOS to an authentic state after corruption or illegal modification (recovery).

The three pillars – protection, detection, and recovery – are also considered as the main mitigation. The assets we need to consider for the BIOS are flash content, boot flow, S3 resume, Management Mode, and Build Tool. We need to perform an analysis for each asset.

Flash Content

NIST SP800-147 and SP800-147B provide system firmware protection guidelines, including the detailed information on system firmware protection and update. NIST SP800-193 provides platform firmware resiliency guidelines. It extends protection to three principles: protection, detection, and recovery. It also enlarges the scope from system firmware (BIOS) to all the firmware on the platform.

The flash content here includes both firmware code (e.g., Pre-EFI Initialization (PEI), Driver Execution Environment (DXE), and Boot Device Selection (BDS), etc.) and firmware data (e.g., UEFI variables, Microcode, etc.). See Tables 2-3, 2-4, and 2-5 for the threat, adversary, and mitigation of the flash content.

Table 2-3. *Threat for Asset – Flash Content*

Threat	Example
Spoofing	N/A
Tampering	If the firmware is not protected or locked, the attacker might modify the firmware directly.
	If the firmware update process is not authenticated, the attacker might send a malicious firmware update image for update.
Repudiation	If the firmware does not implement the event logging correctly, the malicious program may erase or truncate the log.
Information disclosure	If the system software stores the secret in the firmware, the attacker may read the firmware content and get the secret.
Denial of service	If the attacker can modify the firmware content (code or data) and cause the firmware to crash, the system might no longer boot. It becomes a permanent denial of service.
Elevation of privilege	If the attacker can modify the firmware content (code or data) and store a Trojan in firmware, the Trojan may hide itself and gain the higher privilege.

Table 2-4. *Adversary for Asset – Flash Content*

Adversary	Example
Network attacker	If the network is enabled before X86 system management mode (SMM) lock and flash lock, the attacker may send malformed network packets.
Unprivileged software attacker	The attacker may trigger a firmware update or write the UEFI variable.
System software attacker	The attacker may access a silicon register to unlock the flash access register. The attacker may create a race condition to break the flash write protection or flash update authentication.
Simple hardware attacker	The attacker may press the power button during flash update or recovery, or the attacker may set a jumper to modify the system boot mode from normal boot to recovery or even manufacturing mode.The attacker may attach a PCILeech to perform DMA attack during flash update or recovery. The attacker may hijack the SPI bus to read or write to the chip data.
Skilled hardware attacker	N/A

Table 2-5. *Mitigation for Asset – Flash Content*

Mitigation	Example
Protection	For the code region, the flash write protection must always be applied. During the flash update, the new firmware image must be authenticated, and the version must be checked to prevent a rollback attack. In order to mitigate time-of-check/time-of-use (TOC/TOU) attacks, the new image must be copied to a secure environment before the check. The DMA protection must be enabled during flash update.
	For the data region, the UEFI authenticated variable write must happen in an isolated execution environment. The authenticated variable data must be authenticated, and the rollback protection must be applied. Just as in code region protection, in order to mitigate TOC/TOU attacks, new variable content must be copied to a secure environment before the check, and DMA protection must be applied to this environment.
	In addition, the secret must not be saved to the firmware code or data region.
Detection	The detection happens in the next boot.
	For the code region, the industry may have different solutions to make sure the initial boot code is unmodified, such as Project Cerberus, Intel Boot Guard, and so on.
	For the data region, the UEFI variable driver needs to detect if the variable region is modified without using UEFI variable services.
Recovery	If something wrong is detected, the entity which detects the failure needs to start the recovery process, and the recovery data must be in a known good and secure configuration and be delivered from a trusted and always available source.

Boot Flow

The main system firmware work is to initialize the silicon and then transfer control to an operating system. Because the firmware is almost the first component running on the system, another responsibility of the system firmware is to maintain the secure boot chain defined in the Unified Extensible Firmware Interface (UEFI) specification and the trusted boot chain defined by the Trusted Computing Group (TCG).

Here the secure boot chain means that the first entity needs to verify if the second entity is good before running it and not run the second entity if the verification fails. The trusted boot chain means that the first entity needs to measure the second entity before running it and then always runs the second entity. The attestation may happen later. The system firmware needs to maintain both boot flows carefully. The verification and measurement must not be bypassed.

In addition, the system firmware may need to authenticate the end user to determine if the user is authorized to perform some action. For example, the user may be asked to input a hard drive password to continue the boot. Or the user may be asked to input an administrator password to enter a setup page. Those actions must not be bypassed as well.

Table 2-6. *Threat for Asset – Boot Flow*

Threat	Example
Spoofing	If the firmware needs to authenticate the user, the attacker may spoof the identity or bypass the authentication check.
Tampering	The attacker may want to modify the secure boot logic or trusted boot logic (either code or configuration data) to bypass the verification or measurement.
Repudiation	N/A
Information disclosure	The user identity and device password are secret information. The attacker may want to steal them.
Denial of service	The attacker may modify the secure boot configuration data to cause a system crash during verification.
Elevation of privilege	If the attacker bypasses the user authentication, they may enter the firmware setup page to modify the configuration. If the attacker bypasses the secure boot verification, they may run the unauthorized third-party code in the ring 0 environment.

Table 2-7. *Adversary for Asset – Boot Flow*

Adversary	Example
Network attacker	The attacker may send malformed network packets to inject code into the system.
	The attacker may send a bad UEFI image to bypass or break the secure boot logic.
Unprivileged software attacker	The attacker may write a malformed UEFI authenticated variable to break the secure boot configuration.

(continued)

Table 2-7. (*continued*)

Adversary	Example
System software attacker	The attacker may send a command to the isolated execution environment in order to modify the secure boot configuration.
	The attacker may enable a side channel to get secrets from memory.
Simple hardware attacker	The attacker may attach PCILeech to perform DMA attack to read the secret from memory or write the code region to bypass the verification.
Skilled hardware attacker	The attacker may hijack the memory bus to read secrets from memory or write the code region to bypass the verification.

Table 2-8. *Mitigation for Asset – Boot Flow*

Mitigation	Example
Protection	Check for untrusted external input before use (such as a network packet, option ROM, OS loader, and UEFI authenticated variable). Do not run any untrusted third-party code before verification.
	If a secret is generated, it must be cleared after use (such as temporary input from HII). If a secret needs to be stored, the choices include to save secret to hardware directly (such as TCG OPAL password), to save hash plus salt to a UEFI variable (such as user password), or to save the secret in an isolated environment (such as TCG TPM MOR2). Side channel prevention must be applied in this case.
	DMA protection must be enabled. Memory encryption must be used if the memory bus attack is in scope.
Detection	N/A
Recovery	N/A

See Tables 2-6, 2-7, and 2-8 for the threat, adversary, and mitigation of the boot flow.

S3 Resume

S3 resume is a special boot flow. It is defined by the Advanced Configuration and Power Interface (ACPI) specification. During S3 resume, the system restores the configuration from a normal boot and jumps to the OS waking vector.

All protection applied to the normal boot must also be applied in an S3 resume boot flow. See Tables 2-9, 2-10, and 2-11 for the threat, adversary, and mitigation of the S3 resume.

Table 2-9. *Threat for Asset – S3 Resume*

Threat	Example
Spoofing	N/A
Tampering	The attacker may try to modify the S3 configuration, also known as S3 boot script.
Repudiation	N/A
Information disclosure	If the S3 configuration includes a secret (such as Advanced Technology Attachment [ATA] HDD password), the attacker may want to steal the secret.
Denial of service	The attacker may destroy the S3 configuration to prevent the system from booting.
Elevation of privilege	The attacker may disable the protections stored in the S3 configuration such as register lock.

Table 2-10. *Adversary for Asset – S3 Resume*

Adversary	Example
Network attacker	N/A
Unprivileged software attacker	The attacker may write a malformed UEFI variable to break the S3 configuration.
System software attacker	The attacker may send a command to the isolated execution environment to modify the S3 configuration. If there is a secret saved in the isolated environment, the attacker may send a command to get the secret or use a side channel to steal the secret.
Simple hardware attacker	N/A
Skilled hardware attacker	N/A

Table 2-11. *Mitigation for Asset – S3 Resume*

Mitigation	Example
Protection	The S3 configuration data must be saved to a secure place. Examples of secure location for storage may include embedded into a read-only code region, a read-only variable, an isolated execution environment, or a LockBox.
	If the S3 configuration data is secret, then it must be saved in an isolated execution environment or a LockBox to prevent unauthorized reads.
Detection	N/A
Recovery	N/A

Management Mode

Management mode is a special system execution environment. X86 systems have system management mode (SMM), and ARM has ARM TrustZone. The firmware code in management mode is considered as a secure world and having high privilege. See Tables 2-12, 2-13, and 2-14 for the threat, adversary, and mitigation of the management mode.

Table 2-12. *Threat for Asset – Management Mode*

Threat	Example
Spoofing	N/A
Tampering	The attacker may update the management mode memory to inject code or data.
Repudiation	N/A
Information disclosure	The management mode may contain a secret (such as password, TPM MOR2 entropy) or its own information (code and data structure location). This information may be exposed to the normal world.
Denial of service	The management mode only has limited resources (such as memory). The attacker may send a command to management mode code to make it run out of resource.
Elevation of privilege	The attacker may gain unauthorized execution rights in management mode. For example, if the management code calls the normal world code, the attacker may replace the original code with malicious code to gain privileged execution.
	The attacker may construct a confused deputy attack for management mode. For example, the OS kernel may send a command to management mode to let it modify the hypervisor memory or management mode memory.

Table 2-13. *Adversary for Asset – Management Mode*

Adversary	Example
Network attacker	N/A
Unprivileged software attacker	N/A
System software attacker	The attacker may take advantage of an implementation flaw in the management mode code to read or modify the management mode content, or content of a higher-privilege environment, such as a hypervisor.
	The attacker may use a side channel to steal a secret in the management mode memory.
Simple hardware attacker	N/A
Skilled hardware attacker	N/A

Table 2-14. *Mitigation for Asset – Management Mode*

Mitigation	Example
Protection	The management mode code must lock the management mode after it is constructed no later than third-party code running.The management mode code must not call out to the normal world code.
	The system must remove unnecessary management mode handlers.The required management mode handler must verify the untrusted external input before use, including the communication buffer, the pointer inside of the communication buffer, the general-purpose register serving as the communication buffer pointer, and the hardware base address register. The checked content must be copied into management mode memory to prevent TOC/TOU.
	The management mode handler must prevent unauthorized access to itself and highly privileged content such as hypervisor or OS kernel memory.
	The management mode handler must prevent side channel attacks to ascertain any secrets. The management mode handler must not allocate more resources to serve the request. If additional sources are allocated, they must be freed before the handler returns to the normal world.

(continued)

Table 2-14. (*continued*)

Mitigation	Example
Detection	N/A
Recovery	N/A

Build Tool

In 1983, Ken Thompson received the Turing Award with Dennis Ritchie. There, he delivered a speech – "Reflections on Trusting Trust" – and demonstrated how to inject a Trojan Horse into the compiler. Afterward, the compiler generated a buggy binary. It is not impossible to have attacks on tools. This is not a traditional attack to the final system, but it represents an attack to the tool chain in the build environment.

The mitigation is to only trust the tool chain from a trusted source with the source code and thereafter protect the tool chain in the build environment.

Note   Not all firmware share the same threat model as in the preceding text. Some host firmware might not support S3 resume. As such, the S3 resume asset does not exist. Some device firmware might not support management mode. As such, the management mode asset does not exist. For the non-host firmware, the runtime service may become another asset.

Non-host Runtime Service

Runtime service is the service provided by the non-host firmware. It coexists with the normal host OS environment, for example, the Baseboard Management Controller (BMC) for server platform or Embedded Controller (EC) for client platform. The runtime service may provide the local service to the host OS or provide the out-of-band (OOB) service to the remote system.

See Tables 2-15, 2-16, and 2-17 for the threat, adversary, and mitigation of the BMC as examples.

Table 2-15. *Threat for Asset – Non-host Runtime Service*

Threat	Example
Spoofing	The attacker may break the user authentication flow to access the BMC internal data.
Tampering	The attacker may update the BMC internal memory to inject code or data.
Repudiation	The attacker may truncate the event log saved in BMC.
Information disclosure	The BMC may include sensitive information (such as user management data). This information may be exposed to the normal world.
Denial of service	The BMC OOB network service may have risk on network DOS.
Elevation of privilege	The attacker may get the BMC internal privilege data in the memory or on the SPI flash.

Table 2-16. *Adversary for Asset – Non-host Runtime Service*

Adversary	Example
Network attacker	The attacker may send a malformed packet to the BMC runtime out-of-band (OOB) service via the RedFish interface and/or Intelligent Platform Management Interface (IPMI).
Unprivileged software attacker	N/A
System software attacker	The attacker may send a malformed packet to the BMC runtime in-band service via the RedFish interface and/or Intelligent Platform Management Interface (IPMI) or via a special local bus between the host and the BMC.
Simple hardware attacker	N/A
Skilled hardware attacker	N/A

Table 2-17. *Mitigation for Asset – Non-host Runtime Service*

Mitigation	Example
Protection	All network packets from OOB or in-band shall be validated before use.
	The network stack in BMC shall resist network DOS.
	The user authentication shall be done before accessing a BMC resource. The authentication shall not be bypassed in any way.
	The privilege of administrator and normal user shall be separated. The management work shall only be done with the administrator account.
	Sensitive information shall not be saved to BMC flash in plain text.
	The command from the local bus of the host shall also be validated.
Detection	N/A
Recovery	N/A

Security Architecture and Design

Once we have identified the threat and mitigation, we need to design the firmware. "The protection of information in computer systems" provided the general security design guideline, which can still be used today, such as economy of mechanism, fail-safe defaults, complete mediation, open design, separation of privilege, least privilege, least common mechanism, and psychological acceptability.

We can start with the trust region. Different trust regions are isolated by a trust boundary. The trust boundary can be temporal or spatial. Let's take a system firmware boot flow shown in Figure 2-2 as an example. The vertical line shows a temporal trust boundary, and the horizontal line shows a spatial trust boundary.

1) Recovery Trust Region: After the platform is out of reset, it enters the Recovery Trust Region. It is treated as root-of-trust for recovery (RTRec). The Recovery Trust Region does the basic initialization and loads the next component – the Main Trust Region. The Main Trust Region can be from the main flash area or the recovery flash area based upon the boot mode.

2) Main Trust Region: This is the biggest trust region. All the system initialization should be done in this trust region. This region only executes the Original Equipment Manufacturer (OEM) code. No

third-party code should be executed in this region. Usually this region is treated as root-of-trust for update. After this region exits, the flash should be locked. The flash update shall be finished inside of this region. This region loads the Boot Trust Region as the next phase. A red line is put here, because it is the last opportunity to lock down the required interface before any third-party code commences execution.

3) Boot Trust Region: After the system initialization is done, it starts to boot to an operating system (OS). Third-party code may be run here, such as the OS loader or a PCI option ROM. As a final step, the OS loader transfers control to OS and enters the OS Trust Region.

4) Management Mode (MM) Trust Region: All three preceding trust regions are transient. The MM Trust Region is available at runtime. It may be loaded by the Main Trust Region. Only the management mode code may run in the MM Trust Region, such as X86 system management mode (SMM) or ARM TrustZone. The data processed in the MM may be trusted by the Recovery Trust Region or the Main Trust Region because the MM Trust Region is considered as a secure world. The secure world can be trusted by the nonsecure world.

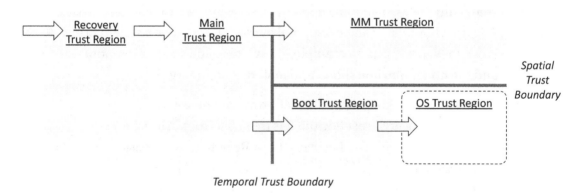

Figure 2-2. Trust Region in Platform Firmware

To match the trust region to the UEFI/PI BIOS, we may see the picture flow shown in Figure 2-3. The Security (SEC) and Pre-EFI Initialization (PEI) phase can be treated as the Recovery Trust Region. It detects the boot mode and decides where to launch. The Driver Execution Environment (DXE) is the Main Trust Region. It loads drivers and initializes SMM, which is considered as a MM Trust Region. Later the system boots to the Boot Device Selection (BDS) phase. The BDS chooses if to boot to a UEFI OS or a legacy OS. We separate the Boot Trust Region and Legacy Trust Region because the UEFI secure boot is enabled in the Boot Trust Region. As such, the chain-of-trust is maintained during OS boot. In the Legacy Trust Region, no verification is performed, and the chain-of-trust is broken. In Figure 2-3, we draw a red vertical line after the Main Trust Region. This is an architecture point that the platform exits the manufacture's auth state and starts running the third-party code. In the UEFI PI specification, this event is named as EndOfDxe. A horizontal line between the MM Trust Region and Boot Trust Region shows the isolation of the high-privilege MM execution environment and normal execution environment.

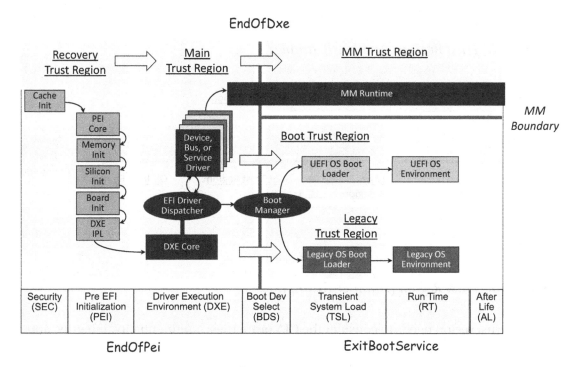

Figure 2-3. *Trust Region Mapped to UEFI Firmware*

Figure 2-3 is a typical system firmware boot flow, although different systems may choose variants thereof. For example, the MM Trust Region may be loaded by the Recovery Trust Region directly in the S3 resume phase or in StandaloneMM mode for the X86 system.

Another example is that the system can have a special MM Recovery Trust Region to load the MM Trust Region and a normal Recovery Trust Region. An ARM system with trusted firmware may use this model. See Figures 2-4 and 2-5.

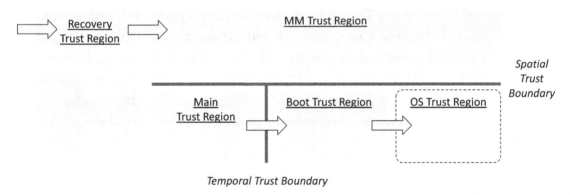

Figure 2-4. *Trust Region (Another Example)*

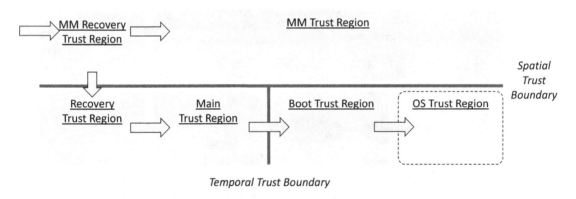

Figure 2-5. *Trust Region (Another Example)*

Each trust region needs to consider the CIA properties: confidentiality, integrity, and availability.

For **confidentiality**, the trust region shall not expose any secrets outside of the region. For example, the password or a secret shall not be saved to the non-volatile storage in plain text.

For **integrity**, each trust region shall only trust the input from the previous trust region and the current trust region, but it cannot trust the input from other trust regions. For example, the MM Trust Region cannot trust any input from the Boot Trust Region or the Legacy Trust Region, such as the MM communication buffer. The Recovery Trust Region cannot trust any input from the OS Trust Region, such as the UEFI variable set in the OS. Verification is always required. The untrusted input includes but is not limited to the new firmware image, the recovery image from the external storage, the MM communication buffer, the network package, the third-party images such as the OS loader and PCI option ROM, the file system and the disk partition, and, finally, the hardware input such as a USB descriptor or a Bluetooth advertisement message.

Each trust region shall also lock the system configuration within the current trust region and not expose the insecure configuration to the next trust region. For the MM Trust Region as an example, if the Main Trust Region loads the MM Trust Region, the Main Trust Region needs to lock MM configuration. If the Recovery Trust Region loads the MM Trust Region, then the Recovery Trust Region needs to lock the MM configuration. Another example is the flash content lock where the Recovery Trust Region does the boot mode detection and shall lock the flash content in a normal boot mode. If the system is in update mode, then the Recovery Trust Region leaves the flash region open and transfers control to the Main Trust Region if the Main Trust Region is the root-of-trust for update. The Main Trust Region performs the new flash image authentication and updates the flash content. Finally, the Main Trust Region shall lock the flash content.

For **availability**, each transient trust region shall make sure the system can continue booting to the next trust region even if it receives unexpected input. The runtime trust region shall make sure the provided service handler is always available. For example, there is a system management mode (SMM) service handler in X86 systems, a TrustZone service in ARM systems, or the management service in the server Baseboard Management Controller (BMC). These service handlers need to make sure no resource leaks exist in the implementation.

Beyond having the threat model and security architecture, there are the social aspects of ensuring that the threat model and the security architecture are sufficient. To that end, the threat model and security architecture review is part of the security development lifecycle (SDL) that involves reviewing the specific mitigations for threats. This process spans the range of formal to semiformal and to informal reviews. These reviews are often led by the originator of a new security feature who presents details of the design to some set of subject matter experts.

Security Test Strategy Planning

Once we have done the threat modeling and the security architecture, the next step in the process includes defining a means by which to assess if the security-specific components match the design intent. This can include system-level testing all the way down to the components. The security test should be based upon the threat model analysis and focus on the asset and the attack point. For example, the test method shown in Figure 2-6 may be considered.

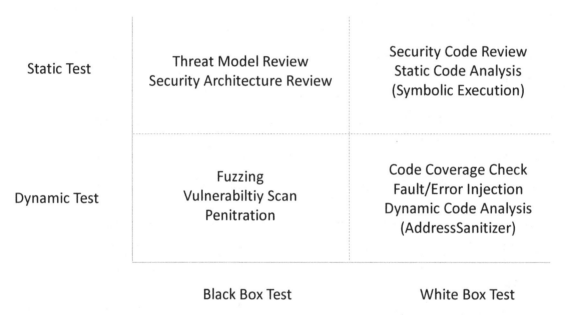

Figure 2-6. *Security Test Classification*

Real Example

Let's see a real example. In EDK II UEFI firmware, we need support for the S3 resume feature. From end users' point of view, they can click OS Start Menu ➤ Sleep. Then the machine enters sleep state. When they click the power button again, the system wakes up quickly and goes back to its original state. How do we do threat model analysis?

Step 0: Do the Control Flow Analysis and Data Flow Analysis for the Feature

In normal boot flow, when the silicon modules do the initialization, they also called the BootScriptSave module to save the silicon register information. In S3 resume boot flow, no silicon initialization modules are needed, because the S3 resume module calls the BootScriptExecutor module and the latter replays the silicon register configuration. Then the firmware jumps to OS waking vector to wake up the system. The purpose of this design is to make sure the S3 resume can be done much faster than a normal boot. Figure 2-7 shows the control flow analysis.

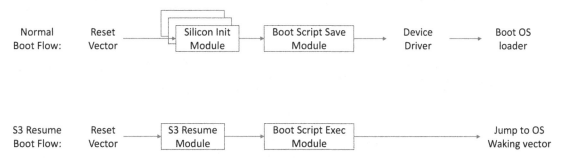

Figure 2-7. *S3 Resume – Control Flow Analysis*

Figure 2-8 shows the data flow analysis in the first version of S3 resume implementation. During normal boot, the SiliconInit module passes the BootScript entry to the BootScriptSave module as the parameter in a function call. Each BootScript entry includes register type, register address, and register value. Then the BootScriptSave module collects all BootScript entries and saves them into a big BootScript table. The BootScript table is in an ACPI NonVolatileStorage (NVS) memory, so that that it won't be overridden by the operating system. At the same time, the BootScriptSave module saves the pointer of BootScriptTable into a UEFI variable. In S3 resume boot, the S3Resume module can get the BootScriptTablePtr UEFI variable, know the address of the BootScript table, and execute the BootScript from the ACPI NVS memory.

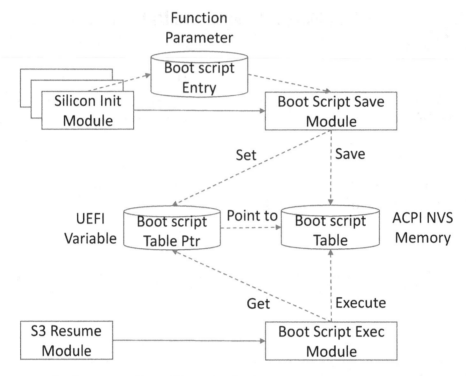

Figure 2-8. *S3 Resume – Data Flow Analysis*

Then we scope them into different trust regions. See Figure 2-9. Here the SiliconInit module and BootScriptSave module are in the Main Trust Region. The S3Resume module and BootScriptExecutor module are in the Recovery Trust Region. The UEFI variable BootScriptTable pointer and the BootScriptTable in ACPI memory are in the Boot Trust Region or OS Trust Region, because the code in OS bootloader or OS may modify the UEFI variable and ACPI NVS memory.

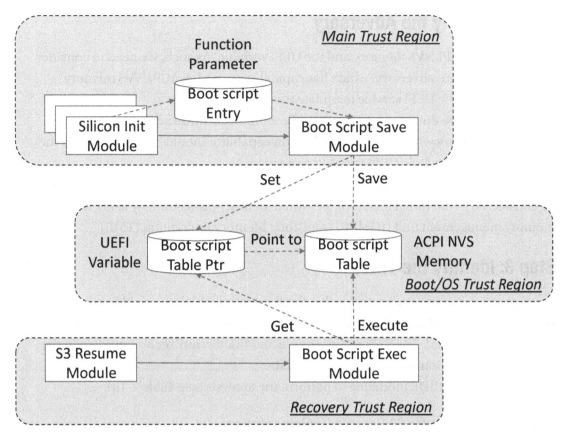

Figure 2-9. *S3 Resume – Trust Region Mapping*

Step 1: Identify the Feature-Specific Asset

From the data flow analysis, we believe the BootScriptTablePtr UEFI variable and BootScriptTable in ACPI NVS memory are the primary asset, because they hold the silicon register setting information.

The code such as the SiliconInit module, BootScriptSave module, S3Resume module, and BootScriptExecutor module are part of the firmware code. They are asset from the whole UEFI firmware point of view. But they are NOT asset for this specific feature. So we don't need to consider them in this S3 resume threat model analysis. The code module should be considered in the threat model of the whole UEFI firmware flash protection.

Step 2: Identify the Adversary

The asset is in ACPI NVS memory and the UEFI variable. As such, we need to consider the system software adversary, which has capability to modify ACPI NVS memory directly and call the UEFI service to update the variable.

In this case, we don't want to consider the simple hardware adversary. A simple hardware adversary with variable modification capability should be considered in the threat model of the whole UEFI variable protection.

A simple hardware adversary with memory content modification capability should be considered in the threat model of the whole memory protection, by using device I/O memory management unit (IOMMU) and Total Memory Encryption (TME).

Step 3: Identify the Threat

From previous discussion, we notice that the BootScriptTablePtr variable and BootScriptTable in ACPI NVS are in the Boot Trust Region or OS Trust Region. As such, they may be modified. The S3Resume module and BootScriptExecutor module in the Recovery Trust Region shall not trust those data.

Now we use STRIDE modeling to perform the analysis (see Table 2-18).

Table 2-18. *Threat for S3 Resume Implementation*

Threat	Yes/No	Comment
Spoofing identity	No	Assume there is no user identity involved in S3.
		The only user identity involved in BIOS is user authentication, which does not happen in S3 resume.
Tampering with data	Yes	The attacker may modify BootScriptTable in ACPI NVS memory directly or use UEFI variable services to modify the BootScriptTablePtr UEFI variable.
Repudiation	No	N/A
Information disclosure	No	Assume there is no secret/password saved in the boot script.
		The hard drive password unlock might be needed in S3 resume, but the password should NOT be saved in the S3 script. It should be covered by the threat model of hard drive password solution.

(continued)

Table 2-18. (*continued*)

Threat	Yes/No	Comment
Denial of service (DoS)	Yes	DOS could be the consequence of tampering with data. With the modified BootScript data, the system cannot resume successfully.
		It may cause permanent denial of service (PDoS), with a bad implementation that performs the flash part locking in the BootScript. The attacker may skip the lock setting and program a bad image in the flash.
Elevation of privilege	Yes	It could be the consequence of tampering with data, with a bad implementation of the system management mode (SMM) lock in the BootScript. The attacker may skip the SMM lock and update the SMM content to get execution privilege in SMM.

The Common Vulnerability Scoring System (CVSS) is a good way to decide the priority of the vulnerability. The basic score includes the following areas:

Attack Vector (AV): Network(N), Adjacent(A), Local(L), Physical(P)

Attack Complexity (AC): Low(L), High(H)

Privileges Required (PR): None(N), Low(L), High(H)

User Interaction (UI): None(N), Required(R)

Scope (S): Unchanged(U), Changed(C)

Confidentiality (C): None(N), Low(L), High(H)

Integrity (I): None(N), Low(L), High(H)

Availability (A): None(N), Low(L), High(H)

If we have an S3 boot script saved in ACPI NVS without any protection and the flash lock and SMM lock relying on the boot script, then the CVSS score could be **CVSS:3.0/ AV:L/AC:L/PR:H/UI:N/S:C/C:N/I:H/A:H: 7.9 (HIGH)**.

We do need a mitigation plan.

Step 4: Create the Mitigation

Creating a mitigation is the final step of the threat model analysis. We need to come up with the basic idea on how to mitigate the threat and then figure out a detailed design for the solution. Table 2-19 shows the basic idea.

Table 2-19. *Security Objective for S3 Resume Implementation*

Threat	Yes/No	Security Objective
Spoofing identity	No	N/A
Tampering with data	Yes	1. Protect the BootScriptTable content in ACPI NVS memory.
		2. Protect the BootScriptTablePtr UEFI variable.
Repudiation	No	N/A
Information disclosure	No	N/A
Denial of service (DoS)	Yes	3. Lock the flash part even if the boot script is tampered.
Elevation of privilege	Yes	4. Lock the SMM even if the boot script is tampered.

1. Protect the BootScriptTable content.

The ACPI NVS is an OS-accessible memory, and it cannot be marked as read-only from BIOS. In order to protect the BootScriptTable, we can move the BootScriptTable into the MM Trust Region where it is not accessible by the OS Trust Region. In X86 systems, it can be implemented by system management mode (SMM). There are two possible ways to achieve that implementation solution:

1) Move BootScriptTable into SMRAM and let it stay there. The BootScriptExecutor will execute the system management RAM (SMRAM) copy of BootScriptTable.

2) Save BootScriptTable into SMRAM and restore the content from SMRAM to ACPI NVS during S3 resume. The BootScriptExecutor will execute the ACPI NVS copy of BootScriptTable.

We choose the second option because we need to follow the security design principle of least privilege. Executing BootScriptTable does not require SMM privilege. As such, there is no reason to execute that in SMRAM.

Care must be taken that just copying the BootScriptTable into SMRAM is sufficient because the BootScriptTable may include a DISPATCH OPCODE. Figure 2-10 shows how

DISPATCH OPCODE works. The BootScriptExecutor will execute a function entry point in the BootScript entry with a parameter. Both the entry point and parameter address are in ACPI NVS memory too. They may be tampered with by an attacker. In order to achieve the security goal, we need to also save the S3 image, which includes the code executed by DISPATCH OPCODE and the associated parameter, into SMRAM and restore them during the S3 resume boot.

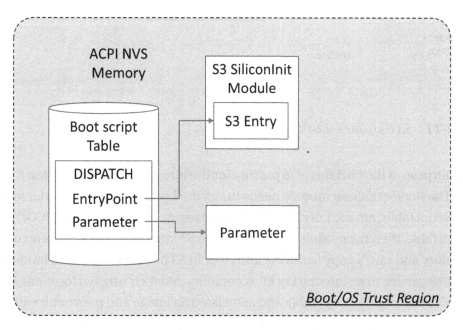

Figure 2-10. *S3 Resume – Boot Script DISPATCH OPCODE*

Now we have multiple components that need to be saved into SMRAM and restored thereafter. It is a burden if we let every module perform the save/restore by themselves. We need to create a service for that – LockBox. See Figure 2-11.

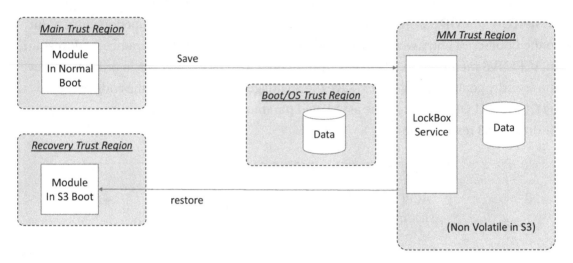

Figure 2-11. *S3 Resume – LockBox Service*

The purpose of the LockBox is to provide for the integrity of data across the S3 resume. The BootScriptSave module needs to call the LockBox service in order to save the BootScriptTable into the LockBox. If a module registers a DISPATCH OPCODE in the BootScriptTable, then the module needs to put the S3 image and the parameter in ACPI NVS memory and save a copy to the LockBox too. In S3 boot, the S3resume module calls the LockBox service to restore the LockBox contents into their original location. As such, any modification of BootScriptTable and associated S3 image and parameter will be reverted to the original known good copy.

The LockBox implementation uses system management mode (SMM) because SMM may provide both integrity and confidentiality support.

   2.   Protect the BootScriptTablePtr variable.

We can use the Variable Lock service to make the BootScriptTablePtr variable to be read-only.

   3.   Lock the flash part even if the boot script is tampered.

The flash lock action shall be moved from the boot script to early S3 silicon initialization code. The purpose of the boot script is to reduce the silicon reinitialization time. Since the flash lock is so simple, the writing of lock register in the code does not impact the S3 resume time. Locking the flash part shall happen before BootScript execution. As such, the vulnerability in BootScript won't impact the integrity of the flash part.

   4.   Lock the SMM even if the boot script is tampered.

The SMM lock action shall be moved from the boot script to early S3 silicon initialization code. For the same reason as flash lock, it does not impact S3 resume time. Locking SMM shall also happen before BootScript execution.

Step 5: Summarize the Final Threat Model and Security Architecture

Table 2-20 shows the summary of S3 resume threat model analysis.

Table 2-20. *Summary for S3 Resume Threat Model Analysis*

Asset	1. BootScriptTable and associated S3 image and parameter 2. BootScriptTablePtr variable
Adversary	System software attack
Threat	1. Tampering with data: The attacker may modify BootScriptTable in ACPI NVS memory directly or use the UEFI variable service to modify the BootScriptTablePtr variable. 2. Denial of service (DoS): It could be the consequence of tampering with data. With the modified BootScript data, the system cannot resume successfully. It may cause permanent denial of service (PDoS), with a bad implementation that performs the flash part lock in BootScript. The attacker may skip the lock setting and program a bad image in flash. 3. Elevation of privilege: It could be the consequence of tampering with data, with a bad implementation of the system management mode (SMM) lock in BootScript. The attacker may skip the SMM lock and update the SMM content to achieve privileged execution in SMM.
Security objective	1. Protect the BootScriptTable content in ACPI NVS memory. 2. Protect the BootScriptTablePtr variable. 3. Always lock the flash part in S3 resume. 4. Always lock the SMM even in S3 resume.
Mitigation	1. Design a LockBox, which can provide the integrity for data across S3 resume. Save the BootScriptTable and associated S3 image and parameter to the LockBox, and restore them during S3 resume. 2. Use the Variable Lock service to lock the BootScriptTablePtr variable to be read-only. 3. Lock the flash part in early S3 silicon initialization code before BootScriptExecution. 4. Lock the SMM in early S3 silicon initialization code before BootScriptExecution.

Figure 2-12 shows the final system architecture.

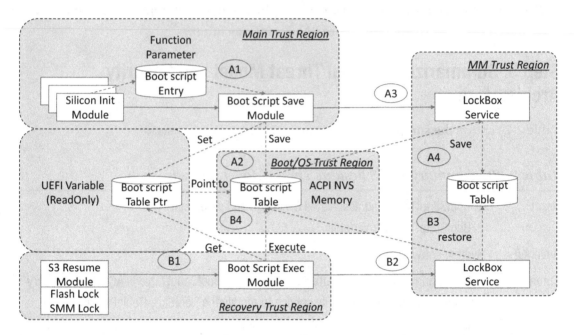

Figure 2-12. *S3 Resume – Final System Architecture*

In normal boot, the silicon initialization module calls the BootScriptSave module to save the BootScript entry. Once the BootScriptSave module collects all BootScriptEntry, it saves to BootScriptTable in ACPI NVS memory and calls the LockBox service to save a copy into the LockBox. The BootScriptSave module also saves the BootScriptTable pointer to a UEFI variable and uses the variable service to lock it.

In a S3 resume boot, the S3 resume module locks the flash part and SMM. Then it calls the BootScriptExecutor module to restore the silicon configuration. BootScriptExecutor calls the LockBox service to restore all the LockBox content to the original ACPI NVS memory. Then it calls the variable service to get the BootScriptTable pointer and execute the BootScriptTable.

Note   The flow in Figure 2-12 shows an example of how we do threat model analysis and derive the security architecture for the boot script–based silicon register restoration. In the full S3 resume, there will be more components involved. We need to perform a similar analysis for all those components involved in S3, such as LockBox, Variable Lock, Memory Configuration Restoration, hard drive password unlock, and so on.

Step 6: Create Security Test Strategy

Now, let's take a look at the picture from test engineer's point of view. We start from the asset and the attack surface:

1) BootScriptTable and associated S3 image and parameter

   We need to make sure the code does save the BootScriptTable. The whole table shall be saved, instead of a portion of the table. We need to make sure the table is saved at the right time. The saving shall be done in the Main Trust Region instead of the Boot Trust Region. The save action shall be done during any boot mode, such as normal boot, S4 resume, recovery, firmware update, or even manufacturing mode. Just in case that the system may boot to the OS and someone does an S3 suspend/resume, we also need to make sure no code adds a new entry to the BootScriptTable in the Boot Trust Region or OS Trust Region.

   Besides the BootScriptTable, we need to test the S3-related image and parameter. If some code adds a DISPATCH OPCODE in BootScriptTable, the whole PE image providing the entry point in the BootScript entry shall be saved into ACPI NVS memory and synced to the LockBox. If the parameter for the entry point is used, the whole parameter buffer and its reference shall be put in the ACPI NVS memory and synced to the LockBox. Similar to the normal boot script entry, the save action shall be done at the right time and during any boot mode.

We did have a security issue before that a platform only saved the normal BootScriptTable to SMM, but the implementation did not save the S3 image from ACPI NVS to SMM.

2)   BootScriptTablePtr variable

Whenever a UEFI variable is used in a solution, we need to think about the attribute. According to the UEFI specification, the variable may have NON_VOLATILE, BOOT_ SERVICE, RUNTIME_SERVICE, and AUTHENTICATED attributes. The EDK II adds a special feature to lock a variable as read-only in the Boot Trust Region and OS Trust Region. According to the threat model analysis, this BootScriptTablePtr variable needs to be set as read-only. As such, we need to make sure that the Variable Lock action is done at the right time and during any boot mode.

We did have a security issue before that a platform only set the Variable Lock in normal boot but skipped the action during a S4 resume.

Note   There is no need to define a test strategy for LockBox, Variable Lock, Memory Configuration Restoration, and hard drive password unlock in this S3 resume task, although they are related and involved in the S3 resume path. We need to use a "Divide and Conquer" strategy. Each of these features shall have its own threat model analysis, mitigation, and security test strategy. We don't need to combine all features together. Here we can assume that those features (LockBox, Variable Lock) are well designed and can be used directly in the S3 resume. From the final production BIOS point of view, all features involved in the BIOS shall have a similar analysis.

In the real world, one big feature may involve several small features. As such, the granularity of the feature shall be considered. On one side, we don't want to put all small features into one and review them. It may cost too much time, and it may bring some distraction. On the other hand, we don't want to split all features into small pieces. That will make it hard to find the relationship for those features.

As an example, it might be possible to merge LockBox into the S3 resume feature because LockBox is designed for S3 resume usage, although it is a standalone feature. However, it does not make sense to merge the Variable Lock or hard drive password feature into S3 resume because even if a platform does not support S3 resume, the Variable Lock and hard drive password feature may still be required.

Development Phase

After we have clear architecture and design, we can start writing code to implement the feature.

Secure Coding Practice

Most of the firmware is developed with the C programming language. As such, it inherits the security vulnerabilities of C, such as buffer overflows and integer overflow. We need to follow all the secure coding practices in C language.

The firmware may also have some specialties compared with general software because of its own special execution environment. We will discuss more details in Chapter 14.

Security Unit Test

Once we have finished the coding work, we need to perform some unit testing. Besides the function unit test, a security unit test is preferred, such as fuzzing. Currently, we have lots of existing tools running in the OS environment to test the OS application. We will discuss more details in Chapter 21 on how to use this tool to perform the security unit test in the OS.

Security Code Review

Secure code review is a special activity compared to normal code review. The normal code review may focus on software quality, such as usability, reusability, and maintainability, while the secure code review needs to focus on the software security, such as confidentiality, integrity, and availability (CIA).

Usually when people perform the secure code review, there will be a checklist regarding which area should be reviewed. Also, there will be a "top five" or "top ten" list regarding where the review should be focused. According to "A Process for Performing Security Code Reviews," the priority of common software code is as follows:

1. Old code

2. Code that runs by default

3. Code that runs in an elevated context

4. Anonymously accessible code

5. Code listening on a globally accessible network interface

6. Code written in C/C++/assembly language

7. Code with a history of vulnerabilities

8. Code that handles sensitive data

9. Complex code

10. Code that changes frequently

We believe the preceding list is still valid for today's firmware world.

Once we have identified the priority, we need to start reviewing the code. We may take the following three steps:

1. Rerun all available code analysis tools.

2. Look for common vulnerability patterns, such as

    a. Integer arithmetic vulnerabilities

    b. Buffer overrun vulnerabilities

    c. Cryptographic vulnerabilities

    d. Structured Query Language (SQL) injection vulnerabilities (if it is database related)

    e. Cross-site scripting vulnerabilities (if it is web related)

3. Dig deep into risky code, such as the following:

    a. Are there logic or off-by-one errors (e.g., ">" vs. ">=" or "||" vs. "&&")?

    b. Is the data correctly validated?

    c. Are buffer lengths constrained correctly?

    d. Are integer values range-checked correctly?

    e. Are pointers validated?

f. Can the code become inefficient (e.g., $O(N^2)$) due to some malformed data (e.g., a hash table lookup becomes a list lookup)?

g. Are errors handled correctly?

Besides "A Process for Performing Security Code Reviews," Ransome provided some good suggestions in the book *Core Software Security: Security at the Source* on how to perform the SDL activity, including a security code review.

The preceding list is from the software perspective. However, the firmware code has some specialty. We performed an analysis from the previous firmware vulnerability list and defined eight categories:

1) External input: External input describes data that can be controlled by an attacker. Examples include UEFI capsule image, boot logo in Bitmap (BMP) or Joint Photographic Experts Group (JPEG) format, contents of file system partitions, read/write (RW) variables, system management mode (SMM) communication buffer, network packets, and so on.

2) Race conditions: There are two typical race conditions found in firmware – race condition in a data buffer and race condition in a register unlocking mechanism.

3) Hardware input: Hardware input is a special class of external input. If an attacker controls hardware, the input from hardware is considered to be untrusted. This includes, but is not limited to, memory mapped input/output (MMIO), cache, Direct Memory Access (DMA), Universal Serial Bus (USB) descriptors, and Bluetooth Low Energy (BLE) advertisement data.

4) Secret handling: In some cases, the users are required to input passwords in the firmware, such as setup administrator password, hard drive password, and Trusted Computing Group (TCG) OPAL password. Sometimes the firmware also includes some password or access key. We need a good way to handle these secrets.

5) Register lock: When the system powers on, most of the silicon registers are unlocked. The firmware code needs to configure the system and lock the critical resources by setting the lock bit in a silicon register. Examples include but are not limited to flash chip lock, SMM lock, SMI lock, MMIO BAR configuration lock, model-specific register (MSR) configuration lock, and so on.

6) Secure configuration: For security features, it is not a good idea to use variables to control the behavior because they can be altered by an attacker to bypass protection. The general configuration also includes the system state, memory configuration, different boot mode, and so on.

7) Replay/rollback: Replay is the ability to use a previously used credential that was designed for one-time approval to access protected content beyond the first instance. Typically, a timestamp, nonce value, or monotonic counter can be used to detect replay. Rollback is the ability to start at a newer level of a release and go back to a forbidden earlier level of a release. Typically, the firmware needs to use a lowest support version (LSV) or secure version number (SVN) to control the update.

8) Cryptography: Cryptography is also an indicator we need to consider when we design a proper solution. Choosing the right cryptographic algorithm is important. A checksum or cyclic redundancy check (CRC) value is no longer considered to be strong protection. Cryptographic key management must be considered as part of a complete security solution.

When doing the code review or design review, keep asking the questions shown in Table 2-21.

Table 2-21. *Security Review for Eight High-Risk Areas*

Category	Review Detail
External input	What is the external input?
	How is the external input checked?
	Does the check happen in all possible paths?
	What is the action if the check failed?
	If SMM is involved, how does the SMI handler do the check for the communication buffer?
	If a variable is involved, how is it consumed?
	Is ASSERT used?
Race condition	What is the critical resource?
	If SMM is involved, can the BSP and AP access the same resource?
	Does the trust region code access resources in the untrusted region?
Hardware input	What is the hardware input?
	How is the hardware input checked?
	Does the check happen in all possible paths?
	If MMIO is involved, how is the MMIO bar checked?
Secret handling	Where is the secret?
	How is the secret cleared after use?
	Does the cleanup function clear all secrets in all places, such as stack, heap, global data, communication buffer, ASCII < = > Unicode, Setup Browser, and key buffer?
	Is the secret saved into a variable?
	Does the password follow the general rules, such as strong password requirement, retry time, history, and so on?
	What if the user forgets the password?
	Is the default password/key used?
	Is the password/key hardcoded?
	Does the key comparison algorithm compare entire data?
	Are side channel guidelines followed?

(*continued*)

Table 2-21. (*continued*)

Category	Review Detail
Register lock	What registers need to be locked? When is the register locked? Is the register lock controlled by some policy? Is the register lock controlled by a variable? Is there any way to bypass the lock? Is the register locked in normal boot, S3, or S4? Is the register locked in capsule or recovery? Is the register locked in manufacturing mode?
Secure configuration	Is a variable used to control the policy? Is a PCD used to control the policy? If so, what is the PCD type? What is the default configuration? What is the behavior in S3, S4, capsule, recovery, manufacturing, or debug mode?
Replay/rollback	Is LSV or SVN used? Where is the LSV or SVN stored? How are timestamps, nonce, or monotonic counters used?
Cryptograph	Is a signing verification algorithm used? Is a deprecated algorithm used? Is cyclic redundancy check (CRC) or checksum used? Should the solution use hash or hash-based message authentication code (HMAC)? Should the solution use symmetric encryption or asymmetric encryption? When is the key deployed and destroyed? Where is the key located? How is the key protected? Is the key root key or session key used to encrypt the data?

For the system firmware EDK II, we have detailed suggestion on how to handle these areas in the development phase and in the testing phase described in "EDK II Secure Code Review Guide." We also suggest adding a decoration tag for the critical functions. As such, the code review can identify the critical function easily.

ASSERTs are removed in release builds but exist in debug builds. An ASSERT is a condition that should never happen in a released system. Some issues found in the past included detection of errors in the ASSERT macro that were omitted during runtime, thus allowing for the error to imperil the product.

Test Phase

Once the code passes the unit test and code review, the code is checked in. Now it is the test engineer's work.

Fortunately, most general software security testing techniques can be used in the firmware area.

Fuzzing

Fuzzing is an automated test tool to provide invalid, unexpected, or random data as input for the program. Because the fuzzing input is random, the fuzzing test design is extremely simple.

However, fuzzing has a test oracle problem – a test must be able to distinguish expected (normal) from unexpected (buggy) program behavior. Crash, hang, or ASSERT is a simple and objective measurement for fuzzing. However, the absence does not indicate the absence of a vulnerability. As such, sanitizers can be used to inject assertions in fuzzing.

Some most widely used fuzzing tools include American Fuzzy Lop (AFL), LibFuzzer, and Peach. All of them are open source tools.

Fuzzing is important for security testing. However, most of the fuzzing tools run in the OS environment. In order to run a fuzzing tool for the firmware code, we have different options:

- Port the fuzzing tool from the OS to the firmware environment and run it in the firmware environment. The porting effort is large, based upon our analysis. It also means that continuous porting is required if we need to keep the fuzzing tool up to date.

- Create an agent in firmware and let the agent accept the mutated data from the OS fuzzing tool. It is doable. However, we might run into performance problems because some time is wasted in the communication between OS and UEFI.

- Make the firmware code run in the OS environment and use the OS fuzzing tool directly. It is the easiest way. If we can build firmware code and run it in the OS environment, we can reuse the OS fuzzing tool directly.

Static Code Analysis

Static code analysis is to supplement secure code review. Static code analysis is performed by an automated tool. Not all the security analysis tools are the same. Different static code analysis tools may detect different problems. Static code analysis may have false positives and false negatives because of the complexity of the program. In that case, we still need humans to do the manual review.

If the firmware supports multiple tool chains and supports customization, then it can be configured to support a static code analysis tool, such as Klocwork, Coverity, or Clang Static Analyzer.

Dynamic Code Analysis

Dynamic code analysis entails performing the analysis when the code is running. It may have the ability to identify the false negatives in static code analysis.

Address Sanitizer is a good tool to detect memory corruption bugs, such as heap buffer overflow, stack buffer overflow, global buffer overflow, and heap use-after-free. Currently it is implemented in Clang, GNU CC (GCC), and Xcode. Besides Address Sanitizer (ASan), the compiler also supports Memory Sanitizer, Thread Sanitizer, Undefined Behavior Sanitizer (UBSan), Leak Sanitizer, Data Flow Sanitizer, and Control Flow Integrity Sanitizer.

Because dynamic code analysis may only cover part of the code, we need a code coverage tool to know which code is covered. Currently there is some commercial code coverage tools, such as Bullseye. Some compilers also add code coverage capability, such as GCOV.

Based upon the result, the uncovered lines of code may be executed by fault injection. The dynamic code analysis may require firmware code support. For example, the EDK II BIOS code supports heap guard, stack guard feature, data execution protection, memory leak detection, and SMI Profile feature.

Vulnerability Scan

Currently, CHIPSEC is a framework for analyzing the security of X86 platforms including hardware, system firmware (BIOS/UEFI), and platform components.

Release and Maintenance Phase

Now the production is released. But the security work is not finished.

Security Incidence Response

After the production is released, we might get a security issue report. Security incidence response is a process developed to handle the security report.

Take the EDK II community as an example. The EDK II community has a closed version of Bugzilla. That is only accessible by a small group named the TianoCore InfoSec group. This allows for reporting issues that are not publicly visible. Every month, members of the EDK II Bugzilla InfoSec group scrub the issues. There is a flow where the group decides if an issue is a security flaw in the EDK II code or a defect in an external architecture specification, such as the UEFI specification. In the latter case, the issue is sent to the UEFI Security Response Team (USRT). Examples of the latter include monotonic counter-based authenticated variable interaction with UEFI secure boot that ultimately led to the deprecation of this type of variable. Once the issue is deemed a security issue in code, the Common Vulnerability Scoring System (CVSS) grading occurs, and a patch is created. If the issue has a sufficiently low CVSS grading or is deemed not a security flaw, it becomes a public Bugzilla. In the case that it is deemed sufficiently severe from a security perspective, an embargo period occurs wherein the bug is held in the closed list for some number of weeks or months. After the embargo expires, the bug is made public; and an entry in the Tiano Security Advisory Document is created that lists the location of the bug fix, its severity, the submitter, and a description of the problem.

Existing tools such as CVSS provide a way to capture the principal characteristics of a vulnerability and produce a numerical score reflecting its severity.

If a third-party module is used in the project, we need to keep eye on the Security Advisory Document of this third-party module, such as the cryptography library – openSSL or mbed TLS.

People Education

People are always the important resource in a software/firmware project. We need to make sure the people involved in the project do understand security.

Before the Project Starts

Security is not a feature in the product. Security is part of every feature in the product, no matter whether it is a security feature (e.g., UEFI secure boot) or a non-security feature (e.g., the file system).

Security should not be assigned to one or two developers to finish. Security should be considered by every developer during the development – architect who designs the solution, developer who implements the solution, and test engineer who validates the solution.

A culture of "security experts" who continually say "no" to certain features creates a climate of us-vs.-them. Instead, security acumen should be instilled in each member of the development team.

After the Project Release

Having a security issue after release means we need to spend a lot of resources to deploy a fix. At the same time, please do use this opportunity to educate people again in order for them to avoid making mistakes the next time.

The best thing is to learn from other people's mistakes. The good thing is to learn from our own mistakes. The worst thing is not to learn from mistakes.

Fallacy and Pitfall

In order to help other people avoid some common misbeliefs or misconceptions, we list some fallacies (misbeliefs), and pitfalls (easily made mistakes).

Security Technology

Fallacy: We are using secure boot, so our firmware is secure.

The secure boot feature just provides a secure infrastructure from an architectural point of view. The implementation of secure boot is also important. A bug in the secure boot feature may cause a critical security issue.

Fallacy: We have a platform Root-of-Trust to perform resiliency and measurement, so our platform is secure and trusted.

The platform Root-of-Trust (RoT) module must be properly implemented. Otherwise, the hacker may attack the platform RoT to break the resiliency and measurement, such as trust anchor attack.

Fallacy: We disable the secure boot feature by default, because people will enable it if needed.

Most people just use the default configuration. Security by default should be followed.

Fallacy: We are using standard cryptograph algorithm, so our firmware is secure.

Using standard cryptography is necessary but not sufficient. We also need to consider if we use that cryptographic protocol correctly (see *Applied Cryptography*) or if the key is stored correctly. The starbleed attack defeats the bitstream encryption. It uses standard AES and standard HMAC algorithm, but builds a vulnerable solution.

Fallacy: We have done fuzz testing, so our firmware is secure.

Testing can only show the presence of a bug, not the absence. So do security testing and fuzz testing. Fuzz testing is important, but it just finds some input issues. There are also some security issues related to configuration, design, information leaks, and so on. It is hard to expose that by fuzzing.

Security Process

Fallacy: Nobody cares about firmware. Most hackers focus on software.

Today we have seen more and more attacks against the firmware. All systems boot from firmware, and having a rootkit in firmware is hard to detect.

Fallacy: We can trust my device on the board. Only software is insecure.

Today we have seen more and more attacks to devices, such as keyboard controller, battery, printer, router, embedded controller (EC), baseboard management controller (BMC), network interface card (NIC), Xbox 360, IP phone, automotive, supervisory control and data acquisition (SCADA) device, even complex programmable logic device (CPLD), field programmable gate array (FPGA), digital signal processing (DSP). There are also more and more attacks from devices to the host system, such as PCI DMA attack and USB attacks. We need to consider all the firmware on the board.

Fallacy: This feature is not a security feature, so we don't need to care about security.

Some security issues are exposed by a non-security feature. For example, ThinkPwn used a vulnerability in a server management feature.

Pitfall: Having a dedicated security team can do all security work.

Having a dedicated security team is possible, but it is impossible to let them do all the work. Everyone in the development team should acquire security knowledge. As such, they can develop security bug-free features.

Pitfall: Have dedicated people to fix all security issues.

If a security bug is found in one feature, we need to let the original developer fix it. As such, this developer learns and will not make the same mistake. If we ask another person to fix, the original feature owner will not learn and may make the same mistake in the future.

Pitfall: Close all SDL tasks one time before release.

SDL tasks should be done at the right time in the development lifecycle. It is far more than letting some people check the box to mark it is done.

Fallacy: We have fixed this reported security issue, so our work is done.

A security issue is just reported in one place. But sometimes the similar issue may exist in another place. Think of the Microsoft ANI bug issue (CVSS 9.3 HIGH). The first issue (MS05-002) was found in 2005. But after the fix, the same issue (MS07-017) was found in 2007.

Fallacy: This code worked for 10 years so it should be secure.

Legacy code works, maybe just because no one attacks them. We have seen some examples of attacker finding issues more than 10 years ago, for example, the AMT network issue was introduced in AMT2.0.

Summary

In this chapter, we discussed the overall proactive firmware security development process – requirement phase, threat model and architecture phase, development phase, test phase, and release and maintenance phase. The threat model analysis and security architecture are the most importance activities because they give the direction for the feature development. In Part II, we will introduce the security architecture and design for the firmware features.

References

Book

[B-1] Tony UcedaVelez, *Risk Centric Threat Modeling: Process for Attack Simulation and Threat Analysis*, Wiley, 2015

[B-2] Brook S. E. Schoenfield, *Securing Systems: Applied Security Architecture and Threat Models*, CRC Press, 2015

[B-3] James Ransome and Anmol Misra, *Core Software Security: Security at the Source*, CRC Press, 2014

[B-4] Adam Shostack, *Threat Modeling: Designing for Security*, Wiley, 2014

[B-5] David Kleidermacher, *Embedded System Security – Practical Methods for Safe and Secure Software and Systems Development*, Newnes, 2012

[B-6] Gary McGraw, *Software Security: Building Security In*, Addison-Wesley Professional, 2006

[B-7] Frank Swiderski, Window Snyder, *Threat Modeling*, Microsoft Press, 2004

[B-8] Michael Howard and David LeBlanc, *Writing Secure Code (2nd)*, Microsoft Press, 2003

[B-9] Ted Huffmire, Cynthia Irvine, Thuy D. Nguyen, Timothy Levin, Ryan Kastner, Timothy Sherwood, *Handbook of FPGA Design Security*, 2010, Springer

Conference, Journal, and Paper

[P-1] Jerome Saltzer, Schroeder Michael, "The protection of information in computer systems," *Proceedings of the IEEE*, 1975, vol. 63, no. 9, pp. 1278–1308, available at http://web.mit.edu/Saltzer/www/publications/protection/

[P-2] Richard Smith, "A Contemporary Look at Saltzer and Schroeder's 1975 Design Principles." IEEE Security Privacy (September 2012), pp. 20–25

[P-3] Michael Howard, "A Process for Performing Security Code Reviews." *IEEE Security & Privacy (2006, July–August)*, pp. 74–79

[P-4] Jiewen Yao, Vincent Zimmer, "EDK II Secure Coding Guide," Intel whitepaper, 2019, available at https://github.com/tianocore/tianocore.github.io/wiki/EDK-II-Security-White-Papers

[P-5] Jiewen Yao, Vincent Zimmer, "EDK II Secure Code Review Guide," Intel whitepaper, 2019, available at https://github.com/tianocore/tianocore.github.io/wiki/EDK-II-Security-White-Papers

[P-6] Jiewen Yao, Vincent Zimmer, "A Tour Beyond BIOS Security Design Guide in EDK II," Intel whitepaper, 2016, available at https://github.com/tianocore/tianocore.github.io/wiki/EDK-II-Security-White-Papers

[P-7] Vincent Zimmer, Shiva Dasari, Sean Brogan, "Trusted Platforms: UEFI, PI, and TCG-based firmware," Intel/IBM whitepaper, 2009, available at `www.cs.berkeley.edu/~kubitron/courses/cs194-24-S14/hand-outs/SF09_EFIS001_` `UEFI_PI_TCG_White_Paper.pdf`

Specification and Guideline

[S-1] NIST SP800-193, "Platform Firmware Resiliency Guidelines," 2018, available at `https://csrc.nist.gov/publications/sp800`

[S-2] NIST SP800-147B, "BIOS Protection Guidelines for Servers," 2014, available at `https://csrc.nist.gov/publications/sp800`

[S-3] NIST SP800-147, "BIOS Protection Guidelines," 2011, available at `https://` `csrc.nist.gov/publications/sp800`

[S-4] Trusted Computing Group, "TCG PC Client Platform firmware Profile Specification," 2019, available at `https://trustedcomputinggroup.org/`

[S-5] Trusted Computing Group, "Trusted Platform Module Library," 2016, available at `https://trustedcomputinggroup.org/`

[S-6] Trusted Computing Group, "Device Identifier Composition Engine (DICE) Architectures," 2018, available at `https://trustedcomputinggroup.org/`

[S-7] GB/T 36639, "Trusted Computing Specification: Trusted Support Platform for Server," 2018, available at `http://openstd.samr.gov.cn`

[S-8] GB/T 29829, "Functionality and Interface Specification of Cryptographic Support Platform for Trusted Computing," 2013, available at `http://openstd.samr.gov.cn`

[S-9] GB/T 29827, "Trusted Computing Specification: Motherboard Function and Interface of Trusted Platform," 2013, available at `http://openstd.samr.gov.cn`

[S-10] UEFI Organization, "UEFI Specification," 2019, available at `www.uefi.org/`

[S-11] UEFI Organization, "UEFI Platform Initialization Specification," 2019, available at `www.uefi.org/`

[S-12] UEFI Organization, "ACPI Specification," 2019, available at `www.uefi.org/`

[S-13] ARM, "ARM Platform Security Architecture Security Model (PSA-SM)," 2019, available at `https://developer.arm.com/architectures/security-architectures/` `platform-security-architecture`

[S-14] ARM, "ARM Platform Security Architecture Firmware Framework (PSA-FF)," 2019, available at `https://developer.arm.com/architectures/security-` `architectures/platform-security-architecture`

[S-15] ARM, "ARM Platform Security Architecture Trusted Boot and Firmware Update (PSA-TBFU)," 2019, available at `https://developer.arm.com/architectures/` `security-architectures/platform-security-architecture`

[S-16] ARM, "ARM Trusted Base System Architecture for M (TBSA-M)," 2019, available at `https://developer.arm.com/architectures/security-architectures/platform-security-architecture`

[S-17] ISO, "ISO-26262: Road vehicles – Functional safety," 2018

Web

[W-1] ARM Trusted Firmware, available at `www.trustedfirmware.org/`

[W-2] EDK II UEFI Firmware, available at `www.tianocore.org/`

[W-3] coreboot firmware, available at `www.coreboot.org/`

[W-4] U-Boot, available at `www.denx.de/wiki/U-Boot`

[W-5] CLANG Address Sanitizer, available at `http://clang.llvm.org/docs/AddressSanitizer.html`

[W-6] CLANG Static Analyzer, available at `http://clang-analyzer.llvm.org/`

[W-7] LLVM LibFuzzer, available at `https://llvm.org/docs/LibFuzzer.html`

[W-8] KLEE – symbolic virtual machine, available at `https://klee.github.io/`

[W-9] AFL – American Fuzz Loop, available at `http://lcamtuf.coredump.cx/afl/`

[W-10] Peach Fuzzer, available at `www.peach.tech/resources/peachcommunity/`

[W-11] CHIPSEC – Platform Security Assessment Framework, available at `https://github.com/chipsec/chipsec`

[W-12] Common Vulnerability Scoring System (CVSS), `www.first.org/cvss/calculator/3.0`

[W-13] OpenSSL, available at `www.openssl.org/`

[W-14] mbed TLS, PolarSSL, available at `https://tls.mbed.org/`

[W-15] Microsoft Security Bulletin MS05-002, available at `https://docs.microsoft.com/en-us/security-updates/securitybulletins/2005/ms05-002`

[W-16] Microsoft Security Bulletin MS07-017, available at `https://docs.microsoft.com/en-us/security-updates/securitybulletins/2007/ms07-017`

[W-17] Starbleed, `www.xilinx.com/support/answers/73541.html`

PART II

Security Architecture

According to the secure software development lifecycle, we need to collect security requirements, analyze the threat model, and derive a security architecture in the architecture phase. Based upon the functional features and security policies required in the system, we need to identify the trusted computing base (TCB) for these items to enforce the security policies. Multiple design choices should be determined immediately. The general principle is to minimize the TCB as much as possible. Therefore, a thorough examination of the TCB is feasible later in the development phase and testing phase, such as code inspection and formal verification.

CHAPTER 3

Firmware Resiliency: Protection

Firmware resiliency includes three elements: protection, detection, and recovery. Protection means the protection of the firmware components from attacks. Protection is a proactive aspect of firmware resiliency, while detection and recovery are reactive mechanisms. For resiliency, the main threat is from both the software attacker and the hardware attacker.

Resiliency Building Block

The resiliency building block includes three parts:

1) Resiliency target: It is a mutable engine, which includes code and data.

2) Resiliency engine: An immutable engine to provide service for the resiliency target, such as protection, verification, update, or recovery.

3) Resiliency authority: An entity that authorizes the resiliency engine to perform the service on a resiliency target.

Inside of the resiliency engine, there are three major blocks:

1) Secure Execution Environment (SEE): This is a safe execution place to stand to ensure that a compromised resiliency target cannot affect the recovery.

2) Protection Latches such as write lock or read lock: This is to ensure the persistent storage in the resiliency engine cannot be tampered by a compromised resiliency target.

© Jiewen Yao and Vincent Zimmer 2020
J. Yao and V. Zimmer, *Building Secure Firmware*, https://doi.org/10.1007/978-1-4842-6106-4_3

3) Watchdog Timers: This is to ensure the compromised resiliency
    target cannot impact the resiliency engine to perform the recovery
    action.

Figure 3-1 shows the resiliency building block.

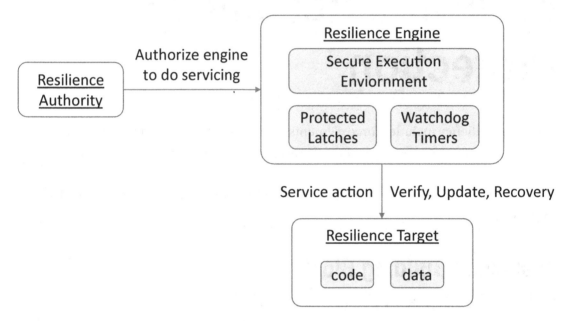

Figure 3-1. *Resiliency Building Block*

To support firmware resiliency, we need to define a set of roots-of-trust (RoTs). These
RoTs include a root-of-trust for update (RTU), root-of-trust for detection (RTD), and
root-of-trust for recovery (RTRec). Some of the functionality can also be implemented
in a chain-of-trust (CoT) anchored in the RoT. We also need to define the corresponding
chain-of-trust for update (CTU), chain-of-trust for detection (CTD), and chain-of-trust
for recovery (CTRec). Those roots-of-trust for resiliency (RTRes) are in the resiliency
engine and provide services such as protection and update, detection, and recovery. We
will discuss them one by one in Chapters 3, 4, and 5.

- A platform may have different firmware components. We classify
  them as follows:

- Immutable ROM (including code and data)

- Updatable firmware (including code and data)

- Configurable data
- Based on these classifications, we may use different protection mechanisms.

Immutable ROM

An Immutable ROM is the non-upgradable logic in the system. It is considered a root-of-trust (RoT). The immutable ROM may include both code and data. Typically, the scope of the immutable ROM should be small enough for review and audit in order to make sure it is bug-free. The advantage is that the protection policy is simple – ROM must always be locked. The disadvantage is that once there is a security issue found in the immutable ROM, there is no chance to fix, and the device shall be discarded.

Integrity

The basic security requirement is the integrity of the ROM. Once the ROM is locked, no one can write it. Usually, this protection is done from the hardware side to prevent a software attack. But we also need to consider the hardware attack. The hardware attacker may hijack the system bus on the platform to bypass the protection. The platform may lock the Serial Peripheral Interface (SPI) flash part in the SPI controller. As such, no one can send a command to the SPI devices, but a hardware attacker may add a flash programmer to the SPI chip directly and burn the whole SPI chip. Or the hardware attacker might attach a supplementary SPI chip that provides alternate code and data. As a mitigation, the platform needs to make the ROM internal and not expose any programmable interface.

Confidentiality

The confidentiality shall also be considered. If the immutable ROM includes a private key, the key shall not be exposed at any time. According Kerckhoffs's principle, the whole immutable ROM can be exposed except the private key. For a highly critical device or system, the whole immutable ROM may also be encrypted or may not be read out because keeping the ROM secret may make it harder to break the device or the system. The internal details may only be exposed for audit purposes.

Case Study

Now, let's take a look at some real cases for the immutable ROM.

Immutable ROM in Mobile, Desktop, and Server

The immutable ROM may exist in a personal computer or server. The X86 CPU Microcode in the on-die ROM is immutable. There might be a CPU Microcode update to patch the Microcode at runtime via patch RAM, but the basic CPU microcode inside of the chip is immutable.

A platform may design a standalone chip as a root-of-trust (RoT). The immutable ROM on the chip verifies the system firmware and some device firmware; thus, it is creating a chain-of-trust (CoT). Examples include the Google-designed Titan chip, Apple-designed T2 chip, AMD-designed AMD Platform Secure Processor, Open Compute Project (OCP)-defined Cerberus Security Architecture, and Intel Platform Firmware Resiliency (PFR). See Figure 3-2 for a traditional X86 system. This RoT firmware verifies the main BIOS and boot-critical firmware such as management engine (ME) firmware, baseboard management controller (BMC) firmware for a server system, and embedded controller (EC) firmware for a client system. Then the main BIOS verifies the non–boot-critical firmware (e.g., Non-Volatile Memory Express (NVMe) firmware, sensor firmware, and audio firmware).

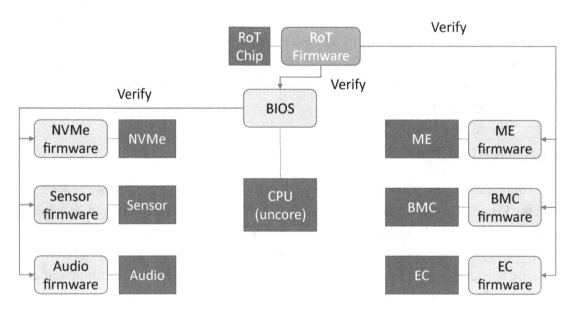

Figure 3-2. *Platform Components in Mobile, Desktop, and Server*

We will discuss more details of the RoT and CoT in Chapter 4.

Immutable ROM in the Embedded and IoT Area

In the embedded area, ARM defines the platform security architecture (PSA) for both A-profile (application processor, AP) and M-profile (microcontroller) to provide guidance for Internet of Things (IoT) devices. The PSA Root-of-Trust (PSA-RoT) includes the hardware and immutable firmware. Trusted-Firmware-A is the reference implementation for the trusted firmware design for the ARM system A-profile (see Figure 3-3). A trusted ROM is the immutable firmware. At power-on, the application processor (AP) executes the trusted ROM at the reset vector. Then the trusted ROM verifies and loads the trusted firmware. The trusted firmware verifies and loads the additional portions of the runtime firmware and nonsecure firmware. The trusted firmware may also verify the system control processor (SCP) firmware if it is present.

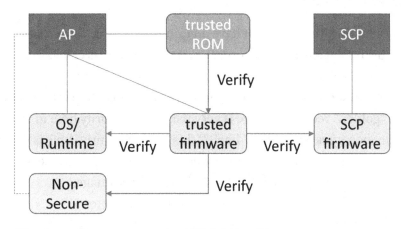

Figure 3-3. *Platform Components in ARM A-Profile*

The Trusted-Firmware-M is the reference implementation for the trusted firmware design for the ARM system M-profile (see Figure 3-4). Because the microcontroller (MC) has a restricted execution environment, the boot flow is much simpler. The microcontroller executes MCUBoot ROM at the reset vector. The MCUBoot verifies all reset firmware including the secure firmware's Secure Partition Manager (SPM) and the non-secure firmware.

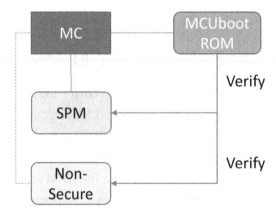

Figure 3-4. *Platform Components in ARM M-Profile*

We will discuss the PSA in more detail in Chapter 4.

Golden Recovery Image

Usually, the system firmware does not have an immutable part. To fix a security issue, all firmware must be upgradable. The only possible exception is called the "golden" recovery image. The golden recovery image is firmware that is only used in the recovery phase in cases when the current system firmware is not bootable. However, making an immutable "golden" recovery image is very risky. Any security hole in the golden system firmware becomes an Achilles' heel. If this kind of security hole is exposed, all the attacker needs to do is to remove the power during the update process to trigger the recovery process. Then they can attack the golden recovery image.

We will discuss more details of recovery handling in Chapter 5.

Attack and Mitigation

Now, let's take a look at some real cases for the attacks against the immutable ROM and possible mitigations.

Secret

The immutable ROM may include a secret – a platform root key that is used to derive the rest of the keys or a private key used to prove identity. This secret must NOT be exposed in any way. For example, if the secret is saved to an external non-volatile storage or exposed on a bus such as the DRAM or SPI bus, it might represent a risk.

Updatable Firmware

Usually, the system firmware is upgradable. The platform manufacturer may release new firmware to fix a functional issue or security issue. The device firmware for one of the on-board devices may be upgradable. This new device firmware may be a standalone package released by the device manufacturer or integrated as part of a whole system update package by the platform manufacturer.

According to NIST SP800-193, the protections for upgradable firmware are based upon three principles:

- Authenticated update mechanism

- Integrity protection

- Non-bypassability

Authenticated Update Mechanism

The guidelines for an authenticated update mechanism are as follows:

- The update image shall be signed with an approved digital signature algorithm.

- The update image shall be signed by an authorized entity, such as a device manufacturer, a platform manufacturer, or a trusted third party.

- The update image shall be verified by a root-of-trust prior to the non-volatile storage being updated.

When we choose a digital signature algorithm, we need to consider the algorithm requirements and the key length requirements from the government. When we design a solution, we need to consider crypto agility. As such, when the requirements are changed, it is easy to migrate to a new algorithm. In practice, using PKCS#7 is a good option because it defines a syntax for describing a cryptographic message. The different algorithms, such as RSA2048/RSA3072 or SHA256/SHA384, can be described by the PKCS#7 certificate. The code does not need to explicitly choose which algorithm to use. However, PKCS#7 may include a X.509 certificate, and parsing the X.509 certificate is complicated and needs a lot of memory. In a resource-constrained environment, such as SRAM only or limited DRAM, it may be necessary to use the algorithm directly without any wrapper.

Note   Checksums or CRCs mean nothing in the security world. They can only be used to detect simple mistakes, not attacks.

Both authentication and update shall happen in a trusted execution environment. The trusted execution environment may be in the early boot phase without executing any third-party or untrusted code, or it may be a processor-specific isolated environment, such as Intel system management mode (SMM) or ARM TrustZone, or it might use a server's Baseboard Management Controller (BMC). We will discuss more details of a trusted execution environment and management mode in Chapter 17.

The firmware update may happen in the OS environment. For example, both Windows and Linux provide guidance on how to initiate a system firmware update using the UEFI-defined capsule format from the OS environment.

In addition to system firmware, device firmware might also need to support update. IETF created the "Software Updates for Internet of Things (SUIT)" group to provide the guidance for IOT devices which have ~10 KiB RAM and ~100 KiB flash. TCG embedded working group provided "TCG Guidance for Secure Update of Software and Firmware on Embedded Systems". DMTF published "Platform Level Data Model (PLDM) for Firmware Update Specification" to define the messages and data structures for updating firmware components in a device of a platform management subsystem.

Case Study

Now, let's take a look at some real cases for the authenticated update mechanism.

Signed UEFI Capsule Update

For security reasons, most system firmware supports updating flash, but it may lock the flash to protect the flash from writes at some point during boot to provide integrity protection (see Figure 3-5). As such, updating flash directly might not be possible.

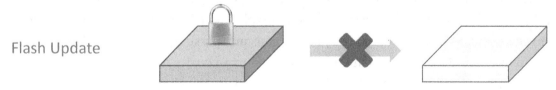

Flash Update

Figure 3-5. *Flash Update Forbidden in Normal Boot*

The UEFI specification defines the capsule mechanism to let the OS pass a new firmware image capsule to the current firmware and issue a reset. A reset forces the system to begin execution in the system firmware. On this next boot, the firmware detects the pending firmware image capsule, and then it will keep the flash part unlocked and process the update request (see Figure 3-6). The firmware image capsule must be put in a read/write non-volatile storage because the content must be preserved across a reset. Candidates include system memory, the hard drive, non-volatile dual in-line memory modules (NVDIMMs), or even a temporary flash storage area. The integrity of the non-volatile storage does not need to be guaranteed because the firmware must validate the firmware image capsule before the update process.

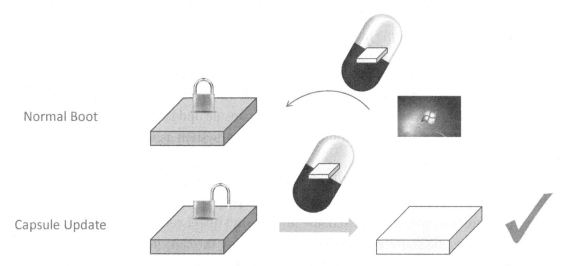

Figure 3-6. *Flash Update Allowed in Update Mode*

The following is the EDK II BIOS implementation of the UEFI capsule update. See Figure 3-7 for the capsule image in memory.

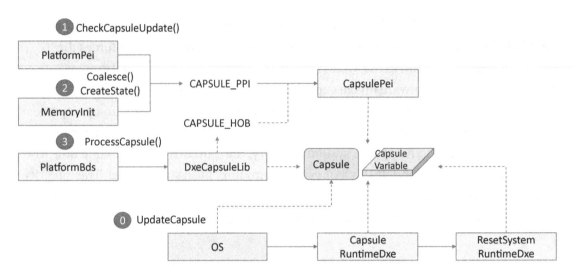

Figure 3-7. *UEFI Capsule Update Flow (Capsule in Memory)*

Step 0: During system boot, the CapsuleRuntimeDxe driver exposes the UEFI runtime UpdateCapsule service. The OS agent loads the capsule image into memory, and then it calls this runtime service to trigger the capsule update. Finally, it places the capsule information to the UEFI variable and resets the system using the ResetSystem runtime service.

Step 1: In the next boot, the PlatformPei module detects the presence of the firmware image capsule and sets the boot mode to "capsule update."

Step 2: After memory is initialized, the MemoryInit driver calls the capsule PEI driver to coalesce the scattered capsule fragments. After the capsule is coalesced, the new capsule location is reported in a capsule Handoff Block (HOB), which passes the information forward to the DXE phase. Then the MemoryInit installs permanent system memory.

Step 3: After all the drivers are dispatched in the Driver Execution Environment (DXE) phase, the system enters the Boot Device Selection (BDS) phase. If the boot mode is set to "capsule update," the PlatformBds driver will process the capsule image reported in the capsule HOB. Then, the new firmware image will be validated, and the flash part will be updated.

The capsule-in-memory solution requires that the memory contents be preserved across the reset. If a system supports S3 resume or a memory content–preserving warm reset, we can use this method. However, some embedded systems and servers do not support those options. In this case, we may put the capsule on the hard drive. This method is sometimes referred as capsule on disk.

See Figure 3-8 for the capsule image on disk.

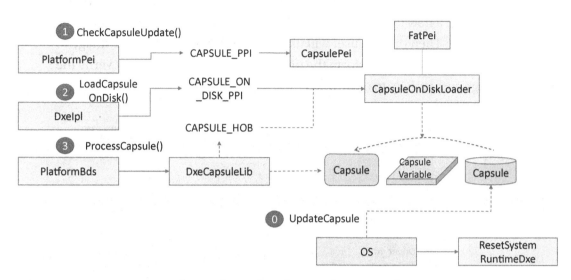

Figure 3-8. *UEFI Capsule Update Flow (Capsule on Disk)*

Step 0: The OS agent puts the capsule image on the disk and sets a flag in a UEFI variable to indicate there is a new capsule on the hard disk that is ready to process. Then the OS agent calls the ResetSystem UEFI runtime service to reset the system.

Step 1: In the next boot, the PlatformPei detects the presence of the firmware image capsule by reading the UEFI variable and sets the boot mode to "capsule update."

Step 2: Because the capsule is not in memory, the memory initialization flow is not impacted by the capsule-on-disk method. Before the Pre-EFI Initialization (PEI) phase is done, the DxeIpl module calls the CapsuleOnDiskLoader function to load the capsule from the disk to the memory. The new capsule location is reported in a capsule HOB.

Step 3: After all the drivers are dispatched, the system enters the BDS phase. In "capsule update" boot mode, the PlatformBds driver will process the capsule image in the capsule HOB. Then, the new firmware image will be validated, and the flash part will be updated.

Whether the capsule-in-RAM or the capsule-on-disk approach is used, the capsule (disk or RAM) and the capsule UEFI variable are considered as external input. As such, the UEFI variable must be checked before use, and the capsule content must be signed. The signed capsule format is defined in the UEFI specification.

The UEFI specification defines the EFI_FIRMWARE_MANAGEMENT_PROTOCOL (FMP) as a standard interface for the system firmware or the device firmware update process. Figure 3-9 describes the data structure of the UEFI FMP capsule image. If the UEFI FMP capsule–based update is used, the platform vendor or the device vendor will release a new firmware image following the data structure defined in the UEFI specification. Then the end user will use the OS interface to send the image to the platform firmware to let it perform the update. The old firmware must verify the firmware image authenticity to ensure it is from a trusted source.

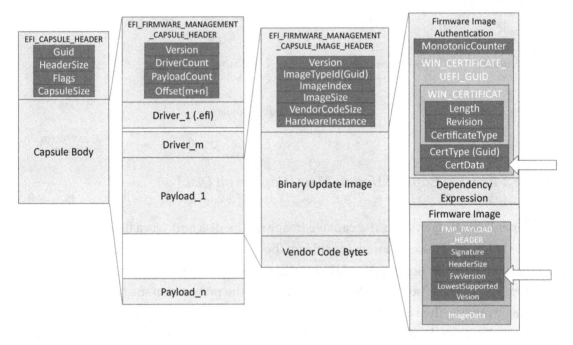

Figure 3-9. *UEFI Capsule Data Structure*

"A Tour Beyond BIOS: Capsule Update and Recovery in EDK II" describes the whole update flow in more detail.

The security verification for the new firmware image shall consider two parts: signature verification and version verification. The firmware update capsule must be signed so that the update mechanism can check the integrity of the contents. The UEFI FMP capsule expects the EFI_FIRMWARE_IMAGE_AUTHENTICATION structure before the actual payload image, and it requires the certificate type to be EFI_CERT_TYPE_PKCS7_GUID. The authentication information is the PKCS7 signature. The capsule update mechanism extracts the "Trusted Cert" from the firmware and uses the "Trusted Cert" to verify the PKCS7 signature. If a capsule does not have the EFI_FIRMWARE_IMAGE_AUTHENTICATION structure or the signing verification fails, this capsule must be ignored.

Besides the signature verification, the update mechanism should also check the capsule version to prevent a rollback attack. The version check requires that the Version in the capsule image must be greater than or equal to the LowestSupportedImageVersion in the current firmware. The version check requires that the Version in the capsule image must be greater than or equal to the LowestSupportedImageVersion in the current firmware. The current UEFI specification does not define how the Version and LowestSupportedImageVersion values are stored in the capsule image. The EDK II implementation defines FMP_PAYLOAD_HEADER before the image data. If the Version in the FMP_PAYLOAD_HEADER is lower than the LowestSupportedImageVersion in the current firmware, this capsule should be ignored.

OS Runtime Update

The previous capsule update flow needs to include a system reset. Sometimes the system reset takes a long time. If the time is too long for the system's use case, a runtime update may be desired. To maintain the integrity, the authentication and update flow must be in a trusted execution environment (TEE), such as the system management mode (SMM) for X86 systems or the TrustZone secure world for ARM systems. Figure 3-10 shows the SMM-based OS runtime update process.

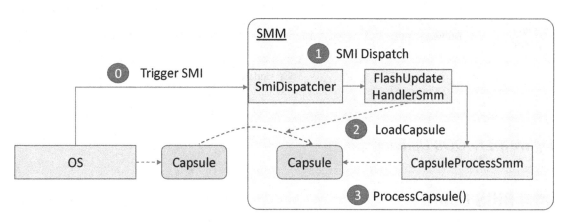

Figure 3-10. *OS Runtime Update*

Out-of-Band (OOB) Update

Server platforms are usually located in a server room. When the flash update is required, we may want to use remote capabilities for the system-initiated update. The DMTF RedFish specification provides the remote management capability and supports the remote firmware update via the RedFish protocol over the network. If a server has a

BMC which supports RedFish, the remote system may send the new firmware image to the BMC via an out-of-band network port. The BMC saves the firmware image to local BMC memory. The BMC may update the flash with the new image directly if the BMC can access the system firmware flash part. Or the BMC may keep the firmware and wait for the next boot of the BIOS. The BIOS RedFish driver may get the new firmware image from the BMC via an in-band port and process the firmware image. Because the new firmware image is from an untrusted source, the image authentication is required by either the BMC or the BIOS before the flash part is updated with the new image. Figure 3-11 shows the BMC-based OOB update for the BIOS.

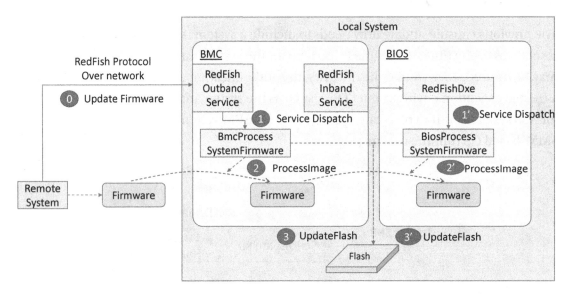

Figure 3-11. *OOB Update*

Intel BIOS Guard

In the preceding solution, the BIOS, the TEE (SMM, TrustZone), or the management controller (BMC) is treated as a root-of-trust for update (RTU). However, they might be a part of a much larger piece of code which might provide a large attack surface and, thus, more potential vulnerabilities. A vulnerability in this RTU may impact the integrity of the firmware. Unfortunately, there have already been actual examples of this happening. For example, attackers broke the capsule coalesce process and updated the BIOS. Attackers compromised the SMM protections and updated the BIOS (ThinkPwn). As such, a smaller RTU is desired so that the attack surface is reduced.

Intel BIOS Guard is a defense in-depth solution for firmware update. It only allows the flash device to be programmed by the Intel BIOS Guard AC module (BGMod) in the SMM environment. This module performs firmware verification and updates in an Authenticated Code RAM (ACRAM) environment. This is designed to prevent issues early in the firmware boot process or SMM from impacting the verification and update flow (see Figure 3-12).

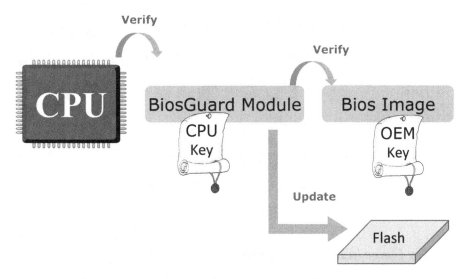

Figure 3-12. *Intel BIOS Guard–Based Firmware Update*

Intel BIOS Guard defines the following data structure (see Figure 3-13):

- BIOS Guard Directory: This is a dynamically built data structure in SMM. It records the address of the BiosGuard module, the BGPDT, the BGUP, and the BGUPC.

- BIOS Guard Platform Data Table (BGPDT): This is a dynamically built data structure in SMM. It records the platform information, secure version number (SVN), embedded controller (EC) descriptor, and signed flash address map (SFAM). The EC descriptor is only required for a platform with an embedded controller (EC).

- BIOS Guard Update Package (BGUP): This includes the BIOS image data and flash update script. It should be created at build time.

- BIOS Guard Update Package Certificate (BGUPC): This is the signing certificate of the BGUP. It should be created at build time.

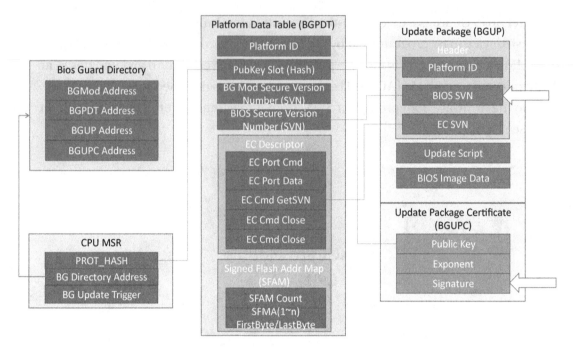

Figure 3-13. *Intel BIOS Guard Diagram*

Table 3-1. *Key Usage in Intel BIOS Guard*

Key	Verifies	Storage	Verified by
BG mod key	BIOS Guard module	CPU	Microcode
BIOS Guard public key	BGUP	CPU MSR PROT_HASH, programmed during boot	BIOS Guard module

Figure 3-14 shows the Intel BIOS Guard–based firmware update. Table 3-1 shows the keys used in Intel BIOS Guard.

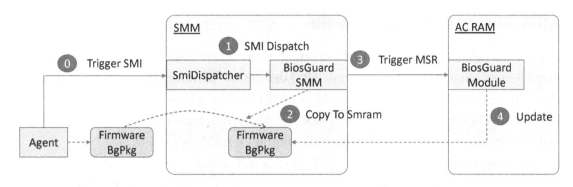

Figure 3-14. *Intel BIOS Guard Flow*

Step 0: The flash update agent loads the BIOS Guard Update Package (BGUP) and Certificate (BGUPC) into memory and triggers SMI.

Step 1: The SMI is processed by the BiosGuardSmm driver.

Step 2: The BiosGuardSmm driver copies the BGUP/BGUPC to SMM RAM (SMRAM) and then creates the Platform Data Table (BGPDT) and BIOS Guard Directory. The BIOS Guard Directory holds the pointers of BGMod/BGPDT/BGUP/BGUPC.

Step 3: The BiosGuardSmm puts the BG Directory to the BG parameter MSR and writes to the BG Update trigger MSR.

Step 4: The CPU verifies the signature of the BiosGuard module. If the verification passes, the CPU loads the BiosGuard module into Authenticated Code RAM (ACRAM). The BiosGuardModule uses the BiosGuardDirectory to get the BGUP and the BGUPC. The BiosGuardModule does the verification based upon the certificate and the version information. Then the BiosGuardModule executes the update script to update the flash region.

Because the final verification and flash update is performed by the BiosGuard module in ACRAM, even if the SMM region is compromised, the verification cannot be bypassed.

Microcode Update

X86 CPUs have on-die microcode and patch RAM that allows for microcode patching or updating. This update can occur during the early boot via features like patch at reset where the microcode patch is discovered by the Firmware Interface Table (FIT). Alternately, the patch may be loaded by the BIOS using, for example, a DXE driver that uses the PI multiprocessor protocol to apply the update for each CPU. Beyond applying the patch from the BIOS, the OS may also apply the patch. As the patch RAM is volatile, the patch update must be executed in all platform boot modes.

ARM Trusted Firmware Update

In the embedded and IoT area, the flash update mechanism is different from the one in traditional client or server platforms. ARM defines the platform security architecture (PSA) for Trusted Boot and Firmware Update (TBFU). It provides the guidance for secure firmware update for ARM systems. Besides the specification, the open source ARM Trusted Firmware is the reference implementation for ARM PSA TBFU.

There are two types of ARM Trusted Firmware in GitHub. Trusted-Firmware-A is for ARM A-profile application processor, and Trusted-Firmware-M is for ARM M-profile microcontroller.

Trusted-Firmware-A defines a set of bootloaders:

- BL1: AP Trusted ROM (S-EL3)

- BL2: Trusted Boot Firmware (S-EL1)

- BL31: EL3 Runtime Software (S-EL3)

- BL32: Secure-EL1 Payload (Trusted OS) (S-EL1)

- BL33: Non-Secure Firmware, such as UEFI or U-Boot

- SCP_BL1: System Control Processor (SCP) Boot ROM

- SCP_BL2: System Control Processor (SCP) RAM Firmware

It also defines a firmware update image:

- BL2U: AP Firmware Update Config

- NS_BL1U: AP Firmware Update Boot ROM

- NS_BL2U: AP Firmware Updater

- SCP_BL2U: System Control Processor (SCP) Firmware Update Config

The detailed trusted boot flow will be described in Chapter 4. Here we just discuss the firmware update–related information.

In the Trusted-Firmware-A, the BL1 is the root-of-trust for update (RTU). The BL1 Boot ROM Secure Monitor Call (SMC) handler supports the firmware update. This handler interacts with the NS_BL1U Non-Secure World Boot ROM to verify BL2U/NS_BL2U/SCP_BL2U. After the verification passes, the BL1 Boot ROM loads the corresponding BL2U to let BL2U do some configuration to complete the firmware update operation. The BL2U image also transfers the SCP_BL2U to SCP RAM and lets SCP_BL2U do some configuration to complete the firmware update operation. Figure 3-15 shows the Trusted-Firmware-A update flow.

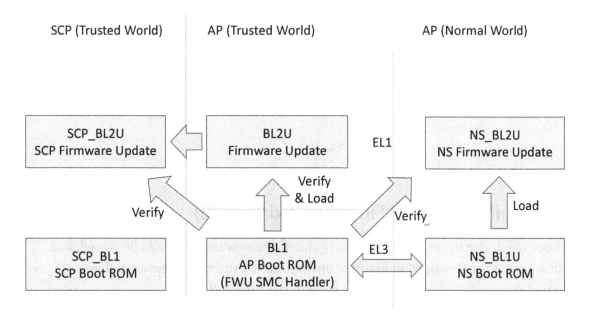

Figure 3-15. *ARM Trusted-Firmware-A Update Support*

The Trusted-Firmware-M uses a different method for firmware update. It defines the following bootloaders:

- BL2 MCUBoot: MCB Boot ROM

- Secure Partition Manager (SPM): Secure World Firmware

- Non-Secure World Firmware

The MCUBoot is the root-of-trust for update (RTU). The flash is divided into the immutable ROM, Slot 0, Slot 1, and the scratch area (see Figure 3-16). The BL2 MCUBoot is in an immutable area. The current image (secure firmware and non-secure firmware) is in an active image – called Slot 0. The new image (secure firmware and non-secure firmware) is put into a staging area – called Slot 1. During the system boot, the BL2 MCUBoot checks if there is a new image in Slot 1 and verifies the new image if it is present. If the new image passes the authentication, the MCUBoot swaps Slot 0 and Slot 1 as the update process.

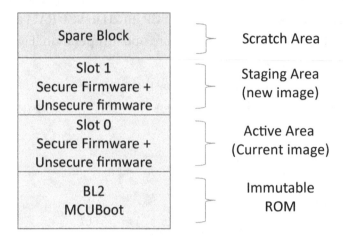

Figure 3-16. *ARM Trusted-Firmware-M Update Support*

Microsoft Component Firmware Update (CFU)

When the device firmware needs to be updated, the new image should be signed, and the update should happen in a trusted environment. Currently, there are different ways to update a device component on the system (see Table 3-2).

Table 3-2. *Component Update Mechanism*

Mechanism	Pros	Cons
Standalone tool	Supports component-specific protocol.	Requires the user to find and download the tool and find out if the update is available and applicable.
UEFI Update Capsule driver	Can be pushed through the OS update process (Windows or Linux).	Can only update the components during boot time, but the components might not be available or attached at that time.
Component-specific update drivers	Can run whenever the device is enumerated.	Bring burden for writing a firmware update driver for each component-specific protocol.

Microsoft defines the component firmware update (CFU) model to unify the different ways to update the device firmware in the OS environment (see Figure 3-17).

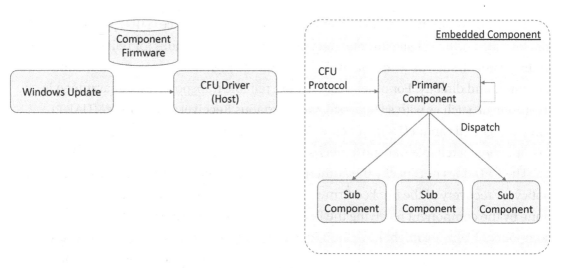

Figure 3-17. *Component Firmware Update*

In CFU, the new component firmware is sent by Windows Update (WU) to the primary component. The primary component may dispatch the new firmware image to the subcomponents to which the component is connected.

The CFU protocol defines a set of commands for the firmware update, as shown in Table 3-3.

Table 3-3. *CFU Command List*

Command	Description
GET_FIRMWARE_VERSION	Gets the current firmware versions of the primary component and its subcomponents.
FIRMWARE_UPDATE_OFFER	Determines whether the primary component accepts or rejects a firmware.
FIRMWARE_UPDATE_OFFER (Information)	Offers information only from the host to the component. It allows the host to provide specific information to the device such as START_OFFER_LIST, END_OFFER_LIST, and START_ENTIRE_TRANSACTION.
FIRMWARE_UPDATE_OFFER (Extended)	Offers command from the host to the device firmware. It allows for extensibility and a way for the host to provide specific information to the device.
FIRMWARE_UPDATE_ CONTENT	Provides the firmware content (i.e., the firmware image). The entire image file is not expected to fit in a single command. The host must split the image into smaller blocks, and each command sends one block of the image at a time.

The CFU command is based upon a Human Interface Device (HID) protocol, and it can be transported via any interconnect buses. If the bus provides for reliable transport in the protocol, such as with USB and Bluetooth, the higher layer can just transmit the command directly. For other buses, where reliable transport is not guaranteed in the protocol, such as with a Universal Asynchronous Receiver/Transmitter (UART), Inter-Integrated Circuit (I2C), or Serial Peripheral Interface (SPI), the higher layer needs to implement a reliable transport mechanism on top of the lower-level protocol.

The CPU does not specify the authentication policy, encryption policy, rollback policy, or recovery of the bricked firmware. The firmware image verification must be done by the component receiving the image instead of by the host CPU driver. Some component firmware might have limited battery power, and downloading firmware might draw a lot of current. As such, the CFU can specify specific properties of the image as part of its offer, such as version, hardware platform, and so on, before it is downloaded. If the component rejects the offer, the downloading can be avoided. But even if the component accepts the offer, the downloaded image may be rejected later due to integrity verification failure.

The whole update flow is shown in Figure 3-18.

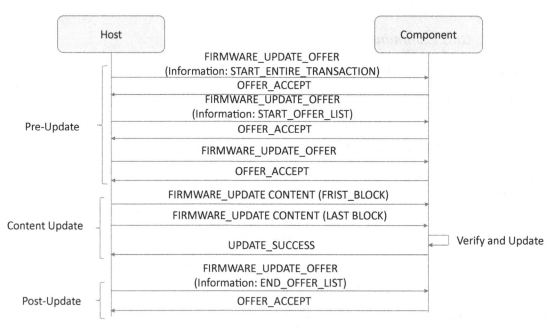

Figure 3-18. *Component Firmware Update Flow*

Project Cerberus

On a server platform, Project Cerberus addresses the firmware protection, detection, and recovery. With Cerberus solution, the firmware flash area is divided into three areas: active, recovery, and staging areas (see Figure 3-19). The active area is to store working firmware. The recovery area is to store the recovery image. The staging area is a scratch buffer to put any new content. If the BIOS flash image or BMC image needs to be updated, an update application puts the new image into the staging area and triggers a platform reset. In the next boot, the Cerberus chip detects the new image in the staging area. Then the Cerberus chip does the new firmware image authentication and updates the new image to the active area if the authentication passes. That image update happens before any BIOS or BMC code running when the Cerberus is the only master of the flash chip.

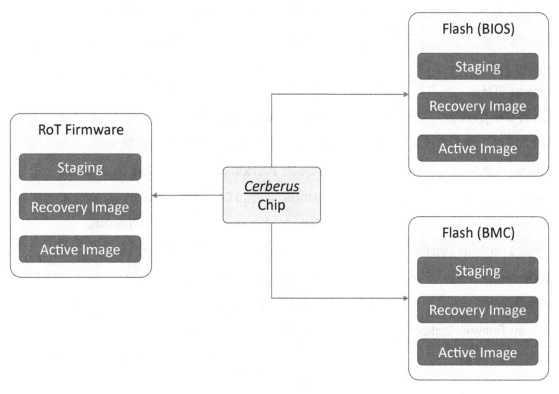

Figure 3-19. *Cerberus Image Layout*

Besides the BIOS and BMC firmware, the Cerberus defines a set of root-of-trust (RoT) commands that can be used to support device firmware update (see Table 3-4).

Table 3-4. *Cerberus RoT Command List*

Register Name	RoT	Description
Get PFM ID	PA	Get Platform Firmware Manifest (PFM) information.
Get PFM Supported	PA	Retrieve the PFM.
Prepare PFM	PA	Prepare PFM payload on Platform Active Root-of-Trust (PA-RoT).
Update PFM	PA	Set the PFM.
Activate PFM	PA	Force activation of supplied PFM.
Get CFM ID	PA	Get Component Firmware Manifest (CFM) ID.
Prepare CFM	PA	Prepare component manifest update.
Update CFM	PA	Update component manifest.
Activate CFM	PA	Activate Component Firmware Manifest update.
Get CFM Supported	PA	Retrieve supported CFM IDs.
Get PCD ID	PA	Get Platform Configuration Data (PCD) ID.
Prepare PCD	PA	Prepare Platform Configuration Data (PCD) update.
Update PCD	PA	Update Platform Configuration Data.
Activate PCD	PA	Activate Platform Configuration Data update.
Prepare Firmware Update	PA	Prepare for receiving the firmware image.
Update Firmware	PA	Firmware update payload.
Update Status	PA	PFM/CFM/DFM status.
Activate Firmware Update	PA	Activate received FW update.
Get Config IDs	PA/AC	Get manifest IDs and signed digest of request nonce and response IDs.

The device firmware image update takes the following steps (see Figure 3-20):

1) Send new image: First, the new image must be put to the staging area. This is done by RoT commands "Prepare Firmware Update" and "Update Firmware." Since the image verification will be done later, no verification is required in these commands.

2) Activate update: This is done by the RoT command "Activate Firmware Update." After the image is put to staging area, the device can be notified to use the new image. The device needs to verify the new image in the staging area and copy the new image into the active area only after the verification passes. After the update is complete, the RoT will start running the new image. The current context will be retained, and no reset is required ideally. Any active session should still be active, and the boot-time initialization will not be rerun.

Other component updates include these:

1) Signing certificate update: A firmware update may involve a signing certificate update. If the certificate is revoked, the firmware image must be signed with a new certificate. Care must be taken for the recovery image. If the recovery image is signed with an old certificate, this recovery image will become invalid once the old certificate is revoked. As such, the recovery image must also be updated when the certificate is revoked.

2) Recovery image update: A firmware update may carry some additional options, for example, force updating the recovery image. If this option is used, then the image in the recovery area is updated. The recovery image can be updated via "Prepare Recovery Image," "Update Recovery Image," and "Activate Recovery Image" commands.

3) Platform Firmware Manifest (PFM) update: The Cerberus RoT firmware accesses a manifest detailing the firmware allowed for the other devices in the platform. That manifest is called PFM. As new firmware becomes available for these components, the PFM needs to be updated for those components, but there is

no need to update the entire Cerberus firmware to achieve this update. Therefore, Cerberus IoT provides commands to only update PFM. Updating PFM is similar to updating the firmware image. The new PFM must be sent via "Prepare PFM Update" and "Update PFM" commands. After the device receives the "Activate PFM" command, the device verifies the new PFM and copies it to the active PFM area.

4) Component Firmware Manifest (CFM) update: To manage attestation for component devices, a PA-RoT needs information about these devices. The CFM is the configuration file that provides this information. Management of CFMs happens in a very similar way to PFM management.

5) Platform Configuration Data (PCD) update: The PCD provides static information that is specific to a platform that Cerberus RoT firmware needs to operate correctly. Management of this configuration data is very similar to PFM management.

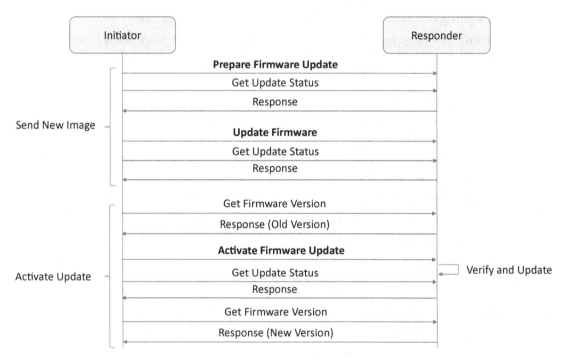

Figure 3-20. *Cerberus Firmware Update*

FPGA Bitstream Download

An Field Programmable Gate Array (FPGA) bitstream is a file that contains the programming information for an FPGA. During the FPGA development phase, we need to download a bitstream to an FPGA device to make it behave as the expected hardware device. In order to maintain the confidentiality for the hardware intelligent property (IP) and the integrity and authenticity of the FPGA device, the FPGA bitstream is encrypted and appended with a message authentication code (MAC). The FPGA device includes a configuration engine. This engine will decrypt the bitstream and check the MAC of the bitstream and then program to the FPGA fabric. See Figure 3-21.

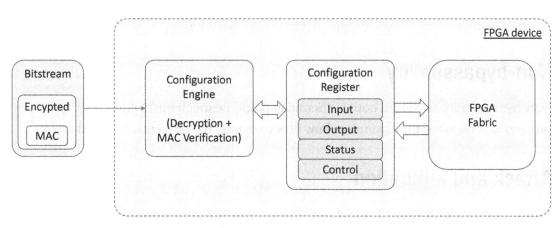

Figure 3-21. *FPGA Bitstream Decryption and Verification*

Integrity Protection

Integrity protection means to lock the flash part, protecting it from writes or erases if the platform is not in the update boot mode or the recovery mode. The lock shall happen as early as possible, at least no later than any third party's code running. Today, flash controllers and flash chips define sets of lock registers to lock the whole flash chip or parts of a flash chip. Those lock registers shall be set during the system boot. The main purpose of those lock registers is to resist the software attack.

The hardware attack to the updatable firmware should also be considered, and it is even more challenging. In order to support local physical recovery, most system firmware on a SPI chip can be updated with a flash programmer. As such, we may have to leverage the detection and recovery to resist the hardware attack.

Case Study

Now, let's take a look at some real cases for protecting the flash part integrity.

BIOS Write Protection

Some silicon registers are locked at boot and only unlocked after the next system reset. Some silicon registers are locked in the normal execution environment and can be unlocked in a trusted execution environment, such as system management mode (SMM) or Authenticated Code RAM (ACRAM). This update only in the trusted execution environment (TEE) is designed for runtime update.

See Chapter 18 for details on silicon secure configuration.

Non-bypassability

Non-bypassability applies to both authenticated update mechanism and integrity protection. The following examples show how to bypass the authenticated update.

Attack and Mitigation

Now, let's take a look at some actual cases for the attack to the updatable firmware and mitigation.

No Lock, No Authentication

In early days, the firmware update was considered an advanced topic. Only a few people knew how to do firmware updates. Updating firmware with the wrong firmware image might brick the system. As such, the flash was not locked, and the firmware update was not authenticated. We had seen lots of small IoT devices that took this approach, such as Embedded Controllers (EC), Human Interface Device (HID) keyboards, printers, routers, and so on. The device is not locked, and the device update may happen in any environment. The reason might be to make it easy for update by the end user. But it also makes it easy for an attacker. In some implementations, even a platform Root-of-Trust with a Field Programmable Gate Array (FPGA) or Complex Programmable Logic Device (CPLD) may be updated without authentication.

Data Used Before Verification

Ideally, if there is a way to verify the data, the data should be verified before it is used. In Xilinx 7-Series FPGAs, the bitstream is interpreted by the configuration engine before the MAC validation. As such, the attacker can modify the bitstream to let the configuration engine do something. Unfortunately, the Xilinx FPGA has a non-volatile register – WBSTAR – which will not be cleared to 0 by the reset procedure. In the starbleed attack, the attacker modified the bitstream to let FPGA write the decrypted data into the WBSTAR content and then reset the FPGA. Then the malicious program can read the decrypted data out from the WBSTAR register. With one reset, the attacker can read out 32-bit decrypted data. When they repeat the attack, all decrypted data can be read out. This is the first phase of the starbleed attack. See Figure 3-22.

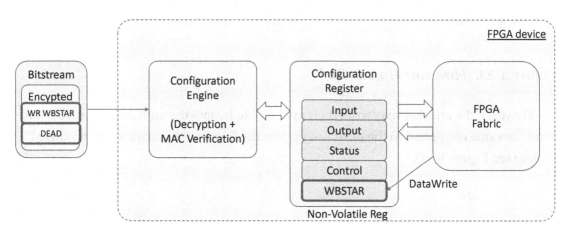

Figure 3-22. *FPGA Starbleed Attack*

In the second phase, the attack can get the MAC key because it is included in the encrypted data. Once the data is decrypted, the MAC key is also exposed. Then the attack can construct a valid bitstream with the correct MAC key to break the authenticity.

Authentication or Update in Non-TEE

Even if a vendor implemented authentication, the environment to do the authentication might be wrong. Authentication or update in a non-secure environment is as bad as no authentication. The reason is that the authentication can be bypassed easily or the update may be vulnerable to a Time-of-Check/Time-of-Use (TOC/TOU) attack.

For example, a vendor may implement an OS update tool and perform the authentication in the OS and then send the command to the device to update the firmware (see Figure 3-23). It is easy to enable such a solution without adding additional complexity in the device.

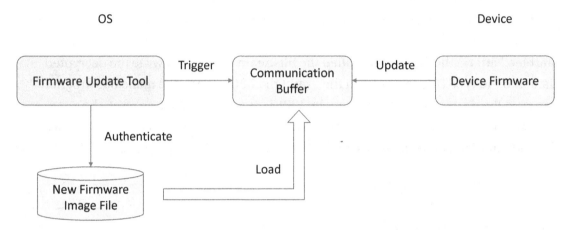

Figure 3-23. *Firmware Update Tool*

However, the attacker may write their own tool to bypass the authentication flow and send the same command to the device to update the firmware but with a compromised image (see Figure 3-24).

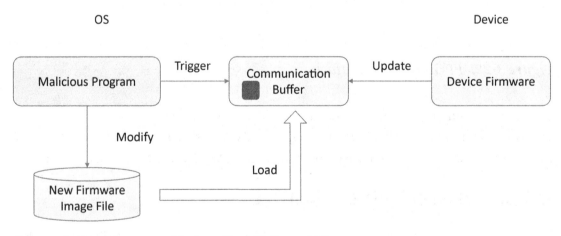

Figure 3-24. *Firmware Update Tool Vulnerability*

Unlock and Update Separation

Ideally, the device firmware should be locked by the root-of-trust and only be unlocked by the root-of-trust. The authentication and update are an atomic operation from the untrusted environment perspective. However, some implementations may separate the unlock and update operations into two commands (see Figure 3-25).

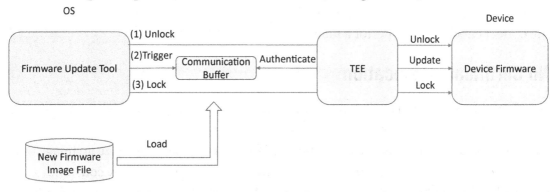

Figure 3-25. *Firmware Update Unlock API*

That allows a possible attack where the attacker just sends the unlock command to the device, which bypasses the authentication and then sends a malicious image to the device to update the firmware in an untrusted environment (see Figure 3-26).

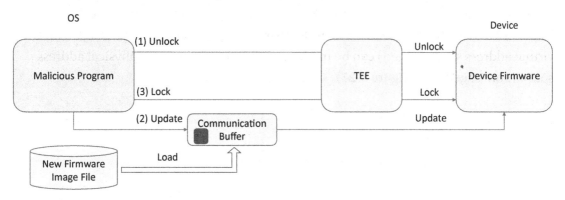

Figure 3-26. *Firmware Update Unlock API Vulnerability*

Weak Integrity Check

To verify the integrity of the firmware, the digital signature shall be present. However, implementing a signature verification in the device might add additional hardware logic and additional cost. Some vendors just use a single checksum verification or a cyclic redundancy check (CRC) to verify the image. The problem is that checksums or CRCs are meaningless from a security perspective, because it is trivial for the attacker to reproduce the correct checksum or CRC for a malicious image.

No Certificate Revocation

Certificate revocation is a challenging topic, especially when a device might not have Internet access. That makes it almost impossible to use the Online Certificate Status Protocol (OCSP) to check the status of a certificate used to authorize an image. Certificate Revocation Lists (CRLs) might be a possible way, but they may consume too much non-volatile storage memory to store the whole list. These lists might also be vulnerable to a configuration rollback attack. A passive update should be required in order to keep the certification always up to date.

Malformed Input

The update image is input from the OS. It might include the additional data structures to describe the image. For example, UEFI capsule images are a data structure that implements a scatter/gather list. It helps to restructure the image so that its layout in a virtual address space (paged) can be mapped to the same layout in a physical address space (non-paged) (see Figure 3-27).

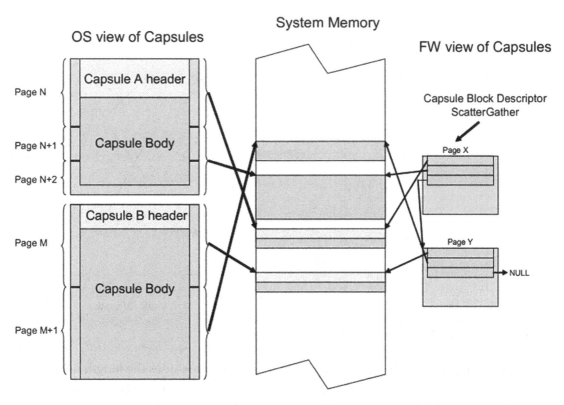

Figure 3-27. *UEFI Capsule Layout in Memory (Source: UEFI Specification)*

In runtime, the scattered list needs to be coalesced into a continuous memory (see Figure 3-28). This work is performed by the PeiCapsulePei driver.

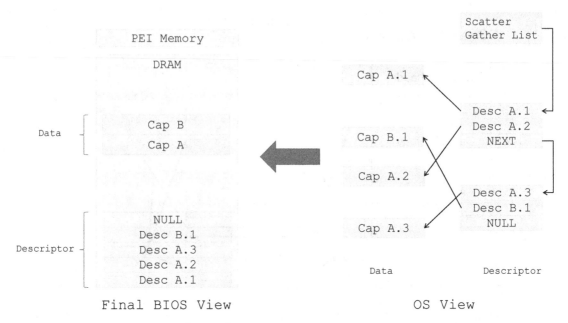

Figure 3-28. *UEFI Capsule Coalesce*

The scatter/gather list is a good attack point because it includes the length field and the address field. Giving an invalid address field may cause the CPU to generate an exception. Giving an invalid length field may cause an integer overflow or buffer overflow and get control from attack or shellcode. For example, Listing 3-1 from the capsule coalesce has an integer overflow issue.

Listing 3-1.

```
===========================
EFI_STATUS
EFIAPI
CapsuleDataCoalesce (
  IN EFI_PEI_SERVICES           **PeiServices,
  IN EFI_PHYSICAL_ADDRESS       *BlockListBuffer,
  IN MEMORY_RESOURCE_DESCRIPTOR *MemoryResource,
  IN OUT VOID                   **MemoryBase,
  IN OUT UINTN                  *MemorySize
  )
```

```
{
  //...
    if (*MemorySize <= (CapsuleSize + DescriptorsSize)) {
      return EFI_BUFFER_TOO_SMALL;
    }
  //...
}

EFI_STATUS
GetCapsuleInfo (
  IN EFI_CAPSULE_BLOCK_DESCRIPTOR    *Desc,
  IN OUT UINTN                       *NumDescriptors OPTIONAL,
  IN OUT UINTN                       *CapsuleSize OPTIONAL,
  IN OUT UINTN                       *CapsuleNumber OPTIONAL
  )
{
//  ...
    } else {
      Size += (UINTN) Desc->Length;
      Count++;
  ...
}
==========================
```

With this vulnerability, the attacker may construct a malicious capsule block descriptor and finally get control in the PEI phase (see Figure 3-29). The details of this exploit are discussed in "Extreme Privilege Escalation on Windows 8/UEFI Systems."

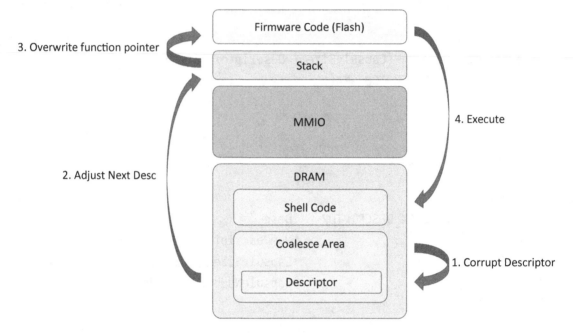

Figure 3-29. *Attacking UEFI Capsule Coalesce*

To mitigate this threat, before the code performs the addition, the code must use the subtraction to check if the addition will cause an integer overflow (see Figure 3-30). Also, we shall define a valid memory range and limit the capsule block descriptor only to reference memory in the valid memory range.

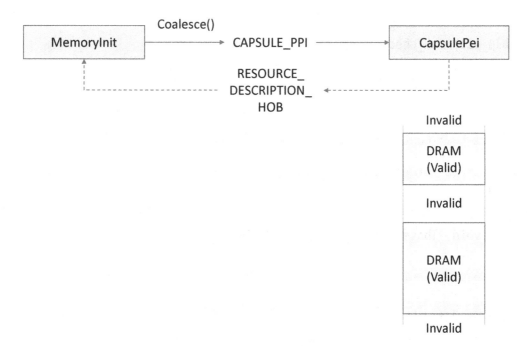

Figure 3-30. *Mitigation in UEFI Capsule Coalesce*

Malformed input is also a threat for ARM Trusted Firmware. For example, Trusted-Firmware-A had a similar problem previously. The attacker may input a large value for `block_size`, and this could result in an integer overflow, thus causing an unexpected large memory copy from the nonsecure world into the secure world (see Listing 3-2).

Listing 3-2.

```
============================
/*
 * If last block is more than expected then
 * clip the block to the required image size.
 */
if (image_desc->copied_size + block_size >
    image_desc->image_info.image_size) {
  block_size = image_desc->image_info.image_size -
      image_desc->copied_size;
  WARN("BL1-FWU: Copy argument block_size > remaining image size."
      " Clipping block_size\n");
}
```

```
/* Make sure the image src/size is mapped. */
if (bl1_plat_mem_check(image_src, block_size, flags)) {
    WARN("BL1-FWU: Copy arguments source/size not mapped\n");
    return -ENOMEM;
}

INFO("BL1-FWU: Continuing image copy in blocks\n");

/* Copy image for given block size. */
base_addr += image_desc->copied_size;
image_desc->copied_size += block_size;
memcpy((void *)base_addr, (const void *)image_src, block_size);
...
```

============================

Rollback Attack

Updating to an earlier firmware image is called rollback. The rollback attack entails an update to an earlier firmware image which contains a known security issue. To mitigate a rollback attack, the system needs to maintain a firmware security version number (SVN). The SVN might be different from the normal firmware version. A new firmware image always has a new version. If the new firmware does not include any security fixes, the security version might be the same as the previous one. Once the new firmware fixes a security issue, the security version must be increased. During the authentication update process, the root-of-trust for update (RTU) code must validate the new firmware security version. If the new security version is lower than the current security version, the update request must be rejected (see Figure 3-31). The security version shall be included in the firmware image with signing protected or be in trusted storage.

Take Qualcomm Achilles vulnerability as example. The attacker can load an old signed library to the Qualcomm Hexagon DSP device, because the DSP only performs the signature verification but no version check or key revocation. Then the attacker can send a malicious payload to the vulnerable library in DSP to gain the persistency.

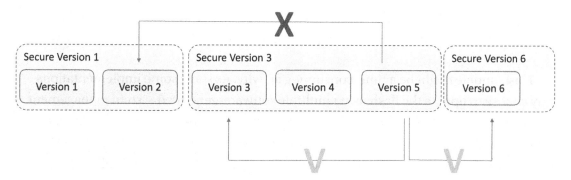

Figure 3-31. *Mitigation for Rollback Attack*

TOC/TOU Attack

Time-of-Check/Time-of-Use (TOC/TOU) is a typical attack to bypass the authentication check. Some of the authentication checks may happen in a trusted execution environment (such as SMM). If the check handler checks the image outside of the trusted environment, the attacker may modify the image after the check and before the new image is updated to non-volatile storage (see Figure 3-32).

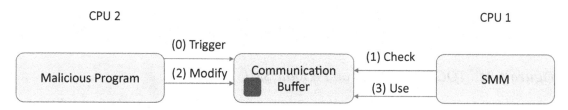

Figure 3-32. *TOC/TOU Attack on SMM Communication Buffer*

To mitigate this, the check handler must copy the image into the trusted environment and then perform the check and update immediately (see Figure 3-33).

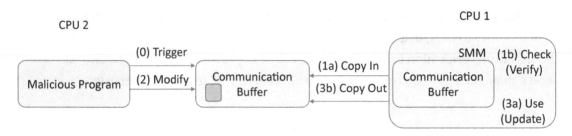

Figure 3-33. *Mitigation for TOC/TOU Attack on SMM Communication Buffer*

Flash update might be a time-consuming activity. As such, some implementations may choose to update the flash using multiple software-generated system management interrupts (SMIs). In each of the SMI activations, the flash update handler just updates a portion of the flash area. An improper implementation may allow another TOC/TOU attack. If the handler to check and the handler to use are separated, the malicious program may modify the image in the communication buffer after it has been checked and then trigger the second SMI. Then the handler will update the modified image to the flash (see Figure 3-34).

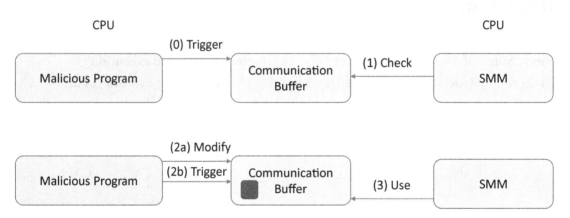

Figure 3-34. *TOC/TOU Attack on Periodic SMI*

To mitigate such an attack, the handler must copy the image to the trusted execution environment (TEE) to do the check. Then in the rest of the SMI, the handler to update the flash area shall always use the TEE internal copy. As such, the modification to the communication buffer will not be used (see Figure 3-35).

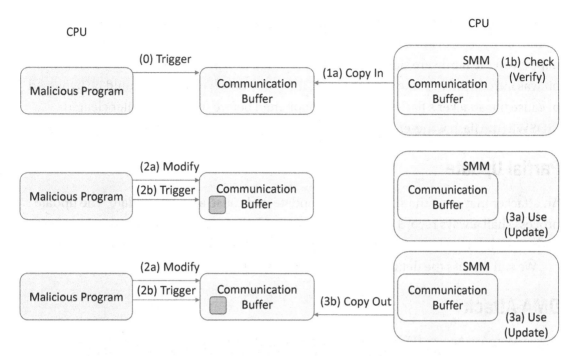

Figure 3-35. *Mitigation for TOC/TOU Attack on Periodic SMI*

Race Condition Attack

The hardware lock register may have a race condition problem. In the trusted execution environment, the lock register may be unlocked to perform runtime update. If another CPU is running in the non-trusted execution environment, this CPU may run some code to update the flash chip without authentication (see Figure 3-36). If we need to unlock a register in a trusted environment, we need make sure all the processors are in the trusted environment.

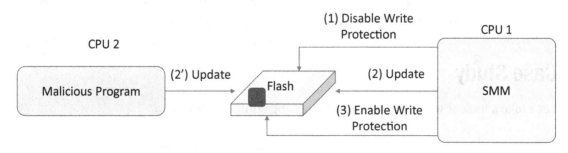

Figure 3-36. *Race Condition Attack on SMM-Based Flash Protection*

Besides firmware, the hardware design also needs to guarantee the protection cannot be bypassed. SpeedRacer is an example showing that the race condition may happen on the hardware side if the flash protection is bypassed. Before the SMM_BWP bit was introduced in some Intel chipsets, the SMM-based protection could be bypassed because the attacker's flash write access happened before the SMI handler cleared BIOSWE (the flash write-enable control bit).

Partial Update

An attacker may reset the system during update and cause a partial update. The update process shall always record the current status, and this information is used for recovery in the next boot.

We will discuss the detailed recovery support in Chapter 5.

DMA Attack

Direct Memory Access (DMA) attacks are another way to bypass the update security. After the host CPU authenticates the update image, the malicious device can generate a DMA transaction to modify the memory of the update image before the CPU sends the command to update the non-volatile storage with the new image. In the real world, PCILeech is an open source tool to perform DMA attacks. The mitigation is to make sure that the image is in DMA-protected memory or that all device DMA is blocked during the update.

We will discuss the details of a DMA attack and mitigations in Chapter 8.

Configurable Data

User-configurable data is designed to be updatable by the end user. We cannot protect it by signing and verification, but we can do some other checks for it.

Case Study

Let's take a look at some actual cases protecting configuration data.

User Authentication

The system BIOS setup configuration is probably the most common user-configurable data. For example, a user may change the boot option from "boot from hard drive" to "boot from USB device." A user may set a password for entering the setup page. As such, only the authenticated users may enter the setup page and modify the configuration.

We will discuss the details of the user authentication in Chapter 10.

User Confirmation

User confirmation is a method to make sure the configuration is from a local user instead of a remote user or a program. For example, the Trusted Platform Module (TPM) owner clear is one possible configuration action in the OS environment. However, a compromised OS may set the TPM owner clear. To protect the TPM from an attack in the OS, the "TPM owner clear" command in the OS is just a request. The real TPM owner clear action happens during the next boot. The firmware detects the request and shows the detailed request information on the screen to let a local user confirm. If the local user accepts the change request, the TPM owner clear happens. If the local user rejects the change request, the TPM owner clear does not happen.

We will discuss the details of the TCG Physical Presence in Chapter 7.

Configuration Correctness Check

No matter whether user authentication is used or not, we may do a correctness check to see if the format of the new setting is valid. The reason is that this configuration may be saved in a normal UEFI variable and exposed in the OS or for the remote configuration via an out-of-band (OOB) channel. For example, the user may set the hard drive controller to disabled, legacy Integrated Drive Electronics (IDE) mode, Serial ATA Advanced Host Controller Interface (AHCI) mode, or Redundant Arrays of Independent Drives (RAID) mode. As such, the hard drive controller mode may only be configured as an integer – 0 (disable), 1 (legacy IDE), 5 (AHCI), or 6 (RAID). Then setting the mode to 4 or a string is considered as an invalid configuration, and it must be rejected.

We will discuss the details of the UEFI variable configuration correctness check in Chapter 11.

Configuration Variable Lock

Besides user configuration variables, the system may need to record the current platform data for the next boot, such as the memory initialization training data. Memory training is time-consuming, and the training data is the same across the warm reset or S3 resume. As such, there is no need to train the memory again. We may save the training data to non-volatile storage and restore the configuration directly during a warm reset or S3 resume.

How can we make sure the configuration data is not modified by other entities? The easiest way is just to lock the variable to make it unchangeable after some point in the time.

We will discuss the details of the UEFI variable configuration lock in Chapter 11.

Secure by Default

Secure by default is one of the fundamental security principles. The system must be in a secure state if the default configuration is used. As an example, review the TCG memory override (MOR) feature. In this feature, the TCG group defined a UEFI variable – L"M emoryOverwriteRequestControl": MEMORY_ONLY_RESET_CONTROL_GUID. This variable indicates to the platform that secrets are present in memory and that the platform firmware must clear memory upon a reset. In some corner cases, such as the first boot after flash image update, the variable might not be present. The platform needs to act as if a MOR request is present and always clear memory.

Attack and Mitigation

Now, let's take a look at some real cases for the attack to the configuration data and mitigation.

Flash Wear-Out Attack

Since the users are free to set the configuration at any time, the malicious attacker may change the configuration in a dramatic way and trigger the flash erase again and again. When the number of flash erases reaches the limit, the flash is unusable. In order to prevent this from happening, the erase shall be disabled at OS runtime. As such, the attacker has to boot the system again and again to perform the wear-out attack.

We will discuss the details of the flash wear-out protection in Chapter 11.

Summary

In this chapter, we discussed the first part of the firmware resiliency – protection. We described different types of protection for the immutable ROM, the updatable firmware, and the configuration data. In the next chapter, we will continue the discussion on the second part of the firmware resiliency – detection.

References

Conference, Journal, and Paper

[P-1] Rob Spiger, "TCG Cyber Resilient Technologies," TCG 2019, https://trustedcomputinggroup.org/wp-content/uploads/TCG-Cyber-Resilient-Technologies-%E2%80%93-Rob-Spiger-Microsoft.pdf

[P-2] Ronald Aigner, Paul England, Andrey Marochko, Dennis Mattoon, Rob Spiger, Stefan Thom, "Cyber-Resilient Platform Requirements," Microsoft Whitepaper, 2017, available at www.microsoft.com/en-us/research/publication/cyber-resilient-platform-requirements/

[P-3] Paul England, Ronald Aigner, Andrey Marochko, Dennis Mattoon, Rob Spiger, Stefan Thom, "Cyber-Resilient Platforms Overview," Microsoft Whitepaper, 2017, available at www.microsoft.com/en-us/research/publication/cyber-resilient-platforms-overview/

[P-4] Zachary Bobroff, "Secure Firmware Update," in *UEFI Plugfest 2012*, available at https://uefi.org/learning_center/presentationsandvideos

[P-5] Jiewen Yao, Vincent Zimmer, "A Tour Beyond BIOS- Capsule Update and Recovery in EDK II," Intel whitepaper, 2016, available at https://github.com/tianocore/tianocore.github.io/wiki/EDK-II-Security-White-Papers

[P-6] Bing Sun, "BIOS Boot Hijacking," in *Power of Community 2007*, available at http://powerofcommunity.net/poc2007/sunbing.pdf

[P-7] K. Chen, "Reversing and exploiting an Apple firmware update," in *Blackhat US 2009*, available at www.blackhat.com/presentations/bh-usa-09/CHEN/BHUSA09-Chen-RevAppleFirm-SLIDES.pdf

[P-8] Ralf-Philipp Weinmann, "The hidden nemesis," in *27th Chaos Communication Congress (27C3) 2010*, available at https://comsecuris.com/slides/rpw-27c3-thmbec.pdf

[P-9] Ang Cui, Salvatore Stolfo, "Print me if you dare," in *COMMUNICATIVE EVENTS 2011*, available at https://academiccommons.columbia.edu/doi/10.7916/D8QJ7RG3

[P-10] Charlie Miller, "Battery Firmware Hacking," in *BlackHat US 2011*, available at https://media.blackhat.com/bh-us-11/Miller/ BH_US_11_Miller_Battery_Firmware_Public_Slides.pdf

[P-11] Mickey Shkatov, Jesse Michael, "Scared Poopless – LTE and *your* laptop," DEFCON 23, 2015, https://paper.seebug.org/papers/Security%20Conf/Defcon/2015/ DEFCON-23-Mickey-Shkatov-Jesse-Michael-Scared-poopless-LTE-a.pdf

[P-12] Corey Kallenberg, Xeno Kovah, John Butterworth, Sam Cornwell, "Extreme Privilege Escalation on Windows 8 UEFI System," in *Blackhat US 2014*, available at www.mitre.org/sites/default/files/publications/ 14-2221-extreme-escalation-presentation.pdf

[P-13] Corey Kallenberg, Rafal Wojtczuk, "Speed Racer: Exploiting an Intel Flash Protection Race Condition," in *Congress 2014*, available at https://fahrplan.events.ccc.de/congress/2014/Fahrplan/system/ attachments/2565/original/speed_racer_whitepaper.pdf

[P-14] Alex Matrosov, Alexandre Gazet, "Breaking Through Another Side," in *Blackhat US 2019*, available at http://i.blackhat.com/USA-19/Thursday/us-19- Matrosov-Breaking-Through-Another-Side-Bypassing-Firmware-Security- Boundaries-From-Embedded-Controller.pdf

[P-15] Sheila Ayelen Berta , "Backdooring Hardware Devices by Injecting Malicious Payloads on Microcontrollers," in Blackhat US 2019, available at http://i.blackhat. com/USA-19/Thursday/us-19-Berta-Backdooring-Hardware-Devices-By-Injecting- Malicious-Payloads-On-Microcontrollers.pdf

[P-16] Jatin Kataria, Rick Housley, Joseph Pantoga, Ang Cui, "Defeating cisco trust anchor: A case-study of recent advancements in direct FPGA bitstream manipulation," in USENIX, WOOT 2019, available at www.usenix.org/system/files/ woot19-paper_kataria_0.pdf

[P-17] Maik Ender, Amir Moradi, Christof Paar, "The Unpatchable Silicon: A Full Break of the Bitstream Encryption of Xilinx 7-Series FPGAs," in USENIX 2020, available at www.usenix.org/system/files/sec20fall_ender_prepub.pdf, https://bit.ly/ Starbleed

[P-18] Trammell Hudson, "SPISPY: open source SPI flash emulator," in CCC Camp 2019, https://trmm.net/Spispy, https://github.com/osresearch/spispy

[P-19] David Garske, Daniele Lacamera, "wolfSSL – Secure Bootloader," in *RISC-V Workshop*, 2019, https://riscv.org/wp-content/uploads/2019/06/13.55-RISC-V- Workshop-Secure-Bootloader.pdf

Specification and Guideline

[S-1] NIST SP800-193, "Platform Firmware Resiliency Guidelines," 2018, available at `https://csrc.nist.gov/publications/sp800`

[S-2] NIST SP800-147B, "BIOS Protection Guidelines for Servers," 2014, available at `https://csrc.nist.gov/publications/sp800`

[S-3] NIST SP800-147, "BIOS Protection Guidelines," 2011, available at `https://csrc.nist.gov/publications/sp800`

[S-4] IETF, "Software Update for Internet of Things (SUIT) Architecture," 2019, available at `https://datatracker.ietf.org/group/suit/documents/`

[S-5] Trusted Computing Group, "TCG Guidance for Secure Update of Software and Firmware on Embedded Systems," 2019, available at `https://trustedcomputinggroup.org/resource/tcg-guidance-for-secure-update-of-software-and-firmware-on-embedded-systems/`

[S-6] DMTF org, "Platform Level Data Model (PLDM) for Firmware Update Specification," 2018, available at `www.dmtf.org/standards/pmci`

[S-7] OCP, "Project Cerberus Architecture Overview Specification," 2018, available at `https://github.com/opencomputeproject/Project_Olympus/blob/master/Project_Cerberus`

[S-8] OCP, "Project Cerberus Firmware Challenge Specification," 2019, available at `https://github.com/opencomputeproject/Project_Olympus/blob/master/Project_Cerberus`

[S-9] OCP, "Project Cerberus Firmware Update Specification," 2019, available at `https://github.com/opencomputeproject/Project_Olympus/blob/master/Project_Cerberus`

[S-10] OCP, "Project Cerberus Processor Cryptography Specification," 2018, available at `https://github.com/opencomputeproject/Project_Olympus/blob/master/Project_Cerberus`

Web

[W-1] "Windows UEFI firmware update platform," available at `https://docs.microsoft.com/en-us/windows-hardware/drivers/bringup/windows-uefi-firmware-update-platform`

[W-2] "Microsoft Component Firmware Update," available at `https://github.com/Microsoft/CFU`

[W-3] Linux Vendor Firmware Service (LVFS), available at LVFS: `https://fwupd.org`

[W-4] The Update Framework (TUF): `https://theupdateframework.github.io/`

[W-5] ThinkPwn, `http://blog.cr4.sh/2016/06/`
`exploring-and-exploiting-lenovo.html`

[W-6] ARM Trusted Firmware A, available at `https://github.com/ARM-software/`
`arm-trusted-firmware/`

[W-7] ARM Trusted Firmware M, available at `https://git.trustedfirmware.org/`
`trusted-firmware-m.git/`

[W-8] Xilinx, "Using Encryption to Secure a 7 Series FPGA Bitstream,"
2018, `www.xilinx.com/support/documentation/application_notes/`
`xapp1239-fpga-bitstream-encryption.pdf`

CHAPTER 4

Firmware Resiliency: Detection

Detection is the second element in firmware resiliency. Even if we use multiple ways to protect the firmware, a vulnerability in software or hardware may still cause the firmware component to be modified or corrupted. As such, we need to have a way to inform the root-of-trust for detection (RTD) to perform the integrity detection in the boot flow. The detection may happen for the mutable code and data components or just the configurable data. Similar to protection, the main threat is from both the software attacker and the hardware attacker.

Secure Boot

The detection is done by the RTD or the Chain-of-Trust for detection (CTD). When using the RTD, the RTD verifies all platform components at the same time. With the CTD, the boot components are checked one by one. Every new component is verified by the current component so that it is trusted. This flow is also called secure boot. If the verification of a new component fails, the current component knows that the system is under an attack. In this case, the current component will stop booting the new component and may start the recovery process.

Detectability

As a prerequisite, when the RTD or CTD does the verification check, it must protect itself and the policy to identify the attack (such as hash value or public certificate) by using one of the mechanisms introduced in the previous chapter. If the attack happens, the RTD or CTD needs to have the capability to detect the attack. For example, if a hash is used to check the layer X firmware component, this hash must be kept in a layer (x-1) firmware component.

© Jiewen Yao and Vincent Zimmer 2020
J. Yao and V. Zimmer, *Building Secure Firmware*, https://doi.org/10.1007/978-1-4842-6106-4_4

The RTD or CTD must also have a way to distinguish the attacked state from the good state. A digital signature (such as Rivest-Shamir-Adleman [RSA] or SM2) or a cryptographic hash (such as SHA or SM3) is a good way, while a checksum or a cyclic redundancy check (CRC) is a bad way. The attacker may be able to create a correct checksum or CRC, but the hacker cannot easily create a digital signature without knowing the private key or create the same hash value with the modified content. Symmetric encryption (such as AES) is another good way to provide the detectability proof. One downside compared with the digital signature and the hash is the encrypted firmware code cannot support execution in place (XIP), which is a requirement for some early boot code. As such, the encryption option only has limited usage. See Table 4-1 for a more detailed comparison of these different options.

Table 4-1. *Detectability for Secure Boot*

Mechanism	Pros	Cons	TCB	Example
Digital signature	It provides XIP capability. PKCS7 may provide flexibility for crypto agility. New component update requires no RTD update.	If the PKCS7 schema is used, the algorithm may require more resources to perform the verification task.	Verification code + the public key or its hash.	UEFI secure boot Project Cerberus Google verified boot Apple secure boot Intel Authenticated Code Module (ACM)
Hash	It supports XIP. Algorithm is simple. Suitable for the resource-constrained environment.	Hash value needs an update if the new component is updated.	Verification code + the hash value of the new component.	Intel Boot Guard
Encryption	It provides additional confidentiality. New component update requires no RTD update.	It cannot support XIP code.	Verification code + the encryption key	Intel microcode patch Intel BIOS Guard module Some IOT boot firmware FPGA bitstream

Version

In order to prevent a rollback attack, the secure version number (SVN) check is required. The SVN number of the new component must be equal to or greater than the current SVN. The current SVN information must be stored in the non-volatile memory of the RTD. It could be stored in the initial Boot ROM or some trusted storage, such as a TPM.

Policy Revocation

Sometimes there might be multiple secure boot policies stored in the RTD. For example, the UEFI secure boot feature defines a signature certificate database. This database includes a set of public certificates. If the certificate of the UEFI image matches any of the certificates in this database, the verification passes. However, some certificates may be considered as invalid later. In this case, we need a way to revoke an invalid certificate. One possible way is just to remove the certificate from the original database. Removal is complicated because we need to read the larger database out, remove the invalid entry, and then write the new database. The UEFI specification defines another way: a forbidden signature certificate database. This forbidden database holds any revoked certificate. As such, when we need to revoke an old certificate, we just need to append this to the forbidden database.

Non-bypassability

The detection process must not be bypassed. The detection must happen in all possible boot paths, including normal boot, S3 resume, S4 resume, warm reboot, code reboot, firmware update mode, recovery mode, and even manufacturing mode or "safe" mode. During the detection phase, the protection shall be applied at the same time. For example, the system must enable the IOMMU to prevent a DMA attack. Without DMA protections, the attacker may attach a device such as the PCILeech device and update the firmware code after it has passed the verification.

Another way to bypass the detection is to use a Time-of-Check/Time-of-Use (TOC/TOU) attack against the firmware flash device. After the firmware code on the flash is loaded to memory and passes verification, the attacker may attach a flash programmer and update the code on the flash device. If there is a vulnerability in the code such that some code reads the flash content again, this code will read the modified content. The modified content could be code or data, and it may impact the further boot flow.

Additional Capability

Besides the detectability, the RTD or CTD may provide additional capabilities, such as informing the end user that the verification fails or recording this failure in the event log. The event log may be saved as part of the RTD/CTD or be forwarded to a remote system via some out-of-band (OOB) mechanism.

Case Study

Now, let's take a look at some real cases of secure boot implementation.

UEFI Secure Boot

UEFI (Unified Extensible Firmware Interface) secure boot is a feature defined in the UEFI specification. The platform system firmware needs to verify any third-party firmware code before launching it. A system firmware image is created by the platform manufacturer – the Original Equipment Manufacturer (OEM). It is treated as part of the Trusted Computing Base (TCB). During boot, the system firmware may need to execute a PCI option ROM created by an Independent Hardware Vendor (IHV) or an OS loader created by an operating system vendor (OSV). Those other pieces of firmware are not part of the TCB. The platform OEM will choose which OSVs and IHVs they want to trust by enrolling the public certificate of the OSVs and IHVs in the firmware image signature database. The end user may also choose to enroll and revoke entries in the security database.

The UEFI specification supports the Portable Executable (PE) image format. The signature of the image is appended to the same PE image with a signing tool (see Figure 4-1).

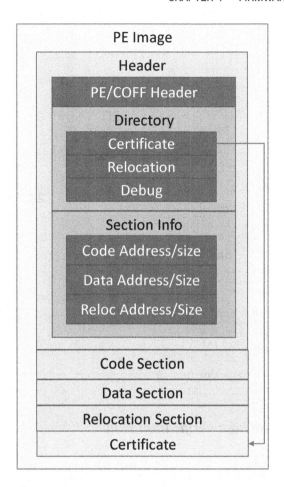

Figure 4-1. *PE Image Layout*

Figure 4-2 shows the UEFI secure boot verification flow. Table 4-2 shows the key/Image Security Database used in UEFI secure boot.

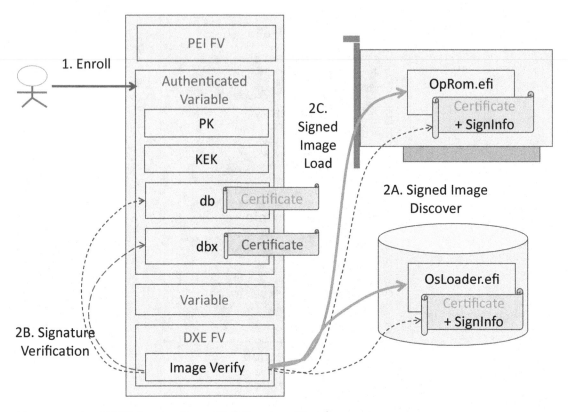

Figure 4-2. *UEFI Secure Boot Verification Flow*

Table 4-2. *Key Usage in UEFI Secure Boot*

Key	Verifies	Update Is Verified by	Comment
PK	New PK New KEK New db/dbx/dbt/dbr New OsRecoveryOrder New OsRecovery####	PK	Platform key
KEK	New db/dbx/dbt/dbr New OsRecoveryOrder New OsRecovery####	PK	Key exchange key

(continued)

Table 4-2. (*continued*)

Key	Verifies	Update Is Verified by	Comment
db	UEFI image (OS loader/option ROM)	PK/KEK	Authorized image database
dbx	UEFI image (OS loader/option ROM)	PK/KEK	Forbidden image database
dbt	UEFI Image + dbx	PK/KEK	Timestamp database
dbr	New OsRecoveryOrder New OsRecovery#### (OS recovery image)	PK/KEK	Recovery database

In UEFI secure boot, the untrusted data is any third-party firmware code, including the OS bootloader, PCI option ROMs, or a tool such as the UEFI shell. The component provider needs to sign these images with their private key and publish the public key to let the OEM or the end user enroll it.

The OEM or the end user may enroll the public key as trusted data (UEFI Secure Boot Image Security Database). The database is stored in a UEFI Authenticated Variable. The database may be updated during boot time. It can be read by anyone but only written using a signed updated value.

The UEFI specification defines multiple security databases. The detailed usage of these databases is described in the UEFI specification:

- db: The allowed image signature database

- dbx: The forbidden image signature database

- dbt: The timestamp signature database

- dbr: The recovery image signature database

During boot, the Image Verification Procedure verifies the third-party firmware code, checking their signatures against those in the preceding databases. If the verification passes, the third-party firmware code is executed. If the verification fails, the third-party firmware code is discarded.

Figure 4-3 shows a verification flow using db/dbx.

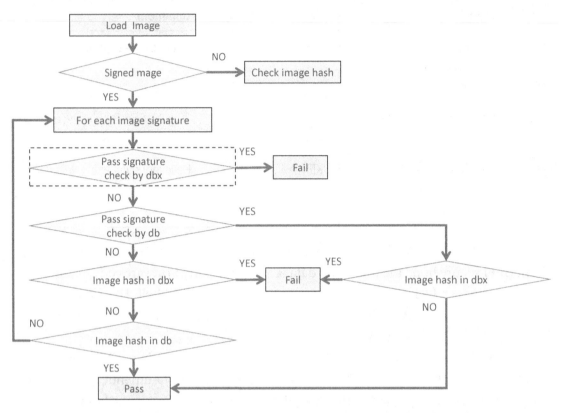

Figure 4-3. *Image Verification with an Image Signature Database*

Figure 4-4 shows a verification flow introducing dbt. An additional check is required based on dbx signature.

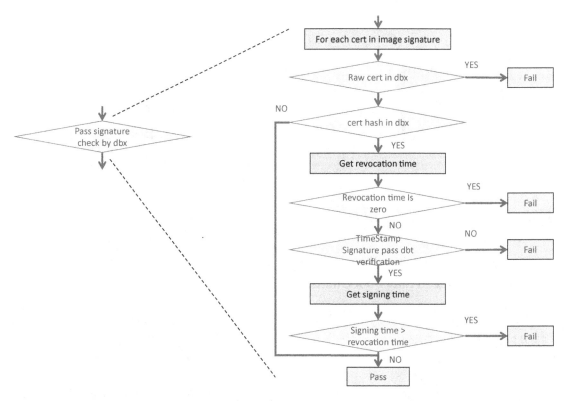

Figure 4-4. *Image Verification with a Timestamp Signature Database*

Intel Boot Guard

UEFI secure boot assumes the OEM platform firmware is a Trusted Computing Base (TCB) and trusts it implicitly. This assumption is only valid for a software attack. However, it is invalid for the simple hardware attack. A hardware attacker may have physical access to the system motherboard and update the flash by using a programmer. An improved implementation would be to use a hardware RoT to verify the OEM platform firmware. A solution can be implemented by using the Intel Boot Guard (see Figure 4-5). This feature verifies the entire OEM platform firmware image by using two components:

- Intel Authenticated Code Module (ACM): It verifies the OEM initial boot block (IBB).

- CPU Microcode: It verifies the Intel ACM binary.

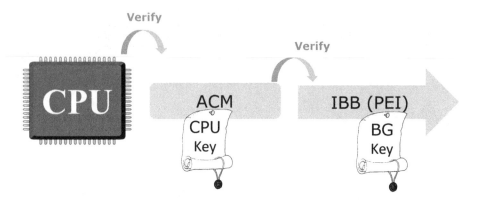

Figure 4-5. *Intel Boot Guard Flow*

Figures 4-6 and 4-7 show the components involved in Intel Boot Guard. Table 4-3 shows the key usage in Intel Boot Guard.

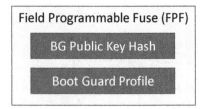

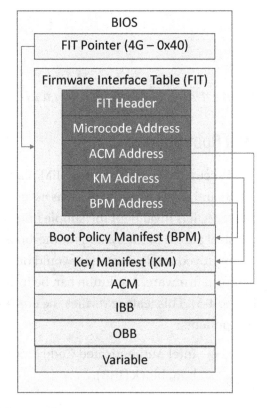

Figure 4-6. *Intel Boot Guard Diagram (in Memory)*

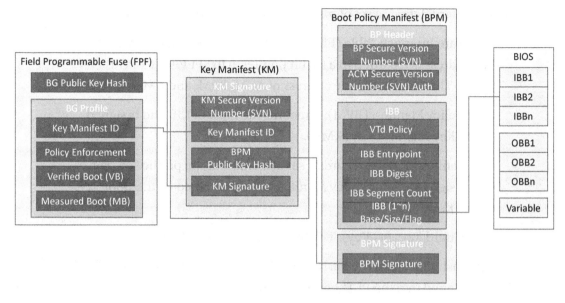

Figure 4-7. *Intel Boot Guard Diagram (Relationship)*

Table 4-3. *Key Usage in Intel Boot Guard*

Key	Verifies	Storage	Verified by
ACM Key	ACM	CPU	Microcode
Key Hash	Boot Guard Key	PCH	ACM
Boot Guard Key	Key Manifest (KM)	Key Manifest (Flash)	ACM
Key Manifest Key	Boot Policy Manifest (BPM)	Key Manifest (Flash)	ACM
IBB Hash	IBB	Boot Policy Manifest (Flash)	ACM

Intel introduced the Intel Boot Guard Authenticated Code Module (ACM), which is a module signed by Intel. The ACM's responsibility is to verify OEM platform firmware before the host CPU transfers control to OEM firmware. Because verifying the entire image is time-consuming, the ACM only verifies the initial boot block (IBB) code. The IBB is then responsible for verifying the OEM boot block (OBB).

Intel Boot Guard defines a set of manifests to record the signature information:

- Firmware Interface Table (FIT): This is a table in firmware image. The FIT address is recorded in a 64-bit pointer at 0xFFFFFFC0 (4 GiB – 64 bytes). The FIT records the address of ACM, BPM, and KM.

- Boot Policy Manifest (BPM): It records the hash of IBB and is signed by the Key Manifest Key (KMK).

- Key Manifest (KM): It records a set of hashes for the public key pair which signs the Boot Policy Manifest, and it is signed by the Boot Guard Key.

- Boot Guard Key (BG Key): The key to sign the Key Manifest.

- Key Hash: It records the hash for the public of Boot Guard Key. It is provisioned into the PCH hardware.

The Key Hash is read-only. It cannot be updated. The Boot Policy Manifest and the Key Manifest can be updated by the firmware. The hash of the ACM public key is inside of the CPU. A debug ACM is signed with the debug key. A production ACM is signed with the production key.

During runtime, the CPU Microcode finds the ACM location from the Firmware Interface Table (FIT) and loads the ACM into an authenticated code execution area in the CPU's cache. Then the CPU Microcode performs the verification of the ACM. If the verification passes, the ACM starts executing. The ACM IBB verification gets the Key Hash from PCH and verifies the Key Manifest. If this verification passes, the ACM gets the Key Hash from the Key Manifest and verifies the Boot Policy Manifest. If this verification passes, the ACM gets the IBB Hash from the Boot Policy Manifest and verifies the firmware's IBB code. If the final verification passes, then the firmware's IBB becomes trusted, and the ACM transfers control to the IBB.

Intel Boot Guard only verifies the initial boot block (IBB) portion of the whole OEM firmware. To make sure the whole OEM firmware is unmodified, the IBB then needs to verify the rest of the OEM boot block (OBB). The OBB public key hash must be stored into the IBB to make sure it is validated by the ACM. As an implementation choice, the OEM may store the OBB hash directly in the IBB rather than using a public key. The OBB verification code is inside of the IBB. If the OBB passes the verification, the OBB is invoked by the IBB. If the OBB fails the verification, the OBB is skipped. Figure 4-8 shows a complete secure boot chain constructed using Intel Boot Guard, OBB verification, and UEFI secure boot.

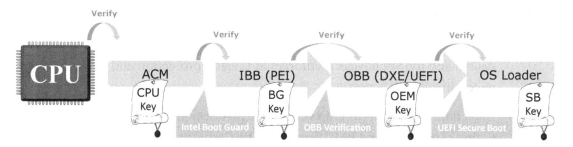

Figure 4-8. *Secure Boot Verification Flow*

Project Cerberus

On a server platform, there are more firmware elements, such as the firmware for the Baseboard Management Controller (BMC), the network interface card (NIC), Redundant Arrays of Independent Drives (RAID) controllers, Non-Volatile Memory Express (NVMe) storage devices, and so on. The existing secure boot solution cannot verify all these devices' firmware because the secure boot logic only verifies the integrity of the system firmware. As such, we need a new solution to verify all firmware on a board in order to meet the NIST SP800-193 requirement. The server BMC may have the capability to access other firmware on the board. However, the BMC is too big, and it includes lots of manageability functionality. As such, we need a smaller TCB.

The Open Compute Project (OCP) defines the Cerberus Security Architecture. It is a hierarchical root-of-trust (RoT) architecture. In this architecture, a Cerberus chip is the key element. It is a dedicated secure microprocessor with internal SRAM and flash. It can access all the firmware on the board via various interfaces such as the Serial Peripheral Interface (SPI) or the System Management Bus (SMBus)/Inter-Integrated Circuit (I2C). It owns the reset control logic for the platform, so unless it is satisfied with the security status of the platform, the platform cannot turn on. From a security perspective, the Cerberus chip is a Device Identifier Composition Engine (DICE). It is physically unclonable, and it is tamper-resistant.

The Cerberus chip supports the NIST SP800-193 requirements in the areas listed here:

1) Protection: The Cerberus chip interposes itself between the system and the SPI device. It enforces SPI region protection and rejects invalid SPI accesses.

2) Detection: The Cerberus chip verifies the platform firmware, such as that of the BIOS and BMC firmware. The Cerberus chip may also verify the component firmware, such as that of the Power Supply Unit (PSU). The Cerberus may also provide the attestation capability. See Chapter 7 for details of the DICE-related attestation concept.

3) Recovery: The Cerberus chip may automatically recover the BIOS or BMC from a known good image if the corruption is detected. See Chapter 5 for details of recovery.

Figure 4-9 describes the Cerberus components. When the system is powered on, the Cerberus chip gets powered on first, and it holds the CPU and BMC in reset. Then the Cerberus chip verifies the digital signature of the UEFI flash and the BMC flash. Only after the verification passes will the Cerberus chip allow flash access, and it then releases CPU and BMC reset.

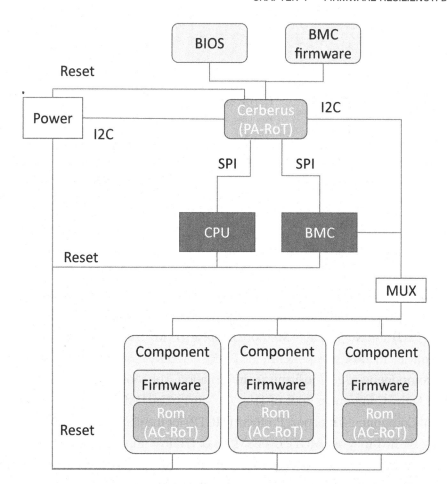

Figure 4-9. *Cerberus Components*

Figure 4-10 shows the Cerberus authentication flow inside of the Cerberus chip. Cerberus internally has an immutable ROM acting as a RoT, a Key Manifest to describe the image attributes, a Cerberus bootloader, and Cerberus firmware. During boot, the immutable Cerberus ROM authenticates the Key Manifest, selects the key from the manifest to verify the Cerberus bootloader, and passes control to the bootloader. Then the Cerberus bootloader selects the key from the manifest to verify the Cerberus firmware. This Cerberus firmware will do the rest of protection, detection, and recovery work for the platform firmware. The platform firmware is described with a Platform Firmware Manifest (PFM). The PFM includes the firmware information such as read-only regions, read/write regions, version, digest of read-only regions, and public certificates. The Cerberus maintains the PFM, verifies the firmware based upon the PFM, and provides the secure update for the PFM.

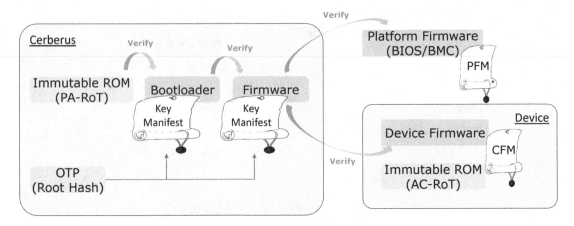

Figure 4-10. *Cerberus Authentication Flow*

The Cerberus is a root-of-trust for the platform. We call this solution a Platform Active Root-of-Trust (PA-RoT). A platform may include different components, such as a Power Supply Unit (PSU) and Non-Volatile Memory Express (NVMe) storage devices. In order to verify the firmware in those components, the PA-RoT needs to communicate with a root-of-trust in the components to get the firmware information. The root-of-trust in the component is named an Active Component Root-of-Trust (AC-RoT). The DMTF forum defines the Management Component Transport Protocol (MCTP) for the communication between two components. PA-RoT may use MCTP over SMBus or I2C to communicate with the AC-RoT to get the device firmware digest or certificates. Similar to the PFM, the component firmware information is also described in a manifest named the Component Firmware Manifest (CFM). The Cerberus solution maintains the CFM, verifies the component firmware based upon CFM, and provides secure update for the CFM. See Table 4-4 for the keys used in the Cerberus. We will discuss the details of MCTP and device authentication in Chapter 8.

Table 4-4. *Key Usage in Cerberus*

Key	Verifies	Storage	Verified by
Root hash	Key Manifest	Cerberus OTP	Cerberus ROM
Key Manifest	Cerberus bootloader	Cerberus NV	Cerberus ROM
Key Manifest	Cerberus firmware	Cerberus NV	Cerberus bootloader
PFM	Platform firmware (BIOS, BMC)	Cerberus NV	Cerberus
CFM	Active components (NVMe, PSU, and so on)	Cerberus NV	Cerberus

There might be several components on a platform. Not all firmware needs to be verified by the Cerberus solution. The Cerberus solution may maintain a Chain-of-Trust to let a verified firmware image or even a verified OS verify the rest of the component firmware.

Intel Platform Firmware Resiliency (PFR)

To reduce firmware-related security risks, Intel developed Intel PFR for server platforms. This feature protects critical firmware from attacks during boot and runtime. It is an implementation of Project Cerberus for NIST SP800-193.

Now we have heard about Intel Boot Guard, Intel BIOS Guard, and Intel PFR. Table 4-5 shows the difference between the three features.

Table 4-5. *Comparison for Intel Boot Guard, Intel BIOS Guard, and Intel PFR*

Feature	Intel Boot Guard	Intel BIOS Guard	Intel PFR
Standalone coprocessor	NO	NO	YES
Protection/ update	NO	YES. The Intel BIOS Guard module updates the BIOS image or EC image on SPI flash. It is triggered by MSR write in SMM.	YES. PFR CPLD updates the whole BIOS image, Server Platform Service (SPS) image, or BMC image.
Detection	YES. Intel Boot Guard ACM checks BPM/KM and verifies the hash of IBB.	NO	YES. PFR CPLD verifies the whole BIOS image, SPS image, and BMC image. Intel PFR relies on Intel Boot Guard ACM to do the check.
Recovery	NO. Intel Boot Guard itself does not provide recovery capability. It may trigger Intel ME to do the recovery.	NO	YES. PFR CPLD may recover to a known good BIOS image, SPS image, or BMC image.

Intel PFR includes the following hardware components:

1) PFR CPLD (Complex Programmable Logic Device): The CPLD is the root-of-trust in a system that is designed based on Intel's PFR. It is used to detect the integrity of other platform firmware components.

2) Firmware connected to PCH SPI's flash controller: This includes the BIOS and Server Platform Service (SPS) image. This area is protected by PFR. The SPS image is equivalent to the Intel Management Engine (ME) image as used for clients' platforms.

3) Firmware connected to BMC SPI flash: BMC image. This area is protected by PFR.

4) Firmware connected via SMBus: Power Supply Unit (PSU), Digital Voltage Regulator (VR), Hot Swap Back Plane (HSBP), Radio Frequency (RF) NVRAM.

5) SPI Mux: Allows selection of the master of BMC SPI flash and PCH SPI flash. In the platform's preboot environment (T-1), the PFR CPLD is the master of BMC flash and PCH flash because it needs to read the flash content and do the check. In normal mode (T0), BMC and PCH are the masters of their flash devices.

Figure 4-11 shows the Intel PFR system diagram.

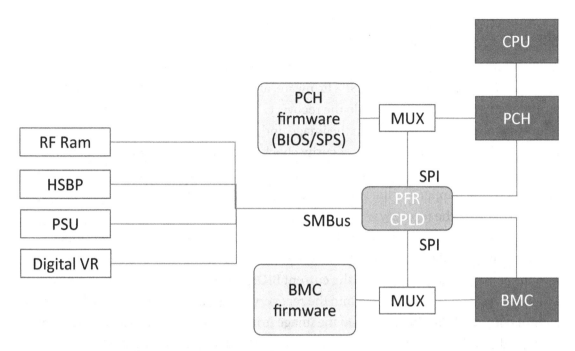

Figure 4-11. *Intel PFR Component*

Figure 4-12 shows the Intel PFR boot flow.

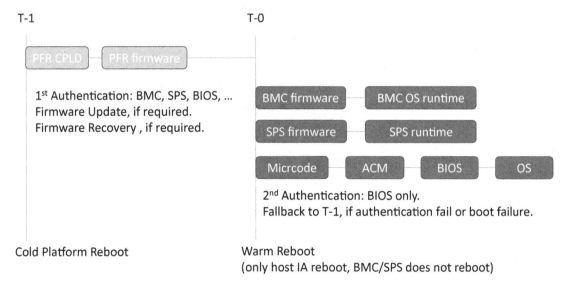

Figure 4-12. *Intel PFR Boot Flow*

After AC power-on, the system enters the preboot environment (T-1). Only PFR CPLD has power. All other components are quiesced. The PFR CPLD ROM performs internal authentication and loads the PFR firmware. Then the PFR firmware authenticates the BIOS, SPS firmware, and BMC firmware. If the PFR CPLD authentication fails, the PFR will do the recovery. The PFR CPLD may also check if there is any update request and perform the image update after the authentication for the new image. Only after all the preceding security check passes the system transitions from T-1 to normal mode (T0). In this mode, the CPLD monitors the platform boot progress. If any boot failure happens or the watchdog is triggered, the system switches back to T-1 mode to perform the recovery.

The Intel PFR feature needs the flash to be divided into three areas – active image, recovery image, and staging areas (see Figure 4-13). The current working firmware is put into the active image area, such as the current BIOS, SPS firmware, and BMC firmware. The recovery backup image is put into the recovery image area. If the working firmware cannot boot, the PFR CPLD can load the image from the recovery image to override the corrupted working firmware. The staging area is to hold the new image for the update purpose. The PFR CPLD needs to check if there is a new image in the staging area and perform the authentication and version check. If all checks have passed, the PFR CPLD will copy the new image from the staging area to the working area.

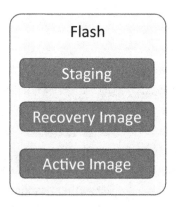

Figure 4-13. *Intel PFR Flash Layout*

Google Titan

Google developed a hardware root-of-trust solution for Google Cloud Platform (GCP), named Titan. The Titan is a low-power microcontroller. Titan provides first-instruction integrity. After the platform has AC power, Titan is the first component to get power.

During the boot time, Titan immutable Boot ROM code verifies the boot firmware on the flash part. During runtime, Titan interposes the access between PCH/BMC and SPI flash. Any illegal SPI command will be rejected. See Figure 4-14 for the Titan verified boot.

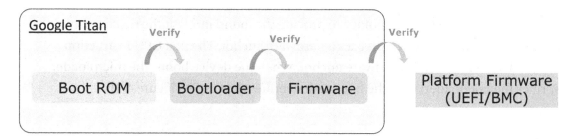

Figure 4-14.   *Titan Verified Boot*

The design of Titan is similar to the Cerberus Security Architecture. "Titan in depth: Security in plaintext" and "Titan silicon root of trust for Google Cloud" provide more detailed information on Titan.

Recently, Google created the OpenTitan project to make the silicon RoT design and implementation more transparent, trustworthy, and secure for enterprises, platform providers, and chip manufacturers.

Apple T2

Apple developed a Secure Enclave coprocessor, named T2, to provide the foundation for Apple File System (APFS) encrypted storage, secure boot, and Touch ID on Mac.

The T2 macOS secure boot chain is similar to other secure boot solutions. The chip executes code from an immutable Boot ROM as the root-of-trust. Then the Boot ROM verifies the iBoot bootloader. The latter verifies the T2 kernel, which subsequently verifies the UEFI firmware. Figure 4-15 shows the T2 macOS secure boot chain.

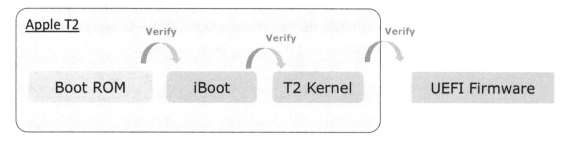

Figure 4-15.   *T2 macOS Secure Boot Chain*

"Apple T2 Security Chip Overview" and "Inside the Apple T2" provide more information on the T2 chip.

Cisco Trust Anchor

Cisco uses Trust Anchor technology to provide the foundation for the Cisco trustworthy system. Cisco secure boot chain uses a hardware anchor. The first CPU instruction is stored in an immutable hardware anchor. When the device boots, the microloader verifies the bootloader; then the bootloader verifies the OS. See Figure 4-16.

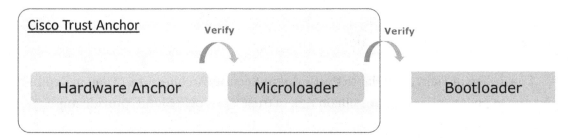

Figure 4-16. *Cisco Trust Anchor*

Besides secure boot, Cisco Trust Anchor Module (TAm) can also be used to verify that the hardware is authentic. The OS can check the TAm for a secure unique device identifier (SUDI) that could have come only from Cisco.

Amazon Nitro RoT

Amazon developed the Nitro security chip as a hardware Root-of-Trust for its cloud platforms. The Nitro security chip is a custom microcontroller that can trap all I/O to the non-volatile storage area starting with the system's power-on. Any unauthorized write access to the non-volatile storage is blocked in the hardware. As such, EC2 servers can't update their firmware. The only way to update firmware is by Amazon Web Services (AWS) through the Nitro System. When the Nitro System starts, it checks every firmware system on the server to ensure that none of them have been modified.

AMD Secure Boot

AMD introduced the Platform Security Processor (PSP) to the platform. The PSP is based upon the ARM TrustZone architecture. It provides a hardware-based root-of-trust and the trusted execution environment. The PSP includes an immutable on-chip Boot ROM, and this Boot ROM verifies an off-chip bootloader. Then the PSP bootloader authenticates the first block of the BIOS and transfers control to it. See Figure 4-17 for the PSP verification flow.

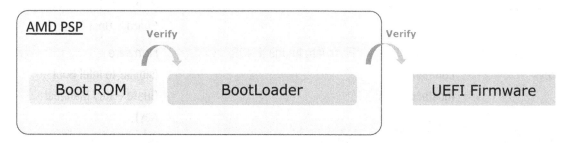

Figure 4-17. *AMD PSP Verification Flow*

Besides boot verification, the PSP also manages the S3 power suspend and resume. In S3 suspend, the PSP saves the context for CPU cores. During S3 resume, the PSP loads and verifies the BIOS, restores the context for CPU cores directly, and then transfers control to the BIOS.

OpenPOWER Secure Boot

IBM OpenPOWER servers implement secure boot to ensure the integrity of the platform firmware image and the OS. The OpenPOWER secure boot function consists of two security domains: the firmware domain and the operating system domain. The key management and verification flow in the firmware domain are similar to the one in the Intel Boot Guard. The key management and verification flow in the operating system domain are similar to the one in the UEFI secure boot (see Table 4-6).

Table 4-6. *Key Usage in IBM OpenPOWER*

Key	Verifies	Storage	Domain
Hardware (HW) root keys Hash	HW root keys	Serial electrically erasable programmable read-only memory (SEEPROM)	Firmware (similar to Intel Boot Guard – Boot Guard Key Hash)
Hardware (HW) root keys	FW keys	Firmware image (PNOR)	Firmware (similar to Intel Boot Guard – Boot Guard Key)
Firmware (FW) keys	Firmware components (hostboot, OPAL, Petitboot)	Firmware image (PNOR)	Firmware (similar to Intel Boot Guard – Key Manifest Key)
Platform key (PK)	KEK	TPM NVRAM	Operating system (similar to UEFI secure boot – platform key)
Key exchange keys (KEK)	DB	Firmware image (PNOR)	Operating system (similar to UEFI secure boot – key exchange key)
Software key database (DB) keys	Operating system (Linux)	Firmware image (PNOR)	Operating system (similar to UEFI secure boot – image database db)

The boot and verification flow of IBM OpenPOWER is shown in Figure 4-18.

1) After the system powers on, the first part of the processor's self-boot engine (SBE) code runs. The first SBE is stored in the processor one-time programmable read-only memory (OTPROM). It is considered as immutable. The first SBE initializes the pervasive bus and jumps to the second part of SBE.

2) The second part of the SBE is stored in the serial electrically erasable programmable read-only memory (SEEPROM). The SEEPROM also includes the hash of the hardware (HW) root keys. The SBE initializes the processor and loads the Hostboot Base (HBB) module from the processor NOR (PNOR) flash memory to the L3 cache and executes the HBB. The SBE needs to verify the HW RootKey reported in the firmware image with the HW root key hash stored in the SEEPROM. Then it verifies the signature of the FW keys signed by the HW root keys and the signature of the loaded image signed by the FW keys. Only after all three verification steps pass is the loaded image authorized to run.

3) The HBB module provides the general execution environment such as task control, memory management, and interrupt support. HBB then verifies and loads the hostboot extended image.

4) The hostboot extended image performs the rest of system initialization such as initializing the Powerbus, initializing the memory controller, building the device tree, loading the Hostboot Runtime (HBRT) Service, and so on. Finally, hostboot verifies and loads the Open Power Abstraction Layer (OPAL).

5) The OPAL initializes the PCIe bus and provides a standard interface to POWER platform services for the operating system. Then the OPAL verifies and loads the Petitboot loader.

6) The Petitboot loader discovers the boot device and verifies and loads the OS. Because the OS kernel is in the operating system domain, the DB keys should be used in the verification instead of FW keys.

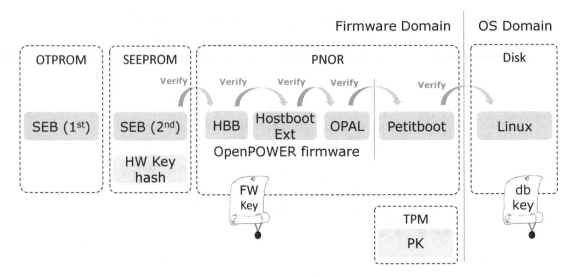

Figure 4-18. IBM OpenPOWER Secure Boot Verification Flow

ARM Platform Security Architecture (PSA)

So far, we have discussed the different technologies used in the traditional mobile, desktop, and server segments. For the embedded and IoT segments, the same challenges exist. In order to address the needs of security, ARM defines a set of specifications for the platform security architecture (PSA), such as Trusted Base System Architecture (TBSA), Trusted Boot and Firmware Update (TBFU), and security model (SM). ARM also provides the Trusted Board Boot Requirement (TBBR) client and Server Base Security Guide (SBSG) for the ARM-based systems.

The PSA defines some terms:

- Secure Processing Environment (SPE), which contains the following:

  - PSA Root-of-Trust (PSA-RoT) provides the root-of-trust in the privileged mode. PSA-RoT acts as the Trusted Computing Base (TCB) for the SPE. It may include the trusted hardware device, the trusted firmware, the trusted bootloader, the trusted OS, or a Secure Partition Manager (SPM).

  - Application Root-of-Trust (ARoT) provides the root-of-trust in the non-privileged mode. It includes the application in the ARM TrustZone system.

- Non-Secure Processing Environment (NSPE) is defined for the general-purpose functionality that is not security critical. On an ARM TrustZone system, the NSPE is the normal world. On other systems, NSPE may be isolated from the SPE, and the NSPE may not access any hardware or software resource owned by the SPE.

See Figure 4-19 for the ARM SPM prior to v8.4 and Figure 4-20 for the ARM SPM after v8.4.

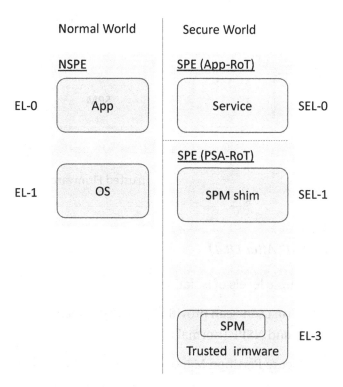

Figure 4-19. *ARM SPM (Prior to v8.4)*

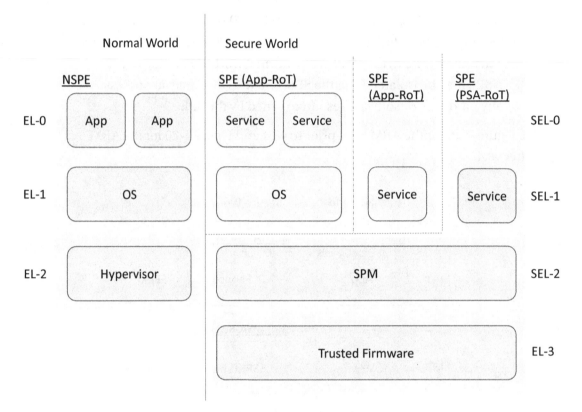

Figure 4-20. *ARM SPM (After v8.4)*

The PSA defines multiple levels of isolation:

- Level 1: ARM TrustZone can provide the isolation between the SPE (secure world) and NSPE (normal world).

- Level 2: The Secure Partition Manager (SPM) is designed to provide isolation between PSA-RoT and ARoT. This can be achieved by the exception-level (EL) isolation.

- Level 3: The SPM may also provide additional isolation for different Security Partitions in ARoT. A virtual machine monitor may be needed to support this.

The SPM is a concept. It can be in S-EL3 with a simple SPM-Shim in S-EL1 for ARM prior to v8.4. Since ARMv8.4 with the virtualization extensions, SPM can be in S-EL2 directly. The details of SPM runtime will be discussed in Chapter 17. Here let's focus on how to create this secure environment in the firmware.

ARM created trusted firmware projects, such as Trusted-Firmware-M and Trusted-Firmware-A. These follow the TBFU standard. The "Trusted Boot" term in the TBFU covers both verification and measurement. Similar to secure boot in X86 systems, ARM systems have an immutable ROM as the root-of-trust. This ROM verifies the next firmware component before executing it. Then a chain-of-trust is created.

Trusted-Firmware-A is for the ARM A-profile (application processors). It includes the following bootloaders:

- BL1: AP Trusted ROM (S-EL3)

- BL2: Trusted Boot Firmware (S-EL1)

- BL31: EL3 Runtime Software (S-EL3)

- BL32: Secure-EL1 Payload (Trusted OS) (S-EL1)

- BL33: Non-Secure Firmware, such as UEFI or U-Boot

- SCP_BL1: System Control Processor (SCP) Boot ROM

- SCP_BL2: System Control Processor (SCP) RAM Firmware

The boot flow of Trusted-Firmware-A is shown in Figure 4-21. The reset vector is in the BL1 AP Trusted ROM. BL1 is executed at EL3. The data is copied to SRAM. BL1 verifies BL2 and loads BL2 to EL1. BL2 follows the same process to verify BL31, BL32, and BL33.

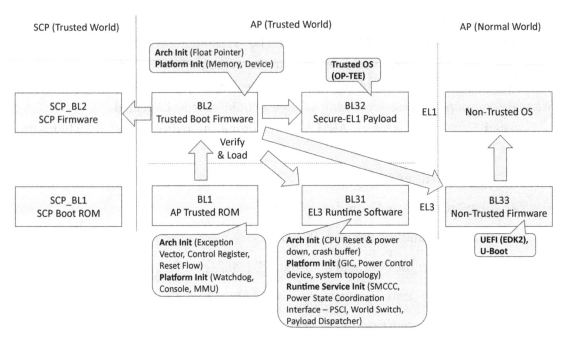

Figure 4-21. *ARM Trusted-Firmware-A Boot Flow*

PSA-TBSA-M defines some special requirements for the ARM M-profile device. The limitation of these devices includes 1) less than 1 M flash, 2) less than 256 K RAM, 3) no MMU, and 4) limited power budget. To deal with these limitations, the boot flow of the Trusted-Firmware-M is totally different from the Trusted-Firmware-A. It includes the following bootloaders:

- BL2 MCUBoot: MCB Boot ROM

- Secure Partition Manager (SPM): Secure World Firmware

- Non-Secure World Firmware

In the M-profile, the secure firmware and the nonsecure firmware are combined in one slot. The BL2 MCUBoot verifies both firmware slots together and only loads the secure firmware. Then the secure firmware loads the nonsecure firmware (see Figure 4-22).

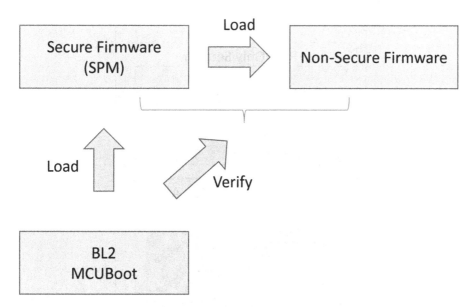

Figure 4-22. *ARM Trusted-Firmware-M Boot Flow*

coreboot Security

EDK II is the implementation for the UEFI specification. Today many mobiles, desktops, and servers are using EDK II-based BIOS. coreboot is another open source system firmware implementation for embedded and some platforms. It also implements the verified boot feature to make sure that all firmware is verified before being loaded.

The coreboot firmware includes two parts: the read-only (RO) section and the read/write (RW) section.

The read-only section includes the reset vector, the boot block, the verification stage code, and the Google Binary Block (GBB). The read/write section includes the ROM stage code, the RAM stage code, the payload for OS-required interfaces, and the verified boot block (VBLOCK). The read/write section also includes the components required for silicon initialization, such as CPU Microcode and the firmware support package (FSP).

The root-of-trust is the read-only section. The read-only section needs to verify the read/write section to build the Chain-of-Trust. See Figure 4-23 for the coreboot image layout.

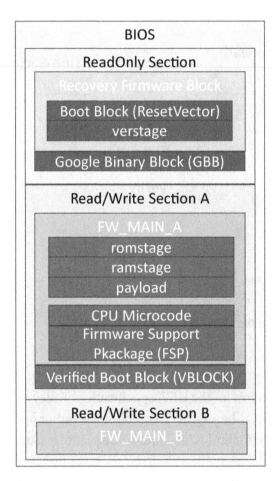

Figure 4-23. *coreboot Image Layout*

The most important data structures involved in the verified boot are the GBB and VBLOCK (see Figure 4-24). The GBB includes the public root key used to verify the VBLOCK area. The VBLOCK area includes the key and signature used to verify the read/write section.

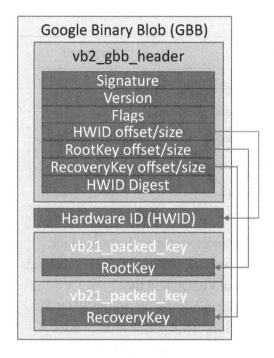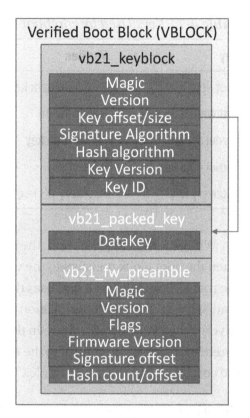

Figure 4-24. *coreboot Image GBB and VBLOCK*

The whole verified boot flow is shown in Figure 4-25. Table 4-7 shows keys used in the verified boot flow.

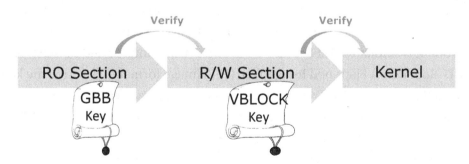

Figure 4-25. *coreboot Verified Boot*

Table 4-7. *Keys Used by coreboot Verified Boot*

Key	Verifies	Storage	Versioned
Root key	Firmware data key	RO firmware (GBB)	NO
Firmware data key	RW firmware	RW FW header (VBLOCK)	YES
Kernel subkey	Kernel data key	RW firmware	YES (as FW)
Kernel data key	OS kernel	OS kernel header	YES
Recovery key	Recovery OS kernel	RO firmware	NO

When the system powers on, the CPU jumps to the reset vector in the boot block. Then the boot block transfers to the verification stage (verstage). The verstage code reads the root key from the GBB and uses that key to verify the VBLOCK in the read/write section. If the verification passes, the verstage reads the key from VBLOCK to verify the FW_MAIN firmware in the read/write section. If the verification passes, coreboot transfers the control to the FW_MAIN firmware code. If the verification fails, the coreboot enters recovery mode.

Verified U-Boot

U-Boot (Universal Boot Loader) is another OS bootloader, targeting the embedded system. It supports multiple system architectures, such as PowerPC, ARM, X86, and MIPS.

Embedded systems have similar secure boot requirements. The root-of-trust needs to have a way to verify the loaded software – such as the OS kernel. U-Boot introduced verified boot. It is similar to UEFI secure boot. Since ARM Linux added device tree support, U-Boot uses a Flattened Image Tree (FIT) image format to describe the kernel image and a Flattened Device Tree (FDT). In order to support secure boot, the kernel, the FDT, and the configuration must include a hash node or a signature node. When U-Boot processes the FIT, then it can verify the kernel, FDT, and configuration. See Figure 4-26 for the U-Boot FIT layout.

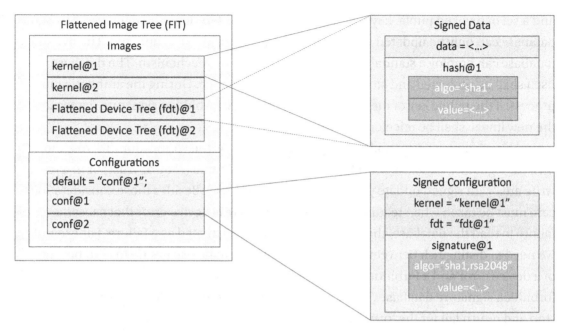

Figure 4-26. *U-Boot FIT Layout*

Attack and Mitigation

Now, let's take a look at some real cases for attacking secure boot and mitigation strategies.

Secure Boot Configuration Attack

Probably the easiest way to attack secure boot is to disable this feature. In some early implementations, the UEFI secure boot enable/disable setting was saved to an unprotected UEFI non-volatile variable. As such, the attacker could just use a normal UEFI runtime service to update this configuration to disable UEFI secure boot.

The mitigation is to remove the runtime setting or to use an authentication mechanism to only allow authorized users to update the setting. We will discuss the user authentication in Chapter 11.

Signature Database Attack

Signature verification is normally based upon a provisioned public key database. The database may be static and include only one or more public keys. Or the database may be dynamic and include a set of allowed public keys, which we call a signature database, and a set of revoked public keys, which we call a forbidden signature database. The static database can only be updated when the whole firmware image is updated. The dynamic database can employ a standalone authenticated update mechanism. The database itself shall be protected and stored in a non-volatile storage. During the authentication process, if the public key of the new image matches the forbidden signature database, the new image shall be rejected immediately.

An attacker may try to modify the database to bypass the verification. To mitigate this, the signature database must be kept in a read-only area (root-of-trust) or in a read/write area with signed update protection (Chain-of-Trust). Besides those considerations, care must be taken when reading the database. If there is device error that causes a failure to read the database, the authentication shall be treated as a failure. For example, we need to distinguish between a forbidden signature database failure to read because of a device error and a forbidden signature database failure to read because there is no forbidden signature database. The authentication shall continue for the latter, but it shall stop and return fail for the former.

Malformed Input: Unsigned Data

In some implementations, only part of the update image might be signed. For example, if the update uses the UEFI/PI-defined signed section (see Figure 4-27), then only the data inside of the section is signed. The firmware volume (FV) header, the firmware file system (FFS) header, and the section header are unsigned. UEFI/PI also defines a signed firmware volume (see Figure 4-28). It is better than a signed section, but the firmware volume header is still unsigned.

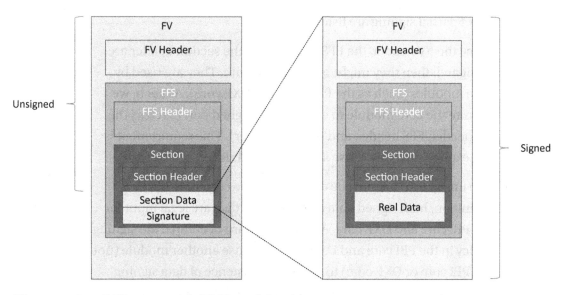

Figure 4-27. *PI Image with PI Signed Section*

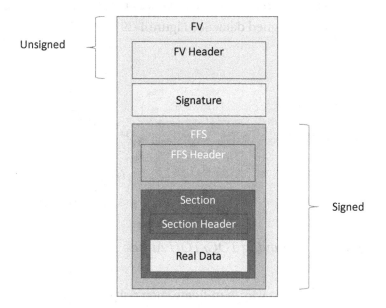

Figure 4-28. *PI Image with PI Signed FV*

The risks of partial signing are listed here:

1) Since the FV header, the FFS header, and the section header are unsigned, then they might be tampered with. They are used by core modules (such as the PEI core and DXE core). As such, we require the core module to verify the unsigned part (such as the FV header, FFS header, and section header). This requirement is not explicit and may cause some potential risk.

2) The unsigned data must be detected. In the current UEFI/PI definition, both signed data and unsigned data are legal input for the PEI core and DXE core. As such, it is hard to enforce the signing policy in the PEI core and DXE core. If we use another module (not the PEI core or DXE core) to detect the existence of data signing, there is a risk of a TOC/TOU attack because the attacker may remove the data signature and mark the data as unsigned after the verification passes. Then, when the PEI core or DXE core parses the data later, it gets unsigned data. See Figure 4-29 for the TOC/TOU attack.

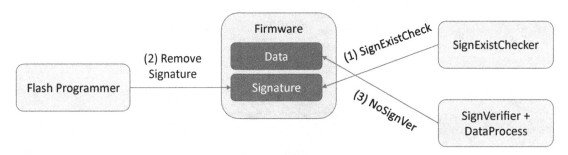

Figure 4-29. *Signature Removing TOC/TOU Attack*

As such, the best and easiest way to mitigate such risk is just to make sure all data is signed or hashed, including the FV header, the FFS header, and the section header.

Malformed Input: Use Unverified Data

This is another TOC/TOU attack wherein the attacker may modify the data after the verification. For example, the Intel Boot Guard ACM loads the BIOS IBB data from the flash to the cache before the memory is initialized and verifies the content in the cache. After the memory initialization is done, the data is migrated from cache to the permanent memory. Then the cache is disabled and re-enabled for the permanent memory only. See Figure 4-30 for the flow.

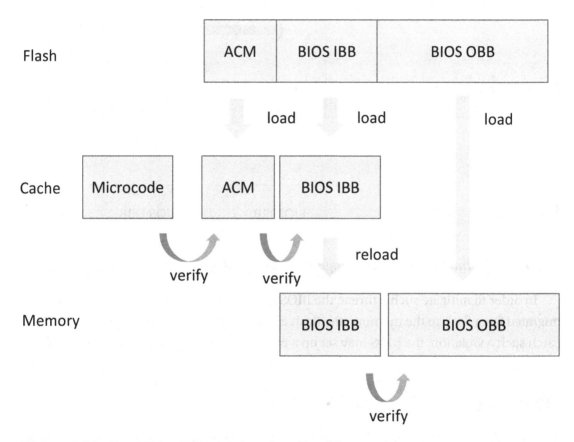

Figure 4-30. *Intel Boot Guard Image Loading Flow*

However, if a program still refers to the data in the flash region, this program may get the malicious data because the content in the flash area may be updated by the attacker after the verification. See Figure 4-31 for the TOC/TOU attack.

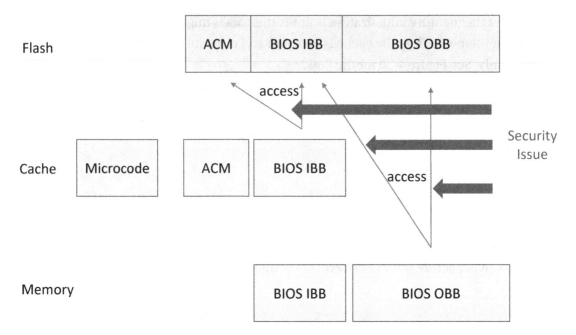

Figure 4-31. *Intel Boot Guard Image TOC/TOU Attack*

In order to mitigate such a threat, the BIOS needs to ensure that after the data is migrated from flash to the memory, the flash content is never accessed again. In order to catch such a violation, the BIOS may set up a page table to mark the flash region as not present.

Malformed Input: Unsigned Storage

Although the data can be signed, the storage to hold the data might still be unsigned. For example, if the BIOS needs to load an OS loader from a disk, the OS loader can be signed, while the file system and the disk partition are unsigned. As such, the attacker may choose to attack the file system or the disk partition.

Listing 4-1 is the old implementation for the GPT (GUIDed Partition Table) partition driver. At first, the PartEntry is allocated with a fixed size – sizeof(EFI_PARTION_ENTRY). But later, this fixed buffer is used to copy a buffer with a variable size – (PrimaryHeader->SizeOfPartitionEntry). As such, the attack may just change the SizeOfPartitionEntry with a big size and cause buffer overflow in the firmware boot.

Listing 4-1.

```
================
  PartEntry = AllocatePool (PrimaryHeader->NumberOfPartitionEntries *
  sizeof (EFI_PARTITION_ENTRY));
  if (PartEntry == NULL) {
    DEBUG ((EFI_D_ERROR, "Allocate pool error\n"));
    goto Done;
  }

  Status = DiskIo->ReadDisk (
                  DiskIo,
                  MediaId,
                  MultU64x32(PrimaryHeader->PartitionEntryLBA, BlockSize),
                  PrimaryHeader->NumberOfPartitionEntries*
                  (PrimaryHeader->SizeOfPartitionEntry),
                  PartEntry
                  );
  if (EFI_ERROR (Status)) {
    GptValidStatus = Status;
    DEBUG ((EFI_D_ERROR, " Partition Entry ReadDisk error\n"));
    goto Done;
  }
================
```

In order to mitigate this, the firmware code shall not trust any data from external storage – not only the file itself but also the file system and partition. Verification for the file system is required.

Secure Configuration

Secure boot can only verify code and read-only data. For the data that is designed to be configurable by the end user, secure boot is not an option. We need some other way to detect the integrity of the data.

Detectability

Similar to secure boot, we may use a different way to detect the configuration data change (see Table 4-8).

Table 4-8. *Detectability of Configuration*

Mechanism	Method	Limitation	Example
Digital signature	Sign the configuration at runtime. The signature and data can be stored in the same place. The signing private key cannot be exposed as plain text.	We may rely on the other secure coprocessor to do the signing work or other secure storage to hold the private key.	TPM, Hardware Security Module (HSM), Management Engine
Hash	Create a hash for the configuration at runtime. The hash of data cannot be stored in the same place.	We need to save the hash value to another secure place to validate the integrity of configuration. We may have the secure storage size limitation.	TPM non-volatile storage
HMAC	Create an HMAC for the configuration at runtime. The HMAC can be stored in the same place. The HMAC key cannot be exposed as plain text.	We may rely on the other secure coprocessor to calculate the HMAC or other secure storage to hold the HMAC key.	Management Engine
Encryption	Encrypt and decrypt the configuration data at runtime. It can support both integrity and confidentiality. The encryption key cannot be exposed as plain text.	We may rely on the other secure coprocessor to encrypt the data and decrypt the data or other secure storage to hold the encryption key.	Management Engine

The detection mainly focuses on the threat introduced by the simple hardware attacker, instead of the system software attacker. As such, we allow any program to modify the configuration via exposed interface. We just do not allow the attacker to modify the configuration by attaching a flash programmer to update the flash content directly.

For the threat from the system software attacker, we need to add correctness checks when the system updates the configuration; see Chapter 3.

Attack and Mitigation

Now, let's take a look at some real cases for the attack to secure configuration and mitigation.

Rollback Attack

For configuration data, we need to prevent a rollback attack or replay attack. The attack may save the current configuration as the known good configuration and restore the good configuration sometime later.

A hardware-based monotonic counter can be used to mitigate such a threat. For example, we may associate the whole configuration variable region with a monotonic counter and increase the monotonic counter whenever there is configuration variable update. As such, the old version configuration data does not match the latest monotonic counter.

We will discuss the details of rollback protection in Chapter 11.

Partial Update Attack

An attacker may choose to power off the system during the configuration data update. As such, the configuration is partially updated. The BIOS must have a way to detect such a scenario based upon the hardware limitations. If the hardware can guarantee the data update at the block level, the detection mechanism can be in the block-based mechanism, such as a Replay Protected Memory Block (RPMB) device. If the hardware can guarantee the data update at the byte level, the detection mechanism shall be at the byte level, such as a Replay Protected Monotonic Counter (RPMC)–capable SPI device.

We will discuss the details of partial update detection in Chapter 11.

Summary

In this chapter, we discussed the second part of the firmware resiliency – detection. We showed the security property of the secure boot and secure configuration and explained the real cases from the industry. In the next chapter, we will continue the discussion on the third part of the firmware resiliency – recovery.

References

Conference, Journal, and Paper

[P-1] Jeff Bobzin, "UEFI Secure Boot," in *UEFI Plugfest 2011*, available at https://uefi.org/learning_center/presentationsandvideos

[P-2] Jiewen Yao, Vincent Zimmer, "Understanding the UEFI Secure Boot Chain," in *EDKII Whitepaper 2019*, available at https://legacy.gitbook.com/book/edk2-docs/understanding-the-uefi-secure-boot-chain/details

[P-3] Jessie Frazelle, "Securing the Boot Process," in *ACM Queue November/December 2019*, available at https://queue.acm.org/detail.cfm?id=3382016

[P-4] Bryan Kelly, "Project Cerberus Hardware Security," in *OCP Summit 2018*, available at https://f990335bdbb4aebc3131-b23f11c2c6da826ceb51b46551bfafdc.ssl.cf2.rackcdn.com/images/fbbdd5feceb6e6328373417e1ab7c06a13a2ef2c.pdf

[P-5] Scott Johnson, "Titan silicon root of trust for Google Cloud," in *Secure Enclaves Workshop 2018*, available at https://keystone-enclave.org/workshop-website-2018/slides/Scott_Google_Titan.pdf

[P-6] Mikhail Davidov, Jeremy Erickson, "Inside the Apple T2," in *Blackhat US 2019*, available at http://i.blackhat.com/USA-19/Thursday/us-19-Davidov-Inside-The-Apple-T2.pdf

[P-7] Doug Stiles, "The Hardware Security Platform Behind Azure Sphere," in HC30, www.hotchips.org/hc30/1conf/1.13_Microsoft_Hardware_Security_Platform_Behind_Azure_Sphere.pdf

[P-8] Roger Lai, "AMD Secure and Server Innovation," in *UEFI Plugfest 2013*, available at www.uefi.org/sites/default/files/resources/UEFI_PlugFest_AMD_Security_and_Server_innovation_AMD_March_2013.pdf

[P-9] Dong Wei, "UEFI Updates and Secure Software Isolation on Arm," in *UEFI Plugfest 2018*, available at https://uefi.org/learning_center/presentationsandvideos

[P-10] Tamas Ban, "Trusted Firmware M – Trusted Boot," in *Linaro HKG18 2018*, available at `http://connect.linaro.org.s3.amazonaws.com/hkg18/presentations/hkg18-223.pdf`.

[P-11] Simon Glass, "Verified boot in Chrome OS and how to make it work for you," in *Embedded Linux Conference Europe 2013*, available at `https://static.googleusercontent.com/media/research.google.com/en//pubs/archive/42038.pdf`

[P-12] Randall Spangler, "Verified boot surviving in the internet of insecure things," in *coreboot conference 2016*, available at `www.coreboot.org/images/c/ce/Verified_Boot_-_Surviving_in_the_Internet_of_Insecure_Things.pdf`

[P-13] JagannadhaSutradharudu Teki, "U-Boot: Verified RSA Boot on ARM Target," in *U-Boot Mini Summit 2013*, available `www.denx.de/wiki/pub/U-Boot/MiniSummitELCE2013/U-Boot_verified_RSA_boot_flow_on_arm_target.pdf`

[P-14] Dave Heller, Nageswara Sastry, "OpenPOWER secure and trusted boot, Part 2: Protecting system firmware with OpenPOWER secure boot," IBM Whitepaper, 2019, `https://developer.ibm.com/articles/protect-system-firmware-openpower/`

[P-15] Leendert van Doorn, "Secure Hardware and the Creation of an Open Trusted Ecosystem," in Trusted Computing Conference 2013, available at `https://classic.regonline.com/custImages/360000/369552/TCC%20PPTs/TCC2013_VanDoorn.pdf`

[P-16] Jim Mann, "System Firmware – The Emerging Malware Battlefront," NIST Computer Security Resource Center, 2015, available at `https://csrc.nist.gov/CSRC/media/Presentations/System-Firmware-The-Emerging-Malware-Battlefront/images-media/day1_trusted-computing_100-150.pdf`

[P-17] Anthony Ligouri, "Powering Next-Gen EC2 Instances: Deep Dive into the Nitro System" in *AWS re:Invent* 2018, `www.slideshare.net/AmazonWebServices/powering-nextgen-ec2-instances-deep-dive-into-the-nitro-system-cmp303r1-aws-reinvent-2018`

[P-18] Nilo Redini, Aravind Machiry, Dipanjan Das, Yanick Fratantonio, Antonio Bianchi, Eric Gustafson, Yan Shoshitaishvili, Christopher Kruegel, and Giovanni Vigna, "BootStomp: On the Security of Bootloaders in Mobile Devices," in *the Proceedings of the 26th USENIX Security Symposium 2017*, `www.usenix.org/system/files/conference/usenixsecurity17/sec17-redini.pdf`

[P-19] John Heasman, "Hacking the Extensible Firmware Interface," in *Blackhat 2007*, available at `www.blackhat.com/presentations/bh-usa-07/Heasman/Presentation/bh-usa-07-heasman.pdf`

[P-20] Alexander Ermolov, "Safeguarding Rootkits: Intel Boot Guard," in *Zeronights 2016*, available at `https://github.com/flothrone/bootguard/blob/master/Intel%20BootGuard%20final.pdf`

[P-21] Alexander Ermolov, "Safeguarding Rootkits: Intel Boot Guard, (part2)," in *DC 2017*, available at https://github.com/flothrone/bootguard/blob/master/ Intel%20BG%20part2.pdf

[P-22] Alex Matrosov, "Betraying the BIOS," in *Blackhat 2017*, available at www.blackhat.com/docs/us-17/wednesday/us-17-Matrosov-Betraying-The-BIOS-Where-The-Guardians-Of-The-BIOS-Are-Failing.pdf

[P-23] Alex Matrosov, "Modern Secure Boot Attacks," in *Blackhat 2019*, available at http://i.blackhat.com/asia-19/Fri-March-29/ bh-asia-Matrosov-Modern-Secure-Boot-Attacks.pdf

[P-24] Trammell Hudson, Peter Bosch, "Now You See It: TOCTOU Attacks Against Secure Boot and BootGuard," in HITBSecConf 2019, https://conference.hitb.org/ hitbsecconf2019ams/materials/D1T1%20-%20Toctou%20Attacks%20Against%20 Secure%20Boot%20-%20Trammell%20Hudson%20&%20Peter%20Bosch.pdf

[P-25] Corey Kallenberg, Xeno Kovah, John Butterworth, Sam Cornwell, "All your boot are belong to us," in *CSW 2014*, available at https://cansecwest.com/ slides/2014/AllYourBoot_csw14-mitre-final.pdf

[P-26] Hao Xu, "Attack Secure Boot of SEP," in *MOSEC 2020*, https://www.mosec. org/en/2020/

Specification and Guideline

[S-1] NIST SP800-193, "Platform Firmware Resiliency Guidelines," 2018, available at https://csrc.nist.gov/publications/sp800

[S-2] UEFI Organization, "UEFI Specification," 2019, available at www.uefi.org/

[S-3] OCP, "Project Cerberus Architecture Overview Specification," 2018, available at https://github.com/opencomputeproject/Project_Olympus/blob/master/ Project_Cerberus

[S-4] OCP, "Project Cerberus Firmware Challenge Specification," 2019, available at https://github.com/opencomputeproject/Project_Olympus/blob/master/ Project_Cerberus

[S-5] OCP, "Project Cerberus Firmware Update Specification," 2019, available at https://github.com/opencomputeproject/Project_Olympus/blob/master/ Project_Cerberus

[S-6] OCP, "Project Cerberus Processor Cryptography Specification," 2018, available at https://github.com/opencomputeproject/Project_Olympus/blob/master/ Project_Cerberus

[S-7] Microsoft, "Microsoft Portable Executable and Common Object File Format Specification," 2019, available at `https://docs.microsoft.com/en-us/windows/win32/debug/pe-format`

[S-8] Microsoft, "Windows Authenticode Portable Executable Signature Format," 2008, available at `https://download.microsoft.com/download/9/c/5/9c5b2167-8017-4bae-9fde-d599bac8184a/Authenticode_PE.docx`

Web

[W-1] Titan in depth security in plaintext, available at `https://cloud.google.com/blog/products/gcp/titan-in-depth-security-in-plaintext`

[W-2] Google, "OpenTitan: Open source silicon root of trust (RoT)," `https://opentitan.org/`

[W-3] Apple T2 Security Chip Overview, available at `www.apple.com/mac/docs/Apple_T2_Security_Chip_Overview.pdf`

[W-4] Amazon, "AWS Nitro System," `https://perspectives.mvdirona.com/2019/02/aws-nitro-system/`

[W-5] Cisco Secure Boot and Trust Anchor Module Differentiation Solution Overview, `www.cisco.com/c/en/us/products/collateral/security/cloud-access-security/secure-boot-trust.html`

[W-6] What is Azure Sphere, `https://docs.microsoft.com/en-us/azure-sphere/product-overview/what-is-azure-sphere`

[W-7] Microsoft, Anatomy of a secure MCU, `https://azure.microsoft.com/en-us/blog/anatomy-of-a-secured-mcu`

[W-8] Intel Platform Firmware Resilience, `https://blog.csdn.net/zdx19880830/article/details/84190005`

[W-9] IBM, "Open Power Firmware document," `https://github.com/open-power/docs/`

[W-10] ARM Trusted Firmware: A trusted board boot, available at `https://github.com/ARM-software/arm-trusted-firmware/blob/master/docs/design/trusted-board-boot.rst`

[W-11] ARM Trusted Firmware M secure boot HW key integration, available at `https://git.trustedfirmware.org/trusted-firmware-m.git/tree/docs/design_documents/secure_boot_hw_key_integration.rst`

[W-12] vboot – Verified Boot Support, available at `https://doc.coreboot.org/security/vboot/index.html`

[W-13] Verified U-Boot, available at `https://lwn.net/Articles/571031/`

[W-14] U-Boot Signature, available at `https://github.com/wowotechX/u-boot/blob/x_integration/doc/uImage.FIT/signature.txt`

[W-15] Checkm8, `https://github.com/axi0mX/ipwndfu`

CHAPTER 5

Firmware Resiliency: Recovery

This chapter describes a critical aspect of platform resiliency – recovery. This supports the availability aspect of the CIA triad of confidentiality, integrity, and availability. If the platform detects that the integrity of components, including code or data, is broken, the platform needs to restore the components to a known good state. This process is called recovery. It is the last element in firmware resiliency. The recovery process is a variant of the update process. It updates the system to an old state. As such, all guidelines for the update should be followed in the recovery process, such as signature checking and version checking.

Image Recovery

The recovery process is performed by the root-of-trust for recovery (RTRec) or the Chain-of-Trust for recovery (CTRec). The RTRec and CTRec shall be the immutable code or the known good code. If the RTRec or CTRec cannot be established, then the end user must perform a manual recovery. For example, if the whole flash chip is corrupt or erased, even the first CPU instruction fetched is an invalid opcode. In this case, the end user might have to attach a flash programmer to the flash chip and burn a new image or be required to ship the machine back to the manufacturer for repair.

RTRec Selection and Recovery Policy

The RTRec and CTRec may be the same as the root-of-trust for detection (RTD) and Chain-of-Trust for detection (CTD), or they may be different. Based upon the relationship between the RTRec and RTD, the platform may use different ways to perform the recovery (see Table 5-1).

163

© Jiewen Yao and Vincent Zimmer 2020
J. Yao and V. Zimmer, *Building Secure Firmware*, https://doi.org/10.1007/978-1-4842-6106-4_5

Table 5-1. *Recovery Policy*

Mechanism	RTRec/RTD Relationship	Detail	Example
Immediate recovery	The RTRec and RTD are the same.	Once the RTD detects the unauthorized change, the RTD invokes the RTRec, and the RTRec starts doing recovery immediately.	EDK II signed recovery. coreboot recovery. HP Sure Start. Project Cerberus. Intel PFR cold reboot.
Reset recovery	The RTRec runs before the RTD/CTD.	Once the RTD/CTD detects the unauthorized change, the RTD/CTD sets the platform state to be "recovery mode" and resets the system. On the next boot, the RTRec detects the "recovery mode" and does the recovery.	Intel PFR warm reboot.
Downgrade boot and late recovery	The RTRec runs after the RTD/CTD.	Once the RTD/CTD detects the unauthorized change, the RTD/CTD continues booting the system with a detectable indicator on the verification failure, such as a TPM measurement. The platform RTRec may have a chance to recover the system to a normal state later.	Intel Boot Guard with the enforcement policy set as timeout shutdown.
Halt and out-of-band recovery	The RTD and RTRec are in different domains.	Once the RTD/CTD detects the unauthorized change, the RTD/CTD halts the system immediately without any in-band recovery capability. As such, only out-of-band (OOB) RTRec can recover the system.	Intel Boot Guard with the enforcement policy set as immediate shutdown.

Recovery Image Selection

The recovery image might be an immutable ROM on the system, a last known good image on the system provided by the manufacturer vendor, or an image saved by the end user. If the recovery image is mutable, the recovery image update must follow the same process as the normal image update, such as image protection, signature check, version check, and so on (see Table 5-2).

Table 5-2. *Recovery Image Selection*

Mechanism	Pros	Cons
Immutable ROM	There is no way to break the immutable ROM.	If immutable ROM has a vulnerability, this vulnerability is permanent.
Last known good image	The platform keeps the recovery image up to date automatically, and the platform ensures there is no known security vulnerability in the recovery image.	It is hard to define what the "good" means. Maybe the platform saves an image which has some functional issue.
End user saved image	End user has the freedom to decide which image to use for recovery.	End user interaction is required. The end user may select a vulnerable image.

The solution to automatically save the last known good image poses a challenge because the definition of "good" cannot be precisely defined. Can we say the new image is "good" when the firmware successfully transfers to the OS loader? Or when the OS is fully booted up? Or when the OS device drivers are all started up? Or when the business application starts working in the OS? Or when the OS has passed a certification test? There is no universal answer, and the platform designer needs to make a decision to balance the OS functionality needed to prove the system is in a good state.

Recovery Image Location

The recovery image might be in the system ROM such as a flash device, on a non-removable disk such as a hard drive, or on a removable disk such as a USB key or CDROM/DVDROM or transmitted from a remote location via a transport such as a serial port or network or even from an out-of-band management device (see Table 5-3).

Table 5-3. *Recovery Image Location*

Mechanism	Pros	Cons	Example
Flash ROM	The recovery image is always present.	The cost is higher.	On the same flash device or a different flash device.
Non-removable disk	There is no cost increase.	The recovery image itself needs to be protected, and only allow authorized recovery image update.	Hard drive (hard disk drive (HDD), solid-state disk (SSD), NVMe, and so on) – hidden partition or system partition.
Removable disk	The recovery image cannot be attacked because it is not attached to the system in a normal boot.	User interaction is required. End user guarantees the correctness of the recovery image.	CDROM/DVDROM, USB key.
Transmitted from remote	There is no need to touch the local machine.	The network driver stack must be in the RTRec. A recovery server needs to be set up.	Network (Ethernet, Wi-Fi, Bluetooth, and so on), serial port.
Transmitted via out-of-band (OOB)	It is easy for remote management.	The OOB engine needs to have flash access.	Baseboard Management Controller (BMC), Manageability Engine (ME).

Case Study

Now, let's take a look at some real cases for the image recovery.

PCH: Top Swap (TS)

During a normal boot, the silicon will map the two 64 KB top boot blocks of the flash chip to the address [0xE0000, 0xFFFFF). When the CPU starts from the reset vector – 0xF000:0xFFF0 – the CPU can execute the instruction directly on the flash. These same boot blocks are also mapped to [0xFFFE0000, 0xFFFFFFFF) because the typical 16-bit real mode boot block code switches to the 32-bit protected mode immediately to access the whole flash region, which may be bigger than 1 MB. See Figure 5-1.

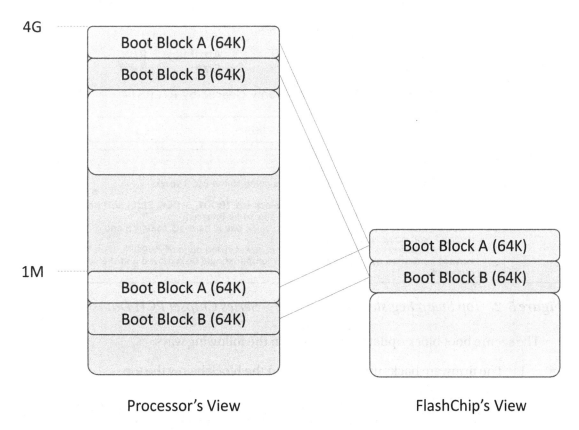

Figure 5-1. *Flash Chip Mapping*

Top Swap (TS) is a feature which swaps the top block of the Firmware Hub or SPI flash (also known as boot block) with another location (see Figure 5-2). This is designed to allow safe update of the boot block. When it is enabled, the PCH will invert the address for cycles going to the two top blocks of the flash. For example, if the block size is 64 K, accessing FFFF_0000h–FFFF_FFFFh MMIO address becomes accessing FFFE_0000h–FFFE_FFFFh flash address and vice versa.

BUC—Backed Up Control Register

Offset Address: 3414h   Attribute: R/W
Default Value: 0000000xb   Size: 8-bit

All bits in this register are in the RTC well and only cleared by RTCRST#.

Bit	Description
0	**Top Swap (TS)**—R/W. 0 = PCH will not allow invert the boot block. 1 = PCH will allow boot block invert, for cycles going to the BIOS space. **Note:** If Top Swap is enabled (TS = 1b): 1. If booting from SPI, then the BIOS boot block size (BOOT_BLOCK_SIZE) **soft strap** determines if A16, A17, A18, A19 or A20 should be inverted. 2. If booting from LPC (FWH), then the boot-block size is hard-set to 64 KB and only A16 is inverted (soft strap is ignored in this case). 3. If PCH is strapped for Top Swap (GPIO55 is low at rising edge of PWROK), then this bit **cannot** be cleared by software. The strap jumper should be removed and the system rebooted.

Figure 5-2. *Top Swap Register (Source: Intel 9 Series Chipset PCH Datasheet)*

The secure boot block update can be used in the following ways:

1.   The firmware backs up the top block to the block below the top (the swap block).

2.   The firmware enables Top Swap. This will invert the appropriate address bits for the cycles going to the Low Pin Count (LPC) or Serial Peripheral Interface (SPI) bus. This bit is stored in the RTC well.

3.   The firmware erases the top block and writes the new top block.

4.   The firmware disables Top Swap.

If there is any power failure reset during step 3, the system will boot from the boot block backed up in step 1 and perform the recovery. See Figure 5-3.

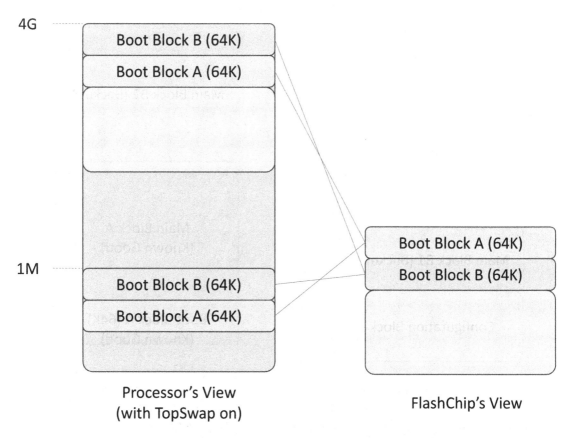

Figure 5-3. *Flash Chip Mapping with Top Swap Enabled*

The BIOS may implement different ways for Top Swap–based recovery to work because the boot block B may control the different code flows. For example, the RTD (such as an ACM or Embedded Controller) may check the boot block A before transferring control. If the RTD finds there is something wrong, the RTD may choose to set the Top Swap and reset the system. On the next boot, the RTD may check the boot block B. If the check passes this time, the boot block B owns the reset vector. It is in recovery mode now. The boot block B may launch the main block B1 from the flash image. The main block B1 may include an external storage driver and load the main block B2 from there. Finally, the main block figures out a way to flash a known good image to boot block A and main block A, clears the Top Swap, and resets the system. Now the next boot becomes the normal boot again. See Figure 5-4 for the flash image layout to support Top Swap recovery.

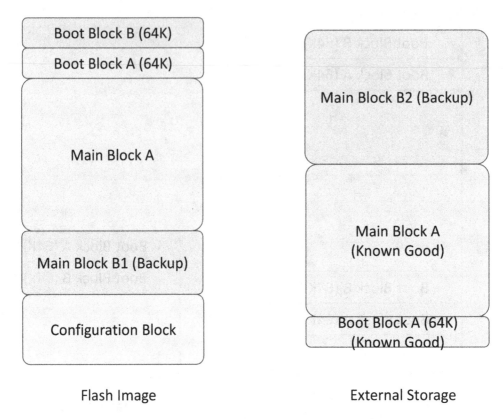

Figure 5-4. Flash Image Layout to Support Top Swap Recovery

PCH: Boot BIOS Strap (BBS)

Boot BIOS Strap (BBS) is a feature to select where the BIOS boots from (see Figure 5-5). It could be from the LPC bus or SPI bus. The platform manufacturer may choose to connect the flash via the LPC bus or SPI bus. Previous generations even had the capability to boot the BIOS from the PCI bus. If the PCI bus is selected, the top 16 MB of the memory below 4GB (FF00_0000h to FFFF_FFFFh) is accepted by the primary side of the PCI-to-PCI bridge and forwarded to the PCI bus. This allows the system recovery from a plug-in PCI card. For example, if the platform owner finds the whole BIOS region is corrupt, they can set a jumper and plug in a PCI card with a known good BIOS on the card. The jumper may route BIOS accesses to the PCI bus. Once the system boots, the platform owner may update a new image to the BIOS connected to the LPC or SPI bus. This boot from the PCI feature is not present in more recent chipsets.

GCS—General Control and Status Register

Offset Address: 3410–3413h   Attribute: R/W, R/WLO
Default Value: 00000yy0h (yy = xx0000x0b)   Size: 32-bit

Bit	Description
31:12	Reserved

11:10	**Boot BIOS Straps (BBS)**—R/W. This field determines the destination of accesses to the BIOS memory range. The default values for these bits represent the strap values of GPIO51 (bit 11) at the rising edge of PWROK and SATA1GP/GPIO19 (bit 10) at the rising edge of PWROK.
	
	    Bits 11:10 **Description**
	       00b LPC
	       01b Reserved
	       10b Reserved
	       11b SPI
	
	When SPI or LPC is selected, the range that is decoded is further qualified by other configuration bits described in the respective sections.
	The value in this field can be overwritten by software as long as the BIOS Interface Lock-Down (bit 0) is not set.
	Boot BIOS Destination Select to LPC by functional strap or using Boot BIOS Destination Bit will not affect SPI accesses initiated by Intel Management Engine or Integrated GbE LAN.

0	**BIOS Interface Lock-Down (BILD)**—R/WLO. 0 = Disabled. 1 = Prevents BUC.TS (offset 3414, bit 0) and GCS.BBS (offset 3410h, bits 11:10) from being changed. This bit can only be written from 0 to 1 once.

Figure 5-5. *Boot BIOS Strap Register (Source: Intel 9 Series Chipset PCH Datasheet)*

coreboot Recovery

The coreboot firmware has two partitions – read-only one (including boot block, verstage, and a recovery image) and read-write one (including romstage + ramstage + payload). The read-only partition is the RTD and RTRec. After the boot block sets up the temporary RAM, the verstage tries to verify and load read/write firmware A. If it fails, the firmware tries to verify and load firmware B. If it fails again, it tries to verify and load the recovery firmware. The recovery image is included in the read-only portion; and it has a full copy of romstage, ramstage, and payload for the recovery mode. See Figure 5-6 for the coreboot recovery flash image layout.

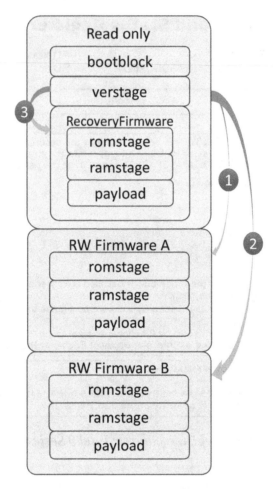

Figure 5-6. *coreboot Recovery Flash Image Layout*

EDK II Signed Recovery

In the EDK II signed recovery solution, the Pre-EFI Initialization (PEI) firmware
volume (FV) works as the RTRec. The PEI components check the Driver Execution
Environment (DXE) main FV and decide the boot mode. The PEI FV may load a recovery
version of the DXE main FV in the recovery boot mode. The recovery DXE main FV
can be loaded from external storage, such as HDD, USB key, CDROM, and so on. See
Figure 5-7 for EDK II signed recovery flow.

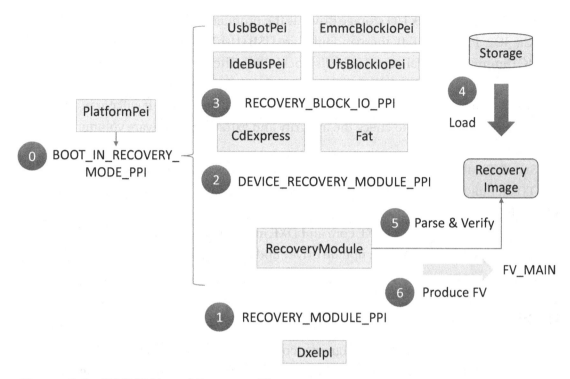

Figure 5-7. *EDK II Signed Recovery Flow*

Step 0: During system boot, a platform PEI module detects the boot mode and sets BOOT_IN_RECOVERY_MODE if recovery is required. It also installs the EFI_PEI_BOOT_IN_RECOVERY_MODE_PPI so that modules with the recovery dependency are dispatched in recovery mode.

Step 1: As the final step of the PEI phase, the DxeIpl tries to load the recovery image via EFI_PEI_RECOVERY_MODULE_PPI.LoadRecoveryCapsule if the system boot mode is in BOOT_IN_RECOVERY_MODE.

Step 2: A RecoveryModule is the producer of EFI_PEI_RECOVERY_MODULE_PPI. It consumes EFI_PEI_DEVICE_RECOVERY_MODULE_PPI.

Step 3: The PEI file system driver is the producer of the EFI_PEI_DEVICE_RECOVERY_MODULE_PPI. In EDK II, these modules include CDROM/DVDROM (CdExpressPei) and FAT file system (FatPei). They consume the EFI_PEI_RECOVERY_BLOCK_IO2_PPI.

Step 4: The PEI block I/O storage driver is the producer of EFI_PEI_RECOVERY_
BLOCK_IO2_PPI. In EDK II, these modules are USB (UsbBotPei), HDD (IdeBusPei),
eMMC (EmmcBlockIoPei), and UFS (UfsBlockIoPei). These PEIMs are the modules to
load the recovery capsule image from a storage device into memory.

Step 5: Once the RecoveryModule retrieves the recovery image, it will parse and
verify the recovery image to check the integrity and extract the firmware volume for the
DXE phase.

Step 6: Finally, the RecoveryModule installs the extracted firmware volume (FV)
for DXE. It builds EFI_HOB_FIRMWARE_VOLUME and installs EFI_PEI_FIRMWARE_
VOLUME_INFO2_PPI.

Then DxeIpl can find the DXE core and DXE main FV and transfer control to
DXE. Later, the DXE phase flash update driver updates the DXE FV in the flash region to
finish the recovery.

HP Sure Start

The coreboot recovery and EDK II signed recovery solution assume that the RTD/RTRec
and other mutable images are in one single device. It simplifies the board design and
lowers the cost. However, in some cases, there is no guarantee that the boot block is
really read-only. It can still be updatable. As such, the previous solution does not work.

HP Sure Start technology includes a standalone chip as the root-of-trust for
protection, detection, and recovery. This chip has the self-healing capability, which
provides automatic recovery from the corruption of the whole BIOS as well as firmware
protection against permanent denial of service (PDoS) attacks. After power-on, the HP
Sure Start chip checks the boot block. If the boot block is corrupted, the HP Sure Start
chip recovers it from a known good image. The boot block then checks the rest of the
system BIOS image. See Figure 5-8 for the flow.

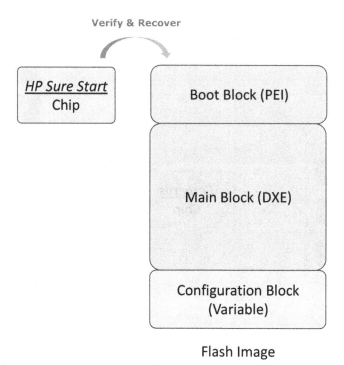

Figure 5-8. *HP Sure Start Detection and Recovery Flow*

Project Cerberus

Cerberus Security Architecture is a server platform solution for protection, detection, and recovery defined by Open Compute Project (OCP). Its scope extends from the host firmware to the baseboard management controller (BMC) firmware. As discussed in Chapter 4, the Cerberus chip connects to the BIOS flash chip and the BMC flash chip. Each flash chip includes three areas: active image, recovery image, and staging image (see Figure 5-9). If the active firmware cannot boot, the Cerberus chip can trigger the recovery process to load the image from the recovery image to overwrite the corrupted active firmware. The recovery can be triggered via the "Recover Image" command as well. See Table 5-4. Of course, the Cerberus chip needs to protect the recovery image from tampering by the active image.

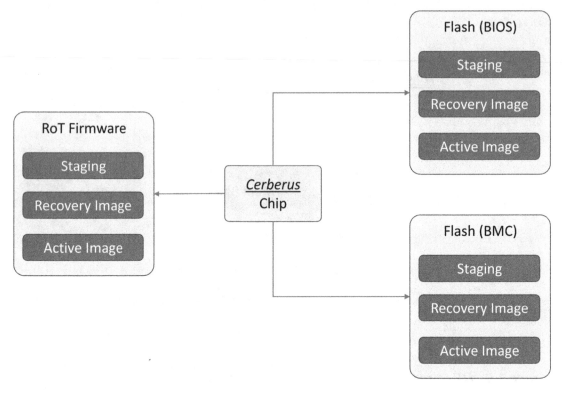

Figure 5-9. *Cerberus Image Layout*

Besides the BIOS and BMC firmware, the Cerberus root-of-trust (RoT) commands can be used to support device firmware update and recovery image update, once the Cerberus finds the device component firmware has been corrupted.

Table 5-4. *Cerberus RoT Command List*

Register Name	RoT	Description
Recovery firmware	Platform Active (PA) RoT/Active Component (CA) RoT	Restore Firmware Index using backup.
Prepare Recovery Firmware	Platform Active (PA) RoT/Active Component (CA) RoT	Prepare storage for recovery image.
Update Recovery Firmware	Platform Active (PA) RoT	Updates the recovery image.
Activate Recovery Firmware	Platform Active (PA) RoT	Activates the received recovery image.

ARM Trusted Boot Firmware

The recovery implementation in ARM Trusted-Firmware-A is platform specific. A platform may choose to boot to a valid flash image saved in the other position of the flash image, if a recovery boot is required. This action may be combined with a firmware update flow to use the recovery image to overwrite the active image region.

ARM Trusted-Firmware-M uses the swap mechanism for update, as we discussed in Chapter 3. This swap mechanism is also used for recovery. If the new image boots fail, the system does a reboot, reverts to an old stable image, and sets the rollback flag. See Figure 5-10.

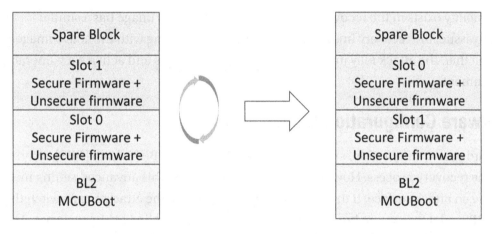

Figure 5-10. *ARM Trusted-Firmware-M Swap Mechanism for Update and Recovery*

Attack and Mitigation

Now, let's take a look at some real cases for the attacks to the image recovery and mitigation of those attacks.

Recovery Image Attack

Since the recovery image is another BIOS image, all hardware attack for the working image may also be applied to the recovery image. If the recovery image is in flash, the flash region must be protected. If the recovery image is on the system partition of the non-removable disk, it is more challenging. This partition must be a protected partition or a hidden partition.

Updating the recovery image is another attack surface. All the rules applied to active image update must be applied to recovery image update too, such as authentication check, version check, non-bypassability, and so on.

Image Downgrade Attack

The recovery image must not have any known security vulnerability. It might be different from the active image and not have the same full functionality as the active image since the major function of the recovery image is to recover the system to a state that can update to a new active image.

When an active image is updated, the platform owner must decide if the vulnerability exists in the recovery image too. If the recovery image has a similar security issue, the recovery image must also be updated along with the active image. Without that, the attack may just trigger the recovery process and activate a vulnerable environment.

Hardware Configuration Attack

The hardware configuration, such as Top Swap (TS) or Boot BIOS Strap (BBS), may help the recovery process. However, the improper usage of this advanced setting may become an attack surface. If those registers are not locked, the attacker can switch the TS or BBS to let the system boot from the other source controlled by the malware. All hardware settings related to security must be locked before the system exits the platform manufacturer authentication phase.

Configuration Recovery

Besides the executable code, the configuration data may also be tampered with or corrupted. If that is detected, the configuration data also needs to perform recovery.

Recovery Configuration Selection

The configuration might be the manufacturer default, a last known good configuration saved by the manufacturer/vendor, or a configuration saved by the end user. If the recovery configuration is mutable, the recovery configuration update must follow the same process as the normal configuration update process. See Table 5-5.

Table 5–5. *Recovery Configuration Selection*

Mechanism	Pros	Cons
Manufacture default	There is no way to break the manufacturer default value, which should be stored in the immutable region or within the recovery image region.	If the manufacturer default value is not a secure configuration, it has to be updated together with the whole recovery image update.
Last known good configuration	The platform keeps the last configuration data automatically.	Similar to the last known good image, it is hard to define what the "good" means.
End user saved configuration	End user has freedom to decide which configuration to recover.	End user may save a non-bootable configuration by mistake.

Usually, a manufacturer provides the default configuration value. If the configuration is not end user changeable such as Vital Production Data (VPD), it should be treated as a part of the recovery image instead of the recovery configuration. If the configuration is end user changeable, such as setup variable policy data or secure boot configuration data, there could be two sets of default values – one is platform manufacturer default, and the other is the end user saved configuration in the setup page. The end user may choose to load the end user saved configuration in the setup page or to load the platform manufacturer default. Figure 5-11 shows the flow.

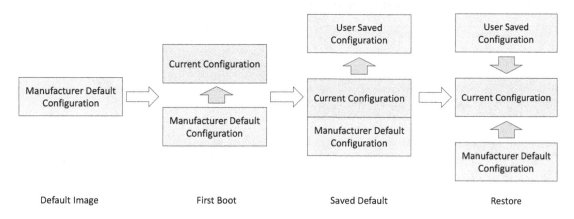

Figure 5-11. *Configuration Recovery*

Attack and Mitigation

Now, let's take a look at some real cases for the attacks to the configuration recovery and mitigation of those attacks.

Configuration Data Attack

Most of the attacks to the recovery configuration are similar to the attacks to the recovery image. The configuration data itself shall be protected.

Configuration Rollback Attack

If the default configuration is not secure enough and the current configuration updates that, the attacker may choose to trigger a recovery to load the default insecure configuration. For example, the default image may include a secure boot forbidden database – dbx1. If the platform appends the new secure boot forbidden database into dbx1, then the current forbidden database – dbx2 – includes more entries than the default forbidden database, dbx1. In order to allow the vulnerable signed image to run, the attacker needs to figure out a way to remove the new entry from the secure boot forbidden database. With recovery enabled, they may trigger a platform recovery to load the manufacturer's default configuration – dbx1. Figure 5-12 shows the concept.

In order to mitigate such an attack, if a platform needs any configuration update to a secure state, the platform must update the current configuration, the saved configuration, and the default configuration.

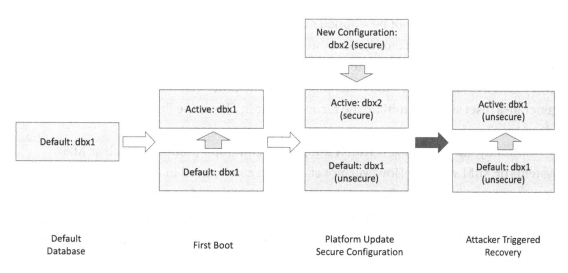

Figure 5-12. *Configuration Rollback Attack*

Watchdog

In the case of a normally operating environment, we expect that the root-of-trust for detection (RTD) can detect instances of firmware corruption and subsequently trigger or initiate the recovery process. However, in some special cases, the firmware may hang due to a configuration data attack which is not detected by the RTD. In the latter scenario, we still want to have an auto recovery mechanism. A watchdog is a hardware device to assist the recovery process in such a case to resist the denial-of-service attack. See Figure 5-13 for a typical watchdog design.

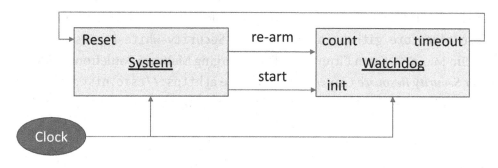

Figure 5-13. *Watchdog*

In the resiliency solution, the watchdog should be part of the resiliency engine, such as the platform Root-of-Trust. The watchdog should be started during the platform root-of-trust and should not be stopped or tampered by any exposed vulnerability in the system. In a normal scenario, the system should rearm the watchdog periodically to prevent it from timing out. If the system runs into a corrupted state or hangs, then the system will fail to rearm the watchdog. When the timer elapses, the watchdog will generate a reset signal to initiate the recovery action. This is the firmware equivalent of a "dead man's switch."

Currently, the watchdog is widely adopted in computer platforms, such as X86 systems or ARM systems. However, not all of them can be used in the resiliency usage because of the special requirement that the watchdog should be tamper-resistant against a vulnerable resiliency target. A cyber resiliency watchdog should be a latchable watchdog or authenticated watchdog. Only the root-of-trust for resiliency (RTRes) can control it.

Summary

In this chapter, we discussed the third part of the firmware resiliency – recovery. We covered both image recovery and configuration recovery. In the next chapter, we will discuss the OS/loader resiliency.

References

Conference, Journal, and Paper

[P-1] Jiewen Yao, Vincent Zimmer, "A Tour Beyond BIOS- Capsule Update and Recovery in EDK II," Intel whitepaper, 2016, available at https://github.com/tianocore/tianocore.github.io/wiki/EDK-II-Security-White-Papers

[P-2] Jim Mann, "System Firmware – The Emerging Malware Battlefront," *NIST Computer Security Resource Center, 2015*, available at https://csrc.nist.gov/CSRC/media/Presentations/System-Firmware-The-Emerging-Malware-Battlefront/images-media/day1_trusted-computing_100-150.pdf

[P-3] Andrew Thoelke, "ARM Trusted Firmware for ARMv8-A," Linaro Connect US 2013, available at www.slideshare.net/linaroorg/arm-trusted-firmareforarmv8alcu13

[P-4] Andrew Thoelke, "Adopting ARM Trusted Firmware," Linaro Connect Asia 2014, available at www.slideshare.net/linaroorg/lca14-102-adoptingarmtrustedfirmware

[P-5] Dan Handley, "ARM Trusted Firmware – from Enterprise to Embedded," Linaro Connect Las Vegas 2016, available at `http://s3.amazonaws.com/connect.linaro.org/las16/Presentations/Thursday/LAS16-402%20-%20Arm-TF%20From%20Embedded%20To%20Enterprise%20v1.0%20%281%29.pdf`

[P-6] Dan Handley, Charles Garcia-Tobin, "Trusted Firmware Deep Dive," available at `www.linaro.org/app/resources/Connect%20Events/Trusted_Firmware_Deep_Dive_v1.0_.pdf`

[P-7] Sun Bing, "BIOS Boot Hijacking and VMware Vulnerabilities Digging," in Power Of Community 2007, available at `http://powerofcommunity.net/poc2007/sunbing.pdf`

[P-8] Alexander Ermolov, "Safeguarding Rootkits: Intel Boot Guard," in *Zeronights 2016*, available at `https://github.com/flothrone/bootguard/blob/master/Intel%20BootGuard%20final.pdf`

[P-9] Alexander Ermolov, "Safeguarding Rootkits: Intel Boot Guard, (part2)," in *DC 2017*, available at `https://github.com/flothrone/bootguard/blob/master/Intel%20BG%20part2.pdf`

[P-10] Ronald Aigner, Paul England, Andrey Marochko, Dennis Mattoon, Rob Spiger, Stefan Thom, "Cyber-Resilient Platform Requirements," Microsoft Whitepaper, 2017, available at `www.microsoft.com/en-us/research/publication/cyber-resilient-platform-requirements/`

[P-11] Frank Stajano, Ross Anderson, "The Grenade Timer: Fortifying the Watchdog Timer Against Malicious Mobile Code," in Proceedings of 7th International Workshop on Mobile Multimedia Communications, 2000 available at `www.cl.cam.ac.uk/~rja14/Papers/grenade.pdf`

Specification and Guideline

[S-1] NIST SP800-193, "Platform Firmware Resiliency Guidelines," 2018, available at `https://csrc.nist.gov/publications/sp800`

[S-2] OCP, "Project Cerberus Architecture Overview Specification," 2018, available at `https://github.com/opencomputeproject/Project_Olympus/blob/master/Project_Cerberus`

[S-3] OCP, "Project Cerberus Firmware Challenge Specification," 2019, available at `https://github.com/opencomputeproject/Project_Olympus/blob/master/Project_Cerberus`

[S-4] OCP, "Project Cerberus Firmware Update Specification," 2019, available at `https://github.com/opencomputeproject/Project_Olympus/blob/master/Project_Cerberus`

[S-5] OCP, "Project Cerberus Processor Cryptography Specification," 2018, available at https://github.com/opencomputeproject/Project_Olympus/blob/master/Project_Cerberus

[S-6] Intel, "Intel® 9 Series Chipset Platform Controller Hub (PCH) Datasheet," 2015, available at www.intel.com/content/www/us/en/products/docs/chipsets/9-series-chipset-pch-datasheet.html

Web

[W-1] Google, "Firmware Boot and Recovery," www.chromium.org/chromium-os/chromiumos-design-docs/firmware-boot-and-recovery?tmpl=%2Fsystem%2Fapp%2Ftemplates%2Fprint%2F&showPrintDialog=1

[W-2] Checkm8, https://github.com/axi0mX/ipwndfu

CHAPTER 6

OS Resiliency

In a personal computer or server, when the host firmware finishes the initial boot, it transfers the control to the host operating system (OS) loader. Then the host OS loader transfers the control to the final operating system (OS). The OS may be installed by the manufacturer, by the enterprise information technology (IT) department, or by the end user. The typical OS is Windows or Linux. For mobile devices, there may be other types of general-purpose OS, such as Chromium, Android, or iOS. They are created and customized by the platform manufacturer as a part of the whole mobile device solution. In an embedded system or microcontroller, the OS is tightly coupled with the firmware or even a part of the firmware. Some of these solutions include a real-time OS (RTOS), such as FreeRTOS, RT-Thread, Contiki OS, mbed OS, ThreadX, uC/OS, LiteOS, TinyOS, and so on.

Because the OS is the environment which provides the real services, the OS is a major target for attacks. If a Windows or Linux OS instance in a personal computer is attacked, the end user may need to reinstall a new one. But if an Android or iOS instance in a mobile phone is attacked, how can the user install a new one? Not to mention an RTOS running in an embedded system, of which the end user is unaware. From the whole solution perspective, the concept of "resiliency" should be extended from the firmware to the OS.

Similar to firmware resiliency, the OS resiliency also includes three parts: protection, detection, and recovery. Because this book focuses on firmware, we will not introduce all aspects of resiliency in the OS but only focus on the firmware-related part.

© Jiewen Yao and Vincent Zimmer 2020
J. Yao and V. Zimmer, *Building Secure Firmware*, https://doi.org/10.1007/978-1-4842-6106-4_6

Protection

Automated Update

Most of the current commercial OSs, such as Windows, Linux, Android, and iOS, support automated component update. An update service is provided by the OS vendor, and it runs in the background. Whenever the OS vendor provides a new release, the end user will receive a notification, and the patch will be deployed automatically.

The benefit of automated update is that the OS software version is always up to date. The vulnerability of the OS software can be fixed immediately once the patch is available.

Detection

Image Signing

Image signing verification is an effective detection mechanism. UEFI secure boot is one of the solutions that use this mechanism in UEFI firmware. The image signing verification is extended from the firmware to the OS kernel. Some OSs such as Windows 10 enforce the code signing policy to maintain the execution code integrity.

Case Study

Now, let's take a look at some real cases of secure boot for the OS/loader.

Linux Machine Owner Key (MOK)

The UEFI secure boot defines the key hierarchy. A platform key (PK) is provided by the platform owner. Here, the platform owner typically refers to the platform manufacturer who creates the machine, although it might be someone else, such as the end user. The PK is used to sign the key exchange key (KEK) which is provided by the operating system vendor. The KEK is used to sign the allowed image database and forbidden image database. Current platforms are typically required to enable UEFI secure boot by default. Since the end user does not have the PK or KEK, they cannot enroll any new image into the database. This design is good for an end user who just wants to use the OS. But in the Linux world, a developer is considered as the owner of the machine. What if the developer updates the OS loader or OS kernel and tests the update on their own machine with UEFI secure boot enabled?

The developer may disable UEFI secure boot. According to the Windows logo requirements for using UEFI, UEFI secure boot can be disabled with physical user presence. The UEFI specification itself is silent upon disabling the feature. However, once UEFI secure boot is disabled, malware may be installed on the system before UEFI secure boot is enabled again, which is a potential risk.

The minimum secure boot requirements for Linux are as follows: 1) The OS loader must be signed with a key enrolled in the firmware and verified by the firmware. 2) The OS kernel must be signed with a key trusted by the OS loader and verified by the OS loader. One option is to enroll a Linux key for all firmware, similar to the one used by the UEFI Certificate Authority (CA) and Microsoft that lets all other firmware enroll the UEFI CA/Windows key. But that brings a scalability issue.

The other option is to let the UEFI Certificate Authority sign one Linux program as a shim. Then this shim can be used to construct a new key hierarchy in the Linux world, using what is known as the Machine Owner Key (MOK). The differences between MOK and UEFI secure boot key are listed in Table 6-1.

Table 6-1. *MOK and UEFI Secure Boot Key*

Key	Provided by	Enrolled by	Signing	Storage
UEFI secure boot key (PK)	Platform owner – platform manufacturer	Platform owner – platform manufacturer	KEK	UEFI Authenticated Variable
UEFI Secure Boot Key (KEK)	OS vendor – UEFI Certificate Authority (CA), Microsoft	Platform owner – platform manufacturer	db/dbx	UEFI Authenticated Variable
UEFI secure boot key (db/dbx)	OS vendor – UEFI Certificate Authority (CA), Microsoft	Platform owner – platform manufacturer	UEFI option ROM, UEFI Loader (Windows OS loader), Linux shim	UEFI Authenticated Variable
Linux MOK	Machine owner – end user	Machine owner – end user	Linux OS loader, Linux OS kernel	UEFI Boot Service Variable (not authenticated)

With Linux MOK, the boot flow is as shown in Figure 6-1. The UEFI firmware uses the UEFI secure boot key – db – to verify the Linux shim. The shim can embed a default Linux key database such as the SUSE key. As such, the Linux shim can verify a Linux's Grub2 loader and a Linux kernel signed with the SUSE key.

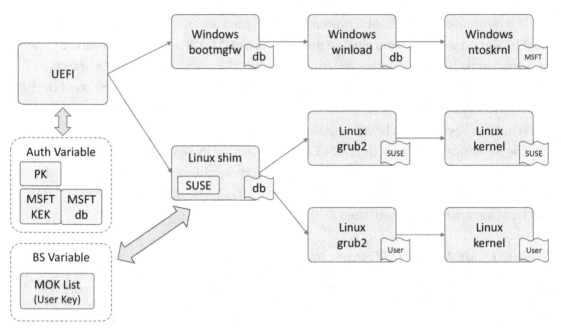

Figure 6-1. *Signing Verification with MOK*

If a Linux developer wants to create a new Grub2 or Linux kernel, they can create a Machine Owner Key (MOK) in the Linux environment and sign the Grub2 and Linux kernel. The user needs to use a MOK utility to enroll the MOK with a password and reboot the system. On the next boot, the MOK manager detects the change request and lets the user input the password to confirm the MOK enrollment. Once the user confirms the update, the MOK takes effect. The Linux shim uses the MOK list to verify the new Linux Grub2 and Linux kernel.

The benefit of the Linux MOK system is that it maintains the secure boot chain from the platform to the Linux kernel, with the flexibility that the end user can enroll the secure boot key for the kernel development.

Chromium OS Verified Boot

Secure boot security can also be implemented in a non-UEFI OS. Take Google Chrome, for example, where the verified firmware solution is extended to the Chromium OS verified boot. The goal of verified boot is to ensure that only a Google-signed Chromium OS can be loaded by the firmware. Table 6-2 shows the keys used by the Chromium verified boot.

Table 6-2. *Keys Used by Chromium Verified Boot*

Key	Verifies	Storage	Versioned
Root key	Firmware data key	RO firmware (GBB)	NO
Firmware data key	RW firmware	RW FW header (VBLOCK)	YES
Kernel subkey	Kernel data key	RW firmware	YES (as FW)
Kernel data key	OS kernel	OS kernel header	YES
Recovery key	Recovery OS kernel	RO firmware	NO

We discussed the coreboot secure boot flow in Chapter 4. Now let's combine them together. The read-only (RO) portion of the firmware works as the root-of-trust of the platform. The RO firmware contains the boot block and a Google Binary Block (GBB), which includes a root key. When the system boots, the boot block code finds the root key in the GBB and uses the root key to verify the read/write (RW) firmware's key block. Inside of the firmware key block, there is a firmware data key which is used to verify the RW firmware preamble. The firmware preamble includes the signature of the firmware body, firmware version, and a subkey for the kernel. Once the firmware body passes the signature verification, the RO firmware transfers control to the RW firmware body. Then the firmware body uses the kernel subkey to verify the kernel's key block. Inside of the kernel key block, there is a kernel data key, which is used to verify the kernel preamble. The kernel preamble includes the signature of the kernel body, kernel version, and related bootloader information. Once the kernel body has passed the signature verification, the RW firmware passes the control to the kernel. See Figure 6-2 for the whole process.

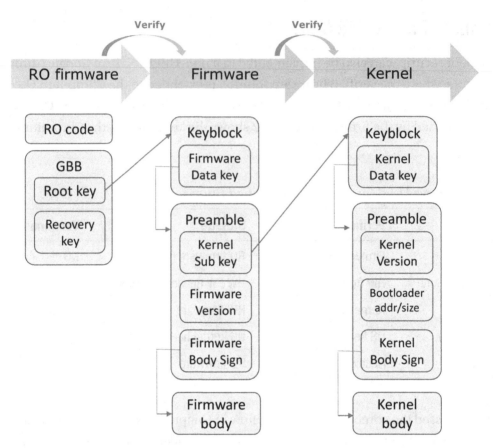

Figure 6-2. *Signing Verification in Chromium Verified Boot*

Besides the OS kernel, Chromium OS uses the device-mapper-verity (dm-verity) to verify the read-only root file system. dm-verity performs integrity checking of block devices and helps prevent persistent rootkits that can hold onto root privileges and compromise devices. The Chromium kernel image also contains a rootfs hash which is used to verify the bundle of disk block hashes. The bundle of disk block hashes is used to verify the blocks of the rootfs when they are read from disk to memory. See Figure 6-3.

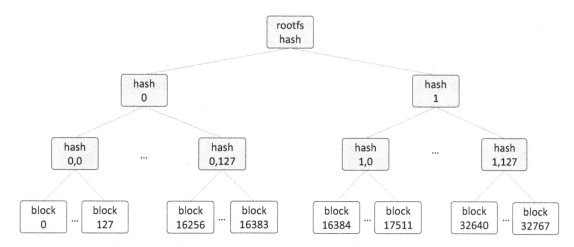

Figure 6-3. *rootfs Hash Verification in Chromium Verified Boot*

The verified boot feature works well in normal boot mode for an end user. But what if the kernel is under development? In order to make the development work easier, Chromium OS supports a special developer mode. This is a built-in "jailbreak mode" to turn verification off. In order to prevent unnecessary user mistakes, the user gets a warning message on the screen if the verification is turned off. When the system switches between the developer mode and normal verified boot mode, the device state is cleared. For example, the Trusted Platform Module (TPM) ownership is cleared.

Chromium OS supports rollback protection. The firmware and kernel key versions are stored in the TPM non-volatile RAM (NVRAM). An image is rejected if its version is smaller than the one recorded in the TPM NVRAM.

Android Verified Boot

The Android system is widely used in mobile phone devices. Android versions 8.0 and higher include Android Verified Boot (AVB) which is also known as the Verified Boot 2.0 reference implementation. The AVB's goal is to ensure the integrity of the software code running on the device. All executed code must come from a trusted source instead of an attacker.

After the system is powered on, a hardware-protected bootloader uses the embedded root key to verify the vbmeta partition. The vbmeta image includes the hash value of the other partitions. For the small partitions, such as the boot partition (including the kernel) and the dtbo partition (including the device tree), the entire content is loaded into memory, and the hash value can be calculated one time. As such, the hash value of the partition is calculated in order to compare with the expected hash. For the large partitions, such as a file system, it is hard to load the entire content into the memory. Only the root hash of the hash tree is calculated to compare with the expected root hash value. A special dm-verity driver is used to verify the large partitions. See Figure 6-4 for the whole verification process.

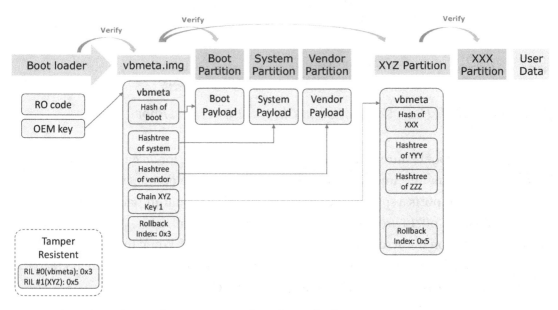

Figure 6-4. *Hash Verification in Android Verified Boot*

The vbmeta structure supports the chained structure. For example, a user can define an XYZ partition which includes the vbmeta structure (the hash of XXX partition, YYY partition, and ZZZ partition) and is signed with key 1. The user includes the public of key 1 in the vbmeta.img. During launch, once the vbmeta.img is verified, the chain XYZ key 1 can be used to verify the vbmeta of the XYZ partition.

The Android Verified Boot also supports rollback protection. Each vbmeta structure has a rollback index location (RIL) number, and each vbmeta structure includes the rollback index number. The rollback index number increases for each image which has a security fix. A system uses the tamper-resistant storage to store all the rollback index numbers with the RIL number. During the runtime check, the vbmeta is rejected if the rollback index is smaller than the stored rollback index in the tamper-resistant storage.

Recovery

Automated Recovery

If the verification fails, the system needs to have a way to restore the known good environment. Since the normal image cannot be used to continue the boot, a special recovery image is used in this case. Ideally, this recovery process can be designed to run automatically and requires minimal user interaction.

Case Study

Now, let's take a look at some real cases for the recovery of the OS/loader.

UEFI Boot Option Recovery

The UEFI specification specifies normal boot options and recovery boot options. A UEFI boot option is recorded in a UEFI variable. The variable contains the description of the boot option, the attributes of the boot option, and, the most important part, the location of the bootable image. The boot option variable name follows the "Boot####" format, where # is a hexadecimal number. Because the typical boot image is provided by the operating system (OS) vendor, the secure boot image verification is required for the boot images.

UEFI recovery includes two parts: OS recovery and platform recovery. If the system needs to perform the recovery, the boot manager will try the OS recovery options first and then try to boot all normal boot options. OS recovery is performed first because it may be necessary to recover boot options. If all normal boot options still fail, the boot manager will try platform recovery as the last option. This platform recovery may include the service reconfiguration and diagnostic options. In order to differentiate OS recovery and platform recovery options from a normal boot, the UEFI specification has separate UEFI variables for them. The OS recovery feature uses the "OSRecovery####" variables, and the platform recovery feature uses the "PlatformRecovery####" variables. One special feature of OS recovery is that the OS recovery image signature database is NOT the standard image signature database (db) but rather a separate recovery image signature database (dbr). The reason is that the recovery image is typically signed with a different key. Table 6-3 shows different types of UEFI recovery.

Table 6-3. *UEFI Boot Option Recovery*

Action	Provided by	Purpose	Image	Image Signature Database
Normal boot	Operating system vendor	Boot to OS.	Defined in "Boot####" variable.	db/dbx/KEK/PK.
OS recovery	Operating system vendor	Allow OS to recover boot options or launch the full OS recovery.	Defined in "OSRecovery####" variable.	dbr/dbx/KEK/PK (dbr is the recovery image signature database).
Platform recovery	Platform manufacturer	Run the remediation as the last resort when no OS is found.	Defined in "PlatformRecovery####" variable.	N/A if it is internal image. Or follow the same UEFI secure boot rule – db/KEK/PK.

Chromium OS Recovery

OS recovery is also supported by non-UEFI OSs, such as Chromium OS. In these systems, the recovery mode can be triggered when the verification fails during normal boot, or it can be triggered when the end user pressed a recovery button.

In the recovery boot mode, the read-only firmware finds the recovery key in the GBB instead of the root key. Since the read-only firmware includes fully functional recovery firmware, the read/write firmware is skipped. The fully functional recovery image uses the recovery key to verify the recovery kernel image. The verification flow is similar to that of the normal boot. It includes the recovery kernel data key verification, the recovery kernel preamble verification, and the recovery kernel body verification. The recovery kernel image also includes a bundle of hashes to verify the rootfs from the recovery media. See Figure 6-5 for the recovery mode boot.

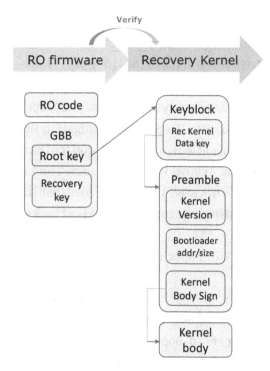

Figure 6-5. *Signing Verification in Chromium Recovery Boot*

Summary

In this chapter, we discussed the OS/loader resiliency including protection, detection, and recovery. In the next chapter, we will discuss the trusted boot, which complements the secure boot.

References

Conference, Journal, and Paper

[P-1] Murali Ravirala, "Windows Boot Environment," in UEFI Plugfest 2007, available at `https://uefi.org/sites/default/files/resources/UEFI-Plugfest-WindowsBootEnvironment.pdf`

[P-2] Olaf Kirch, "UEFI Secure Boot," SUSE presentation, available at `www.suse.com/media/presentation/uefi_secure_boot_webinar.pdf`

[P-3] "Chrome OS Verified Boot," 2016, available at https://docs.google.com/
presentation/d/14haBMrbpc2zlgdWmiaTlp_iDG_A8t5PTTXFMz5kqHSM/
present?slide=id.g11a5e5b4cf_0_140#slide=id.g34551fb06_0121

[P-4] David Weston, "Advancing Windows Security," in *Platform Security Summit
2019*, available at www.platformsecuritysummit.com/2019/speaker/weston/

[P-5] Yunhai Zhang, "Liar Game: The Secret of Mitigation Bypass Techniques," in
Bluehat Shanghai 2019, available at www.microsoft.com/china/bluehatshanghai/2019/

[P-6] Tony Chen, "Guarding Against Physical Attacks: The Xbox
One Story," in *Bluehat Seattle 2019*, www.slideshare.net/MSbluehat/
bluehat-seattle-2019-guarding-against-physical-attacks-the-xbox-one-story

Specification and Guideline

[S-1] UEFI Organization, "UEFI Specification," 2019, available at www.uefi.org/

Web

[W-1] "Ubuntu Secure Boot," https://wiki.ubuntu.com/UEFI/SecureBoot

[W-2] "Chromium OS Verified Boot," www.chromium.org/chromium-os/
chromiumos-design-docs/verified-boot

[W-3] "Chromium OS Recovery Mode," www.chromium.org/chromium-os/
chromiumos-design-docs/recovery-mode

[W-4] "Chromium firmware boot and recovery," www.chromium.org/chromium-os/
chromiumos-design-docs/firmware-boot-and-recovery

[W-5] "Chromium OS verified boot data structures," www.chromium.org/
chromium-os/chromiumos-design-docs/verified-boot-data-structures

[W-6] "Android A/B (Seamless) System Updates," https://source.android.com/
devices/tech/ota/ab

[W-7] "Android Verified Boot," https://source.android.com/security/
verifiedboot

[W-8] "Android Verified Boot 2.0," https://android.googlesource.com/platform/
external/avb/+/master/README.md

[W-9] "Android Verified Boot 2.0," https://blog.csdn.net/rikeyone/article/
details/80606147

[W-10] "Android dm-verity," https://source.android.com/security/
verifiedboot/dm-verity

[W-11] "Practical Windows Code and Driver Signing," www.davidegrayson.com/
signing/

CHAPTER 7

Trusted Boot

The CIA triad of confidentiality, integrity, and availability should always be of top importance for the developer. Regarding "integrity," secure boot is a valuable feature to help maintain integrity claims of a platform. It is also called verified boot. When secure boot is enabled, one component will verify the next component before it executes it. If the verification fails, the next component will not be executed. It seems very useful. But how does the other software know if the secure boot is enabled and enabled correctly? How does the other software know if the secure boot was not disabled by mistake?

Today, even if we believe a system is secure, we still want to let other entities have a way to confirm such secure attributes. Once the system has a way to prove it possesses such attributes, we can say it is trusted.

NOTE   The definition for "trust" is different from "secure." From the Trusted Computing Group (TCG) definition, an entity can be trusted if it always behaves in the expected manner for the intended purpose. A trusted system might not be a secure system. For example, if we know a system is infected by a virus and the virus scans the C disk at 5 PM every day and uploads the all doc files to a specific URL via http protocol, we can say this system is trusted and it is not secure.

TCG defines a way to let other software check if the system has booted into a trusted environment. The process is called TCG trusted boot.

© Jiewen Yao and Vincent Zimmer 2020
J. Yao and V. Zimmer, *Building Secure Firmware*, https://doi.org/10.1007/978-1-4842-6106-4_7

Static Root-of-Trust for Measurement (SRTM)

TCG specification defines special hardware – a Trusted Platform Module (TPM). A TPM has a set of cryptographic engines, non-volatile memory, volatile memory, and a set of Platform Configuration Registers (PCRs). The TCG specification defines a set of Roots-of-Trust (RoTs):

- Root-of-Trust for measurement (RTM): The RTM does the initial measurement process. The RTM is some code on the host side. In the real implementation, we have two different types of RTM – static RTM (SRTM) or dynamic RTM (DRTM). We will discuss them later. The RTM may include many components. In those components, the Core-RTM (CRTM) means the component to run the first code after platform reset.

- Root-of-Trust for reporting (RTR): The RTR reports the measured information via a TPM PCR and provides the capability to attest to the authenticity of the PCR based upon the TPM identities.

- Root-of-Trust for storage (RTS): The RTS provides a protected storage area for keys and data.

Trusted Platform Module (TPM)

A TPM includes all of the trusted capabilities except the root-of-trust for measurement. This book focuses on how to use TPM in the firmware. Refer to the TPM specification or books listed in the references for the detailed introduction to TPM hardware and its capabilities.

The TPM's Platform Configuration Registers (PCRs) hold the value of the final measurement. The measurement follows the equation given here. This operation is PCR extend:

$$PCR_{(new)} = HASH (PCR_{(old)} \| HASH(Data))$$

PCR extend is the only way to modify the PCR value. If a platform extends a PCR multiple times, all data is hashed into the PCR.

When the platform uses the SRTM, the C-SRTM is the firmware boot block code. Boot block firmware could be the PEI firmware volume in the UEFI/PI BIOS. It could also be the ROM stage in a coreboot BIOS. Or it could be the Intel Boot Guard ACM if Intel Boot Guard capability is enabled. See Figure 7-1. The RTM needs to measure all other components based upon the TCG Platform Firmware Profile Specification.

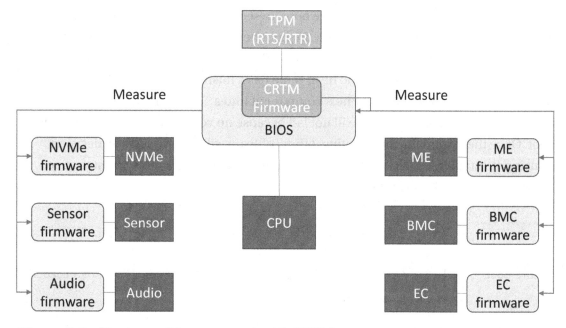

Figure 7-1. *Firmware Measurement with SRTM*

This C-SRTM must measure itself into PCR0, and the rest of components (code or data) must be measured into the corresponding PCRs by the chain-of-trust, based upon the TCG Platform Firmware Profile Specification. See Table 7-1.

Table 7-1. *SRTM PCR Measurement*

PCR Index	Usage
0	SRTM, BIOS, Host Platform Extensions, embedded option ROMs, and PI Drivers
1	Host Platform Configuration
2	UEFI driver and application code
3	UEFI driver and application configuration and data
4	UEFI Boot Manager Code (or Initial Program Loader (IPL) in legacy Master Boot Record (MBR)) and Boot Attempts
5	Boot Manager Code Configuration and Data (for use by the Boot Manager Code) and GUID Partition Table (GPT) (or legacy MBR Partition Table)
6	Host Platform Manufacturer Specific
7	Secure boot policy

Trusted boot is different from secure boot. In secure boot, one component needs to authenticate the next component. Secure boot needs to check the signature or the hash value before loading the next component. Secure boot will stop the platform boot if the signature is invalid or the hash value has a mismatch. In trusted boot, one component needs to measure the next component into a TPM PCR before loading the next component. Measured boot will not fail because no verification is performed during boot. Once the system finishes booting, other software will make a security decision by using attestation to check if the current state is the same as the previous state. See Figures 7-2 and 7-3 for the difference.

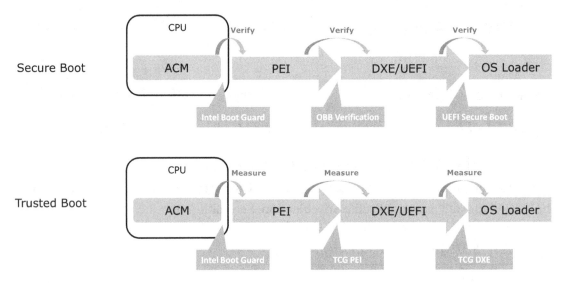

Figure 7-2. *Secure Boot and Trusted Boot Flow*

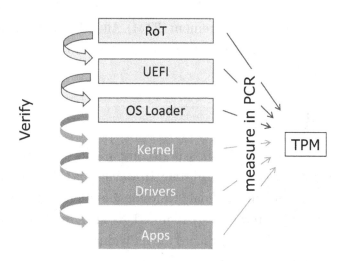

Figure 7-3. *Secure Boot vs. Trusted Boot*

TPM Device Type

The first TPM production followed TPM specification version 1.2, also known as TPM1.2. However, overtime it became clear that the TPM1.2 specification had some limitations. For example, TPM1.2 only supports the SHA1 hash algorithm and the RSA asymmetric algorithms. Once the ownership of TPM1.2 is taken by OS, the platform BIOS may not use the TPM.

In order to resolve those limitations, TCG defines the TPM specification family 2.0, also known as TPM2.0. TPM2.0 supports cryptography agile. A TPM2.0 device may support SHA1, SHA256, SM3_256, or future algorithms such as SHA3_256 or SHA3_384. TPM2.0 defines a dedicated platform hierarchy for the platform firmware usage. The OS manages storage hierarchy which is independent from the platform hierarchy. TPM2.0 provides a uniform framework for using authorization capabilities and expands the authorization method – clear text password and hash-based message authentication code (HMAC).

Besides TPM1.2 and TPM2.0, the Chinese government defines Trusted Cryptography Module (TCM). TCM provides the root-of-trust for report (RTR) and the root-of-trust for storage (RTS) and supports the trusted boot. It is similar to TPM from the functionality perspective. For example, TCM defines the Platform Configuration Register (PCR), non-volatile memory, endorsement key, identity key, and so on. TCM only supports Chinese cryptography – SM2, SM3, and SMS4.

Similar to TPM, the Trusted Cryptography Module (TCM) is also a passive device. In order to support active measurement, the Chinese government standard defines the Trusted Platform Control Module (TPCM). In addition to RTR and RTS, the TPCM provides the root-of-trust for measurement (RTM). After the system powers on, the TPCM measures the platform BIOS and records the result to PCRs; then TPCM transfers control to the host CPU.

Measurement Report

The PCRs hold the final hash of the measured components (code and/or data). It can be used to present the current platform state. However, it is infeasible to obtain the individual measurements from the final PCR value. But there might be a situation where the individual measurements are required. As such, the TCG defines the integrity measurement event log to record the individual measurement hashes and the description for the measurement. See Figure 7-4.

Figure 7-4. *TCG Measurement Event and PCR*

During system boot, whenever the firmware records a measurement into a PCR, a corresponding event is appended to the event log. Finally, the event log is passed to the operating system (see Figure 7-5).

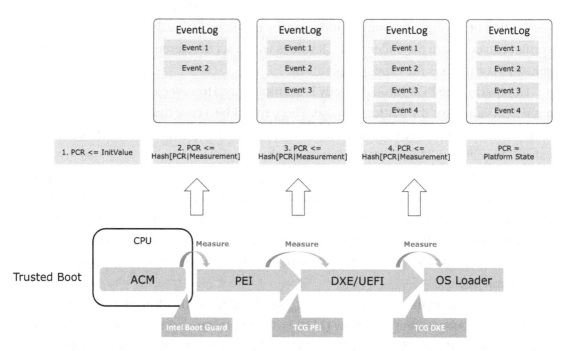

Figure 7-5. *TCG Measurement Event Log Recording During Boot*

Care must be taken since the event log cannot be trusted because the event log is in volatile memory and this memory is not the root-of-trust for reporting or the root-of-trust for storage. Only PCRs from the TPM chip can be trusted. While consuming the event log, the verifier must extract each TCG event and reconstruct the PCR value from the event log and then compare it with the PCR value from the TPM chip. If there is a mismatch, the TCG event log cannot be trusted. If they match, the digest value from the TCG event log can be trusted.

Attestation

Attestation is the presence of the evidence on the machine (the attester) for another entity (appraiser or verifier) to verify. With a TPM, the evidence is the PCR values. If a verifier wants to check if the system is in a known good state, it must trust the authenticity of the PCR values. This may happen in the local platform or in the remote

verifier. If the PCR value is transmitted through an untrusted environment, such as
a software stack or a network, then we need the TPM_Quote operation to provide
the protection. The TPM_Quote is a command to sign a set of PCR values with the
TPM private key and provide the digital signature. Then the verifier can perform the
verification of the digital signature and trust the collected PCR values. At this point, the
verifier can compare the collected PCR values with a set of reference PCR measurement
values to see if this is the expected platform.

Comparing the PCR values directly is a simple way. However, the TPM only provided
eight PCR values for the platform to use. There might be a case that a platform wants to
assert some of the measurement values in one PCR and skip some other measurement
values. As such, the TCG event log can be used.

In the TCG event log–based verification, the first step is also to verify the authenticity
of the PCR values. Then the verifier needs to reconstruct the PCR value from the event
log to verify the authenticity of the measurement in the event log. Finally, the verifier
may compare the collected integrity measurement event log with a list of golden
reference measurements. Now partial compare can be supported based upon the
verification policy.

Figure 7-6 shows the example of verification defined in NIST SP800-155. The
Measurement Assessment Authority (MAA) – the appraiser – collects the event log and
PCR from the endpoint device, the attester. The MAA also gets the golden measurement
derived from a set of supported provisioned authorities, such as the Original Equipment
Manufacturer (OEM) and Value-Added Reseller (VAR). Then the MAA compares the
event log with the golden measurement to see if they match. If there is a mismatch, the
MAA may let the endpoint device start the remediation.

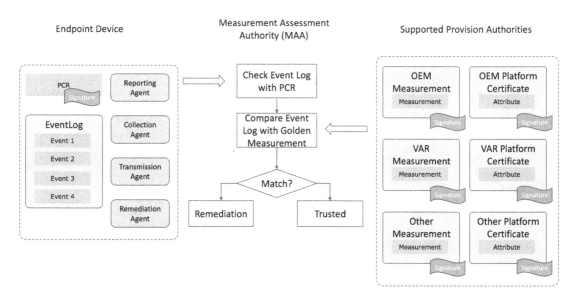

Figure 7-6. *Measurement Assessment with Golden Reference Measurement*

The detail of message exchange is shown in Figure 7-7. First, the MAA gets the Quote from the endpoint device. The Quote is a list of TPM PCR values signed with the TPM attestation key (AK). The Quote is proof of the current platform state. Once the MAA gets the Quote, the MAA uses the public attestation key to verify the Quote value – this is called remote attestation. Then the MAA collects the full event log from the client and replays the event log to generate a list of PCRs. If the generated PCRs match the Quote PCRs, that means the event log is not tampered. This event log can be used to compare with the golden measurement.

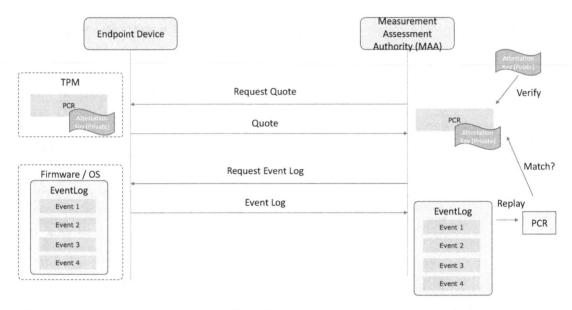

Figure 7-7. *TCG Remote Attestation Flow*

The complete remote attestation also includes a process to verify the TPM by using the TPM endorsement key (EK). Each TPM contains a unique EK pair in a shielded location on the TPM. The public key of the EK is included in the EK certificate. An EK Credential is to assist attestation CAs to issue the attestation key (AK) for signing purposes only. The EK Credential can be used to provide evidence that the AK is on the same TPM as the EK.

S3 Resume

In order to support power efficiency, a platform may support sleep, also known as S3 resume per the definition in the Advanced Configuration and Power Interface (ACPI) specification. If the system needs to enter the S3 state, the operating system saves the current system configuration, sets an OS waking vector, and writes a silicon-specific register. Then the platform hardware enters the S3 state. The CPU and most devices are off. The system memory is in a self-refresh state to keep the memory content viable. After an end user wakes up the system, the SRTM – BIOS starts running. The BIOS initializes the system according to the saved configuration and jumps to the OS waking vector.

In a normal system shutdown and system startup, the OS sends a TPM_Shutdown(CLEAR) command to the TPM, and BIOS sends a TPM_Startup(CLEAR) to the TPM which resets the TPM context to the default initialization state. S3 resume is different. In order to maintain the trust chain, the OS needs to send a TPM_Shutdown(STATE) command before putting the system into S3. Then the TPM saves the current context including all PCR values. When the BIOS starts up, the BIOS sends a TPM_Startup(STATE) command to resume the TPM to the original state before entering S3, including all PCR values. There is no requirement to perform a PCR extend for the SRTM in a normal S3 resume.

However, if the TPM_Startup(STATE) fails due to some reason, the SRTM needs to try TPM_Startup(CLEAR) to restart the TPM. If the TPM is restarted successfully, the SRTM needs to extend an error code to the PCRs because the SRTM runs in a different boot path in S3 and it is impossible to replay the normal boot flow to create the same PCR.

Device Identifier Composition Engine (DICE)

The TPM is widely adopted in personal computing, mobile, and server platforms. However, the Internet of Things (IoT) market may have different solutions with challenging power, security, resource, and other constraints. Not all IoT systems and components adopt the TPM. As such, the TCG created the Device Identifier Composition Engine (DICE) working group to develop new approaches to enhancing security and privacy with minimal silicon requirements. Even the tiniest microcontrollers can afford DICE support to establish the device identity and perform attestation and secure firmware update.

Figure 7-8 shows the fundamental idea of the DICE. The immutable ROM – DICE hardware engine combines a unique device secret (UDS) and the hash of the startup code to create a hash-based message authentication code (HMAC). This HMAC is used as the Compound Device Identity (CDI) of the device.

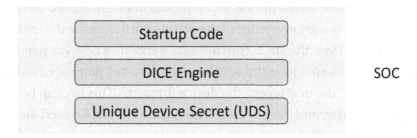

Figure 7-8. *DICE SOC*

The equation is

$$CDI = HMAC(UDS, Hash(Code))$$

If the firmware startup code is updated, a new CDI is automatically generated. This may be a feature. However, if the old CDI is used for device identity, the new CDI on the patched device will not be recognized. It may bring some manageability problems. A better solution is to build the code into layers. See Figure 7-9.

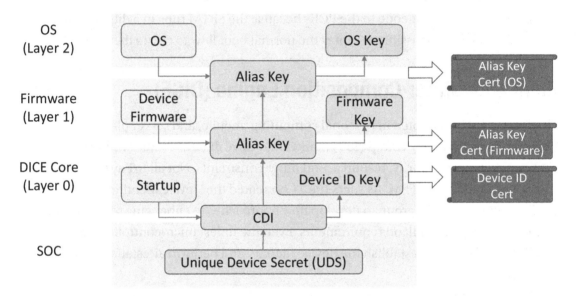

Figure 7-9. *Layered DICE Architecture*

The CDI is generated from SOC hardware with the UDS and the hash of the startup code. Then the DICE core (layer 0) uses the CDI to derive a device ID key pair. The device ID key pair is the identifier of the device, and it should not be disclosed outside of the DICE core. In order to prove knowledge of the private portion of the device ID without exposing the device ID key, the DICE core needs to generate a new key pair for the next layer. This key pair is referred to as the alias key. The alias key pair is derived from the CDI and the identity of the next layer – the device firmware. This key can be passed to the device firmware layer, and the private portion of the key can be used during the device firmware lifetime. The device firmware needs to make sure the alias key is not disclosed outside of the device firmware. The device firmware update will cause the alias key pair update without impacting the device ID key pair. The DICE core also creates the certificate for the alias key signed with the device ID private key and a self-signed device

ID certificate. The device ID certificate does not change for the life of the device, while the alias key certificate changes more frequently when the firmware is updated.

The DICE core implementation can be easily extended to a multilayered boot. Each layer creates a new alias key and an alias certificate for the next layer. The alias certificates issued to the next layer are signed with the alias key granted to the current layer.

DICE and a TPM use different mechanisms for key protection. In a TPM solution, the key is stored and used in an isolated environment provided by a combination of hardware and software, and the key is available for use at any time. This is referred to as *spatial* protection. The *DICE* design relies on *temporal* protection for keys. The key is received from the previous component in the boot chain, used only in the current component, and then deleted from memory before transferring control to the next component. The crypto operations using the key can only be performed for a limited time. Figures 7-10 and 7-11 show the difference.

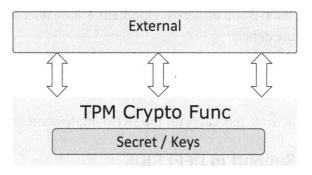

Figure 7-10. *TPM Key Protection*

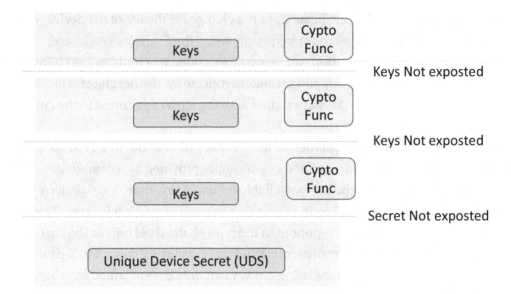

Figure 7-11. *DICE Key Protection*

The DICE specification is still under development. Please refer to the latest DICE documentation for more details.

Case Study

Now, let's take a look at some real cases for the SRTM implementation.

Measured Boot Support in UEFI BIOS

Current UEFI BIOS implementations, such as those based on EDK II, support TCG trusted boot. The UEFI BIOS measures the required components, such as PEI modules, DXE modules, SMM modules, UEFI drivers, and data such as setup variables, to the appropriate PCR. Figure 7-12 and Table 7-2 show the components in the platform and their corresponding PCR values.

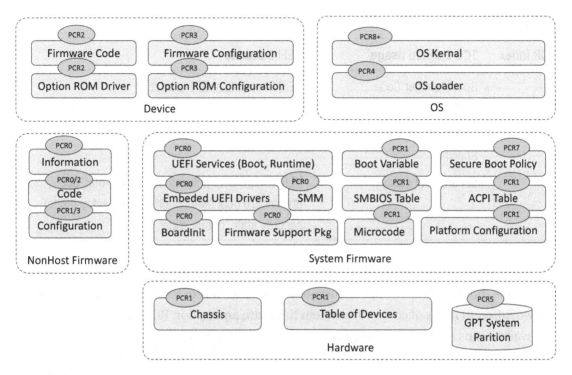

Figure 7-12. *PCR Mapping in UEFI BIOS*

Table 7-2. *PCR Measurement in UEFI BIOS*

PCR Index	TCG Defined Usage	UEFI Example
0	CRTM, Host Platform Code	CRTM, platform firmware (PEI, DXE, SMM, UEFI Boot Services, UEFI runtime services, Embedded Driver), presence of non-host firmware (type, version)
1	Host Platform Configuration	CMOS configuration, UEFI boot variable, UEFI setup variable, ACPI table, SMBIOS table, Microcode, chassis
2	UEFI driver code	Option ROM, device firmware, non-host firmware
3	UEFI driver configuration and data	Option ROM configuration, device firmware configuration, non-host firmware configuration
4	UEFI Boot Manager Code	OS loader

(continued)

Table 7-2. (*continued*)

PCR Index	TCG Defined Usage	UEFI Example
5	Boot Manager Code Configuration and Data	UEFI Boot Action, GPT partition
6	Host Platform Manufacturer Specific	N/A
7	Secure boot policy	UEFI secure boot policy (PK, KEK, db, dbx, dbt, dbr, secure boot state, audit mode, deploy mode), security state, debug state

The system firmware contributes most of the PCR measurements. Any running code on the non-host firmware or device should also be measured. For a device, there might be two different kinds of code – the system firmware and option ROMs. The system firmware means the code running on the device which provides the services to the host. The option ROMs are a special type of firmware that runs on the host side and works as a device driver in the BIOS environment before the operating system driver is available. Typically, PCI storage cards, PCI graphic cards, or PCI network cards may have an option ROM.

After the system firmware finishes initialization, it measures the OS loader and transfers control to the OS loader. Then the OS loader measures the OS kernel and the boot parameters, and then the OS loader transfers control to the OS kernel. In order to let the OS loader reuse the measurement code from the BIOS, the BIOS needs to expose a measurement interface, such as the legacy INT 1A TCPA service, the EFI_TCG_PROTOCOL for TPM1.2, or the EFI_TCG2_PROTOCOL for TPM2.0.

The BIOS also needs to provide a way to let the OS get the TCG event log. For TPM1.2, the event log is passed in the TCPA ACPI table. TPM2.x supports multiple hash algorithms, whereas a TPM1.2 only supports the SHA1 hash algorithm. When TPM2.x was introduced, TCG added a second type of event log. One is compatible with TPM1.2 and only supports SHA1. The other uses a new format and supports multiple hash algorithms. Today, since SHA1 is deprecated, only the new format of the event log is used. It can be retrieved by TCG2_PROTOCOL's GetEventLog() function or from the TPM2 ACPI table.

To map to the real world, Table 7-3 shows how the BIOS interacts with the operating system during the TCG trusted boot flow.

Table 7-3. *PCR Measurement Step During OS Boot*

Steps	Legacy OS (Windows/Linux)	UEFI Windows	UEFI Linux	Customized BIOS/OS
The BIOS will measure the "OS bootloader."	The legacy BIOS measures the Master Boot Record (MBR) content.	The UEFI BIOS measures bootmgr.efi.	The UEFI BIOS measures grub.efi.	BIOS internal behavior. It should know where the OS loader is and what the format is. It needs to measure it before passing the control to it.
BIOS exposes "the measurement service" to the OS bootloader.	INT 1A TCPA (16-bit real mode) for TPM1.2.	EFI_TCG_PROTOCOL. HashLogExtendEvent() for TPM1.2. EFI_TCG2_PROTOCOL. HashLogExtendEvent() for TPM2.0.	EFI_TCG_PROTOCOL. HashLogExtendEvent() for TPM1.2 EFI_TCG2_PROTOCOL. HashLogExtendEvent() for TPM2.0.	It might not be required, if the OS loader knows how to interact with the measurement device.
BIOS exposes the TCG event log to OS.	TCPA ACPI table for TPM1.2.	TCPA ACPI table for TPM1.2 EFI_TCG2_PROTOCOL. GetEventLog() and FINAL_EVENTS_TABLE or TPM2 ACPI table for TPM2.0.	TCPA ACPI table for TPM1.2. EFI_TCG2_PROTOCOL. GetEventLog() and FINAL_EVENTS_TABLE or TPM2 ACPI table for TPM2.0.	ACPI table or a private interface may be used.

(continued)

Table 7-3. (*continued*)

Steps	Legacy OS (Windows/Linux)	UEFI Windows	UEFI Linux	Customized BIOS/OS
The OS bootloader may use the BIOS measurement service to "extend the OS kernel" before the OS driver is ready to use.	The legacy bootloader (MBR and extension) measures the rest of the OS kernel.	bootmgr.efi measures the Windows OS kernel.	grub.efi measures the command and kernel file.	The vendor-specific loader measures the vendor-specific kernel.
Once the control is transferred to the OS, the BIOS service is not available. The OS will use its own driver to extend more components.	Legacy OS kernel measures the rest.	Windows OS kernel measures the rest.	Linux OS kernel measures the rest.	Kernel measures the rest.

"A Tour Beyond BIOS: Implementing TPM2 Support in EDKII" describes more details about TPM support in the EDK II BIOS.

Intel Boot Guard

The UEFI implementation described earlier assumes that the PEI code is the root-of-trust for measurement. If a platform enables Intel Boot Guard, the Boot Guard ACM is the root-of-trust. The Boot Guard ACM not only verifies the initial boot block (IBB), but it also measures the IBB into the TPM PCR. The PCRs extended by the Boot Guard ACM are listed in Table 7-4. In brief, the PCR[0] records the details, and the PCR[7] records the authorities.

Table 7-4. *PCR Measurement in Intel Boot Guard*

PCR Index	TCG Defined Usage	Boot Guard ACM Example
0	CRTM, Host Platform Code	Detail: ACM Policy Status (measured boot, verified boot), ACM Secure Version Number (SVN), ACM Signature, KeyManifest Signature, BootPolicyManifest Signature, Initial Boot Block (IBB) Hash
1	Host Platform Configuration	N/A
2	UEFI driver code	N/A
3	UEFI driver configuration and data	N/A
4	UEFI Boot Manager Code	N/A
5	Boot Manager Code Configuration and Data	N/A
6	Host Platform Manufacturer Specific	N/A
7	Secure boot policy	Authorities: ACM Policy Status (measured boot, verified boot), ACM Secure Version Number (SVN), ACM Public Key Hash, KeyManifest Public Key Hash, BootPolicyManifest Public Key Hash

Since the Boot Guard ACM needs to use a TPM, it must start the TPM. If the Boot Guard ACM starts the TPM in locality 3, a TCG_EFI_STARTUP_LOCALITY_EVENT must be created to record such information.

Measured Boot Support in coreboot

coreboot also supports TCG trusted boot. However, the coreboot solution does not use the TCG Platform Firmware Profile but instead uses the TPM in its own way. Table 7-5 shows the PCR usage in coreboot.

Table 7-5. *PCR Measurement in coreboot*

PCR Index	TCG Defined Usage	coreboot Example
0	CRTM, Host Platform Code	Google VBoot GBB flags
1	Host Platform Configuration	Google VBoot GBB HWID
2	UEFI driver code	Core root-of-trust for Measurement which includes all stages, data, and blobs, such as COREBOOT CBFS (boot block, fallback/verstage), FW_MAIN CBFS (fallback/romstage, fspm, fallback/postcar, fallback/ramstage, cpu_microcode_blob, fsps, vbt, fallback/dsdt.aml, fallback/payload), RO_VPD, GBB, SI_DESC, SI_GBE
3	UEFI driver configuration and data	Runtime data like hwinfo.hex or MRC cache, such as SI_ME, RW_NVRAM
4	UEFI Boot Manager Code	N/A
5	Boot Manager Code Configuration and Data	N/A
6	Host Platform Manufacture Specific	N/A
7	Secure boot policy	N/A

Similar to UEFI, the coreboot solution uses the ACPI table to pass the event log information. The TCPA ACPI table includes the event log information for TPM1.2, and the TPM2 ACPI table includes the event log information for TPM2.0.

Windows BitLocker

BitLocker is a feature to provide the disk encryption in the Windows operating system. The TPM is used as a hardware solution to assist the key protection without user interaction. The TPM can store some data locked by PCRs and only unlock the data if the PCRs match. This is called sealing. This sealing process is used to save the BootLocker key encryption key during the provisioning phase. During each boot, the BitLocker tries to unseal a key from the TPM and use that key to decrypt the disk encryption key. This unsealing process guarantees that the key is decrypted if and only if the current system state (as recorded in PCRs) is the same as the state when the key was provisioned. See Figure 7-13.

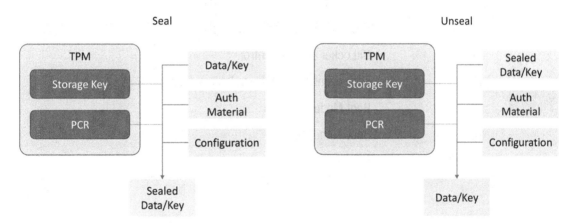

Figure 7-13. *TPM Seal/Unseal with PCR*

By default, BitLocker binds the key to PCRs 0, 2, and 4 which record the code running on the platform. Because the system firmware update causes the PCR0 value to change, BitLocker recovery will be triggered, and the end user needs to provide either the recovery password or the recovery key to unlock the device. As such, BitLocker binds the key to PCR7, if UEFI secure boot is enabled, and PCR7 is properly extended. The BitLocker leverages the secure boot to do the integrity verification. Table 7-6 shows the PCR usage in a Windows OS. For more details about BitLocker, please refer to Microsoft BitLocker documentation.

Table 7-6. *PCR Measurement in BitLocker*

PCR Index	Windows Operating System
0	Core System Firmware executable code
1	Core System Firmware data
2	Extended or pluggable executable code
3	Extended or pluggable firmware data
4	Boot manager/Legacy MBR
5	GPT/Partition Table/Legacy MBR Partition Table
6	Resume from S4 and S5 Power State Events
7	Secure boot state
8	Reserved/Legacy NTFS Boot Sector
9	Reserved/Legacy NTFS Boot Block
10	Reserved/Legacy Boot Manager
11	BitLocker access control
12	Data events and highly volatile events
13	Boot Module Details
14	Boot Authorities
15~23	Reserved

Grub

Grub is the default OS loader of most Linux systems. If a TPM is present in the system, Grub measures the executed commands and files into TPM. Table 7-7 shows the PCR usage in Grub.

Table 7-7. *PCR Measurement in Grub*

PCR Index	Grub
8	Grub command line:
	All executed commands (including those from configuration files) will be logged and measured as entered with a prefix of "grub_cmd:"
	Kernel command line:
	Any command line passed to a kernel will be logged and measured as entered with a prefix of "kernel_cmdline:"
	Module command line:
	Any command line passed to a kernel module will be logged and measured as entered with a prefix of "module_cmdline:"
9	Files:
	Any file read by Grub will be logged and measured with a descriptive text corresponding to the filename.

Linux Integrity Measurement Architecture

The Linux Integrity Measurement Architecture is designed for kernel integrity. The goal of kernel integrity is to detect if files have been modified accidentally or maliciously, compare a file's measurement value to the golden value, and enforce local file integrity.

Integrity Measurement Architecture (IMA) was first introduced in Linux 2.6.30 kernel. It includes three components: IMA-measurement, IMA-appraisal, and IMA-audit. IMA maintains a list of runtime measurements and the aggregated PCR values in the TPM. The benefit of having the aggregated values in the TPM is that if the list is modified, then the modification can be detected by reconstructing the PCR values. The IMA uses the PCR[10] to record the measurement of the files.

OpenPOWER Trusted Boot

IBM OpenPOWER servers implement the trusted boot process to let a customer verify that the server is running only authorized firmware components from IBM or another trusted vendor. The PCR usage in OpenPOWER is similar to the one defined by TCG. PCR[0,1] are for the host platform; PCR[2,3] are for the add-in component; PCR[4,5] are for the boot state transition. Table 7-8 shows the PCR usage in OpenPOWER.

Table 7-8. *PCR Measurement in OpenPOWER*

PCR Index	TCG Defined Usage	OpenPOWER Example
0	CRTM, Host Platform Code	Hostboot and other firmware components
1	Host Platform Configuration	Configuration data and firmware container metadata
2	UEFI driver code	IBM Coherent Accelerator Processor Interface (CAPI) code
3	UEFI driver configuration and data	IBM Coherent Accelerator Processor Interface (CAPI) data
4	UEFI Boot Manager Code	Open Power Abstraction Layer (OPAL) firmware, static OS (Linux kernel and initramfs)
5	Boot Manager Code Configuration and Data	TPM enabled flags, Open Power Abstraction Layer (OPAL) container metadata, boot sequence, static OS configuration (Linux kernel command line)
6	Host Platform Manufacturer Specific	Reserved
7	Secure boot policy	Reserved

Supply Chain Validation

A supply chain is a network between a company and its suppliers to produce and distribute a specific product to the final buyer. An attacker may tamper with the components (hardware, firmware, or software) after the supplier ships the product and before the final buyer receives the product. How can the buyer make sure the product received is the product shipped from the supplier?

NIST SP800-155 provides guidelines for the BIOS integrity measurement, reporting, collection, and transmission. The Measurement Assessment Authority (MAA) can judge if the system is as expected, which has been discussed in the Verification and Attestation section. Besides the reference measurements, TCG also defines the platform certificate which should be provided by an OEM and/or VAR. This certificate describes the EK certificate, platform attributes such as platform manufacture string, platform model, platform version, and TPM and platform assertions such as MeasurementRootType. That concept is shown in Figure 7-6.

The National Security Agency (NSA) open sourced a prototype named Host Integrity at Runtime and Startup (HIRS) to illustrate the supply chain validation capability. The platform manufacturer creates the Base Platform Certificate. The system integrators and Value-Added Resellers create the Delta Platform Certificate. An Attestation Certificate Authority (ACA) can provision the TPM with an Attestation Identity Credential (AIC). At runtime, the ACA can perform the Endorsement Credential Certificate Chain Validation to verify if the endorsement key used by the TPM is placed there by the Original Equipment Manufacturer (OEM) and the Platform Credential Certificate Chain Validation to verify the provenance of the system's hardware components, such as the motherboard and chassis, by comparing measured component information against the manufacturers, models, and serial numbers listed in the Platform Credential.

Intel Transparent Supply Chain is another implementation for supply chain verification. It enables platform- and component-level traceability for Intel vPro systems.

Project Cerberus

The Cerberus platform requires the active components support a hardware and firmware combined identity through the Device Identifier Composition Engine (DICE). See Figure 7-14. The measurement of each DICE layer can be

$$Measurement = HMAC(Seed, Hash(Code))$$

221

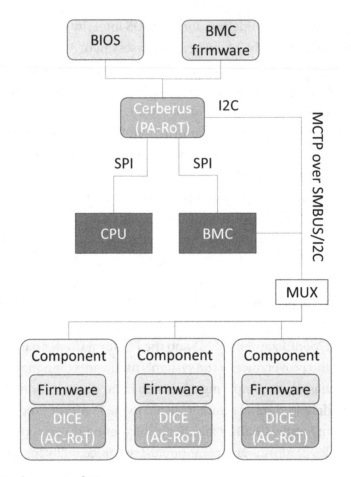

Figure 7-14. *Cerberus Architecture*

The seed is typically derived from the measurement of the previous layer or the alias key certificate. As such, the final measurement is a chained measurement of all the layers.

The Platform Active RoT (PA-RoT) may use attestation messages to communicate with the Active Component RoT (AC-RoT). The attestation message interface uses the Management Component Transport Protocol (MCTP) over the SMBus/I2C message protocol. The PA-RoT is always the MCTP master. The AC-RoT can be configured as endpoint or endpoint and master. By using MCTP RoT commands, the PA-RoT and AC-RoT may establish a platform-level RoT. Table 7-9 lists a set of RoT commands that can be used by PA or AC. For more detailed information, please refer to the Cerberus specification. Part of the commands are also the same as the Security Protocol and Data Model (SPDM) messages which we will discuss in Chapter 8.

Table 7-9. *Cerberus RoT Command List*

Register Name	RoT	Description
Firmware Version	PA/AC	Retrieves firmware version information.
Device Capabilities	PA/AC	Retrieves device capabilities.
Device ID	PA/AC	Retrieves device ID.
Export Certificate	PA/AC	Exports certificate signing request (CSR).
GET_DIGESTS	PA/AC	PA-RoT retrieves session information.
GET_CERTIFICATE	PA/AC	PA-RoT sets session variables based on Session Query.
CHALLENGE	PA/AC	PA-RoT retrieves and verifies AC-RoT certificate.
Key Exchange	PA	Exchanges pre-master session keys.
Get Log	PA	Retrieves debug, attestation, and tamper log.
Platform Configuration Register	PA	Returns the Platform Measurement.
Extend Platform Configuration Register	PA	Extends Platform Measurements.
Unseal Message	PA/AC	Unseals attestation challenges.
Unseal Message Result	PA/AC	Gets unsealing status and result.

Microsoft Azure Sphere: Pluton

Microsoft Azure Sphere is a secured high-level application platform with built-in communication and security features for Internet-connected devices. It comprises a secured, connected, crossover microcontroller unit (MCU). The Pluton secure subsystem is the tamper-resistant hardware-based root-of-trust for Azure Sphere. It has a cryptographic engine and provides services for secure boot verification.

Besides secure boot, the Pluton secure subsystem also supports measured boot and remote attestation in silicon. During boot, the Pluton records the hash of all boot components. When an Azure Sphere device connects to the Azure Sphere Security Service (AS3), the device verifies the server authentication by using a locally stored certificate. At the same time, AS3 also authenticates the device itself via remote attestation. The Pluton returns the hash value and the signature of the hash value with the attestation key. Because AS3 has the device attestation key, then the AS3 can determine whether the device is authentic and whether the device boots with genuine software.

Cisco Trust Anchor

Cisco uses Trust Anchor technology to provide the foundation for the Cisco trustworthy system. Besides secure boot, the Cisco Trust Anchor Module (TAm) can be used to verify that the hardware is authentic. The OS can check the TAm for a secure unique device identifier (SUDI) that could have come only from Cisco. The SUDI is permanently programmed into the TAm in the manufacturing processes to support the supply chain verification.

Attack and Mitigation

Now, let's take a look at some real cases for the attacks to the SRTM and mitigation.

Attack on Completeness

Completeness is the biggest challenge of trusted computing. The final solution must measure any mutable component and configuration for the verification. In practice, some firmware might not measure all the firmware code. A change in that code would not be detected. Also, some firmware might not measure all the security-related settings. If the security settings were turned off, it would not be detected.

Non-host firmware is also problematic. Researchers have demonstrated the capability to replace the keyboard firmware, embedded controller (EC) firmware, baseboard management controller (BMC) firmware, battery firmware, and other system board firmware. As such, the hacker may record the user's keystrokes, remotely control the system, or control the battery charging. However, those devices' firmware might not be measured in the most current systems.

Take Stuxnet as another example. The virus Stuxnet is typically introduced into the supply network via an infected USB flash drive by a person with physical access to the system. The worm then travels across the network, scanning software on computers controlling a programmable logic controller (PLC). Stuxnet introduces the infected rootkit onto the PLC modifying the code and giving unexpected commands to the PLC while returning a loop of normal operation value feedback to the users. The questions are as follows: Should we measure if the USB port is blocked? Should we measure the USB flash device firmware? Should we measure the content on the USB flash device? Should we measure the software which controls the PLC device? Should we measure the PLC code?

Any missing part of the measurement is a potential attack point.

Attack S3 Resume

As we discussed before, the normal S3 resume process includes TPM_Shutdown(STATE) and TPM_Startup(STATE). If the OS is hacked, then the OS can skip the TPM_ Shutdown(STATE) command when it puts the system in S3 state. In S3 resume, when the BIOS SRTM sends TPM_Startup(STATE) command to the TPM, the TPM fails. If a bad SRTM implementation forgets to send TPM_Startup(CLEAR) or forgets to extend the error code, then the TPM PCR is all zero when the system boots. Then the TPM PCR value can be forged by the attacked OS later. Remote TPM quote operations will show the system is trusted, based upon the PCR value. But actually, the system is already attacked. See Figure 7-15 for the boot flow.

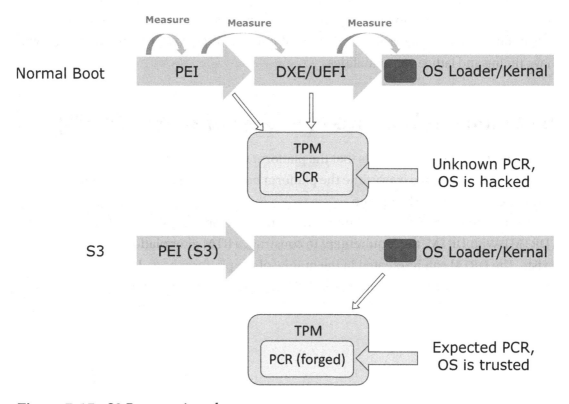

Figure 7-15. *S3 Resume Attack*

Hijack the Device

The TPM is attached to the platform board. It may be connected via the Low Pin Count (LPC) bus, Serial Peripheral Interface (SPI) bus, or I2C bus. The TCG Platform TPM Profile Specification describes the TPM hardware interface. Currently hackers have demonstrated how to hijack the LPC bus or I2C bus between the TPM and the platform board. A high-assurance platform may choose to not expose the TPM connection. Or if the TPM connection is exposed, then all the commands need to use authorization sessions, and the TPM EK certificate verification is required.

Attack the TPM Device

By definition, the TPM device should be tamper-resistant. However, the TPM implementation may have security flow. For example, there have been examples of firmware TPM (fTPM) implementations with security issues related to remote code execution via crafted EK certificate. The fTPM or discrete TPM (dTPM) implementations have timing and lattice vulnerabilities.

Dynamic Root-of-Trust for Measurement (DRTM)

The biggest problem for SRTM is that the platform must make sure every required component is measured every time the platform boots. One missing measurement may cause the trust chain to be broken.

In order to mitigate this, TCG introduced another type of RTM – dynamic RTM (DRTM). With DRTM, the requirement to construct a RTM after platform reset no longer exists. The DRTM can be created in the middle of the platform boot. In contrast, the static root-of-trust for measurement (SRTM) requires a platform restart to build the root-of-trust from the beginning. See Figure 7-16 for the differences between SRTM and DRTM.

SRTM V.S. DRTM

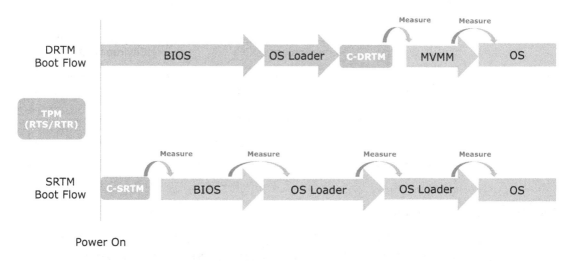

Figure 7-16. *DRTM vs. SRTM Boot Flow*

CPU-Based Dynamic Root-of-Trust

TCG defines some new concepts for the dynamic root-of-trust for measurement (DRTM). DRTM Configuration Environment (DCE) is the software that executes the dynamic launch CPU instruction and transfers the control to a Dynamically Launched Measured Environment (DLME). The DCE is launched by the DCE preamble, which is the code that starts the DRTM process by calling a DRTM CPU instruction. The DCE also checks if the current environment can meet the trusted execution requirement. If this requirement cannot be satisfied, the DCE fails to enter DLME and returns back for the remediation. If all checks pass, the DCE calls the DLME entry point. The DLME is the software executed after the DCE checks and sets up the environment. The DLME launches a measured virtual machine monitor (MVMM). Then the MVMM launches the guest OS and monitors the system behavior. Figure 7-17 shows the DRTM launch flow. Typically, the DCE is provided by the CPU silicon vendor, and the DLME is provided by the operating system vendor.

DRTM Boot

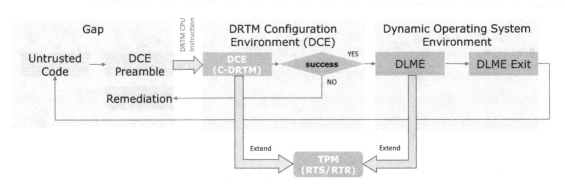

Figure 7-17. *DRTM Launch Flow*

After the system enters DLME, the BSP needs to wake up all APs to make them rendezvous in the final execution environment. Figure 7-18 shows one implementation. Once the BSP enters the DCE, the BSP pulls all the halted APs into DCE and waits there. After the DCE transfers the control to the DLME, the DLME uses another CPU instruction to wake up APs by giving an AP wakeup vector in the DLME. Once the APs in the DCE receive the instruction, they jump to the new address to rendezvous with BSP in the DLME.

AP Join

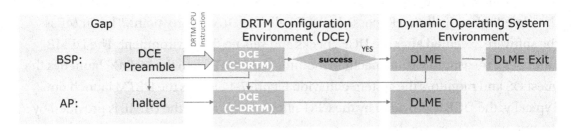

Figure 7-18. *DRTM Application Processor Launch Flow*

The TCG DRTM specification defines a set of special PCRs for DRTM usage (see Table 7-10). Both DCE and DLME may extend to the TPM PCRs.

Table 7-10. *DRTM PCR Measurement*

PCR Index	TCG Defined Usage
17	Detail:
	Used to record detailed measurements of all components involved in the DRTM process, including components provided by the chipset manufacturer, the platform manufacturer, and the operating system vendor.
18	Authorities:
	Used to record the authority measurements of the chipset manufacturer components and the platform manufacturer components.
19	DLME.Authority:
	Used to record the authority of the DLME launched at the end of the DRTM process.
20~22	For the DLME/MVMM.

The measurement report and the verification flow of DRTM are similar to the ones of SRTM. DRTM extends the TPM PCR value and generates the event log for future attestation.

A system may choose to use the SRTM solution or the DRTM solution based upon need. In SRTM, the system needs to add the OEM BIOS into the TCB or Chain-of-Trust. If the first instruction is the BIOS reset vector, then the initial boot block (IBB) of the BIOS is the C-SRTM. In this case, the IBB needs to measure itself and the rest of the BIOS into a PCR. If we don't trust the OEM BIOS IBB, a processor-based C-SRTM may be used, such as Intel Boot Guard or AMD secure boot.

If we don't trust the OEM BIOS, then we may use DRTM. The DRTM solution requires a measured virtual machine monitor (MVMM) and relies on the measured VMM monitoring the system.

S3 Resume

The S3 resume in DRTM is different from SRTM. In SRTM, before a platform enters S3 state, the OS sends TPM_Shutdown(STATE) to let the TPM save the context. When resuming from S3, the BIOS sends the TPM_Startup(STATE) to let the TPM restore the context. The TPM context includes all the SRTM PCRs, but does not include the DRTM PCRs. After resume, all DRTM PCRs are reset to 0xFF.

The DCE preamble must rerun the DRTM instruction to enter the DCE. The DCE must recheck the environment and remeasure itself and the DLME into TPM. Later the DLME must also remeasure the required components and restore the original execution environment. The whole process is very similar to the normal boot.

Care must be taken when the dynamic OS calls DLME_Exit. The DLME_Exit does not modify any PCR values. As such, the dynamic OS must extend some garbage value to the DRTM PCR to prevent the untrusted environment from unsealing data protected by DRTM PCR values.

The DLME must also make sure there is no secret in the memory. If there is a secret that needs to be saved, the DLME may choose to seal the data to the TPM or encrypt the data and seal the key into TPM.

DEC's Execution Environment

The DCE is responsible for ensuring the platform is in a trustworthy state as defined by the CPU, chipset, and platform manufacturer. For example, when the DCE is executed, then all interrupts must be disabled, including external interrupts, non-maskable interrupts, and the system management interrupt. Only the Boot Strap Processor (BSP) is allowed to execute this dynamic launch instruction. All other application processors (APs) must be halted. The Direct Memory Access (DMA) controller should be stopped, and the DCE process will prohibit the DMA access to the critical memory involved in the DCE state transition.

System management mode (SMM) is a special host CPU execution mode. In this special mode, the SMM code may access all memory or I/O resources. The normal VMM cannot trap any access from SMM. The SMM code must protect itself from being tampered with by other hardware devices. The SMM code and the BIOS code that sets up the SMM environment should be measured into a SRTM PCR. Then this SRTM PCR should be referenced in the attestation phase. If we don't want to rely on a SRTM PCR, then the DCE may block the SMM code execution or let the DLME set up another special VMM in the SMM environment, such as SMI Transfer Monitor (STM), to monitor the SMM behavior (see Figure 7-19). This special SMM VMM should be treated as part of MVMM and measured into a DRTM PCR. We will discuss the details of SMM and STM in Chapter 17.

Figure 7-19. *DLME and STM*

Direct Memory Access (DMA) devices are devices that can access the system memory with DMA. The DMA device is outside of the Trust Computing Base (TCB) in DRTM. The DCE should turn off the DMA for the device or set up a I/O memory management unit (IOMMU) to block the DMA from the device.

If a hardware device can be restricted from accessing the platform, DCE, or DLME's memory or I/O resource, it is called a peripheral device. On the other hand, if a hardware device cannot be restricted from accessing the platform, DCE, or DLME's memory or I/O resource, it is called a non-host platform (NHP). The NHP usually consists of a separate CPU or microcontroller that executes the firmware and the software. If the NHP is immutable, it is called fixed NHP. If the NHP is mutable, it is called an updatable NHP. If the state of an updatable NHP can be reliably reported by the DCE, then it is a DCE-verifiable NHP. If the DCE cannot reliably report on an NHP, then it is a DCE-unverifiable NHP. The DCE shall measure or verify the DCE-verifiable NHP. If an NHP is unverifiable, the DCE has to trust it, and the NHP update mechanism must include signing verification.

Hot Plug

By design, if DRTM is chosen, the BIOS is outside of the Trusted Computing Base (TCB), and the BIOS measurement is not required. However, there might be some special cases where we still need some BIOS code in the TCB. SMM is one of the examples. Now let's take a look at another example – CPU hot plug. The normal CPU may follow the preceding flow to launch the MVMM. A hot added CPU cannot run the code in the measured environment directly. The hot added CPU needs to run a CPU reset vector like the normal CPU. As such, the initial boot block of the BIOS code must be trusted and measured. More precisely, any code that the hot added CPU runs before it joins the existing measured environment must be measured. See Figure 7-20. As such, both

DRTM PCRs and SRTM PCRs need to be referenced for a hot plug capable system. For example, a RAS server platform may choose to measure SMM and the initial BIOS code into the SRTM PCR[0] and refer to the SRTM PCR[0]. A client platform without RAS capability may choose to support VMM in SMM, and then no PCR[0] record needs to be referred.

CPU Hot Plug

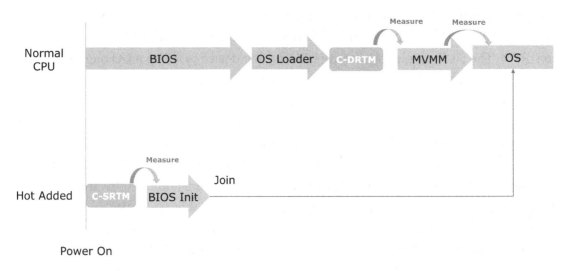

Figure 7-20. *DRTM Hot Plug Support*

Case Study

Now, let's take a look at some real cases for the DRTM implementation.

Intel Trusted Execution Technology (TXT)

Trusted Execution Technology (TXT) is a DRTM implementation on an Intel processor. The DCE code is provided by the Intel SINIT Authenticated Code Module (ACM). The CPU instruction to enter SINIT-ACM is SENTER. TXT names the DLME to be a Measured Launch Environment (MLE). When the CPU executes the SENTER instruction, it verifies the signature of SINIT-ACM and executes the code in the SINIT-ACM. The SINIT-ACM validates the system state and transfers the control to the MLE. In a TXT launch, the ACM measures the ACM information, STM, and MLE into the TPM PCRs 17 and 18. Table 7-11 shows the PCR measurement in Intel TXT.

Table 7-11. *PCR Measurement in Intel TXT*

PCR Index	TCG Defined Usage	Intel TXT Example
17	Detail	BIOS-ACM registration information, SCRTM status code, platform owner (PO) policy PolicyControl field, all matching elements of the policy, STM, OsSinit table capability field, MLE
18	Authorities	Public key of SINIT-ACM, SCRTM status code, OsSinit table capability field, platform owner (PO) policy PolicyControl field, all matching elements of the Launch Control Policy (LCP)
19	DLME.Authority	N/A

Besides platform hardware status check, the SINIT-ACM uses a Launch Control Policy (LCP) to verify if the software launched meets the predefined criteria, such as ACM version, STM enabling state, and MLE hash. The LCP is also extended to PCRs 17 and 18. The configuration of LCP is complicated. Please refer to Intel 64 and IA-32 Architectures Software Developer Manuals and Intel TXT software development guide for details.

AMD Secure Virtual Machine (SVM) Architecture

Secure Virtual Machine (SVM) Architecture is a DRTM implementation on AMD processors. The DCE code can be referred to as AMD Secure Loader (SL). The CPU instruction to enter AMD-SL is SKINIT. When the CPU executes the SKINIT instruction, it verifies the SL and executes the code in the SL. The SL is in the Security Loader Block (SLB) memory. The SL validates the system state and initializes a secure kernel (SK). Finally, the SL transfers the control to the SK. During SL launch, the contents of the SLB are measured into PCR 17. Table 7-12 shows the PCR measurement in AMD SVM.

Table 7-12. *PCR Measurement in AMD SVM*

PCR Index	TCG Defined Usage	AMD SVM Example
17	Detail	Secure Loader Block (SLB)
18	Authorities	N/A
19	DLME.Authority	N/A

Please refer to AMD64 Architecture Programmer's Manual for more detailed information.

Both Intel TXT and AMD SVM implemented the dynamic launch (DL) event via a CPU instruction. Table 7-13 shows the Intel TXT and AMD SVM mapping to the TCG DRTM definition.

Table 7-13. *DRTM Concept Mapping*

TCG	Intel TXT	AMD SVM
Dynamic launch (DL) event	GETSEC[SENTER]	SKINIT
DRTM Configuration Environment (DCE)	SINIT Authenticate Code Module (ACM)	Secure Loader (SL)
Dynamically Launched Measured Environment (DLME)	Measured Launch Environment (MLE)	Secure kernel (SK)

tboot

Both Intel and AMD support the DRTM DCE component. Now the question is, where is the DLME component? Trusted Boot (tboot) project is the first open source DLME project that may be used in Xen or Linux.

During tboot launch, TPM PCRs are also extended by tboot. See Table 7-14.

Table 7-14. *PCR Measurement in tboot*

PCR Index	TCG Defined Usage	tboot Example
17	Detail	tboot policy control value, hash of tboot policy, hash of the first module in grub.conf (e.g., Xen or Linux kernel), hash of all modules (other than the first one)
18	Authorities	tboot policy control value, hash of tboot policy
19	DLME.Authority	N/A

Let's take a Linux VMM system as an example. The BIOS boots using Grub as the OS loader. The Grub loads a Xen hypervisor. Then the Xen hypervisor loads the guest Linux OS. However, when the Xen hypervisor starts, there is no guarantee that Xen is running in a trusted environment. tboot helps to bridge the gap. tboot runs between the Grub and the Xen hypervisor. It helps to establish a trusted environment and transfer control to the Xen hypervisor. The first stage of tboot is untrusted code. It is known as a gap according to the TCG DRTM specification. Then the tboot code executes the SENTER instruction to launch the SINIT-ACM. This ACM is the C-DRTM, and it measures the tboot into TPM PCR and then transfers control to the tboot second stage – DLME, which is considered to be trusted code. Then the tboot DLME code measures the Xen hypervisor into TPM PCR again and transfers control to Xen. The Xen hypervisor or a remote agent may use attestation to know if the Xen runs in a trusted environment later. Figure 7-21 shows the tboot flow.

tboot

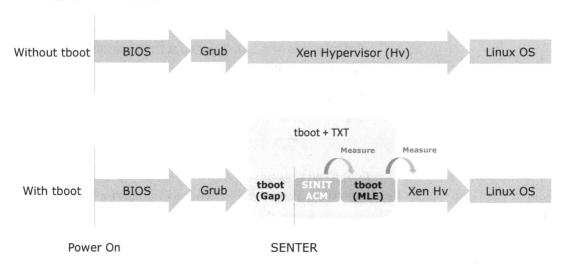

Figure 7-21. *tboot Flow*

Currently tboot only supports Intel TXT, but there are other open source projects that support AMD SVM, such as OSLO – The Open Secure Loader – or TrenchBoot. tboot only supports Linux and does not support Windows.

TrenchBoot

tboot is a good reference implementation for DRTM. However, there are some limitations when using tboot. For example, tboot only supports Intel TXT. TrenchBoot is a secure launch project to support DRTM in Linux. It supports both Intel TXT and AMD SVM. For example, in AMD's SVM, the SKINIT instruction launches the SL module. This SL module is the C-DRTM, and it measures the TrenchBoot LandingZone and then transfers control to the LandingZone. Then the LandingZone code measures the trusted bootloader into TPM PCR 17 and transfers control to the bootloader. Figure 7-22 shows the TrenchBoot flow.

TrenchBoot

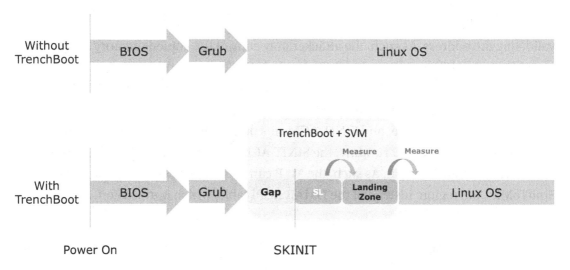

Figure 7-22. *TrenchBoot Flow*

Windows Defender System Guard Secure Launch

In 2019, Microsoft announced the "Windows Defender System Guard Secure Launch" in Windows 10 version 1809. This is the first official DRTM implementation on the Windows operating system. It allows untrusted UEFI firmware code to boot the system and securely transfer to the Windows OS in a trusted and measured state. This seems to be the implementation for the Next-Generation Secure Computing Base (NGSCB), code name Palladium, which was announced in 2003.

Attack and Mitigation

Now, let's take a look at some real cases for the attack to the DRTM and related mitigations.

Malicious Software Input for DCE

The DCE plays an important role in establishing the DRTM. It must check the current running environment, and it must not trust any input from the system because it is the DCE that creates the root-of-trust environment. However, since DCE is also software, it may have vulnerabilities. It is an attack surface in DRTM.

Take Intel SINIT-ACM as an example. The SINIT-ACM needs to parse the DMA remapping (DMAR) ACPI table to set up the I/O memory management unit (IOMMU) to protect the memory from DMA attack. The DMAR ACPI table is untrusted input, and it may be modified by the malicious attacker. However, the DMAR table is used before validating the address. As such, the attacker may control the copied memory length and override the Intel Trusted Executable Technology (TXT) heap and SINIT-ACM itself.

See Figure 7-23. The left-hand side is the normal flow. The BiosData, OsMleData, OsSinitData, and SinitToMleData are all in the TXT heap region. The first three are set up by the DCE gap code, and SINIT-ACM sets up the SinitToMleData to pass the verified data to the MLE. At runtime, the SINIT-ACM needs to copy the DMAR table into SinitToMleData and verify it. As such, the MLE can use the verified DMAR table in the SinitToMleData region, instead of the DMAR ACPI table, which is untrusted.

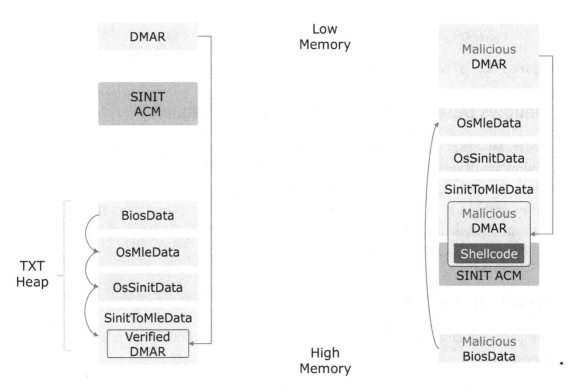

Figure 7-23. *SINIT-ACM Attack via the DMAR ACPI Table*

The right-hand side is how the flow is attacked. Because the BiosData, OsMleData, and OsSinitData on the TXT heap are untrusted, the attacker may give a negative value for the BiosData size. It makes the SINIT-ACM calculate that the OsMleData and

OsSinitData are above the SINIT-ACM. SINIT-ACM also puts the SinitToMleData above the SINIT-ACM. With the DMAR table hacked, the SINIT-ACM copies the malicious DMAR into SinitToMleData, because the check of the DMAR table's length is missing. The SINIT-ACM copies the big chunk of the DMAR table and overwrites the beginning of the SINIT-ACM with shellcode.

In order to prevent this software attack, the DCE must carefully check all external input.

Malicious Hardware Configuration for DCE

In addition to software input, malicious hardware configuration for the DCE might also be fatal. Here is one more example of an attack on SINIT-ACM. Because the SINIT-ACM needs to make sure the IOMMU engine in the DMAR table is reported correctly, the SINIT-ACM checks the hardware configuration – including the memory controller hub (MCH) base address register (BAR) value. See the left-hand side of Figure 7-24.

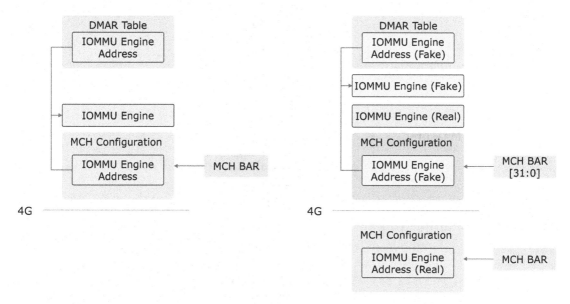

Figure 7-24. *SINIT-ACM Attack via MCH-BAR Reconfiguration*

The MCH-BAR is 36 bits according to the silicon definition. In most systems, this MCH-BAR is configured below 4GB because the early boot code runs in 32-bit protected mode. Unfortunately, the SINIT-ACM only checks the lower 32 bits of the MCH-BAR. If the attacker assigns some real value above 4GB but allocates a fake IOMMU engine and reports it in the fake MCH configuration below 4GB, then the check may pass, but the IOMMU engine does not work to prevent DMA attack. See the right-hand side of Figure 7-24.

The DCE must not make any assumptions on the hardware configuration, and it must read the full register value to do the check.

Attack the DLME Completeness

The completeness problem may also exist in DRTM. It is a little better because DRTM measures less components than SRTM. But if some critical component is missing, the trust chain is also broken.

Take tboot for example. The tboot image is a typical executable image which includes code section, read-only data sections, initialized data sections, and uninitialized data sections. However, the attacker may find that only the code section and the read-only data sections are measured. However, the initialized data section is not measured, but there may be function pointers in the initialized data section. As such, the hacker may overwrite the function pointer to the shellcode to forge the measurement. See Figure 7-25.

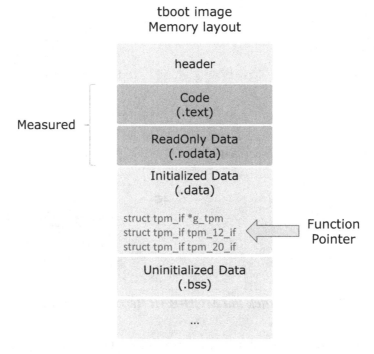

Figure 7-25. *tboot Attack – Image Layout*

The hash value extended to TPM can be forged, instead of the real hash value from the measured data. This is not detectable by the TPM attestation process because TPM quotes the PCR value in the hardware, instead of recreating how the hash value is calculated from the data. See Figure 7-26. The left-hand side is the expected flow. The right-hand side shows how the measurement is forged in S3 resume boot path.

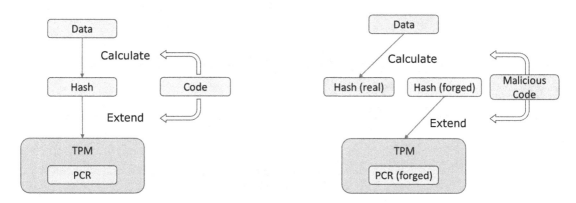

Figure 7-26. *tboot Attack – PCR Forge*

Attack via SMM

As we discussed in the DCE's execution environment, a DRTM solution may choose to monitor the SMM or trust the SMM. In most current platforms, the SMM monitor is not present. As such, trusting SMM is the only choice. However, a vulnerability in SMM may break the trust chain. For example, the Grub OS loader may take advantage of an SMM vulnerability to inject shellcode into SMM. After the tboot measures the Xen and loads it into memory, the SMM may inject the evil code into the Xen hypervisor. This is not detectable because the SMM code is measured during boot before Grub infects SMM and the Xen code is also measured by tboot before the SMM infects the Xen. All measurements show the correct value, but the real content is not expected. See Figure 7-27.

SMM attack

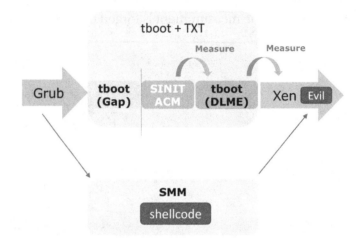

Figure 7-27. *Intel TXT Attack Via SMM*

Attack via Hardware Configuration

We will discuss malicious hardware configuration in Chapter 18.

The DCE must check the hardware configuration and register locks.

Attack via Peripheral or NHP

We will discuss the DMA attack in Chapter 8.

The DCE must enable DMA protection when it executes.

TCG Memory Overwrite

Many people assume that a computer's memory is erased immediately when it loses power. However, typical DRAMs lose their contents gradually over a period of seconds, even for minutes or hours if the chips are kept at low temperatures. As such, the attackers may suddenly reset the system, giving the trusted OS no opportunity to clear the secrets in the memory. Then on the next boot, after the memory controller is initialized, a malicious program may read the contents of the memory to steal the secret.

In order to mitigate the reset attack, the TCG defines a memory overwrite mechanism. When the BIOS boots, the BIOS sets a UEFI variable MOR as 0 to indicate no memory overwrite request. If the OS wants to create the secret in the memory, the OS writes the MOR variable to 1 to indicate that there is a secret and the memory needs to be overwritten on the next boot. If the system shuts down normally, the OS needs to remove the secret from the memory and reset the MOR variable to 0. This is to save the boot time since overwriting all system memory may be time-consuming work.

However, if the attacker triggers a malicious reset with a secret in memory, the BIOS will find there is memory override request in the MOR variable. Then the BIOS clears all the system memory after the DRAM controller is initialized, giving a later program no chance to dump the secret from the DRAM. Once the BIOS clears the secret, the BIOS resets the MOR variable to 0, same as the normal boot flow. Figure 7-28 shows the boot flow with or without secret in the memory.

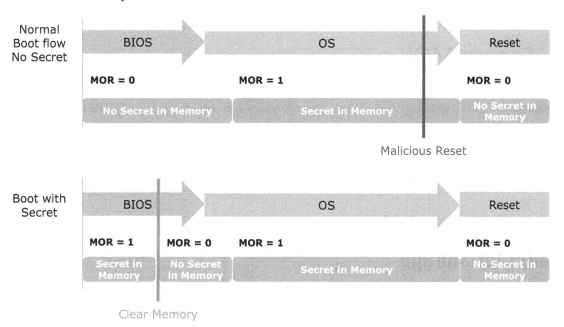

Figure 7-28. *MOR Flow*

Secure MOR

If the system includes a hypervisor and an OS, things become more complicated. The secret might be set up by the hypervisor, but the OS may have capability to read and write the UEFI variable, including the MOR variable. Even if the hypervisor sets the MOR variable to indicate a memory overwrite request, the malicious OS may clear the MOR variable later and trigger a reset to read the secret from the hypervisor.

In order to mitigate this, a MOR control variable is introduced. This MOR control variable is used to lock the MOR variable. The hypervisor sets a random value as the key to the MOR control variable, to indicate lock action. Once MOR is locked, no one can modify the value. Later after the hypervisor clears the secret, it may want to clear the MOR value. The hypervisor sets the same random value again to the MOR control variable, to indicate unlock action. Then the MOR becomes read/write again. Since the malicious OS does not know the random value from the hypervisor, the malicious OS cannot control the MOR variable unlock and cannot write to the MOR variable. Figure 7-29 shows the secure MOR flow.

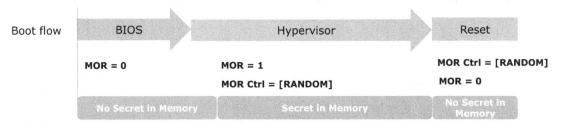

Figure 7-29. *Secure MOR Flow*

MOR for Storage

If there is an MOR request, the BIOS needs to not only clear the memory but also send the TCG Trusted Peripheral (TPer) Reset command to the storage device through the IEEE 1667 protocol or through the native TCG storage protocol. This TPer Reset command is to make sure the protected ranges are locked on the abnormal reset.

Putting them all together, please see Figure 7-30. The memory initialization module gets the MOR variable and clears the memory if the MOR was requested. The TCG MOR module gets the MOR variable and sends the TPer reset if MOR is requested. The OS may set or clear the MOR request via the ACPI ASL interface. The hypervisor can control the MOR setting via the MOR control variable.

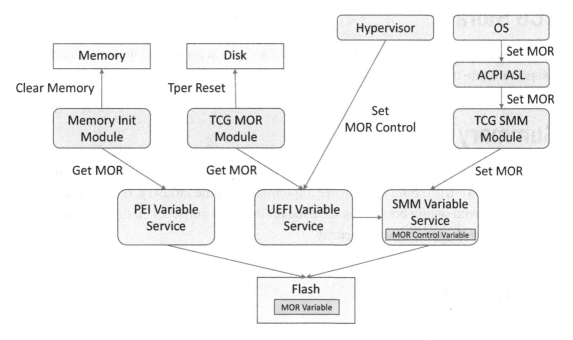

Figure 7-30. *Memory Overwrite Component*

Attack and Mitigation

Now, let's take a look at some real cases for the attack to the TCG memory overwrite and mitigation.

Default MOR Policy

The BIOS code needs to read the MOR variable to figure out if there is memory overwrite request or not. There might be a case that the BIOS code cannot find any MOR variable. A bad BIOS implementation may interpret this as no memory overwrite request. That gives the attacker a chance to manipulate the flash region to make the variable not available to the BIOS. Then the memory overwrite will not happen. The right behavior shall be to always treat the MOR request as present if the MOR variable is not available.

TCG Physical Presence Configuration

The TCG specification defines the physical presence interface, which lets the user configure the TPM. We will discuss this in Chapter 10.

TCG Storage

TCG defines a set of storage extensions to allow a physical presence interface which lets users configure the TCG storage. We will discuss this in Chapter 10.

Summary

In this chapter, we discussed the two forms of trusted boot – static root-of-trust and dynamic root-of-trust. Both of them are implemented in the industry. We compared trusted boot with secure boot. They are used for different purposes. In the next chapter, we will discuss device firmware security.

References

Book

[B-1] Sean W. Smith, *Trusted Computing Platforms: Design and Applications*, Springer, 2004

[B-2] Graeme Proudler, Liqun Chen, Chris Dalton, *Trusted Computing Platforms: TPM2.0 in Context*, Springer, 2016

[B-3] Ariel Segall, *Trusted Platform Modules: Why, when and how to use them*, The Institution of Engineering and Technology, 2016

[B-4] Will Arthur, David Challener, *A Practical Guide to TPM2.0*, Apress, 2015

[B-5] David Challener, Kent Yoder, Ryan Catherman, David Safford, Leendert Van Doom, *A Practical Guide to Trusted Computing*, IBM Press, 2008

[B-6] William Futral, James Greene, *Intel Trusted Execution Technology for Server Platforms: A Guide to More Secure Datacenters*, Apress, 2013

[B-7] David Grawrock, *Dynamics of a trusted platform: a building block approach*, Intel Press, 2009

[B-8] David Grawrock, *The Intel Safer Computing Initiative Building Blocks for Trusted Computing*, Intel Press, 2006

Conference, Journal, and Paper

[P-1] David Safford, Mimi Zohar, Reiner Sailer, "Using IMA for Integrity Measurement and Attestation," IBM 2009, available at `https://blog.linuxplumbersconf.org/2009/slides/David-Stafford-IMA_LPC.pdf`

[P-2] Jiewen Yao, Vincent Zimmer, "A Tour Beyond BIOS with the UEFI TPM2 Support in EDKII," Intel whitepaper, 2014, available at `https://github.com/tianocore/tianocore.github.io/wiki/EDK-II-Security-White-Papers`

[P-3] Tom Dodson, "Intel Transparent Supply Chain process," in *Software and Supply Chain Assurance Forum 2017*, available at `https://csrc.nist.gov/CSRC/media/Projects/Supply-Chain-Risk-Management/documents/ssca/2017-winter/TuePM1_3_%20Intel.pdf`

[P-4] Eduardo Cabre, Tom Dodson, "Secure Your Business: End-to-End Supply Chain Traceability," *Intel Whitepaper 2019*, available at `https://tsc.intel.com/documents/TSCBlockchain_white_paperFINAL.PDF`

[P-5] Paul England, Andrey Marochko, Dennis Mattoon, Rob Spiger, Stefan Thom, David Wooten, "RIoT – A Foundation for Trust in the Internet of Things," *Microsoft Whitepaper 2016*, available at `www.microsoft.com/en-us/research/publication/riot-a-foundation-for-trust-in-the-internet-of-things/`

[P-6] Ronald Aigner, Paul England, Kevin Kane, Andrey Marochko, Dennis Mattoon, Rob Spiger, Stefan Thom, and Greg Zaverucha, "Device Identity with DICE and RIoT: Keys and Certificates," *Microsoft Whitepaper 2017*, available at `www.microsoft.com/en-us/research/publication/device-identity-dice-riot-keys-certificates/`

[P-7] Rob Spiger, Stefan Thom, "Trusted Computing and Securing Devices," in *International Trusted Computing and Security Innovation Summit 2017*, available `https://trustedcomputinggroup.org/wp-content/uploads/3.4_Trusted-Computing-and-Securing-Devices-2017.04.06-Final.pdf`

[P-8] Bryan Kelly, "Project Cerberus Hardware Security," in *OCP Summit 2018*, available at `https://f990335bdbb4aebc3131-b23f11c2c6da826ceb51b46551bfafdc.ssl.cf2.rackcdn.com/images/fbbdd5feceb6e6328373417e1ab7c06a13a2ef2c.pdf`

[P-9] Doug Stiles, "The Hardware Security Platform Behind Azure Sphere," in HC30, `www.hotchips.org/hc30/1conf/1.13_Microsoft_Hardware_Security_Platform_Behind_Azure_Sphere.pdf`

[P-10] Dave Heller, Tim Block, "OpenPOWER secure and trusted boot , Part 1: Using trusted boot on IBM OpenPOWER servers," *IBM Whitepaper, 2017*, `https://developer.ibm.com/articles/trusted-boot-openpower/`

[P-11] Joseph Cihula, "Trusted Boot: Verifying the Xen Launch," in *Xen Summit 2007*, available at `www-archive.xenproject.org/files/xensummit_fall07/23_JosephCihula.pdf`

[P-12] Bernhard Kauer, "OSLO: Improving the security of Trusted Computing," in *USENIX Security 2007*, available at `http://os.inf.tu-dresden.de/papers_ps/kauer07-oslo.pdf`

[P-13] Piotr Krol, "TrenchBoot – Open DRTM implementation for AMD platforms," in OSFC 2019, `https://osfc.io/talks/trenchboot-open-drtm-implementation-for-amd-platforms`

[P-14] Daniel Kiper, Daniel P. Smith, "TrenchBoot How to nicely boot system with Intel TXT and AMD SVM," in Linux Security Summit 2019, `https://static.sched.com/hosted_files/lssna19/75/trenchboot_ot_lss_20190815.final.ds.dk.pdf`

[P-15] Seunghun Han, Jun-Hyeok Park, "I don't want to sleep tonight: Subverting Intel TXT with S3 Sleep," in *Blackhat 2018*, available at `https://i.blackhat.com/briefings/asia/2018/asia-18-Seunghun-I_Dont_Want_to_Sleep_Tonight_Subverting_Intel_TXT_with_S3_Sleep.pdf`

[P-16] Seunghun Han, Jun-Hyeok Park, "Finally I can sleep tonight: catching sleep mode vulnerabilities of the TPM with the napper," in *Blackhat 2019*, available at `http://i.blackhat.com/asia-19/Thu-March-28/bh-asia-Seunghun-Finally-I-Can-Sleep-Tonight-Catching-Sleep-Mode-Vulnerabilities-of-the-TPM-with-the-Napper.pdf`

[P-17] Seunghun Han, Wook Shin, Jun-Hyeok Park, and HyoungChun Kim, "A Bad Dream: Subverting Trusted Platform Module While You Are Sleeping," in *USENIX Security 2018*, available at `www.usenix.org/system/files/conference/usenixsecurity18/sec18-han.pdf`

[P-18] Seunghun Han, Jun-Hyeok Park "BitLeaker: Subverting BitLocker with One Vulnerability," in *Blackhat EU 2019*, available at `https://i.blackhat.com/eu-19/Thursday/eu-19-Han-BitLeaker-Subverting-BitLocker-With-One-Vulnerability.pdf`

[P-19] Sven Turpe, Andreas Poller, Jan Steffan, Jan-Peter Stotz, Jan Trukenmuller, "Attacking the BitLocker Boot Process," *International Conference on Trusted Computing, Trust 2009 Trusted Computing*, pp 183-196 available at `http://citeseerx.ist.psu.edu/viewdoc/download?doi=10.1.1.149.5116&rep=rep1&type=pdf`

[P-20] Evan R. Sparks, "A Security Assessment of Trusted Platform Modules," *Computer Science Technical Report TR2007-597, Dartmouth College, 2007*, available at `https://pdfs.semanticscholar.org/b6a1/802e356f7f900bbbe8b5dc0d8d3aa7fb0ad9.pdf`

[P-21] Johannes Winter, Kurt Dietrich, "A Hijacker's Guide to the LPC bus," in *EuroPKI'11 Proceedings of the 8th European conference on Public Key Infrastructures, Services, and Applications, 2011, Pages 176-193*, available at `https://link.springer.com/content/pdf/10.1007/978-3-642-29804-2_12.pdf`, PPT available at `https://online.tugraz.at/tug_online/voe_main2.getvolltext?pCurrPk=59565`

[P-22] Johannes Winter, Kurt Dietrich, "A hijacker's guide to communication interfaces of the trusted platform module," in *Journal Computers & Mathematics with Applications Volume 65 Issue 5, March, 2013, Pages 748-761*, available at `www.sciencedirect.com/science/article/pii/S0898122112004634`

[P-23] Johannes Winter, "Eavesdropping Trusted Platform Module Communication," in *4th European Trusted Infrastructure Summerschool, ETISS, 2009*, available at `http://citeseerx.ist.psu.edu/viewdoc/download?doi=10.1.1.464.6048&rep=rep1&type=pdf`

[P-24] Jeremy Boone, "TPM Genie," in *CanSecWest 2018*, available at `https://github.com/nccgroup/TPMGenie/blob/master/docs/CanSecWest_2018_-_TPM_Genie_-_Jeremy_Boone.pdf`

[P-25] Denis Andzakovic, "Extracting BitLocker Keys From a TPM," in 2019, available at `https://pulsesecurity.co.nz/articles/TPM-sniffing`

[P-26] K. Chen, "Reversing and exploiting an Apple firmware update," in *Blackhat US 2009*, available at `www.blackhat.com/presentations/bh-usa-09/CHEN/BHUSA09-Chen-RevAppleFirm-SLIDES.pdf`

[P-27] Ralf-Philipp Weinmann , "The hidden nemesis," in *27th Chaos Communication Congress (27C3) 2010*, available at `https://comsecuris.com/slides/rpw-27c3-thmbec.pdf`

[P-28] Charlie Miller, "Battery Firmware Hacking," in *BlackHat US 2011*, available at `https://media.blackhat.com/bh-us-11/Miller/BH_US_11_Miller_Battery_Firmware_Public_Slides.pdf`

[P-29] Nico Waisman, Matias Sebastian Soler, "The Unbearable Lightness of BMCs," in *BlackHat US 2018*, available at `http://i.blackhat.com/us-18/Wed-August-8/us-18-Waisman-Soler-The-Unbearable-Lightness-of-BMC.pdf`

[P-30] Joanna Rutkowska, Rafal Wojtczuk, "Preventing and Detecting Xen Hypervisor Subversions," in *BlackHat US 2008*, available at `https://invisiblethingslab.com/resources/bh08/part2-full.pdf`

[P-31] Rafal Wojtczuk, Joanna Rutkowska, "Attack Intel TXT," in *BlackHat DC 2009*, available at `www.blackhat.com/presentations/bh-dc-09/Wojtczuk_Rutkowska/BlackHat-DC-09-Rutkowska-Attacking-Intel-TXT-slides.pdf`

[P-32] Rafal Wojtczuk, Joanna Rutkowska, Alexander Tereshkin, "Another Way to Circumvent Intel® Trusted Execution Technology," in *invisiblethingslab whitepaper 2009*, available at `https://invisiblethingslab.com/resources/misc09/Another%20TXT%20Attack.pdf`

[P-33] Rafal Wojtczuk, Joanna Rutkowska, "Attacking Intel TXT via SINIT Hijacking," in *invisiblethingslab whitepaper 2011*, available at `https://invisiblethingslab.com/resources/2011/Attacking_Intel_TXT_via_SINIT_hijacking.pdf`

[P-34] Joseph Sharkey, "Breaking Hardware-Enforced Security with Hypervisors," in *BlackHat US 2016*, available at `www.blackhat.com/docs/us-16/materials/us-16-Sharkey-Breaking-Hardware-Enforced-Security-With-Hypervisors.pdf`

[P-35] J. Alex Halderman, Seth D. Schoen, Nadia Heninger, William Clarkson, William Paul, Joseph A. Calandrino, Ariel J. Feldman, Jacob Appelbaum, and Edward W. Felten, "Lest We Remember: Cold Boot Attacks on Encryption Keys," in *Proc. 17th USENIX Security Symposium 2008*, available at `www.usenix.org/legacy/event/sec08/tech/full_papers/halderman/halderman.pdf`

[P-36] Yuriy Bulygin, "Evil Maid Just Got Angrier: Why Full-Disk Encryption With TPM is Insecure on Many Systems," in *CanSecWest 2013*, available at `www.c7zero.info/stuff/Evil%20Maid%20Just%20Got%20Angrier.pdf`

[P-37] "AMD PSP: fTPM Remote Code Execution via crafted EK certificate," 2018, `https://seclists.org/fulldisclosure/2018/Jan/12`

[P-38] Daniel Moghimi, Berk Sunar, Thomas Eisenbarth, Nadia Heninger, "TPM-FAIL: TPM meets Timing and Lattice Attacks," in *29th USENIX Security Symposium 2020*, available at `https://arxiv.org/abs/1911.05673`

[P-39] Matus Nemec, Marek Sys, Petr Svenda, Dusan Klinec, Vashek Matyas, "The Return of Coppersmith's Attack: Practical Factorization of Widely Used RSA Moduli," in ACM CCS 2017, available at `https://crocs.fi.muni.cz/_media/public/papers/nemec_roca_ccs17_preprint.pdf`, `https://crocs.fi.muni.cz/_media/public/papers/ccs-nemec-handout.pdf`

[P-40] Paul England, Butler Lampson, John Manferdelli, Marcus Peinado, Bryan Willman, "A Trusted Open Platform," in *IEEE Computer Society 2003*, available at `www.microsoft.com/en-us/research/wp-content/uploads/2016/11/68-TrustedOpenPlatform.pdf`

[P-41] Magnus Nystrom, Martin Nicholes, Vincent Zimmer, "UEFI Networking and Pre-OS Security," in *Intel Technology Journal – UEFI Today: Bootstrapping the Continuum*, Volume 15, Issue 1, available at `https://www.techonline.com/electrical-engineers/education-training/tech-papers/4231173/UEFI-Networking-and-Pre-OS-Security`

Specification and Guideline

[S-1] NIST SP800-155, "BIOS Integrity Measurement Guidelines," 2011, available at `https://csrc.nist.gov/publications/sp800`

[S-2] Trusted Computing Group, "Trusted Platform Module Library," 2016, available at `https://trustedcomputinggroup.org/resource/tpm-library-specification/`

[S-3] Trusted Computing Group, "TCG PC Client Platform firmware Profile Specification," 2019, available at `https://trustedcomputinggroup.org/resource/pc-client-specific-platform-firmware-profile-specification/`

[S-4] Trusted Computing Group, "TCG PC Client Platform TPM Profile (PTP) Specification," 2019, available at `https://trustedcomputinggroup.org/resource/pc-client-platform-tpm-profile-ptp-specification/`

[S-5] Trusted Computing Group, "TCG Server Management Domain Firmware Profile," 2020, available at `https://trustedcomputinggroup.org/wp-content/uploads/TCG_ServerManagementDomainFirmwareProfile_v1p00_11aug2020.pdf`

[S-6] Trusted Computing Group, "TCG PC Client Platform Reset Attack Mitigation Specification," 2019, available at `https://trustedcomputinggroup.org/resource/pc-client-work-group-platform-reset-attack-mitigation-specification/`

[S-7] Trusted Computing Group, "TCG EFI Protocol Specification," 2016, available at `https://trustedcomputinggroup.org/resource/tcg-efi-protocol-specification/`

[S-8] Trusted Computing Group, "TCG ACPI Specification," 2017, available at `https://trustedcomputinggroup.org/resource/tcg-acpi-specification/`

[S-9] Trusted Computing Group, "TCG Trusted Attestation Protocol (TAP) Information Model," 2019, available at `https://trustedcomputinggroup.org/resource/tcg-tap-information-model/`

[S-10] Trusted Computing Group, "TCG Platform Certificate Profile," 2018, available at `https://trustedcomputinggroup.org/resource/tcg-platform-attribute-credential-profile/`

[S-11] Trusted Computing Group, "TCG EK Credential Profile," 2018, available at `https://trustedcomputinggroup.org/resource/tcg-ek-credential-profile-for-tpm-family-2-0/`

[S-12] Trusted Computing Group, "TCG Reference Integrity Manifest (RIM) Information Model," 2019, available at `https://trustedcomputinggroup.org/wp-content/uploads/TCG_RIM_Model_v1-r13_2feb20.pdf`

[S-13] Trusted Computing Group, "TCG PC Client Reference Integrity Manifest," 2020, available at `https://trustedcomputinggroup.org/wp-content/uploads/TCG_PC_Client_RIM_r0p15_15june2020.pdf`

[S-14] Trusted Computing Group, "TCG PC Client Platform Firmware Integrity Measurement," 2019, available at `https://trustedcomputinggroup.org/wp-content/uploads/TCG_PC_Client-FIM_v1r24_3feb20.pdf`

[S-15] Trusted Computing Group, "Hardware Requirements for a Device Identifier Composition Engine," 2018, available at `https://trustedcomputinggroup.org/resource/hardware-requirements-for-a-device-identifier-composition-engine/`

[S-16] Trusted Computing Group, "Implicit Identity Based Device Attestation," 2018, available at `https://trustedcomputinggroup.org/resource/implicit-identity-based-device-attestation/`

[S-17] Trusted Computing Group, "Symmetric Identity Based Device Attestation," 2020, available at `https://trustedcomputinggroup.org/resource/symmetric-identity-based-device-attestation/`

[S-18] Trusted Computing Group, "TCG DICE Layering Architecture," 2020, available at `https://trustedcomputinggroup.org/resource/dice-layering-architecture/`

[S-19] Trusted Computing Group, "TCG DICE Certificate Profile," 2020, available at `https://trustedcomputinggroup.org/resource/dice-certificate-profiles/`

[S-20] Trusted Computing Group, "TCG Mobile Trusted Module Specification," 2010, available at `https://trustedcomputinggroup.org/resource/mobile-phone-work-group-mobile-trusted-module-specification/`

[S-21] Trusted Computing Group, "TPM 2.0 Mobile Reference Architecture Specification," 2014, available at `https://trustedcomputinggroup.org/tpm-2-0-mobile-reference-architecture-specification/`

[S-22] Trusted Computing Group, "TPM 2.0 Mobile Common Profile," 2015, available at `https://trustedcomputinggroup.org/tcg-tpm-2-0-mobile-common-profile/`

[S-23] Trusted Computing Group, "TCG TPM 2.0 Mobile Command Response Buffer Interface Specification," 2014, available at `https://trustedcomputinggroup.org/resource/tpm-2-0-mobile-command-response-buffer-interface-specification/`

[S-24] Trusted Computing Group, "TCG Runtime Integrity Preservation in Mobile Devices," 2019, available at `https://trustedcomputinggroup.org/wp-content/uploads/TCG_MPWG_RIP_r105_pubrev.pdf`

[S-25] Trusted Computing Group, "TCG Remote Integrity Verification: Network Equipment Remote Attestation System," 2019, available at `https://trustedcomputinggroup.org/wp-content/uploads/TCG-NetEq-Attestation-Workflow-Outline_v1r9b_pubrev.pdf`

[S-26] Trusted Computing Group, "TCG D-RTM Architecture," 2013, available at `https://trustedcomputinggroup.org/resource/d-rtm-architecture-specification/`

[S-27] GB/T 36639, "Trusted Computing Specification: Trusted Support Platform for Server," 2018, available at `http://openstd.samr.gov.cn`

[S-28] GB/T 29829, "Functionality and Interface Specification of Cryptographic Support Platform for Trusted Computing," 2013, available at `http://openstd.samr.gov.cn`

[S-29] GB/T 29827, "Trusted Computing Specification: Motherboard Function and Interface of Trusted Platform," 2013, available at `http://openstd.samr.gov.cn`

[S-30] NISTIR 8060, "Guidelines for the Creation of Interoperable Software Identification (SWID) Tags," 2016, available at `https://csrc.nist.gov/publications/nistir`

[S-31] AMD, "AMD Architecture Programmer's Manual," 2019, available at `www.amd.com/en/support/tech-docs`

[S-32] Intel, "Intel 64 and IA-32 Architecture Software Developer Manuals," 2019, available at `https://software.intel.com/en-us/articles/intel-sdm`

[S-33] Intel, "Intel TXT Software Development Guide," 2017, available at `www.intel.com/content/www/us/en/software-developers/intel-txt-software-development-guide.html`

[S-34] Microsoft, "Secure MOR implementation," 2017, available at `https://docs.microsoft.com/en-us/windows-hardware/drivers/bringup/device-guard-requirements`

[S-35] Microsoft, "DICE – Device Identifier Composition Engine," 2015, available at `www.microsoft.com/en-us/research/project/dice-device-identifier-composition-engine`

[S-36] OCP, "Project Cerberus Architecture Overview Specification," 2018, available at `https://github.com/opencomputeproject/Project_Olympus/blob/master/Project_Cerberus`

[S-37] OCP, "Project Cerberus Firmware Challenge Specification," 2019, available at `https://github.com/opencomputeproject/Project_Olympus/blob/master/Project_Cerberus`

[S-38] DMTF org, "MCTP Base Specification," 2016, available at www.dmtf.org/standards/pmci

[S-39] DMTF org, "Management Component Transport Protocol (MCTP) SMBus/I2C Transport Binding Specification," 2017, available at www.dmtf.org/standards/pmci

[S-40] DMTF org, "Security Protocol and Data Model Specification," 2019, available at www.dmtf.org/standards/pmci

[S-41] DMTF org, "SPDM over MCTP Binding Specification," 2019, available at www.dmtf.org/standards/pmci

[S-42] DMTF org, "Secure MCTP Message over MCTP Binding Specification," 2020, available at https://www.dmtf.org/standards/pmci

[S-43] DMTF org, "Secure Messages using SPDM Specification," 2020, available at https://www.dmtf.org/standards/pmci

Web

[W-1] BitLocker Group Policy settings, https://docs.microsoft.com/en-us/windows/security/information-protection/bitlocker/bitlocker-group-policy-settings

[W-2] Secure the Windows 10 boot process, https://docs.microsoft.com/en-us/windows/security/information-protection/secure-the-windows-10-boot-process

[W-3] Windows Defender System Guard Secure Launch, https://docs.microsoft.com/en-us/windows/security/threat-protection/windows-defender-system-guard/system-guard-how-hardware-based-root-of-trust-helps-protect-windows

[W-4] Microsoft Discusses Details of Next-Generation Secure Computing Base, https://news.microsoft.com/2003/05/07/at-winhec-microsoft-discusses-details-of-next-generation-secure-computing-base/

[W-5] What is Azure Sphere, https://docs.microsoft.com/en-us/azure-sphere/product-overview/what-is-azure-sphere

[W-6] Microsoft, Anatomy of a secure MCU, https://azure.microsoft.com/en-us/blog/anatomy-of-a-secured-mcu

[W-7] Cisco Secure Boot and Trust Anchor Module Differentiation Solution Overview, www.cisco.com/c/en/us/products/collateral/security/cloud-access-security/secure-boot-trust.html

[W-8] Intel® Trusted Execution Technology (Intel® TXT) Enabling Guide, https://software.intel.com/en-us/articles/intel-trusted-execution-technology-intel-txt-enabling-guide

[W-9] Intel Security Libraries for Data Center, www.intel.com/content/www/us/en/architecture-and-technology/security-libraries-for-data-center-article.html

[W-10] coreboot measured boot, `https://doc.coreboot.org/security/vboot/measured_boot.html`

[W-11] GNU GRUB Manual, `www.gnu.org/software/grub/manual/grub/grub.html`

[W-12] Trusted GRUB2, `https://github.com/Rohde-Schwarz/TrustedGRUB2`

[W-13] Linux Integrity Measurement Architecture, `http://linux-ima.sourceforge.net/`

[W-14] Trusted Computing Supply Chain Validation – Host Integrity at Runtime and Startup, `https://github.com/nsacyber/hirs`

[W-15] RIoT Reference Architecture, `https://github.com/Microsoft/RIoT`

[W-16] Google, "OpenTitan: Open source silicon root of trust (RoT)," `https://opentitan.org/`

[W-17] tboot, `https://sourceforge.net/p/tboot`

[W-18] TrenchBoot, `https://github.com/TrenchBoot`

[W-19] OSLO – The Open Secure LOader, `http://os.inf.tu-dresden.de/~kauer/oslo/`

[W-20] the real story of Stuxnet, `https://spectrum.ieee.org/telecom/security/the-real-story-of-stuxnet`

CHAPTER 8

Device Security

A hardware device is an important component in the solution. It can be one part of a platform with other devices on a board, such as a Trusted Platform Module (TPM) device, a Baseboard Management Controller (BMC), a Power Supply Unit (PSU), and so on. Or it can be a standalone one, such as a Universal Serial Bus (USB) device, graphic card device, network card device, hard disk drive, and so on.

Device Firmware Resiliency

The "Seven Properties of Highly Secured Devices" introduces the following design principles:

1. Hardware-based root-of-trust

2. Small trusted computing base

3. Defense in depth

4. Compartmentalization

5. Certificate-based authentication

6. Renewable security

7. Failure reporting

Principles 3 and 4 are similar to the general secure software design principles. Principles 1, 2, 5, 6, and 7 are hardware/firmware resiliency related. The device firmware resiliency should follow the same rules as host firmware resiliency. The protection, detection, and recovery should be considered. This has been discussed in Chapters 3, 4, and 5.

© Jiewen Yao and Vincent Zimmer 2020
J. Yao and V. Zimmer, *Building Secure Firmware*, https://doi.org/10.1007/978-1-4842-6106-4_8

Secure Device Communication

During system boot, the host needs to communicate with the device in order to exchange information. This communication channel might be attacked by a hardware adversary. The attack mechanisms might include but are not limited to interception, modification, eavesdropping, and masquerading.

Authentication and Measurement

Similar to host firmware, a platform may want to define a way to perform attestation for the device, not just support device firmware resiliency. This includes the authentication of the device hardware identity and the measurement of the device firmware identity.

Figure 8-1 shows an example of how to use asymmetric cryptography to achieve that. Each device is provisioned with a certificate. The public portion of the certificate is known by the Platform Active Root-of-Trust (PA-RoT). The private portion of the certificate is kept as a secret in the device immutable ROM, acting as the Active Component Root-of-Trust (AC-RoT). During the system boot, the platform RoT works as the initiator to send a message to the device RoT (the responder), and the device sends a response back.

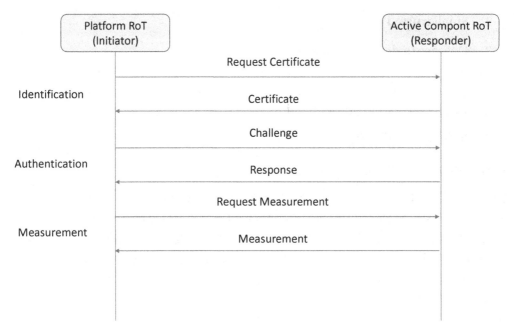

Figure 8-1. *Device Authentication and Measurement Flow*

During the identification phase, the platform RoT requests the device certificate, and the device RoT returns the public certificate of the device. Then the platform RoT can know which device is on the platform.

Next, during the authentication phase, the platform RoT sends a challenge message to the device RoT, and the device RoT encrypts the challenge value with its private certificate as a response. With challenge/response, the platform RoT can know that the device is genuine.

Finally, during the measurement phase, the platform RoT requests the device measurement, including the measurements of the immutable ROM, mutable firmware, hardware configuration, and firmware configuration. Once the device RoT returns this information back, the platform RoT may save that information to a TPM device (root-of-trust for storage and reporting) for further platform attestation.

Secure Communication Channel

Once the platform RoT authenticates the device, it may need to exchange messages. The platform RoT trusts the device, but the platform RoT might not trust the link between them. An attacker might hijack the hardware bus to attack the link between the platform RoT and the device. The connection on the platform motherboard is similar to today's Internet – two endpoints need to create a secure channel in an untrusted world. The most famous secure channel for the Internet is Transport Layer Security (TLS). TLS can provide authentication during the handshake phase and provide confidentiality and integrity during the application phase. The original TLS is a protocol on top of a connection-oriented protocol such as Transmission Control Protocol (TCP). The TLS concept can also be used in other protocols such as Extensible Authentication Protocol (EAP). A variant of TLS – Datagram TLS (DTLS) – can be used on top of a connectionless protocol such as User Datagram Protocol (UDP).

The secure channel may include three phases: handshake, application, and termination (see Figure 8-2). In the handshake phase, the initiator and responder need to exchange the key and crypto parameters and do the authentication. At the end of the handshake phase, both the initiator and responder can calculate a set of session keys used to encrypt the message and calculate the message authentication code (MAC) of the message. In the application phase, the initiator and the responder can exchange the application layer messages, encrypted by the session encryption key and MACed by the session MAC key. Later when the communication is finished, the session is closed.

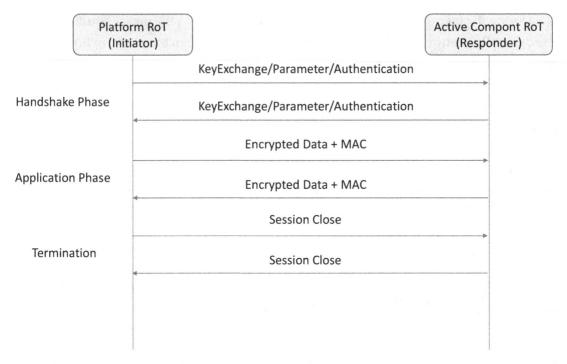

Figure 8-2. *Device Secure Communication*

Device Identifier Composition Engine (DICE)

We have discussed the DICE in Chapter 7. Here the Active Component RoT (AC-RoT) could be a DICE device. Each DICE device includes a unique device secret (UDS), and the DICE core generates the DICE certificate based upon the UDS. This DICE certificate can be used as the identity of the device. Figure 7-9 in Chapter 7 shows the DICE certificate generation.

Case Study

Now, let's take a look at some real cases for secure device communication.

Security Protocol and Data Model (SPDM)

The Distributed Management Task Force (DMTF) Platform Management Components Intercommunication Working Group published the "Security Protocol and Data Model (SPDM) Specification" to define messaging between two entities, including how to exchange information for device authentication and device measurement. Table 8-1 shows the commands defined in the SPDM 1.0 specification. With these commands, the host can authenticate the device and extend the device measurement to TPM PCRs.

Table 8-1. *SPDM 1.0 Command List for Authentication and Measurement*

Command/Response	Category	Description
GET_VERSION/VERSION	Capability discovery and negotiation	Retrieves an endpoint's SPDM version.
GET_CAPABILITIES/CAPABILITIES		Retrieves an endpoint's security capabilities.
NEGOTIATE_ALGORITHMS/ ALGORITHMS		Negotiates cryptographic algorithms.
GET_DIGESTS/DIGEST	Hardware identity authentication	Retrieves the certificate chain digests.
GET_CERTIFICATE/ CERTIFICATE		Retrieve the certificate chains.
CHALLENGE/ CHALLENGE_AUTH		Authenticates an endpoint through the challenge-response protocol.
GET_MEASUREMENTS/ MEASUREMENTS	Firmware measurement	Retrieves firmware measurements.

TLS is a good protocol to provide a secure channel on the Internet. However, it might be overcomplicated for the link on a platform board. As such, the SPDM 1.1 specification adds a special command for a secure communication channel on the platform. These commands model TLS 1.3 in a simplified way by assuming that the transport layer provides reliability in transmission and reception of data and that either the transmission of data is in order or the order of data can be reconstructed at reception. See Table 8-2. In the handshake phase, the two entities may use certificate-based asymmetric key session creation or pre-shared key (PSK)–based session creation. Because the embedded device may be in a resource-constrained environment, the PSK can be used for endpoints that do not support asymmetric key cryptography or certificate processing. In the application phase, the two entities can maintain the session by sending a heartbeat message or updating the session key message. Once the session is no longer needed, the two entities use an "end session" message to close the session.

Table 8-2. *SPDM 1.1 Command List for Secure Communication Channel*

Command/Response	Category	Description
KEY_EXCHANGE/ KEY_EXCHANGE	Session Handshake: Asymmetric key–based session creation	Initiates the handshake between the requester and the responder intended to authenticate the responder, negotiate cryptographic parameters (Diffie-Hellman Ephemeral), and establish shared keying material.
FINISH/FINISH		Completes the handshake between the requester and responder initiated by a KEY_EXCHANGE.
PSK_BASED_EXCHANGE/ PSK_BASED_EXCHANGE	Session Handshake: Symmetric key–based session creation	Allows a requester and a responder to performmutual authentication and session key establishment with symmetric key cryptography, based upon pre-shared key (PSK).
PSK_BASED_FINISH/ PSK_BASED_FINISH		Proves to the responder that the requester knows the PSK and has derived the correct session keys.
HEARTBEAT/HEARTBEAT	Session Application: Session maintenance	Keeps a session alive.
KEY_UPDATE		Updates session keys, especially when the per-record nonce will soon reach its maximum value and rollover.
GET_ENCAPSULATED_ REQUEST/ ENCAPSULATED_ REQUEST	Session Application: Message initiated by the responder (Potential Mutual Authentication)	Retrieves an SPDM request message from the responder.
DELIVER_ENCAPSULATED_ RESPONSE/ ENCAPSULATED_ RESPONSE_ACK		Provides a response to a responder's request.
END_SESSION/ENS_ SESSION_ACK	Session Application: Session termination	Terminates a session.

SPDM 1.0 can only support one-way authentication – the requester to authenticate the responder. SPDM 1.1's encapsulated message can be used for mutual authentication. The responder can send messages to the requester, such as GET_DIGEST/GET_CERTIFICATE or even CHALLENGE, to verify the identity of the requester.

USB Authentication

The SPDM defines the data exchange model. The SPDM messages can be sent via different hardware interfaces. The USB Organization published the "USB Authentication Specification" to describe how to exchange SPDM messages for a USB device on top of the USB bus.

PCI Express Component Measurement and Authentication

SPDM messages can also be sent via a PCIe device. Intel published the "PCIe Device Security Enhancements Specification" as one approach. The PCI-SIG is augmenting that material with the "ECN - Component Measurement and Authentication (CMA)" and "ECN - Data Object Exchange (DOE)" specifications to describe how to exchange SPDM messages for PCIe devices on top of the PCI express bus and provide a mechanism to verify the component configuration and firmware/executables (Measurement) and hardware identities (Authentication).

PCI Express Integrity and Data Encryption

The PCI-SIG published "ECN - Integrity and Data Encryption (IDE)" specifications to describe how to provide confidentiality, integrity, and replay protection for Transaction Layer Packets (TLPs) transmitted and received between two ports. The security model considers threats from physical attacks on links, including cases where an adversary uses lab equipment, purpose-built interposers, malicious extension devices, etc. to examine data intended to be confidential, modify TLP contents, reorder and/or delete TLPs.

The IDE document defines IDE stream, which is a port to port connection to secure TLP traffic between the two ports. There are two types of IDE stream. Selective IDE Stream means that the IDE TLPs flow through switches without affecting their security, while Link IDE Streams means that the two ports must be connected without intervening switches. The SPDM secure session messages are used to establish IDE stream and programming keys.

Other hardware interfaces, such as Computer Express Link (CXL), are also adopting SPDM messages.

SPDM over Management Component Transport Protocol (MCTP)

The DMTF organization defines the Management Component Transport Protocol (MCTP). It is used for the intercommunication between intelligent devices within the platform management subsystem of a managed computer system. For example, MCTP provides for communication between management controllers, intelligent management devices, network controllers, and system firmware. MTCP may be transported over SMBus/I2C, USB, PCIe Vendor Defined Message, and so on. SPDM messages can also be transported over MTCP. As such, MCTP devices can exchange SPDM messages. As we discussed in Chapter 7, the Cerberus project uses this mechanism to let the Platform Active Root-of-Trust (PA-RoT) authenticate the device Active Component Root-of-Trust (AC-RoT).

EDK II Device Security

The EDK II project is adding device firmware security features to its UEFI BIOS implementation. The device authentication and measurement activities are similar to the UEFI image authentication and measurement. See Figures 8-3 and 8-4.

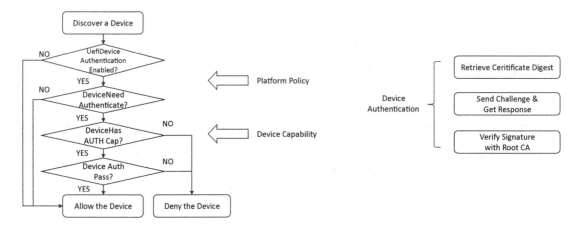

Figure 8-3. *EDK II Device Authentication*

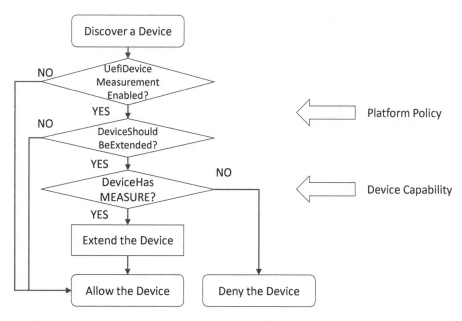

Figure 8-4. *EDK II Device Measurement*

Take the PCI bus as an example. After the PCI enumeration process discovers a device, the PCI bus driver checks if UEFI device authentication or measurement is enabled. If it is enabled, then the PCI bus driver leverages platform policy to determine if this device needs to be authenticated or measured. This step is required to maintain compatibility since only a limited number of devices support such a feature in the market today. If the platform policy requires authentication or measurement of this device, the PCI bus driver checks the device's capabilities and then performs the authentication or measurement. Only after the device authentication passes and measurements are collected will the PCI bus driver allow the device to be enabled or used. If the device does not have the required capability or the authentication fails, the PCI bus treats it as a policy violation and will deny the device. Here the "allow" means the PCI bus driver allocates resources (MMIO, I/O, bus) for the device and makes it discoverable via EFI_PCI_IO_PROTOCOL, and "deny" means the PCI bus driver does not allocate resources and does not install the EFI_PCI_IO_PROTOCOL.

The Trusted Computing Group (TCG) PC Client working group is adding the device firmware measurement into its "TCG PC Client Platform Firmware Profile Specification" to describe how the measurement of the device is collected, the measurement is extended into the TPM, and the measurement is recorded in the event log.

Putting all involved components together, we get Figure 8-5. The NIST SP800-193 provides the general platform firmware resiliency guide. The NIST SP800-155 specification provides the general platform integrity measurement guideline. The host CPU may communicate with the device to do the authentication and measurement via SPDM messages over PCIe or USB. The measurement of the device is extended to a TPM, and the corresponding event log is created. A standalone platform Root-of-Trust device may communicate with boot-critical devices to do the authentication and measurement via SPDM messages over MCTP on top of SMBus or I2C.

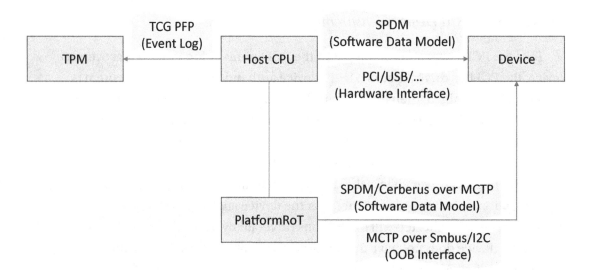

Figure 8-5. *Platform Device Security Summary*

Attack and Mitigation

Now, let's take a look at some real cases of secure communication attacks and mitigation.

Security Policy Configuration Attack

In UEFI secure boot, one attack is just to disable the UEFI secure boot capability. This can also be applied to device security. The platform policy to enable/disable device authentication or measurement should be a static setting or else a runtime setting requiring physical user confirmation.

The device signature database in device authentication is similar to the image signature database in UEFI's secure boot. It is a database to record the allowed device certificates and the forbidden device certificates. This database is saved in UEFI variables, and records can be enrolled or revoked. When a user wants to update the device signature database, the new database must be signed or updated with the physical user presence.

Device selection is a new attack surface. Because device authentication is a new concept, not all existing devices support it. A platform may choose to use a policy to only authenticate some devices but not all devices. As such, the platform needs to have a way to record which devices need to be authenticated or which devices can be left unauthenticated. If this information is saved as a UEFI variable, it must be locked, or the attacker may just update the device selection configuration to bypass the authentication flow.

Malformed Input: SPDM Response

Before the device is authenticated, we don't know if the device is good or malicious. A compromised device or a malicious device may send malformed response messages to the initiator, including a malformed header, malformed certificate, malformed signature, malformed measurement, and so on. See Figure 8-6. Those attacks may cause buffer overflow in the initiator's software. Care must be taken when parsing the response from the device.

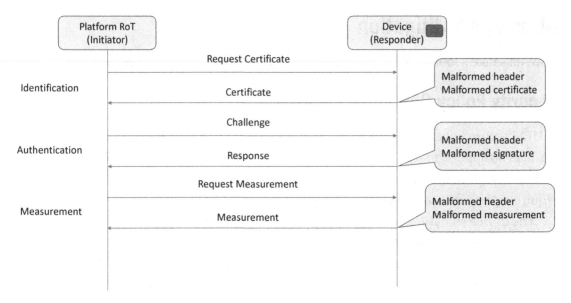

Figure 8-6. *Attack Surface for SPDM Message*

Device Attack Prevention

Before secure communication is established, basic, insecure communication might already have happened. As such, it is important to be careful to prevent the attacks to the device.

Device Identifier Data

Device authentication and measurement are new technologies. The existing devices might not support those features. As such, all messages from the device should be checked to make sure their format is correct. When the host software discovers a new device, the host software needs to know which device it is, what the supported features are, and what the attributes are. The information is typically defined in the device specification and reported in a type-length-value (TLV) format. However, malicious devices do not follow the specification and may send out malformed TLV data in order to cause a buffer overflow or other parsing-based vulnerabilities in the host software.

Attack and Mitigation

Now, let's take a look at some real cases of device identifier data attacks and mitigation.

USB Descriptor Attack

A USB descriptor is used to report the USB device attributes. The USB specification defines a set of standard descriptors, including device descriptor, binary device object store (BOS) descriptor, configuration descriptor, interface descriptor, and endpoint descriptor. A length field in the beginning of each indicates the total size of the descriptor.

   If a software just follows the structures defined in the USB specification to allocate a buffer for the descriptor data structures, a malicious USB device may provide a very large length field value and cause a buffer overflow in the software (see Figure 8-7).

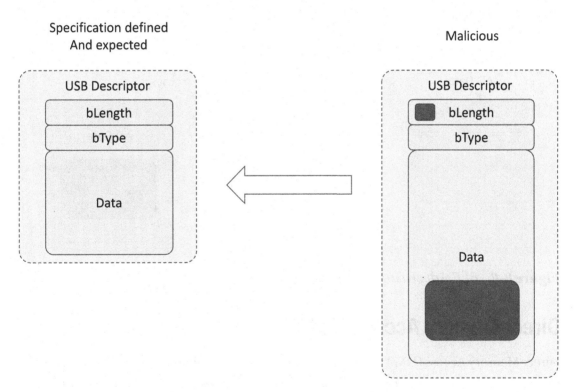

Figure 8-7. *USB Descriptor Attack*

Bluetooth Advertisement Attack

Bluetooth advertisement is a message sent by a Bluetooth slave device to report information to a Bluetooth master device. The advertising data (AD) starts with a length field followed by a type and data. If the host software makes assumptions about the AD structure and just copies the data based on the length field, a malicious Bluetooth device may inject bad advertising data by using large length field values in order to cause a buffer overflow in the host software (see Figure 8-8).

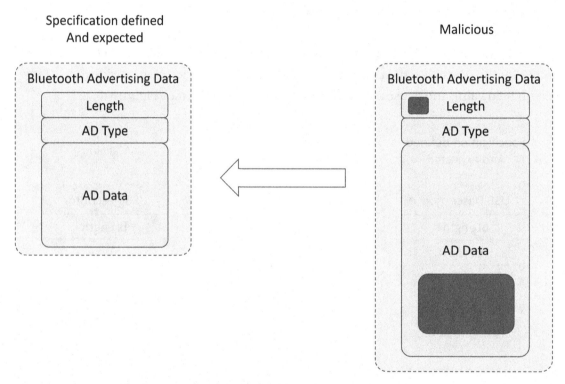

Figure 8-8. *BLE Advertising Data Attack*

Direct Memory Access (DMA)

Direct Memory Access (DMA) is one mechanism to let a device communicate with the host. With permission from the host, a device may access any system memory to exchange the information, independent of the host CPU. In the host environment, most architectures support a memory management unit (MMU) to provide virtual address/

physical address translation for the CPU. For the device, the system may use an I/O memory management unit (IOMMU) to perform the device address/physical address translation. See Figure 8-9.

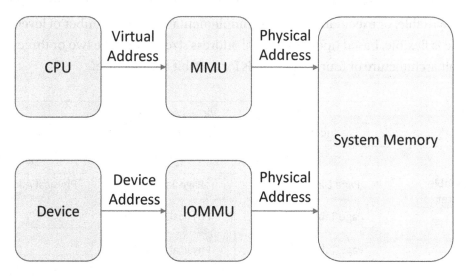

Figure 8-9. *MMU and IOMMU Translation*

The IOMMU is an optional feature. Without an IOMMU, the system may treat the device address to be the same as the memory physical address. An IOMMU provides two features:

1) Address translation: Remap the device address to a different physical address. For example, a device may only support 32-bit device addresses, with a maximum address of 4 GiB. With an IOMMU, the device addresses can be mapped to an above–4 GiB 64-bit physical address. If the system does not have a large contiguous physical address, the IOMMU can map a contiguous device address to fragmented physical addresses.

2) Access control: The IOMMU can control which system memory can be read or written by which device. This is important to prevent a malicious device from attacking the system memory.

With the MMU, a page table translates the virtual address to a physical address. Take Figure 8-10 as an example, where a page table pointer is the address of a page directory. The CPU uses the upper part of the virtual address as the index of the page directory to retrieve an address of a page table. Then, the CPU uses the middle part of the virtual address as the index of the page table to retrieve the physical page address, plus the lower part of the virtual address as the physical page offset. That is the final physical address. Each page table entry has precise privilege control as to whether the page is readable, writable, or executable. In actual implementations, the number of levels of a page table is flexible, based upon the virtual address size. It could be two or three levels for a 32-bit architecture or four or five levels for a 64-bit architecture.

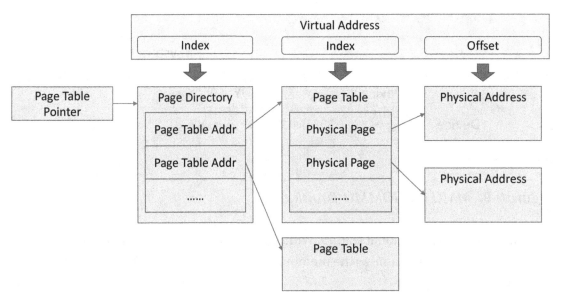

Figure 8-10. *MMU Address Translation*

If a hypervisor is enabled in a platform, the hypervisor controls the final physical address access (see Figure 8-11). Modern virtualization technology supports two different translation tables. One translation table is in the guest operating system. It is controlled by a guest OS to translate the guest virtual address to the guest physical address. This guest translation table is the same as the one without virtualization. The other translation table is in the virtual machine monitor. It is controlled by the hypervisor to translate the guest physical address to the host physical address. The advantage of the two-layers translation is to enable different controls in different domains.

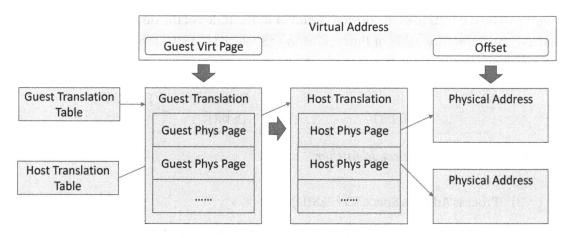

Figure 8-11. *MMU Address Translation in the Hypervisor*

The translation process for an IOMMU is more complicated because an IOMMU needs to consider more things:

1) IOMMU engine

A platform may have multiple IOMMU engines. Each IOMMU engine manages a set of PCI devices. In most cases, each PCI segment has its own IOMMU engine. Within one PCI segment, there can also be multiple IOMMU engines. For example, on X86 client systems, the graphic controller may have a dedicated IOMMU engine. All other PCI devices are managed by another IOMMU engine. This is determined by the hardware design. A platform needs to report PCI device scope information in an IOMMU ACPI table. For the non-PCI system, each device has a unique ID, and the ID is also reported in the IOMMU ACPI table. Each IOMMU engine has a device table base address.

2) Device source identifier

Each device should have its own translation table. The two devices may refer to the same device address, but the IOMMU should be able to set up different physical addresses for the two devices. In an IOMMU, the device source identifier is used to identify the device. A PCI device can be identified with segment number, bus number, device number, and function number (see Figure 8-12). If each segment has its own IOMMU engine, the bus/device/function number can be used as the device source identifier for the current device in this segment. The whole source identifier is 16 bits, including an 8-bit bus number, a 5-bit device number, and a 3-bit function number. Although this is designed for a PCI device, a non-PCI device also has the identifier number. The IOMMU uses the device identifier as the index of the device table to retrieve the translation table or Process Address Space ID (PASID) table.

| Bus (8 bit) | Device (5 bit) | Function (3 bit) |

Figure 8-12. *Device Source Identifier*

3)   Process Address Space ID (PASID)

PASID is a feature defined in the PCI express specification. With PASID, a device can be shared with multiple processes and provides each process a complete 64-bit virtual address space. The implementation of PASID requires that a PCIe Transaction Layer Packet's (TLP) prefix contain a 20-bit PASID that is added to memory transaction TLPs. If a system supports PASID, the address in the device table is the PASID table address. The IOMMU uses the PASID as the index of the PASID table to retrieve the address of the translation table. The non-PCI system also has similar concepts. Each process can use a unique ID to indicate its own translation table.

4)   Nested translation table

Each device has a unique translation table. The data structure of the translation table is similar to the one in the MMU. The upper part of the device address is used as the index to find the next-level page table. The IOMMU uses the address of the leaf page table as the final physical page address, plus the lower part of the device address as the final physical page offset.

In a hypervisor environment, the IOMMU engine may choose to use two translation tables. This optional feature is called nested translation. One guest translation table set for the guest OS is to translate the device address to the guest physical address. Then the other host translation table for the hypervisor is to translate the guest physical address to the host physical address. The advantage of this two-layer translation in an IOMMU is that it aligns with current virtualization design in most hypervisors where different domains have different controls.

Similar to the MMU, each page table entry has precise privilege control if the page is readable, writable, and executable or even not present. If the device access violates the predefined policy control in the translation table, the access will be denied, and an error will be generated by the IOMMU engine.

Figure 8-13 shows the full IOMMU address translation flow.

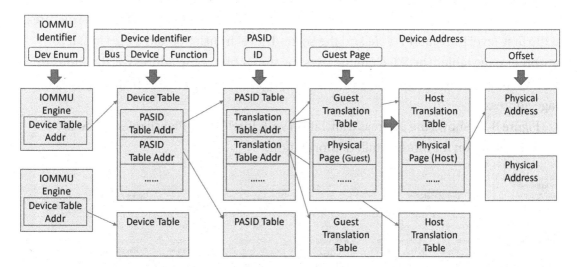

Figure 8-13. *IOMMU Address Translation*

Case Study

Now, let's take a look at some real cases of DMA protection.

Intel VT-d

Intel Virtualization Technology for Directed I/O (VT-d) is an IOMMU implementation. It supports the DMA address translation feature. The VT-d engine uses two-level device tables. Each VT-d engine has only one root table. When doing the address translation, the VT-d uses the upper 8 bits (bus number) as the index to a root table to retrieve an address of the context table. Then the VT-d uses the lower 8 bits (device number and function number) as the index to the context table to retrieve an address of the next translation table. It could be a PASID table or device translation table if PASID is unsupported.

If a system supports PASID, the address in the context table is the PASID directory. If the device sends the memory access request with 20-bit PASID, VT-d uses the PASID[19:6] as the index of the PASID directory to retrieve the address of the PASID table. Then VT-d uses the PASID[5:0] as the index of the PASID table to retrieve the address of the device translation table.

VT-d supports nested translation. The guest translation table is called the first-level translation table. The host translation table is called the second-level translation table. Both addresses of translation tables are included in the PASID table entry. The structures of the first-level translation table and the second-level translation table are similar to any other page table. The VT-d engine uses the upper bits of the address as the index to retrieve the next-level page table until the leaf page where it contains the final physical page address.

Figure 8-14 shows the address translation with Intel VT-D. Please refer to the Intel VT-d specification for more detailed information.

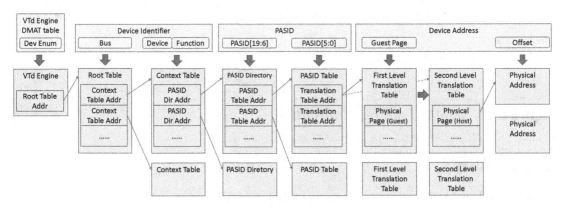

Figure 8-14. *Intel VT-d Address Translation*

In general, the DMA access can be blocked by two ways: translation and exclusion. Besides the translation page table, VT-d includes two sets of registers to provide the DMA exclusion. The register is called the Protected Memory Register (PMR). One register set is below 4GB – Protected Low Memory Register (PLMR). The other is above 4GB – Protected High Memory Register (PHMR). A region covered by the PMR is not a DMA capable region (see Figure 8-15). This DMA exclusion mechanism is useful in a simple and resource-constrained environment, such as an early boot phase in the system firmware or in the Authenticated Code Module (ACM).

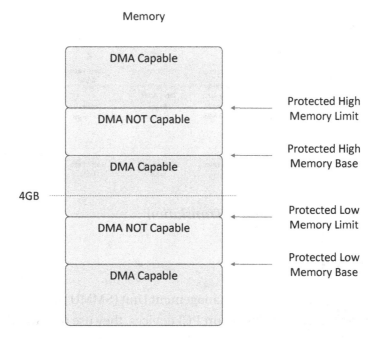

Figure 8-15. *Intel VT-d PMR*

AMD I/O Virtualization

An AMD IOMMU has the DMA translation capability but with a different data structure. The IOMMU engine may have multiple device table segments. Each device table is just a one-level table. Nested translation is supported. Each device table entry includes two translation table addresses: Guest CR3 (GCR3) table and host page table. The Guest CR3 table is for the PASID translation, and it can be multilevel. The IOMMU uses the PASID as the index to retrieve a guest page table address in the final Guest CR3 level 1 table. Then the IOMMU uses the guest page table to translate the guest device address to the guest physical address and uses the host page table to translate the guest physical address to the system physical address.

Besides the DMA translation, AMD also supports DMA protection via the DMA exclusion – Device Exclusion Vector (DEV). The DEV table is a contiguous array of bits in the physical memory, and each bit corresponds to one 4 K page.

Figure 8-16 shows the address translation with AMD IOMMU. Please refer to the AMD IOMMU specification for more detailed information.

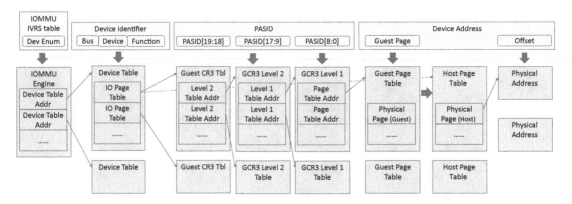

Figure 8-16. *AMD IOMMU Address Translation*

ARM System MMU

ARM systems use the System Memory Management Unit (SMMU) for DMA remapping. Because most ARM systems do not support PCI devices, they use the StreamID as the device identifier and the SubStreamID as the PASID. The StreamID namespace is per-SMMU. Devices behind different SMMUs may be assigned with the same StreamID. A device might emit traffic with more than one StreamID, which represents that the data streams are differentiated by device-specific state. SubStreamID differentiates streams of traffic originating from the same logical block in order to associate different application address translations to each. Each SMMU has a stream table. The SMMU uses the StreamID as the index to get the Stream Table Entry (STE) from the stream table. The Stream Table Entry includes an address of a Stage 1 Context Table (S1ContextPtr) and an address of a Stage 2 Translation Table (S2TTB). Then the SMMU uses the SubStreamID as the index to get the Context Descriptor (CD) from the Stage 1 Context Table. The Context Descriptor includes the address of the Stage 1 Translation Table (TTB0/TTB1). The Stage 1 and Stage 2 Translation Tables support the nested translation as we discussed before. The Stage 1 Translation Table translates the guest virtual address to an intermediate physical address, and the Stage 2 Translation Table translates the intermediate physical address to the final physical address.

Figure 8-17 shows the address translation with ARM SMMU. Please refer to the ARM SMMU specification for more detailed information.

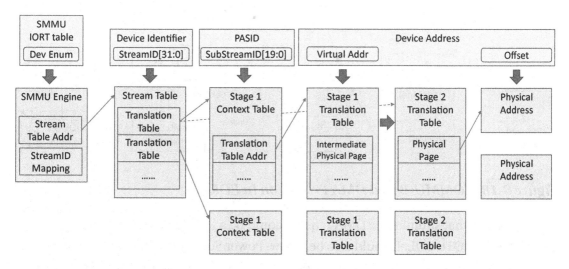

Figure 8-17. *ARM SMMU Address Translation*

EDK II IOMMU Support

EDK II implemented an IOMMU protocol for system firmware (see Figure 8-18). The
IOMMU protocol abstracts IOMMU access. A typical IOMMU driver includes the four
components:

1) IOMMU ACPI table parser: The platform reports the presence of
an IOMMU via the ACPI table. A platform-agnostic IOMMU driver
parses the ACPI table for the IOMMU location and the devices
managed by the IOMMU.

2) IOMMU engine manager: The driver needs to control the IOMMU,
enabling it, disabling it, and flushing the translation table.

3) Translation table manager: The driver also needs to update the
translation table based upon the request from the device. By
default, no memory should be DMA capable after the IOMMU
is initialized. When a device requests a DMA buffer, the IOMMU
driver allows DMA access in the IOMMU's translation table. Once
the DMA buffer is released, the IOMMU driver needs to revoke the
access rights in the IOMMU's translation table.

4) IOMMU protocol services: The driver provides a software
interface in order to let other device drivers submit DMA requests.

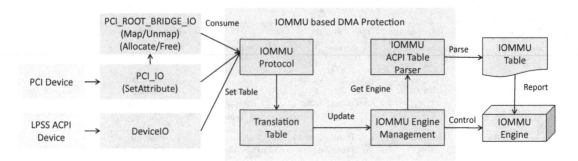

Figure 8-18. *IOMMU-Based DMA Protection in EDK II*

The device that submits the DMA request could be a PCI device which uses the EFI_PCI_IO_PROTOCOL. It could also be a Low-Power Subsystem (LPSS) ACPI device, such as a Universal Asynchronous Receiver/Transmitter (UART), or a device connected via the Serial Peripheral Interface (SPI) or Inter-Integrated Circuit (I2C) bus or Secure Digital Input and Output (SDIO) bus. These use a device-specific I/O interface. Take a PCI driver as an example in Figure 8-19. Here, the PCI driver uses the AllocateBuffer/FreeBuffer to manage a common DMA buffer for both reads and writes, or it may allocate system memory and then use Map/Unmap to use it as a read DMA buffer or a write DMA buffer. All those actions are hooked by the IOMMU driver. The IOMMU driver allocates the DMA buffer in the AllocateBuffer/FreeBuffer/Map/Unmap function. Later the PCI driver uses the SetAttributes function in the IOMMU protocol to inform the IOMMU driver of the access rights and modifies the access right in the DMA translation table. The translation table is per device so that the IOMMU driver can identify the device by the device handle. The IOMMU translation table is set up for fine-grained protection. Since the IOMMU driver can identify the device by the UEFI device handle, each device will be assigned a translation table.

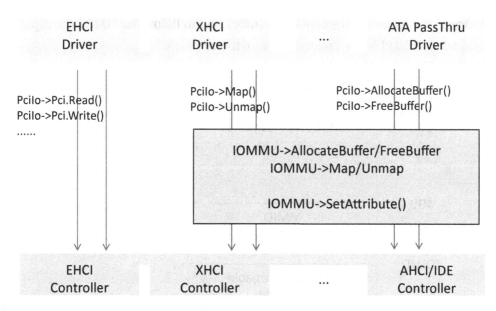

Figure 8-19. *IOMMU Hook in EDK II*

The UEFI environment does not enable virtualization by default, and it does not enable PASID for PCI devices. As such, the IOMMU engine only needs to use the device table and host translation table. The PASID table and guest translation table are not required.

Before the UEFI environment is set up, the Pre-UEFI Initialization (PEI) phase can also use the IOMMU after the memory is initialized (see Figure 8-20). The PEI phase is a simple and resource-constrained execution environment. There is no device handle concept. As such, all the devices share one single translation table. Some architectures may provide a set of registers to define a global DMA capable region or a global DMA non-capable region. Those registers can be used to set the protected region and leave a small region as a DMA buffer. That simplifies the firmware code. Taking Intel VT-d as an example, the Protected High Memory Base and Limit Register (PHMB/PHML) and the Protected Low Memory Base and Limit Register (PLMB/PLML) can be used in the PEI phase. The PEI IOMMU driver can set the PHMB/PHML registers to cover the region from the 4 GiB to the Top of Upper Usable DRAM (TOUUD). For the below–4 GiB memory, some MMIO regions are naturally not DMA capable, such as the flash, Advanced Programmable Interrupt Controller (APIC), and PCI express configuration space. Even below the Top of Low Usable DRAM (TOLUD), some special regions are also not DMA capable, such as system management Ram (SMRAM). As such, the PEI

IOMMU driver can leave a DMA capable memory region below the DMA non-capable region and set PLMB/PLML to cover the rest of memory.

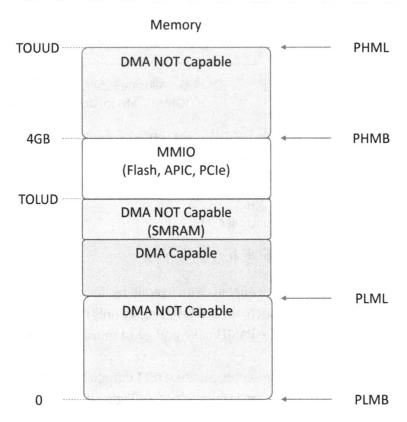

Figure 8-20. *Protected Memory Solution in PEI*

Figure 8-21 shows the DMA protection mechanism in EDK II. There might be a gap between the firmware exit (ExitBootServices event in normal boot and EndOfPei in S3 resume) and the OS IOMMU driver taking control. If the OS cannot take control of the IOMMU directly from the firmware, the firmware must disable IOMMU-based protection. If the OS can seamlessly take control of the IOMMU, the firmware may keep IOMMU enabled.

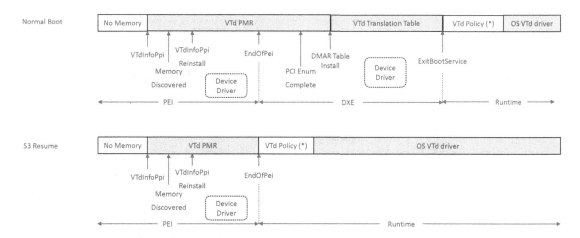

Figure 8-21. *DMA Protection in EDK II*

"Using IOMMU for DMA Protection in UEFI Firmware" describes the IOMMU design in EDK II in more detail.

Attack and Mitigation

Now, let's take a look at some real cases of DMA attacks and their mitigation.

DMA Attack from Device

A Direct Memory Access (DMA) attack is one way to bypass firmware security features such as secure boot or authenticated update. After the host CPU authenticates the image, the malicious device may generate DMA traffic to modify the memory of the image before the CPU executes the image or reads the image. DMA attacks may also be used to steal secrets in memory, such as the BIOS password and hard disk drive (HDD) password. PCILeech and microblaze are an open source tool that can perform just such a DMA attack. Figure 8-22 shows the possible DMA attack.

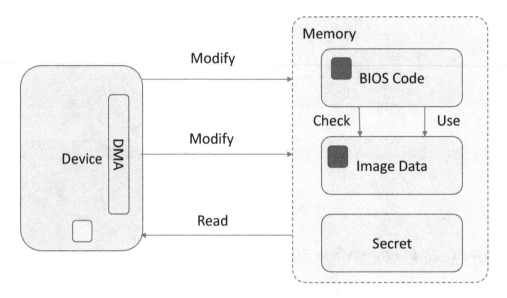

Figure 8-22. *Possible DMA Attack*

Because the malicious DMA is generated from a malicious device, the first thought of mitigation is to disable the DMA from the device. A PCI device has a Bus Master Enable (BME) bit in the PCI configuration space. This bit can be used to control whether DMA is allowed for this PCI device. Ideally, the firmware can prevent DMA attack by not setting the BME bit. However, there are limitations:

1) Some internal PCI devices or non-PCI devices do not have the BME bit. DMA is always enabled.

2) If a device under a bridge needs DMA, all bridges on the path need to set the BME enable bit.

3) The EDK II PCI bus driver needs to enable the BME bit to test whether BME can be enabled or disabled. This allows the device driver to know if it needs to set BME to enable DMA.

4) A platform may choose to only enable the BME for the devices which are required in the boot, such as one storage and one graphic device. But the device must be present and work first before the end user selects them. If there are multiple devices present, the BME bits of those devices are already enabled by the device driver. If one device is malicious, it is useless to clear the BME bit after enabling the BME bit because the attack has already happened.

Usually, the IOMMU engine is set up by the OS to prevent DMA attacks on the OS kernel (see Figure 8-23). Here the firmware can use the IOMMU to resist DMA attacks as well. The system memory is not DMA capable by default. Only after a device driver sends a request for a DMA buffer will this DMA buffer be allocated by the IOMMU for this particular device. Once the DMA is finished, the IOMMU resets the memory to not DMA capable.

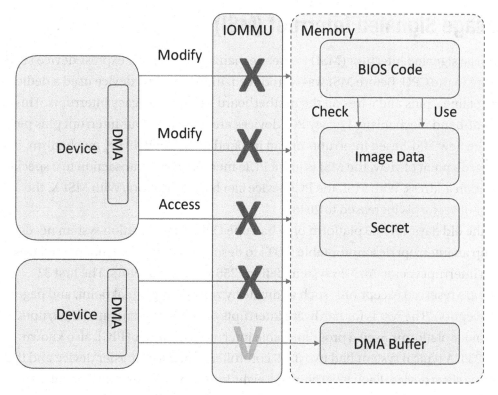

Figure 8-23. *DMA Attack Mitigated by IOMMU*

ACPI Table Bypass

As we have seen, the IOMMU is an efficient way to prevent DMA attacks to a device. For a platform that has already adopted IOMMU-based protection, one possible attack is to remove the IOMMU ACPI table reporting. As such, the host software thinks that there is no IOMMU available on the system.

This attack can be mitigated by enabling UEFI secure boot. As such, there is no way to run untrusted third-party code. Another option is to enable TCG trusted boot. For example, with DRTM, Intel TXT enabled, the SINIT-ACM will verify the DMAR ACPI table. If the DMAR ACPI table is missing or the information in the DMAR table is not expected, the SINIT-ACM will trigger TXT reset for the platform. If the expected DMAR table is created, the SINIT-ACM will copy the DMAR table to the TXT heap's SINIT-to-MLE region. Then the hypervisor can get the verified DMAR table from the TXT heap instead of from the normal ACPI table region.

Message Signaled Interrupt (MSI)

A message signaled interrupt (MSI) is one mechanism to let a PCI express device send an interrupt to the CPU. Before MSI was introduced, the legacy PCI device used a dedicated interrupt line – pins and wires on the motherboard – to signal legacy interrupts. This is an out-of-band mechanism. Legacy PCI devices are limited to four interrupt pins per card. The new MSI-based interrupts are an in-band interrupt delivery mechanism. From the device's point of view, the MSI is just a PCIe memory write transaction to a special destination address. With MSI, the PCI device can have 32 vectors. With MSI-X, the number of vectors is increased to 2048.

In the old days, an X86 platform only had one CPU. The operation system needed to set up an interrupt descriptor table (IDT) to describe the interrupt handler address of each interrupt vector. An X86 system defines 256 interrupt vectors. The first 32 vectors are reserved exceptions, such as divide by zero, debug, breakpoint, and page fault exception. The rest is for hardware interrupts or software-generated interrupts. These older platforms used a programmable interrupt controller (PIC), also known as an 8259. A typical system had two 8259 controllers – one as a master device and the other as a slave device. Each 8259 chip has eight Interrupt Request (IRQ) inputs. This gives a system 16 IRQ inputs. Each 8259 chip can be programmed with an interrupt vector base by the software. As such, each IRQ can be mapped to interrupt vectors by the PIC. Unfortunately, legacy systems had already assigned certain IRQs to specific devices. For example, IRQ0 is for the Timer, IRQ1 is for the PS2 Keyboard, IRQ2 is for the 8259 Slave, IRQ3 is for Serial Port A, IRQ4 is for Serial Port B, IRQ5 is for Parallel Port A, IRQ6 is for the Floppy Disk, IRQ7 is for Parallel Port B, IRQ8 is for the CMOS/RTC Alarm, IRQ12 is for the PS2 Mouse, IRQ13 is for the Arithmetic Processor, IRQ14 is for the Legacy Primary IDE Controller, and IRQ15 is for the Legacy Secondary IDE Controller.

That leaves only a limited number of IRQs which can be assigned to the PCI devices. According to the PCI specification, each PCI device may have four interrupt pins (INTA#,

INTB#, INTC#, INTD#). Each function of a PCI device has one pin. Now we need a way to map the PCI device interrupt pins to the limited IRQs. This is done by the Programmable Interrupt Router. A system typically had eight PCI Interrupt Request (PIRQ) routing control registers (PIRQA, PIRQB, PIRQC, PIRQD, PIRQE, PIRQF, PIRQG, PIRQH) in the Low Pin Count (LPC) controller. For a PCI device, INTA/B/C/D was usually hardcoded. The PIRQ registers mapped the pin on the chipset to a specific IRQ. The wires on the board determined whether INTA/INTB/INTC/INTD mapped to PIRQA/PIRQB/PIRQC/PIRQD/PIRQE/PIRQF/PIRQG/PIRQH except for built-in devices. Figure 8-24 shows the interrupt flow with 8259.

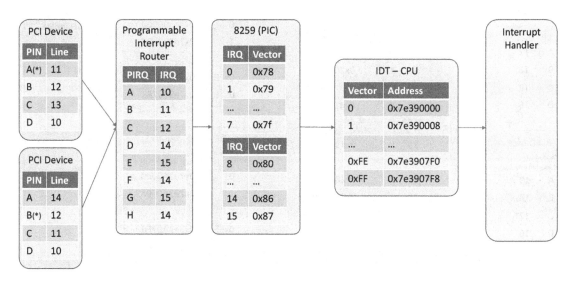

Figure 8-24. *Interrupt Flow with PIC/8259*

A single CPU is no longer the trend. Most of today's systems include multiple CPUs. Each CPU has its own IDT table. The PIC is not enough because it cannot indicate which interrupt vector is for which CPU. The X86 system introduced the Advanced Programmable Interrupt Controller (APIC). The APIC is divided into various parts – a local APIC which is inside of a CPU and IOAPIC which serves the similar purpose as the legacy PIC. Let's focus on the IOAPIC first. An IOAPIC supports 24 APIC interrupts. Each interrupt has a unique vector assigned by the software in an interrupt redirection table. The first 16 interrupts are mapped to the 16 legacy IRQs (IRQ0 ~ IRQ15). The next eight interrupts (indexes 16 ~ 23) are dedicated for the eight PCI IRQs (PIRQA ~ PIRQH). One advantage of an IOAPIC is that we don't need to struggle to assign IRQ numbers for PCI IRQs. The other advantage of an IOAPIC is that we can specify which IRQ is delivered to which CPU in the interrupt redirection table. Each entry in the interrupt redirection table has a destination ID. The destination ID matches the APIC ID in the local APIC of the CPU. The APIC ID is also an identifier for a CPU in a multiple-CPU system. In APIC mode, the PCI device just needs to indicate which APIC index (16 ~ 23) is the interrupt line. Of course, if a system needs to support many PCI devices, it may include multiple IOAPICs. With a second IOAPIC, all 24 interrupts can be used for PCI IRQs. Figure 8-25 shows the interrupt flow with IOAPIC.

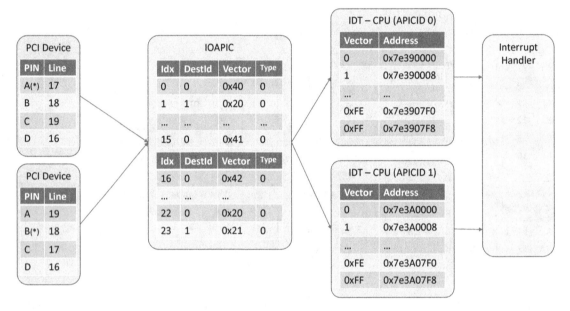

Figure 8-25. *Interrupt Flow with IOAPIC*

Besides PCI devices, CPUs may need to talk to each other via inter-processor interrupts (IPIs) in a multiple-CPU environment. This can be done using the local APIC. Each local APIC has an interrupt command register (ICR). Accessing the ICR is just a memory write operation. Software can fill the destination ID and vector number of other CPUs by writing to the ICR. Then the hardware will send the interrupt via the local APIC bus to the other CPU. Figure 8-26 shows the interrupt flow with a local APIC.

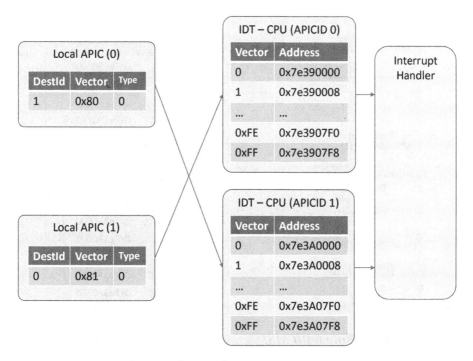

Figure 8-26. *Interrupt Flow with Local APIC*

With the local APIC, software can write an address to trigger an interrupt. Can we use a similar mechanism for the PCI device? The answer is yes, with message signaled interrupts (MSIs). A PCI device may provide the message address register and message data register in the PCI configuration space. The software programs the destination ID in the message address register and vector in the message data register. Once the PCI device requests an interrupt, the device just needs to write the message data to the message address. Then the local APIC can interpret this message and invoke the corresponding interrupt handler. This operation does not rely on any interrupt pins. This design removes the pin number limitations and provides low latency and high efficiency. See Figure 8-27.

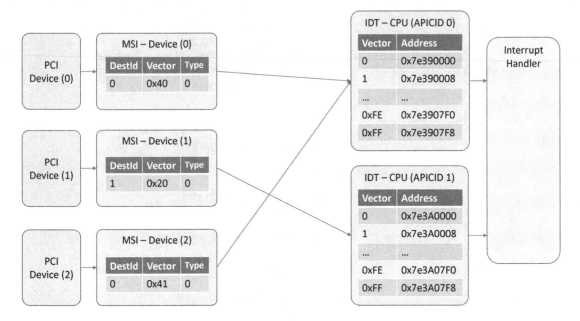

Figure 8-27. *Interrupt Flow with MSI*

MSI provides flexibility. However, a device may send a malicious interrupt message directly to the system bus and break the system, such as a startup message, system interrupt call, or Alignment Check (#AC) exception. As such, we need a way to prevent this from happening.

The basic mitigation idea is borrowed from the protection mechanism of privilege ring switches from user mode to supervisor mode. The supervisor mode code sets up a call gate or interrupt gate with the service handler address and the gate number. The user mode can only invoke the gate to switch to the service handler code, instead of arbitrarily selecting which piece of code to invoke.

The new MSI interrupt format is called remappable format. The key difference between the remappable format and the original compatible format is that the remappable format does allow specifying various detailed properties such as destination ID and vector number. The information is programmed in the interrupt remapping table (IRT). The remappable MSI format only allows the programming of the index of the interrupt remapping table. See Figure 8-28.

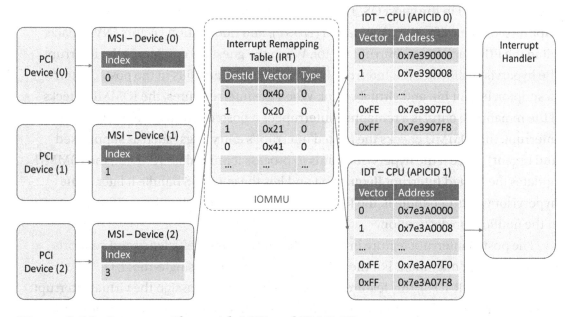

Figure 8-28. *Interrupt Flow with MSI and IOMMU*

The IRT can be supported by a system IOMMU engine as well. It provides the interrupt isolation and interrupt migration capability.

Case Study

Now, let's take a look at some real cases for the interrupt protection.

Intel VT-d

The Intel VT-d engine supports interrupt remapping. Each VT-d engine has one interrupt remapping table. When an MSI is generated, the MSR address and MSR data field include the handle and sub-handle information. The IOMMU uses those two fields as the index of the remapping entry in the remapping table. The remapping entry includes the destination ID and vector information. The IOMMU generates a new Interrupt Request according to the information in the remapping entry.

Besides normal interrupt remapping, the VT-d engine also has support for posted interrupt remapping. The posted interrupt is a feature in virtualization technology. It allows the APIC to inject the interrupt to the guest OS directly without a VM exit. During the initialization phase, the hypervisor sets up a posted interrupt descriptor (PID) for each virtual CPU in the guest OS. The PID includes the Posted Interrupt Request (PIR), suppressed bit, notification destination (NDST), and notification vectors (NVs). Each bit in the PIR maps to an interrupt vector. When the guest OS configures the interrupt, the hypervisor allocates the Interrupt Remapping Entry and fills in the posted interrupt descriptor, urgent bit, and virtual vector. When the interrupt fires, the IOMMU checks if the remapping entry is a remapped interrupt or a posted interrupt. If it is a posted interrupt, the IOMMU checks the posted interrupt's entry flags (such as suppressed and urgent) to see if the hypervisor wants to process it immediately. If not, the IOMMU updates the Posted Interrupt Request bit and lets the guest OS handle it later. If the hypervisor wants to handle it, the IOMMU signals an interrupt to the notification vector at the notification destination.

The posted interrupt feature improves the virtualization efficiency and supports virtual interrupt migration. For the PCI device that supports single-root I/O virtualization (SR-IOV), this feature allows the hypervisor to assign the virtual interrupt to a virtual function (VF) directly. It resolves the interrupt vector scalability problem, because each VF can have its own virtual vector number.

Figure 8-29 shows the interrupt remapping in Intel VT-d. Please refer to the Intel VT-d specification for more detailed information.

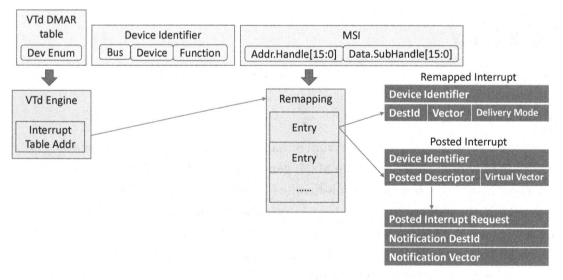

Figure 8-29. *Interrupt Remapping in Intel VT-d*

AMD I/O Virtualization

AMD IOMMU supports the interrupt remapping in the device level. Each device table entry includes an interrupt remapping table address. The IOMMU uses the MSI data bits 10~0 as the index of the interrupt remapping table to get an entry. The remapping entry includes destination ID and vector information. Finally, the IOMMU regenerates the Interrupt Request and sends it out.

Figure 8-30 shows the interrupt remapping in AMD IOMMU. Please refer to the AMD IOMMU specification for more detailed information.

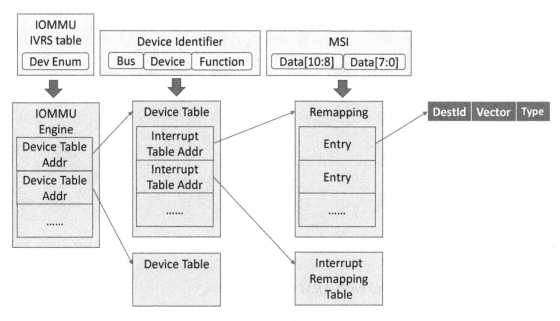

Figure 8-30. *Interrupt Remapping in AMD IOMMU*

ARM Generic Interrupt Controller (GIC)

Different from X86 systems, the ARM system uses a different architecture for interrupt controller, following the Generic Interrupt Controller (GIC) specification. See Figure 8-31. The GICv2 supports 1024 interrupt number (INTID). The INTID 0~15 is for software-generated interrupt (SGI). The INTID 16~32 is for Private Peripheral Interrupt (PPI). Both SGI and PPI are local to a CPU interface. The INTID 1020~1023 is for special purposes. The rest is for Shared Peripheral Interrupt (SPI). This is a hardware pin-based mechanism. The PPI and SPI are managed by the Distributor component in the GICv2. The PPIs are CPU core specific. The SPIs are sharable, and the Distributor provides the routing configuration of SPIs. Once arbitration is finished, the Distributor sends the interrupt to the corresponding CPU interface in the GICv2. The CPU interface sends interrupt messages via IRQ (Interrupt Request) or FIQ (Fast Interrupt Request) to the corresponding CPU core. The GICv2 supports a maximum of eight processing elements (PEs). It might be enough for client systems, but the server platform may need to support more cores.

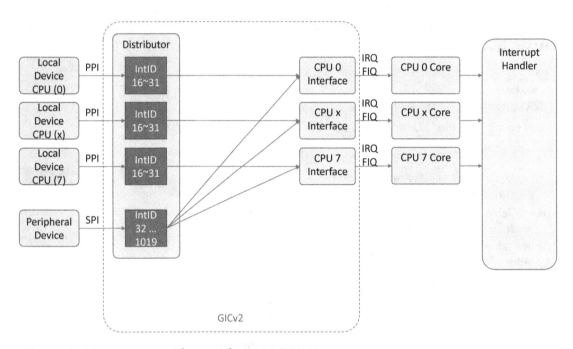

Figure 8-31. *Interrupt Flow with ARM GICv2*

The GICv3 defines an affinity hierarchy to support more cores, separates the CPU interfaces, and adds a Redistributor between the Distributor and the CPU interface (see Figure 8-32). Each CPU interface has an associated Redistributor. Now the Distributor manages SPIs and sends them to the Redistributor. The Redistributors manages the PPIs and sends the interrupt to the CPU interface via the Interrupt Routing Infrastructure (IRI) command. Finally, the CPU interface sends IRQs and FIQs to the CPU core.

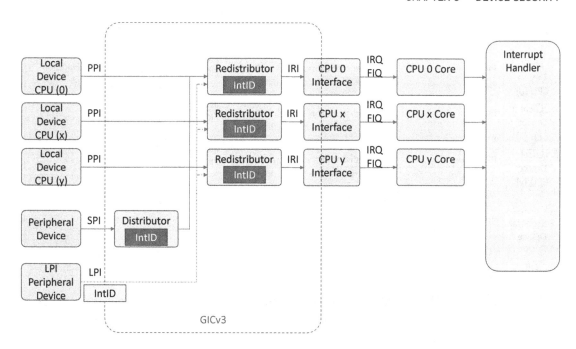

Figure 8-32. *Interrupt Flow with ARM GICv3*

The GICv3 introduces a new message-based interrupt – Locality-Specific Peripheral Interrupt (LPI). It can reduce the number of wires in the system. Similar to MSI, a memory-based Set LPI Pending Register (GICR_SETLPIR) is provided by the Redistributor in the GICv3. An LPI-capable device can write the IntID message to the register to trigger the LPI. Then the LPI is delivered to the Redistributor.

The GICv3 also introduces Interrupt Translation Service (ITS). See Figure 8-33. The LPI device can send an EventID information to the ITS Translation Register (GITS_TRANSLATER) instead of IntID. Then the ITS translates the EventID to the final IntID and sends the IntID to the final Redistributor. In ARM system the interrupt remapping is done by the ITS in the GIC.

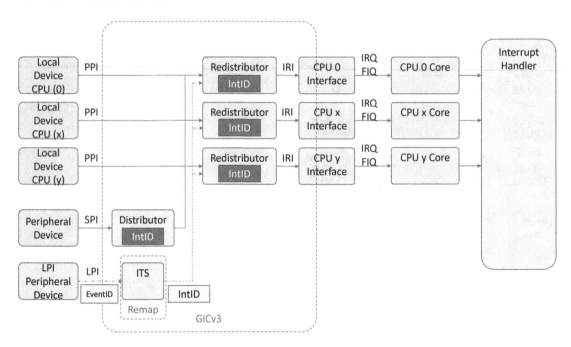

Figure 8-33. *Interrupt Flow with ARM GICv3 ITS*

The ITS includes an address of a device table. When a device sends the LPI, the ITS uses the DeviceID as the index of the device table to retrieve the address of the Interrupt Translation Table (ITT). Then the ITS uses the EventID as the index of the ITT to retrieve the interrupt translation entry (ITE). For the physical interrupt, ITE includes IntID and the Interrupt Collection Number (ICID). The ITS derives a Collection TableID from the ICID and uses the TableID as index to select a Collection Table (CT) entry that describes the target Redistributor. Finally, the ITS delivers the IntID to the Redistributor. For the virtual interrupt supported in GICv4, the ITE includes virtual IntID (vIntID) and the virtual Processing Element ID (vPEID). The ITS uses the vPEID as index of a vPEID table to get the real Redistributor and delivers the vIntID to the Redistributor.

Figure 8-34 shows the interrupt remapping in ARM GIC. Please refer to the ARM GIC specification for more detailed information.

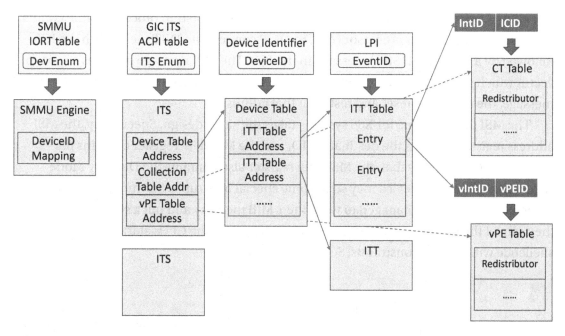

Figure 8-34. *Interrupt Remapping in ARM GIC*

Attack and Mitigation

Now, let's take a look at some real cases for the interrupt attack and mitigation.

MSI Attack

Because the MSI is generated by the device, a malicious device may generate a malicious MSI on the system bus to attack the system. If there is no interrupt remapping, the device has the capability to decide the CPU destination ID and interrupt vector. Just generating a normal interrupt is not interesting. It can be handled by the normal interrupt handler. However, there are some special interrupt handlers that can be used to attack the system, such as the startup inter-processor interrupt (SIPI), the syscall INT service, and Alignment Check (#AC) exception. Those special interrupt handlers can be used to attack a trusted domain from an untrusted domain. Let's take a look one by one:

1) SIPI attack

In X86 systems with multiple processors, the CPU needs to send special interrupts such as the system management interrupt, non-maskable interrupt, INIT, an startup. This information is included in the interrupt command register (ICR) of a local APIC.

It is named as Delivery Mode (DM). For example, if the bootstrap processor (BSP) wants to restart the application processor (AP), the BSP can send an INIT message in the ICR followed by a startup IPI (SIPI) message in the ICR. The SIPI message includes a startup vector which points to a 4 K aligned address below 1 MiB. When the AP received the message, the AP will be reset and restart at that address.

The MSI message type for X86 systems takes the same design. Specifically, the MSI address register contains the destination ID, and the MSI data register contains the interrupt vector. Besides that, the MSI data register also contains the Delivery Mode (DM). That means the device may send some special interrupts. Startup IPI (SPI) is one of them. If the attacker managed to write the 1 MiB memory and put a shellcode there, they can let the device send an MSI message to let one of the CPUs start executing the shellcode without any constraints. See Figure 8-35.

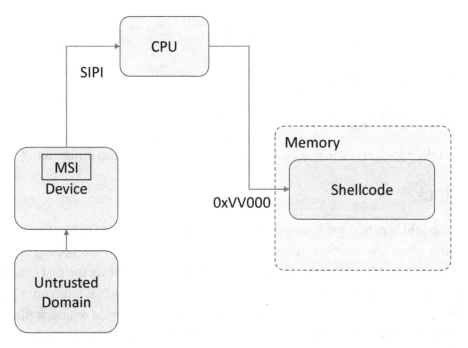

Figure 8-35. *MSI SIPI Attack*

2)   Syscall injection attack

The hypervisor usually provides the hypercall (a software interrupt, such as INT 0x80 or 0x82) for the trusted domain to provide the services. In order to prevent the hypercall from the untrusted domain, the hypervisor checks the execution context. If the current context is not the trusted domain, the hypercall will be rejected. If the attacker managed to let the device send MSI (the hypercall software interrupt) when the trusted domain is active, then the hypervisor thinks the hypercall is sent by the trusted domain. With a carefully prepared parameter, the attacker can take advantage of the hypercall to let the hypervisor grant more privilege to the untrusted domain. See Figure 8-36.

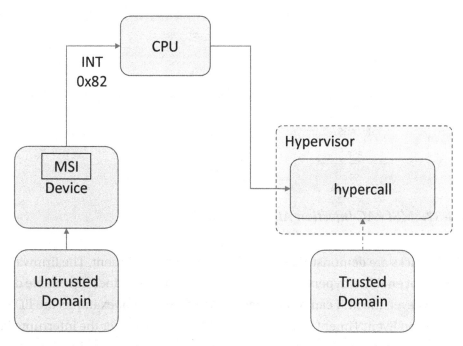

Figure 8-36. *MSI Syscall Injection Attack*

3) Alignment Check (#AC) exception injection attack

The MSI data message includes the interrupt vector. The vector number can be from 0x10 to 0xFF. However, the vector number from 0x10 to 0x1F is the exception number. When the exception happens, the CPU may put an error code to the top of the stack to provide additional information for the exception. The error code is exception specific. Some exceptions have the error code, and some exceptions do not. Unfortunately, the Alignment Check exception (#AC, vector 0x11) has the error code. The #AC handler assumes there is error code on the top and parses the data structure. However, the CPU never puts the error code for the hardware interrupt. If a device indicates to generate MSI with vector number 0x11, there is no error code on the top of the stack. When the #AC exception handler parses the data and returns, it treats the CS to be the RIP and RFLAGS to be the CS. If the attacker managed to control the RFLAGS and CS and put a shellcode to the low memory pointed by the RFLAGS:CS, then they can control the code execution in the privileged environment. See Figure 8-37.

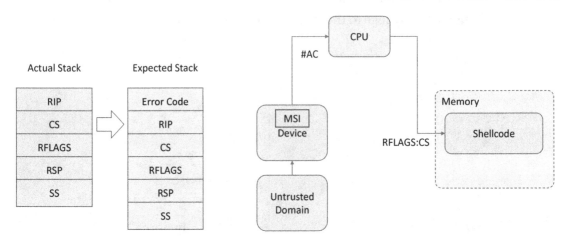

Figure 8-37. *MSI #AC Injection Attack*

All MSI attacks are demonstrated in the hypervisor environment. The firmware usually does not enable a hypervisor. And the firmware usually does not enable device interrupt. However, the MSI can be enabled in the firmware. For example, the EDK II High-Precision Event Timer (HPET) can be configured to deliver the interrupt via IOAPIC or MSI. Just in case more privileged control is enabled in the firmware, care must be taken to prevent the untrusted domain from enabling device MSI to attack the trusted domain.

Server RAS (Reliability, Availability, and Serviceability)

The reliability, availability, and serviceability (RAS) are the term that describes the robustness of a server platform. Originally, it comes from the IBM mainframe computers. And now it is an important attribute in server computers. The RAS capability is a system-level concept including hardware, software, and firmware. Each server provider may have its own RAS solution. Introducing full RAS features is out of the scope of this book. Here we just focus on the security impact with the advanced RAS features.

Case Study

Now, let's take a look at some real cases for the server RAS.

CPU Hot Add

CPU Hot Add (as known as CPU on-lining) is a RAS feature to add a new CPU hardware to a running system without shutting down the machine. The CPU Hot Add needs

1) Hardware support: The hardware internal logic needs to support the transaction with the newly added CPU.

2) Firmware support: The firmware need to provide initialization routing in the BIOS, CPU synchronization routing in the system management mode (SMM), and ACPI routing to help the operating system (OS) bring up the machine.

3) Software support: The OS needs to support the ability to add a new CPU.

We have described the CPU Hot Add high-level flow in Chapter 7. When the normal CPU is running in the OS, it receives the Hot Plug event and quiesce. The hot added CPU needs to run a CPU reset vector like the normal CPU to finish the CPU initialization and memory configuration. Then the normal CPU releases the quiesce and brings the hot added CPU into the OS environment. The details of CPU rendezvous might be implementation specific. Figure 8-38 shows one example.

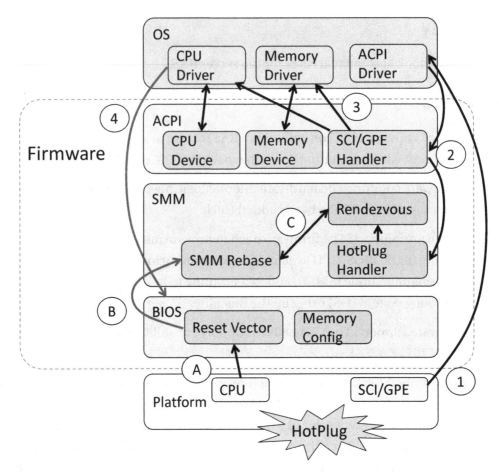

Figure 8-38. *CPU Hot Add Flow*

From the host existing CPU side:

> Step 1: The platform generates a System Control Interrupt (SCI)
> or General-Purpose Event (GPE). The event is captured by the OS
> ACPI driver.

> Step 2: The OS ACPI driver runs the SCI/GPE handler provided
> by the firmware. And ACPI code triggers a system management
> interrupt (SMI) to wait for the rendezvous in system management
> mode (SMM).

From the newly added CPU side:

> Step A: The newly added CPU executes the system reset vector as the normal flow and does the basic memory configuration.

> Step B: The newly added CPU performs the SMM rebase to change the default SMI handler address from 0x38000 to the system management Ram (SMRAM).

> Step C: The newly added CPU does SMM rendezvous with other existing CPUs in SMM. Then the new CPU waits for the wakeup message from the OS.

From the host existing CPU side:

> Step 3: When the SMM rendezvous finishes, the host CPU returns to the ACPI code. The ACPI handler notifies the OS CPU driver that the new CPU is added.

> Step 4: The OS sends out the startup message to the new CPU and brings the new CPU into the OS. Now all the CPUs can work in the OS environment.

Memory Online Sparing and Memory Hot Plug Mirroring

The memory subsystem is also involved in the server RAS design. For example, the Error Correcting Code (ECC) technology can detect and correct single-bit or multi-bit memory error in the DRAM chip. Some advanced memory protection technologies require firmware support, such as Online Spare Memory and Hot Plug Mirror Memory.

The Online Spare Memory is the complement of the ECC (see Figure 8-39). The DIMM can design a special rank as the Online Spare rank. If one of the DIMMs exceeds a threshold rate of the correctable memory errors, the affected rank of memory within the DIMM is taken offline, and the data is copied to the Online Spare rank. This technology maintains the availability of the server and the reliability of the memory without a server shutdown.

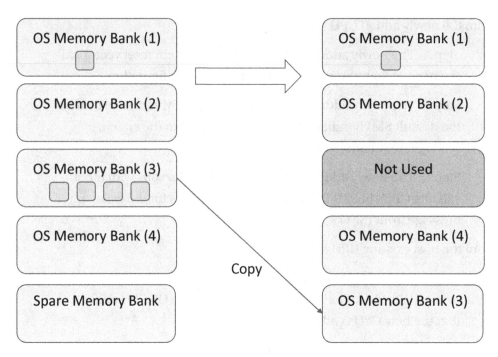

Figure 8-39. *Online Spare Memory*

The Mirror Memory is a fault-tolerant solution which provides more availability than the Online Spare Memory (see Figure 8-40). The basic idea is that the user designates half of the memory as the system memory and the other half of the memory to be mirrored memory. The same data is written to both system memory and mirrored memory, and the data is read only from the system memory. But if the DIMM reaches the predefined threshold of memory error, the system will read the data from the mirrored memory. The Mirror Memory can be Non-Hot Plug or Hot Plug. If the Hot Plug Mirror Memory is used, the user can hot-replace the failed DIMM without shutting down the server.

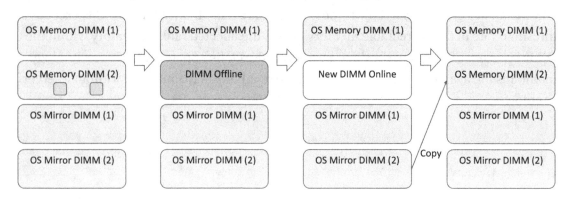

Figure 8-40. *Hot Plug Mirror Memory*

304

Both Online Spare Memory and Hot Plug Mirror Memory are supported by the hardware and the system firmware. No operating system or special software support is required.

Attack and Mitigation

Now, let's take a look at some real cases for the server RAS attack and mitigation.

CPU Hot Plug Attack

In an X86 system, if a CPU is hot added, it executes the instruction from the BIOS reset vector and initial boot block. It also needs to perform the SMM rebase from the default SMI handler at 0x38000 to the SMRAM top segment (TSEG). This action is mandatory because the 0x38000 is the normal DRAM region. It is not the SMRAM, and it is not protected by the system architecture. Now, if the attacker owns the system, they can write a shellcode and copy to the 0x38000 region or use a malicious device to generate a DMA transaction to write data into 0x38000 (see Figure 8-41). Once the hot added CPU does the SMM rebase, the CPU runs the malicious code in the SMM. This is dangerous because the shellcode in SMM owns the whole system including updating the flash region or injecting a Trojan Horse into protected SMRAM.

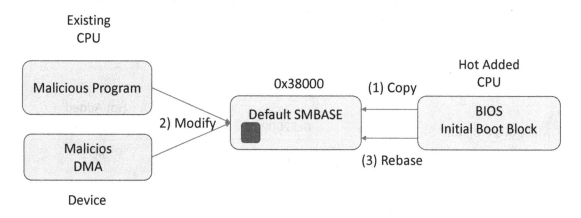

Figure 8-41. *CPU Hot Add Attack to SMM Rebase*

In order to prevent the SMM rebase attack, the platform needs to rendezvous all active CPUs in SMM and then let this hot added CPU reinitialize the handler in the default SMBASE and then perform the SMM rebase. A DMA attack should also be considered. Server silicon introduced the GENPROTRANGE register. The firmware needs to set 0x38000 into GENPROTRANGE to make it a non-DMA capable region (see Figure 8-42). With those protections, no malicious program can run, and no malicious DMA can attack the default SMBASE.

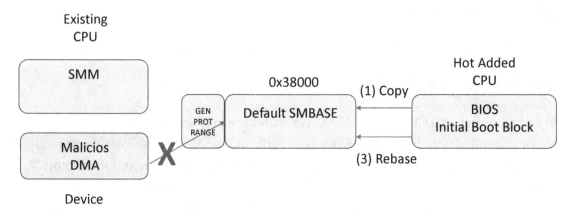

Figure 8-42. *CPU Hot Add Attack Prevention*

Another attack point is the wakeup vector. When the OS brings the new CPU into the environment, the OS sends out a startup IPI message with vector number 0xE2 which means to let the new CPU execute the code at address 0xE2000. The similar protection mechanism can be used to maintain the integrity of the system, including DMA protection and integrity verification. See Figure 8-43.

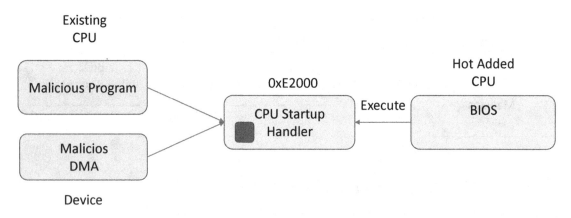

Figure 8-43. *CPU Hot Add Attack to SIPI Handler*

Memory RAS Threat

The system firmware is a key element to support the Online Spare Memory and Hot Plug Mirror Memory. This work is done by the system management mode (SMM) during the OS runtime. Because the SMM code needs to help to copy the OS memory to a good DIMM bank, the SMM code needs 1) to read the OS memory and 2) write to the OS memory. The read action may break the confidentiality, and the write action may break the integrity. As such, the SMM RAS handler must be carefully reviewed, and the platform manufacturer needs to ensure there is no vulnerability there.

For more details on the SMM security, please refer to Chapter 17.

Summary

In this chapter, we discussed the device security–related topics including secure device design principle, secure communication, and device attack prevention, such as DMA and interrupt. In next chapter, we will move our focus to the system firmware and discuss the S3 resume boot path.

References

Conference, Journal, and Paper

[P-1] Galen Hunt, George Letey, Edmund B. Nightingale, "The Seven Properties of Highly Secure Devices," in *Microsoft Whitepaper 2017*, available at `www.microsoft.com/en-us/research/wp-content/uploads/2017/03/SevenPropertiesofHighlySecureDevices.pdf`

[P-2] Jiewen Yao, Vincent Zimmer, "A Tour Beyond BIOS Using IOMMU for DMA Protection," *Intel Whitepaper 2017*, available at `https://firmware.intel.com/sites/default/files/Intel_WhitePaper_Using_IOMMU_for_DMA_Protection_in_UEFI.pdf`

[P-3] Anthony Ligouri, "Powering Next-Gen EC2 Instances: Deep Dive into the Nitro System," in *AWS re:Invent 2018*, available at `www.slideshare.net/AmazonWebServices/powering-nextgen-ec2-instances-deep-dive-into-the-nitro-system-cmp303r1-aws-reinvent-2018`

[P-4] Shelia Berta, "Backdooring Hardware Devices By Injecting Malicious Payloads On Microcontrollers," in *Blackhat US 2019*, available at `http://i.blackhat.com/USA-19/Thursday/us-19-Berta-Backdooring-Hardware-Devices-By-Injecting-Malicious-Payloads-On-Microcontrollers.pdf`

[P-5] Damien Aumaitre, Christophe Devine, "Subverting Windows 7 x64 Kernel with DMA attacks," in *HITB SecConf 2010*, available at `https://conference.hitb.org/hitbsecconf2010ams/materials/D2T2%20-%20Devine%20&%20Aumaitre%20-%20Subverting%20Windows%207%20x64%20Kernel%20with%20DMA%20Attacks.pdf`

[P-6] Jeff Forristal, "Hardware Involved Software Attacks," *Whitepaper 2011*, `http://forristal.com/material/Forristal_Hardware_Involved_Software_Attacks.pdf`

[P-7] Fernand Lone Sang, Vincent Nicomette, Yves Deswarte, "I/O Attacks in Intel-PC Architectures and Countermeasures," in *LAAS-CNRS 2011*, available at `www.syssec-project.eu/media/page-media/23/syssec2011-s1.4-sang.pdf`

[P-8] P. Stewin and I. Bystrov. "Understanding DMA Malware," in *Detection of Intrusions and Malware, and Vulnerability Assessment (DIMVA'12), 2012*, available at `https://pdfs.semanticscholar.org/88ad/913424405ac32657a8557f74003b22e9be3c.pdf`

[P-9] Russ Sevinsky, "Funderbolt – Adventures in thunderbolt DMA attacks," in *Blackhat US 2013*, available at `https://media.blackhat.com/us-13/US-13-Sevinsky-Funderbolt-Adventures-in-Thunderbolt-DMA-Attacks-Slides.pdf`

[P-10] Sergej Schumilo, "Don't trust your USB," in *Blackhat 2014*, available at `www.blackhat.com/docs/eu-14/materials/eu-14-Schumilo-Dont-Trust-Your-USB-How-To-Find-Bugs-In-USB-Device-Drivers.pdf`

[P-11] Trammell Hudson, "Thunderstrike," in *31C3 2015*, available at `https://trmm.net/Thunderstrike_31c3`

[P-12] Trammell Hudson, Xeno Kovah, Corey Kallenberg, "Thunderstrike 2," in *Blackhat 2015*, available at `www.blackhat.com/docs/us-15/materials/us-15-Hudson-Thunderstrike-2-Sith-Strike.pdf`

[P-13] Mickey Shkatov, Jesse Michael, "Scared Poopless – LTE and *your* laptop," in *DEFCON23 2015*, available at `https://paper.seebug.org/papers/Security%20Conf/Defcon/2015/DEFCON-23-Mickey-Shkatov-Jesse-Michael-Scared-poopless-LTE-a.pdf`

[P-14] Alex Ionescu, "Getting Physical With USB Type-C – Windows 10 RAM Forensics and UEFI Attacks," in Recon 2017, available at `http://alexionescu.com/publications/Recon/recon2017-bru.pdf`

[P-15] Ben Blaxil, Joel Sandin, "PicoDMA: DMA Attacks at Your Fingertips," in Blackhat US 2019, available at `http://i.blackhat.com/USA-19/Wednesday/us-19-Sandin-PicoDMA-DMA-Attacks-At-Your-Fingertips.pdf`

[P-16] Rafal Wojtczuk, Joanna Rutkowska, "Following the White Rabbit: Software attacks against Intel(R) VT-d technology," *invisiblethingslab whitepaper 2011*, `https://invisiblethingslab.com/resources/2011/Software%20Attacks%20on%20Intel%20VT-d.pdf`

[P-17] Cuauhtemoc Chavez-Corona, Jorge Gonzalez-Diaz, Rene Henriquez-Garcia, Laura Fuentes-Castaneda, Jan Seidl, "Abusing CPU Hot-Add weaknesses to escalate privileges in Server Datacenters," in *CanSecWest 2017*, available at `https://cansecwest.com/slides/2017/CSW2017_Cuauhtemoc-Rene_CPU_Hot-Add_flow.pdf`

[P-18] HPE, "Memory technology evolution: an overview of system memory technologies Technology brief," HPE Whitepaper, available at `https://support.hpe.com/hpsc/doc/public/display?docId=emr_na-c01552458`

[P-19] HPE, "HP Advanced Memory Protection technologies," HPE Whitepaper, available at `http://service1.pcconnection.com/PDF/AdvMemoryProtection.pdf`

[P-20] Daniel Henderson, "POWER8® Processor-Based Systems RAS," IBM Whitepaper 2016, available at `www.digitaltrend.it/wp-content/uploads/2017/05/Il-processore-RAS-del-Power8.pdf`

[P-21] Galen Hunt, George Letey, Edmund B. Nightingale, "The Seven Properties of Highly Secure Devices," Microsoft Whitepaper 2017, `www.microsoft.com/en-us/research/wp-content/uploads/2017/03/SevenPropertiesofHighlySecureDevices.pdf`

Specification and Guideline

[S-1] DMTF org, "MCTP Base Specification," 2016, available at `www.dmtf.org/standards/pmci`

[S-2] DMTF org, "Security Protocol and Data Model Specification," 2019, available at `www.dmtf.org/standards/pmci`

[S-3] DMTF org, "SPDM over MCTP Binding Specification," 2019, available at `www.dmtf.org/standards/pmci`

[S-4] DMTF org, "Secured MCTP Messages over MCTP Binding Specification," 2019, available at `www.dmtf.org/standards/pmci`

[S-5] DMTF org, "Platform Level Data Model (PLDM) for Firmware Update Specification," 2018, available at `www.dmtf.org/standards/pmci`

[S-6] IETF, "RFC 8446 – The Transport Layer Security (TLS) Protocol Version 1.3," 2018, available at `https://tools.ietf.org/html/rfc8446`

[S-7] IETF, "RFC 6347 – Datagram Transport Layer Security Version 1.2," 2012, available at `https://tools.ietf.org/html/rfc6347`

[S-8] USB org, "USB Authentication Specification," 2019 available at `www.usb.org/documents`

[S-9] PCI-SIG, "PCI Local Bus Specification," 2004, available at `https://pcisig.com/specifications`

[S-10] PCI-SIG, "PCI Express Base Specification," 2019, available at `https://pcisig.com/specifications`

[S-11] PCI-SIG, "Data Object Exchange (DOE) ECN," 2019, available at `https://pcisig.com/specifications/review-zone`

[S-12] PCI-SIG, "Component Measurement and Authentication (CMA) ECN," 2019, available at `https://pcisig.com/specifications/review-zone`

[S-13] PCI-SIG, "Integrity and Data Encryption (IDE) ECN," 2020, available at `https://pcisig.com/specifications/review-zone`

[S-14] CXL org, "The CXL Specification," 2019, available at `www.computeexpresslink.org/`

[S-15] Trusted Computing Group, "TCG Guidance for Secure Update of Software and Firmware on Embedded Systems," 2019, available at `https://trustedcomputinggroup.org/`

[S-16] Trusted Computing Group, "TCG Runtime Integrity Protections in Mobile Devices," 2019, available at `https://trustedcomputinggroup.org/`

[S-17] OCP, "Project Cerberus Architecture Overview Specification," 2018, available at `https://github.com/opencomputeproject/Project_Olympus/blob/master/Project_Cerberus`

[S-18] OCP, "Project Cerberus Firmware Update Specification," 2019, available at `https://github.com/opencomputeproject/Project_Olympus/blob/master/Project_Cerberus`

[S-19] UEFI Organization, "ACPI Specification," 2019, available at `www.uefi.org/`

[S-20] AMD, "AMD Architecture Programmer's Manual," 2019, available at `www.amd.com/en/support/tech-docs`

[S-21] AMD, "AMD I/O Virtualization Technology," 2016, available at `https://support.amd.com/TechDocs/48882_IOMMU.pdf`

[S-22] ARM, "ARM® System Memory Management Unit Architecture Specification," 2017, available at `https://static.docs.arm.com/ihi0070/b/SMMUv3_architecture_specification_IHI0070B.pdf`

[S-23] ARM, "I/O Remapping Table," 2018, available at `https://static.docs.arm.com/den0049/d/DEN0049D_IO_Remapping_Table.pdf`

[S-24] ARM, "ARM® Generic Interrupt Controller Architecture Specification," 2017, available at `https://static.docs.arm.com/ihi0069/d/IHI0069D_gic_architecture_specification.pdf`

[S-25] Intel, "Intel 64 and IA-32 Architecture Software Developer Manuals," 2019, available at `https://software.intel.com/en-us/articles/intel-sdm`

[S-26] Intel, "Intel Scalable I/O Virtualization Specification," 2018, available at `https://software.intel.com/en-us/download/intel-scalable-io-virtualization-technical-specification`

[S-27] Intel, "Virtualization Technology for Directed I/O specification," 2019, available at `https://software.intel.com/en-us/download/intel-virtualization-technology-for-directed-io-architecture-specification`

[S-28] Intel, "PCIe Device Security Enhancements Specification," 2018, available at `www.intel.com/content/www/us/en/io/pci-express/pcie-device-security-enhancements-spec.html`

[S-29] Intel, "Intel® 9 Series Chipset Platform Controller Hub (PCH) Datasheet," 2015, available at `www.intel.com/content/www/us/en/products/docs/chipsets/9-series-chipset-pch-datasheet.html`

[S-30] Intel, "Multi Processor Specification," 1997, available at `https://pdos.csail.mit.edu/6.828/2018/readings/ia32/MPspec.pdf`

Web

[W-1] Microsoft, "Hardware Compatibility Specification for Systems for Windows 10," `https://docs.microsoft.com/en-us/windows-hardware/design/compatibility/systems`

[W-2] Microsoft, "Blocking the SBP-2 driver and Thunderbolt controllers to reduce 1394 DMA and Thunderbolt DMA threats to BitLocker," `http://support.microsoft.com/kb/2516445`

[W-3] Microsoft, "Kernel DMA Protection for Thunderbolt," `https://docs.microsoft.com/en-us/windows/security/information-protection/kernel-dma-protection-for-thunderbolt`

[W-4] Microsoft, "Windows Hardware Error Architecture (WHEA) design guide," `https://docs.microsoft.com/en-us/windows-hardware/drivers/whea/`

[W-5] Microsoft, "Component Firmware Update," `https://github.com/Microsoft/CFU`

[W-6] Microsoft, "Component Firmware Update Protocol Specification," `https://github.com/microsoft/CFU/blob/master/Documentation/CFU-Protocol/Component%20Firmware%20Update%20Protocol%20Specification.docx`

[W-7] Microsoft, "Introducing Component Firmware Update," 2018, `https://blogs.windows.com/windowsdeveloper/2018/10/17/introducing-component-firmware-update/`

[W-8] EDKII, "SPDM based Device Firmware Security in EDKII," 2019, https://edk2.groups.io/g/devel/files/Designs/2019/1018/EDKII-Device%20Firmware%20Security%20v2.pdf, https://github.com/jyao1/openspdm

[W-9] Amazon, "AWS Nitro System," https://aws.amazon.com/ec2/nitro/

[W-10] Nigel Edwards, Theo Koulouris, Michael Krause, "PCIe Component Authentication," 2019, https://pcisig.com/pcie%C2%AE-component-authentication

[W-11] Intel, "Intel® Virtualization Technology for Directed I/O (VT-d): Enhancing Intel platforms for efficient virtualization of I/O devices," https://software.intel.com/en-us/articles/intel-virtualization-technology-for-directed-io-vt-d-enhancing-intel-platforms-for-efficient-virtualization-of-io-devices

[W-12] "Thunderbolt™ 3 and Security on Microsoft Windows® 10 Operating system," https://thunderbolttechnology.net/security/Thunderbolt%203%20and%20Security.pdf

[W-13] Ulf Frisk, "Attacking UEFI and Linux," 2017, http://blog.frizk.net/2017/01/attacking-uefi-and-linux.html

[W-14] Ulf Frisk, "DMA attacking over USB-C and Thunderbolt 3," 2016, http://blog.frizk.net/2016/10/dma-attacking-over-usb-c-and.html

[W-15] Ulf Frisk, "macOS FileVault2 Password Retrieval," 2016, http://blog.frizk.net/2016/12/filevault-password-retrieval.html

[W-16] "PCILeech," https://github.com/ufrisk/pcileech

[W-17] Microblaze, https://github.com/Cr4sh/s6_pcie_microblaze

[W-18] "Facedancer," http://goodfet.sourceforge.net/hardware/facedancer21/

CHAPTER 9

S3 Resume

The Advanced Configuration and Power Interface (ACPI) specification defines a set of power states (see Figure 9-1). These power states include the following:

- G0 (S0) – the working state: The running firmware or OS is in S0 state.

- G1 – the sleep state

  - S1 – standby: All system context is preserved, except the CPU cache. All CPUs are halted. Other devices are still in a working state. The system resumes from the next instruction when the system is suspended.

  - S2 – similar to S1: Not used today.

  - S3 – suspend to memory: The system context is saved into the platform memory. The devices stop working. Only DRAM is flushed to preserve the content. The system resumes from the firmware reset vector and jumps to the OS waking vector. Afterward, the OS restores the context from memory. When a user chooses the "sleep" option, the system enters S3 state. This can also be initiated by actions such as closing the lid in a laptop.

  - S4 – suspend to disk: The system context is saved into the disk. All devices stop working. The system resumes from the firmware reset vector and boots the OS as normal boot. Afterward, the OS restores the context from disk. When a user chooses the "hibernation" option, the system enters the S4 state.

© Jiewen Yao and Vincent Zimmer 2020
J. Yao and V. Zimmer, *Building Secure Firmware*, https://doi.org/10.1007/978-1-4842-6106-4_9

- There is one option named S4 BIOS, which means the BIOS saves a copy of memory to disk and then initiates the hardware S4. When the system wakes, the firmware restores memory from disk and wakes the OS by transferring control to the OS waking vector. Today this is not used in most platforms since this is an OS-independent art from early advanced power management (APM) that predates ACPI.

- G2 (S5) – the soft off state: When a user chooses the "shutdown" option, the system enters S5 state.

- G3 – the power off state: When a user powers off the machine, the machine is in G3 state.

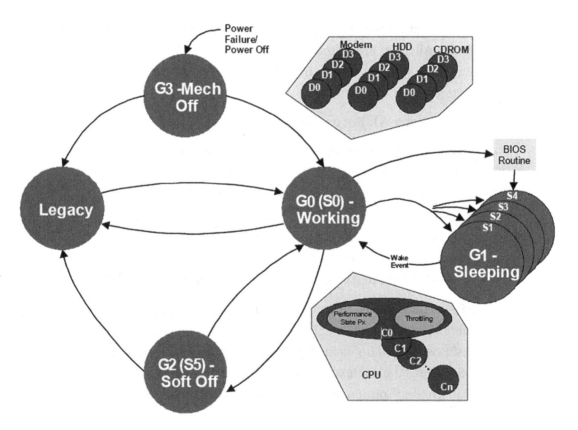

Figure 9-1. *Global System Power States and Transitions (Source: ACPI Specification)*

The system firmware is involved in the Sx suspend and resume. S1 resume is handled inside the OS directly. S4 resume and S5 resume are similar to a normal boot. S3 resume is a special boot path and has significant differences from the normal boot path. These differences create unique security challenges that we will focus on in this chapter.

Threat Model

S3 means "suspend to memory." The OS context is in memory, and some firmware S3 context is also in memory. If malicious code can access the OS or firmware S3 context used in an S3 resume, it may impact the system's confidentiality, integrity, and availability.

The assets of the S3 resume are shown in Table 9-1. The assets include but are not limited to the flash content, memory content, silicon register settings, TPM device state, and storage device configuration. The assets may require integrity, availability, or confidentiality properties.

Table 9-1. *S3 Resume Asset*

Asset	Integrity	Availability	Confidentiality
Flash	Firmware code Firmware configuration	Firmware code Firmware configuration	N/A
Memory	SMRAM	OS waking vector	SMRAM
Silicon	Locked Register	Silicon register Memory configuration data	N/A
TPM state	TPM2 platform hierarchy	TPM device state	N/A
Storage disk	TCG storage BlockSID HDD Freeze	N/A	Disk password

The S3 resume attacker could use a software attack (such as writing code to modify the system context) or hardware attack (such as using a flash programmer to access the flash area, using a device to perform DMA attack and trigger power failure). The attack surface could be flash access, memory access, silicon register, or a TPM command. See Table 9-2 for the S3 attack surface.

Table 9-2. *S3 Attack Surface*

Attack Surface	Software Attack	Hardware Attack
Flash access	Read/write configuration (variable)	Firmware code Firmware configuration
Memory access	ACPI non-volatile storage (NVS) ACPI reserved memory	ACPI non-volatile storage (NVS) ACPI reserved memory
Silicon register	Read/write silicon register (I/O, MMIO, PCI)	N/A
TPM command	TPM device state (shutdown command)	N/A

The attack may be performed during S3 suspend (such as modifying ACPI memory in the OS, sending malicious TPM command, or not sending a specific TPM command), in S3 state (such as updating the firmware code using a flash programmer), or during S3 resume (such as attaching a malicious PCI device for DMA access).

In order to mitigate these attacks, the S3 resume implementation should implement defenses. See Table 9-3. Some S3 mitigations are similar to the ones used in normal boot, such as flash image verification in S3 and setting up the IOMMU or another DMA protection to resist DMA attacks in S3. Some S3 mitigations are device specific, such as preserving the TPM device state. These technologies have been discussed in previous chapters. One major category of S3 mitigation is secure storage to save the settings used during S3 resume, including 1) CPU configuration data in memory such as CPU state, SMM environment – page table, and SMBASE, 2) silicon register configuration data such as the register settings of the chipset and PCI express device, and 3) the device configuration data such as TCG storage BlockSID state and the hard disk unlock password. We refer to this type of secure storage as the LockBox.

Table 9-3. *S3 Attack Mitigation*

Asset	Prevention	Detection	Recovery
Flash	Flash Device Lock. Variable Lock/Authentication.	Flash image verification in S3. Variable Check/RPMC.	Switch to normal boot for recovery.
Memory	IOMMU in S3. Save data to LockBox(*).	Power loss detection.	Switch to normal boot.
Silicon	Save configuration data to the LockBox(*). Register lock in the code.	N/A	N/A
TPM state	Send TPM2_HierarchyChangeAuth().	Check TPM2_Startup().	Cap PCRs.
Storage disk	Save configuration data to LockBox(*).	N/A	N/A

LockBox

The LockBox is an abstraction of secure storage for usage during S3 resume. In a normal boot or during the S3 suspend phase, the authorized firmware component saves the current configuration to the LockBox. In the S3 resume phase, the authorized firmware component retrieves the configuration from the LockBox, configures the system, and boots to the OS waking vector. See Figure 9-2.

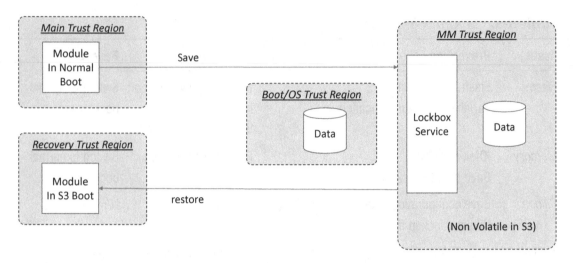

Figure 9-2. *LockBox Usage in S3 Resume*

The LockBox may provide confidentiality, integrity, and availability support. For confidentiality considerations, only an authorized entity can read the LockBox content. For integrity, only an authorized entity can write the LockBox content. For the availability concern, the LockBox should always be present. It is difficult to prevent hardware attacks because the hardware attack may include just removing power to destroy the contents of the memory or using a flash programmer to erase the contents of the flash.

Platforms have many options to implement the LockBox, including but not limited to a Trusted Execution Environment (TEE) such as system management mode (SMM), UEFI variables (with Variable Lock for integrity and variable encryption for confidentiality), TPM non-volatile storage, or coprocessor-based mechanisms such as the Intel Converged Security and Management Engine (CSME), AMD Platform Secure Processor (PSP), server Baseboard Management Controllers (BMCs), and so on. See Table 9-4 for the summary of LockBox implementation choices.

Table 9-4. *S3 LockBox Implementation*

Mechanism	Integrity	Availability	Confidentiality	Comment
TEE (SMM)	Yes	Yes, for software attacks. No, for hardware attack.	Yes	Maybe unsupported before memory initialization.
Variable	Requires Variable Lock or authentication.	Yes, for software attacks. No, for hardware attack.	Requires variable encryption.	Flash size limitation.
TPM NV	Requires auth session or lock.	Yes	Requires auth session.	TPM device dependency, NV size limitation.
Coprocessor	Yes	Yes	Yes	Coprocessor device dependency.

Case Study

Now, let's take a look at some real use cases for the LockBox implementation.

TEE-Based LockBox

The goal of the S3 resume process is to restore the platform to its preboot configuration. The UEFI PI Architecture still needs to restore the platform in a phased fashion just as it does in a normal boot path. Figure 9-3 shows the phases in an S3 resume boot path.

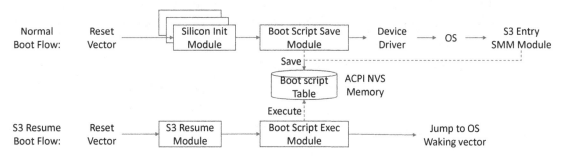

Figure 9-3. *PI Architecture S3 Resume Boot Path*

In a normal boot, the PEI phase is responsible for initializing enough of the platform's resources to enable the execution of the DXE phase, which is where the majority of platform configuration is performed by different DXE drivers.

In the S3 resume phase, bringing DXE in and making a DXE driver boot path aware is very risky for the following reasons:

- The DXE phase hosts numerous services, which makes it rather large.

- Loading DXE from flash is very time-consuming.

Instead, the PI Architecture provides a boot script that lets the S3 resume boot path avoid the DXE phase altogether, which helps to maximize S3 resume performance. The boot script is a set of entries such as IO_WRITE(Port, Data), MMIO_WRITE(Address, Data), and PCI_WRITE(Segment, Bus, Device, Function, Register, Data). It is a lightweight way to configure the silicon registers. During a normal boot, such as powering on from S5, DXE drivers record the platform's configuration in the boot script, which is saved in NVS. During the S3 resume boot path, a boot script engine executes the script, thereby restoring the configuration.

The ACPI specification only requires the BIOS to restore chipset and processor configuration. The chipset configuration can be viewed as a series of memory, I/O, and PCI configuration operations which DXE drivers record in the PI Architecture boot script. During an S3 resume, a boot script engine executes the boot script to restore the chipset settings.

In a normal boot, the boot script is saved in the following fashion:

1) In the DXE phase, the silicon/platform driver saves the register configuration to the boot script. This is the boot-time S3 script.

2) In SMM, the silicon/platform driver can continue saving the register configuration to the table, even during OS runtime. A typical implementation is that when the OS triggers entry into S3, the system enters SMM. A special SMI handler collects the runtime silicon register settings such as PCI configuration and saves the information to the boot script. This is the runtime S3 script.

During S3 resume, the boot script is executed as follows:

3) In PEI, a boot script execution engine gets the boot script and replays the saved boot scripts to restore the system configuration. Both the boot-time S3 scripts and runtime S3 scripts are executed.

In practice, the boot script is large because it contains all of the silicon settings from the chipset as well as PCI express devices. Saving the boot script to a UEFI variable or TPM NV is not always practical because of limitations in the storage available in the TPM or in flash. Using the SMM environment is one architectural solution used by the EDK II BIOS to implement the SMM-based LockBox as the default one for boot script.

Besides the boot script usage, we also need to save the hard disk password to the LockBox to unlock the disk automatically. As such, the SMM-based LockBox needs to consider both integrity and confidentiality.

The integrity rules for an SMM-based LockBox are as follows:

- Before the SmmReadyToLock event, any driver can use the DXE LockBox or SMM LockBox interface to save information into the LockBox. Restoring information from the LockBox is also supported, although it is seldom used.

- After the SmmReadyToLock event, the DXE code is no longer trusted. Attempts to save information into the LockBox by DXE code are rejected. The SMM code is already available, and the SMM code can use the SMM LockBox to save the runtime boot script.

- During S3 resume, there is no need to save information to the LockBox. Therefore, the PEI LockBox does not provide the ability to save information into the LockBox.

With these rules, only the platform manufacturer's code can save information into the LockBox. Third-party code cannot save information into the LockBox.

The confidentiality rules for an SMM-based LockBox are as follows:

- By default, the LockBox does not provide any confidentiality support. The DXE/PEI/SMM instances can restore the LockBox contents.

- If a LockBox requires confidentiality, the creator needs to set the LOCK_BOX_ATTRIBUTE_RESTORE_IN_S3_ONLY attribute for the LockBox.

- If the LOCK_BOX_ATTRIBUTE_RESTORE_IN_S3_ONLY attribute is set, this LockBox can only be restored

  - Before the SmmReadyToLock event (or)

  - Between the time that the system enters S3 (S3Entry event) and the end of S3 resume (EndOfS3Resume event)

With this rule, secrets can only be restored before the platform exits the platform manufacturer's authentication phase or during the firmware S3 resume phase. Third-party code cannot restore a secret from the LockBox.

In EDK II, the LockBox provides the following services:

1) SaveLockBox(): Send data to the LockBox. A LockBox can be uniquely identified by a Globally Unique Identifier (GUID).

2) UpdateLockBox(): Update data in the LockBox.

3) SetLockBoxAttributes(): Set LockBox attributes.

   a) LOCK_BOX_ATTRIBUTE_RESTORE_IN_PLACE means this LockBox can be restored to its original address with RestoreAllLockBoxInPlace().

   b) LOCK_BOX_ATTRIBUTE_RESTORE_IN_S3_ONLY means this LockBox can be restored in the S3 resume path only. This is used to provide confidentiality support.

4) RestoreLockBox(): Get data from the LockBox to a caller-provided buffer address or the original buffer address.

5) RestoreAllLockBoxInPlace(): Restore data from all LockBoxes which have the LOCK_BOX_ATTRIBUTE_RESTORE_IN_PLACE attribute.

Not all LockBox services are available in all BIOS phases. A full summary is shown in Figure 9-4.

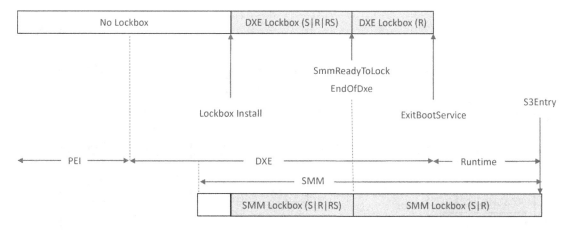

Figure 9-4(1). *SMM-Based LockBox Features in Each Phase (Normal Boot)*

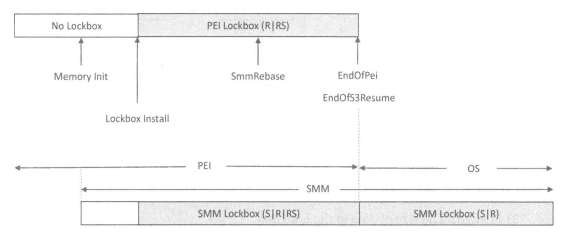

Figure 9-4(2). *SMM-Based LockBox Features in Each Phase (S3)*

S means LockBox Save.

R means LockBox Restore.

RS means LockBox Restore for the Secret.

The SMM-based LockBox implementation saves all LockBox contents inside of SMRAM. See Figure 9-5.

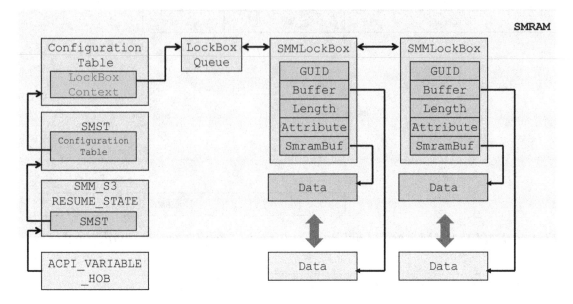

Figure 9-5. *SMM-Based LockBox: Internal Data Structure*

The LockBoxQueue is the head of the SmmLockBox's linked list. Every LockBox uses the following data structure:

1) GUID: Identifies the LockBox.

2) Buffer: A pointer to the original data buffer. This is used when a caller requests to restore to the original buffer address.

3) Length: The size of data in the LockBox.

4) Attribute: The attributes of the LockBox.

5) SmramBuffer: The data buffer in SMRAM.

The address of the LockBoxQueue is also saved as an SMM configuration table pointed to by the SMST. The reason is that if the SMI is not enabled yet, the PEI phase LockBox library can search the SMRAM region to get the LockBoxQueue and get all of the LockBox content. This makes the PEI LockBox service available before SMM is ready in the S3 resume phase.

The DXE phase LockBox library calls the SMM_COMMUNICATION protocol to communicate with the SMM LockBox service provider. The SmmLockBox driver provides the LockBox software SMI handler to service the request from the DXE instance.

Let's take the boot script as an example (see Figure 9-6): When an SMM version boot script library requests a LockBox service, the code calls into the LockBoxSmmLib. The SMM instance allocates SMRAM, saves the data, and returns immediately. When the DXE version of the boot script library requests a LockBox service, the code calls SMM_COMMUNICATE.Communicate(). Then a software SMI is triggered. The SmmCore dispatches to the handler registered by the SmmLockBox driver. The LockBox SMM handler calls into the SMM LockBox instance to allocate SMRAM and save the data, and then the handler returns from SMM.

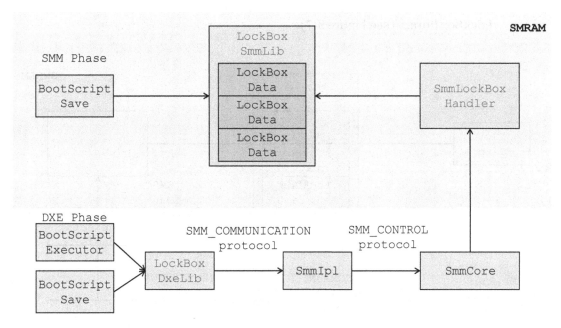

Figure 9-6. *SMM-Based LockBox: DXE/SMM Phase Usage*

The DXE LockBox library supports five LockBox services before the SmmReadyToLock event. After the signaling of the SmmReadyToLock event, SaveLockBox(), UpdateLockBox(), and SetLockBoxAttribute() are closed and will reject further calls for security reasons. RestoreLockBox() can only restore the LockBoxes that do not have the LOCK_BOX_ATTRIBUTE_RESTORE_IN_S3_ONLY attribute. Otherwise, the call is also rejected.

The SMM LockBox library supports five LockBox services as well. It also records the current execution phase. After the SmmReadyToLock event, the firmware exits the platform manufacturer's auth state. The LockBox save request from the DXE environment will be rejected after SmmReadyToLock. Before the system enters the S3, the platform signals the S3Entry event via the EFI_SMM_SX_DISPATCH2 protocol. Then the system goes into the S3 state. After the system wakes up, the PEI S3 resume drivers restore the environment. Before the firmware calls the OS waking vector, it signals an EndOfS3Resume event. The SMM LockBox only allows the LockBox secret restoration between the S3Entry event and EndOfS3Resume event.

The PEI LockBox library has two ways to communicate with the LockBox in SMRAM:

1) Using the SMM_COMMUNICATION PPI to communicate with the SmmLockBox service provider, similar to the behavior of the DXE LockBox library (see Figure 9-7).

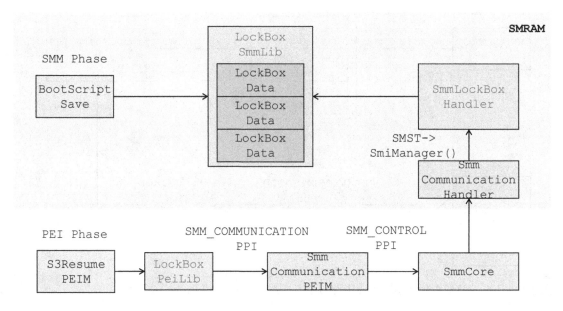

Figure 9-7. *SMM-Based LockBox: PEI Phase Usage*

2) If the PEI LockBox library is used before SMM is ready, the SMM_COMMUNICATION PPI will return EFI_NOT_STARTED. In this case, the PEI LockBox library can search the SMRAM region directly to find the LockBox content. The LockBox internal data structure is shown in Figure 9-5. The PEI LockBox library can find the ACPI_VARIABLE_HOB to get the SMM_S3_RESUME_STATE location and then retrieve the SMM System Table (SMST) pointer. The address of the LockBoxQueue is saved as the

SmmConfigurationTable entry in the SMM System Table (SMST). Care must be taken when PEI is 32 bits while SMM/DXE is 64 bits – all UINTN/VOID * defined in SMST must be parsed as UINT64 even in a 32-bit PEI execution environment.

The PEI LockBox library only supports two LockBox services in the S3 phase – RestoreLockBox() and RestoreAllLockBoxInPlace().

Secure Boot Script Implementation

Once we have the LockBox, the boot script implementation should use the lock to protect the silicon configuration data and the boot script execution engine itself. The following content must be saved into the LockBox:

1) Boot script execution engine

The boot script engine executes the S3 boot script in S3 the resume phase.

The boot script engine may be in the TEE such as SMM. If so, there is no need to save it to the LockBox. Since SMM is a high-privilege environment, a platform might not want to give this level of privilege to the boot script engine.

Therefore, the current implementation lets the boot script be executed in the normal execution environment. During the normal boot, the boot script engine is loaded into the reserved memory. During S3 resume, the boot script engine executes from the reserved memory.

Reserved memory is not a secure place because the OS may modify its contents. Therefore, the boot script engine should save the boot script itself into a LockBox during normal boot and restore it from the LockBox to the reserved memory during S3 resume. The LockBox for the boot script engine needs to use the LOCK_BOX_ATTRIBUTE_ RESTORE_IN_PLACE. As such, the contents can be restored automatically when the S3 resume module calls RestoreAllLockBoxInPlace().

2) Boot-time S3 script and runtime S3 script

Conceptually, a platform may have two boot scripts – a boot-time S3 script and a runtime S3 script. A boot-time S3 script includes the silicon settings recorded during the BIOS boot. The information must be collected before the EndOfDxe event. The runtime S3 script provides additional silicon configuration when the OS triggers the S3 suspend. A special SMI handler traps the S3 suspend action and saves the runtime silicon settings as additional data to the runtime S3 script.

The boot script driver implementation may choose to separate the two tables or combine them into one table. Both the boot-time S3 script and runtime S3 script are in ACPI non-volatile storage (NVS) memory and should be saved into the LockBox.

The LockBox for the S3 script should also have the LOCK_BOX_ATTRIBUTE_ RESTORE_IN_PLACE attribute. As such, it can be automatically restored in the S3 resume phase. Then the boot script engine just needs to execute the boot script content in the ACPI NVS memory.

3)   S3 script metadata

The boot script implementation may allocate additional memory to record the metadata of the boot-time S3 script and runtime S3 script, including the table address, the table length, the last boot script entry, and so on. The metadata is in ACPI NVS memory and should also be saved into the LockBox. Figure 9-8 shows the S3 script and metadata in EDK II.

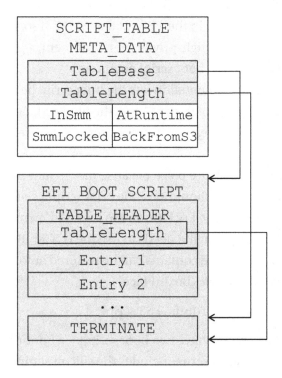

Figure 9-8. *Boot Script and Metadata*

4)   Special handling for DISPATCH OPCODE

The boot script defines a set of opcodes for register access such as IO_WRITE, IO_READ_WRITE, IO_POLL, MEM_WRITE, MEM_READ_WRITE, MEM_POLL, PCI_ CONFIG_WRITE, PCI_CONFIG_READ_WRITE, PCI_CONFIG_POLL, and so on. The boot script also supports two special opcodes: DISPATCH_OPCODE and DISPATCH_2_ OPCODE. These two DISPATCH OPCODEs support the ability to run arbitrary code during boot script execution. These code objects include an EntryPoint and a Context parameter. The EntryPoint is just a pointer to the code to be run, and the Context is the argument to be passed into the EntryPoint. See Figure 9-9.

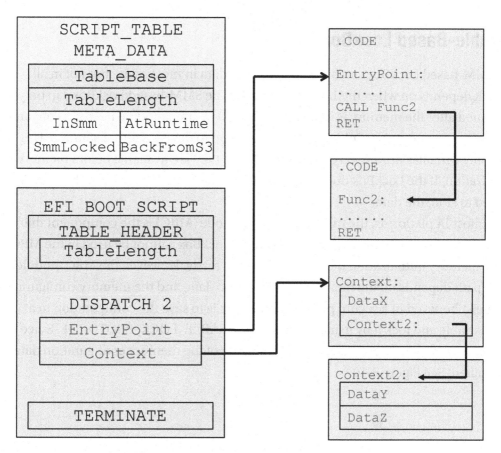

Figure 9-9. *Boot Script: DISPATCH_2_OPCODE*

The EntryPoint associated with the DISPATCH_2_OPCODE is an 8-byte address in the boot script. Saving the 8-byte EntryPoint in the LockBox cannot protect all of the code used by the EntryPoint. Therefore, the driver that produces the 8-byte EntryPoint must use the LockBox services to protect the code used by the EntryPoint. If that function calls other functions, all code of the other functions must also be protected by the LockBox.

The Context associated with the DISPATCH_2_OPCODE is also an 8-byte address in the boot script. For the same reason, the driver that produces the 8-byte EntryPoint must use the LockBox services to protect the data referred to by the Context parameter. If the Context contains another data pointer, all the data referenced must also be protected by the LockBox.

This is described in more detail in the article "Implementing S3 Resume in EDK II" which describes the LockBox and S3 resume design in EDK II.

Variable-Based LockBox

The SMM-based LockBox can be used to protect data in most cases, but not in all cases. It depends on when the LockBox is ready. The SMM-based LockBox can only be consumed after the memory is initialized. If the S3 resume module needs to consume data before the memory is initialized, then we need to devise another solution. UEFI read-only variables are a good candidate because they are available before memory initialization. If the LockBox does not require confidentiality, the read-only variable can be used to store the data.

In most IA platforms, the memory reference code (MRC) is the component that initializes the system memory. The SMM-based LockBox cannot be used in the MRC before memory initialization because SMM is not ready. However, the MRC module in the S3 path depends on the memory configuration data, and the memory configuration data must be saved in a secure place. The solution is to save the configuration to a UEFI variable and lock it by using the EDKII_VARIABLE_LOCK_PROTOCOL. Since this variable is read-only after EndOfDxe, the integrity of the memory configuration data is maintained. See Figure 9-10.

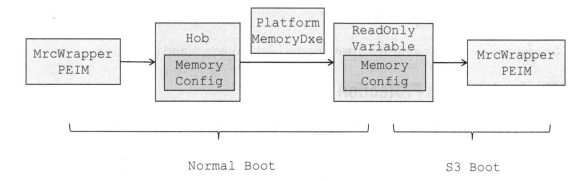

Figure 9-10. *Read-Only Variable Usage for Memory Configuration Data*

Coprocessor-Based LockBox

Besides a local TEE-based LockBox, a secure coprocessor such as an AMD Platform Secure Processor (PSP) may also help to save and restore the silicon configuration.

The AMD PSP is an ARM-based processor that resides in the same chipset as the AMD64 cores. In the S3 suspend action, after an SMI handler traps the S3 command, the SMI handler notifies the PSP of the S3 entry event. The PSP saves the CPU core context. Then the SMI handler sends the S3 command to the system. During S3 resume, the PSP restores the S3 save state of the CPU core and then transfers control to the BIOS and continues the S3 resume path. Figure 9-11 shows the AMD PSP–assisted S3 resume flow.

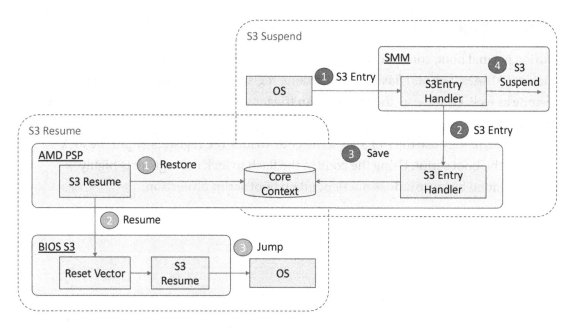

Figure 9-11. *AMD PSP–Assisted S3 Resume*

Attack and Mitigation

Now, let's take a look at some real cases for the LockBox attack and mitigation.

Missing LockBox Protection

Some firmware implementations include the register lock in the S3 boot script. If the script is not protected, the attacker may modify the boot script to inject some malicious opcode or remove the lock register access in the S3 resume. The boot script must be saved into the LockBox.

Besides the boot script, if the firmware uses the DISPATCH OPCODE, the firmware should also save the image that produces the DISPATCH EntryPoint to the LockBox and save the context data to the LockBox. Otherwise, the attacker can modify the DISPATCH function to inject malicious code.

Incorrect LockBox Attribute

The LockBox should also be used to save secrets used during S3 resume, such as hard disk storage passwords. For secrets like these, the LockBox must use the LOCK_BOX_ ATTRIBUTE_RESTORE_IN_S3_ONLY attribute. Otherwise, the attacker may dump the LockBox content during normal boot.

Missing Register Lock

During normal boot, some silicon registers are locked to maintain the system integrity such as SMRAM lock and flash lock. The same registers must be locked during S3 resume as well. Otherwise, the attacker can trigger a S3 resume to put the system into an unsafe state.

A platform may use the PEI S3 resume code to lock the registers or put the lock action in the boot script. Using the code in the flash to lock the register is highly recommended because it does not depend on boot script protection.

Summary

In this chapter, we discussed the S3 resume path and focused on LockBox design. In the next chapter, we will discuss access control in the firmware.

References

Conference, Journal, and Paper

[P-1] Jiewen Yao, Vincent Zimmer, "A Tour Beyond BIOS Implementing S3 Resume with EDK II," Intel Whitepaper 2015, `https://github.com/tianocore-docs/Docs/raw/master/White_Papers/A_Tour_Beyond_BIOS_Implementing_S3_resume_with_EDKII_V2.pdf`

[P-2] Roger Lai, "AMD Secure and Server Innovation," in *UEFI Plugfest 2013*, available at `www.uefi.org/sites/default/files/resources/UEFI_PlugFest_AMD_Security_and_Server_innovation_AMD_March_2013.pdf`

[P-3] Rafal Wojtczuk, Corey Kallenberg, "Attacks on UEFI Security," in CanSecWest 2015, available at `https://cansecwest.com/slides/2015/AttacksOnUEFI_Rafal.pptx`

[P-4] Oleksandr Bazhaniuk, Yuriy Bulygin, Andrew Furtak, Mikhail Gorobets, John Loucaides, Alex Matrosov, Mickey Shkatov, "Attacking and Defending BIOS in 2015," in RECon 2015, available at `www.c7zero.info/stuff/AttackingAndDefendingBIOS-RECon2015.pdf`

[P-5] Yuriy Bulygin, Mikhail Gorobets, Oleksandr Bazhaniuk, Andrew Furtak, "FRACTURED BACKBONE: BREAKING MODERN OS DEFENSES WITH FIRMWARE ATTACKS," in BlackHat US 2017, `www.blackhat.com/docs/us-17/wednesday/us-17-Bulygin-Fractured-Backbone-Breaking-Modern-OS-Defenses-With-Firmware-Attacks.pdf`

Specification and Guideline

[S-1] UEFI Organization, "ACPI Specification," 2019, available at `www.uefi.org/`

[S-2] UEFI Organization, "UEFI Platform Initialization Specification," 2019, available at `www.uefi.org/`

CHAPTER 10

Access Control

Access control is an important security mechanism to control how the subject accesses the object. The subject here usually means an end user, but the subject could also be a computer or a running process. The object means the computer systems or services. The object could be the hardware, such as a network or a storage device. The object could also be the software, such as an operating system or a database. Finally, the object could be data, such as a file, a registry entry, or memory content. The typical access means to read, write, or execute. The access taxonomy also includes other actions, such as modify, create, delete, append, extend, and so on. Access control can protect the system and resources from unauthorized usage. That is also true in the firmware area.

Figure 10-1 shows the potential subject and object sets in the BIOS. For example, the user is asked to input the user password to continue the boot or input the admin password to enter the setup User Interface (UI) page. The user needs to input the WIFI password in order to enable the wireless network usage in the BIOS. The platform BIOS extends the firmware component measurement into Platform Configuration Registers (PCRs) so that Microsoft BitLocker can unseal a disk encryption key from the Trusted Platform Module (TPM) device. Only after the correct PCR value is extended to the TPM can the platform access the storage device. The Trusted Execution Environment (TEE) may only be accessed by the early firmware which creates the TEE. This early-boot open access is sometimes referred to as temporal isolation. Once the TEE is constructed, non-TEE code cannot access the TEE environment anymore.

© Jiewen Yao and Vincent Zimmer 2020
J. Yao and V. Zimmer, *Building Secure Firmware*, https://doi.org/10.1007/978-1-4842-6106-4_10

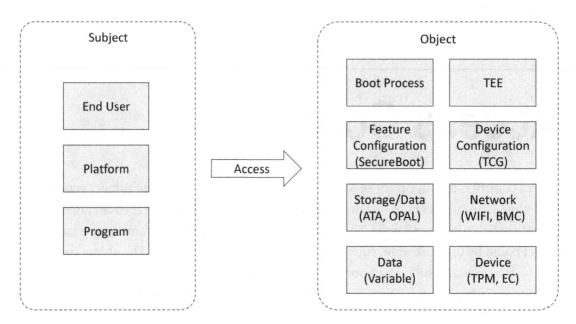

Figure 10-1. *Subject and Object in Firmware*

For the object, the three major security principles are CIA – confidentiality, integrity, and availability. For this topic, what we need to consider is IAA – identification, authentication, and authorization. Identification is the means by which a subject claims to have a specific identity. For example, a user possesses the username, email address, or cellphone number as the identity. Authentication is a process that a system employs to verify the identity of the subject. The three typical means of authentication include (1) use what subject knows, such as a password; (2) use what subject has, such as a smart card; and (3) use what subject is, such as a fingerprint. The identification and the authentication information make up the credentials of the subject. The credentials are compared to the pre-saved credential for this subject. If they match, the subject is authenticated.

Once the subject passes authentication, the system needs to determine which object resources can be accessed by the subject. It can be a predefined access matrix or the security label of the object. If the system determines the subject can access the object, it authorizes the subject.

The identification, authentication, and authorization in firmware may be simplified. For example, if the system only supports one user, user identification can be skipped, and only authentication is required. The authorization can also be simple – just continue the boot.

In the next sections, we will discuss the access control capabilities one by one from the object's perspective.

Boot Access Control

One of the main roles and responsibilities of a BIOS is to boot the system. The BIOS may add some boot access control to only allow some people to boot the system.

What a User Knows: Password

The BIOS password was introduced early in the history of the PC. Typically, the BIOS supports a user password and administrator (admin) password. When the system boots up, it pops up a dialog to let the end user input a user password. If the user password is correct, the system continues to boot; if not, the system rejects the boot request and resets or shuts down the system. When the end user wants to enter the BIOS setup User Interface (UI) page, the BIOS may pop up a dialog and require the end user to input an admin password. If the admin password is correct, the BIOS shows the setup page to let the user modify the BIOS configuration. If the admin password is not correct, the BIOS does not enter the setup page. This feature is called BIOS password or BIOS user authentication.

Password Storage

The password information must be stored in non-volatile storage. The legacy BIOS typically uses the CMOS RAM as the non-volatile storage (NVS). The standard CMOS RAM only has 128 bytes, and the extended CMOS RAM has another 128 bytes. The CMOS RAM can be read/written via I/O port 70/71 and I/O port 72/73. The memory of the CMOS RAM is maintained by the CMOS battery. If an end user removes the CMOS battery, the CMOS contents are cleared.

The CMOS region is not tamper-resistant. If the password is stored in CMOS, it can easily be attacked. The attacker may write to port 70/71 to update the CMOS RAM directly or clear the CMOS contents by removing the CMOS battery.

Today, the UEFI BIOS no longer uses CMOS RAM for non-volatile storage because of the above-listed security issues. A tamper-resistant storage device must be used to store the encrypted password. Most UEFI BIOS implementations use the flash device as the non-volatile storage for storing the password in UEFI variables. The integrity protection must be guaranteed for the portion of the flash device used for the password.

Password Encryption

The password should not be stored in the non-volatile storage directly as plain text. Rather, it must be encrypted to maintain its confidentiality so that the password cannot be guessed from the value stored in the non-volatile storage. Typically, the password is encrypted using a one-way function – a hash. This hash (not the password) is stored in the NV storage. The password verification process calculates the hash of the input password with the same one-way function and compares the results between the calculated value and the stored value.

However, just storing the hash of the password is vulnerable to a rainbow table attack. The rainbow table is a database of precalculated hash values for common passwords. With a rainbow table, the attacker just needs to compare the value in the rainbow table and the stored value, which is much faster than hash calculation.

In order to mitigate the rainbow table attack, a salt value should be appended to the password before performing the hash calculation. The password verification process is as follows: get the salt value from the stored area, calculate the hash of the input password and salt, and then compare the calculated value with the stored value. When using the salt value, the fixed rainbow table is useless. The salt should not be a fixed value. It must be as random as possible. For example, each platform should generate the salt value at runtime to make sure it is different between platforms. When a user changes the password, a new salt value can be generated.

The purpose of adding the salt is to make sure that the hash reverse calculation time is closer to that of a brute force attack rather than the much lower time required when using rainbow table lookups.

Another method to increase hash reverse calculation time is to increase the hash iteration count. The hash iteration count is the number of times that the output of the hash function is then used as input and the result is calculated again and again. With a large iteration count such as 1000, the attacker needs to spend much more time to calculate the final result for each password in the dictionary. But the impact to one password calculation is negligible compared to the time the user spends to input the password.

When choosing the one-way function for calculating the hash, a slow hash function should be used, for example, Password-Based Key Derivation Function 2 (PBKDF2). The slower time means that an attacker must spend more time to create the rainbow table to perform the attack.

The recommended encryption algorithm is shown in Figure 10-2. The BIOS should adopt all good practices for a BIOS password solution.

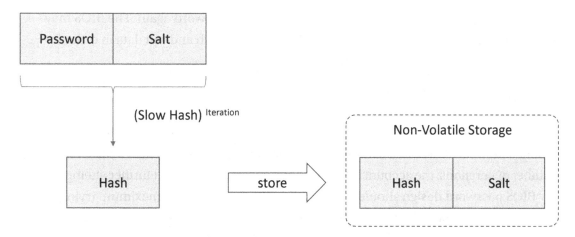

Figure 10-2. *Password Encryption*

Strong Password Enforcement

Even today, people are still inclined to use a simple password, such as 123456. When inputting or provisioning the password, the BIOS should enforce strong password requirements. Examples include the length of the password must be greater than or equal to eight, and also there must be at least one lowercase/uppercase letter, number, and symbol in the password. The BIOS should enforce the strong password requirements and reject weak passwords during provisioning.

Password Update Enforcement

Some computer systems have mandatory password change requests. The user is required to change the password of the system after a period of time, such as three months. This requirement may also be implemented in the BIOS. For example, the BIOS can save the date when the password is created along with the password storage and compare the current date with the stored value. However, it might be a burden for an end user to keep changing the BIOS password. Also, the PC typically doesn't support a trusted time source, so enforcement of this requirement could be bypassed by an attacker.

Password History

Password history is the hash of previous passwords, such as the three latest passwords or five latest passwords. If the user is asked to change to a new password, some systems check if the new password has been used before by comparing the hash to the previous ones. This is a way to prevent a user from using an old password again. The BIOS may also implement this feature by saving the old password hash and salt data in order to compare the new password hash with them.

Password Retry Limit

In the normal OS or web login pages, the user is only allowed to attempt the password entry a limited number of times, such as three times or five times. After failing the predefined number of iterations, the account will be locked for a while to prevent further attempts.

BIOS password design should use a similar mechanism. If the maximum trying count is reached, the BIOS should stop accepting any further password input. The user needs to reset the system before trying again.

Password Lost

Sometimes the user really forgets their password. Most web pages support the reset password option. After a user clicks the forget password link, the system sends a new link to the end user's registered email or cellphone. However, it is hard to implement such a solution in the BIOS because it requires a full network stack in the BIOS, a full user registration process, and a dedicated database for BIOS user management. Those are huge burdens for a BIOS implementation and the system manufacturer.

The platform designer must balance between the usability and security of the system. A high-assurance platform may request the platform be sent back to the manufacturer to unlock, such as with a return merchandise authorization (RMA) process. An alternative solution is to let the user submit a password reset request via another machine with the proper user identification and allow the remote administrator to clear password via an out-of-band (OOB) method. A low-end platform may allow the end user to press a special key combination or enter a recovery mode to clear a new password with the assertion of physical user presence if the person who touches the machine is assumed to be the owner of the machine.

Password Verification

Password verification or update must be in a trusted execution environment, for example, system management mode (SMM) or the early UEFI environment before any third-party code is running. If the password needs to be updated, the old password verification and new password update must happen in the same trusted execution environment, and there must be no interruption between them.

Password Management

The typical BIOS password is stored in the local NV storage area. However, the system password may be managed by a dedicated key server in an enterprise environment. For example, Kerberos is a network authentication protocol used in operating systems such as Windows or Linux. With Kerberos, the client sends the user identity and credential to the remote Kerberos server. The user information and password are stored in the Kerberos server, and the authentication happens in the Kerberos server.

The BIOS may implement the Kerberos client. Once a user inputs the password credential, the BIOS Kerberos client communicates with the remote Kerberos server to finish the user authentication. Care must be taken for the location of the remote Kerberos server. If the server location is saved in the UEFI NV storage region, this data must be protected. Otherwise, the attacker may try to modify the location of the Kerberos server and redirect the action to a fake server.

BIOS Update Mode

If the encrypted user password is saved in the NV storage area, this password information should be preserved during the BIOS update process.

S3 Resume Mode

S3 resume is a resource-constrained execution environment because the primary goal of a S3 resume boot mode is to restore the system configuration and return to the OS as soon as possible. As such, a typical S3 environment does not have the keyboard device driver or the graphic device driver. It is hard to authenticate a user in the S3 resume phase.

Recovery Boot Mode

Recovery boot is another special environment where the UEFI variables might not be available. If the user information and credential are saved to the UEFI NV storage area, they cannot be retrieved during recovery mode. As such, the user authentication may be skipped. If the user authentication is important for an authorized capability, such as continuing to boot, then the authorized capability will be disabled in recovery mode.

What a User Has: Token

Besides passwords, a BIOS may support the device token-based authentication, such as a smart card or a cellphone. The BIOS may include a smart card driver to retrieve the information from the card or include a Bluetooth Low Energy (BLE) driver to exchange messages with a cellphone.

With a password and token, a BIOS may support multifactor authentication (MFA).

What a User Is: Biometrics

The BIOS may also support biometrics-based authentication, such as the fingerprint, if the BIOS includes a fingerprint reader. Or the BIOS may include the ability to perform voice recognition or facial recognition. The issue that needs to be resolved for biometrics is that the BIOS needs to have a way for data sampling, which is not an easy task in the BIOS environment.

Other Considerations

Besides user authentication, the BIOS may consider some other aspects of user management.

User Enroll Enforcement

Some systems or web pages may enforce the enrollment of a username and password at the first boot or at the first web visit. The BIOS password may use this policy as well to enforce user input of a password during the first boot.

Multiple-User Management

A typical BIOS may support the user password and the administrator password. To support multiple users requires more work because the BIOS needs to save the user identity. The purpose of enabling multiple users is to assign different privileges for different users. For example, user A can boot Windows, and user B can boot Linux. If all users have the same authority to boot the OS, then multiple-user support is not required.

Single Sign-On

Single Sign-On (SSO) may be a use case for the multiple users in the BIOS. Once the user authentication is done in the BIOS, the BIOS may pass the user identity and credential to the OS. There are a couple of technical issues that need to be considered. For example, how does the BIOS protect the credential in the memory when the BIOS passes the information to the OS? How does the BIOS handle the situation when the user changes the password in the OS environment? How does the OS trust the information from the OEM BIOS?

Case Study

Now, let's take a look at some real use cases for boot access control.

EDK II User Authentication

The EDK II BIOS provides a reference implementation for user authentication. A user needs to input a password to enter the BIOS setup UI page to change the BIOS settings, for example, to change the boot option from "boot from hard drive" to "boot from USB device." As such, only the authorized user is allowed to change such settings.

The EDK II user authentication solution includes two parts. The first part is a password User Interface (UI). It accepts the end user input, puts the password into the SMM communication buffer, and triggers the system management interrupt (SMI). The second part is the password verification. It is inside of the trusted execution environment – the system management mode (SMM). Once the SMI is triggered to call the password verification handler, the handler copies the password from the SMM communication buffer into the SMM environment. Then the password verification handler reads the password salt value and stored hash value from the UEFI variable. Next, the verification handler calculates the real hash value from the salt and the real password. Finally, the password verification handler compares the real hash with the stored hash. If they are the same, then the password verification passes. If they are different, the password verification fails. See Figure 10-3.

The password update follows a similar process. The user needs to input an old password and a new password twice. All of these passwords need to be put into the SMM communication buffer. The password verification handler copies these passwords to the SMM environment and verifies the old password. Once the verification passes, the password driver creates a new salt and calculates the new password hash based upon the new salt and new password. Finally, the new salt and new password hash are saved to the NV storage area. The old salt and password hash are moved to the history variable. See Figure 10-4.

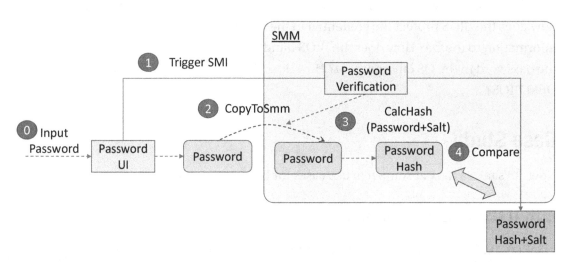

Figure 10-3. *EDK II User Authentication*

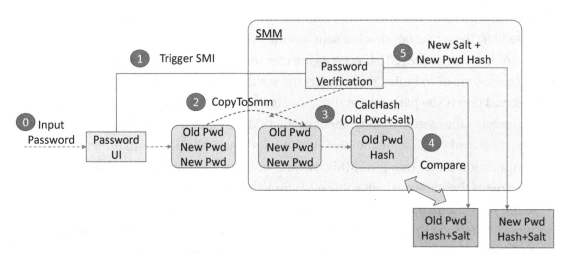

Figure 10-4. *EDK II User Password Update*

EDK II User Authorization

In the traditional BIOS, a user is authorized to boot the system, and an administrator is authorized to enter the BIOS setup page and modify the setup options. It is also possible that a BIOS may authorize the user to view the BIOS setup page information or authorize the user to modify some basic BIOS settings, such as the boot options.

Attack and Mitigation

Now, let's take a look at some real cases for the password attack and mitigation.

Traditional Password Attack

The traditional password attacks include brute force attack against a weak password, dictionary attacks, and a rainbow table attack. There might also be a non-standard password encryption algorithm attack.

The following best practices must be followed for passwords:

1) The password update MUST be in a secure environment, such as SMM, or before EndOfDxe.

2) The password in firmware MUST meet common best password criteria (strength, update, algorithm, retry time, old password check, password lost, and so on).

3) The password in memory MUST be cleared after use. The secret MAY be in a global data region, stack, or heap.

4) The password MUST NOT be hardcoded in the code.

5) If the code needs to compare the plain text password, the code MUST always compare all characters of the string, instead of breaking on the first mismatch. This guarantees that comparison times are always identical whether it is a match or mismatch, preventing timing-based password attacks.

6) Salt MUST be added to the password to resist rainbow table attacks.

7) Hash generation MUST add enough iterations to make sure the hash calculation is slow.

8) Password encryption MUST use a standard encryption algorithm such as PBKDF2, bcrypt. Do not use XOR or any weak hash algorithm.

Some firmware-specific attacks are as follows.

Password Memory

The password is input from the end user via a keyboard. The keystroke is saved in the keyboard-specific memory. If the keyboard memory is not cleared, the attacker can read the whole keyboard memory. In legacy systems, the keystroke is saved in a fixed BIOS data area (BDA). That key buffer in the BDA must be cleared.

The UEFI BIOS does not use BDA. The keystroke is saved in the keyboard driver directly. However, the UEFI BIOS uses Unicode to save the key data. The Unicode buffer needs to be converted to an ASCII buffer and input to the SMM communication buffer. When the final code clears the key buffer, both the Unicode buffer and the ASCII buffer need to be cleared. It could be in a global data region, stack, or heap.

Encrypted Password Storage

The password storage must be tamper-resistant. If the legacy BIOS uses the non–tamper-resistant storage, such as the CMOS region, then the attacker can easily modify the password storage area or clear the password area in order to log into the system.

The UEFI variable storage is tamper-resistant. When the variable is deleted, though, the UEFI variable implementation does not erase the whole variable buffer but instead sets a bit to indicate that the variable is deleted. This is designed because of the hardware attribute of NOR SPI flash. The NOR flash can easily write a bit value of 1 to 0 but cannot write a bit location of value 0 to 1. If the NOR flash needs to set a bit value of 0 to 1, it needs to send an erase command to erase the flash section or block whose size is 4 K or 64 K instead of 1 bit or 1 byte.

If the UEFI solution needs to save the password plain text in the variable region and then delete it, the password content will be in the variable region. As a mitigation, the password plain text should never be put in the variable region.

TEE Access Control

The trusted execution environment (TEE) needs access control. Otherwise, any module can update the TEE content. The details of the TEE will be discussed in Chapter 17.

Feature Configuration Control

The BIOS may allow a user to update the feature configuration. Some features are security related and require special control for the configuration update.

User Physical Presence

In firmware, some feature configuration is saved in a UEFI variable. The update for the configuration requires the user to assert physical presence. This is designed to prevent the configuration being updated by a malicious program automatically.

However, the evidence of the user's physical presence is a platform-specific design element. Normally, user presence is detected by console input. If there is input from the console, that is good enough to prove a physically present user. For example, the user inputs a password and enters the setup page.

The console could be local or remote. The local console output could be a local graphic device such as Video Graphics Array (VGA), Digital Visual Interface (DVI), High-Definition Multimedia Interface (HDMI), or a local serial port such as a COM port. The remote console output could be via a remote serial port such as Intel Active Management Technology (AMT) Serial Over LAN (SOL) or a remote graphic device such as KVM (Keyboard Video Mouse) redirection. The platform can decide to only treat the local console input as valid for determining physical user presence or both local and remote console inputs as valid. Other implementations of user presence can include a special jumper setting, a special hot key, or a chassis intrusion detection circuit.

UEFI Variable

The UEFI variable is the architectural non-volatile storage that holds firmware configuration settings. In order to prevent malicious access to the UEFI variable, we introduce several ways to control the access to the UEFI variable region. We will discuss these in detail in Chapter 11.

Case Study

Now, let's take a look at some real cases for the feature configuration control.

UEFI Secure Boot

The UEFI secure boot feature requires executable image verification using an image signature database. The image signature database can be updated with authorization. According to the UEFI specification, the update of the image signature database needs to be signed by the platform key (PK) provided by the platform vendor or the key exchange key (KEK) provided by the operating system vendor. Otherwise, the platform needs to have a secure platform-specific implementation of this update. The EDK II uses the physical user presence as the secure platform-specific means by which to authorize the update of the secure boot image signature database. See Figure 10-5 for the two update methods.

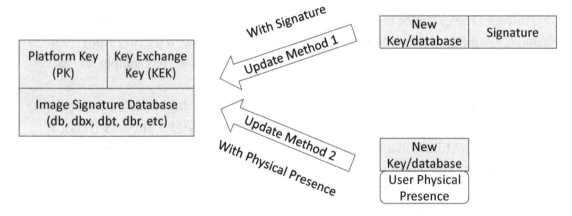

Figure 10-5. *UEFI Secure Boot Signature Database Update*

In EDK II, the variable driver uses the AuthVariableLib to control the secure boot–related authentication variable update (see Figure 10-6). The AuthVariableLib invokes the PlatformSecureLib UserPhysicalPresence() function to determine if the physical presence is asserted or not.

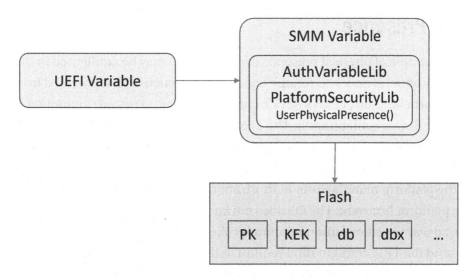

Figure 10-6. *UEFI Secure Boot Variable Component*

Attack and Mitigation

Now, let's take a look at some real cases for the feature configuration attack and mitigation.

PCD-Based Attack

The physical user presence check may happen in the trusted execution environment (TEE), such as system management mode (SMM). As such, the physical user presence function in SMM must not refer to any non-TEE data or function, such as the UEFI Platform Initialization (PI) specification–defined Platform Configuration Database (PCD). The PCD interface is a DXE service only. Referencing the PCD service at SMM runtime causes the typical SMM callout issue. The one possible mitigation is to get the PCD value at the SMM driver entry point and save it as a global variable. Afterward, this global variable can be used during the SMM runtime.

Device Configuration Control

The BIOS may allow a user to update the device configuration. Some features are security related and require special controls for the configuration update.

Physical Presence

As another example of physical presence usage, a device may be configured in the firmware environment only and require access control, such as that provided by a Trusted Platform Module (TPM)'s device configuration and Trusted Computing Group (TCG) storage device configuration. The TPM device may need to be configured in the OS environment, such as clearing the TPM or changing the Platform Configuration Register (PCR) bank. However, making such configuration change in the TPM device requires the platform manufacturer authorization value. This authorization value is only set by the platform firmware. The OS does not know the auth value.

A typical way to achieve this operation is called user confirmation. The end user needs to send the TPM configuration request in the OS, and the platform firmware records this request in non-volatile storage. After the system resets, when the platform firmware finds there is a pending request from the OS, the firmware pops up a User Interface (UI) page to let the end user confirm if this was a real request submitted by the end user. After the end user confirms the request, the platform firmware performs the configuration of the device and resets the system to make the new configuration take effect.

Care must be taken regarding the difference between the physical presence as defined by UEFI secure boot and as defined by TCG TPM devices and TCG storage. A platform may use different ways to implement the physical presence feature for each although the name is the same. For UEFI secure boot, the solution needs proof that the user is present – a simple GPIO setting or a keystroke. For TCG's physical presence feature, the solution requires that the end user confirm that this is exactly the request submitted from the OS.

Secure Console

If user confirmation is required, the output device and input device must be trusted. A trusted console means the console device connected by the platform BIOS runs before any third-party code, such as that provided by a PCI option ROM or OS application. All the code must be provided by the platform manufacturer. A trusted console might be an 1) integrated device such as a PS2/USB keyboard/mouse without any option ROM, 2) a chipset-integrated video device which is soldered to the system board and whose driver is inside of the BIOS instead of in a separate PCI option ROM flash container, and 3) a third-party video device which is soldered to the system board and whose driver is inside of the BIOS instead of in a PCI option ROM flash container. 4) If a remote console is used as a trusted console, additional authentication may be used, such as a request for an administrator password.

Case Study

Now, let's take a look at some real use cases for the device configuration control.

TCG Physical Presence

The TCG Physical Presence (PP) configuration is defined in the TCG specification. Table 10-1 shows the possible operation code of the TCG PP feature for the TPM2.0 device and TCG storage device.

Table 10-1. *TCG Physical Presence for TPM2.0 and TCG Storage*

Opcode	Operation Name	Device	Management Flags	When PP Confirmation Is Required (SetPPRequired XXX Is Set)
0	No option			
1~95 for TPM2 management				
1	Enable	TPM		TurnOn
2	Disable	TPM		TurnOff
5	Clear	TPM		Clear
14	Enable + Clear	TPM		Clear or TurnOn
17	SetPPRequiredFor Clear_True		TPM Flags	
18	SetPPRequiredFor Clear_False		TPM Flags	Always
21	Enable + Clear	TPM		Clear or TurnOn
22	Enable + Clear	TPM		Clear or TurnOn

(*continued*)

Table 10-1. (*continued*)

Opcode	Operation Name	Device	Management Flags	When PP Confirmation Is Required (SetPPRequired XXX Is Set)
23	SetPCRBanks	TPM		ChangePCRs
24	ChangeEPS	TPM		ChangeEPS
25	SetPPRequiredFor ChangePCRs_False		TPM Flags	Always
26	SetPPRequiredFor ChangePCRs_True		TPM Flags	
27	SetPPRequiredFor TurnOn_False		TPM Flags	Always
28	SetPPRequiredFor TurnOn_True		TPM Flags	
29	SetPPRequiredFor TurnOff_False		TPM Flags	Always
30	SetPPRequiredFor TurnOff_True		TPM Flags	
31	SetPPRequiredFor ChangeEPS_False		TPM Flags	Always
32	SetPPRequiredFor ChangeEPS_True		TPM Flags	
33	LogAllDigests	TPM		
34	DisableEndorsement EnableStorageHierarchy	TPM		TurnOn or TurnOff
96~127 for TCG storage management				
96	Enable_BlockSIDFunc	Storage		EnableBlockSIDFunc
97	Disable_BlockSIDFunc	Storage		DisableBlockSIDFunc
98	SetPPRequiredFor Enable_BlockSIDFunc_True		Storage Flags	

(*continued*)

Table 10-1. (*continued*)

Opcode	Operation Name	Device	Management Flags	When PP Confirmation Is Required (SetPPRequired XXX Is Set)
99	SetPPRequiredFor Enable_BlockSIDFunc_False		Storage Flags	Always
100	SetPPRequiredFor Disable_BlockSIDFunc_True		Storage Flags	
101	SetPPRequiredFor Disable_BlockSIDFunc_False		Storage Flags	Always
>=128 for TCG vendor-specific extension				

Operations 1~95 are for TPM2 management. All of these commands need platform auth and must be executed by the platform firmware. The physical presence check can prevent the TPM2 device from being compromised by a malicious program.

Operations 96~127 are for TCG storage devices. The physical presence check can prevent a malicious entity from taking ownership of a SID credential that is still set to its default value of MSID.

TCG defines two ways to control the device state configuration:

1) Physical presence control: A platform operator who is physically present at the platform must press a key to authorize an action.

2) Software control: An OS or other software controlling the system manages the device without the need for a physically present operator to approve changes.

The pros and cons for each option are obvious. With physical presence control, a malicious software entity cannot control the system. It is proper for a high-assurance system. Software control, on the other hand, makes it easier for configuration automation. See Figure 10-7 for the two update methods.

The TCG Physical Presence (PP) also defines a set of operations to control the two options. For example, the user may perform the SetPPRequiredForClear_False operation and confirm the action. Then, the next time the software sends the TPM clear command, no user confirmation is required.

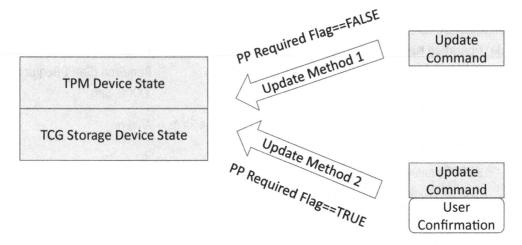

Figure 10-7. *TCG PP Configuration Update*

In EDK II, the TCG2PhysicalPresenceLib uses the PP variable to manage the TPM2 or TCG storage (such as OPAL, Opalite, Pyrite, or Ruby) device state. There are two PP variables – one is PP request variable that records the PP request and PP parameters, and the other is PP flags variable that records the PP management flags and the device states. The PP request variable is a read/write variable because everyone can send the PP request. The PP flags variable is a read-only variable because it records the final user-confirmed flags or states, which is used to set the TPM2 or TCG storage device state. Figure 10-8 shows the TCG PP Configuration Component Design.

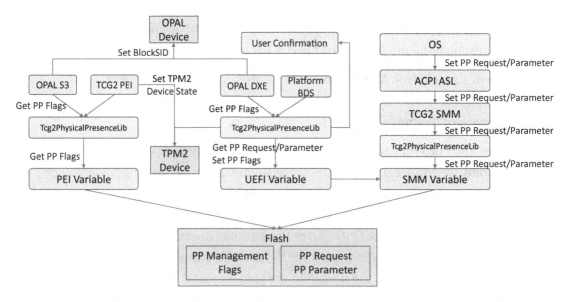

Figure 10-8. *TCG PP Configuration Component Design*

According to the TCG PP specification, the PP request is submitted from the OS via the ACPI ASL interface. Typically, the ASL generates a software SMI whose handler records the PP request and its parameters to the PP request variable. On the next boot, BDS processes the TCG PP request via the Tcg2PhysicalPresenceLib. The Tcg2PhysicalPresenceLib pops up a UI to let the user confirm the request based upon the request. Once the PP request is confirmed, the Tcg2PhysicalPresenceLib has two ways to process the PP request. 1) If the request takes effect once, such as to clear TPM or set the TPM PCR bank, the PP library sends the command to the device immediately. 2) If the request takes effect on every boot, such as setting the BlockSID auth, disabling the TPM, or changing PPRequiredForXXX flags, the PP library records the information in the PP flags variable. Whether or not there has been a PP request, the PP flags variable should always be locked. On every subsequent boot, the TCG2 PEIM and the OPAL storage driver consume the PP flags variable information in order to set the TPM2 device state and set the BlockSID auth.

Attack and Mitigation

Now, let's take a look at some real use cases for the device configuration attack and mitigation.

PP Flags Variable Attack

The PP flags variable records the expected device state and the need to request user confirmation. An attack may try to update the variable to bypass the user confirmation. Ideally the PP flags variable should be locked on every system boot.

One vulnerability we have seen before is when the PP flags variable is not locked during S4 resume. Because the TCG PP specification requires skipping the TCG PP process on the S4 resume path, the PP library might accidentally skip everything during S4 resume including locking the TCG PP flags variable.

Another vulnerability is during S3 resume. The OPAL PEI S3 driver uses a special read/write variable to record the TCG BlockSID request. As such, the attacker may change that variable to cause the driver to modify the TCG OPAL device state.

The mitigation is to make any TCG PP variable a read-only variable and lock the PP variable in every possible boot mode.

Storage Access Control

Today, data is one of the most important resources for both end users and enterprises. Storage device access controls are an important way to prevent data leakage. From the endpoint device perspective, the storage devices such as the hard disk drive (HDD), solid-state disk (SSD), and Non-Volatile Memory Express (NVMe) drives are attached to a platform device and used by an end user. As such, we may bind the storage device to the platform or the end user. Table 10-2 shows the difference between the two solutions.

***Table 10-2.** Storage Device Binding*

Mechanism	PROs	CONs	Solution	Example
Bind to a platform (provided by TPM)	User interaction is not required to unlock the disk.	Any user can access the storage if they can touch the platform hardware.	The OS supports full disk encryption with the key sealed in the TPM with PCR.	Microsoft TPM-based BitLocker.
Bind to an end user (provided by the storage device)	Different users cannot access the disk.	User interaction is required.	The storage device supports the password-based unlock.	ATA password, TCG OPAL password.

We have discussed the Windows BitLocker solution for binding the storage to the platform in Chapter 7. Now we will focus on the second part – binding the storage to the end user.

Hard Drive Password

The hard drive password solution must follow all the same password best practices as the user password authentication solution. For example, the solution should not save the password plain text in the NV storage area. The password memory must be cleared after verification. If the password verification fails, the system should reset instead of continuing to boot. The only difference is that the entity that does the verification is the hard drive hardware rather than the platform firmware.

Fast Boot Impact

The hard drive password unlock should happen in the BIOS. As such, all locked hard drives should be unlocked; then all hard drives should be discovered and connected in the BIOS.

Because the BIOS does not know if a hard drive needs to be unlocked or not, the BIOS has to connect all hard drives in the system irrespective of whether a password unlock is needed. That brings a burden for the BIOS fast boot feature because the BIOS fast boot requires that it only connect the devices required for the OS boot. Connecting any additional device adds unnecessary additional boot time.

Unlock in a Warm Reset

Ideally the hard drive is locked after reset, and password verification is required during the next boot. However, if a platform reset is a warm reset, the hard drive might or might not be reset. Without reset, the hard drive remains in the unlocked state. In this case, there is no way to let hardware verify the password.

On the other hand, there does need to be a way to verify the password because the password needs to be saved by the BIOS in order to unlock the drive during S3 resume. This is due to the fact that there is no console during S3 resume by default. As such, asking a user to input a password during S3 resume is not a desired option.

In order to achieve this, we have two options depending upon the device's capability:

1) Hardware solution: If the device can support the lock command, the BIOS can send the lock command at first; then try to use the new password to unlock.

2) Software solution: If the device does not support the lock command, the BIOS can save the encrypted verified hard drive password to the NV storage and compare the encrypted new password with the stored value in the NV storage.

Auto Unlock in S3

Most platform BIOS do not have a User Interface during S3 resume. However, the hard drive is locked in the S3 state because of the power loss. As such, the BIOS needs to have a secure way to save the hard drive password during the normal boot and send the unlock command during S3 resume. In order to achieve this, the solution needs to do the following: 1) always get the password during a normal boot, and 2) save the password in a secure place with confidentiality and integrity protection.

We have discussed the solution to always get the password in a normal boot in a previous section. Even if the hard drive is unlocked, we still have a way to verify the password.

The secure place to store the password could be the Trusted Execution Environment (TEE) or any other environment. EDK II BIOS designed the "LockBox" concept to abstract such a secure place. Any driver can put some data into the LockBox during a normal boot and restore the same content during S3 resume. The LockBox implementation can guarantee the data integrity (no lower-privilege driver is allowed to modify the contents) and the data confidentiality (no lower-privilege driver is allowed to read the contents). We have discussed LockBox in Chapter 9.

Runtime D3 impact

A storage device may support the runtime D3 feature. Runtime D3 means putting the device into the D3 hot/cold low-power state while the rest of the system is still in the S0 working state. If the hard drive is in a D3 cold state, it loses power and it is locked. If the system needs to bring the hard drive back to the D0 working state, there must be an entity to input the password and unlock it.

This work can be done by the BIOS or by the operating system. But both solutions have limitations. If the BIOS needs to unlock the hard drive, the runtime BIOS code (SMM) needs to access the device registers. There is a potential MMIO resource conflict between the BIOS and the OS because the OS owns all system resources at runtime, including the MMIO resources. Another potential conflict is DMA access because sending a command to the hard drive needs to use DMA. However, the OS owns the DMA/IOMMU controller. If the OS needs to unlock the hard drive, then the end user is required to input the hard drive password again at OS runtime because the OS does not know the password that the user input while in the BIOS. This adds an extra burden on the end user.

Maybe the best solution is to disable the hard drive password feature for the devices that support runtime D3.

Password Update

The user may update the hard drive password. This work must be done in a trusted execution environment. If the system BIOS does not treat the BIOS setup User Interface (UI) as a trusted execution environment, the system BIOS cannot let the user perform the password update there.

One possible solution is to let the user submit the password update request in the BIOS setup UI and then reboot the system. During the next boot, the password driver can pop up a dialog box to let the end user change the password.

User Password vs. Master Password

An end user needs to set a hard drive user password. With the user password, the hard drive is unlocked, and the end user can use the data on the disk.

An administrator may set a hard drive master password as well. With the master password, the administrator can delete the user password and erase the data on the disk. But the administrator cannot read the disk data with the master password. This is purposely designed for the scenario that a user returns the disk to an administrator in the enterprise still locked with the user password.

Retry Count

The hard disk drive maintains a password attempt count internally. Once the retry count is reached, the device will return a command abort for any further access to the device until next boot.

Hard Drive Freeze

Sometimes, the BIOS does not want to set a hard drive password and also does not want the password to be set by the operating system. As such, the BIOS needs to send a Freeze Lock command to freeze the disk security features, thus preventing a malicious program in the OS from setting a random password to the hard drive.

Secure Console

Hard drive unlock has similar strict secure console requirements.

Case Study

Now, let's take a look at some real use cases for storage access control.

ATA Password

The Advanced Technology Attachment (ATA)/AT Attachment with Packet Interface (ATAPI) Command Set Standard defines the security features. The security-related ATA commands are shown in Table 10-3.

Table 10-3. *ATA/ATAPI Security Commands*

ATA/ATAPI Command	Usage
SECURITY SET PASSWORD	Set a new user/master password for the hard drive.
SECURITY UNLOCK	Unlock the hard drive.
SECURITY ERASE PREPARE	Erase the user content.
SECURITY ERASE UNIT	Prepare for the erase command.
SECURITY FREEZE LOCK	Freeze the disk and prevent password setting attack.
SECURITY DISABLE PASSWORD	Disable hard drive password.

This feature is implemented in EDK II. Once the hard disk drive (HDD) is discovered, the HddPassword driver pops up a dialog to let the end user input the password. The HddPassword driver uses the password to unlock the hard drive and then saves the password hash and salt into the UEFI variable for a warm reset. The password and the device information are also saved into the LockBox for use during S3 resume. See Figure 10-9.

If the hard disk drive is already unlocked by the warm reset, the HddPassword driver needs to encrypt the password and compare it with the encrypted password stored in the UEFI variable. Then the password and the device information are also saved in the same LockBox for S3 resume. See Figure 10-10.

During S3 resume, the PEI HddPassword driver retrieves the password from the LockBox and uses it to unlock the hard drive. This action does not need any user interaction. See Figure 10-11.

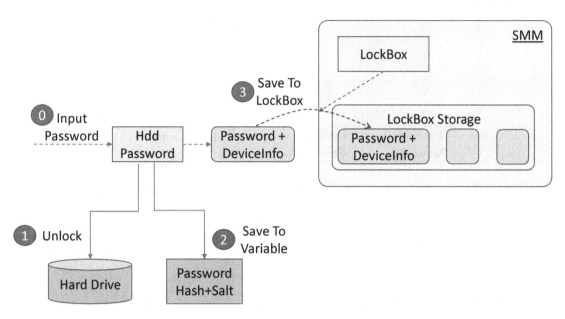

Figure 10-9. *HDD Password Solution in Cold Reboot*

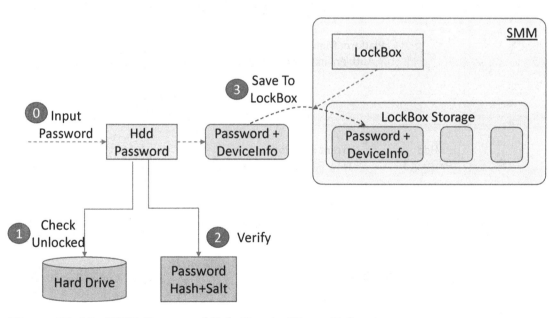

Figure 10-10. *HDD Password Solution in Warm Reboot*

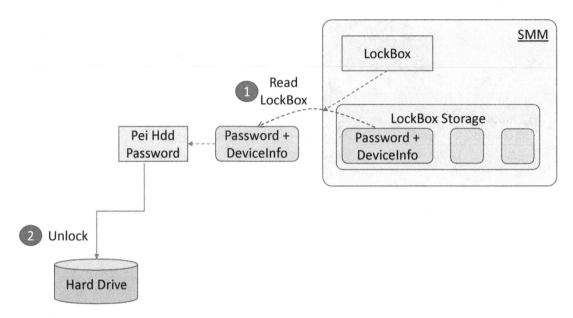

Figure 10-11. *HDD Password Solution in S3 Resume*

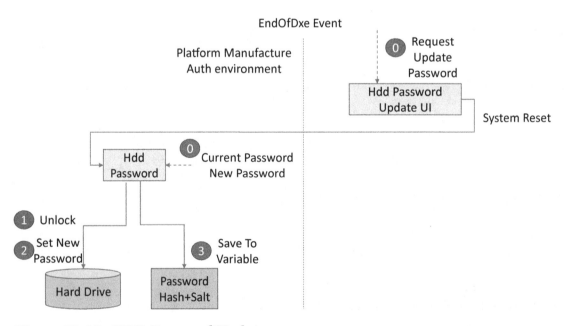

Figure 10-12. *HDD Password Update*

The user may want to update the HDD password in the BIOS setup page. Because the BIOS setup UI is not in the platform manufacturer auth environment, setting a new HDD password is not allowed. As such, the user can only send the password update request and reset the system. During the next boot, the HddPassword driver detects the password update request and processes it. It shows a dialog to let the user input the current password and the new password. The current password is used to unlock the device. The new password is used to lock the device. Once that is done, the encrypted new password is saved into a UEFI variable, and the new password is saved into the LockBox. See Figure 10-12.

TCG Storage Password

The ATA/ATAPI command set is only for ATA/ATAPI devices. However, there are other storage devices such as those attached to other buses, such as the Small Computer System Interface (SCSI), Universal Serial Bus (USB), Non-Volatile Memory Express (NVMe), and so on. How can we support the similar security features on those storage devices? The Trusted Computing Group (TCG) storage group defines common security services that allow all storage devices to support the storage device password.

The TCG-defined storage device includes the Trusted Peripheral (TPer). The TPer manages trusted storage-related functions and data structures. Two main aspects of the TPer use cases are

1) Data confidentiality and access control over TPer features and capabilities, including the data area readability and writability

2) TPers and hosts' bilateral enrollment and connection for the permissions and authorizations

The TPer may contain one or more Security Providers (SPs). A Security Provider is a set of tables and methods that control the persistent trust state of the SP or TPer. Each SP has its own storage, functional scope, and security domain. A Security Provider includes tables, table content, methods, authorities, access control lists (ACLs), and access control elements (ACEs). See Figure 10-13.

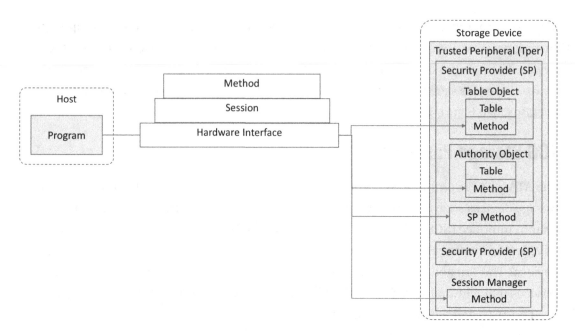

Figure 10-13. *TCG Storage Device Architecture*

The only way to communicate with an SP is via a session. Only the host is able to open a session. Methods are invoked within sessions. In order to start a session, the host needs to indicate the 8-byte SP Unique Identifier (UID) – which SP the host wants to communicate – the 8-byte Host Signing Authority UID, and the host challenge data for the Host Signing Authority. Within the session, the host may invoke the method provided by the SP, and the host needs to indicate the 8-byte invoking ID (such as session manager, this SP, table UID, object UID) and 8-byte method ID – the method provided by the invoking ID and the method parameters.

Let's take a look at some examples:

1)   TCG storage unlocks.

See Figure 10-14. In order to unlock the TCG storage, the TcgOpalPassword driver needs to create a session for communication with OPAL_UID_LOCKING_SP with the Signing Authority being OPAL_LOCKING_SP_ADMIN1_AUTHORITY and host challenge data being the user input password. To start a session, the TcgOpal driver sends a CALL method with the invoking ID being TCG_UID_SMUID and the method being TCG_UID_SM_START_SESSION. The parameters of the start session method are SP UID, Signing Authority ID, host challenge, and so on. After the session is created, the TcgOpalPassword sends the second CALL method with the invoking ID being

OPAL_LOCKING_SP_LOCKING_GLOBALRANGE and method ID being TCG_UID_
METHOD_SET. The parameter is ReadLocked=FALSE and WriteLocked=FALSE. After
this command is received by the device, the device is unlocked. Finally, the
TcgOpalPassword driver sends the ENDSESSION token to the device to close the session.

Compared with ATA security features, the TCG defines a more complicated method
of host/device communication. The benefit of this approach is that device functionality
is abstracted as the method within the SP.

Session	SP UID	Signing Authority ID	Host Challenge
OPAL storage unlocks	OPAL_UID_LOCKING_SP	OPAL_LOCKING_SP_[ADMIN1|USER1]_AUTHORITY	Password

Operation	Token	Invoking ID	Method ID	Method Parameter
Start Session	CALL (Method)	TCG_UID_SMUID	TCG_UID_SM_START_SESSION	SP UID, Signing Authority ID, Host Challenge
Set Locking Global Range	CALL (Method)	OPAL_LOCKING_SP_LOCKING_GLOBALRANGE	TCG_UID_METHOD_SET	ReadLocked, WriteLocked
EndSession	ENDSESSION			

Figure 10-14. *TCG Storage Unlock*

2)   TCG storage set admin password.

Figure 10-15 shows the second example, to set a new admin password. This is a more
complicated case. Totally three sessions are involved. First, the TcgOpalPassword driver
creates a session with OPAL_UID_LOCKING_SP with OPAL_LOCKING_SP_ADMIN1_
AUTHORITY and old password. The purpose of this step is to verify the password. If the
password verification fails, the driver will stop and pop up an error message to the end user.

Second, after the verification passes, the TcgOpalPassword driver creates the second
session with OPAL_UID_ADMIN_SP with the OPAL_ADMIN_SP_SID_AUTHRITY and
the old password. After the session is created, the TcgOpalPassword driver invokes the
CALL method with invoking ID being OPAL_UID_ADMIN_SP_C_PIN_SID and the
method ID being TCG_UID_METHOD_SET. The parameter is the PIN column number
and the new password. This session is to update the PIN in the ADMIN_SP.

Third, the TcgOpalPassword driver updates the PIN for the LOCKING_SP. It creates
a session with OPAL_UID_LOCKING_SP again and invokes a new CALL method with
invoking ID being OPAL_LOCKING_SP_C_PIN_ADMIN1 and method ID being TCG_
UID_METHOD_SET. The parameter is the PIN column number and the new password.

After those steps, the PIN is updated in both the ADMIN_SP and the LOCKING_SP.

Session	SP UID		Signing Authority ID		Host Challenge
verify password	OPAL_UID_LOCKING_SP		OPAL_LOCKING_SP_ADMIN1_AUTHORITY		Old Password
Operation	**Token**	**Invoking ID**	**Method ID**		**Method Parameter**
Start Session	CALL (Method)	TCG_UID_SMUID	TCG_UID_SM_START_SESSION		SP, Authority, Challenge
End Session	ENDSESSION				
Set Admin Password	OPAL_UID_ADMIN_SP		OPAL_ADMIN_SP_SID_AUTHORITY		Old Password
Method	**Token**	**Invoking ID**	**Method ID**		**Method Parameter**
Start Session	CALL (Method)	TCG_UID_SMUID	TCG_UID_SM_START_SESSION		SP, Authority, Challenge
Set Admin Password	CALL (Method)	OPAL_UID_ADMIN_SP_C _PIN_SID (Row)	TCG_UID_METHOD_SET		Colume: PIN New Password
End Session	ENDSESSION				
Set Locking Password	OPAL_UID_LOCKING_SP		OPAL_LOCKING_SP_ADMIN1_AUTHORITY		Old Password
Method	**Token**	**Invoking ID**	**Method ID**		**Method Parameter**
Start Session	CALL (Method)	TCG_UID_SMUID	TCG_UID_SM_START_SESSION		SP, Authority, Challenge
Set Locking Password	CALL (Method)	OPAL_LOCKING_SP_C_PIN_ ADMIN1 (Row)	TCG_UID_METHOD_SET		Colume: PIN New Password
End Session	ENDSESSION				

Figure 10-15. *TCG Storage Set Admin Password*

The CALL method or the ENDSESSION are the token in the data buffer. The OpalPassword driver adds three headers – TcgComPacket, TcgPacket and TcgSubPacket before the data buffer and constructs the whole data block. Once the data block is passed to the storage driver, the storage driver adds the storage secure command block (IF-SEND or IF-RECV, Security Protocol ID 0x1, ComId) and sends the whole message to the TPer device. See Figure 10-16.

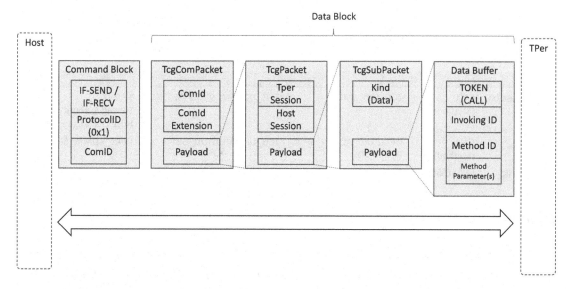

Figure 10-16. *TCG Storage Interface Data Block*

TCG Storage – SID (Secure Identifier)

The Security Identifier (SID) authority is used by TPer owner, also known as the storage device owner, to authenticate to the Admin SP. After getting the device, the user may take the ownership by changing the SID Personal Identification Number (PIN). Figure 10-15 shows how to set the admin password.

TCG Storage – MSID (Manufactured SID)

When a TCG Storage device is shipped, it may carry a Manufactured SID (MSID) credential set at the manufacturing time by the storage device vendor. The MSID does not have any associated authority and it may be read by anybody. The MSID value can be used as the device initial SID value – the device owner's password. Once the user takes ownership, the user may input the MSID value to the SID authority in the admin SP then set a new SID value to replace the default MSID value.

See Figure 10-17. To perform the MSID read, the OpalPassword driver communicates with OPAL_UID_ADMIN_SP with NULL authority and NULL host challenge, and then the driver invokes the OPAL_UID_ADMIN_SP_C_PIN_MSID read method with column OPAL_ADMIN_SP_PIN_COL to read the MSID data from the device.

Session	SP UID	Signing Authority ID	Host Challenge
Read MSID	OPAL_UID_ADMIN_SP	TCG_UID_NULL	NULL

Operation	Token	Invoking ID	Method ID	Method Parameter
Start Session	CALL (Method)	TCG_UID_SMUID	TCG_UID_SM_START_SESSION	SP UID, Signing Authority ID, Host Challenge
Revert	CALL (Method)	OPAL_UID_ADMIN_SP_C_PIN_MSID	TCG_UID_METHOD_GET	OPAL_ADMIN_SP_PIN_COL
EndSession	ENDSESSION			

Figure 10-17. *TCG Storage Read MSID*

At this point we can enable the admin password for the first time by using the MSID credential (See Figure 10-18). The OpalPassword driver communicates with OPAL_UID_ADMIN_SP with OPAL_ADMIN_SP_SID_AUTHORITY and MSID as the host challenge. Then the OpalPassword driver invokes the CALL method with invoking ID being OPAL_UID_ADMIN_SP_C_PIN_SID and method ID being TCG_UID_METHOD_SET. The parameter is the PIN column number and the new password. This session is to update the PIN in the ADMIN_SP.

After that, in the same session the OpalPassword invokes the CALL method with invoking ID being OPAL_UID_LOCKING_SP and method ID being OPAL_ADMIN_SP_ACTIVATE_METHOD, to activate the locking SP.

Session	SP UID	Signing Authority ID	Host Challenge
Set Admin Password (First)	OPAL_UID_ADMIN_SP	OPAL_ADMIN_SP_SID_AUTHORITY	MSID

Method	Token	Invoking ID	Method ID	Method Parameter
Start Session	CALL (Method)	TCG_UID_SMUID	TCG_UID_SM_START_SESSION	SP, Authority, Challenge
Set Admin Password	CALL (Method)	OPAL_UID_ADMIN_SP_C_PIN_SID (Row)	TCG_UID_METHOD_SET	Colume: PIN New Password
Activate locking SP	CALL (Method)	OPAL_UID_LOCKING_SP	OPAL_ADMIN_SP_ACTIVATE_METHOD	
End Session	ENDSESSION			

Figure 10-18. *TCG Storage use MSID to set first Admin password*

TCG Storage – BlockSID

Sometimes, the ownership of the TCG storage device is not taken. The SID PIN is the default MSID. In order to prevent a malicious program from taking ownership with default MSID, the BIOS needs to block SID setting. The storage driver uses the storage secure command block (IF-SEND or IF-RECV, Security Protocol ID 0x2, ComId 0x0005 BlockSID) and sends the message to the TPer device to enable the BlockSID. See Figure 10-19.

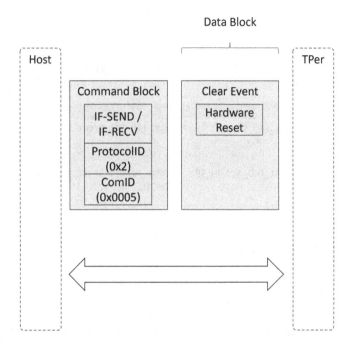

Figure 10-19. *TCG Storage BlockSID*

From the BIOS perspective, there is a policy that determines whether the BIOS needs to send the BlockSID command or not. TCG storage reuses the TCG Physical Presence solution to process the BlockSID enable/disable request from the OS and uses a read-only variable to store the policy information. See Table 10-1.

TCG Storage – PSID (Physical Presence SID)

If a user or an admin forgets the TCG storage password and still wants to use the device, he or she may use the Physical Presence SID (PSID) revert. The PSID revert resets the SID PIN to the default MSID and may erase all media encryption keys. As a consequence, the user data is destroyed. The PSID feature was designed so that if the user forgets the password, the user may input the PSID credential value to revert the device. The PSID delivery method is vendor specific. One simple solution is to print the PSID credential value on the device label. Any physical user who can touch the device can get the PSID value.

See Figure 10-20. To perform the PSID revert, the OpalPassword driver communicates with OPAL_UID_ADMIN_SP with OPAL_ADMIN_SP_PSID_AUTHORITY and PSID as the host challenge, then sends the OPAL_ADMIN_SP_REVERT_METHOD to revert the data on the device.

Session	SP UID	Signing Authority ID	Host Challenge
PSID revert	OPAL_UID_ADMIN_SP	OPAL_ADMIN_SP_PSID_AUTHORITY	PSID

Operation	Token	Invoking ID	Method ID	Method Parameter
Start Session	CALL (Method)	TCG_UID_SMUID	TCG_UID_SM_START_SESSION	SP UID, Signing Authority ID, Host Challenge
Revert	CALL (Method)	OPAL_UID_ADMIN_SP	OPAL_ADMIN_SP_REVERT_METHOD	
EndSession	ENDSESSION			

Figure 10-20. *TCG Storage PSID revert*

TCG Storage – TPer Reset

The platform reset attack may get the secret in the memory. In order to mitigate the reset attack to memory, the TCG defines the Memory-Only Reset (MOR) feature to inform the BIOS to clear memory after an abnormal reset. We have discussed that feature in Chapter 7. The storage device may experience a similar platform reset attack because the protected region may be unlocked after the platform reset. In order to mitigate the attack to the storage device, the BIOS needs to issue a TPer Reset command once the BIOS detects the MOR request. After TPer reset, all protected regions are locked again.

The storage driver uses the storage secure command block (IF-SEND or IF-RECV, Security Protocol ID 0x2, ComId 0x0004 TPerReset) and sends the message to the TPer device to issue TPerReset. See Figure 10-21.

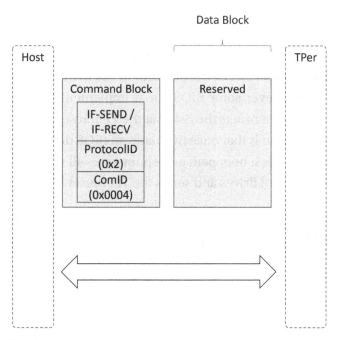

Figure 10-21. *TCG Storage TPer Reset*

Attack & Mitigation

Now, let's take a look at some real use cases for the attack for the storage access control and mitigation.

No HDD Freeze Lock / TCG BlockSID

The HDD Freeze Lock and the TCG BlockSID feature are designed to prevent the attack by a malicious program in the operating system (OS) to take ownership of a device. The OS may want to take ownership of the storage device, or the OS might not take ownership by setting a new password to the storage device. This is a policy set by the OS. The TCG defines the physical presence (PP) interface for the policy passing from the OS to the BIOS via the ACPI method. Similar to the TPM PP interface, the storage PP interface also saves the storage management flag to a UEFI variable. This UEFI variable must be locked in any boot mode, including normal boot and S3 resume.

One vulnerability we have found before is that the BlockSID command is only sent in a normal boot, but not sent during S3 resume. Then the malicious program just needs to trigger an S3 resume then takes owner control of the device. The TCG storage driver should consume this storage management flag variable to send the BlockSID command in S3 resume as well if necessary.

No TCG TPer Reset

TPer Reset commands should be sent when the BIOS detects the MOR request. In order to issue a TPer reset to all hard drives, the platform needs to detect all the hard disks and restart all of them. However, some BIOSes may implement a fast boot path and only connect the boot device. That brings the risk that the TPer reset is not sent to the rest of the devices. The mitigation is that once the platform BIOS detects the MOR request, the platform BIOS quits the fast boot path and enumerates all the hard drives. Then the MOR driver discovers all hard drives and sends the TPer reset to all of them.

Network Access Control

A UEFI BIOS may include a full TCP/IP network stack to support the Preboot Execution Environment (PXE) boot or HTTP boot. Network access control may be needed in this case.

Case Study

Now, let's take a look at some real cases for network access control.

WIFI network

The physical layer of the network could be a wired network device or a wireless network such as Wireless-Fidelity (WIFI). In order to support connecting to a WIFI network, the user may be asked to input credentials for authentication. In client mode, the WIFI network uses the pre-shared key (PSK), also known as WIFI password, for authentication. In enterprise mode, the WIFI network uses IEEE 802.1X port authentication and the Extensible Authentication Protocol (EAP) authentication method.

For the PSK use-case, the user needs to input the WIFI password to connect the network. The question is if the BIOS needs to store the WIFI password. On the one hand, if the BIOS does not store any WIFI password, then the user is required to input the WIFI password whenever he or she wants to connect to the same WIFI network. That is a different user experience compared with the OS environment. On the other hand, if the BIOS stores the WIFI password in a UEFI variable or a configuration file, the plain text data may be exposed to any program. This solution may bring a security concern. The

BIOS may choose to encrypt the WIFI password with a key. Now the problem is how to get the key in the boot. If the user is asked to input the key, we go back to the original problem – user interaction is required.

There is no simple answer on how to handle a WIFI password in the BIOS. The solution must balance the usability and the security.

Bluetooth

A UEFI BIOS may include Bluetooth support, such as a Bluetooth keyboard or mouse. Bluetooth device connection may also require authentication, such as numeric comparison, passkey entry, or an out-of-band mechanism. Once the device and host pairing is successful, a pairing key is generated. The UEFI implementation may choose to save the pairing key for future use. However, the integrity and the confidentiality of the pairing key might be a concern if the platform saves the pairing key plain text to a UEFI variable. That should be considered when implementing a Bluetooth auto-reconnection feature.

TCP/IP Network Security

Because the firmware may include the TCP/IP network stack, the network security features could also be implemented, such as Transport Layer Security (TLS) or Internet Protocol Security (IPSec). For the TLS example in Figure 10-22, the UEFI BIOS acts as a TLS client and initiates the connection with a remote server via a normal TLS session. The UEFI implementation may choose no-authentication, one-way authentication or mutual authentication. 1) If the TLS session uses no-authentication, the client and server won't send any certification to each other. 2) If the TLS session uses one-way authentication – the client needs to authenticate the server. The UEFI client needs to provision the server public certificate in the UEFI authenticated variable. After the server sends the server certification and signing data in the handshake, the client will compare the server certificate and verify the server signature in order to finish the server authentication. 3) If the TLS session needs mutual authentication, things become complicated because the UEFI BIOS does not have an architectural way to save the client private certificate to sign the data. The UEFI variable cannot be used because the UEFI variable does not provide confidentiality support. One possible solution is that the client needs a special Trusted Execution Environment (TEE) feature to save the client private certificate. Then the BIOS gets the private certificate from the TEE at boot time and signs the client data to allow the server to authenticate. The TEE needs to close the service to return the private certificate after the BIOS boot.

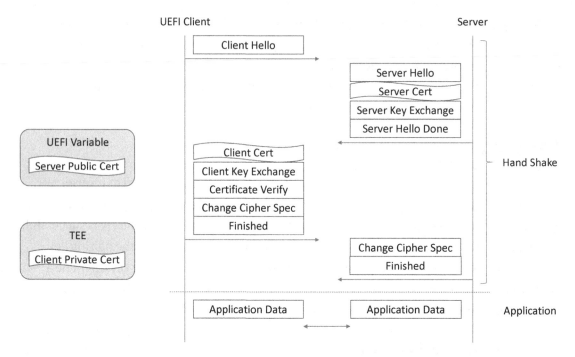

Figure 10-22. *TLS Handshake*

Attack & Mitigation

Now, let's take a look at some real use cases for the attack for the network access control and mitigation.

Private Certificate Storage Attack

The management of the private certificate or private key in the UEFI BIOS is always a big challenge. If it is saved in the UEFI Variable region, it becomes a problem because the UEFI Variable only provides the integrity support but not confidentiality support according to the UEFI Specification. Adding the certification management in the UEFI Variable might be an overhead because we may enable data encryption with the user password, which means user interaction is required. As an alternative, we can leverage the TPM non-volatile storage and key hierarchy to manage the private key, with the option to bind to a platform instead of a user. Another choice is to let a TEE maintain the private key, such as the Intel Converged Security and Management Engine (CSME). Care must be taken to keep the key service in the BIOS only accessible before any third-party code running and close the service before booting into the OS.

TLS Hostname Attack

The network security in the UEFI BIOS supports peer authentication. The UEFI client side may need to authenticate the server. One TLS issue in EDK II that has arisen before is about the peer hostname verification. Here is the issue: The server certificate has a Common Name (CN) for the subject. This name is used to match the hostname of the server site. The expected behavior from the client side is 1) to verify the hostname (identification), 2) to verify the certificate (authentication). The early version of UEFI TLS only verified the server certificate, but not the hostname, which brings in the potential of a man-in-the-middle attack.

Device Access Control

One of the main roles and responsibilities of a BIOS is to initialize the devices on the motherboard. Different devices may have different mechanisms for the device access control.

Case Study

Now, let's take a look at some real use cases for the device access control.

TPM2 Hierarchy Auth Value

The TPM2 specification defines three hierarchies. Each hierarchy has its own authorization policy and authorization value. The hierarchy can be enabled or disable independently.

1) Platform hierarchy – Controlled by the platform manufacturer. It is used by the platform BIOS.

2) Storage Hierarchy – Controlled by the platform owner. The owner could be an end user or the IT administrator. It is used for the key or data storage.

3) Endorsement Hierarchy – Controlled by the privacy administrator, who might be an end user. It is used for privacy sensitive actions, such as providing device attestation.

During system boot, the platform BIOS needs to take over the platform hierarchy by sending TPM2_HierarchyChangeAuth (TPM_RH_PLATFORM) command with a platform auth value. After this command is executed, the further access to the platform hierarchy requires the platform auth value. Usually the BIOS just creates a random value whose length is the same as the size of the TPM supported hash algorithm, uses this random value as the platform auth value, and discards the random value after the command is sent. This is to prevent a malicious program from controlling the platform hierarchy at the OS runtime.

EC Access Passcode

An Embedded Controller (EC) is a microcontroller in a system to control various devices such as keyboard, thermal, battery, Light Emitting Diode (LED), and so on. Some EC implementations require a passcode to unlock the EC to allow the EC firmware update (see Figure 10-23). This is designed to prevent the malicious program from performing an EC firmware update directly. Ideally, the platform BIOS generates an ephemeral value and programs the value to the EC as the passcode. The passcode should be discarded in the BIOS environment but saved in a TEE environment. Later when there is a need to update the EC, the TEE should use the saved passcode to unlock the EC and perform the update.

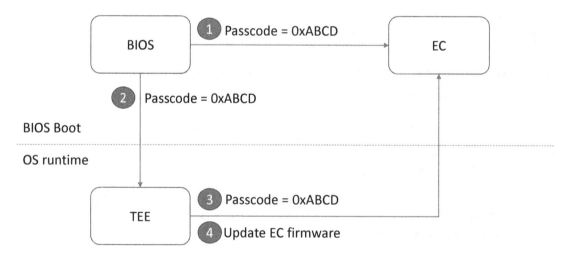

Figure 10-23. *EC Firmware Update with Passcode*

Smart Battery Access Code

Battery systems provide the power for a laptop. The smart battery system (SBS) specification defines the interface to let other programs communicate with the battery device. A battery device may have different access modes:

1) sealed mode: support standard SBS read-only command. This should be default mode when the device is shipped.

2) unsealed mode: support some SBS read/write command. Firmware update should be performed in this mode.

3) full access mode: support all read/write commands. With this mode, the program can enter BootROM and configuration mode. Then the program can tell the battery what level of current, voltage, temp and so on.

In order to prevent malicious access to the device, the smart battery requires an access code to switch the battery mode from sealed mode to unsealed mode, and from unsealed mode to full access mode. Only after the program sends out the right access code can the battery mode can be switched.

Attack & Mitigation

Now, let's take a look at some real use cases for the attack for the device access control and mitigation.

Default Password or Static Password

If a platform uses the default manufacturer password or a hardcoded static password to unlock the device, the password can be easily retrieved by the attacker if the attacker searches the device data sheet or reverse engineers the firmware code. A platform should always apply the best practices for the device password, such as not hardcoding a password in the firmware, do not use the same manufacturer password for the device, use different passwords for different devices and different platforms.

S3 Resume Attack

The platform BIOS needs to send a TPM2_HierarchyChangeAuth (TPM_RH_PLATFORM) command to take over the TPM2 platform hierarchy in the normal boot to prevent a malicious program from controlling the platform hierarchy. This action should also be considered in the S3 resume because the malicious program may perform the S3 attack against the TPM2 device. If the TPM2 device is suspended successfully, the BIOS uses the TPM2_Startup(State) to resume the TPM2 state. However, if the attack performs the system reset without letting the OS suspend the TPM2 device, the TPM2_Startup(State) will fail in the BIOS S3 resume. A typical BIOS will send TPM2_Startup(CLEAR) to restart the TPM2. Then the platform auth is reset to NULL. In this case, the BIOS must send the TPM2_HierarchyChangeAuth (TPM_RH_PLATFORM) again to initiate a random platform auth value.

Summary

In this chapter, we discussed the access control methods in the firmware, including the boot access control, feature configuration control, device configuration control, storage access control, network access control, device access control. In the next chapter we will discuss the firmware configuration.

References

Conference, Journal, and Paper

[P-1] Jonathan Brossard, "Bypassing Pre-boot Authentication Passwords", in *DEFCON16 2008*, available at www.defcon.org/images/defcon-16/dc16-presentations/brossard/defcon-16-brossard-wp.pdf

[P-2] Charlie Miller, "Battery Firmware Hacking", in *BlackHat US 2011*, available at https://media.blackhat.com/bh-us-11/Miller/BH_US_11_Miller_Battery_Firmware_Public_Slides.pdf

[P-3] Alex Matrosov, Alexandre Gazet, "Breaking Through Another Side", in *Blackhat US 2019*, available at http://i.blackhat.com/USA-19/Thursday/us-19-Matrosov-Breaking-Through-Another-Side-Bypassing-Firmware-Security-Boundaries-From-Embedded-Controller.pdf

[P-4] Jeff Bobzin, "Strategies for Firmware Support of Self-Encrypting Drives", in *UEFI Plugfest 2011*, available at https://members.uefi.org/learning_center/UEFI_Plugfest_JBOBZIN_2012Q1_V2.pdf

[P-5] Trusted Computing Group, "TCG Storage Integration Guide", 2016, available at https://trustedcomputinggroup.org/wp-content/uploads/TCG_Storage_ReferenceDocument_Opal_Integration_Guidelines_v1.00_r1.00.pdf

[P-6] Trusted Computing Group, "TCG TPM v2.0 Provisioning Guidance", 2017, available at https://trustedcomputinggroup.org/wp-content/uploads/TCG-TPM-v2.0-Provisioning-Guidance-Published-v1r1.pdf

[P-7] sata-io, "Serial ATA Device Sleep (DevSleep) and Runtime D3 (RTD3)", sata-io whitepaper 2012, available at https://sata-io.org/sites/default/files/documents/SATADevSleep-and-RTD3-WP-037-20120102-2_final.pdf

[P-8] Microsoft, "Encrypted Hard Drive Device Guide", 2011, available at http://download.microsoft.com/download/8/9/1/891EB055-F1FA-4601-82B4-5FEC784A69EA/encrypted-hard-drive-device-guide.docx

[P-9] Frederick Knight, Sridhar Balasubramanian, "TCG SSC: Key Per IO," in USENIX Vault '20, https://www.usenix.org/sites/default/files/conference/protected-files/vault20_slides_balasubramanian_0.pdf

Specification and Guideline

[S-1] NIST SP800-56A, "Recommendation for Pair-Wise Key-Establishment Schemes Using Discrete Logarithm Cryptography", 2018, available at https://csrc.nist.gov/publications/sp800

[S-2] NIST SP800-56B, "Recommendation for Pair-Wise Key-Establishment Using Integer Factorization Cryptography", 2019, available at https://csrc.nist.gov/publications/sp800

[S-3] NIST SP800-56C, "Recommendation for Key-Derivation Methods in Key-Establishment Schemes", 2018, available at https://csrc.nist.gov/publications/sp800

[S-4] NIST SP800-57 Part1, "Recommendation for Key Management, Part 1: General", 2019, available at https://csrc.nist.gov/publications/sp800

[S-5] NIST SP800-57 Part2, "Recommendation for Key Management: Part 2 – Best Practices for Key Management Organizations", 2019, available at https://csrc.nist.gov/publications/sp800

[S-6] NIST SP800-57 Part3, "Recommendation for Key Management, Part 3: Application-Specific Key Management Guidance", 2015, available at https://csrc.nist.gov/publications/sp800

[S-7] NIST SP800-63-3, "Digital Identity Guidelines", 2017, available at `https://csrc.nist.gov/publications/sp800`

[S-8] NIST SP800-63A, "Digital Identity Guidelines: Enrollment and Identity Proofing", 2017, available at `https://csrc.nist.gov/publications/sp800`

[S-9] NIST SP800-63B, "Digital Identity Guidelines: Authentication and Lifecycle Management", 2017, available at `https://csrc.nist.gov/publications/sp800`

[S-10] NIST SP800-63C, "Digital Identity Guidelines: Federation and Assertions", 2017, available at `https://csrc.nist.gov/publications/sp800`

[S-11] NIST SP800-90A, "Recommendation for Random Number Generation Using Deterministic Random Bit Generators", 2015, available at `https://csrc.nist.gov/publications/sp800`

[S-12] NIST SP800-90B, "Recommendation for the Entropy Sources Used for Random Bit Generation", 2018, available at `https://csrc.nist.gov/publications/sp800`

[S-13] NIST SP800-90C, "Recommendation for Random Bit Generator (RBG) Constructions", 2016, available at `https://csrc.nist.gov/publications/sp800`

[S-14] NIST SP800-107, "Recommendation for Applications Using Approved Hash Algorithms", 2012, available at `https://csrc.nist.gov/publications/sp800`

[S-15] NIST SP800-108, "Recommendation for Key Derivation Using Pseudorandom Functions", 2009, available at `https://csrc.nist.gov/publications/sp800`

[S-16] NIST SP800-131A, "Recommendation for Transitioning the Use of Cryptographic Algorithms and Key Lengths", 2019, available at `https://csrc.nist.gov/publications/sp800`

[S-17] NIST SP800-132, "Recommendation for Password-Based Key Derivation", 2010, available at `https://csrc.nist.gov/publications/sp800`

[S-18] NIST SP800-133, "Recommendation for Cryptographic Key Generation", 2019, available at `https://csrc.nist.gov/publications/sp800`

[S-19] NIST SP800-135, "Recommendation for Existing Application-Specific Key Derivation Functions", 2011, available at `https://csrc.nist.gov/publications/sp800`

[S-20] FIPS 140-3, "Security Requirements for Cryptographic Modules", 2019, available at `https://csrc.nist.gov/publications/fips`

[S-21] Trusted Computing Group, "TCG PC Client Platform Physical Presence Interface Specification", 2015, available at `https://trustedcomputinggroup.org/resource/tcg-physical-presence-interface-specification/`

[S-22] Trusted Computing Group, "TCG Storage Architecture Core Specification", 2015, available at `https://trustedcomputinggroup.org/resource/tcg-storage-architecture-core-specification/`

[S-23] Trusted Computing Group, "TCG Storage Interface Interactions Specification", 2018, available at https://trustedcomputinggroup.org/resource/storage-work-group-storage-interface-interactions-specification/

[S-24] Trusted Computing Group, "TCG Storage Work Group Storage Security Subsystem Class: Opal", 2015, available at https://trustedcomputinggroup.org/resource/storage-work-group-storage-security-subsystem-class-opal/

[S-25] Trusted Computing Group, "TCG Storage Work Group Storage Security Subsystem Class: Opalite", 2015, available at https://trustedcomputinggroup.org/resource/tcg-storage-security-subsystem-class-opalite/

[S-26] Trusted Computing Group, "TCG Storage Work Group Storage Security Subsystem Class: Pyrite", 2018, available at https://trustedcomputinggroup.org/resource/tcg-storage-security-subsystem-class-pyrite/

[S-27] Trusted Computing Group, "TCG Storage Work Group Storage Security Subsystem Class: Enterprise", 2015, available at https://trustedcomputinggroup.org/resource/storage-work-group-storage-security-subsystem-class-enterprise-specification/

[S-28] Trusted Computing Group, "TCG Storage Work Group Storage Security Subsystem Class: Ruby", 2020, available at https://trustedcomputinggroup.org/resource/tcg-storage-security-subsystem-class-ruby-specification/

[S-29] Trusted Computing Group, "TCG Storage Feature Set: Block SID Authentication", 2015, available at https://trustedcomputinggroup.org/resource/tcg-storage-feature-set-block-sid-authentication-specification/

[S-30] Trusted Computing Group, "TCG Storage Opal SSC Feature Set: PSID", 2015, available at https://trustedcomputinggroup.org/resource/tcg-storage-opal-feature-set-psid/

[S-31] Trusted Computing Group, "TCG Storage Opal SSC Feature Set: PSK Secure Messaging", 2015, available at https://trustedcomputinggroup.org/resource/tcg-storage-opal-ssc-feature-set-psk-secure-messaging/

[S-32] Trusted Computing Group, "TCG Storage Opal SSC Feature Set: Configurable Namespace Locking", 2019, available at https://trustedcomputinggroup.org/resource/tcg-storage-opal-ssc-feature-set-configurable-namespace-locking/

[S-33] Trusted Computing Group, "TCG Storage Opal SSC Feature Set: Single User Mode", 2015, available at https://trustedcomputinggroup.org/resource/tcg-storage-opal-ssc-feature-set-single-user-mode/

[S-34] Trusted Computing Group, "TCG Storage Opal SSC Feature Set: Additional DataStore Tables", 2012, available at `https://trustedcomputinggroup.org/resource/tcg-storage-opal-ssc-feature-set-additional-datastore-tables/`

[S-35] Trusted Computing Group, "TCG Storage Enterprise SSC Feature Set: Locking LBA Ranges Control Specification", 2014, available at `https://trustedcomputinggroup.org/resource/tcg-storage-opal-ssc-feature-set-additional-datastore-tables/`

[S-36] Trusted Computing Group, "TCG Storage Opal Family Feature Set: Shadow MBR for Multiple Namespaces", 2019, available at `https://trustedcomputinggroup.org/wp-content/uploads/TCG_SWG_Feature_Set_ShadowMBR_for_Multiple_Namespaces_v1p00_r1p06_pubrev.pdf`

[S-37] IEEE 1667, "Standard Protocol for Authentication in Host Attachments of Transient Storage Devices", 2018, `https://standards.ieee.org/standard/1667-2018.html`

[S-38] T13 org, "Information technology – ATA Command Set – 4 (ACS-4)", 2016, `www.t13.org/`

[S-39] UEFI Organization, "ACPI Specification", 2019, available at `www.uefi.org/`

[S-40] PCI-SIG, "PCI Express Base Specification", 2019, available at `https://pcisig.com/specifications`

[S-41] IEEE 802.11i, "Wi-Fi Protected Access II", 2004, available at `http://standards.ieee.org/getieee802/download/802.11i-2004.pdf`

[S-42] IEEE 802.1X, "Port Based Network Access Control", 2010, available at `http://standards.ieee.org/getieee802/download/802.1X-2010.pdf`

[S-43] Bluetooth Org, "Bluetooth Core Specification", 2019, available at `www.bluetooth.com/specifications/bluetooth-core-specification/`

[S-44] IETF, "RFC 8446 – The Transport Layer Security (TLS) Protocol Version 1.3", 2018, available at `https://tools.ietf.org/html/rfc8446`

[S-45] IETF, "RFC 6347 – Datagram Transport Layer Security Version 1.2", 2012, available at `https://tools.ietf.org/html/rfc6347`

[S-46] Trusted Computing Group, "Trusted Platform Module Library", 2016, available at `https://trustedcomputinggroup.org/resource/tpm-library-specification/`

[S-47] SBS forum, "Smart Battery Data Specification", 1998, available at `http://sbs-forum.org/specs/`

Web

[W-1] "server certificate with invalid domain name (CN) accepted in HTTPS-over-IPv6 boot", `https://bugzilla.tianocore.org/show_bug.cgi?id=960`

CHAPTER 11

Configuration

User-configurable data can be used to control the firmware behavior with the same firmware code. The configuration data is designed to be updatable and mutated by the end user, whereas the firmware code is typically only editable by the platform manufacturer. As such, the protection of configuration data is different from the protection of the firmware code.

A UEFI variable is a way to store the UEFI firmware configuration. Let's take UEFI variables as an example to describe the different protection mechanisms. These mechanisms can be used for alternate implementation choices to implement the firmware configuration data.

UEFI Variables

According to the UEFI specification, UEFI variables are intended to store the data that is passed between the UEFI components, such as components from the platform manufacturer, UEFI applications, or UEFI OS loaders. The classic CIA (confidentiality, integrity, availability) security attributes should be considered properties of UEFI variables. The adversaries attacking UEFI variables can be categorized as software attackers and hardware attackers. Software attack can be performed via calling UEFI SetVariable/GetVariable API and using code to directly read/write the area where the variables are stored or cached, and hardware attack can be performed via powering off the system during variable update or using a flash programmer to read/write the flash region where the variables are stored. See Table 11-1 for the UEFI variable protection mechanisms. We will describe them one by one.

J. Yao and V. Zimmer, *Building Secure Firmware*, https://doi.org/10.1007/978-1-4842-6106-4_11

Table 11-1. *UEFI Variable Protection Mechanisms*

Mechanism	Resist Software Attack	Resist Hardware Attack
Integrity protection	Variable authentication	Variable with RPMB
	Trusted Execution Environment	Variable with RPMC
	Variable Lock	Variable with TPM storage
	Variable Sanity Check	
Availability protection	Variable quota management	Variable atomicity
	Flash wear-out protection	Fault-tolerant write (FTW)
Confidentiality protection	User Key Encrypted Variable	Platform Key Encrypted Variable
		User Key Encrypted Variable

Integrity Protection

Variable Authentication

The purpose of variable authentication is to ensure the entity that calls the SetVariable() API to update the UEFI variable has the authority to update the variable. According to the UEFI specification, the caller needs to provide the updated variable with the signed certificate in order to update an authenticated variable.

There are three kinds of authenticated variable formats:

1) Count-based authenticated variable, if the EFI_VARIABLE_ AUTHENTICATED_WRITE_ACCESS attribute is set (this is deprecated)

2) Time-based authenticated variable, if the EFI_VARIABLE_TIME_ BASED_AUTHENTICATED_WRITE_ACCESS attribute is set (currently used)

3) Extensible authenticated variable (time based or nonce based), if the EFI_VARIABLE_ENHANCED_AUTHENTICATED_WRITE_ ACCESS attribute is set (new)

When a user calls the SetVariable() API, the authenticated variable input data format is used. There is a timestamp or a nonce associated with the authentication descriptor. For the certificate type field, only PKCS7 is accepted for a time-based authenticated variable or extensible authenticated variable. The certificate is DER-encoded PKCS#7 version 1.5 SignedData. The most important fields are the signer's DER-encoded X.509 certificate, SHA256 hash of the metadata (VariableName, VariableGuid, Attributes), second descriptor (timestamp or nonce), optional additional nonce, optional additional certificate, and new variable data content. The descriptor is an extensible structure to identify a unique X.509 cert associated with a given variable. It could be a timestamp or a nonce value. The Authenticated Variable driver will check the authentication descriptor before updating the variable content. Figures 11-1 and 11-2 show the format of a time-based auth variable input and a nonce-based authenticated variable input. (* means the field is optional.)

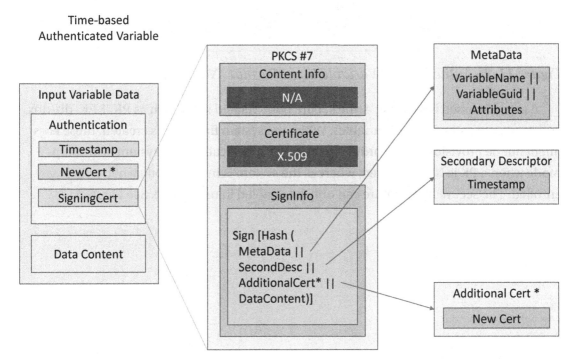

Figure 11-1. *Authenticated Variable Input Format (Time Based)*

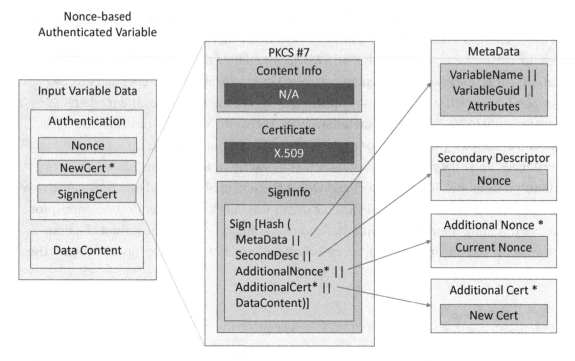

Figure 11-2. *Authenticated Variable Input Format (Nonce Based)*

As we discussed in Chapter 4, the secure boot–related keys, such as PK, KEK, db/dbx, and so on, are authenticated variables. When the system firmware is created, these keys might not be provisioned. According to the UEFI specification, the system is in setup mode when a PK is NOT enrolled, whereas the system is in user mode when a PK is enrolled. The secure boot feature can only be enabled in user mode. See Figure 11-3.

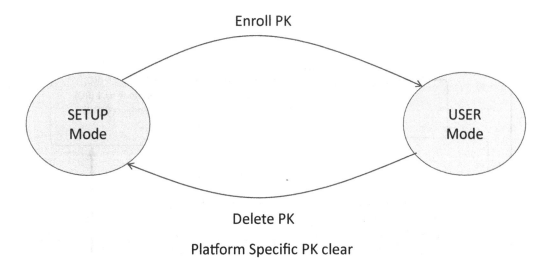

Figure 11-3. *UEFI Secure Boot Setup Mode vs. User Mode*

In the UEFI 2.5 specification, two additional modes were added – deployed mode and audit mode (see Figure 11-4). Audit mode is an extension for setup mode. Audit mode enables programmatic discovery of signature list combinations that successfully authenticate installed EFI images without the risk of rendering a system unbootable. Chosen signature list configurations can be tested to ensure the system will continue to boot after the system is transitioned out of audit mode. After transitioning to audit mode, signature enforcement is disabled such that all images are initialized and enhanced Image Execution Information Table (IEIT) logging is performed including recursive validation for multi-signed images.

Deployed mode is an extension for user mode. Deployed mode is the most secure mode. By design, both user mode and audit mode support unauthenticated transitions to Deployed Mode. However, to move from deployed mode to any other mode requires a secure platform-specific method, or deleting the PK, which is authenticated.

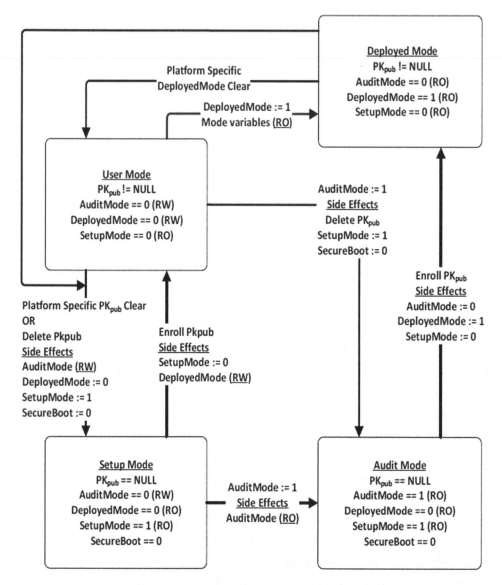

Figure 11-4. *UEFI2.5 Secure Boot Modes (Source: UEFI Specification)*

Updating the secure boot keys (PK, KEK, db/dbx, etc.) requires signing verification. However, it prevents the end user from updating the secure boot keys because the end user does not have the PK or KEK. As such, EDK II introduced two special secure boot modes (see Figure 11-5):

1) Standard secure boot mode: The default mode to follow the UEFI specification

2) Custom secure boot mode: Allows more flexibility as specified in the following:

- PK variable update need NOT be signed by an old PK.

- KEK variable update need NOT be signed by a PK.

- Image signature database (db/dbx), timestamp database (dbt), and recovery database (dbr) update need NOT be signed by PK or KEK.

The switch between standard mode and custom mode needs user physical presence, as we discussed in Chapter 10. There must be a platform-specific way to detect if a physical user is present in order to perform such an action.

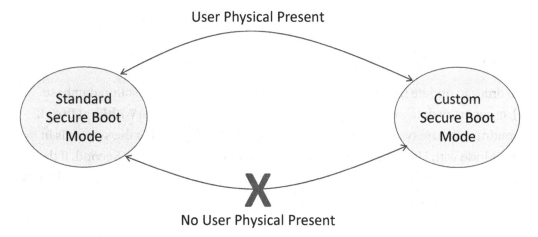

Figure 11-5. *Standard Secure Boot Mode vs. Custom Secure Boot Mode*

In order to update the PK or KEK, the following authentication flow is used. First, if the system is in CustomMode with UserPhysicalPresent, no authentication is needed. Second, if the system is in setup mode, no authentication is needed with the PK. Third, if the system is in user mode, authentication with the PK is performed. Last, if the system is in setup mode to enroll the PK, authentication with this payload is performed. See Figure 11-6.

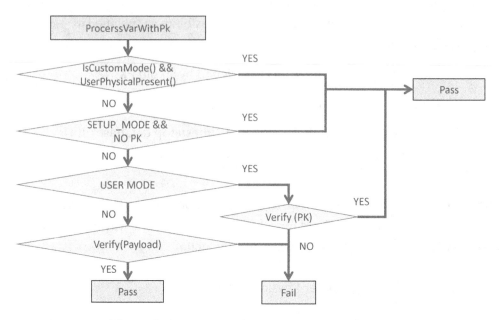

Figure 11-6. *Variable Authentication Flow – ProcessVarWithPk*

In order to update the image signature database (db/dbx), timestamp database (dbt), or recovery database (dbr), the system will invoke ProcessVarWithPk at first. If this routine fails, the system will invoke ProcessVarWithKek. First, if the system is in CustomMode with UserPhysicalPresent, no authentication is needed. Second, if the system is in setup mode, no authentication is needed. Last, authentication with KEK is performed. See Figure 11-7.

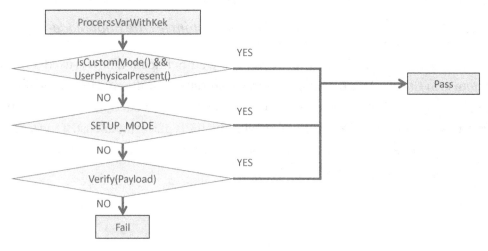

Figure 11-7. *Variable Authentication Flow – ProcessVarWithKek*

Other authenticated variables (other than those secure boot related) do not require the PK/KEK verification. The verification flow is different. First, if the variable requires physical presence, but the user is not physically present, the update request is rejected. Second, if the variable is a time-based authenticated variable, authentication with time and the creator's key is performed. Last, if an old variable has an AUTHENTICATED attribute which does not patch the current one, the update request is rejected. Or it means no authentication is needed. See Figure 11-8.

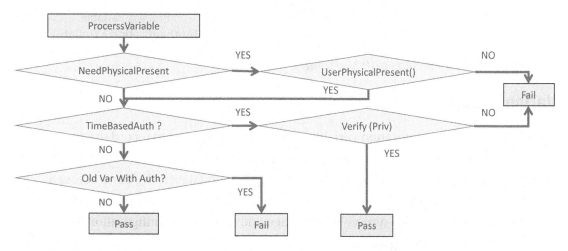

Figure 11-8. *Variable Authentication Flow – ProcessVariable*

Trusted Execution Environment

Similar to firmware image signing verification, the variable authentication and update requires a trusted execution environment. That achieves the non-bypassability of the capability.

The UEFI or OS runtime is not a trusted execution environment. For X86 systems, system management mode (SMM) is used for the implementation of the variable authentication services. The UEFI runtime service SetVariable puts the variable data and signature into an SMM communication buffer and triggers an SMI. Then the SetVariableHandler is invoked. It copies the communication buffer data into SMM and then processes the variable by performing the authentication and update. See Figure 11-9.

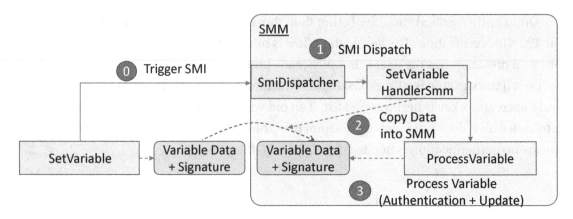

Figure 11-9. *TEE-Based Auth Variable Update*

Variable Lock

In addition to user configuration variables, the system may need to record the current platform data at runtime. For example, it can include the memory initialization training data. Memory training is time-consuming, and the training data is the same across a warm reset or S3 resume. As such, there is no need to train the memory again. We may save the training data to the non-volatile storage and restore the configuration directly after a warm reset or during a S3 resume.

How can we can make sure the configuration data is not modified by another entity? The easiest way is just to lock the variable and make it unchangeable at some point in time.

EDK II implements the EDKII_VARIABLE_LOCK_PROTOCOL to support marking some variables READ ONLY, by adopting the following rules:

- Before the EndOfDxe event, the EDKII_VARIABLE_LOCK_ PROTOCOL.RequestToLock() API is used to submit a Variable Lock request.

- This lock request itself is volatile. That means RequestToLock() must be called each boot.

- After the EndOfDxe event, the RequestToLock() API is closed.

Variable Lock policy rules are as follows:

- Before the EndOfDxe event, Variable Lock does not take effect because only the OEM BIOS code is executed and trusted.

- After the EndOfDxe event, Variable Lock takes effect in the DXE or OS runtime phase because the third-party code is not trusted. A locked variable cannot be deleted or updated. A locked variable cannot be created if it has not existed before.

- Variable Lock does not have any effect in SMM because SMM is constructed by the OEM BIOS and there is no non-platform code in SMM. Inside SMM, the variable can still be updated.

A full summary is shown in Figure 11-10.

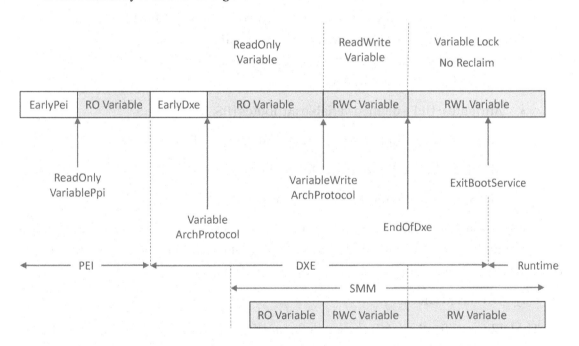

Figure 11-10. *Variable Features in Each Phase*

RO means read-only.

RW means read/write.

RWC means read/write, with reclaim feature.

RWL means read/write, with lock feature.

The UEFI specification also defined other attributes such as RUNTIME (RT).

Variables with the RT attribute are not accessible after the Exit Boot Service event.

Variable Sanity Check

A platform may define a setup variable that can be used by the UEFI Human Interface Infrastructure (HII) so that users can control the platform settings by updating a setup User Interface (UI). For example, a user can configure a SATA controller to be in IDE mode or AHCI mode or RAID mode. A setup variable field SataMode is used. 1 means IDE mode, 5 means AHCI mode, and 6 means RAID mode. Other values, such as 0, 2, 3, 4, or 7, are considered as invalid input.

The problem is that there is no way to check if some variable fields are valid and reject invalid variable updates. In the preceding example, when the code calls SetVariable() to update a setup variable, we hope the variable driver can check SataMode to see if the setting is valid (1, 5, or 6) and reject the variable update if the setting is invalid.

In order to resolve this problem, EDK II introduced "Variable Check" – the capability of checking variable contents based on a predefined policy.

In order to check a variable, a driver can register a SetVariable check handler to define properties for a specific variable:

- Attributes: UEFI-defined variable attributes (BS, RT, NV, etc.)

- Property: Non–UEFI-defined variable attributes (READ_ONLY)

- MinSize: The minimum size of the variable data

- MaxSize: The maximum size of the variable data

A system can have multiple variable checkers. Two examples of checkers are a UEFI Human Interface Infrastructure (HII)–based checker and a UEFI Platform Initialization (PI) Platform Configuration Database (PCD)–based checker:

1) HII-based checker

The UEFI specification's HII section defines HII opcodes that allow the setting UI to be linked with UEFI variable storage. Some other setup options go through the HII_CONFIG_ACCESS_PROTOCOL. They could link to a variable or some other storages. If a variable is associated with a setup option, we can use data in HII IFR opcode to check the legal configuration of variable content. For example, the variable mapped to the ONE_OF_OP, NUMERIC_OP, ORDERED_LIST_OP, or CHECKBOX_OP must be in a predefined range.

In order to achieve preceding checks, the VarCheckHii handler needs to get HII data from two sources:

- Static HII data: HII data built inside of the firmware volume. The EDK II build tool generates HII information into an FFS raw section (see Figure 11-11) or a UEFI-specific PE/COFF resource. The typical usage is setup configuration data. The information can be retrieved even if some special setup data is not installed into the HII database due to the current hardware configuration.

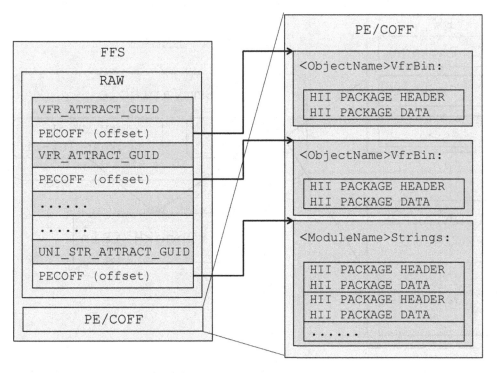

Figure 11-11. *HII Build Time Info*

- Dynamic HII data: HII data exposed by the HII_DATABASE_ PROTOCOL. This is the UEFI-defined way to get HII data from the HII database. The platform code or third-party option ROM may construct HII data dynamically from C code. All HII data is exposed by the HII_DATABASE_PROTOCOL.

Figure 11-12 shows the VarCheckHii process during system boot. During initialization, VarCheckHiiGen() collects HII information from the FV and HII_DATABASE_PROTOCOL and generates VarCheckHiiBin – a compact data structure to store the ONE_OF, NUMERIC, and CHECKBOX information. During runtime, SetVariableCheckHandlerHii() refers to VarCheckHiiBin to check if the variable content is legal. If variable attributes are different, data size is different, or the content does not satisfy the HII question, the variable content is treated as illegal, and EFI_SECURITY_VIOLATION is returned to the SetVariable() call to reject the variable update.

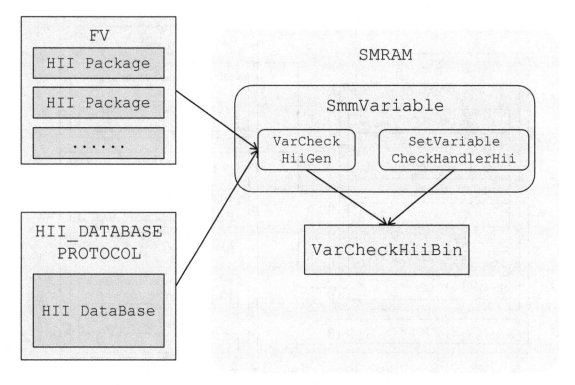

Figure 11-12. *Variable Check HII*

The EDK II VarCheckHii handler just uses a simple policy for ONE_OF, NUMERIC, and CHECKBOX opcodes because they are the most popular questions used for platform setup. A known limitation is that the inconsistent error checking opcodes are not supported, because evaluating these opcodes would require IFR expression parser support or reading other variable storage or buffer storage. The implementation might be too complicated.

2) PCD-based checker

EDK II PCDs are mapped to a UEFI variable if it is instantiated using the PcdDynamicHii access type. The EDK II PCD implementation also supports defining a set of valid configurations for a specific PCD in a DEC file, for example:

- @ValidList: Variable data must be in the list.

- @ValidRange: Variable data must be in the range.

Therefore, we have a way to check if the PCD-mapped variable is legal.

The EDK II build tool generates the information, and the information may be encoded in binary form in an FFS raw section. See Figure 11-13. During initialization, LocateVarCheckPcdBin () gets the VarCheckPcdBin binary from the FFS raw section. During runtime, SetVariableCheckHandlerPcd() refers to VarCheckPcdBin to check if the variable contents are legal. If variable attributes are different, variable size is too small, or the content does not satisfy the valid list or valid range for the PCD, then the variable content is treated as illegal, and the EFI_SECURITY_VIOLATION status code is returned.

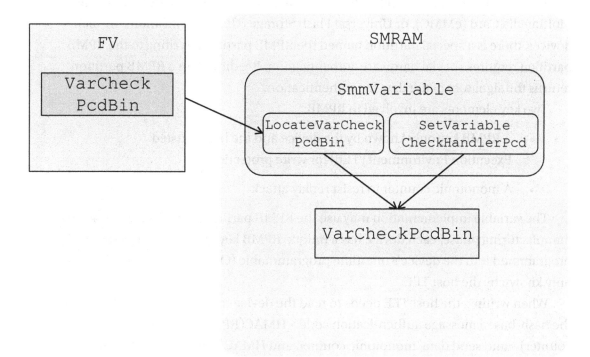

Figure 11-13. *Variable Check PCD*

PCDs include the offset in the variable but not the variable's size. We can only check if a variable is too small, but we cannot determine if a variable is too large. This is a known limitation of VarCheckPcd.

The EDK II VarCheckPcd handler uses a simple policy for @ValidList and @ValidRange. A known limitation is that PCD's @Expression validity check is unsupported, since this needs expression parser support. The implementation might be too complicated.

The variable checker only checks the variable format in SetVariable() API. It does not check variable format in GetVariable() API, assuming that if variable data is checked on Set, it must be correct on Get.

This assumption is true if our adversary is a software attacker, but it is not true for the hardware attacker, which we will discuss in the following section.

Variable with Replay Protected Memory Block (RPMB)

Some storage devices support Replay Protected Memory Block (RPMB) capability, such as those conforming to the Non-Volatile Memory Express (NVMe), Embedded Multimedia Card (eMMC), or Universal Flash Storage (UFS) specifications. In such devices, there is a special partition named the RPMB partition. Writing to the RPMB partition requires special hardware authentication. Reading from a RPMB partition returns the signature of the data for authentication.

Two key elements are involved in RPMB:

- A RPMB key only known by the device and the host Trusted Execution Environment (TEE) for write protection.

- A monotonic counter to resist replay attack

The variable implementation may use the RPMB partition (see Figure 11-14). In the manufacturing phase, each device has a unique RPMB key generated, and that key is programmed into the device's one-time programmable (OTP) area. The RPMB key is only known by the host TEE.

When writing, the host TEE needs to read the device monotonic counter, calculate the hash-based message authentication code – HMAC(RPMB key, data || monotonic counter) – and send data, monotonic counter, and HMAC to the device. The device will check if the monotonic counter is the same as the current one. If they are the same, then the device will verify the HMAC value. Only after the HMAC verification passes the device writes the data into the RPMB area and increases the monotonic counter.

When reading, the host TEE generates a random value and sends the read request to the device. The device reads out the data, calculates the HMAC(RPMB key, data || random value), and sends the data, random value, and HMAC to the host. After the host gets the data, the host will check whether the random value is the same as the current one. If they are the same, then the host will verify the HMAC value. Only after the HMAC verification passes the host can then make sure the data is from the real RPMB device.

One RPMB-capable device may have multiple RPMB partitions. Each RPMB partition can only have one owner. If we save UEFI variables into a RPMB partition, the BIOS is the owner for this partition. The SMM and Management Engine (ME) can be used as a TEE. In the manufacturing phase, the ME can generate a unique RPMB key and provision it to the RPMB device. During runtime, the SMM variable driver can get the RPMB key from the ME and get the monotonic counter from the RPMB device. When a UEFI runtime service is used to set a new variable, it sends a request to the SMM variable driver. The SMM variable driver then calculates the HMAC and sends both data and HMAC to the RPMB device. Then the RPMB device verifies the HMAC and writes the data onto the RPMB storage area.

UEFI Variable in RPMB

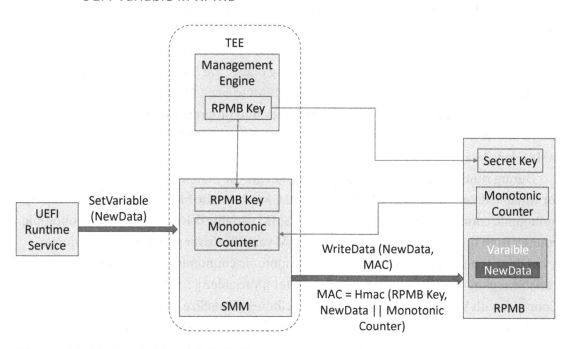

Figure 11-14. *Variable with RPMB*

The hardware attack to the variable won't succeed since the attacker does not know the RPMB key. As such, they cannot create a HMAC for the new variable data.

The replay attack can also be mitigated based upon the fact that the HMAC includes a monotonic counter. Writing old data will be rejected because the counter in the old HMAC does not match the current one.

Variable with Replay Protected Monotonic Counter (RPMC)

RPMB requires special storage devices. If a system does not have such a RPMB-capable device but only has a traditional SSD and SPI flash, then the enhanced SPI flash with Replay Protected Monotonic Counter (RPMC) capability can be used.

The RPMC device has a monotonic counter. A unique RPMC key is required to increment the monotonic counter. In the manufacturing phase, each RPMC device has a unique RPMC key generated and programmed into the device's one-time programmable (OTP) area. The RPMC key is only known by the host TEE. As such, the host TEE can increment the monotonic counter with the MAC-based authentication.

RPMC SPI devices have no flash write authentication capability. The host TEE can access the RPMC-capable SPI device like a normal SPI device. The value of the RPMC SPI device that it provides a monotonic counter which can help to resist the replay attack.

The variable implementation may leverage the RPMC counter and a platform key in the ME (see Figure 11-15). In the manufacturing phase, the ME can generate a unique RPMC root key and provision the key into the RPMC device. During system initialization, the ME can generate a random RPMC HMAC key and program the RPMC HMAC key to the RPMC device via the UpdateHmacKey() command with HMAC(RPMC root key, new HMAC key data).

During runtime, the SMM variable driver can get the platform key from the ME for variable data MAC and get the RPMC HMAC key from the ME to increment the monotonic counter of the RPMC device. The SMM variable driver also gets the monotonic counter from the RPMC device. When the SMM variable driver gets a request to update a variable, it uses the platform key and the monotonic counter to create a HMAC for the variable region – HMAC(platform key, Variable1 || Variable2 || ... || VariableN || Monotonic Counter), with VariableX = Name || Guid || Attributes || DataSize || Data. Then the SMM variable driver saves both the data and the HMAC to the flash device. This HMAC is saved as the variable metadata. Because the HMAC is calculated with the platform key, the attacker cannot tamper with the HMAC. Finally, the SMM variable driver sends the IncrementCounter() command to the RPMC device with HMAC(RPMC Hmac Key, monotonic counter). On the next boot, the variable driver reads all of the variable data and the metadata. The variable driver calculates the HMAC with the platform key, all variable data, and the monotonic counter. Then the variable driver compares the calculated HMAC with the variable metadata. If they are the same, then the variable region is good. Otherwise, the variable region has been updated by an unauthorized entity. After such a mismatch is found, the recovery process is triggered.

UEFI Variable in RPMC

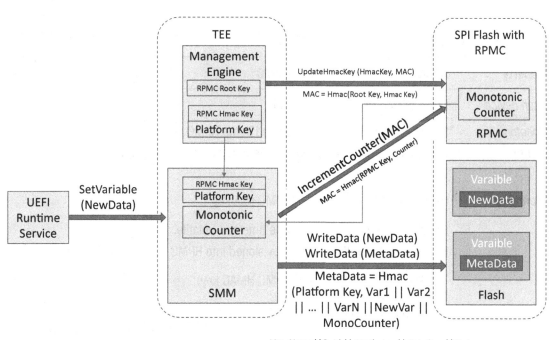

Var=Name||Guid || Attributes || DataSize || Data

Figure 11-15.   *Variable with RPMC*

Hardware writes to the variable region will succeed. However, this attack will be detected on the next boot based upon the variable's metadata and based upon the fact that the attacker does not have the platform key and cannot create the valid HMAC. Once the attack is detected, the system firmware must trigger the variable recovery process. The firmware settings for recovery have been discussed in Chapter 5.

The replay attack can also be mitigated based upon the fact that the HMAC includes a monotonic counter. Writing the same old data will be rejected because the counter in the old HMAC does not match the current one. Also, the attacker cannot send the command to increment the RPMC monotonic counter, based upon the fact that the attacker does not have the RPMC root key and RPMC HMAC key.

Compared with RPMB, the RPMC solution is more difficult to implement because the SMM variable driver needs to calculate a metadata variable to store the MAC for the variable region and also needs increment the monotonic counter. The advantage of the RPMC solution is that there is no flash device dependency – the SPI device can be used. The difference between RPMC-based SPI flash solution and RPMB-based NVMe/eMMC/UFS flash storage solution is in Table 11-2.

Table 11-2. *Variable with RPMB vs. RPMC*

Property	RPMB	RPMC
Flash device	NVMe/eMMC/UFS.	SPI.
Monotonic counter	Stored in the RPMB device. Counter increased for every write.	Stored in the RPMC device. Counter increased for every write.
Secret key	RPMB key:	RPMC root key:
	One time non-volatile. Provisioned into RPMB during manufacture. Host TEE gets the key from the ME during runtime.	One time non-volatile. Provisioned into RPMC during manufacture. RPMC HMAC key: Generated during boot time. Host TEE gets the key from the ME during runtime. Platform key: One time non-volatile. Host TEE gets the key from the ME during runtime.
Content storage	In RPMB device.	In SPI flash device.

(continued)

Table 11-2. (*continued*)

Property	RPMB	RPMC
Security property	Integrity, confidentiality, availability.	Integrity.
Protection (write authentication)	Done by the RPMB device. Write MAC is calculated by the host TEE and verified by RPMB.	No. RPMC SPI flash does not have capability for write authentication. MAC is calculated by the host TEE and stored on the flash device.
Detection (read verification)	Done by the host TEE. Read MAC is calculated by the RPMB device and verified by the host TEE.	Done by the host TEE. MAC is calculated by the host TEE at write operation and verified once during initialization in next boot.
Recovery	Not required.	Required, if the hardware modification is detected on the next boot.

Variable with TPM Storage

Besides the flash device, the TPM non-volatile storage may be used to hold the variable data (see Figure 11-16). Because the TPM chip is tamper proof, the simple hardware attacker may not modify the data in TPM directly. However, the limitation is that because of the TPM non-volatile storage size, we are not able to write very big non-volatile data into TPM.

The alternative is to record a hash of the variable data. As such, the unauthorized modification can be detected later if the attacker updated the variable region directly.

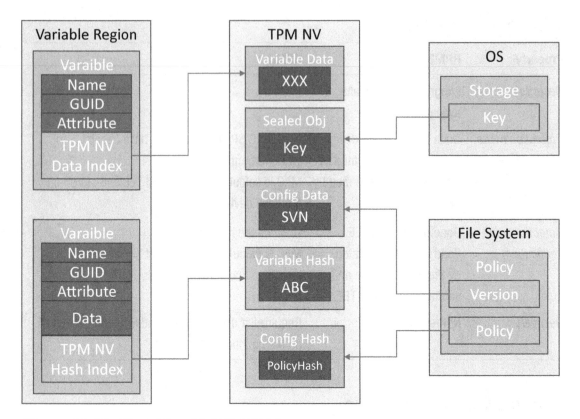

Figure 11-16. *Variable with TPM NV Storage*

The TPM NV storage can be used to save UEFI variable data. It can also be used to save UEFI variable–independent data. As such, the caller needs to use the TPM interface to access the variable data, instead of the UEFI interface. If the TPM NV storage stores the hash, the variable data can be in the UEFI variable or other storage such as the file system, as long as the caller knows where to get the data.

The TPM non-volatile storage can be an NV index or a sealed object.

We have discussed sealing usage in Chapter 7. Here are the steps of sealed object usage. The VariableData is sealed to be a TPM object by the TPM2_Create command with AuthPolicyHash. The output is the public area (outPublic) and the encrypted sensitive area (outPrivate). The PCR value may be used as AuthPolicy. The outPublic and outPrivate are saved in UEFI NV. The outPublic and outPrivate can be used to unseal to the VariableData by the TPM2_Load and TPM2_Unseal commands.

The TPM NV index variable should be defined before it is used. A TPM NV variable must have an index, and index-specific authorization policies, which can be used to authorize reading and writing to the TPM NV. The policy includes a password/key, PCR value, locality value, read/write lock, and so on. These policies can be defined by the TPM2 Enhanced Authorization (EA) commands in a policy session. For a policy session, some commands require checking something at execution time. For example, TPM2_PolicyCounterTimer checks the TPMS_TIME_INFO structure, TPM2_PolicyLocality checks the locality information, TPM2_PolicyPCR checks the PCR value, and TPM2_PolicyPassword checks the password value. TPM2 provides a more flexible policy control via EA, which can be used to create the policy AND or policy OR. For example, one object may be accessed when the PCR value matches and the locality value matches. Another object may be accessed when the PCR value matches or the password value matches. We can store the VariableData into TPM NV with EA command PolicySession for access control. Table 11-3 shows the TPM storage usage. Besides integrity, the TPM storage solution can also provide confidentiality.

Table 11-3. *Variable with TPM Storage*

Property	TPM NV Index (Data)	TPM NV Index (Hash)	TPM Sealed Object (Data)	TPM Sealed Object (Hash)
TPM access control	The TPM NV index has flexible attributes, such as read lock, write lock, write once, and increment-only. The TPM NV can use policy session for access control, such as PCRs, locality, and user password.		The sealed object is bound to TPM PCRs.	
Security property	Integrity, confidentiality, availability.	Integrity.	Integrity, confidentiality.	Integrity.
Use case	Intel ACM/SGX secure version number (SVN). coreboot firmware version number.	Intel TXT Launch Control Policy (LCP) – policy hash.	Windows BitLocker key.	

Availability Protection

Variable Quota Management

Any system resource is limited, including variable storage. A typical platform may allocate around a 128K~256K region for variable storage. Sometimes the variable region may be full, and SetVariable() returns OUT_OF_RESOURCE. It might happen when a QA engineer runs a test in the UEFI shell or a hacker tries to attack the system in the OS. How do we handle that?

Most modern OSs (Linux and Windows) have disk quota management to set a limit for disk storage for a special user or group, give notification if the disk is nearly full, and let the user clean up. In EDK II, we enabled a similar mechanism for variable quota management.

EDK II defines a set of variable size–related PCDs:

- PcdFlashNvStorageVariableSize: The whole variable storage region size on flash

- PcdMaxVariableSize: The maximum size of a single non–HwErr-type variable

- PcdMaxAuthVariableSize: The maximum size of a single authenticated variable

- PcdMaxHardwareErrorVariableSize: The maximum size of a single hardware error record variable

- PcdVariableStoreSize: The size of a volatile buffer

- PcdHwErrStorageSize: The size of reserved HwErr variable space

- PcdBoottimeReservedNvVariableSpaceSize: The size of NV variable space reserved at UEFI boot time

- PcdMaxUserNvVariableSpaceSize: The size of maximum user NV variable space

The last three PCDs are used for quota management (see Figure 11-17).

PcdHwErrStorageSize indicates the space reserved for the UEFI hardware error logging variable only.

PcdBoottimeReservedNvVariableSpaceSize indicates the space reserved for UEFI boot time. Even if a malicious code writes into the variable space until out of resource state at OS runtime, the BIOS can still write a new variable at boot time.

PcdMaxUserNvVariableSpaceSize indicates the maximum space that can be used for a user NV variable. The EDK II variable driver divides variables into two groups: system variables and user variables. The following types of variables will be regarded as a system variable after EndOfDxe:

- UEFI-defined variables (gEfiGlobalVariableGuid and gEfiImageSecurityDatabaseGuid variables at least), for example, L"ConIn", L"ConOut", L"db", and L"dbx"

- Variables managed by the variable driver internally, for example, L"CustomMode" and L"VendorKeysNv"

- Variables that need to be locked and MUST be set by the Variable Lock protocol, for example, L"PhysicalPresenceFlags"

- Important variables during platform boot – their properties SHOULD be set by the VarCheck protocol – for example, L"MemoryOverwriteRequestControl", L"MemoryOverwriteRequestC ontrolLock", and platform setup variable for system configuration

If a variable is not a system variable, it is a user variable.

System variables can be authenticated variables or non-auth variables. User variables can also be authenticated variables or non-auth variables.

The reason the EDK II variable driver supports a limit for user NV variables is that the variable driver wants to make sure there is enough space for system variables. System variables are critical for system boot. User variables are less important.

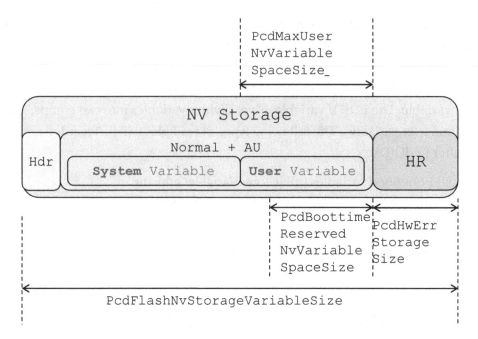

Figure 11-17. *Variable Quota Allocation*

When the quota limitation is hit, the EDK II variable driver needs to record the error. Then a platform owner may take action to recover the system to a good state.

This error information is recorded in the L"VarErrorFlag" variable. The EDK II variable driver uses 1 byte to record the error. 0xFF means no error. 0xEF means system variable out of space. 0xFE means user variable out of space. If the system gets a 0xEE later, it means both system variable and user variable are out of space.

On the next boot, if a platform detects L"VarErrorFlag" is in an error state, it may use a platform-specific way to clean up some unused variables. The system variables can be handled differently than user variables. The possible implementation could be

- System variable out of space: Enter Setup to let the user load default settings; or force clear the variable region and treat as a first boot.

- User variable out of space: Prompt a setup page and list all user variables to let the user select which user variables to be deleted or just delete all user variables.

Flash Wear-Out Protection

The SPI is a NOR flash device. In order to change a bit from 1 to 0, the code can send a WRITE command to the device to update 1 byte. However, in order to change a bit from 0 to 1, the code must send an ERASE command to the device to erase a 4 KiB or 64 KiB block to all 1s and then send a write command to update 1 byte. Ideally, the user is free to set configuration at any time. However, the SPI flash device has the ERASE limitation. When the number of flash ERASE actions reaches the limit, the flash is no longer usable.

The variable driver takes this into account on the variable storage design. The variable exists in a special variable firmware volume (FV). The variable FV can be identified by gEfiSystemNvDataFvGuid in the File System GUID field of the FV header. The Authenticated Variable can be identified by gEfiAuthenticatedVariableGuid in the GUID field of the variable store header. 0x5A in the Format field of a variable store header means this region is formatted. 0xFE in the State field of the variable store header means healthy. Figure 11-18 shows the variable storage format and the individual variable formats.

Each individual variable is saved after the variable storage header. 0x55AA in StartId of a variable header means there is a new variable storage. 0x3F in the State field means it is a valid variable added. 0x3D in the State field means it is deleted. In some rare case, system reset during variable update, a 0x7F in the State field means only the header is valid and no real variable data written. 0x3E in the State field means this variable is in delete transition.

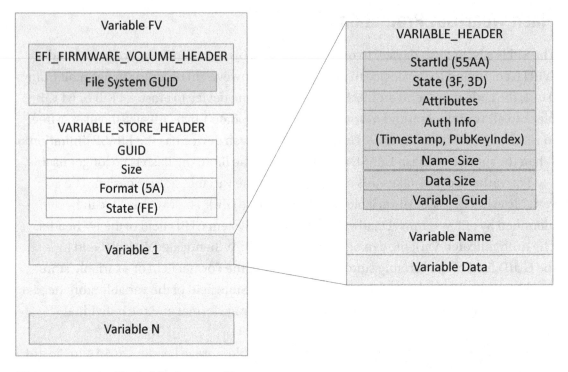

Figure 11-18. *Variable Storage Format*

The State field is extremely useful on variable updates. Figure 11-19 shows the variable update flow:

1) The old variable state is marked as InDeleted.

2) The new variable full header is added with state unchanged (0xFF).

3) The new variable state is changed to Header Valid state.

4) New variable full data is added.

5) The new variable state is changed to Added.

6) The old variable state is marked as deleted.

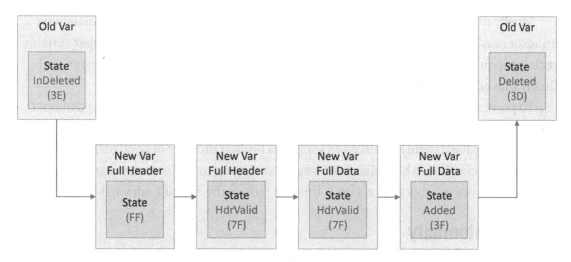

Figure 11-19. *Variable Update Flow*

From the preceding variable update flow, when a variable is updated, it is actually not UPDATED in the original place, but marked as DELETED in the original place and then ADDED in a new place. If a user updates the variable several times, the non-volatile storage will have many DELETED variables which are useless but occupy storage space.

In this case, there is a mechanism called reclaim to reorganize the variable region (see Figure 11-20). Reclaim removes the DELETED variables to save space. Reclaim is triggered in the following conditions:

1) When updating a variable or adding a new variable and there is not enough free space

2) On exiting the OEM phase (EndOfDxe event) and there is not enough remaining free space

3) On initialization and the variable storage free space is not all 0xFF (there must be something wrong)

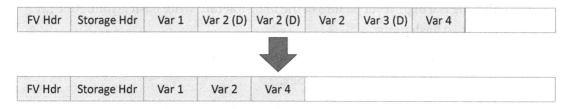

Figure 11-20. *Variable Reclaim*

411

Ideally the variable reclaim should not happen frequently. However, the malicious attacker may manipulate a variable update service in a dramatic way and trigger variable reclaim again and again. Then the flash ERASE command is sent again and again, and finally that action causes the flash device to become broken.

To prevent this from happening, the ERASE command shall be only allowed at boot time within the OEM manufacture code. The ERASE command should be disabled at runtime. Only flash write is allowed to support a limited number of configurations. As such, the attacker has to boot the system again and again to perform the wear-out attack. Because the system reboot needs time, this can reduce the risk of flash wear-out.

Variable Atomicity

As we discussed how to update variable in the preceding section, only 1-byte write from bit 1 to bit 0 can be atomic for the NOR flash device from the hardware perspective. This state is designed to maintain atomicity of individual variables from the software perspective. Each variable exists in ALL-or-NONE state. A partial variable is not allowed. See Figure 11-19.

Fault-Tolerant Write

Individual variable atomicity is maintained by the variable update flow. However, during variable reclaim, the flash block will be erased and written again. In that period of time, if there is a power loss or system shutdown due to a user mistake, the variable firmware volume will be partially destroyed. That means if a variable crosses a flash block, it might be partially correct. The atomicity is broken in this scenario, which is not acceptable.

Fault-tolerant write (FTW) is designed to handle this situation. The EDK II FTW driver is not included in the variable driver. It is a standalone driver to provide the capability of fault-tolerant write. Every flash update driver can consume the FTW protocol API to update the flash part in a safe manner.

The following is a high-level picture of the fault-tolerant write flash layout. An FTW driver requires two flash parts:

1) FTW working block: This is a block to record a write action. It is the record block, not the data block.

2) FTW spare block: This is a real data block to save the data. It must be bigger than the size of the block required to perform the update. In this case, it must be bigger than the variable region.

In the FTW working block, the FTW driver puts a data structure to record the write request and write status. Figure 11-21 shows the fault-tolerant write flash layout.

The signature field of the WORKING_BLOCK_HEADER is used to identify if it is the FTW working block. After the header, there will be multiple WriteQueueEntry's. Each WriteQueueEntry has one WRITE_HEADER and one or more WRITE_RECORDs. The number of WRITE_RECORDs is recorded as the NumberOfWrites fields of the WRITE_HEADER. The most important fields are the Complete field of the WRITE_HEADER, the SpareComplete, and the DestinationComplete of the WRITE_RECORD. Those fields record the status of writes and guarantee the fault tolerance.

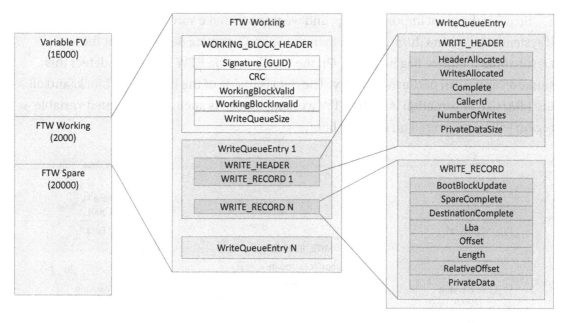

Figure 11-21. *Fault-Tolerant Write Flash Layout*

Now, let's see how FTW->Write() works. Figure 11-22 shows the detailed steps:

1) Step 1: When FTW->Write() is invoked, this API will record the request in the FTW working block.

2) Step 2: This API finds SpareBuf on the FTW spare flash area and backs it up to memory.

3) Step 3: This API writes NewData to the FTW spare block, instead of the variable FV.

4) Step 4: After that, it sets the SpareComplete flag in the FTW working block.

5) Step 5. This API writes NewData from the FTW spare block to the variable FV.

6) Step 6: After that, it sets the DestinationComplete flag in the FTW working block.

7) Step 7: If it is the last WRITE_RECORD associated with WRITE_ HEADER, this API sets the Complete flag in WRITE_HEADER.

8) Step 8: SpareBuf is restored in the FTW spare block. Then FTW->Write() finishes.

Step 5 is the most important step, and we want to make sure it is fault tolerant. If system reset occurs during step 5, then the SpareComplete flag is set, but the DestinationComplete flag is not set. On the next boot, the FTW driver will detect this situation and try to perform recovery. The data is inside of the FTW spare block, and all the LBA/size information is in the FTW working block. As such, the corrupted variable region will be recovered on the next boot.

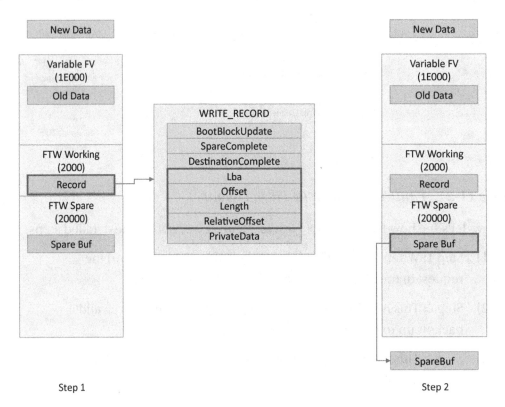

Step 1   Step 2

Figure 11-22(1). *FTW Steps 1 and 2*

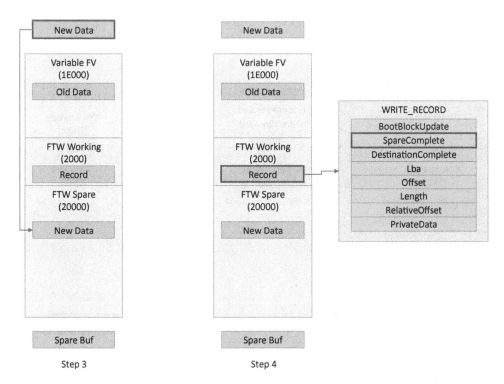

Figure 11-22(2). *FTW Steps 3 and 4*

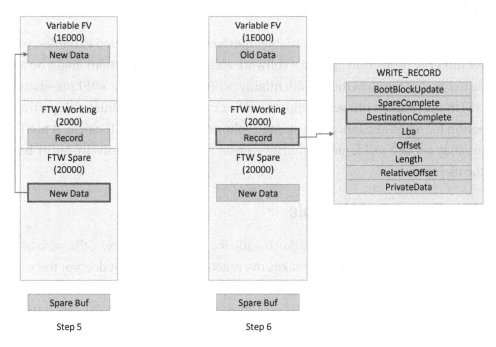

Figure 11-22(3). *FTW Steps 5 and 6*

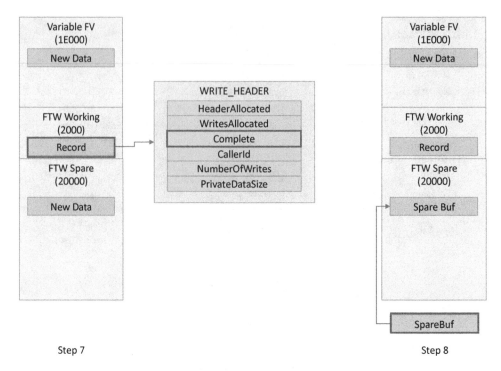

Figure 11-22(4). FTW Steps 7 and 8

Confidentiality Protection

The UEFI specification defines the variable interface for authenticated variables, which provides integrity protection against a software attacker. However, there might be some variable usage that requires the confidentiality protection, such as a WIFI pre-shared key (PSK) in the preboot phase to support further reconnection, a Bluetooth pairing key information for reconnection, and a storage volume key to decrypt the disk. A platform firmware may choose a different authority – a user or a platform hardware entity based upon the use case.

User Key Encrypted Variable

If a user is required to provide the authorization for the variable access, the variable data is bound to a user. If another person takes the machine, they cannot decrypt the variable content. The data migration is easy. If a user copies the data to another machine, they can still access the same data. The only disadvantage is that the physical user must be present to perform the user authentication.

We have discussed the three types of user authentication in Chapter 10: 1) what the user knows, such as password; 2) what the user has, such as hardware token; and 3) what the user is, such as biometrics. Take the user password as an example. In this case, the password itself can be used as a root key to derive the encryption key. Then the encryption key can be used to encrypt or decrypt the variable data.

Platform Key Encrypted Variable

If a platform is required to provide the authorization for the variable access, the variable data is bound to a platform. It is different from the user binding. If another person takes the machine, they may get the decrypted content because the platform authority has zero knowledge on which user is using the machine. If data migration is needed, the user must use the old platform authority to decrypt the data, copy data to a new machine, and use the new platform authority to encrypt the data.

In practice, there could be different platform authorities. For example, the Trusted Platform Module (TPM) Platform Configuration Register (PCR) could be used to seal the variable data or the key to encrypt the variable data. The sealed object is saved in the TPM non-volatile storage. When the firmware wants to get the variable, it just sends an unseal command to the TPM device. It is the TPM hardware that checks and returns the data if the PCR policy matches. We have discussed this in Chapter 7 and previous sections – variable with TPM storage.

The other example is to use a platform key (see Figure 11-23). During the manufacturing phase, each platform can generate a unique platform key and save the key to a secure coprocessor, such as Intel Converged Security and Management Engine (CSME). The platform system firmware can get the platform key at initialization time and save the key in the trusted execution environment. Then this platform key can be used to encrypt and decrypt the variable data.

UEFI Variable Encryption

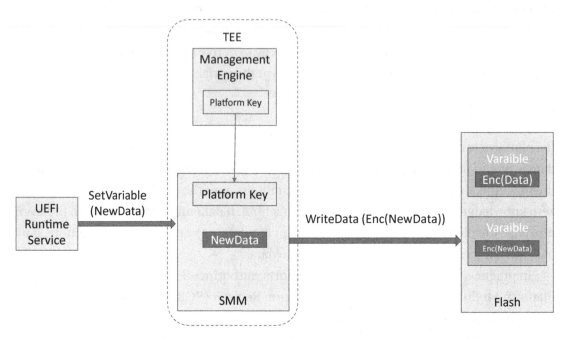

Figure 11-23. *Variable Encryption*

The platform key–based encryption might not able to resist the software attacker because an attacker may just write a software program to call the GetVariable service to ascertain the decrypted data. If this is a threat, the solution needs to use another mechanism to prevent the GetVariable service from being invoked.

The user authority and the platform authority can be combined together to provide more security. For example, a solution can use the TPM NV index to save the variable data with the policy PCR (platform authority) and policy password (user authority). If the PCR matches and the user provides the correct password, only then the variable can be decrypted.

Table 11-4 shows the difference between the user authority and platform authority.

Table 11-4. *Authority of the Confidential Variable*

Property	User	Platform
Authentication mechanism	User authentication, such as what a user knows, what a user has, and what a user is.	Platform property, such as TPM Platform Configuration Register (PCR) and platform key – from a secure coprocessor.
Binding	Bind to a user. If another person takes the machine, they cannot decrypt the variable content.	Bind to a platform. If another person takes the machine, they may get the decrypted content.
User interaction	Required.	Not required.
Data Migration	Easy.	Hard.
Adversary	Software attack, hardware attack	Hardware attack
Example	User inputs password as encryption key.	Management Engine provides the RPMB key. CSME provides the variable encryption key. TPM PCR seals the variable encryption key.

It is possible that we can use a user password or a platform PCR to seal the data encryption key directly. However, a better way is to use a key encryption key (KEK) to protect the encryption key and only bind the KEK to the user or the platform (see Figure 11-24). The data encryption key might be backed up to another source, such as a USB key device, just in case that the user forgets the password or the platform PCRs are changed.

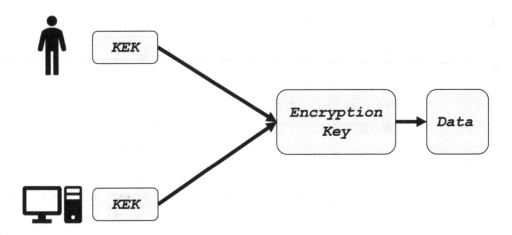

Figure 11-24. *Key Encryption Key*

The key from the user or the platform can also be used as the root key to create a key hierarchy (see Figure 11-25). The root key can be used to encrypt the subkey. It is the subkey that encrypts the final secret variable data. The subkey can be created by the user and saved into the NV storage area. The subkey can also be derived from the root key automatically by using a key deviation function such as the HMAC-based key deviation function (HKDF), for example:

$$VarEncKey = HKDF\_Expand\ (SHA256, RootKey,$$
$$VarName\|VarGuid\|Attributes\|"VAR\_ENC\_KEY")$$

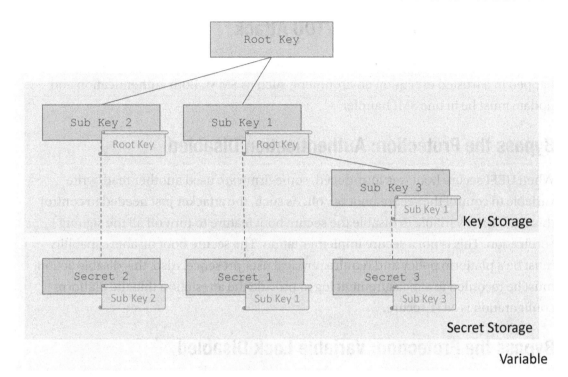

Figure 11-25. *Key Hierarchy*

The encrypted variable data is only on the flash region. For performance considerations, the variable data may save a copy of the decrypted variable data in the memory as a cache to support GetVariable() API. In this case, we need other technologies to resist the hardware attack to the system memory, such as Total Memory Encryption (TME).

Attack and Mitigation

Now, let's take a look at some real use cases for the attack against UEFI variables and mitigation.

Malformed Input

The authenticated variable requires the signature verification. The attacker may construct a malformed variable input data, such as no signing data or bad signing data. The signing verification code should reject the no signing data as well as the bad signing data.

Bypass the Protection: TOC/TOU Attack

Similar to the image signing verification, the variable authentication and update must happen in a trusted execution environment, such as SMM. Both authentication and update must be in one SMI handler.

Bypass the Protection: Authentication Disabled

When UEFI secure boot was introduced, some firmware used another read/write variable to control the secure boot on/off. As such, the attacker just needed to control this read/write variable to disable the secure boot feature to turn off all the signing verification. This is not a secure implementation. The secure boot disable capability must be a platform policy and require physical user presence. Also, this disable action must be recorded to a measurement log to provide the attestation that the platform configuration is NOT secure.

Bypass the Protection: Variable Lock Disabled

Ideally, the read-only variable should be locked in any possible boot path, such as normal boot, S3 resume, capsule update, and so on. If this read-only variable is not locked in a special boot path, then the attack may trigger this patch and modify the variable content.

Replay Attack: Software

The software replay attack means to save a valid variable input data and try to call it later. See Figure 11-26.

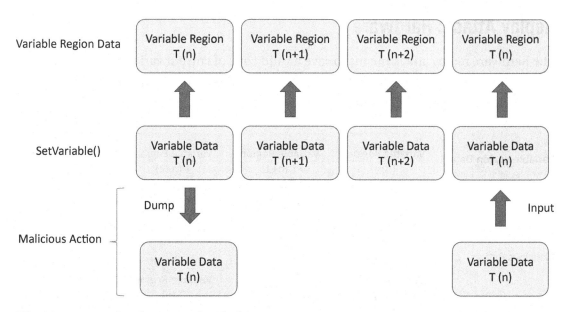

Figure 11-26. *Replay Attack – Software*

In order to prevent the software replay attack, the UEFI authentication variable must be used. It could be a time-based auth variable or nonce-based auth variable. For the time-based auth variable, the new timestamp must be greater than the old one. As such, the signature is invalid because the timestamp is older. For the nonce-based auth variable, the new nonce data must be different from current nonce. As such, the signature is invalid because the nonce value is changed. See Figure 11-27.

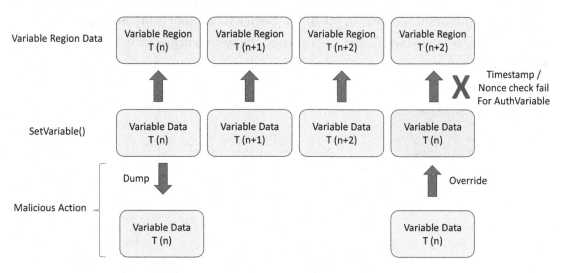

Figure 11-27. *Replay Attack Prevention – Time-Based/Nonce-Based Auth Variable*

423

Replay Attack: Hardware

The hardware replay attack means to save a valid copy of current variable configuration and restore the same configuration later via a flash programmer to update the flash content directly. See Figure 11-28.

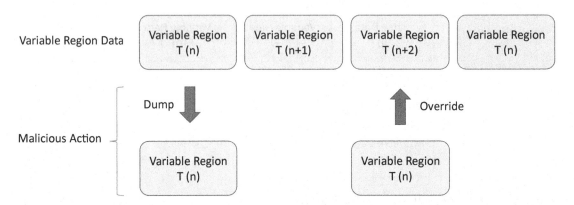

Figure 11-28. *Replay Attack – Hardware*

In order to prevent the hardware replay attack, the UEFI variable may use a hardware-based monotonic counter, such as RPMB or RPMC. For the RPMB-based variable, the flash data write will fail, because the old monotonic counter is smaller than the current RPMB device monotonic counter (see Figure 11-29). For the RPMC-based variable, the flash data write will succeed because of the absence of flash protection. But on the next boot, the attack will be detected. The MAC of the variable region is invalid because the monotonic counter in the RPMC device is different from the one involved in the MAC calculation (see Figure 11-30). Then the system firmware will trigger the recovery process.

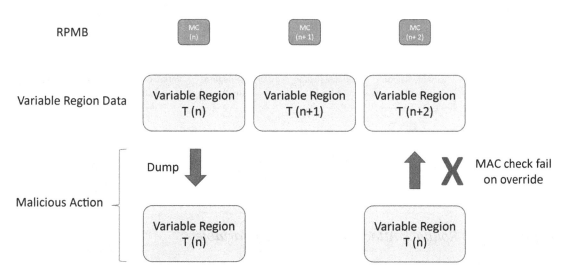

Figure 11-29. *Replay Attack Prevention with RPMB*

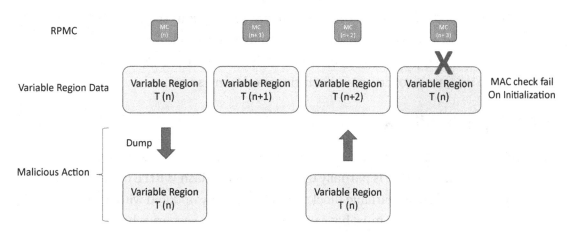

Figure 11-30. *Replay Attack Prevention with RPMC*

Rollback Attack

In the preceding section, we know that the hardware replay attack can be detected with RPMC, with the consequence of variable recovery. This can be used as a special attack to roll back the current UEFI secure boot variable to the old manufacture version (see Figure 11-31). This is very dangerous for UEFI secure boot because the UEFI secure boot variable policy may be updated to add the latest image forbidden database (dbx). The recommendation is that the platform system firmware should update the manufacturer default forbidden database along with the current used forbidden database.

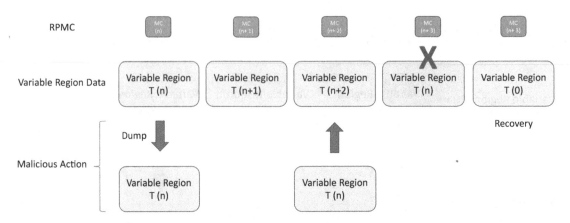

Figure 11-31. *Rollback Attack – RPMC-Based Variable*

Flash Wear-Out Attack

We have discussed the flash wear-out protection in the previous section. The key is to lock the flash erase action after OEM platform manufacture code. Care must be taken that this lock must happen in any boot mode, such as normal boot, S4 resume, S3 resume, flash update, recovery, manufacturing mode, and so on.

Partial Update Attack

An attacker may power off the system during the variable data update. One possibility is that an individual variable is partially updated with the flash WRITE command. The other possibility is that the variable block region is partially updated with the flash ERASE command. The BIOS must have ways to detect both scenarios based upon the hardware limitation. If the hardware can guarantee the data updating at the block level, the detection mechanism shall be in the block-based mechanism, such as a Replay Protected Memory Block (RPMB) device. If the hardware can guarantee the data updating at the byte level, the detection mechanism shall be at the byte level, such as a Replay Protected Monotonic Counter (RPMC)–capable SPI device.

For the individual variable update, the variable atomicity must be guaranteed, which we have discussed in the previous section. Each variable exists in ALL-or-NONE state.

For the variable block region update, the fault-tolerant write must be used, which we have also discussed in the previous section. The variable region can be recovered on the next boot if the corruption is detected.

426

UEFI PI Firmware Volume

Besides UEFI variable, the configuration data can be saved to a UEFI PI firmware volume (FV). See Table 11-5 for the UEFI PI configuration FV protection mechanisms. If a key is used to verify the integrity of the configuration FV data in the update or boot, the key itself must be protected as well to resist the same attack. Otherwise, the attacker can modify the verification key to bypass the protection.

Table 11-5. *UEFI PI Configuration FV Protection Mechanism*

Mechanism	Resist Software Attack	Resist Hardware Attack
Integrity Protection	Flash region lock Signed Update, such as UEFI signed capsule update.	Hardware root-of-trust based verification, such as Intel Boot Guard, Intel Platform Firmware Resilience
Availability Protection	Flash Wear-out Protection Update Version Check	Fault Tolerant Write Default/Golden Configuration Recovery
Confidentiality Protection	User-Key Encryption	Platform-Key Encryption User-Key Encryption

UEFI PI PCD (Platform Configuration Data)

UEFI variables provide read/write configuration data support based upon a name/GUID pair. Besides UEFI variables, the UEFI Platform Initialization (PI) specification defines the Platform Configuration Database (PCD) concept to abstract the configuration data with a token ID. The PCD could be static data fixed at build time or dynamic data editable at runtime.

Static PCD:

- PcdsFeatureFlag: This type of PCD only supports 1/0. The caller uses FeaturePcdGet() to retrieve the value. This type of PCD is mapped to be a MACRO so that a compiler optimization can remove the code scoped by "if(FALSE)". It is not allowed to set as a PcdsFeatureFlag.

- PcdsFixedAtBuild: This type of PCD can be mapped to a global variable if the caller uses PcdGet() or a MACRO if the caller uses FixedPcdGet(). As such, this type of PCD can be used in a data structure definition. It is not allowed to set as a PcdsFixedAtBuild.

427

- PcdsPatchableInModule: This type of PCD is mapped to a global variable. It is allowed for use by both PcdGet and PcdSet. If PcdSet is called, it only changes the module-level PCD value instead of the system-level PCD value. Only the current module sees the PCD change. Other modules still see the original value.

Dynamic PCD:

- PcdsDynamicDefault: PcdsDynamicDefault is mapped to a PPI or protocol. It is allowed for both PcdGet and PcdSet. PcdSet changes the system-level PCD value immediately. This type of PCD value is volatile. The changed value will not be saved on the next boot.

- PcdsDynamicHii: PcdsDynamicHii is mapped to a UEFI variable. It is non-volatile. As such, the changed value can be saved on the next boot. However, the tricky thing is that this PCD value depends on the readiness of the UEFI variable services. If PcdGet is called before UEFI variable services are ready, the default PCD value will be returned instead of the updated PCD value. We suggest that the platform owner be very careful of this trap. If DXE PcdGet is required before the UEFI variable services are ready, we suggest that the platform define the PCD with the access type of PcdsDynamicDefault and then use the value returned by GetVariable in the PEI phase. A nonsecure bootrelated variable can be set in this PCD's value.

- PcdsDynamicVpd: PcdsDynamicVpd is used to map configuration data to a static flash region so that a tool can modify the values after the flash image is generated. This is used by a BIOS that needs to support binary configuration after build. Intel Firmware Support Package (FSP) is an example that uses PcdsDynamicVpd. The dynamic VPD can also be map to a configuration FV and updated via UEFI signed capsule.

- PcdsDynamicEx: PcdsDynamicEx supports external modules for binary build. If a UEFI module (DXE driver or PEIM) is not built with the system firmware, the dynamic PCD must be declared as PcdsDynamicEx. If a platform wants to include this binary EFI module, the binary module INF must be included in the DSC file. As such, the PCD database will include the external PCDs declared in this binary module. This is important since the PCD database only includes PCDs that are used by a module.

Special PCD concepts:

- SkuIds: SkuIds allow the building of one UEFI firmware image that boots on multiple boards with a different configuration in each board. It can support multiple board configurations generated at build time and then support runtime selection to make one configuration active.

- DefaultStores: DefaultStores is a special usage of PCD (gEfiMdeModulePkgTokenSpaceGuid.PcdSetNvStoreDefaultId). The use case of DefaultStores is to create different default stores in different boot modes, such as standard boot mode, manufacturing boot mode, or safe boot mode. The configuration data is set to (gEfiMdeModulePkgTokenSpaceGuid. PcdNvStoreDefaultValueBuffer). All those default stores are configured at build time and selected at runtime according to the boot mode. The default store PCD can be consumed by the HII database to support a BIOS setup "load default" operation.

Static (FeatureFlag or FixedAtBuild) PCD is built in the code. The PcdsDynamicDefault is implemented as a standard PPI or protocol in memory. They have no attack surface. From a security perspective, the only potential attack surface is PcdsDynamicVpd and PcdsDynamicHii.

VPD is used to provide the static configuration data in a flash region. Because the data is not runtime updatable, it is similar to the firmware code. As such, signing-based verification can be used for the VPD region.

Dynamic HII PCDs can be mapped to the UEFI variables. All the protection mechanisms for UEFI variables can also be used for dynamic HII PCDs.

Summary

In this chapter, we discussed firmware configuration. We use UEFI variables as an example. In the next chapter, we will discuss the non-host firmware.

References

Conference, Journal, and Paper

[P-1] Jiewen Yao, Vincent Zimmer, Star Zeng, "A Tour Beyond BIOS Implementing UEFI Authenticated Variables in SMM with EDK II," Intel Whitepaper, `https://github.com/tianocore-docs/Docs/raw/master/White_Papers/A_Tour_Beyond_BIOS_Implementing_UEFI_Authenticated_Variables_in_SMM_with_EDKII_V2.pdf`

[P-2] Yuriy Bulygin, Andrew Furtak, Oleksandr Bazhaniuk, John Loucaides, Corey Kallenberg, Xeno Kovah, John Butterworth, Sam Cornwell, "All your boot are belong to us," in CanSecWest 2014, available at `https://cansecwest.com/slides/2014/AllYourBoot_csw14-mitre-final.pdf`, and `www.c7zero.info/stuff/AllYourBoot_csw14-intel-final.pdf`

[P-3] Yuriy Bulygin, Andrew Furtak, Oleksandr Bazhaniuk, "A Tale of One Software Bypass of Windows 8 Secure Boot," in BlackHat US 2013, available at `www.c7zero.info/stuff/Windows8SecureBoot_Bulygin-Furtak-Bazhniuk_BHUSA2013.pdf`

[P-4] Yuriy Bulygin, John Loucaides, Andrew Furtak, Oleksandr Bazhaniuk, Alexander Matrosov, "Summary of Attacks Against BIOS and Secure Boot," in DEF CON 22, available at `www.c7zero.info/stuff/DEFCON22-BIOSAttacks.pdf`

[P-5] Yoongu Kim, Ross Daly, Jeremie Kim, Chris Fallin, Ji Hye Lee, Donghyuk Lee, Chris Wilkerson, Konrad Lai, Onur Mutlu, "Flipping Bits in Memory Without Accessing Them: An Experimental Study of DRAM Disturbance Errors," in IEEE 2014, available at `http://users.ece.cmu.edu/~yoonguk/papers/kim-isca14.pdf`

[P-6] Mark Seaborn, Thomas Dullien, "Exploiting the DRAM rowhammer bug to gain kernel privileges," in project zero 2015, available at `https://googleprojectzero.blogspot.com/2015/03/exploiting-dram-rowhammer-bug-to-gain.html`

[P-7] Anil Kurmus, Nikolas Ioannou, Matthias Neugschwandtner, Nikolaos Papandreou, Thomas Parnell, "From random block corruption to privilege escalation: A filesystem attack vector for rowhammer-like attacks," in USENIX 2017, available at `www.usenix.org/system/files/conference/woot17/woot17-paper-kurmus.pdf`

Specification and Guideline

[S-1] NVM Express Org, "NVM Express Specification," 2019, available at `https://nvmexpress.org/resources/specifications/`

[S-2] JEDEC Org, "Universal Flash Storage," 2018, available at `www.jedec.org/standards-documents/focus/flash/universal-flash-storage-ufs`

[S-3] JEDEC Org, "e-MMC," 2019, available at `www.jedec.org/standards-documents/technology-focus-areas/flash-memory-ssds-ufs-emmc/e-mmc`

[S-4] Intel, "Serial Flash Hardening Product External Architecture Specification," 2013, available at `www.intel.com/content/www/us/en/support/articles/000020984/software/chipset-software.html`

[S-5] Trusted Computing Group, "Trusted Platform Module Library," 2016, available at `https://trustedcomputinggroup.org/resource/tpm-library-specification/`

[S-6] UEFI Organization, "UEFI Specification," 2019, available at `www.uefi.org/`

[S-7] UEFI Organization, "UEFI Platform Initialization Specification," 2019, available at `www.uefi.org/`

[S-8] Intel, "Intel TXT Software Development Guide," 2017, available at `www.intel.com/content/www/us/en/software-developers/intel-txt-software-development-guide.html`

[S-9] IETF, "RFC 5869 – HMAC-based Extract-and-Expand Key Derivation Function (HKDF)," 2010, available at `https://tools.ietf.org/html/rfc5869`

Web

[W-1] Chromium TPM usage, `www.chromium.org/developers/design-documents/tpm-usage`

[W-2] BitLocker Drive Encryption Overview, `https://docs.microsoft.com/en-us/windows/security/information-protection/bitlocker/bitlocker-device-encryption-overview-windows-10`

[W-3] eCryptfs: An Enterprise-class Encrypted Filesystem for Linux, `www.kernel.org/doc/ols/2005/ols2005v1-pages-209-226.pdf`

[W-4] Windows Quota, `https://docs.microsoft.com/en-us/windows-server/storage/fsrm/quota-management`

[W-5] Linux Disk Quota, `https://access.redhat.com/documentation/en-us/red_hat_enterprise_linux/6/html/storage_administration_guide/ch-disk-quotas`

CHAPTER 12

Security Model

In the previous chapter, we described different security architectures and designs to meet a set of security goals. We may have several questions at the end of that design and architecture discussion. Specifically, how do I know if the design is good enough? Is there any existing framework or scheme that can help me verify the security design works? For those types of questions, a security model can help. A security model is a methodology used to describe the system and a set of security policies to satisfy the security requirements. For example, there is a security requirement for a third-party PCI option ROM – the system firmware cannot trust it. We need to authenticate the PCI option ROM and authorize the execution rights to the PCI option ROM. We found that the Clark-Wilson integrity model can be applied to this security policy. This model defines nine rules for different security properties, such as integrity, access control, auditing, and accountability. Using this model, we can then design a secure solution and adopt those rules to provide the necessary security properties.

Today we have many computer security models. Each security model is developed and used in a particular environment based upon specific security policies. In this chapter, we will introduce some security models and apply them to the firmware security features.

Confidentiality

Confidentiality is an important security property in information technology. For example, in a multilevel security (MLS) system, the information can be at different levels: top secret, secret, confidential, and unclassified. How can we ensure that information remains at the right level and does not flow to a less secure level?

© Jiewen Yao and Vincent Zimmer 2020
J. Yao and V. Zimmer, *Building Secure Firmware*, https://doi.org/10.1007/978-1-4842-6106-4_12

Bell-LaPadula

In the 1970s, David Elliott Bell and Leonard J. LaPadula formalized the US Department of Defense (DoD) multilevel security (MLS) policy and developed the Bell-LaPadula model.

In the Bell-LaPadula model, a subject and an object are associated with a security level or sensitivity level, such as top secret, secret, confidential, and unclassified. The maximum-security level for a subject is known as the clearance level. The security level for an object is known as the data classification level. A subject can view an object (read) or alter an object (write). The main rules defined in the Bell-LaPadula model are as follows:

1) Simple security property: A subject in a clearance level cannot read an object in a higher classification level. This is known as "no read-up" (NRU). See Figure 12-1, left side.

2) * (Star) security property: A subject in a security level cannot write an object in a lower classification level. This is known as "no write-down" (NWD). See Figure 12-1, right side.

   There is a **strong star security property** which means a subject who has read and write access to an object can only perform both functions at the same security level.

3) Discretionary security property: A subject can access an object based upon the access control matrix.

4) Tranquility Principle: A subject cannot change the security level of an object. This rule appeared in the first Bell-LaPadula model but was removed later. In a real environment, the object security level control varies from system to system.

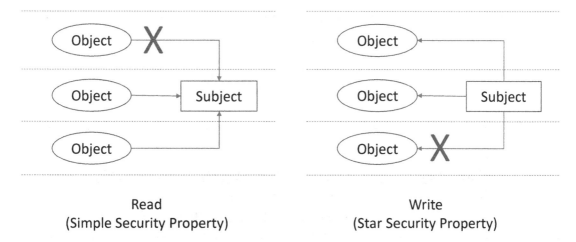

Read
(Simple Security Property)

Write
(Star Security Property)

Figure 12-1. *Bell-LaPadula Model*

The Bell-LaPadula model prevents the flow of data from a high-security level to a low-security level, but it only focuses on the confidentiality property. The model does not consider the integrity of the data. For example, the star property has no write-down, but write-up is allowed, which means the integrity of an object might be tampered. We will discuss that part in the integrity model in the next section.

These properties can be expressed more formally. We begin with the preliminary terms

$$allow: subjects \; x \; access \; x \; objects \rightarrow boolean$$

$$dominates: labels \; x \; labels \rightarrow boolean$$

where the no read-up (NRU) and no write-down (NWD) are as follows:

$$NRU: \forall s \in subjects, o \in objects$$

allow(s,o,read) if and only if label(s) dominates label (o)
and

$$NWD: \forall s \in subjects, o \in objects$$

allow(s,o,write) if and only if label(o) dominates label(s)
where

$$labels = levels \; x \; P(categories)$$

Examples can include

```
levels = {confidential, secret}
categories = {user, owner}
P(categories) = {NULL, {user}, {owner}, {users, owner}}
```

and

```
labels =
{(confidential, {user}), (secret, {user}), (confidential, {owner}),
(secret, {owner}), (confidential, (user, owner)},
(secret, {users, owner}), (confidential, NULL), (secret, NULL)}
```

Integrity

Integrity is the most important security property for the firmware. NIST SP800-193 provides the guidelines for firmware resiliency in order to maintain firmware integrity. NIST SP800-155 provides the guidelines for the integrity measurement and attestation. Now let's see how to apply the integrity model to them.

Biba Model

In 1975, Kenneth J. Biba developed the Biba integrity model which describes a set of access control policies and rules to ensure the integrity of data.

In the Biba model, a subject and an object are associated with an integrity level. For a subject, it is determined by the permitted integrity level range to maintain the minimal integrity level necessary to access the object. For an object, it means the importance of data, such as crucial, very important, and important. A subject can observe an object (read) or modify an object (write). The main rules defined in the Biba model are as follows:

1) Simple integrity property: A subject in an integrity level cannot read an object in a lower-integrity level. This is known as "no read-down." See Figure 12-2, left side.

2) * (Star) integrity property: A subject in an integrity level cannot write an object in a higher-integrity level. This is known as "no write-up." See Figure 12-2, right side.

3) Invocation property: A subject cannot invoke any other subject at
    a higher-integrity level.

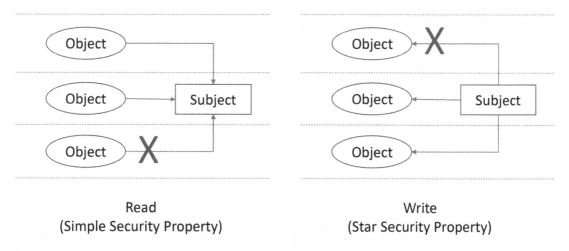

Read
(Simple Security Property)   Write
(Star Security Property)

Figure 12-2. *Biba Model*

The Biba model prevents a data flow from a high-integrity level to a low-integrity
level, but it only focuses on the integrity. It does not consider confidentiality. At some
levels, the Biba model is the reverse of the Bell-LaPadula model. For the simple security
property, the Bell-LaPadula model requires no read-up, and the Biba model requires
no read-down. In the star security property, the Bell-LaPadula model requires no write-
down, and the Biba model requires no read-up.

Security models provide a framework to guide you on how to think about a security
property. A specific security model may have limitations. It might be unnecessary
because some rules might be too strict or conflict with others. It might be inadequate
because it does not cover some real use cases. For example, if a modern commercial
system requires both confidentiality and integrity with policy control, then it needs to
apply the Biba model and Bell-LaPadula model at the same time. Assuming the security
level is aligned with the integrity level, then the rules become read-equal only and write-
equal only. Isolation is probably the best way to achieve this.

Clark-Wilson Model

In 1987, David D. Clark and David R. Wilson developed the Clark-Wilson commercial policy, in contrast to the military security policy listed earlier. It focuses on the commercial security policy for the data integrity problem. The Clark-Wilson model includes the following concepts:

1) Data item:

   A) Constrained Data Item (CDI)

   B) Unconstrained Data Item (UDI)

2) Procedure:

   A) Integrity Verification Procedure (IVP)

   B) Transformation procedures (TPs)

3) Rule:

   A) Certification rule (CR): Integrity monitoring

   C1 - (Basic: IVP Certification): All IVPs must properly ensure that all CDIs are in a valid state.

   C2 - (Basic: Validity): All TPs must be certified to be valid. For each TP and each set of CDIs that it may manipulate, the security officer must specify a "relation" of the form (TP, {CDI}).

   C3 - (Separation of Duty Certification): The list of relations in E2 must be certified to meet the separation of duty requirement.

   C4 - (Journal Certification): All TPs must be certified to write to an append-only CDI (the log), all information necessary to permit the nature of the operation to be reconstructed.

   C5 - (Transformation Certification): Any TP that takes a UDI as an input value must be certified to perform only valid transformations, or no transformations, for any possible value of the UDI. The transformation should take the input from a UDI to a CDI, or the UDI is rejected.

B) Enforcement rule (ER): Integrity preserving

E1 – (Basic: Enforcement of Validity): The system must maintain the list of relations specified in C2 and must ensure that only TPs certified to run on a CDI manipulate that CDI.

E2 – (Enforcement of Separation of Duty): The system must associate a user with each TP and set of CDIs in a list of relations of the form (User, TP, {CDI}). It must ensure that only executions described in one of the relations are performed.

E3 – (User Identity): The system must authenticate the identity of each user attempting to execute a TP.

E4 – (Initiation): Only the agent permitted to certify entities may change the list of such entities associated with other entities, specifically the one associated with a TP. An agent that can certify an entity may not have any execute rights concerning that entity.

Figure 12-3 shows the certification rules and enforcement rules in the Clark-Wilson model.

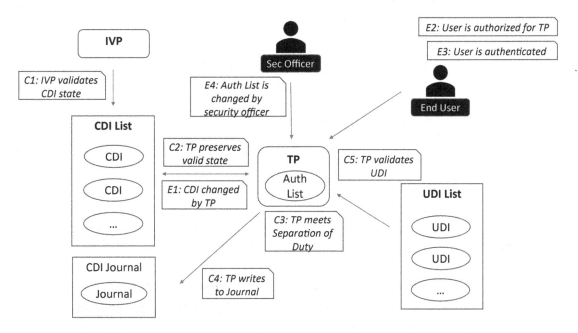

Figure 12-3. *Clark-Wilson model*

This model is based on the relationship between an authenticated principal, a program, and data items. The elements of this relationship are referred to as the "Clark-Wilson Triple" (User, TP, {CDI}). The Clark-Wilson model shows the rules required to meet the security properties of integrity in Table 12-1.

Table 12-1. *Clark-Wilson Model*

Property	Description	Rule
Integrity	An assurance that CDIs can only be modified in constrained ways to produce valid CDIs.	C1, C2, C5, E1, E4
Access control	The ability to control access to resources.	C3, E2, E3
Auditing	The ability to ascertain the changes made to CDIs and ensure that the system is in a valid state.	C1, C4
Accountability	The ability to uniquely associate users with their actions.	E3

Because the Clark-Wilson model focuses on duty and transaction, it is more applicable to business and industry processes. Currently, some papers describe how to apply the Clark-Wilson integrity model to existing systems, such as Windows, Java, or Trusted Computing Group (TCG) security.

Schematically, the Clark-Wilson rules can be shown as follows for data, D

$$D = CDI \cup UDI$$

$$CDI \cap UDI = \varnothing$$

and a transformation procedure (TP)

$$TP : subjects \ x \ D \rightarrow D$$

for a given subject and its data.

Others

Besides Bell-LaPadula, Biba, and Clark-Wilson, there are some other security models, such as the Brewer-Nash Model (as known as Chinese Wall Model), the Graham-Denning Model, the Harrison-Ruzzo-Ullman Model, the Take-Grant Model, the

Noninterference Model, the Lattice Model of Secure Information Flow, and many more. We will not introduce all of them in this chapter and instead just list them in the reference section.

Application

Let's see how to apply the security model to the firmware security features.

Trusted Computing Group Security Model

The Trusted Computing Group (TCG) defines the security model to address the system integrity concerns. A TCG-defined Trusted Platform Module (TPM) is a root-of-trust in the hardware and provides the foundation of the security. The paper "A Comparison of the Trusted Computing Group Security Model with Clark-Wilson" provides a comparison analysis in Table 12-2.

Table 12-2. *Comparison Between Clark-Wilson and TCG Security*

Rule	Clark-Wilson	TCG Security
C1	The system will have an IVP for validating the integrity of any CDI.	The TPM implements protected capabilities for keys, authorization data, sessions, embedded keys, platform configuration registers (PCRs), and flags. The core root-of-trust for measurement (CRTM) and other processes produce measurements of data items. Integrity may be verified using PCRs (in protected capabilities) and an external IVP function. Measurement transforms data into partially controlled data items (PDIs). Data exists outside shielded locations and a hash of the data inside shielded locations.
C2	The application of a TP to any CDI must maintain the integrity of that CDI.	All TPM-managed CDIs are encrypted or signed prior to transferring objects outside the physical boundary of the TPM. Hash values of partially controlled data items (PDIs) are maintained within the TPM. Corruption is detectable, but external TP is needed to recover from corruption of CDI.

(continued)

Table 12-2. (*continued*)

Rule	Clark-Wilson	TCG Security
C3	A CDI can only be changed by a certified TP. Separation of duties/least privilege.	TPMs may be evaluated to ISO-15408 guidelines. Application-level CDI is certified based on external TPs. The TCG distinguishes between key loading (into the TPM) and key usage (signing/encryption). Data can be "sealed" to the operational state establishing an operational least privilege.
C4	TP actions are logged.	The TPM audits TPM command invocations and protects audit record integrity using digital signatures.
C5	TP actions on UDIs result in valid CDIs.	Transitive trust uses TPs to measure UDI containing measurement code. The code measures other UDIs. This inductive process may transform all UDIs to PDIs. Application-level TP transforms PDI to CDI. TPM migration keys are transformed into CDI via TPM storage protected capabilities. Digital signatures applied to UDI produce signed UDI, which can be regarded as CDI for the signing transformation. TPM session protocols use nonce to prevent man-in-the-middle between the TPM and caller.
E1	Only certified TPs may act on CDIs.	Data intended for a particular TPM can be sealed to the TPM key and platform configuration such that only a particular instance of a TPM-implemented protected capability (TP) may be used to unseal. TPM-managed keys can be sealed to a particular TPM ensuring only that instance of the TPM may recover the key.
E2	Subjects may access CDIs only through TPs for which they are authorized.	Subject-owned objects (keys, secrets, passwords, etc.) have associated shared secret authorization data that is managed by the TPM. Knowledge of the secret implies authorization to access the key. Key-Cache-Manager subjects may possess auth data that enables key load/unload into TPM.

(*continued*)

Table 12-2. (*continued*)

Rule	Clark-Wilson	TCG Security
E3	Subjects attempting to execute a TP must first be authenticated.	TPM-managed CDIs are authenticated by the TPM. TPM-managed PDIs are authenticated by an external TP. TPM owner and management operations require session authentication.
E4	Only administrators can specify TP authorizations.	The TCG defines an owner that controls privileged commands, including the ability to change the owner. Physical access implies owner privilege is intrinsic.

Firmware Resiliency (Protection, Detection, Recovery)

According to NIST SP800-193, the system needs to maintain integrity and availability for the firmware. The firmware resiliency includes the protection, detection, and recovery capabilities. Firmware protection means to lock the firmware and only allow for an authenticated firmware update. Firmware detection (as known as secure boot or verified boot) means to use a set of policy objects to verify the next firmware component before execution. Firmware recovery means to launch a recovery firmware image if the verification fails. For example, to match C5, the system uses the TP (verification procedure) to verify the UDI (untrusted firmware component), transforms the UDI into a CDI (trusted firmware component), and performs the proper action such as updating, executing, or recovering.

In contrast, a TCG trusted boot (also known as measured boot) process does not verify the next entity. It only records the digest of the next boot entity to a trusted location, such as a Platform Configuration Register (PCR) in the Trusted Platform Module (TPM). This allows a trusted boot chain to be verified later in the boot process. Many security models use secure boot and trusted boot capabilities in combination for maximum effectiveness. For example, if the system enables secure boot and trusted boot, the secure boot policy is measured into PCR7. Whenever the secure boot verification handler verifies a subsequent component, the policy authority is also measured into PCR7. At a later time, the verifier can know all secure boot policies and know which one is used to verify the firmware component. Table 12-3 lists the Clark-Wilson model in firmware resiliency.

Table 12-3. *Clark-Wilson Model in Firmware Resiliency*

Property	Description	Rule	Firmware Resiliency
Integrity	An assurance that CDIs can only be modified in constrained ways to produce valid CDIs.	C1, C2, C5, E1, E4	Firmware needs to verify the next loaded component, new firmware component, recovery component, policy data, and so on.
Access control	The ability to control access to resources.	C3, E2, E3	There is no user concept in firmware resiliency. Root-of-trust or chain-of-trust can access the resource.
Auditing	The ability to ascertain the changes made to CDIs and ensure that the system is in a valid state.	C1, C4	TCG trusted boot may record the verification information in the TCG event log such as authority.
Accountability	The ability to uniquely associate users with their actions.	E3	There is no user concept in firmware resiliency. Root-of-trust or chain-of-trust can perform the action.

Patterns in the Firmware Resiliency

Definition:

1) Firmware[N]: The N-level firmware binary. Any firmware layer is updatable.

   Firmware[0] means the component verified by hardware.

   Firmware[N] means the component verified by firmware[N-1].

   It may include both code (Firmware[N].Code) and data (Firmware[N].Data).

2) Firmware[N].Code: The code of the N-level firmware binary.

   It may include the verifier (Firmware[N].Code.Verifier).

3) Firmware[N].Data: The data of the N-level firmware binary.

It may include the verification policy (Firmware[N].Data.Policy).

4) Firmware[N].Code.Verifier: The verification function of the N-level firmware binary.

5) Firmware[N].Data.Policy: The policy data inside of the N-level firmware binary.

This data is used by the verification function. Both the verification function and policy data have the following subcategory:

A) Boot: The firmware boot.

B) PolicyUpdate: The policy update. It may or may not exist.

C) FirmwareUpdate: The firmware update (it may or may not include policy data).

D) Recovery: The firmware recovery.

E) Communication: The firmware runtime communication.

6) Hardware: The hardware, including Register Transfer Level (RTL) and registers. The hardware is not updatable. The hardware must be fused when it is shipped to the end user.

There are two types of verification:

1) The verifier for boot (verified boot): The read-only code and read-only data are in this category. This category includes both initial installation and upgrade. For example, UEFI secure boot is for code installation, UEFI Authenticated Variables are for data policy update, signed capsule update is for code/data upgrade, and signed recovery is for code/data reinstallation. In most cases, the verification is based upon a crypto-algorithm, such as Secure Hash Algorithm (SHA) or Rivest-Shamir-Adleman (RSA) Algorithm. The policy data can be the hash value of the firmware or the public key hash of the firmware. Above 5.A, 5.B, 5.C, and 5.D belong to this type.

2)   The verifier for communication (verified communication): The read/write data are in this category. This category is for cross-boundary data passing, such as trusted execution environment (TEE) communication, including the UEFI non-volatile variables. In most cases, the verification is based upon a boundary check, valid range check, and so on. Above 5.E belongs to this type.

Patterns for Verified Boot

Table 12-4 shows the patterns for the verified boot. NOTE: If N == 0, Firmware[-1] means the hardware.

Table 12-4. *Patterns for Verified Boot*

Item	Entity	Provider	Location
TP	Firmware[N].Code.Verifier.Boot (Firmware[N].Data.Policy.Boot, Firmware[N+1])	Firmware[N] owner	Same as Firmware[N]
CDI	Firmware[N]	Firmware[N] owner	Originally on flash, loaded into RAM by Firmware[N-1]
UDI	Firmware[N+1]	Firmware[N+1] owner	Originally on flash, loaded into RAM by Firmware[N]

Patterns for Verified Policy Update

Table 12-5 shows the patterns for the verified policy update.

Table 12-5. *Patterns for Verified Policy Update*

Item	Entity	Provider	Location
TP	Firmware[N].Code.Verifier. PolicyUpdate (Firmware[N].Data.Policy. PolicyUpdate, Firmware[N].Data.Policy:New)	Firmware[N] owner	See in the following.
CDI	Firmware[N].Code.Verifier. PolicyUpdate + Firmware[N].Data.Policy. PolicyUpdate	Firmware[N] owner	In a trusted execution environment. As such, the rest of Firmware[N] cannot tamper with it.
UDI	Firmware[N].Data.Policy:New	Policy data owner	RAM, loaded into the trusted execution environment, by Firmware[N]. Code.Verifier. PolicyUpdate.

Patterns for Verified Firmware Update

Table 12-6 shows the patterns for the verified firmware update.

Table 12-6. *Patterns for Verified Firmware Update*

Item	Entity	Provider	Location
TP	Firmware[N].Code.Verifier.FirmwareUpdate (Firmware[N].Data.Policy.FirmwareUpdate, Firmware[N]:New)	Firmware[N] owner	See in the following.
CDI	Firmware[N]	Firmware[N] owner	Flash unlockable environment, loaded by Firmware[N-1].
UDI	Firmware[N]:New	Firmware[N] owner	Flash unlockable environment, loaded by original Firmware[N].

Patterns for Verified Recovery

Table 12-7 shows the patterns for the verified firmware recovery.

Table 12-7. *Patterns for Verified Recovery*

Item	Entity	Provider	Location
TP	Firmware[N].Code.Verifier.Recovery (Firmware[N].Data.Policy.Recovery, Firmware[N+1]:Recovery)	Firmware[N] owner	See in the following.
CDI	Firmware[N]	Firmware[N] owner	Originally on flash, loaded into RAM by Firmware[N-1].
UDI	Firmware[N+1]:Recovery	Firmware[N+1] owner	Originally on recovery storage (such as flash, USB, hard drive, etc.), loaded into RAM by Firmware[N].

Patterns for Verified Runtime Communication

Table 12-8 shows the patterns for the verified runtime communication.

Table 12-8. *Patterns for Verified Runtime Communication*

Item	Entity	Provider	Location
TP	Firmware[N].Code.Verifier. RuntimeCommunication (Firmware[N].Data.Policy. RuntimeCommunication, Data:New)	Firmware[N] owner	See in the following.
CDI	Firmware[N].Code.Verifier. RuntimeCommunication + Firmware[N].Data.Policy. RuntimeCommunication	Firmware[N] owner	In a trusted execution environment. As such, the rest of Firmware[N] cannot tamper it.

(continued)

Table 12-8. (*continued*)

Item	Entity	Provider	Location
UDI	Data:New	Any	RAM, loaded into a trusted execution environment by Firmware[N]. Code.Verifier. PolicyUpdate. This can be any data, as long as the format is known by the producer and consumer.

Comparing Clark-Wilson and Firmware Resiliency

Table 12-9 illustrates how the firmware resiliency is mapped to Clark-Wilson certification and enforcement rules.

Table 12-9. *Comparison Between Clark-Wilson and Firmware Resiliency*

Rule	Clark-Wilson	Firmware Resiliency
C1	The system will have an IVP for validating the integrity of any CDI.	The integrity may be verified based upon the firmware signature or firmware hash.
C2	The application of a TP to any CDI must maintain the integrity of that CDI.	The firmware flash region should be locked to prevent unauthorized update.
C3	A CDI can only be changed by a certified TP. Separation of duties/least privilege.	If the flash needs to be unlocked for update, the action should be done in a trusted execution environment (TEE).
C4	TP actions are logged.	The firmware resiliency does not include a logging mechanism. The TCG event log can be used here.

(*continued*)

Table 12-9. (*continued*)

Rule	Clark-Wilson	Firmware Resiliency
C5	TP actions on UDIs result in valid CDIs.	The firmware needs to verify the next component in secure boot. The firmware needs to verify the new firmware in a secure update. The firmware needs to verify the recovery image in the secure recovery process. The firmware needs to verify the policy data in the secure policy update, such as a UEFI authenticated variable.
E1	Only certified TPs may act on CDIs.	The verification is in the trusted execution environment or an environment without any third-party code.
E2	Subjects may access CDIs only through TPs for which they are authorized.	No user concept in firmware resiliency. CDI can be accessed by the root-of-trust (RoT) or chain-of-trust (CoT).
E3	Subjects attempting to execute a TP must first be authenticated.	No user concept in firmware resiliency. TP is executed by the root-of-trust (RoT) or chain-of-trust (CoT).
E4	Only administrators can specify TP authorizations.	The platform policy is created by the manufacturer owner when the system is in the manufacturing phase. The owner policy is updatable by the machine owner with the assertion of physical presence.

UEFI Secure Boot Image Verification

In Chapter 4, we have introduced the UEFI secure boot. Here we map the secure boot activity to the Clark-Wilson model in Table 12-10.

Table 12-10. *UEFI Secure Boot Image Verification*

Item	Entity	Provider	Location
TP	UEFI Secure Boot Image Verification	Original Equipment Manufacturer (OEM)	Originally on flash, loaded into DRAM.
CDI	Manufacturer Firmware Code	OEM	Originally on flash, loaded into DRAM.
	UEFI Secure Boot Image Security Database (Policy)	End user (or OEM default)	Originally on flash, authenticated variable region, loaded into DRAM.
UDI	Third-party firmware code (OS bootloader)	Operating system vendor (OSV)	Originally on external storage (e.g., hard drive, USB), loaded into DRAM.
	Third-party firmware code (PCI option ROM)	Independent Hardware Vendor (IHV)	Originally on PCI card, loaded into DRAM.
	Third-party firmware code (UEFI shell tool)	Any	External storage (e.g., hard drive, USB), loaded into DRAM.

Signing

In UEFI secure boot, the UDI is any third-party firmware code, including the OS bootloader, PCI option ROMs, or a UEFI shell tool. The component provider needs to sign these components with a private key and publish the public key.

Public Key Storage

The OEM or end user may enroll the public key as a CDI (i.e., UEFI Secure Boot Image Security Database). The database is in a UEFI Authenticated Variable region. The database can also be updated during runtime. It can be read by anyone but only be written after data authentication. See Table 12-11.

Verification

During boot, the TP (Image Verification Procedure) verifies the UDI (third-party firmware code), according to the CDI (UEFI Secure Boot Image Security Database) as policy. If the verification passes, the UDI is transformed into a CDI, and the third-party firmware code is executed. If the verification fails, the third-party firmware code is discarded.

UEFI Authenticated Variable Verification (Policy Update)

In Table 12-10, the CDI (UEFI Secure Boot Image Security Database) is updatable. The database itself is in the UEFI Authenticated Variable region. Table 12-11 shows the component involved in the UEFI Authenticated Variable Verification.

Table 12-11. *UEFI Authenticated Variable Verification*

Item	Entity	Provider	Location
TP	UEFI Authenticated Variable Verification	OEM	Originally on flash, loaded into TEE-specific RAM.
CDI	Manufacturer Firmware Code in a trusted execution environment (TEE)	OEM	Originally on flash, loaded into TEE-specific RAM.
	UEFI Secure Boot Image Security Database (Policy)	End user (or OEM default)	Originally on flash, loaded into TEE-specific RAM.
UDI	New UEFI Secure Boot Image Security Database	End user	Originally in normal DRAM, loaded into TEE-specific RAM.

Signing

To update the existing image security database (CDI), the new image security database (UDI) needs to be signed if UEFI secure boot is enabled.

Public Key Storage

The signer's public key must be enrolled in system firmware. It is the same as the public key used for UEFI Secure Boot Image Verification. The database is stored in a UEFI Authenticated Variable region.

Verification

During runtime update, the TP (Authenticated Variable Verification Procedure) verifies the UDI (new image security database), according to the CDI (UEFI Secure Boot Image Security Database) as policy. If verification passes, then the UDI is transformed into a CDI, and the new image security database takes effect on the next boot. If verification fails, the new image security data is discarded.

Signed Capsule Update

Platform firmware often requires an update. NIST SP800-193 provides multiple guidelines for authenticated updates. We have introduced the authenticated firmware update mechanism in Chapter 3. Table 12-12 shows firmware update components.

Table 12-12. *Firmware Update Verification*

Item	Entity	Provider	Location
TP	Firmware Update Verification	OEM	Originally on flash, loaded into the flash unlockable environment. (It could be DRAM before the flash is locked or TEE-specific RAM.)
CDI	Firmware Update TCB Code	OEM	Originally on flash, loaded into the flash unlockable environment.
	Firmware Update Signature Database (Policy)	OEM	Originally on flash, loaded into the flash unlockable environment.
UDI	Firmware update package	OEM	Originally on external storage (e.g., hard drive, USB, memory, or read-write flash), loaded into the flash unlockable environment.

Signing

The UDI is the whole new firmware image. As such, the whole firmware binary needs to be signed by the OEM private key.

Public Key Storage

The OEM public key should be embedded in the original firmware. As such, it can be used to verify the new firmware binary.

A policy may be updated along with the new firmware image.

Verification

During the firmware update process, the TP is inside of the original firmware image. The TP will load the new firmware image from external storage into memory. The memory can be normal DRAM (if the update happens before any third-party code is executed) or flash (in an unlocked state). If the update must occur after third-party code execution, the update must occur in a trusted execution environment, such as X86 system management mode (SMM). Care must be taken that both verification and update occur in the same environment, and also ensure that there are no Time-of-Check/Time-of-Use threats or Direct Memory Access (DMA) attacks. If the TP passes verification, the new firmware image is programmed into flash. If verification fails, the flash update process is aborted.

Signed Recovery

If firmware corruption is detected, the firmware can perform recovery to prevent a permanent denial of service (PDoS) attack. We have introduced the authenticated firmware recovery mechanism in Chapter 5. Table 12-13 shows the firmware recovery components.

Table 12-13. *Firmware Recovery Verification*

Item	Entity	Provider	Location
TP	Firmware Recovery Verification	OEM	Originally on flash, loaded into DRAM.
CDI	Firmware Recovery TCB Code	OEM	Originally on flash, loaded into DRAM.
	Firmware Recovery Signature Database (Policy)	OEM	Originally on flash, loaded into DRAM.
UDI	Firmware Recovery Package	OEM	Originally on external storage (e.g., hard drive, USB, memory, or flash), loaded into DRAM.

Signing

The UDI is provided a new firmware image in the same fashion as the UEFI capsule update implementation. The entire firmware binary must be signed using the OEM private key.

Public Key Storage

The OEM public key should be embedded in the original firmware and recovery launcher module.

Verification

If firmware corruption is detected during boot, the recovery boot path is triggered. In this scenario, the TP is the firmware recovery launcher module. This module loads the recovery image from a known source and verifies the signature. If the TP passes verification, the recovery image is loaded, and the recovery launcher module transfers control to the recovery image. If the recovery verification fails, the recovery image is discarded, and the recovery launcher attempts to locate additional recovery images. If all recovery images fail verification, then the recovery process is aborted.

Note   The signed recovery image itself may be updatable even if it is on the flash region.

Trusted Execution Environment (TEE) Runtime Communication

A trusted execution environment (TEE) is an isolated execution environment. It could be a special highly privileged processor execution mode, such as X86 system management mode (SMM). One usage of a TEE is that the firmware may provide some special services in TEE, which is referred to as a TEE handler. The TEE handler uses a shared TEE communication buffer to convey information to the service consumer during OS runtime. The TEE handler may assist the firmware resiliency, such as protection or update. As such, maintaining the integrity of TEE is of great importance. Table 12-14 describes TEE Runtime Communication Verification.

Table 12-14. *TEE Runtime Communication Verification*

Item	Entity	Provider	Location
TP	TEE Communication Verifier Code	OEM	Originally on flash, loaded in TEE-specific RAM.
CDI	TEE handler	OEM	Originally on flash, loaded in TEE-specific RAM.
UDI	TEE communication buffer	Any	DRAM.

The TEE communication buffer is not signed because any program may use the buffer to invoke TEE services. TEE communication is treated as an attack surface, so the TEE handler must verify the contents of the TEE communication buffer. Since there is no signature, common verification is limited to prevent TEE attacks since it cannot verify the originator. We will introduce more details on the TEE in Chapter 17.

Summary

In this chapter, we introduced three basic secure models: Bell-LaPadula model, Biba integrity model, and Clark-Wilson integrity model. Then we used the Clark-Wilson model as an example and mapped the firmware security features to it, including the TCG security model and firmware resiliency (protection, detection, and recovery). In the next chapter, we will introduce the firmware in the virtualization world.

References

Book

[B-1] Matt Bishop, *Computer Security: Art and Science, 2nd edition*, Wiley, 2018

[B-2] Edward Amoroso, *Fundamentals of Computer Security Technology*, Prentice Hall, 1994

[B-3] Dieter Gollmann, *Computer Security, 3rd edition*, Wiley, 2011

[B-4] Ross J. Anderson, *Security Engineering: A Guide to Building Dependable Distributed Systems, 2nd edition*, Wiley, 2008

[B-5] Charles P. Pfleeger, Shari Lawrence Pfleeger, Jonathan Margulies, *Security in Computing, 5th edition*, Prentice Hall, 2015

[B-6] Henry M. Levy, *Capability-Based Computer Systems*, Digital Press, 1984, available at `https://homes.cs.washington.edu/~levy/capabook/`

Conference, Journal, and Paper

[P-1] E. Stewart Lee. "Essays about Computer Security," Centre for Communications Systems Research, Cambridge, 1999, available at `www.cl.cam.ac.uk/~mgk25/lee-essays.pdf`

[P-2] David Elliott Bell, Leonard J. LaPadula, "Secure Computer Systems: Mathematical Foundations," in MITRE Technical Report 1973, available at www-personal.umich.edu/~cja/LPS12b/refs/belllapadula1.pdf

[P-3] David Elliott Bell, Leonard J. LaPadula, "Secure Computer Systems: A Mathematical Model," in MITRE Technical Report 1973, available at `http://citeseerx.ist.psu.edu/viewdoc/download?doi=10.1.1.20.6361&rep=rep1&type=pdf`

[P-4] David Elliott Bell, Leonard J. LaPadula, "Secure Computer Systems: A Refinement of the Mathematical Model," in MITRE Technical Report 1974, available at `https://apps.dtic.mil/dtic/tr/fulltext/u2/780528.pdf`

[P-5] David Elliott Bell, Leonard J. LaPadula, "Secure Computer System: Unified Exposition and Multics Interpretation," in in MITRE Technical Report 1976, available at `https://csrc.nist.gov/csrc/media/publications/conference-paper/1998/10/08/proceedings-of-the-21st-nissc-1998/documents/early-cs-papers/bell76.pdf`

[P-6] David Elliott Bell, "Looking Back at the Bell-La Padula Model," 2005, available at `www.acsac.org/2005/papers/Bell.pdf`

[P-7] K. J. Biba, "Integrity Considerations for Secure Computer Systems," 1975, available at `http://seclab.cs.ucdavis.edu/projects/history/papers/biba75.pdf`

[P-8] David D. Clark, David R. Wilson, "A Comparison of Commercial and Military Computer Security Policies," 1987, available at `http://theory.stanford.edu/~ninghui/courses/Fall03/papers/clark_wilson.pdf`

[P-9] Sonya Q. Blake, "The Clark-Wilson Security Model," SANS Institute Information, May 17, 2000, available at `www.giac.org/paper/gsec/835/clark-wilson-security-model/101747`

[P-10] Ian Welch, Robert Stroud, "Supporting real world security models in Java," in IEEE 1999, available at `http://citeseerx.ist.psu.edu/viewdoc/download?doi=10.1.1.103.7386&rep=rep1&type=pdf`

[P-11] Ned Smith, "A Comparison of the trusted Computing Group Security Model with Clark-Wilson," 2004, available at `www.semanticscholar.org/paper/A-Comparison-of-the-trustedComputing-Group-Model-Smith/fa82426d99b86d1040f80b8bd8e0ac4f785b29a6`

[P-12] Xiaocheng Ge, Fiona Polack, Regine Laleau, "Secure Databases: An Analysis of Clark-Wilson Model in a Database Environment," 2004, available at `www.researchgate.net/publication/220920890_Secure_Databases_An_Analysis_of_Clark-Wilson_Model_in_a_Database_Environment`

[P-13] Umesh Shankar, Trent Jaeger, Reiner Sailer, "Toward Automated Information-Flow Integrity Verification for Security-Critical Applications," 2006, available at `www.cse.psu.edu/~trj1/papers/ndss06.pdf`, `http://www.cse.psu.edu/~trj1/cse544-s10/slides/Info-Flow-NDSS-2006.pdf`

[P-14] David F.C. Brewer, Michael J. Nash, "The Chinese Wall Security Policy," 1989, available at `www.cs.purdue.edu/homes/ninghui/readings/AccessControl/brewer_nash_89.pdf`

[P-15] Dorothy E. Denning, "A Lattice Model of Secure Information Flow," in ACM 1976, available at `https://courses.cs.washington.edu/courses/cse590s/02sp/secure-information-flow.pdf`

[P-16] Michael A. Harrison, Walter L. Ruzzo, Jeffrey D. Ullman, "Protection in operating systems," in ACM 1976, `www.cs.unibo.it/babaoglu/courses/security/resources/documents/harrison-ruzzo-ullman.pdf`

[P-17] Butler W. Lampson, "Protection," in Princeton Conf. on Information Sciences and Systems 1971, available at `https://cseweb.ucsd.edu/classes/fa01/cse221/papers/lampson-protection-osr74.pdf`

[P-18] G. Scott Graham, Peter J. Denning, "Protection – principles and practice," in 1972, available at `https://dl.acm.org/doi/pdf/10.1145/1478873.1478928`

[P-19] J. A. Goguen, J. Meseguer, "Security Policies and Security Models," in 1982, available at `www.cs.purdue.edu/homes/ninghui/readings/AccessControl/goguen_meseguer_82.pdf`

[P-20] R. J. Lipton, L. Snyder, "A Linear Time Algorithm for Deciding Subject Security," in ACM 1977, available at `www.cs.nmt.edu/~doshin/t/s06/cs589/pub/2.JLS-TG.pdf`

[P-21] Butler W. Lampson, Howard E. Sturgis, "Reflections on an operating system design," in ACM 1976, available at `www.microsoft.com/en-us/research/wp-content/uploads/2016/02/acrobat-22.pdf`

[P-22] James P. Anderson, "Computer Security Technology Planning Study," 1972, available at `http://seclab.cs.ucdavis.edu/projects/history/papers/ande72.pdf`

[P-23] Mark S. Miller, Ka-Ping Yee, Jonathan Shapiro, "Capability Myths Demolished," 2003, available at `https://srl.cs.jhu.edu/pubs/SRL2003-02.pdf`

CHAPTER 13

Virtual Firmware

In previous chapters, we talked about the security design for the real firmware in the system. Now let's take a look at the virtual firmware. Figure 13-1 is a typical type-I virtualization architecture. When the system firmware finishes the platform initialization, it launches a hypervisor. Then the hypervisor creates four domains and launches them. Each guest domain has its own virtual firmware. The virtual firmware prepares the required interface for the guest OS and launches the guest OS.

In the real machine, the purpose of the firmware is to initialize the hardware and provide a common interface to the operating system (OS). As such, the OS can be platform agnostic. In the virtual machine, the virtual firmware serves the same purpose. The virtual firmware provides the same common interface to the guest OS. For example, if the guest OS is a UEFI Windows or UEFI Linux, the virtual firmware needs to create the UEFI environment for the guest UEFI OS.

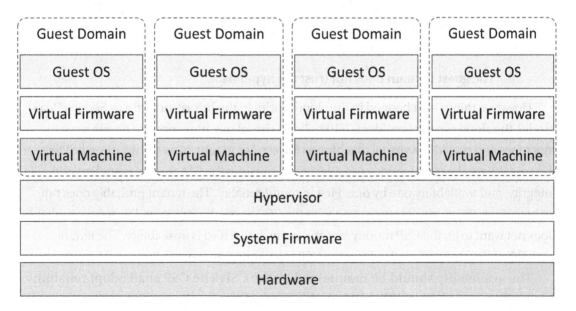

Figure 13-1. *Virtualization Architecture*

© Jiewen Yao and Vincent Zimmer 2020
J. Yao and V. Zimmer, *Building Secure Firmware*, https://doi.org/10.1007/978-1-4842-6106-4_13

New Threats in the Guest Domain

When we talk about security, the first step is to understand the threat model. There are two different threat models for the virtual firmware based upon two different use cases:

1) The guest domain trusts the hypervisor.

In 1972, Anderson mentioned the concept of a "reference monitor" in the technical report "Computer Security Technology Planning Study." The reference monitor is an abstract machine which controls the access from the subjects to the objects. The reference monitor ensures the subjects have the access rights to the objects and protects the objects from unauthorized access. In 1974, Popek and Goldberg published the "Formal Requirements for Virtualizable Third Generation Architectures" and mentioned three properties of a virtual machine monitor (VMM), also known as the hypervisor: 1) efficiency, 2) resource control, and 3) equivalency. Because the VMM could control the system resource, it is a good candidate as the reference monitor. In most of the current virtualization architectures, the VMM can access and control the behavior of guest domains. For example, an IT person may install a hypervisor to protect the guest operating system on a laptop machine sent to the enterprise user. When the end user uses the operating system, they trust the hypervisor.

In this case, the guest relies on the hypervisor to provide for its protection. The virtual firmware can trust the hardware device and the software service provided by the hypervisor. The hypervisor controls everything. No special new threat needs to be considered by the virtual firmware.

2) The guest domain does not trust the hypervisor.

However, things are changed in the cloud world. In the Infrastructure as a Service (IaaS) model, the cloud service provider (CSP) builds a virtual machine monitor on physical machines and provides a virtual machine as the service to rent. Now the question is: Does the tenant trust the cloud service provider? Let's consider the CIA triad of confidentiality, integrity, and availability one by one. First is confidentiality. The tenant probably does not want to share the secret company data with the CSP. Second is integrity. The tenant probably does not want to let the CSP modify any company data. Third is availability. The tenant probably does not want service from the CSP interrupted unexpectedly.

The availability should be maintained by the CSP. The CSP shall adopt reliability, availability, and serviceability (RAS) when providing the cloud service. The untrusted input should be verified before use, such as a network packet or disk image, which is similar to the real system firmware. But if the service is stopped by the CSP due to network disconnection or hypervisor shutdown, the virtual firmware can do nothing.

The confidentiality and integrity are special in this case because the CSP is treated as malicious and the CSP may try to attack the guest domain. For example, the attacker may put a scanner in the hypervisor to scan the guest memory to get the secret. The attacker may put a rootkit in the virtual firmware to control the guest operating system. As such, the guest domain needs a way to protect its data from being attacked by the hypervisor.

At a high level, the VM data can be in three categories: 1) data at rest, 2) data in transition, and 3) data in use. The data at rest can be protected with encryption. The data in transition can be protected by the network protocol such as Transport Layer Security (TLS). The protection of the data in use needs hardware assistance with the help from the virtual firmware.

Case Study

Now, let's take a look at some real cases for the security extension in virtualization.

AMD Secure Encrypted Virtualization (SEV)

When the CPU executes the code or refers to the data, it needs to access the memory in plain text. In most of the current architectures, the data in DRAM is also plain text. That brings a potential risk that if the attacker can hijack the memory bus, they can read the data and modify the data. In order to mitigate this attack, AMD uses Secure Memory Encryption (SME) which encrypts the data sent to DRAM (see Figure 13-2). As such, the data on the memory bus or in the DRAM is ciphertext. Each CPU system on a chip (SOC) includes an AMD Secure Processor (AMD-SP) with an Advanced Encryption Standard (AES) engine to encrypt and decrypt the data. The AES key is randomly generated on each system reset and unavailable outside of the SOC.

This SME feature can be partially enabled based upon the page table. The physical address in the page table has an enCrypted Bit (C-bit) to indicate if this page needs encryption or not. As such, the OS can decide which memory range needs encryption. In order to provide the support for OS which has no knowledge of the new C-bit, the CPU can instead use Transparent SME (TSME). In the TSME mode, all the memory is encrypted regardless of whether the C-bit is set or clear.

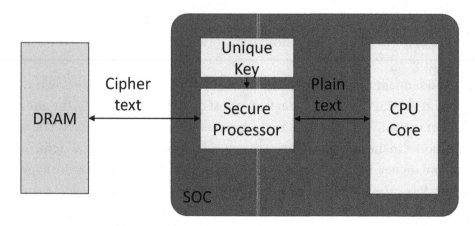

Figure 13-2. *AMD SME Architecture*

The SME feature is good, but it does not resolve all problems in the cloud world because the hypervisor can still access the memory of the guest domain. There is only one key used in SME.

AMD Secure Encrypted Virtualization (SEV) technology uses SME and adds an extension with multiple encryption keys (see Figure 13-3). During launch, each guest domain has a unique virtual machine (VM) address space ID (ASID). The SEV hardware assigns a tag for the data or code with its VM ASID. When the data enters or leaves the SOC, the data is encrypted or decrypted with a unique key based upon the associated tag. As such, the hypervisor or other domains cannot access the memory in a domain.

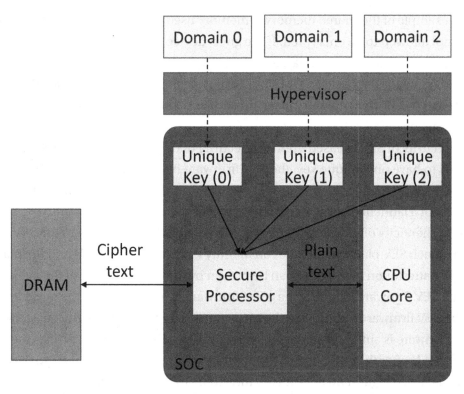

Figure 13-3. *AMD SEV Architecture*

In some cases, the guest domain needs to communicate with the hypervisor for sharing information. As such, the guest may choose to disable encryption for the communication buffer as the share page while leaving other pages encrypted as private pages (see Figure 13-4).

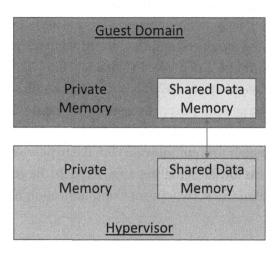

Figure 13-4. *AMD SEV Communication*

One example of the shared memory is memory used for Direct Memory Access (DMA). DMA is not allowed to be encrypted. If the guest device driver needs to use DMA to communicate with a device emulated by the hypervisor or a real hardware device, the device driver needs to allocate a DMA buffer and clear the C-bit. When the DMA buffer is reclaimed to as a normal memory page, this driver needs to clear the C-bit to mark it as a private page.

The security of SEV is based upon the security of the encryption key. Because each VM needs to have one unique key, the SEV firmware needs to provide a key management interface to enforce three security properties: 1) the authenticity of the platform, 2) the attestation of a launched guest, and 3) the confidentiality of the guest data.

The authenticity of the platform can be proven with an identity key in the SEV firmware. Each SEV platform includes an identity key assigned by AMD and the platform owner. The attestation of the guest can be proven by the measurement of the guest image. When the SEV firmware launches the guest firmware, it also measures the guest image. Later, the SEV firmware can provide the measurement to the owner of the guest. Because the SEV firmware is authenticated with the identity key, the guest owner trusts the SEV firmware. Only after the guest owner verifies the measurement and decides to trust this guest image will the guest owner transfer more data to the guest image, such as a disk encryption key to decrypt the VM disk. The confidentiality of the guest data is based upon the memory encryption key which is known by the SEV firmware. The SEV firmware must not expose the encryption key or expose any clue about the encryption key.

AMD SEV provides the encryption of guest memory. But the hypervisor may tamper with the guest execution by modifying the guest registers such as RAX/RBX/RCX/RDX. The AMD SEV Encrypted State (SEV-ES) provides additional protection for the guest register state. During launch, the guest registers are initialized to a known state, and they are encrypted and measured as part of the SEV launch process. The integrity check is done for each VMRUN. A dedicated Virtual Machine Save Area (VMSA) is allocated for the virtual machine with SEV-ES, with information such as the segment state, the control state, the general-purpose register (GPR) state, and the float point unit (FPU) state.

If the guest domain needs to communicate with the hypervisor using a GPR, then the hypervisor must access the guest register area. As such, the guest needs to copy the register to the dedicated Guest Hypervisor Communication Block (GHCB). See Figure 13-5.

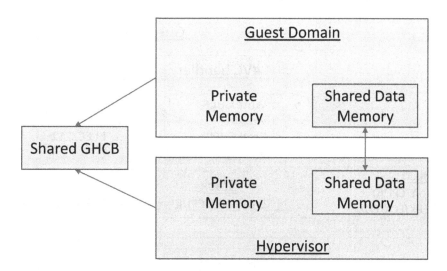

Figure 13-5. *AMD SEV-ES Communication with GHCB*

Let's take one example – the CPUID instruction. The CPUID instruction uses the EAX register for the input and uses the EAX, EBX, ECX, and EDX registers for the output. In the virtualization environment without SEV-ES, when the guest domain executes the CPUID instruction, it triggers a VmExit. The hypervisor parses the VmExit reason to know it was a CPUID instruction that triggered the VmExit. Then the hypervisor gets the EAX value as the CPUID index and sets EAX/EBX/ECX/EDX in the guest general-purpose register fields and resumes the guest.

However, this flow does not work with SEV-ES because the hypervisor is not allowed to read EAX from the guest or write EAX/EBX/ECD/EDX to the guest directly. There are two ways to resolve this problem: 1) The guest software can replace the CPUID instruction with an alternate operation which writes to EAX in the GHCB, triggers VmExit, and reads EAX/EBX/ECX/EDX from the GHCB. This brings compatibility problems with existing guest software binaries. 2) Another way is to leverage a new VMM communication exception (#VC). See Figure 13-6. When the guest software executes CPUID, the CPU hardware triggers a #VC exception with an error code to indicate what the instruction is. Then the guest #VC exception handler can write the instruction (CPUID) and its input parameters (EAX) to the GHCB and trigger VmExit. The corresponding hypervisor handler parses the instruction and input data in the GHCB, writes the output data for the instruction to the GHCB, and resumes to the guest. Then the guest #VC handler reads the output parameters (EAX/EBX/ECX/EDX) of the instruction (CPUID) into the CPU registers. With the help of the new #VC handler, the compatibility is maintained.

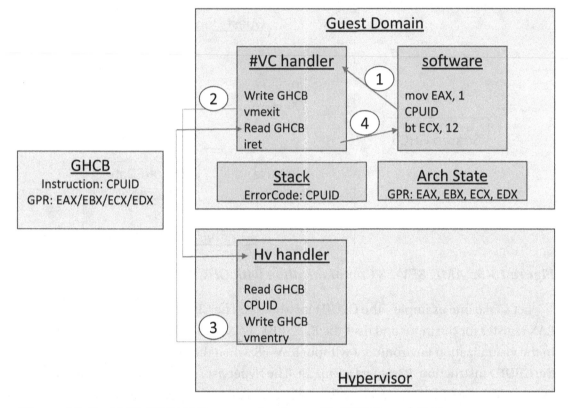

Figure 13-6. *AMD SEV-ES Communication with GHCB and #VC*

This GHCB communication mechanism can be used for instructions that require the hypervisor to parse the guest state, such as CPUID, read MSR, write MSR, I/O read, I/O write, and so on. With SEV-ES, the guest memory and the guest state cannot be tampered by the hypervisor. The guest firmware needs to enable this feature to provide its execution environment.

Please refer to the "AMD Architecture Programmer's Manual" for more detailed information.

Intel Trust Domain Executions (TDX)

Intel provides the memory encryption feature. The Total Memory Encryption (TME) provides the basic memory encryption capability. It is similar to AMD SME. It encrypts the entire physical memory of a system with one ephemeral key. In order to support the guest memory security in the virtualization environment, Intel provides Multi-key Total Memory Encryption (MKTME) in a flexible way. With MKTME, each page can be tagged with a KeyID. During runtime, the different VM is assigned with different KeyIDs by the hypervisor to achieve the domain isolation. Take Figure 13-7 as an example. The hypervisor has a shared KeyID 0 and a private KeyID 1. The guest domain 0 has a shared KeyID 0 with hypervisor, a shared KeyID 4 with domain 1, and a private KeyID 2. The guest domain 1 has a shared KeyID 0 with hypervisor, a shared KeyID 4 with domain 1, and a private KeyID 3.

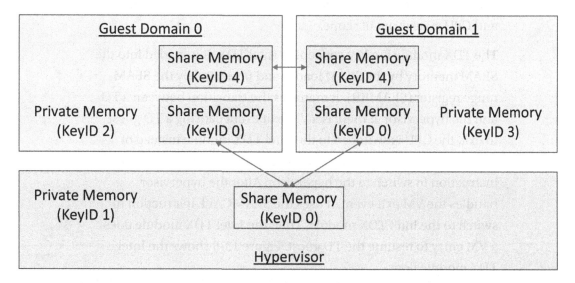

Figure 13-7. *Intel MKTME Communication with KeyID*

For the DMA, the hypervisor can set the KeyID in the IOMMU page table, similar to the way of setting the KeyID in the external page table (EPT) – the host page table. For the physical DMA, the KeyID can be applied to the physical address directly. This design can simplify the guest software.

Please refer to the Intel MKTME specification for more detailed information.

Building upon Intel MKTME and virtualization technology, Intel introduced Trust Domain Executions (TDX). Intel TDX is similar to AMD SEV. It can provide a hardware isolated virtual machine (VM), which is called trust domain (TD). The TD has two capabilities:

1) The confidentiality and integrity of the memory and CPU states. The TD only trusts: Intel TDX module which is executed in the Secure Arbitration Mode (SEAM) mode, Intel Authenticated Code Module (ACM) also known as SEAM loader (SEAMLDR), Intel TD Quoting Enclave (QE) and Intel CPU hardware. The data in a TD is protected to resist an attack from software, such as another

VM or TD, hypervisor, BIOS system management mode (SMM), integrated devices, etc. It also resists attack from hardware, such as offline memory analysis and active memory attacks, including capturing, modifying, relocating, splicing, and aliasing. But a memory replay attack is out of scope. The TD still relies on the hypervisor to setup the resources. The availability of the memory and CPU state is out of scope.

The TDX module is a key concept in Intel TDX. It is loaded into the SEAM memory by the SEAM loader and protected by the SEAM range register (SEAMRR). It manages the transition between a TD and the hypervisor. If there is a VM exit event causing a TD guest to exit, the CPU is switched to the Intel TDX module instead of the hypervisor. The Intel TDX module then uses the SEAMRET instruction to switch to the hypervisor. After the hypervisor handles the VM exit event, it uses the SEAMCALL instruction to switch to the Intel TDX module. Then the Intel TDX module does a VM entry to resume the TD guest. Figure 13-8 shows the Intel TDX module flow.

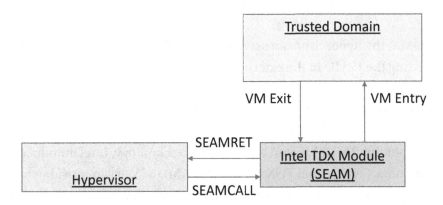

Figure 13-8. *Intel TDX Module Flow*

Figure 13-9 shows how the Intel TDX memory protection works. The TD may access two classes of memory – private memory that contains the confidential data inside of the TD; shared memory that is used to communicate with an untrusted agent outside of the TD, such as a hypervisor service or a device driver's DMA or I/O. With TDX, the highest bit in the guest physical address (GPA) is designated as a "shared" bit. The private memory has the shared bit as 0, and the shared memory has the shared bit as 1. When the TD is executing, there are two different extended page tables (EPT) – a shared EPT is setup by the hypervisor and manages the shared GPA translations with shared keyID; a secure EPT is setup by the Intel TDX module and manages the private GPA translations with private keyID.

Besides the secure EPT, the Intel TDX module also maintains the confidentiality and integrity of the CPU-state. When a TD is created, the Intel TDX module requires additional memory to setup the virtual machine control state (VMCS) and TD state save area etc. These data structures are protected by the TD private key. As such, they cannot be tampered by the hypervisor.

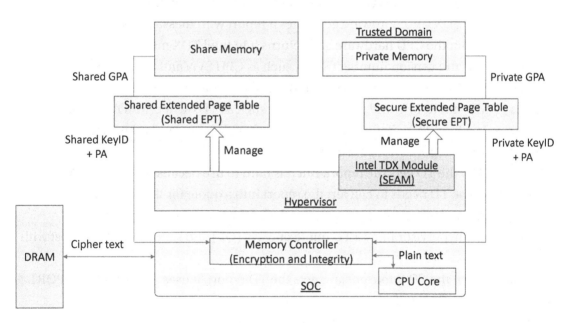

Figure 13-9. *Intel TDX Memory Protection*

2) Remote attestation allows the owner of TD and the consumers of the services in TD to determine the version of the trusted computing base (TCB) in a TD which they are relying on to protect the data. It brings confidence that the service is running inside of a TD on a genuine Intel TDX system.

During a TD creation, the hypervisor allocates private memory and asks Intel TDX module to load the initial memory content. The Intel TDX module also extends the initial memory content and its metadata, such as memory addresses, into a TD measurement register (TDMR). After the TD is launched by the Intel TDX module, the initial TD can continue extending more information, such as additional code and configuration data to a set of runtime extendable measurement registers (RTMR). Both TDMR and RTMR are used in the remote attestation for the TD.

Figure 13-10 shows the remote attestation architecture flow.

Step 1: A challenger sends the challenge request to a TD.

Step 2: The TD asks the Intel TDX module to get a report for the TD.

Step 3: The Intel TDX module invokes SEAMREPORT instruction.

Step 4: The TDX CPU hardware generates a report with message authentication code (MAC) from the CPU hardware and returns it to Intel TDX module. The report includes the secure version number (SVN), such as CPU SVN and SEAMLDR SVN, and the hash of the TD information. The TD information includes the measurement register, such as TDMR and RTMR, and the TD attribute such as TD owner (MROWNER).

Step 5: The Intel TDX module gets the report from hardware, combines the TD information, and reports the full report to the TD.

Step 6: Now the TD gets the report. But it is hard to use because it only uses MAC for the integrity. The TD needs to convert the report into a quote for the attestation. As such, the TD sends the report to the hypervisor and asks for a quote for the report.

Step 7: The hypervisor finds a TD quote enclave (QE) and sends a quote request with the TD report.

Step 8: When the TD quote enclave gets the TD report, it uses the EVERIFYREPORT instruction to let CPU verify the integrity of the report.

Step 9: If the MAC of the report is correct, it means the report is genuine. The CPU hardware returns the information back to quote enclave.

Step 10: Then the TD quote enclave signs the report with an attestation key and returns the quote to the hypervisor.

The attestation key can be verified with the attestation infrastructure. An Intel provisioning certification enclave (PCE) is designed to act as a local certificate authority for the local TD quote enclave. During TD quote enclave launch, it generates its own attestation key and submits to PCE. Then the PCE authenticates the request and issues a certificate like structure for the TD quote enclave and the attestation key. This structure is signed by the provisioning certification key (PCK), which is maintained by Intel.

Step 11: The hypervisor returns the quote back to the TD.

Step 12: The TD now responses the challenge and return the TD quote to the challenger.

Step 13: The challenger can verify the quote by using attestation key certification and verify the attestation key certification with an Intel provision certificate key (PCK). If the verification passes, it means the quote is genuine.

Step 14: The challenger can parse the TD report and get the TD information, such as TD measurement (TDMR and RTMR), to see if they meet the expectation.

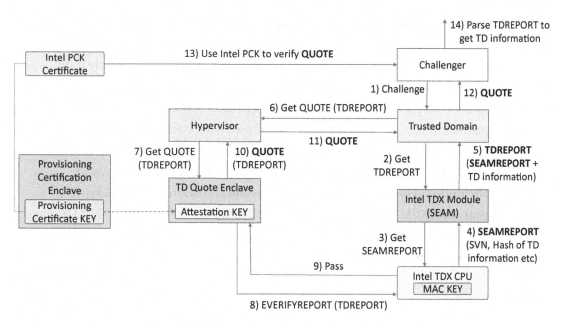

Figure 13-10. *Intel TDX Remote Attestation*

IBM Secure Virtual Machine (SVM)

Similar to AMD Secure Encrypted Virtualization (SEV), IBM enabled Secure Virtual Machine (SVM) on IBM Power Systems. A new mode - ultravisor mode – is introduced to support the SVM. The ultravisor mode has higher privilege than the hypervisor mode. The memory is partitioned into secure memory and normal memory. As part of the secure boot process, the Protected Execution Ultravisor (or Ultravisor) is loaded into secure memory. When the SVM starts, the software in the SVM calls the Ultravisor to move the SVM to secure memory where execution resumes. An SVM uses hypervisor calls (h-calls) to obtain services from the hypervisor and ultravisor calls (u-calls) to the Ultravisor. The Ultravisor filters all calls between an SVM and the hypervisor to assure that only the information required to perform the call is passed to the hypervisor. It also makes sure that only the response from the hypervisor goes back to the SVM. The hardware prevents unauthorized system software and hardware from referencing the secure memory.

An SVM can run only on systems that support the IBM Protected Execution Facility (PEF). The IBM PEF has a public/private key pair. The private key is known only to the system (not be exposed to the owner of the system) and is useable only if the correct, verified, firmware has been launched. The public key of the target system is used to wrap the encryption key of the secure VM when it is created.

The Ultravisor makes an encrypted version of the requested SVM memory page available to the hypervisor. The cryptographic mode used to protect the SVMs is an extension of the Advanced Encryption Standard (AES) called Integrity Aware Parallelizable Mode (IAPM), which can detect any modifications of the encrypted representation of an SVM page by the hypervisor. For device I/O, the virtual I/O bounce buffer is used. The SVM need specify to the Ultravisor that specific pages of its memory are to be shared with the hypervisor without protection.

EDK II Support

EDK II implemented the Open Virtual Machine Firmware (OVMF). In order to support SEV, the OVMF sets the guest page table with C-bit for the private memory. When the guest requires the DMA, the OVMF code needs to clear the C-bit for the shared DMA buffer and set the C-bit again when the DMA buffer is reclaimed to be private memory. In order to support SEV-ES, the OVMF implements the #VC handler to convert the special instruction with the GHCB access.

Attack and Mitigation

One Infrastructure as a Service (IaaS) use case is shown in Figure 13-11. A tenant provides a guest disk which contains an operating system and the application data to the cloud service provider (CSP). Then the CSP allocates memory for the tenant and uses the hypervisor to launch the guest disk image. Now let's assume the CSP/hypervisor is malicious and take a look at the attack point.

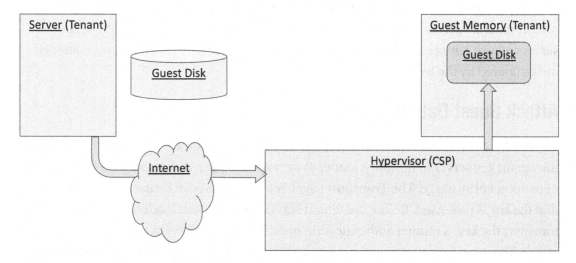

Figure 13-11. *An IaaS Use Case*

Attack Guest Data at Rest

The data at rest is the guest disk image. The hypervisor may read the data on the disk or tamper the data. There are at least two possible ways for the protection:

1) Encryption: If the full disk image is encrypted, then the hypervisor cannot read the content without the key. If the hypervisor modifies the disk image, the decrypted data will be invalid.

2) Measurement: Once the disk image is loaded into memory, the tenant uses a hardware assistant mechanism to measure the disk image. The limitation of measurement is that it cannot prevent the hypervisor from reading the disk content. The process to measure for the whole image in memory is complicated, and it also requires additional root-of-trust for measurement support.

As such, let's assume that the encryption solution is chosen for the disk. Now the question is who does the decryption and how the disk encryption key is transported.

Besides the disk image, the tenant may choose to transmit a guest loader to the hypervisor. The guest loader is so simple that it does not have any secret. As such, the guest loader can be in plain text. The guest loader has a way to communicate with the tenant server to get the disk encryption key, which is used to decrypt the disk. Because the disk loader is simple and has no secret, it is possible to use the measurement and attestation mechanism for the disk loader. During launch, a root-of-trust for measurement, such as SEV firmware, may measure the disk loader. Later, the tenant server can use remote attestation for the guest loader to ensure that the guest loader is not tampered by the hypervisor.

Attack Guest Data in Transition

The data in transition is the disk encryption key. The key should be transmitted from the tenant key server to the guest loader to decrypt the guest disk image. This is a typical network security usage. The Transport Layer Security (TLS) can be used here, to ensure that the key is protected. Before the tenant server and the guest loader create a session to transport the key, a mutual authentication must be done to prevent man-in-the-middle attack. The guest loader may include a server public certificate to verify the key server in the TLS handshake. The tenant key server may use the remote attestation result as the evidence that the guest loader is not tampered.

Attack Guest Data in Use

In order to protect the data in use, memory encryption must be used. Either SEV or MKTME can be used here. As such, the hypervisor cannot access the guest memory. Putting them all together, the solution is in Figure 13-12. The assumption is that the tenant trusts themself and the Independent Hardware Vendor (IHV) and the tenant does not trust the cloud service provider (CSP).

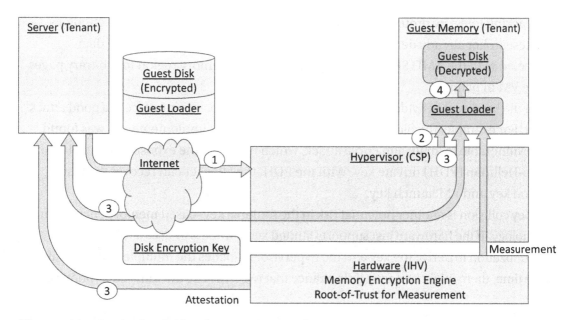

Figure 13-12. *An IaaS Use Case – Protected Guest Domain*

Step 1: The tenant server transmits a guest loader and a guest disk image to the CSP hypervisor.

Step 2: The CSP hypervisor creates a guest environment for the tenant and launches the guest loader. The hardware component is involved in this launch process. The hardware measures the guest load and enables the memory encryption for the guest memory.

Step 3: The guest loader communicates with the tenant server to get the disk encryption key. Before the key is transmitted by the tenant key server, the key server uses remote attestation to communicate with the hardware to ensure that the guest loader is unmodified.

Step 4: The guest loader gets the key, decrypts the guest disk image, and loads it.

Attack the Hardware root-of-trust

In the preceding process, the hardware root-of-trust is one key component. It maintains the memory encryption key for the guest and provides the measurement for the guest domain. If the hardware root-of-trust is broken, the preceding protection does not take effect.

Lacking integrity protection is a weakness of the memory encryption technology. The researcher already demonstrated the SEVered attack to extract the VM data protected with the AMD SEV by remapping the entire memory region to arbitrary pages in the VM in plain text.

If the hardware provides the key management service, this interface is a good attack point. For example, the old AMD SEV elliptic curve (ECC) implementation was found to be vulnerable to an invalid curve attack, which results in the exposure of the platform Diffie-Hellman (PDH) private key. With the PDH, the attacker can recover the whole session key and VM launch key.

Key collision is another potential risk in the multiple key–based memory encryption technology. If the hardware just supports limited key numbers or uses a weak randomization to derive the key and the hypervisor launches the multiple guest domains at same time, there might be a very little chance that two VMs use the same encryption key.

Device Interface

The guest domain runs on top of the hardware emulated by the hypervisor. The virtual device interface varies based upon the implementation, for example:

1) Emulated hardware

The virtual hardware can have the same interface as the real hardware, and the virtual hardware is fully emulated by the hypervisor. This device should be in a full virtualization environment.

2) Synthetic hardware

The virtual hardware can be a hypervisor-specific standard interface, such as the Virtual I/O Device (virtio) with Linux Kernel–Based Virtual Machine (KVM) and Quick Emulator (QEMU) and the Virtual Machine Bus (vmbus) with the Microsoft Hyper-V. This device should be in the para-virtualization environment for better performance.

3) Physical hardware (passthru)

The virtual hardware can be a physical device assigned by the hypervisor in passthru mode, such as the graphic device. This can be supported with hardware partitioning. The hypervisor just lets the guest manage the device with the help of IOMMU.

4) Virtual device interface of a physical hardware (passthru)

The virtual hardware can be a virtual device interface on the physical device and passthru to the physical device, such as the PCI express Single Root I/O Virtualization (SR-IOV) and Intel Scalable I/O Virtualization.

Case Study

Now, let's take a look at some real cases for the device interface support in virtualization.

Single Root I/O Virtualization (SR-IOV)

A SR-IOV device can have one physical function (PF) and multiple virtual functions (VFs). See Figure 13-13. The virtual function is a lightweight PCI express function, and it is assigned with a unique routing ID. The VF has its own dedicated PCI configuration space, base address register (BAR), memory mapped I/O (MMIO) resource, message signaled interrupt (MSI) storage table, function-level reset (FLR), advanced error reporting (AER), power management (PM), and so on. The virtual function must have the same device type as the physical function. Each virtual function can be assigned to a dedicated guest domain by the host VMM. As such, the guest domain can control and use the device directly without the interrupt from VMM. This design can improve the performance and resolve the physical device limitation.

A network interface card may implement the SR-IOV to increase the throughput of the network traffic in the virtualization environment. The Non-Volatile Memory Express (NVMe) also added SR-IOV support in the NVMe specification for the flexible resource management.

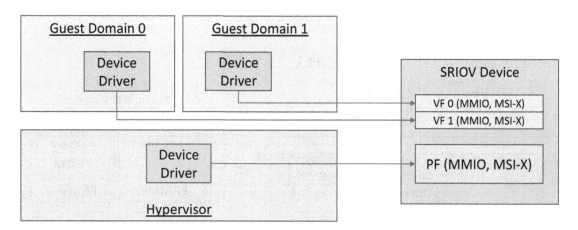

Figure 13-13. *Virtual Function Allocation with SR-IOV*

Scalable I/O Virtualization (Scalable IOV)

The SR-IOV is realized by replicating the hardware/software interface for each virtual function, such as memory mapped I/O (MMIO) resources and message signaled interrupts (MSIs). This replication adds complexity to the device and brings limitations when scaling to large numbers of virtual functions. In order to resolve this problem, Intel brings the Scalable I/O Virtualization (IOV) technology.

The Intel Scalable IOV device organizes the hardware/software interface into two categories: fast path and slow path. The fast-path access focuses on the data transmission at runtime. The slow-path access focuses on initialization, configuration, reset, error handling, and so on. With these categories, the fast-path accesses are mapped to the physical device directly, and the slow-path accesses are emulated by the device-specific host software.

In SR-IOV, the fast-path category is implemented using virtual functions. However, what is really needed is dedicated MMIO resources and interrupt resources. The Intel Scalable IOV uses the Assignable Device Interface (ADI) for the MMIO resources to replace the MMIO base address register (BAR) in the virtual function and the Interrupt Message Storage (IMS) to replace the MSI-X table storage (see Figure 13-14) for interrupts. The ADI is in the physical function's MMIO BAR instead of the virtual function's. All ADIs share the same physical BAR and share the same requester ID (RID) – bus/device/function of the physical function. Each ADI must be assigned with a Process Address Space Identifier (PASID). The difference between RID and PASID is that the RID is used for transaction routing to an I/O fabric, while PASID is used to convey the address space targeted by the memory transaction. The ADI uses the IMS for interrupt storage. The IMS is similar to virtual MSI-X, except that it is realized in the physical function instead of a virtual function.

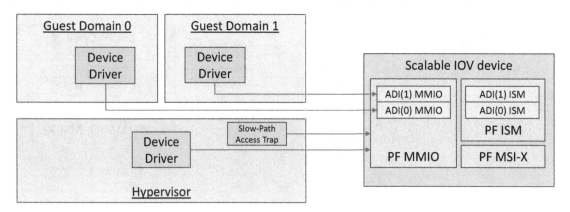

Figure 13-14. *Assignable Device Interface with SR-IOV*

The benefit of this approach is that the high-performance I/O can still be achieved by the fast path (ADI and ISM) and the scalability is achieved by the simpler hardware design with the help of device emulation for the slow path.

Virtual I/O Device (virtio)

With full virtualization, the hypervisor must intercept all the commands to the hardware device and emulate the hardware behavior to send the response back to the guest. It brings a performance impact because of VM exit costs and emulation costs. It also brings a hardware compatibility risk because the hypervisor must emulate all supported hardware. Para-virtualization requires small modifications for the guest OS with the benefit of big performance improvements because it simplifies the hypervisor. With para-virtualization, the guest needs to implement the front side of the device to consume the function, and the hypervisor needs to implement the backend of the device to provide the service.

In order to support interoperability and compatibility, there is a need to define a standard interface between the hypervisor and the guest. The interface just needs to focus on the function of the device, such as storage, network, input, output, and so on.

virtio is one of the standard interfaces on the Linux side (see Figure 13-15). It defines the network device, block device, console device, entropy device, memory balloon device, SCSI host device, GPU device, input device, crypto device, and socket device. The virtio device can be discovered by the guest via standard PCI bus, MMIO, or channel I/O.

The EDK II Open Virtual Machine Firmware (OVMF) implements the virtio device driver and supports transport via the virtio PCI interface. OVMF prepares the data in the shared buffer and sends the I/O request which is intercepted by the Linux Kernel–Based Virtual Machine (KVM). Then the KVM notifies the Quick Emulator (QEMU) about the virtio request. It is QEMU that implements the virtio backend, which parses the data in the shared buffer and sends the response back via the shared buffer.

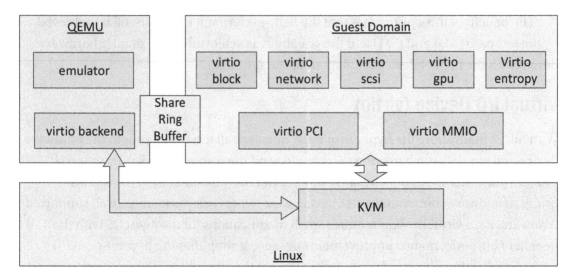

Figure 13-15. *virtio device*

Virtual Machine Bus (vmbus)

vmbus is the guest hypervisor communication channel in the Microsoft Hyper-V (see Figure 13-16). The guest domain can have multiple Virtual Service Clients (VSCs) such as network, video, storage, and Human Interface Device (HID). The VSC can use vmbus to communicate with the Virtual Service Provider (VSP) in the root partition directly to improve the virtualization performance.

With the standard vmbus, a Linux guest may include a vmbus driver (VSC) and run in the Microsoft Hyper-V environment. Vice versa, it is possible that a Windows guest may use the vmbus driver and run in the Linux KVM/QEMU with vmbus and VSP support.

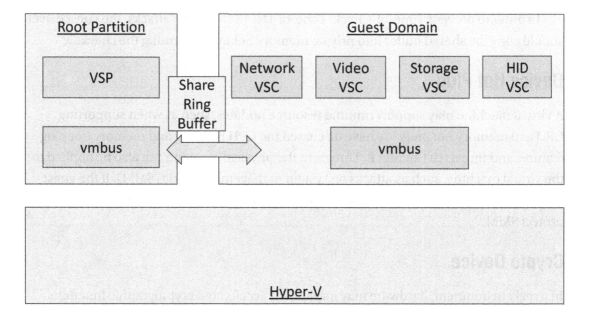

Figure 13-16. *vmbus Device*

Attack and Mitigation

Now, let's take a look at some real cases for the attack from the virtual device or physical device and mitigation.

Device Input

No matter whether the device is physical (direct passthru, SR-IOV, or Scalable IOV) or virtual (virtio or vmbus), it can be used to attack the guest domain. For example, the device identifier data or the DMA input buffer can provide spurious device input. A malicious device may fill the data buffer with malformed data.

Hackers have already demonstrated attacks from the guest domain to the hypervisor by using the shared ring buffer VM escape to cause. The hypervisor may use a similar technique to attack the guest domain.

Similar to what we have discussed in Chapter 8, the guest device driver should

1) Verify the device with the help of the platform Root-of-Trust and set up a secure communication channel.

2) Parse the device data carefully and reject any invalid data.

In order to prevent Time-of-Check/Time-of-Use (TOC/TOU) attacks, the guest driver should copy the shared buffer into private memory before performing the check.

Device Hot Plug

A virtual machine may support runtime resource updates, such as when supporting CPU and memory hot plug. We have discussed the CPU hot plug and memory hot plug features and threats in Chapter 8. Threats to the physical machine can also be applied to the virtual machine, such as attacks on system management mode (SMM). If the guest domain implemented SMM, the guest should use similar protection mechanisms to protect SMM.

Crypto Device

In a real environment, hardware may implement accelerated cryptographic functions. For example, ARMv8 CPUs implement symmetric encryption (AES, SM4), hash (SHA, SHA2, SHA3, SM3), and randomization (RNDR) instructions. Intel CPUs implement randomization (RDSEED, RDRAND), hash (SHA, SHA2), and symmetric encryption (AES) instructions.

In the virtualization world, a virtual device may also provide such support. For example, virtio provides the entropy device to return random data and the crypto device to provide the crypto services, such as symmetric encryption services (ARC4, AES, 3DES), hash services (MD5, SHA1, SHA2, SHA3), message authentication code (MAC) services (HMAC, CMAC, GMAC, CBCMAC), and Authenticated Encryption with Associated Data (AEAD) services (GCM, CCM, ChaCha20-Poly1305).

If the guest treats the hypervisor as malicious, those virtual cryptographic devices should not be used. If the guest trusts the hardware which provides protection for the guest, the guest may choose to use the services provided by the trusted hardware.

Special Feature

Besides booting to a guest OS, virtual firmware may implement some special features. Each feature may have its own special threat model.

Case Study

Now, let's take a look at some real cases for security features.

Trusted Boot

We have discussed the trusted boot implementation in the real world in Chapter 7. The trusted boot can also be used in the virtualization environment to provide the evidence that the boot flow of the guest is unmodified.

In the physical world, the trusted boot can rely on a Trusted Platform Module (TPM), which provides a set of Platform Configuration Registers (PCRs). These act as the root-of-trust for reporting (RTR) to record the system state and support the remote attestation. The TPM also provides the protected storage area as the root-of-trust for storage (RTS) for keys and data. The TPM cannot provide the root-of-trust for measurement (RTM). The RTM should be some code on the host side, on which the Core-RTM (CRTM) measures the component to run after the platform reset.

The guest domain may have a virtual TPM (vTPM) to provide virtual RTR (vRTR) and virtual RTS (vRTS), with a virtual RTM (vRTM) to do the measurement. The vTPM and vRTM must be in the Trusted Computing Base (TCB).

If the guest can trust the hypervisor, the vTPM (vRTR and vRTS) and vRTM can be provided by the hypervisor. Figure 13-17 shows one possible implementation. When the hypervisor launches the virtual firmware, the vRTM may measure the virtual firmware into the vTPM. The measurement process in the guest domain is the same as the process in the physical environment. When a remote challenger wants to use remote attestation to check if the guest environment is trusted, the challenge can use the standard remote attestation process to communicate with an attestation service in the guest domain and get the vTPM PCR quote. In order to verify the authenticity of the vTPM, the challenger also needs to use remote attestation for the hypervisor who provides the vTPM.

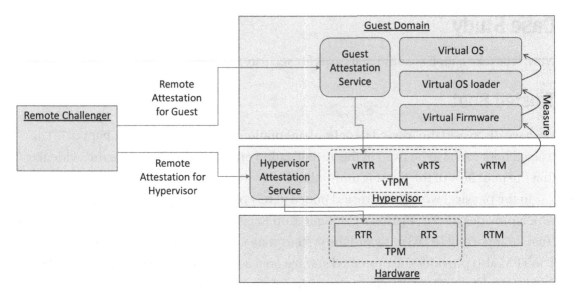

Figure 13-17. *Virtual TPM from the Hypervisor*

If the guest cannot trust the hypervisor, the vTPM (vRTR and vRTS) and vRTM cannot be provided by the hypervisor. Figure 13-18 shows another possible implementation. The vRTR, vRTS, and vRTM are provided by the system on a chip (SOC). When the hypervisor wants to launch a guest domain, the SOC assists the guest launch process. The vRTM records the measurement into vRTR inside of the SOC. The guest may use the measurement service provided by the SOC to extend the data in the guest domain. The SOC must maintain the isolation between the guest domain and the hypervisor as we discussed in the first section of this chapter. As such, the malicious hypervisor cannot tamper the guest execution environment and the guest execution context recorded in the SOC. The vRTR, vRTS, and vRTM must be domain specific and must not be accessed by the hypervisor or other guest domains. When the challenger wants to verify the guest domain, the challenger uses the remote attestation for the guest at first. Then the challenger needs to do the remote attestation for the SOC as well to ensure the authenticity of the SOC.

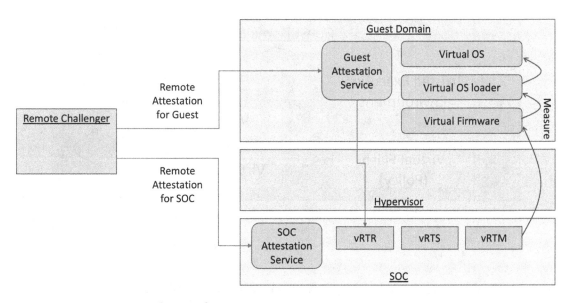

Figure 13-18. *Virtual TPM from SOC*

Secure Boot

The secure boot is used when one component loads the next boot component. If the next component is from a different vendor and it is not trusted, the secure boot can help verify if the next component is unmodified before it is loaded. This is also true in the guest domain. The virtual firmware can use UEFI secure boot to ensure that only the verified guest OS can be loaded. That can mitigate some attacks on the guest OS.

Similar to the one in the real environment, the guest secure boot policy should be stored in a protected storage, and it should only be updated in a trusted execution environment. As such, the other guest software cannot update the secure boot policy without authorization. The secure boot policy may be updated by the root-of-trust, which could either be the hypervisor or the SOC based upon the threat model. If the guest domain trusts the hypervisor, the guest firmware can rely on the hypervisor to emulate the flash device and store the secure boot policy there. The guest firmware should lock the guest flash device so that no other guest software can update it. The hypervisor also needs to emulate a trusted execution environment (TEE) such as system management mode (SMM) and only allows the flash update in the SMM environment. See Figure 13-19.

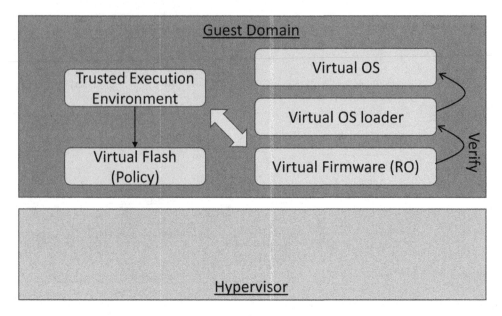

Figure 13-19. *Secure Boot from the Hypervisor*

However, if the guest domain does not trust the hypervisor, the guest domain may store the secure boot policy in a read-only flash device. The secure boot solution needs to work with the trusted boot in this case. When the SOC launches the guest domain, the SOC measures both the code in the virtual firmware and the policy in the virtual flash configuration area. Care must be taken so that if the trusted execution environment (TEE) is emulated by the hypervisor, the TEE cannot be trusted by the guest domain. The TEE for the guest domain can only be trusted if the TEE is provided by the SOC. See Figure 13-20.

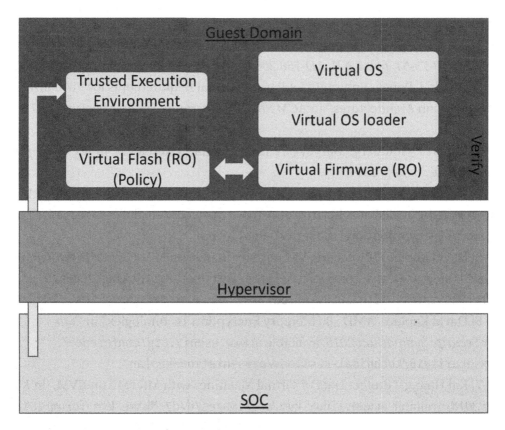

Figure 13-20. *Secure Boot from SOC*

Summary

In this chapter, we discussed virtual firmware security design including hardware security extensions, device interface support, and special security features implemented in the virtual firmware. In Part III, we will introduce the security implementation in the firmware.

References

Book

[B-1] Jim Smith, Ravi Nair, *Virtual Machines: Versatile Platforms for Systems and Processes*, Morgan Kaufmann, 2005

[B-2] Edouard Bugnion, Jason Nieh, Dan Tsafrir, *Hardware and Software Support for Virtualization*, Morgan & Claypool Publishers, 2017

Conference, Journal, and Paper

[P-1] J. P. Anderson, "Computer security technology planning study," in *Technical Report ESD-TR-73-51, vols I & II, AD-758 206, USAF Electronic Systems Division. 1972.*

[P-2] Gerald J. Popek, Robert P. Goldberg, "Formal Requirements for Virtualizable Third Generation Architectures," in *ACM SIGOPS Operating Systems Review 17:412-421, January 1974.*

[P-3] Robert P. Goldberg, "Survey of Virtual Machines Research," in *IEEE Computer, Volume: 7, Issue: 6, June 1974.*

[P-4] David Kaplan, Jeremy Powell, Tom Woller, "AMD Memory Encryption," *AMD Whitepaper 2016*, available at `http://developer.amd.com/wordpress/media/2013/12/AMD_Memory_Encryption_Whitepaper_v7-Public.pdf`

[P-5] David Kaplan, "Protecting VM Register State with SEV-ES," *AMD Whitepaper 2017*, available at `www.amd.com/system/files/TechDocs/Protecting%20VM%20Register%20State%20with%20SEV-ES.pdf`

[P-6] David Kaplan, "AMD x86 Memory Encryption Technologies," in *25th Usenix Security Symposium 2016*, available at `www.usenix.org/conference/usenixsecurity16/technical-sessions/presentation/kaplan`

[P-7] Kai Huang, "Protect Data of Virtual Machines with MKTME on KVM," in *KVM Forum 2018*, available at `www.linux-kvm.org/images/d/d7/Mktme_kvm_forum_2018.pdf`

[P-8] "Intel Trust Domain Extensions," Intel whitepaper 2020, available at `https://software.intel.com/content/www/us/en/develop/articles/intel-trust-domain-extensions.html`

[P-9] Guerney D. H. Hunt, "Protected Execution Facility – Secure computing for Linux on OpenPOWER," in 2018, `https://events19.linuxfoundation.org/wp-content/uploads/2017/12/Protected-Execution-Facility-Guerney-D.-H.-Hunt-IBM-Research.pdf`

[P-10] Guerney Hunt, Richard (Rick) Boivie, Eric Hall, Elaine Palmer, Dimitrios Pendarakis, Enriquillo (Ray) Valdez, "Supporting protected computing on IBM Power Architecture," in IBM whitepaper 2018, available at `https://developer.ibm.com/articles/l-support-protected-computing/`

[P-11] Rodrigo Branco, Shay Gueron, "Blinded random corruption attacks," in *IEEE International Symposium on Hardware Oriented Security and Trust (HOST)*, 2016

[P-12] Mathias Morbitzer, Manual Huber, Julian Horsch, Sascha Wessel, "SEVered: Subverting AMD's Virtual Machine Encryption," in *Proceedings of the 11th European Workshop on Systems Security, 2018*

[P-13] "AMD-SEV: Platform DH key recovery via invalid curve attack," 2019, available at `https://seclists.org/fulldisclosure/2019/Jun/46`

[P-14] Roman Kagan, "VMBus (Hyper-V) devices in QEMU/KVM," in *Linux Foundation Event 2017*, available at `http://events17.linuxfoundation.org/sites/events/files/slides/VMBus%20%28Hyper-V%29%20devices%20in%20QEMU%252FKVM_0.pdf`

[P-15] Alex Ionescu, "Ring 0 to Ring -1 Attacks – Hyper-V IPC Internals," in *SYSCAN 2015*, available at `www.alex-ionescu.com/syscan2015.pdf`

[P-16] Andrea Allievi, "Hyper-V and its Memory Manager," in *Recon 2017*, available at `www.andrea-allievi.com/files/Recon_2017_Montreal_HyperV_public.pptx`

[P-17] Joe Bialek, Nicolas Joly, "A Dive in to Hyper-V Architecture & Vulnerabilities," in *Blackhat US 2018*, available at `http://i.blackhat.com/us-18/Wed-August-8/us-18-Joly-Bialek-A-Dive-in-to-Hyper-V-Architecture-and-Vulnerabilities.pdf`

[P-18] Somnath Chakrabarti, Brandon Baker, Mona Vij, "Intel® SGX Enabled Key Manager Service with OpenStack Barbican," 2017, `https://arxiv.org/ftp/arxiv/papers/1712/1712.07694.pdf`

[P-19] Jordan Rabet, "Hardening Hyper-V through Offensive Security Research," in *Blackhat US 2018*, available at `http://i.blackhat.com/us-18/Thu-August-9/us-18-Rabet-Hardening-Hyper-V-Through-Offensive-Security-Research.pdf`

[P-20] Stefan Berger, Ramon Caceres, Kenneth A. Goldman, Ronald Perez, Reiner Sailer, Leendert van Doorn, "vTPM: Virtualizing the Trusted Platform Module," in *15th Usenix Security Symposium*, available at `www.usenix.org/legacy/event/sec06/tech/full_papers/berger/berger.pdf`

[P-21] Joshua Schiffman, "vTPM: Virtualizing the Trusted Platform Module," in Systems and Internet Infrastructure Security, `www.cse.psu.edu/~pdm12/cse544/slides/cse544-schiffman-vTPM.pdf`

Specification and Guideline

[S-1] AMD, "AMD Architecture Programmer's Manual," 2019, available at `www.amd.com/en/support/tech-docs`

[S-2] AMD, "Secure Encrypted Virtualization API," 2019, available at `https://developer.amd.com/wp-content/resources/55766.PDF`

[S-3] AMD, "Guest Hypervisor Communication Block (GHCB) Standardization," 2019, available at `https://developer.amd.com/wp-content/resources/56421.pdf`

[S-4] AMD, "SEV Secure Nested Paging Firmware ABI Specification," 2020, available at `https://www.amd.com/system/files/TechDocs/56860.pdf`

[S-5] Intel, "Intel 64 and IA-32 Architecture Software Developer Manuals," 2019, available at `https://software.intel.com/en-us/articles/intel-sdm`

[S-6] Intel, "Intel Architecture Memory Encryption Technologies Specification," 2019, available at `https://software.intel.com/sites/default/files/managed/a5/16/Multi-Key-Total-Memory-Encryption-Spec.pdf`

[S-7] Intel, "Intel Scalable I/O Virtualization Specification," 2018, available at `https://software.intel.com/en-us/download/intel-scalable-io-virtualization-technical-specification`

[S-8] Intel, "Virtualization Technology for Directed I/O specification," 2019, available at `https://software.intel.com/en-us/download/intel-virtualization-technology-for-directed-io-architecture-specification`

[S-9] OASIS, "Virtual I/O Device (VIRTIO) Version 1.1," 2019, available at `http://docs.oasis-open.org/virtio/virtio/v1.1/virtio-v1.1.html`

[S-10] Microsoft, "Hypervisor Specification," 2018, `https://docs.microsoft.com/en-us/virtualization/hyper-v-on-windows/reference/tlfs`

[S-11] Trusted Computing Group, "Virtualized Trusted Platform Architecture Specification," 2011, available at `https://trustedcomputinggroup.org/resource/virtualized-trusted-platform-architecture-specification/`

[S-12] PCI-SIG, "PCI Express Base Specification," 2019, available at `https://pcisig.com/specifications`

[S-13] CXL org, "The CXL Specification," 2019, available at `www.computeexpresslink.org/`

Web

[W-1] Amit Singh, "An Introduction to Virtualization," 2004, `www.kernelthread.com/publications/virtualization/`

[W-2] "AMD Secure Encrypted Virtualization," `https://developer.amd.com/sev/`

[W-3] "Windows VirtIo Drivers," `www.linux-kvm.org/page/WindowsGuestDrivers/Download_Drivers`

[W-4] Microsoft, "Hyper-V Architecture," 2018, `https://docs.microsoft.com/en-us/virtualization/hyper-v-on-windows/reference/hyper-v-architecture`

[W-5] Nirmal Sharma, "Understanding Hyper-V VSP/VSC and VMBUS Design," 2013, `www.serverwatch.com/server-tutorials/understanding-hyper-v-vspvsc-and-vmbus-design.html`

[W-6] Gerhart, "Hyper-V Internals," 2015, `http://hvinternals.blogspot.com/2015/10/hyper-v-internals.html`

[W-7] "Hyper-V / VMBus device emulation in Qemu," `https://src.openvz.org/projects/UP/repos/edk2/browse`

[W-8] "Hyper-V enlightenments," `https://github.com/qemu/qemu/blob/master/docs/hyperv.txt`

[W-9] "TPM 2.0 Simulator for Linux/TEE," `https://develop.trustedcomputinggroup.org/2019/05/08/tpm-2-0-simulator-for-linux-tee/`, `https://github.com/stwagnr/tpm2simulator`

[W-10] "TSS.MSR: The TPM Software Stack from Microsoft Research," `www.microsoft.com/en-us/download/details.aspx?id=52507`, `https://github.com/microsoft/TSS.MSR`

[W-11] "IBM's Software TPM 2.0," `https://sourceforge.net/projects/ibmswtpm2/`

[W-12] "QEMU TPM Device," `https://github.com/qemu/qemu/blob/master/docs/specs/tpm.txt`

[W-13] Miriam Zimmerman, "Virtual Trusted Platform Module for Shielded VMs: security in plaintext," 2018, `https://cloud.google.com/blog/products/gcp/virtual-trusted-platform-module-for-shielded-vms-security-in-plaintext`

[W-14] Jason Geffner, "VENOM – Virtualized Environment Neglected Operations Manipulation," available at `https://venom.crowdstrike.com/`, `https://www.crowdstrike.com/blog/venom-vulnerability-details/`

[W-15] Vishnu Dev, "QEMU VM escape," 2019, available at `https://blog.bi0s.in/2019/08/24/Pwn/VM-Escape/2019-07-29-qemu-vm-escape-cve-2019-14378/`, `https://www.secpod.com/blog/qemu-vm-escape/`

[W-16] Tencent Blade Team, "V-gHost : QEMU-KVM VM Escape in vhost/vhost-net," available at `https://blade.tencent.com/en/advisories/v-ghost/`

PART III

Security Development

Being a good security architect is a good start, but it is insufficient to ensure the delivery of a secure system. When we implement the security features or policies, we need to follow the security development best practices to reduce the risk of the vulnerabilities being introduced in the implementation. For example, memory safety issues contribute more than 50% of vulnerabilities in the software and firmware. There are multiple technologies introduced to mitigate those issues, such as compiler defenses, hardware enhancements, new languages, and so on. These items can also be used in the firmware development phase.

CHAPTER 14

Firmware Secure Coding Practice

After we finish the security architecture and design, we need to bring security into the development phase. On the one hand, firmware is still a type of software that is written in a software programming language, such as the C language. Most software secure coding practices are also applicable for firmware development. On the other hand, firmware is a special class of software. Its work is to initialize the silicon to boot the operating system, such as a system firmware, or to provide special runtime services in a hidden execution environment, such as device firmware. Firmware has unique security requirements based upon those usages. Today, there are lots of books introducing software secure coding. Two classic books, *Code Complete* by Steve McConnell and *Writing Solid Code* by Steve Maguire, are highly recommended for C programmers. Newer books, such as *Writing Secure Code* by Michael Howard and David Le Blanc and *Building Secure Software* by John Viega and Gary McGraw, are excellent resources for the secure programming practices in Windows and Linux. We will not duplicate the details of those parts but instead will give examples on how that guidance impacts the firmware. After that, we will introduce the firmware-specific secure coding practices.

Basic Security Practice

First, let's look at the basic secure coding practice and secure design practice.

Secure Coding Practice

The general secure coding practice in the firmware is similar to the one in the software.

© Jiewen Yao and Vincent Zimmer 2020
J. Yao and V. Zimmer, *Building Secure Firmware*, https://doi.org/10.1007/978-1-4842-6106-4_14

Prevent Buffer Overrun

Buffer overrun is one of the top security issues in software. It is also one of the top security issues in the firmware. One cause of the buffer overrun is that the program reads a length field from an untrusted external input and uses it without any checks. Listing 14-1 shows a classic buffer issue in the old implementation of the GUIDed Partition Table (GPT) partition driver in EDK II firmware. At first, the PartEntry is allocated with a fixed size – sizeof(EFI_PARTION_ENTRY). But later, this fixed buffer is used to copy a buffer with a variable size – (PrimaryHeader->SizeOfPartitionEntry). The PrimaryHeader-> SizeOfPartitionEntry is the external data on the disk image, such as a hard disk driver or a USB disk driver. As such, the attack may just change the SizeOfPartitionEntry with a large size and cause a buffer overflow in the firmware boot.

Listing 14-1.

```
================
  PartEntry = AllocatePool (PrimaryHeader->NumberOfPartitionEntries *
  sizeof (EFI_PARTITION_ENTRY));
  if (PartEntry == NULL) {
    DEBUG ((EFI_D_ERROR, "Allocate pool error\n"));
    goto Done;
  }

  Status = DiskIo->ReadDisk (
                  DiskIo,
                  MediaId,
                  MultU64x32(PrimaryHeader->PartitionEntryLBA, BlockSize),
                  PrimaryHeader->NumberOfPartitionEntries* (PrimaryHeader-
                  >SizeOfPartitionEntry),
                  PartEntry
                  );
  if (EFI_ERROR (Status)) {
    GptValidStatus = Status;
    DEBUG ((EFI_D_ERROR, " Partition Entry ReadDisk error\n"));
    goto Done;
  }
================
```

In order to prevent buffer overrun, we need to check the data from external inputs and ensure that the allocated buffer is of sufficient size to contain all of the external data. See Listing 14-2.

Listing 14-2.

```
================
PartEntry = AllocatePool (PrimaryHeader->NumberOfPartitionEntries *
PrimaryHeader->SizeOfPartitionEntry);
if (PartEntry == NULL) {
  DEBUG ((EFI_D_ERROR, "Allocate pool error\n"));
  goto Done;
}

Status = DiskIo->ReadDisk (
              DiskIo,
              MediaId,
              MultU64x32(PrimaryHeader->PartitionEntryLBA, BlockSize),
              PrimaryHeader->NumberOfPartitionEntries* (PrimaryHeader-
              >SizeOfPartitionEntry),
              PartEntry
              );
if (EFI_ERROR (Status)) {
  GptValidStatus = Status;
  DEBUG ((EFI_D_ERROR, " Partition Entry ReadDisk error\n"));
  goto Done;
}
================
```

Listing 14-3 shows another example in the old ACPI table processing of the Intel Authenticated Code Module (ACM), with the reserved pseudo C code. The BiosData and AcpiTable are the external untrusted input for the ACM. Without checks for the BiosData and AcpiTable, the attacker can control DmarDest by giving a malicious variant of the BiosData->Size field and control the AcpiTable and its length. As such, the attacker has the capability to override the ACM memory in the TxtHeap.

Listing 14-3.

```
================
  BiosData = TxtHeapPtr;
  OsMleData = BiosData + BiosData->Size;
  OsSinitData = OsMleData + OsMleData->Size;
  SinitMleData = OsSinitData + OsSinitData->Size;
  DmarDest = SinitMleData + DMAR_OFFSET;

  if (AcpiTable->Header.Signature == 'DMAR') {
    CopyMem (DmarDest, AcpiTable, AcpiTable->Header.Length);
  }
================
```

To mitigate this, the code should check BiosData->Size to ensure it points to the correct TxtHeap and also check the AcpiTable->Header.Length to ensure that there is no buffer overrun in the memory copy.

If the firmware has capability to process network packets, care must be taken to parse the network packet, especially for the type-length-value (TLV) format structure. There are many real cases showing that missing length check in memory copy function causes the buffer overrun, such as openssl heartbleed, BroadPwn, QualPwn, LoRaDawn etc. Listing 14-4 shows the BroadPwn issue. The current_wmm_ie (information element) is allocated with a fixed size 0x2C, but memcpy() function copies ie->len which has the 255 bytes as the maximum size. It overflows 211 bytes.

Listing 14-4.

```
================
  pm = wlc_calloc(0x78);
  wlc->pm = pm;
  current_wmm_ie = wlc_calloc(0x2C);
  wlc->current_wmm_ie = current_wmm_ie;
  ...
  if ( frame_type == FC_ASSOC_RESP ) {
    ...
    if ( wlc->pub->_wme )
    {
```

```
    cfg->flags |= 0x100u;
    memcpy(current_wmm_ie, ie->data, ie->len);
  }
================
```

Prevent Arbitrary Buffer Access and Execution

Sometimes the external buffer includes not only the data but also a pointer or an offset to additional data. In this case, the attack may coerce the pointer to reference an arbitrary location in order to override the data. Listing 14-5 shows a classic arbitrary buffer access issue in the old implementation of the UEFI SMM variable driver in EDK II firmware. The attacker can create a variable buffer read request in the CommBuffer and then request that the system management interrupt (SMI) handler return the variable. Because the attacker can control the CommBuffer address, they can control to which the data is written. For example, if the CommBuffer points to highly privileged system management RAM (SMRAM) or the hypervisor memory, then this is a typical confused deputy attack.

Listing 14-5.

```
================
SmmVariableHandler ()
{
  // ...
  SmmVariableFunctionHeader = (SMM_VARIABLE_COMMUNICATE_HEADER *)CommBuffer;
  switch (SmmVariableFunctionHeader->Function) {
  case SMM_VARIABLE_FUNCTION_GET_VARIABLE:
    SmmVariableHeader = (SMM_VARIABLE_COMMUNICATE_ACCESS_VARIABLE *)
    SmmVariableFunctionHeader->Data;
    Status = VariableServiceGetVariable (
               SmmVariableHeader->Name,
               &SmmVariableHeader->Guid,
               &SmmVariableHeader->Attributes,
               &SmmVariableHeader->DataSize,
               (UINT8 *)SmmVariableHeader->Name + SmmVariableHeader
               ->NameSize
               );
}
```

```
VariableServiceGetVariable (
  IN      CHAR16          *VariableName,
  IN      EFI_GUID        *VendorGuid,
  OUT     UINT32          *Attributes OPTIONAL,
  IN OUT  UINTN           *DataSize ,
  OUT     VOID            *Data OPTIONAL
  )
{
  // ...
  CopyMem (Data, GetVariableDataPtr (Variable.CurrPtr), VarDataSize);
}
```

================

In order to prevent this arbitrary buffer access, the SMI handler code should check the location of the communication buffer pointer in addition to the buffer overflow check. Listing 14-6 shows the full check of address and size used for the communication buffer before the code invokes the GetVariable() service.

Listing 14-6.

================
```
SmmVariableHandler ()
{
  // ...
  if (!VariableSmmIsBufferOutsideSmmValid ((UINTN)CommBuffer,
  TempCommBufferSize)) {
    DEBUG ((EFI_D_ERROR, "SmmVariableHandler: SMM communication buffer in
    SMRAM or overflow!\n"));
    return EFI_SUCCESS;
  }

  SmmVariableFunctionHeader = (SMM_VARIABLE_COMMUNICATE_HEADER *)CommBuffer;
  switch (SmmVariableFunctionHeader->Function) {
  case SMM_VARIABLE_FUNCTION_GET_VARIABLE:
      if (CommBufferPayloadSize < OFFSET_OF(SMM_VARIABLE_COMMUNICATE_
      ACCESS_VARIABLE, Name)) {
        DEBUG ((EFI_D_ERROR, "GetVariable: SMM communication buffer size
        invalid!\n"));
```

```
    return EFI_SUCCESS;
}
//
// Copy the input communicate buffer payload to pre-allocated SMM
variable buffer payload.
//
CopyMem (mVariableBufferPayload, SmmVariableFunctionHeader->Data,
CommBufferPayloadSize);
SmmVariableHeader = (SMM_VARIABLE_COMMUNICATE_ACCESS_VARIABLE *)
mVariableBufferPayload;
if (((UINTN)(~0) - SmmVariableHeader->DataSize < OFFSET_OF(SMM_
VARIABLE_COMMUNICATE_ACCESS_VARIABLE, Name)) ||
    ((UINTN)(~0) - SmmVariableHeader->NameSize < OFFSET_OF(SMM_
    VARIABLE_COMMUNICATE_ACCESS_VARIABLE, Name) + SmmVariableHeader-
    >DataSize)) {
  //
  // Prevent InfoSize overflow happen
  //
  Status = EFI_ACCESS_DENIED;
  goto EXIT;
}
InfoSize = OFFSET_OF(SMM_VARIABLE_COMMUNICATE_ACCESS_VARIABLE, Name)
          + SmmVariableHeader->DataSize + SmmVariableHeader->NameSize;

//
// SMRAM range check already covered before
//
if (InfoSize > CommBufferPayloadSize) {
  DEBUG ((EFI_D_ERROR, "GetVariable: Data size exceed communication
  buffer size limit!\n"));
  Status = EFI_ACCESS_DENIED;
  goto EXIT;
}

//
```

```
    // The VariableSpeculationBarrier() call here is to ensure the
    previous
    // range/content checks for the CommBuffer have been completed before
    the
    // subsequent consumption of the CommBuffer content.
    //
    VariableSpeculationBarrier ();

    if (SmmVariableHeader->NameSize < sizeof (CHAR16) || SmmVariableHeader->
    Name[SmmVariableHeader->NameSize/sizeof (CHAR16) - 1] != L'\0') {
      //
      // Make sure VariableName is A Null-terminated string.
      //
      Status = EFI_ACCESS_DENIED;
      goto EXIT;
    }

    Status = VariableServiceGetVariable (
              SmmVariableHeader->Name,
              &SmmVariableHeader->Guid,
              &SmmVariableHeader->Attributes,
              &SmmVariableHeader->DataSize,
              (UINT8 *)SmmVariableHeader->Name + SmmVariableHeader
              ->NameSize
              );
}
================
```

Besides an X86 SMI handler, the ARM TrustZone system may include a secure
monitor call (SMC) for the same purpose. Listing 14-7 shows the reverse engineering
result of an old implementation of the time querying interface in TEEGlobalTask. The
dword_5E2E0 is the TrustZone SMC communication buffer. The attacker may control
the operation_phys and let the SMC handler write data there.

Listing 14-7.

```
============================
int get_sys_time()
{
  int result; // r0@1
  tag_TC_NS_Operation *v1; // r3@1
  unsigned int v2; // [sp+0h] [bp-10h]@1
  int v3; // [sp+4h] [bp-Ch]@1
  get_time((int)&v2);
  result = 0;
  operation_phys = dword_5E2E0->operation_phys;
  *(int*)(operation_phys+4) = v2;
  *(int*)(operation_phys+8) = 1000 * v3;
  return result;
}
================
```

As a mitigation, the SMC handler should perform the similar check for the TrustZone communication buffer.

Besides arbitrary buffer access, the attacker may also control the arbitrary buffer execution. ThinkPwn is one of the examples. Listing 14-8 shows one of the vulnerabilities exposed in the ThinkPwn attack. The SMI handler sub_AD3AFA54 gets the structure pointer v3 from the communication data and invokes the function at (v3 + 0x8). Since the attacker may control all data in the communication buffer, the attacker achieves execution rights inside of SMM, the highest-privilege mode of the firmware at runtime.

Listing 14-8.

```
============================
EFI_STATUS __fastcall sub_AD3AFA54(EFI_HANDLE SmmImageHandle, VOID
*CommunicationBuffer, UINTN *SourceSize)
{
    VOID *v3; // rax@1
    VOID *v4; // rbx@1

    // get some structure pointer from EFI_SMM_COMMUNICATE_HEADER.Data
    v3 = *(VOID **)(CommunicationBuffer + 0x20);
```

```
    v4 = CommunicationBuffer;
    if (v3)
    {
        /*
            Vulnarability is here:
            this code calls some function by address from obtained v3
            structure field.
        */
        *(v3 + 0x8)(*(VOID **)v3, &dword_AD002290, CommunicationBuffer +
        0x18);

        // set zero value in EFI_SMM_COMMUNICATE_HEADER.Data to indicate
        successful operation
        *(VOID **)(v4 + 0x20) = 0;
    }

    return 0;
}
=================
```

As a mitigation, the SMI handler should never refer to a function pointer from an untrusted source. A design change is required to let the SMI handler retrieve the function pointer from inside of SMRAM.

Avoid Arithmetic Error

The cause of buffer overruns varies. One of the most important is an integer overflow. A typical integer overflow might be caused by multiplication or addition.

Listing 14-9 shows an example of multiplication overflow in the old Bitmap (BMP) parser in the EDK I BIOS. The attacker may input a malicious BMP image file with a large 32-bit PixelWidth and 32-bit PixelHeight in order to cause the BltBufferSize overflow. At that time, a very small GopBlt buffer is allocated. When the code copies the whole BMP buffer to the BltBuffer, the BltBuffer overflows.

Listing 14-9.

```
==========================
EFI_STATUS ConvertBmpToGopBlt ()
{
  /// ...
  if (BmpHeader->CharB != 'B' || BmpHeader->CharM != 'M') {
    return EFI_UNSUPPORTED;
  }
  BltBufferSize = BmpHeader->PixelWidth * BmpHeader->PixelHeight * sizeof
  (EFI_GRAPHICS_OUTPUT_BLT_PIXEL);
  IsAllocated = FALSE;
  if (*GopBlt == NULL) {
    *GopBltSize = BltBufferSize;
    *GopBlt = EfiLibAllocatePool (*GopBltSize);
  }
  BltBuffer = *GopBlt;

......

  for (Height = 0; Height < BmpHeader->PixelHeight; Height++) {
    Blt = &BltBuffer[(BmpHeader->PixelHeight-Height-1) * BmpHeader-
    >PixelWidth];
    for (Width = 0; Width < BmpHeader->PixelWidth; Width++, Image++, Blt++) {
      /* 24bit bmp case */
      Blt->Blue = *Image++;
      Blt->Green = *Image++;
      Blt->Red = *Image;
    }
==========================
```

In order to mitigate this integer overflow, we need to check the input data in order to see if there is any chance to cause an overflow in the final result. Listing 14-10 shows the check for multiplication overflow by using division.

Listing 14-10.

```
==========================
  if (BmpHeader->PixelWidth > MAX_UINT / sizeof (EFI_GRAPHICS_OUTPUT_BLT_
  PIXEL) / BmpHeader->PixelHeight) {
    return EFI_INVALID_PARAMETER;
  }
==========================
```

Listing 14-11 shows an example of addition overflow in the old ARM Trusted-Firmware-A. The attacker may input a large value for block_size, and this could result in an integer overflow, thus causing an unexpected large memory copy from the nonsecure world into the secure world.

Listing 14-11.

```
==========================
/*
 * If last block is more than expected then
 * clip the block to the required image size.
 */
if (image_desc->copied_size + block_size >
    image_desc->image_info.image_size) {
    block_size = image_desc->image_info.image_size -
        image_desc->copied_size;
    WARN("BL1-FWU: Copy argument block_size > remaining image size."
        " Clipping block_size\n");
}

/* Make sure the image src/size is mapped. */
if (bl1_plat_mem_check(image_src, block_size, flags)) {
    WARN("BL1-FWU: Copy arguments source/size not mapped\n");
    return -ENOMEM;
}

INFO("BL1-FWU: Continuing image copy in blocks\n");

/* Copy image for given block size. */
base_addr += image_desc->copied_size;
```

```
image_desc->copied_size += block_size;
memcpy((void *)base_addr, (const void *)image_src, block_size);
...
```

==========================

Listing 14-12 shows the check added for the block_size by using subtraction.

Listing 14-12.

==========================
```
/*
 * If the given block size is more than the total image size
 * then clip the former to the latter.
 */
remaining = image_size - desc->copied_size;
if (block_size > remaining) {
    WARN("BL1-FWU: Block size is too big, clipping it.\n");
    block_size = remaining;
}
```
==========================

Type casting is another potential arithmetic operation. Listing 14-13 shows the Xbox 360 King Kong attack which is an example wherein an improper integer comparison was used by the hypervisor syscall handler.

Listing 14-13.

==========================
```
extern u32 syscall_table[0x61]
void syscall_handler(r0, r3, r4, ...) {
  if((u32)r0 >= 0x61) {
    goto bad_syscall;
  }
  r1 = (void*)syscall_table[(u64)r0];
  r1();
}
```
==========================

We need to make sure that the data used is the same as the data checked. It could be the data without any type cast or the data with the same type cast. See Listing 14-14.

Listing 14-14.

```
===========================
extern u32 syscall_table[0x61]
void syscall_handler(r0, r3, r4, ...) {
  if((u32)r0 >= 0x61) {
    goto bad_syscall;
  }
  r1 = (void*)syscall_table[(u32)r0];
  r1();
}
===========================
```

Eliminate Banned Functions

In the C language, there are some notorious unsafe functions, also known as "banned functions." If the firmware code uses those banned functions, there might be a security risk. Listing 14-15 shows an old web server in the HP iLO4 baseboard management controller (BMC). The sscanf() is a banned function because there is no parameter to indicate the length of the destination buffer https_connection->connection. Unfortunately, the actual buffer implementation of https_connection->connection is very small. As such, the attacker can send a long http_header to override the https_connection buffer.

Listing 14-15.

```
===========================
else if (!strnicmp (request, http_header , "Content - length :", 0xFu) )
{
  content_length = 0;
  sscanf (http_header, "%*s %d", &content_length);
  state_set_content_length (global_struct_, content_length);
}
else if (!strnicmp (request, http_header, "Cookie :", 7u) )
{
```

```
  cookie_buffer = state_get_cookie_buffer (global_struct_);
  parse_cookie (request, http_header, cookie_buffer);
}
else if (!strnicmp (request, http_header, "Connection :", 0xBu) )
{
  sscanf (http_header, "%*s %s", https_connection->connection);
}
===========================
```

As a mitigation, the safe version of sscanf_s() should be used with the size of https_connection->connection as the last parameter.

Microsoft listed the banned functions in MSDN. The new C standard provides the safe version of the C standard library, such as strcpy_s, strcat_s, strncpy_s, strncat_s, and so on. Please be aware that the strncpy() and strlcpy() services are not recommended for use. There are many debates on if they are secure or not. It might be secure if they are used properly, but the biggest concern for strncpy() is that it is not NULL terminated. strlcpy() is better since it is NULL terminated, but it is not in any standard. As such, using strlcpy() is not portable.

The general guideline is that the firmware should NOT need any banned unsafe version of a function. The firmware may create its own specific safe version of the associated function. Some lessons we learned are as follows:

1) The safe version of a function shall include a size of the destination buffer so that the callee can check the buffer size to ensure there is not a buffer overrun.

2) The safe version of a function shall return a NULL-terminated destination buffer for a string so that the caller can use the buffer for the string operation directly.

3) The safe version of a function shall return the error status in case of a runtime verification failure so that the caller can check the return status to know if it has succeeded or not.

4) The safe version of a function should include the source size.

5) The safe version of a function may return the filled destination size.

String operations are always dangerous. Even if a safe function is used, we need to ensure it is used in the correct manner. Listing 14-16 is the old web authorization check in the Intel Active Management Technology (AMT). strncmp() is not a banned function, but it is used in an incorrect fashion. Because the following code takes the user input response length as the length for the string compare, the attacker can just input an empty string to bypass this check.

Listing 14-16.

```
===========================
if (strncmp(computed_response, response.value, response.length))
{
  goto error;
}
return 0;
===========================
```

The length should also be compared with the expected one. See Listing 14-17.

Listing 14-17.

```
===========================
if (computed_response_length != response.length)
{
  goto error;
}
===========================
```

Care must be taken that the safe version of the C standard library is used correctly. Otherwise the program is still unsafe and exploitable. Listing 14-18 shows the vulnerable pseudocode with memcpy_s() in a modern Smartphone Baseband. Ideally, the caller need ensure the second parameters (destination size) of memcpy_s() be correct and not controllable by the attacker. However, in Listing 14-18 the destination size is same as the source size and it is controlled by the attacker, then the check in the memcpy_s() can be bypassed.

Listing 14-18.

```
================
  byte_pos = 0;
  for (index = 1; index < 20; index++) {
    memcpy_s (parsedDst + byte_pos, someControlledLen,
                smsInput + someControlledOffset, someControlledLen);
    byte_pos += someControlledLen;
  }
================
```

Be Aware of Race Conditions

Race conditions may occur in the firmware as well, including race conditions for a data buffer and a race condition in a register unlock function.

The classic race condition for a data buffer is the time-of-check/time-of-use (TOC/TOU) issue. We have discussed this in Chapter 3. Figure 3-29 shows the classic TOC/TOU attack on the SMM communication buffer. The mitigation is to copy the untrusted input buffer to the trusted execution environment and perform the check and usage. Figure 3-30 shows that concept.

Because the firmware may use an isolated trusted execution environment to unlock the flash region and perform a runtime update, there is another race condition on flash region unlock. We have also discussed that in Chapter 3. Figure 3-33 shows the race condition attack on an SMM-based flash protection implementation. The mitigation is to rendezvous all processors in the trusted execution environment before performing the unlock action.

Take Care of Information Leaks

The firmware may need to handle secret information, such as BIOS password. The secret cannot be stored in plain text anywhere, including stack, heap, global variable, and any communication buffer in the code path. After the password is used, the program should clear the temporary buffer used to store the password by using a non-optimized zero memory function.

One common mistake is that the password is not cleared in the key buffer. The legacy BIOS saved the keystroke in the fixed BIOS data area (BDA), which is at 0x400 physical memory. If that region is not cleared before boot, then the attacker in the operating system may steal the password by dumping the BDA region.

The flash region may be used as a temporary buffer as well. Similar to the file system, the delete action for the flash region might not erase the content, but only set a flag to indicate the content is invalid. In that case, the real content is still in the flash region. As such, we cannot use the flash region as the temporary buffer to store any secret data.

If the password needs to be stored in the flash region, then we should follow the best practices for the password to add a salt value and use a time-consuming hash-based algorithm to generate the digest.

Sometimes the device access requires a special passcode. We have seen examples that used a hardcoded passcode comparison in the code. That is not a good idea because the hardcoded passcode can easily be discovered by reverse engineering.

Besides the secrets, such as password or passcode, the firmware should define the secret information in the execution context, such as the important data structure locations in the kernel, hypervisor, or trusted execution environment (TEE). If the address space layout randomization (ALSR) technique is used to prevent the control flow attack, then the content information shall also be treated as secret and not exposed.

A random number may be required in the firmware. The implementation should try to use the hardware-generated random seed, if supported, such as the X86 RDSEED and RDRNG instruction or ARM RNDR and RNDRRS instruction. The RTC is not a good random seed.

Know Bad Compiler Optimizations

For firmware, it is good to enable the compiler optimizations to build a small-sized firmware image. At the same time, we should be aware of the possible side effects.

One common concern in the compiler optimization process is about zero memory for the local variable. Usually, this is used before the function return, and the purpose is to clear the secret in the local buffer. However, the compiler may believe it is useless to zero the local buffer because it is not accessed afterward. Then the compiler just skips the zeroing memory operation and returns directly. That behavior leaves the secret in the local stack. The typical mitigation is to create a non-optimizable version of a zeroing memory function to clear the secret in order to ensure that the secret clear operation always happens, such as memset_s() in C11 extension, SecureZeroMemory() in Windows, and explicit_bzero() in Linux.

Another problem with compiler optimizations is to reorder for the hardware accesses. Consider Listing 14-19 as a simple example. The purpose is to issue a memory mapped I/O (MMIO) command to let the system perform some sanity checking and fill in the Result and then check if the Result is satisfied. However, a compiler may think the MMIO address assignment has no relationship with the Result comparison. In that case, the compiler may optimize the code, as shown in Listing 14-20. In this case, the check is bypassed.

Listing 14-19.

```
=========================
    *(UINT32 *)(TARGET_MMIO_ADDRESS + 4) = Data;
    *(UINT32 *)(TARGET_MMIO_ADDRESS) = Command;
    Status = (Result == 0x1);
    If (Status) {
        // pass
    } else {
        // fail
    }
=========================
```

Listing 14-20.

```
=========================
    Status = (Result == 0x1);
    *(UINT32 *)(TARGET_MMIO_ADDRESS + 4) = Data;
    *(UINT32 *)(TARGET_MMIO_ADDRESS) = Command;
    If (Status) {
        // pass
    } else {
        // fail
    }
=========================
```

If the memory access order is important, the code should tell the compiler the order by using the compiler memory barrier. For example, Microsoft Visual Studio has the _ReadWriteBarrier() function and Linux GCC has asm volatile("" ::: "memory"). See Listing 14-21.

Listing 14-21.

```
===========================
    *(UINT32 *)(TARGET_MMIO_ADDRESS + 4) = Data;
    *(UINT32 *)(TARGET_MMIO_ADDRESS) = Command;
    ReadWriteBarrier();
    Status = (Result == 0x1);
    If (Status) {
        // pass
    } else {
        // fail
    }
===========================
```

Please do not confuse these actions with the hardware memory barrier actions which need the CPU-specific instructions, such as X86 LFENCE, SFENCE, MFENCE or ARM DMB, DSB, ISB.

Use ASSERT the Right Way

ASSERT is very helpful to catch program mistakes. However, the ASSERT macro only exists in the debug build, and it is removed in the release build. As such, the ASSERT is not a replacement for the error checking and error handling.

Code Complete discusses several guidelines for ASSERT usage:

1) Use error handling code for conditions you expect to occur; use assertions for conditions that should never occur.

2) Avoid putting executable code into assertions.

3) Use assertions to document and verify preconditions and postconditions.

4) For highly robust code, assert and then handle the error anyway.

These rules can be used in a UEFI BIOS as well. For the condition that is "expected to occur," the BIOS must use error handling; for the condition that should "never occur," the BIOS can use ASSERT to ensure that condition is satisfied.

In the early boot phase, such as the Security (SEC) phase or Pre-EFI Initialization (PEI) phase, an error might mean a system configuration error or a hardware error.

It might be unrecoverable and should never occur. For example, the memory initialization module may fail to find any valid dual in-line memory module (DIMM). In that case, the best way to handle the scenario is to use the ReportStatusCode to inform the end user of the situation via an LED activation or audible BEEP code. ASSERT() can be used here to let the developer check if the memory initialization module is using the wrong parameters. In another condition, the memory initialization module may find two valid DIMMs wherein one of them passed self-test, while the other did not. Then we should not use ASSERT(). Instead, we should disable the bad DIMM in the error handling logic and boot the system with the good DIMM and then report the DIMM error to the end user via some console message or error log entry.

The UEFI shell environment receives external input from the end user, such as to list a nonexistent file or to copy a file to a read-only location. These actions should be handled by the error handler instead of ASSERT(). The network driver receives network packets from the Internet. It cannot assume the packet is always the correct one. The network driver should not use ASSERT to handle the errant packets. Instead, the proper way is to check the packets and drop malformed ones.

The following are some other examples of ASSERT usage in the system firmware, such as UEFI.

1) For UEFI Variable API

1.1) GetVariable() with non-volatile (NV) and runtime (RT) attributes without the authentication (AU) or read-only (RO) attribute: We should not use ASSERT() but use error handling because the attacker may delete it.

1.2) GetVariable() with the AU or RO attribute: We may use ASSERT() if the driver assumes the variable must exist because the attacker may not modify it.

1.3) SetVariable() with the NV attribute: We should not use ASSERT() but use error handling because the attacker may write the full variable region and trigger an out of resource condition.

1.4) SetVariable() without the NV attribute: We may use ASSERT() before exiting the manufacture auth phase because the attacker cannot control the environment at that time.

2) For resource allocation

   2.1) Memory allocation should not use ASSERT() after exiting the manufacture auth phase because the attacker may allocate all memory.

   2.2) Memory allocation may use ASSERT() before exiting the manufacture auth phase if the allocation failure is critical and prevents the system from booting or processing the next step.

   2.3) Memory mapped I/O (MMIO)/IO allocation for external devices should not use ASSERT() because we never know how many external devices the attacker may choose to plug in.

   2.4) MMIO/IO allocation for the onboard devices may use ASSERT() before exiting the manufacture auth phase because the resources can be precalculated for a given platform. It might be a critical error, and the system may not be able to boot without this critical resource.

3) For the trusted execution environment (TEE), such as SMM or TrustZone

   3.1) The TEE handler should not use ASSERT() for the external input check after exiting the manufacture auth phase because the attacker may inject malicious data in the external input.

   3.2) The TEE driver may use ASSERT() in the entry point to construct the TEE. A failure may be a critical issue and block the system from booting.

ASSERT may be used in the library functions, such as BaseLib, BaseMemoryLib, IoLib, PciLib, and HobLib in EDK II UEFI firmware. If a library accepts the external input, ASSERT must not be used, such as a signature verification function in a CryptoLib. *Writing Solid Code* mentioned a good way for self-test: Once you've written a function, review it and ask yourself, "What am I assuming?" If you find an assumption, either assert that your assumption is always valid, or rewrite the code to remove the assumption. For the former, the caller needs to guarantee the input data is correct; for the latter, the callee needs to guarantee the input data is correct.

Secure Design Practice

Besides the secure coding practice, there are secure design practices in the firmware which are also similar to the ones in software.

Check Input Cross Trust Boundary

In Chapter 2, we discussed the trust boundary definition in firmware. If there is a data flow across the trust boundary, then this data must be validated before use, including data type, length, range, format, and so on. Remember the secure coding practices, such as preventing buffer overrun, preventing arbitrary buffer access and execution, avoiding arithmetic error, eliminating banned functions, being aware of race conditions, and using ASSERT in the correct manner.

Fail Intelligently

If the input validation fails, then the program should fail intelligently. Listing 14-22 shows an old signature verification flow in the HP iLO5. The problem with this code is that the load_signature() function returns SUCCESS if load_legacy_key failed in the index2. The signature fields are left untouched.

Listing 14-22.

```
===========================
load_signature()
{
  steps_mask = 0;
  if ( load_legacy_key(hdr->index1 , &pkey , 0x804) )
  {
    steps_mask = 1;
    if ( decrypt_hash(hdr->sig1 , &sig_size , hdr->sig1 , sig_size , &pkey) )
      goto EXIT_FAILED;
  }
  if ( !load_legacy_key(hdr->index2 , &pkey , 0x804) )
    goto FUCK_YEAH; // <------ !!! NO FFS !!!
  steps = steps_mask | 2;
```

```
if ( decrypt_hash(hdr->sig2 , &sig_size , hdr->sig2 , sig_size , &pkey) )
  goto EXIT_FAILED;

if ( steps == 2 )
  memcpy(hdr->sig1 , sig2 , sig_size); // only sig2 , overwrite sig1

// two sigs ? ensure they match
if ( steps == 3 && memcmp(img_hdr_ ->sig1 , sig2 , sig_size) )
EXIT_FAILED:
  return ERROR;
FUCK_YEAH:
  return SUCCESS;
===========================
```

The right way is to send any unexpected error to the failure case.

A similar issue also exists in the old EDK II image verification function. See Listing 14-23. Ideally, the image verification logic is to initially check the forbidden image database to see if there is a match and then check the allowed image database. However, the problem is that if there are some other errors in the function that prohibit assessing the forbidden database, then the IsSignatureFoundInDatabase() function just returns NOT_FOUND. At this point, the attacker may just trigger this failure condition and bypass the forbidden database check.

Listing 14-23.

```
===========================
BOOLEAN
IsSignatureFoundInDatabase (
  )
{
  Status    = gRT->GetVariable (VariableName, &gEfiImageSecurityDatabaseGuid,
  NULL, &DataSize, NULL);
  if (Status != EFI_BUFFER_TOO_SMALL) {
    return FALSE;
  }
```

```
  Data = (UINT8 *) AllocateZeroPool (DataSize);
  if (Data == NULL) {
    return FALSE;
  }
  ...
}

DxeImageVerificationHandler ()
{
    ...
    // Check forbidden database
    if (IsSignatureFoundInDatabase (EFI_IMAGE_SECURITY_DATABASE1,
    mImageDigest, &mCertType, mImageDigestSize)) {
      Action = EFI_IMAGE_EXECUTION_AUTH_SIG_FOUND;
      IsVerified = FALSE;
      break;
    }
    ...
}
```

==========================

The boothole issue in GRUB2 OS loader is also an example that a vulnerability in error handling causes buffer overflow and the arbitrary code execution. Because Grub2 need parse the input configuration file grub.conf, it uses flex and bison to generate a parsing engine. The parser engine generated by flex includes this define as part of the token processing code. See Listing 14-24. If the code detects that a token is too large to fit into the internal buffer, it calls YY_FATAL_ERROR(). However, the YY_FATAL_ERROR() implementation provided in the GRUB2 just prints an error to the console and returns, instead of aborting the function or halting the system. As the consequence, the flex starts to copy the large buffer to internal and overflow the internal buffer.

Listing 14-24.

==========================

```
#define YY_DO_BEFORE_ACTION \
    yyg->yytext_ptr = yy_bp; \
    yyleng = (int) (yy_cp - yy_bp); \
```

```
    yyg->yy_hold_char = *yy_cp; \
    *yy_cp = '\0'; \
    if ( yyleng >= YYLMAX ) \
        YY_FATAL_ERROR( "token too large, exceeds YYLMAX" ); \
    yy_flex_strncpy( yytext, yyg->yytext_ptr, yyleng + 1 , yyscanner); \
    yyg->yy_c_buf_p = yy_cp;
#define YY_FATAL_ERROR(msg)                        \
  do {                                             \
    grub_printf (_("fatal error: %s\n"), _(msg));  \
  } while (0)
==========================
```

Reduce Attack Surfaces

The firmware may have attack surfaces. Take the trusted execution environment (TEE) as an example. This example includes the system management interrupt (SMI) handler in an X86 system or the secure monitor call (SMC) handler in an ARM system. Usually, the attacker may use fuzz testing to trigger all possible software SMI handlers or SMC handlers in the TEE to see if there is any vulnerability. If a handler in the TEE is not required, it might not be validated. As such, we should remove these unused and unvalidated TEE handlers. It is highly recommended that a firmware implementation should implement a profile feature to list all possible TEE handlers for evaluation purposes.

Use Least Privilege

The firmware may implement features within different privilege levels. For example, normal data processing, such as a Bitmap (BMP) file parser, requires the user mode – ring 3. Modifying the system status, such as a page table or a PCI device configuration state, requires the supervisor privilege – ring 0. Unlocking the flash region and performing a UEFI variable update or BIOS update may require TEE privilege, such as X86 system management mode (SMM) because the flash is protected in the TEE. The best design is to put different functions in different privilege levels. In case there is a vulnerability, the damage is limited to that privilege level only. For example, we can use the TEE handler profiling feature to list all TEE handlers to see if each is really needed to be implemented inside of the TEE. Or if we can have some other way to implement it in a non-TEE. If the TEE privilege is not required, then we should move the feature out of the TEE.

Defense in Depth

Defense in depth is a general way to protect the most critical assets. Take Intel BIOS Guard as the example. In a general X86 system, the flash is protected by the system management mode (SMM) environment. However, if there is an SMM vulnerability, then the attacker may break SMM and thus break the flash protection, such as the ThinkPwn attack. Intel BIOS Guard brings one more layer of protection. In order to update the BIOS, the SMM code must launch a special BIOS Guard module to perform the BIOS flash update. The new BIOS image signature check and flash unlock are performed inside of the BIOS Guard module. Even if the SMM environment is broken, the malicious code cannot update the flash region freely. As such, the platforms which adopt Intel BIOS Guard can resist the flash update attack from the ThinkPwn-style attack.

Another example is the PCI option ROM loading. Because the PCI option ROM is third-party code, it must be signed to meet the UEFI secure boot requirements. However, signing can only guarantee the code is from a trusted source but cannot guarantee there are no bugs. As such, the PCI option ROM is loaded after the platform exits the manufacture auth phase. At that time, the BIOS flash is locked. Even if there is bug in an option ROM code, the attacker cannot take advantage of this flaw to attack the system BIOS flash before it is locked.

Open Design

Open design is based upon the basic cryptography principle – Kerckhoffs's principle: The security of a system should be based upon the key instead of the algorithm. The algorithm should be public. The key should be the only secret. Today, this is referred to as "Obscurity != Security." The security architecture and implementation should be open to the public. We should not rely on hidden design and implementation details to provide the security, such as hiding private keys or passcodes in the firmware image. Results show that the attackers have used reverse engineering to uncover security issues introduced more than ten years ago.

Remove Backdoors

A backdoor refers to an undocumented interface which may be used for special purposes, such as maintenance. The existence of a backdoor violates the secure design practices of reducing attack surfaces and open design. One example is that in Black Hat 2018, Domas demonstrated how to find a hidden instruction to gain supervisor privileges in user mode. He used fuzzing to scan the system and found a special "God Mode Bit" (MSR 1107, BIT 0). Toggling this bit activated a launch instruction (0F03). By using a co-located core with unrestricted access to the core register file, software can send content via Ring 3 to modify a Ring 0 register and obtain hardware privilege escalation.

Keep Code Simple

Simple code makes it easy for testing and code review. The general guideline is that a file should have less than 1000 lines of code and a function should have less than 100 lines of code. One bad example is that in the EDK II UEFI variable driver – MdeModulePkg/ Universal/Variable/RuntimeDxe/Variable.c. The UpdateVariable() routine has more than 600 lines of code and 65 "if" branches. One of the "if" branches misses the "else" branch handling and causes the timestamp field to be filled with a wrong value. This issue had been there for several years. We performed several rounds of code reviews and testing, but no one found this problem. Sixty-five"if" branches in one function is overly complicated.

Boot Firmware Secure Design Practice

Besides general design practices, we list some boot firmware-specific secure design practices.

Firmware Resiliency: Protection, Detection, and Recovery

The firmware should take firmware resiliency into account, such as integrity protection, secure update, secure boot, and secure recovery. We have discussed the firmware resiliency solutions in Chapters 3, 4, and 5.

Firmware Measurement and Attestation

The firmware should report firmware integrity measurements and support attestation. It can use the Trusted Platform Module (TPM)–style measurement and attestation or the Device Identifier Composition Engine (DICE)–style measurement and attestation. We have discussed the firmware trusted boot in Chapter 7.

Device Security

Devices have become a threat these days. On the one hand, the system firmware should authenticate and measure the device firmware, such as using the Secure Protocol and Data Model (SPDM) protocol. On the other hand, the system firmware should not trust the input from the device. For example, it should set up protection for DMA attack and validate the input from the device. We have discussed device security in Chapter 8.

S3 Script

S3 script is used to restore the system configuration in an S3 resume phase. The recommendation is the following:

1) Enable a LockBox for S3 data storage.

2) Save the S3 script itself into the LockBox.

3) Save the S3 script executor into the LockBox.

4) If the S3 script includes a function pointer, save the full function into the LockBox.

5) If the S3 script includes a function parameter, save the full parameter into the LockBox.

6) If a LockBox is not available, use a read-only variable as an alternative.

7) If there is a confidentiality requirement, use the TEE directly, such as X86 SMM RAM (SMRAM).

More details of the S3 resume are discussed in Chapter 9.

Secure Configuration

Sometimes the BIOS provides an option to let the end user enable or disable some feature in the BIOS setup configuration page. The recommendation for the secure configuration includes the following:

1) Do not provide an option to control the protection managed by the manufacturer owner, such as flash protection. It should always be enabled.

2) Require user physical presence to control the protections managed by the machine owner, such as UEFI secure boot or TPM.

More details of system access control are discussed in Chapter 10.

UEFI Variable Use and Misuse

UEFI variables are used to store the non-volatile configuration for the boot firmware. Most UEFI secure variables are read/write. As such, the UEFI variable should also be treated as untrusted input. We should verify the variable data before accessing it. For example, an expected string in the UEFI variable might not be NULL terminated. An expected 8-byte data might only have 1 byte stored, and the remaining 7 bytes contain a random value. The system configuration in the variable might be garbage.

The general recommendation is that

1) If the variable data is not required to be persistent across a reboot, then we should remove the non-volatile (NV) attribute.

2) If the variable data is not required to be accessed at OS runtime, then we should remove the runtime (RT) attribute.

3) If the variable data is critical and we do not expect anyone to modify the data at OS runtime, then we should lock this variable at boot time.

More details of the system configuration are discussed in Chapter 11.

Trusted Execution Environment

Usually, the trusted execution environment (TEE) has the highest privilege to access a system resource, such as X86 system management mode (SMM) or ARM TrustZone. The TEE design should meet the following requirements:

1) The TEE should protect itself from access by the code and I/O out of the TEE.

2) The TEE should not trust any data from outside of the TEE and perform input validation.

3) The TEE should not call any code outside of the TEE.

4) The TEE should not act as a confused deputy to assist the low-privilege nonsecure world to attack the high-privilege secure world.

We will introduce more on the TEE subject in Chapter 17.

Silicon Register Lock

The role of the system firmware is to initialize the silicon and boot to the OS. After the silicon is initialized, the system firmware should lock the configuration to resist any further attack, such as corruption or modification of assets like flash storage, the TEE, and memory mapped I/O (MMIO) configuration base address registers (BARs). This lock action is silicon specific. Chapter 18 provides some examples for the X86 system.

Advanced Secure Coding Topic

Now let's take a look at the advanced secure coding topic. We will discuss the side channel attack and fault injection, followed by the software mitigation.

Side Channel Attack

There is an interesting puzzle named 3 Bulbs and 3 Switches. The puzzle proceeds as follows: "There is a room with a door (closed) and three light bulbs. Outside the room, there are three switches, connected to the bulbs. You may manipulate the switches as you wish, but once you open the door, you can't change them. Please identify each switch with its bulb."

The solution of this puzzle cannot be reduced to a mathematical model. Logically, it seems impossible to identify which switch controls which bulb by entering the room only once because each bulb can only have one of two states – ON or OFF. There is not enough mathematical information to distinguish the different states of three bulbs. In practice, the bulb can have more than two states because of the heat. If we turn on a switch for a while, the bulb becomes hot. Even after we turn off the switch, the bulb is still hot for a while.

The final solution of the puzzle is "Turn on switch X for 5–10 minutes. Turn it off and turn on switch Y. Open the door and touch the light bulb:

1   If the light is on, it is Y.

2   If the light is off and hot, it is X.

3   If the light is off and cold, it is Z."

The heat of the bulb is a typical example of side channel information which is used to distinguish X and Z.

Another side channel example includes the classic numeric keypad wear-out issue. See Figure 14-1 which shows a worn-out numeric keypad. The numbers 3 and 7 are heavily worn out, and the numbers 4 and 8 are slightly worn out. From this, we know that 3, 4, 7, and 8 should be included in the passcode. There is a high probability that multiples of 3 or 7 exist. The wear-out is a typical example of side channel information.

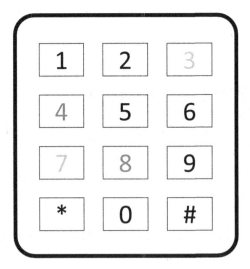

Figure 14-1. *Worn-Out Numeric Keypad*

Traditional Side Channel Attack

The traditional side channel attack can be pure software or hardware assisted. The software side channel attack includes a timing attack and a cache attack. The hardware side channel attack includes simple power analysis (SPA), simple electromagnetic analysis (SEMA), differential power analysis (DPA), differential electromagnetic analysis (DEMA), and so on. Some of these are used to attack the cryptographic library implementation.

Marc Witteman's whitepaper "Secure Application Programming in the Presence of Side Channel Attacks" provides good information on this topic.

Timing Attack

Listing 14-25 shows a typical example of passcode memory compare which can be used to compare the input passcode with the expected passcode.

Listing 14-25.

```
===========================
bool compare_mem(byte *a, size_t a_len, byte *b, size_t b_len) {
  if (a_len != b_len) { // data dependent!
    return false;
  }
  for (size_t i = 0; i < a_len; i++) {
    if (a[i] != b[i]) { // data dependent!
      return false;
    }
  }
  return true;
}
===========================
```

The problem with this approach is that the function execution time is proportional to the number of chars matched in the passcode. In the first round, the attacker can construct a set of strings "a*******", "b*******", "c*******", and so on as input and measure the function execution time. They may observe a significant timing difference between "P*******" and "Q*******" and then conclude the first char is "P." In the second round, the attacker constructs a set of strings "Pa******", "Pb******", "Pc******", and so on as input and measures the function execution time. A significant timing difference can be observed between "P@******" and "P#******". Then they know the second char is "@". Using a similar technique, the attacker uses linear time to attack all chars in the passcode one by one. See Figure 14-2.

	P	@	s	s	w	0	r	d
Round 1	P	*	*	*	*	*	*	*
Round 2	P	@	*	*	*	*	*	*
Round 3	P	@	s	*	*	*	*	*
Round 4	P	@	s	s	*	*	*	*
Round 5	P	@	s	s	w	*	*	*
Round 6	P	@	s	s	w	0	*	*
Round 7	P	@	s	s	w	0	r	*
Round 8	P	@	s	s	w	0	r	d

Figure 14-2. *Timing Attack*

The mitigation is to let the for-loop's execution time become independent of the number of character matches. See Listing 14-26.

Listing 14-26.

```
===========================
bool compare_mem (byte *a, size_t a_len, byte *b, size_t b_len) {
  volatile size_t x = a_len ^ b_len;

  for (size_t i = 0; ((i < a_len) & (i < b_len)); i++) {
    x |= a[i] ^ b[i];
  }

  return (x==0);
}
===========================
```

Cache Attack

A cache side channel attack is based upon the fact that the cache access time is much faster than the memory access time. Figure 14-3 shows a single level of a set-associated cache. Each row in a memory block (memory line) is mapped to the corresponding row in the cache block (cache line). The cache line holds a copy of a subset of the memory line in cases where the memory line is accessed by the CPU. For a new memory line access, if the CPU finds the data in the cache (also known as cache hit), the CPU accesses the data in the cache directly. Otherwise, if the CPU cannot find data in the cache (also known as cache miss), the CPU loads the content from memory to the cache by evicting its previous content. The CPU also provides an instruction to flush the content out of the cache. In this case, it will always cause a cache miss during the next access. There are two common techniques used in last-level cache (LLC)–based attacks: PRIME+PROBE and FLUSH+RELOAD. Let's see them one by one.

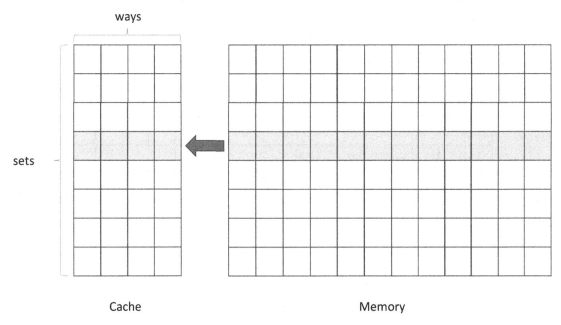

Figure 14-3. A Single Level of Set-Associated Cache

Prime+Probe

The PRIME+PROBE attack exploits resource contention between two processes, thus allowing an attacker process to measure the cache usage of a victim process. A round of attack includes three phases:

1) For phase PRIME, the attacker primes the targeted cache set by accessing the cache lines in its eviction buffer. The monitored cache set is filled with the attacker's data. See Figure 14-4.

2) For phase IDLE, the attacker waits for a while to allow the victim to access the target cache line.

3) For phase PROBE, the attacker probes the cache set by measuring the time to access the cache lines in the eviction buffer. If the victim accesses the target cache line in phase 2, the target cache line will evict an attacker line from the cache; then the PROBE operation will take a longer time. See Figure 14-5.

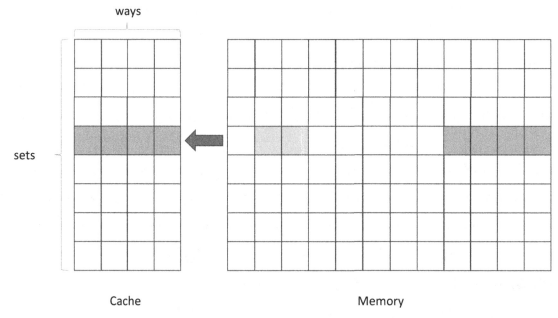

Figure 14-4. *Prime+Probe Attack – PRIME Phase*

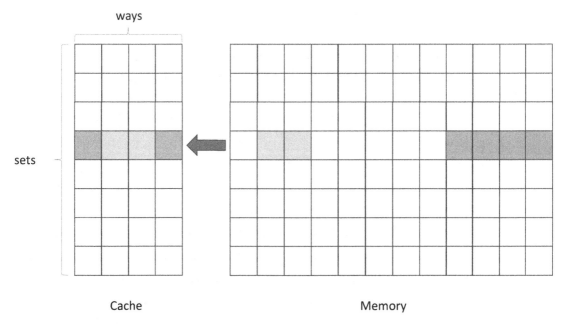

Figure 14-5. *Prime+Probe Attack – PROBE Phase*

One example of the Prime+Probe attack is to monitor the lookup table usage in a bad AES crypto implementation and then derive the key value based upon the side channel information.

The mitigation includes removing the lookup table, using a dynamic lookup table, disabling the cache, hiding timing, and using hardware-assisted cryptographic algorithms.

Flush+Reload

The FLUSH+RELOAD attack relies on a share page between the attacker and victim processes. Both processes must have access to the same resource. A round of attack includes three phases.

1) For phase FLUSH, the attacker flushes the target cache line from the cache hierarchy. For example, this flush can be accomplished by using the clflush instruction. See Figure 14-6.

2) For phase IDLE, the attacker waits for a while to allow the victim to access the target cache line.

3) For phase RELOAD, the attacker reloads the target cache line and measures the time to load. If the victim accesses the target cache line in phase 2, then the RELOAD operation will take a short time. Otherwise, the RELOAD operation takes a longer time. See Figure 14-7.

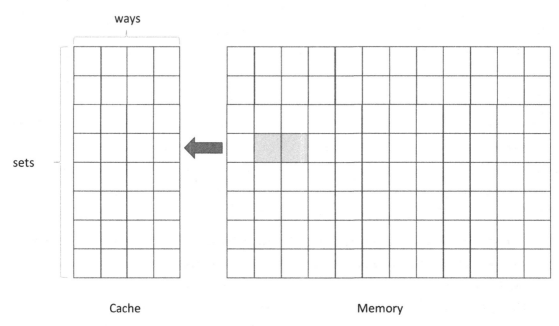

Figure 14-6. *Flush+Reload Attack – FLUSH Phase*

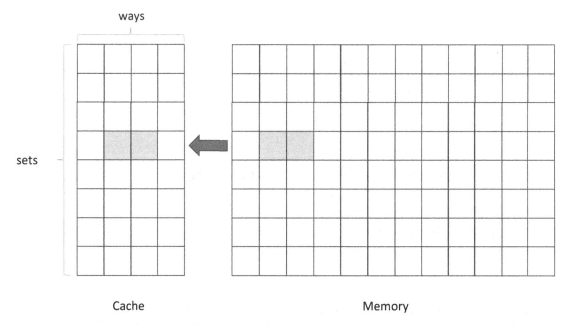

Figure 14-7. *Flush+Reload Attack – RELOAD Phase*

There are some other cache attacks, such as Evict+Time and Evict+Reload. With a cache attack, the attacker can know if the content in a specific memory location is accessed by measuring the time difference between a cache hit and a cache miss.

One example of the Flush+Reload attack is to recognize the Square-Reduce-Multiply-Reduce pattern in the bad GnuPG crypto implementation. With the side channel information, the attacker may recover the bits of the exponent.

The mitigations include but are not limited to preventing page sharing, not using special data-dependent algorithm, disabling the cache, hiding timing, and using hardware-assisted cryptographic algorithms.

Simple Analysis

Simple analysis includes simple power analysis (SPA) and simple electromagnetic analysis (SEMA). The attacker can observe the power consumption difference or the electromagnetic signal difference to distinguish different instruction executions. Special measurement equipment is required to collect such information. ChipWhisperer is one of the open-source toolchains for side-channel power analysis and glitching attacks.

Differential Analysis

Differential analysis includes differential power analysis (DPA) and differential electromagnetic analysis (DEMA). The attacker needs to collect a large number of trace data sets and use statistical analysis to figure out their relationships and then to derive secrets. Similar to the simple analysis, special measurement equipment is required to collect such information.

Principle of Traditional Side Channel–Resistant Coding

Intel's whitepaper "Guidelines for Mitigating Timing Side Channels Against Cryptographic Implementations" describes the principles for the traditional side channel attacks – timing side channel and cache side channel:

1) Secret-independent runtime (SIR)

Timing side channels take advantage of the smallest differences in execution time, sometimes at the resolution of a single clock cycle. We need to ensure algorithms consistently process secret data and only use instructions whose latency is invariant to the data values. The compare_mem() implementation is a typical example.

2) Secret-independent code access (SIC)

The value of a secret, or values derived from a secret, must not affect a conditional branch or the target of an indirect branch. The address sequence of executed instructions must be independent of secret values. For example, if there is special squaring code for the square calculation, then the attacker can deduce the data pattern by using Flush+Reload to monitor if the squaring code has been executed. Using general multiplication to replace square calculation can mitigate this concern.

3) Secret-independent data access (SID)

Secret values should not cause a change to the order of accessed addresses or the data size of loads/stores. For example, don't use a secret value to load a specific location from a table representing an S-box without taking appropriate precautions. Care must be taken for any lookup table usage in the crypto library.

Speculative Execution Attack

Modern CPUs have introduced some advanced techniques to achieve maximum performance, such as branch prediction, speculative execution, out-of-order execution, and so on. The basic idea is to execute the next instruction in the instruction pipeline whenever it is possible and prepare the result. If this instruction needs to be executed finally, the result can be committed directly. If this instruction is not needed, then the result is discarded.

Ideally, once the result is discarded, there will be no impact to the security of the system. Unfortunately, this intermediate result may impact the cache state. Then the cache state can be exposed via the cache side channel attack we discussed in the preceding text, such as the Flush+Reload attack. Spectre and Meltdown are two famous side channel attacks. Let's discuss them one by one.

Spectre Variant 1: Bounds Check Bypass

Spectre breaks the isolation between different applications. It allows an attacker to trick error-free programs, which follow best practices, into leaking their secrets.

The Spectre attack variant 1 is named bounds check bypass. Consider the code example in Listing 14-27 of a function receiving an untrusted input x. The code fragment uses a bound check on x to prevent the buffer overflow access because there might be sensitive information after the array1.

Listing 14-27.

```
=========================

uint8 array1[ARRAY1_SIZE];
int array1_size = sizeof(array1);
uint8 array2[ARRAY2_SIZE];
uint8 secret[SECRET_SIZE];

DataProcess (int x)
{
  if (x < array1_size) {
    y = array2[array1[x] * 256];
  }
}
=========================
```

If the attacker gives x = &secret[0] - &array1, then k = array1[x] = secret[0] is the first byte of secret. With speculative execution, the CPU will read the k from the secret, calculate the y, and save the value k and array2[k * 256] to the cache before the if statement is evaluated. Later after the CPU notices that the value x is out of bound, then it will discard the value y. However, the secret k and the value array2[k * 256] are still in the cache.

Now, the attacker can use the Flush+Reload attack to get the k if the array2 is readable from the attacker's process. In phase FLUSH, the attacker flushes the cache line for the array2. Then they trigger the data process. In phase RELOAD, the attacker can try to load each byte at array2[n* 256], where n is from 0 to 255. When n == k, the reload time is very short because the data is from the cache. Otherwise, the reload time is significantly longer because the data is from memory.

The main mitigation of bounds check bypass is to use a speculation barrier instruction, such as LFENCE instruction in the X86 platform and CSDB instruction in the ARM platform when the code needs to reference the untrusted input as the index. Ideally, we hope the compiler can be smart enough to insert the speculation barrier instruction into the correct location. However, there might be false-positive or false-negative cases. As such, if possible, the developer should be aware of this issue and insert a speculation barrier instruction directly. See Listing 14-28.

Listing 14-28.

```
==========================

uint8 array1[ARRAY1_SIZE];
int array1_size = sizeof(array1);
uint8 array2[ARRAY2_SIZE];
uint8 secret[SECRET_SIZE];

DataProcess (int x)
{
  if (x < array1_size) {
    SpeculationBarrier ();
    y = array2[array1[x] * 256];
  }
}
==========================
```

For the host firmware, the system management mode (SMM) code might be impacted by the bounds check bypass. As such, the speculation barrier instruction is required for the SMM handler if it accepts any untrusted external input as array index.

Spectre Variant 2: Branch Target Injection

The Spectre attack variant 2 is named branch target injection. An indirect branch means the target address of the branch is from a register (such as jmp eax), a memory location (such as jmp [eax] or jmp [0x12345678]), or a stack location (such as ret). Listing 14-29 shows a typical indirect branch in the UEFI firmware.

Listing 14-29.

```
===========================
  gBS->LocateProtocol (&gEfiPciIoProtocol, NULL, &PciIo);
  PciIo->AllocateBuffer (
          PciIo,
          AlloateAnyPages,
          EfiBootServicedData,
          1,
          &HostAddress,
          0
          );
===========================
```

The branch target injection takes advantage of the indirect branch predictors that are used to direct what operations are speculatively executed. By influencing how the indirect branch predictors operate, a malicious attacker can cause malicious code to be speculatively executed and then measure the effects such code has on the processor cache/system memory to infer data values.

According to Intel's whitepaper, an exploit using a branch target injection is composed of five specific elements, all of which are required for successful exploitation. Traditional application software which is not security sensitive needs to be carefully evaluated for all five elements before applying the mitigation:

1) The target of the exploit (the victim) must have some secret data that an exploit wants to obtain. In the case of an OS kernel, this includes any data outside of the user's permissions, such as memory in the kernel memory map.

2) The exploit needs to have some method of referring to the secret. Typically, this is a pointer within the victim's address space that can be made to reference the memory location of the secret data. Passing a pointer of an overt communication channel between the exploit and the victim is a straightforward way to satisfy this condition.

3) The exploit's reference must be usable during execution of a portion of the victim's code which contains an indirect branch that is vulnerable to exploitation. For example, if the exploit pointer value is stored in a register, the attacker's goal is for speculation to jump to a code sequence where that register is used as a source address for a move operation.

4) The exploit must successfully influence this indirect branch to speculatively mis-predict and execute a gadget. This gadget, chosen by the exploit, leaks the secret data via a side channel, typically by cache timing.

5) The gadget must execute during the "speculation window" which closes when the processor determines that the gadget execution was mis-predicted.

The mitigation of branch target injection can be accomplished in two ways:

1) The first mitigation entails directly manipulating the speculation hardware. This requires a CPU microcode update and manipulation of hardware registers.

2) The second mitigation involves indirectly controlling speculation behavior. Retpoline is a software construct for preventing branch target injection. It only impacts element 4 in the preceding five elements, but it is sufficient to stop the branch target injection exploit.

What does retpoline mean? First, let's see Figure 14-8 – speculative execution without retpoline. If the attacker can poison the predicted target address, they can control the speculative path execution to a gadget.

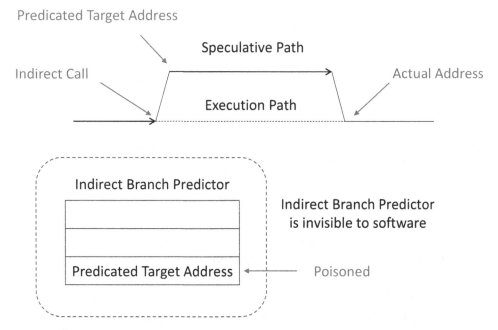

Figure 14-8. *Speculative Execution Without Retpoline*

The indirect branch predictor is an internal CPU structure which is invisible to software. Even operating systems cannot control the behavior of the indirect branch predictor. As such, we need a way to bypass the indirect branch predictor. We know that the prediction of RET instructions differs from that of JMP and CALL instructions because the RET instruction relies on the Return Stack Buffer (RSB). The RSB is a typical last-in-first-out (LIFO) stack which is also a CPU internal structure different from the stack in the memory. The RSB can be controlled by software. The CALL instruction pushes entries, and the RET instruction pops entries. As such, we can convert a JMP or CALL instruction to a RET instruction to force the hardware to use the RSB instead of an indirect branch predictor. See Figure 14-9.

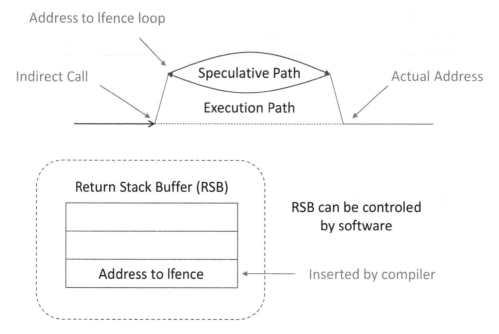

Figure 14-9. *Speculative Execution with Retpoline*

Usually the retpoline is generated by the compiler. In some rare case, we may need to write assembly code directly. As such, we need to know how to write retpoline code.

Listing 14-30 shows a simple JMP indirect branch. Listing 14-31 shows its retpoline replacement.

Listing 14-30.

```
===========================
  jmp [rax]
===========================
```

Listing 14-31.

```
===========================
    call load_label
capture_ret_spec:
    lfence
    jmp capture_ret_spec
load_label:
```

```
  mov [rsp], rax
  ret
=========================
```

Listing 14-32 shows a simple CALL indirect branch. Listing 14-33 shows its retpoline replacement.

Listing 14-32.

```
=========================
  call [rax]
next_instruction:
=========================
```

Listing 14-33.

```
=========================
  jmp label2
label0:
  call label1
capture_ret_spec:
  lfense
  jmp capture_ret_spec
label1:
  mov [rsp], rax
  ret
label2:
  call label0
next_instruction:
=========================
```

When the CALL instruction is executed, the next instruction address is pushed to the stack and the RSB, which is capture_ret_spec. The "mov [rsp], rax" instruction only modifies the content in the stack, but not the RSB. This is very important because the memory stack and RSB differ at this point. Just in case the speculation happens at RET, it will execute the entry in the RSB, which is capture_ret_spec, instead of the rax, and then run into a dead loop. See Figure 14-10.

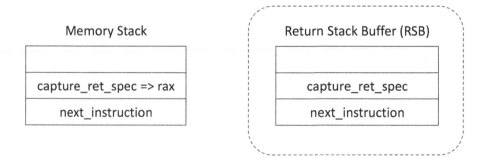

Memory Stack

Return Stack Buffer (RSB)

Figure 14-10. *Memory Stack and RSB*

The RSB is a fixed-size stack implemented in hardware. It can underflow in certain conditions, thus causing undesirable behavior. When the RSB stack is empty on some processors, a RET instruction may speculate based upon the contents of the indirect branch predictor. This latter case is the situation that retpoline is designed to avoid.

According to the Intel whitepaper, there are also a number of events that happen asynchronously from normal program execution that can result in an empty RSB. Software may use a "RSB stuffing" sequence whenever these asynchronous events occur:

1) Interrupts/NMIs/traps/aborts/exceptions which increase call depth

2) System management interrupts (SMIs)

3) Host VMEXIT/VMRESUME/VMENTER

4) Microcode update load (WRMSR 0x79) on another logical processor of the same core

Listing 14-34 shows an example of RSB stuffing sequences.

Listing 14-34.

```
==========================
void rsb_stuff(void)
{
    asm(".rept 16\n"
        "call 1f\n"
        "pause ; LFENCE\n"
        "1: \n"
```

```
        ".endr\n"
        "addq $(8 * 16), %rsp\n");
}
============================
```

The host firmware might not be impacted by the branch target injection if all codes run at the same privilege. On processors with different empty RSB behaviors, SMM code should stuff the RSB with CALL instructions before returning from SMM to avoid interfering with non-SMM usage of the retpoline technique.

Meltdown Variant 3

Meltdown breaks the most fundamental isolation between user applications and the operating system. This attack allows a program to access the memory, and thus also the secrets, of other programs and the operating system.

Meltdown attack takes three steps:

1) Secret read: The attacker accesses a kernel address and loads the content into a register, such as using a MOV instruction. This address is inaccessible because of the privilege. Most modern operating systems use a single page table to map the application space and the kernel space. As such, the kernel space address is present in the page table. Because of out-of-order execution, the CPU loads the kernel data internally at first regardless of the privilege. Later when the MOV instruction retires, the exception is triggered. However, there is a race condition between the raising of the exception and the secret transmit step.

2) Secret transmit: The attacker uses a transient instruction sequence to access a cache line based on the secret content of the register. If this transient instruction sequence is executed before the MOV instruction is retired in the race condition and the transient instruction sequence performed computations based on the secret, it can be utilized to transmit the secret to the attacker.

3) Secret receive: The attacker uses the Flush+Reload attack to determine the accessed cache line and then gets the secret content.

Listing 14-35 shows the code example of the Meltdown attack. With this approach, the application can dump the whole kernel memory content.

Listing 14-35.

```
==========================
  ; rcx = kernel address
  ; rbx = probe array
retry:
  mov al, byte [rcx]
  shl rax, 0xc
  jz retry
  mov rbx, qword [rbx + rax]
==========================
```

The mitigation of Meltdown is to set up dual page tables, also known as kernel page table isolation (KPTI). One page table is designated for the user-level application, with a minimal kernel page for the context switch only. The other page table is only for the OS kernel usage. With the dual page tables, the Meltdown attack will fail in the secret read because the user mode paging does not have a valid address for the OS kernel. There is no way to read the OS kernel content. We will introduce more details in Chapter 16.

If the firmware enables the kernel mode and user mode isolation, the dual page tables should be used to resist the Meltdown attack.

Others

Besides the original Spectre variant 1 and variant 2 and Meltdown variant 3, there are more and more side channel attacks appearing, such as variant 3a, Rogue System Register Read; variant 4, Speculative Store Bypass; SpectreRSB; BranchScope; and so on.

The Spectre and Meltdown website lists all impacted products, including the processors, such as X86 and ARM, and operating systems, such as Linux and Windows. The following documents describe some technical details of the issue and the mitigation:

Intel, "Host Firmware Speculative Execution Side Channel Mitigation"

Intel, "Deep Dive: Analyzing Potential Bounds Check Bypass Vulnerabilities"

Intel, "Deep Dive: Retpoline - A Branch Target Injection Mitigation"

Intel, "Security Best Practices for Side Channel Resistance"

ARM, "Cache Speculation Side-channels"

Google, "Retpoline: a software construct for preventing branch-target-injection"

Linux, "KAISER: hiding the kernel from user space"

Microsoft, "Spectre mitigations in MSVC"

Microsoft, "Mitigating Spectre variant 2 with Retpoline on Windows"

Besides the cache, other micro-architecture may also be vulnerable to the speculative attack, such as Intel Microarchitecture Data Sampling (MDS). Intel MDS involves Microarchitecture Store Buffer Data Sampling (MSBDS), Microarchitecture Fill Buffer Data Sampling (MFBDS), Microarchitecture Load Port Data Sampling (MLPDS), and Microarchitecture Data Sampling Uncacheable Memory (MDSUM). The key concept of MDS is that the CPU microarchitecture includes one or more special data buffer in the memory pipeline besides the CPU cache. These special data buffers are vulnerable to cache speculative attack, such as FLASH+RELOAD. The Rogue In-Flight Data Load (RIDL) showed the attack to leak in-flight data from the line-fill buffer. The fallout demonstrated the attack the data leakage from the store buffer. Those attacks can bypass the existing cache speculative mitigation. Intel whitepaper "Deep Dive: Intel Analysis of Microarchitectural Data Sampling" provides more detailed information on MDS.

Please always refer to the latest side channel mitigation guidelines.

Fault Injection

Fault injection entails the generation of unexpected conditions and triggering of a fault. In general, it includes software fault injection and hardware fault injection. The software fault injection can be compiler time or runtime. The compiler-time fault injection is to add some stub functions to trigger the error path. Usually, it is used to test the robustness and error handling code. The runtime software fault injection is similar to the untrusted external input. It can be used in both the penetration test and real attack. It is already covered in the previous section - "Check Input Cross Trust Boundary."

Hardware fault injection involves the modification of the physical environment by placing the hardware chip in an unusual situation. It could be overvoltage, under-voltage, voltage glitch, electromagnetic pulse, high-energy radiation, high temperature, low temperature, and so on. A typical hardware fault injection brings a transient effect, such as flipping a single bit or a few bits, to skip an instruction or control a branch path. It is very effective to bypass the security check. In the real world, we have seen row hammer attacks or glitch attacks to bypass the security checking and gain privilege. The real open source example includes ChipWhisperer and SySS iCEstick Glitcher, etc. Our focus in this section is to discuss the mitigation for the hardware fault injection.

Let's take a look at Listing 14-36. It is a typical enum definition and the function to use this enum.

Listing 14-36.

```
===========================
typedef enum {
  EfiDriverConfigurationActionNone           = 0,
  EfiDriverConfigurationActionStopController    = 1,
  EfiDriverConfigurationActionRestartController = 2,
  EfiDriverConfigurationActionRestartPlatform   = 3,
  EfiDriverConfigurationActionMaximum
} EFI_DRIVER_CONFIGURATION_ACTION_REQUIRED;

TestDriver ()
{
  EFI_DRIVER_CONFIGURATION_ACTION_REQUIRED  Action;

  Test (&Action);
  // Test and decide action

  switch (Action) {
  case EfiDriverConfigurationActionStopController:
    StopController ();
    break;
  case EfiDriverConfigurationActionRestartController:
    RestartController ();
    break;
```

```
case EfiDriverConfigurationActionRestartPlatform:
  ResetPlatform ();
  break;
default:
  // continue;
  break;
}
```

===========================

This function is vulnerable to the glitch attack if the attack can flip 1 bit between "Test (&Action)" and "switch (Action)." In cases wherein the test function finds some errors and sets Action to be an abnormal one, such as EfiDriverConfigurationActionStopController (1), the attacker can flip the Action bit0 to 0 in order to let this code just continue running. If the test function sets the Action to be EfiDriverConfigurationActionRestartController (2), the attacker can flip the Action bit1 to 0. If the Action is set to EfiDriverConfigurationActionRestartPlatform (3), then the attacker cannot flip the Action to 0. However, the attacker can flip the Action bit31 to 1 to make it invalid. Because the default path in the switch is continued, this code just continues running with the invalid action.

To resist the glitch attack, we need to write code in a more robust fashion. See Listing 14-37.

Listing 14-37.

```
===========================
typedef enum {
  EfiDriverConfigurationActionNone              = 0x5AC33CA5,
  EfiDriverConfigurationActionStopController    = 0xA53CC35A,
  EfiDriverConfigurationActionRestartController = 0xC35AA53C,
  EfiDriverConfigurationActionRestartPlatform   = 0x3CA55AC3,
} EFI_DRIVER_CONFIGURATION_ACTION_REQUIRED;

TestDriver ()
{
  EFI_DRIVER_CONFIGURATION_ACTION_REQUIRED  Action;

  Test (&Action);
  // Test and decide action
```

```
switch (Action) {
case EfiDriverConfigurationActionStopController:
  StopController ();
  break;
case EfiDriverConfigurationActionRestartController:
  RestartController ();
  break;
case EfiDriverConfigurationActionRestartPlatform:
  ResetPlatform ();
  break;
case EfiDriverConfigurationActionNone:
  // continue
  break;
default:
  // impossible case
  ASSERT(FALSE);
  ResetPlatform ();
  break;
}
```

==========================

First, the enum definition should use a non-trivial value with a large Hamming distance. The Hamming distance between two numbers is defined as the number of bits that differ for those numbers. For example, the pair (0, 1) has a Hamming distance 1. (0x5A=0101_1010b, 0x3C=0011_1100b) has a Hamming distance 4. (0x5A=0101_1010b, 0xA5=1010_0101b) has a Hamming distance 8. A large Hamming distance makes it hard for the attacker to change from one value to the other value. Second, we handle the undefined state in the default path and treat it as a failure condition. This makes it difficult for the attacker to take advantage of success by default.

Let's see another example in Listing 14-38. This is a typical flow in authentication routines.

Listing 14-38.

```
===========================
BOOLEAN Authentication ()
{
  BOOLEAN    Result = FALSE;

  Result = ReadPolicyData ();
  if (!Result) {
    return FALSE;
  }
  Result = ReadPublicKey ();
  if (!Result) {
    return FALSE;
  }
  Result = ComparePublicKey ();
  if (!Result) {
    return FALSE;
  }
  Result = VerifySignature ();
  if (!Result) {
    return FALSE;
  }
  return TRUE;
}
===========================
```

This function is also vulnerable to the glitch attack. First, the Result is a BOOLEAN, where zero means FALSE and any other non-zero value means TRUE. As such, the attacker can flip 1 bit in the result to make it pass the verification stage. Second, all checks happen in a fixed order. Ideally the timing is also fixed. It is easy for the attack to hit the data.

Listing 14-39.

```
===========================
typedef enum {
  AuthStateFail    = 0x5AC33CA5,
  AuthStateSuccess = 0xA53CC35A,
} AUTH_STATE;

AUTH_STATE Authentication ()
{
  AUTH_STATE    Result1 = AuthenticationIteration();
  AUTH_STATE    Result2 = AuthenticationIteration(); // redundancy
  if (Result1 != Result2) {
    return AuthStateFail;
  }
  if ((Result1 != AuthStateSuccess) ||
      (Result2 != AuthStateSuccess)) {
    return AuthStateFail;
  }
}

AUTH_STATE AuthenticationIteration ()
{
  AUTH_STATE    Result1 = AuthStateFail;
  AUTH_STATE    Result2 = AuthStateFail;
  AUTH_STATE    Result3 = AuthStateFail;
  AUTH_STATE    Result4 = AuthStateFail;

  Delay (GetRandom() & MAX_DELAY);
  Result1 = ReadPolicyData ();

  Delay (GetRandom() & MAX_DELAY);
  Result2 = ReadPublicKey ();

  Delay (GetRandom() & MAX_DELAY);
  Result3 = ComparePublicKey ();

  Delay (GetRandom() & MAX_DELAY);
  Result4 = VerifySignature ();
```

```
  if ((Result1 != AuthStateSuccess) ||
      (Result2 != AuthStateSuccess) ||
      (Result3 != AuthStateSuccess) ||
      (Result4 != AuthStateSuccess) ) {
    return AuthStateFail;
  }
  return AuthStateSuccess;
}
==========================
```

Listing 14-39 shows the improvement. First, it uses the non-trivial definition for the final result instead of a BOOLEAN. As such, it is hard for the attacker to flip the result. Second, it adds a redundancy check. For example, the authentication function is called twice as a double check. The attacker must flip bits in two different places. Third, it uses a random delay before any check function, which makes it hard for the time-based fault injection.

Mitigation Summary

The basic mitigation for fault injection is the following:

1) Use non-trivial code with a large Hamming distance.

2) Fail the default path in a switch case explicitly.

3) Add redundancy checks.

4) Add random delay in the code.

High-Risk Area in Firmware

In Chapter 2, we mentioned eight high-risk areas in firmware. Now let's revisit to see how to apply the secure coding practice to those areas.

External Input

Checking the untrusted external input across the trust boundary is rule number 1.

What entails untrusted external input should be defined clearly based upon the threat model. You may ask yourself, can the attacker control and modify the data? If yes, then it is untrusted external input. If no, then it is probably trusted data. Some external input data are very clear, such as a BIOS logo Bitmap (BMP) file or Joint Photographic Experts Group JPEG file, a BIOS update image, content in the file system, the trusted execution environment (TEE) communication buffer, network packet, and so on. Some external input data may be trusted or untrusted, such as a recovery image. If the system designer puts the recovery image into an immutable location and only allows manufacturing mode update, then this image could be treated as trusted. If the system designer allows the end user to put a recovery image in any allowed recovery media, such as the hard disk or USB disk, then the input is untrusted. Another example is the flash content. If the threat model includes the simple hardware adversary and assumes the attacker may use a flash programmer to update the flash content directly, then it is untrusted and should be validated by a platform Root-of-Trust. If the threat model does not include simple hardware adversary but only includes a system software adversary, then we can just apply flash write protection in the TEE. The flash content can be treated as trusted in the boot.

The concept of trusted internal input and untrusted external input may change in the production. For example, in old days, the BMP logo file was treated as the internal input. The end user cannot modify the BMP BIOS boot logo file. Later, some BIOS treated it as a feature to allow an end user to customize the BIOS boot logo. Then the BMP logo file becomes an untrusted external input. The universal plug and play (UPnP) protocol is designed to be used in a trusted local area network (LAN) and the protocol does not implement any form of authentication or verification. However, many common Internet-connected devices support UPnP. The attacker found the vulnerabilities, such as CallStranger. Then the Open Connectivity Foundation (OCF) has updated the UPnP specification to address this issue. If the previous assumption is changed, the external input for the production must be reevaluated.

When we perform the input check, the secure coding practices should be followed. Per our observation, buffer overflow, arbitrary buffer access, and arithmetic error such as integer overflow are the top three issues. Care must be taken for them. If the input check is missing or incomplete, there is a high risk of privilege escalation. This usually happens during the firmware update process or in a trusted execution environment (TEE) handler, such as X86 system management interrupt (SMI) handler or ARM secure monitor call (SMC) handler. The input validation is critical for the TEE to resist the confused deputy attack because of the high privilege of the TEE.

Correct error handling is also important. For example, if the check function fails to find the policy, it should return a verification failure instead of a verification pass. Especially in cases where the check function fails to find the revocation policy or denied image policy due to expected system error or hardware error, it should still also return verification fail. Only if the check function fails to find the revocation policy or denied image policy because the policy is valid but empty should it return a verification pass. Missing error handling is not a good choice. ASSERT may be used to define the contract clearly. Before using ASSERT, please always ask yourself: Might this occur when the attacker tries to attack the system and modify the software or hardware state? Or is this a case that never occurs because it is guaranteed by the other code logic or hardware restriction? ASSERT should only be used in the latter case. Error handling should be used for the former case.

The compatibility support might be a burden because the old image format or signature format might be different from the latest one. It is highly recommended to use a different function and different code path to cover the compatibility support instead of mixing the logic with the latest format. We have seen bad examples where the code combines both logic flows together and thus makes it very complicated. With such complexity, a small mistake in the compatibility support logic brings a security hole in the checking function.

The deprecated or banned API should not be used because it may miss a length parameter. Even if you use a safe version of API, you still need to pay much attention to the input parameter, especially the length of the buffer. We have seen bad examples when the project tried to clean up the banned API usage. The developer filled a wrong length parameter to a safe string function, which makes the boundary check in the safe string function useless.

Race Condition

In general, there are two typical race conditions in firmware.

The first one is the race condition for the external data buffer for the check function. This brings a typical time-of-check/time-of-use (TOC/TOU) issue. The right way to handle this type of race condition is as follows: 1) copy the data from an untrusted environment to a trusted environment, 2) verify the data in the trusted environment, and 3) use the data in the trusted environment. The data in the untrusted environment should never be used in steps 2 and 3. One example is the trusted execution environment (TEE) communication buffer. The TEE handler should copy the communication buffer into TEE and then verify and use the data inside of the TEE. Another example is the boot flash content, where a root-of-trust should copy the boot flash to a trusted memory, such as cache, and then verify and use the content in the trusted memory. If the external flash cannot be trusted, then it should not be accessed anymore after verification.

The second one is the race condition for the critical register unlock in the TEE. This is a typical TEE-based protection. The X86 system management mode (SMM)–based flash protection is one example. The flash region is locked, and no flash write is allowed after boot. The flash region can only be unlocked inside of SMM. The normal process is as follows: 1) enter SMM, 2) unlock the flash region, 3) write flash content, 4) lock the flash region again, and 5) exit SMM. These five steps must be in one system management interrupt (SMI). Before the CPU performs the unlock action, this CPU must check the state of other CPUs to see if they are also in SMM running trusted code. If there is one CPU not inside of SMM, then this malicious CPU can perform the flash content write after the flash region is unlocked by the CPU in SMM. As such, if we need to unlock the critical register in the TEE, we must check that all CPUs are in the TEE and running trusted code.

Hardware Input

Hardware input is an extension for the external input class of concern. We list it here independently because it is a new threat and it is easily ignored when we design a solution.

The device-specific data is the hardware input, such as the USB descriptor or Bluetooth Low Energy (BLE) advertisement data. The attacker can easily create malicious data and send the malformed data, such as the USB FaceDancer tool. At the same time, we have seen some implementations just follow the specification and assume that the device sends the data according to the specification. Eventually, the malformed data caused a buffer overflow. The same attack can be on the Serial Peripheral Interface (SPI) bus, Inter-Integrated Circuit (I2C) bus, System Management Bus (SMBus), and so on.

The silicon register is another hardware input because the attacker may program it to a malicious state and attack the TEE. The remap register reprogramming and the memory mapped I/O (MMIO) base address register (BAR) overlapping are two common techniques in the address alias attack. As such, if possible, we should lock the configured silicon register. For the unlockable MMIO BAR register, an overlap check is always required before accessing any data in the MMIO region. The overlap check should cover the TEE, such as SMM, the high-privilege environment such as the hypervisor, or any other high-privilege assets to potentially overlap the MMIO region.

DMA attacks have become more and more popular. The PCI Leech is a tool to generate DMA from a PCI device to attack the system. It could run in both the OS phase and the pre-OS firmware phase. If a DMA attack is included in the threat model, then DMA protection should be included. The time to enable DMA protection should also depend upon the threat model. If only external DMA threats need to be considered, the DMA protection can be enabled before we connect the external device. If the internal DMA threat needs to also be considered, the DMA protection should be enabled before the DRAM initialization. If the internal DMA can access the SRAM, then the DMA protection should be enabled by default when the system powers on.

Secret Handling

If the firmware needs to deal with a secret, such as a password, then the best practices for secret handling must be followed. A common mistake is that the secret is left in the memory, such as the key buffer, temporary local variable to convert the format of the secret from ASCII to Unicode or vice versa, or communication buffer to pass the secret from one environment to the other environment. The secret should be cleared after use in all those places.

When clearing the secret, please pay attention to the compiler optimization. The zeroing memory function might be optimized by the compiler. Please always double-check the final generated binary to confirm the zeroing action is still there.

If the secret needs to be stored in the non-volatile memory, then we should not use plain text. The best practice is to use a slow hash function with salt data. Please pay attention to the special data management attribute of the non-volatile memory because the removal operation might simply be a flag setting on the volatile memory storage to achieve the best performance. One example is the file system. Even after a file is deleted, the content of the file is still on the disk. Saving the secret in such a file system is not a good idea, even as temporary storage.

Register Lock

After the system boots, the firmware should lock down the configuration as much as possible. The most important ones include the flash region lock, the TEE lock such as SMM, and system configuration lock, such as MMIO BAR. A simple check you can do is to read the datasheet to see if there is a lock register. If there is, then probably you need to lock it, unless you are told not to lock with a good justification.

Care must be taken that the lock action might not be a register setting. It might be a command, such as the End Of Post (EOP) command transmitted as an Intel Management Engine (ME) EOP message; a freeze command, such as the ATA SECURITY_FREEZE_LOCK command; or a block command, such as the TCG OPAL BLOCK_SID command.

Secure Configuration

In firmware, some security features are configurable, for example, the secure boot and TPM capability. The configuration can be static or dynamic. For the static configuration, it should be locked by the firmware to prevent any malicious reconfiguration, such as the flash lock, TEE lock, or MMIO BAR lock. For the dynamic configuration, the platform should use an access control mechanism to prevent the malicious configuration, such as the secure boot policy change requiring the authenticated variable update and the TPM configuration change requiring physical user presence.

An attacker may enable the recovery mode or manufacturing mode to bypass some security checks. We should design the solution carefully to apply the same security policy in the special boot modes. For example, skipping the secure boot verification in manufacturing mode is probably not a good idea.

A production implementation should not include any debug-related code or data. A debug message may cause an information leak in the TEE. A debug service handler may expose an unnecessary attack surface. A debug key or test key in the production platform may lead to a bypass of the authentication via a debug tool. All of those should be removed in final production.

An attacker may attach a debugger to the product in order to steal information in order to tamper with the system. The telemetry information is allowed for sending to the debugger, but the private key should never be exposed. Also, a root-of-trust module should detect this behavior and report a different firmware measurement to distinguish a debugger-attached boot from a normal boot. As such, the verifier can know the system is under debug and assert a different trust level.

In the TCG trusted boot solution, the completeness is the most important thing. The firmware must measure all required data into the right Trusted Platform Module (TPM) Platform Configuration Register (PCR). If a firmware forgets to measure one component, the tampering of this component will not be discovered. People have demonstrated how to use this missing measurement in tboot to attack the Intel Trusted Execution Technology (TXT) in S3 resume phase.

S3 resume is another perfect attack point because the system needs to be reconfigured in the S3 phase. All the secure configuration policy in the normal boot should be applied to S3 resume as well.

Replay/Rollback

The firmware usually needs to be updated. One threat in the firmware update is that the attacker may roll back the current firmware to an old known vulnerable version. As such, the version check in the firmware update is as important as the firmware integrity check, such as digital signature. The firmware version must be signed as part of the firmware image. The new firmware image version must not be smaller than the lowest supported version number (LSN) of the current firmware image.

If the firmware supports a data communication protocol, then the old vulnerable communication protocol must be excluded in the implementation. Otherwise, the attacker may try to negotiate with the firmware and downgrade the communication protocol to the older vulnerable one. The SSL Padding Oracle on Downgraded Legacy Encryption (POODLE) attack is such an example. It downgrades the TLS to SSL3.0.

Another example is the Qualcomm Achilles vulnerability. When a Digital Signal Processor (DSP) chip loads a library, the signature of the library is verified. However, there is no version check in the loader of the DSP and there is no device limitation. The attacker may find an old known vulnerable signed library from an old device and load it on a new DSP device. This is a typical downgrade vulnerability.

Cryptography

Assuming most developers are not cryptographic experts, the general recommendations are as follows:

1) Do not invent any cryptographic algorithm or protocol but instead follow the industry standards and guidelines. For example, don't invent a new algorithm to support encryption and MAC. Please use the standard Authenticated Encryption with Associated Data (AEAD) instead.

2) Do not write your own cryptographic library and instead use the existing one, such as openSSL and mbed TLS. The reason is that there were lots of implementation flaws observed in previous implementations and fixed, especially the side channel vulnerability. A new implementation may have the same mistake unless all existing vulnerabilities are well known by the developer.

3) Always ask a cryptography expert to review the crypto-related architecture and implementation.

One important consideration in cryptography is the random number. The common mistakes are

1) Insufficient entropy in the random number seed

2) Weak pseudo random number generation function

As such, if the hardware provides the random seed or random number, we should use the hardware-generated one.

The developer should also be aware of the randomness requirement in different algorithms and protocols, such as initialization vector, nonce, counter, sequence number, and so on. The initialization vector must be uniformly random. Using a fixed value for the initialization vector is a bad idea. A sequence number might not need to be random, but an incremental value needs to be synchronized between the sender and the receiver.

Similar to secret handling, the symmetric key and the private key must be cleared after use.

Summary

In this chapter, we introduced the secure coding practice in firmware. It covers the basic secure coding practice and secure design practice. We also introduced the advanced secure coding topic, including the traditional side channel attacks, such as timing side channel and cache side channel, the speculative execution attack, and the fault injection attack, as well as the mitigations. Finally, we summarized the recommendations for firmware development in the high-risk areas. In the next chapter, we will introduce the compiler defensive technologies to see how we can use those in the firmware development.

References

Book

[B-1] Steve McConnell, *Code Complete: A Practical Handbook of Software Construction*, 2nd Edition, Microsoft, 2004

[B-2] Steve Maguire, *Writing Solid Code: Microsoft's Techniques for Developing Bug-Free C Programs*, Microsoft, 1993

[B-3] Michael Howard, David LeBlanc, *Writing Secure Code: Practical Strategies and Proven Techniques for Building Secure Applications in a Networked World, 2nd Edition*, Microsoft, 2004

[B-4] Michael Howard, David LeBlanc, John Viega, *24 Deadly Sins of Software Security: Programming Flaws and How to Fix Them*, McGraw-Hill, 2009

[B-5] M.G. Graff and K.R. van Wyk, *Secure Coding: Principles and Practices*, O'Reilly, 2002

[B-6] John Viega, Matt Messier, *Secure Programming Cookbook for C and C++: Recipes for Cryptography, Authentication, Input Validation and More*, O'Reilly Media, 2003

[B-7] John Viega, Gary McGraw, *Building Secure Software: How to Avoid Security Problems the Right Way*, Addison-Wesley Professional, 2001

[B-8] Greg Hoglund, Gary McGraw, *Exploiting Software: How to Break Code*, Addison-Wesley Professional, 2004

[B-9] Jon Erickson, *Hacking: The Art of Exploitation, 2nd Edition*, No Starch Press, 2008

[B-10] Christian Collberg, Jasvir Nagra, *Surreptitious Software: Obfuscation, Watermarking, and Tamperproofing for Software Protection*, Addison-Wesley Professional, 2009

[B-11] Wenliang Du, *Computer and Internet Security: A Hands-on Approach*, CreateSpace Independent Publishing Platform, 2019

[B-12] Brian W. Kernighan, Rob Pike, *The Practice of Programming*, Addison-Wesley, 1999

[B-13] Gary Stringham, *Hardware/Firmware Interface Design: Best Practices for Improving Embedded Systems Development*, Newnes, 2009

[B-14] Jacob Beningo, *Reusable Firmware Development: A Practical Approach to APIs, HALs and Drivers*, Apress, 2017

[B-15] Jason Cohen, *Best Kept Secrets of Peer Code Review*, Smart Bear Inc., 2006

[B-16] Daniel P. Freedman and Gerald M. Weinberg, *Handbook of Walkthroughs, Inspections, and Technical Reviews: Evaluating Programs, Projects, and Products*, Dorset House, 1990

[B-17] Tom Gilb and Dorothy Graham, *Software Inspection*, Addison-Wesley Professional, 1994

[B-18] Karl Wiegers, *Peer Reviews in Software: A Practical Guide*, Addison-Wesley Professional, 2001

Conference, Journal, and Paper

[P-1] Rafal Wojtczuk, Alexander Tereshkin, "Attack Intel BIOS," in *BlackHat 2009*, available at www.blackhat.com/presentations/bh-usa-09/WOJTCZUK/BHUSA09-Wojtczuk-AtkIntelBios-SLIDES.pdf

[P-2] Rafal Wojtczuk, Joanna Rutkowska, "Attacking Intel TXT via SINIT Hijacking," in *invisiblethingslab whitepaper 2011*, available at https://invisiblethingslab.com/resources/2011/Attacking_Intel_TXT_via_SINIT_hijacking.pdf

[P-3] Di Shen, "Attacking your Trusted Core – Exploiting Trustzone on Android," in *BlackHat US 2015*, www.blackhat.com/docs/us-15/materials/us-15-Shen-Attacking-Your-Trusted-Core-Exploiting-Trustzone-On-Android.pdf

[P-4] Oleksandr Bazhaniuk, Yuriy Bulygin, "Blue Pill for Your Phone," in BlackHat 2017, available at www.blackhat.com/docs/us-17/wednesday/us-17-Bazhaniuk-BluePill-For-Your-Phone.pdf

[P-5] Dmitriy Evdokimov, Alexander Ermolov, Maksim Malyutin, "Intel AMT Stealth Breakthrough," in *BlackHat 2017*, available at www.blackhat.com/docs/us-17/thursday/us-17-Evdokimov-Intel-AMT-Stealth-Breakthrough.pdf

[P-6] Fabien Perigaud, Alexandre Gazet, Joffrey Czarny, "Backdooring your server through its BMC," in *SSTIC 2018*, available at www.sstic.org/media/SSTIC2018/SSTIC-actes/subverting_your_server_through_its_bmc_the_hpe_ilo/SSTIC2018-Slides-subverting_your_server_through_its_bmc_the_hpe_ilo4_case-gazet_perigaud_czarny.pdf

[P-7] Nico Waisman, Matias Sebastian Soler, "The Unbearable Lightness of BMCs," in *BlackHat 2018*, available at http://i.blackhat.com/us-18/Wed-August-8/us-18-Waisman-Soler-The-Unbearable-Lightness-of-BMC.pdf

[P-8] Fabien Perigaud, Alexandre Gazet, Joffrey Czarny, "Turning your BMC into a revolving door," in ZeroNight 2018, https://airbus-seclab.github.io/ilo/ZERONIGHTS2018-Slides-EN-Turning_your_BMC_into_a_revolving_door-perigaud-gazet-czarny.pdf

[P-9] Vincent Lee, "Hardware Reversing with the BELKIN SURF N300 Router," 2019, available at www.thezdi.com/blog/2019/6/6/mindshare-hardware-reversing-with-the-belkin-surf-n300-router

[P-10] Vincent Lee, "Wipe Out! Hanging (More Than) Ten On Your Old Belkin Surf Router," 2019, available at www.thezdi.com/blog/2019/8/1/wipe-out-hanging-more-than-ten-on-your-old-belkin-surf-router

[P-11] Vincent Lee, "Hardware Reversing with the TP-LINK TL-WR841N Router," 2019, available at www.thezdi.com/blog/2019/9/2/mindshare-hardware-reversing-with-the-tp-link-tl-wr841n-router

[P-12] Vincent Lee, "Hardware Reversing with the TP-LINK TL-WR841N Router – Part 2," 2019, available at www.zerodayinitiative.com/blog/2019/12/2/mindshare-hardware-reversing-with-the-tp-link-tl-wr841n-router-part-2

[P-13] Gal Beniamini, "Over The Air: Exploiting Broadcom's Wi-Fi Stack," in 2017, available at https://googleprojectzero.blogspot.com/2017/04/over-air-exploiting-broadcoms-wi-fi_4.html, https://googleprojectzero.blogspot.com/2017/04/over-air-exploiting-broadcoms-wi-fi_11.html

[P-14] Nitay Artenstein, "Broadpwn: Remotely Compromising Android and IOS via a Bug in Broadcom's Wi-Fi Chipsets," in BlackHat US 2017, available at https://www.blackhat.com/docs/us-17/thursday/us-17-Artenstein-Broadpwn-Remotely-Compromising-Android-And-iOS-Via-A-Bug-In-Broadcoms-Wifi-Chipsets.pdf

[P-15] Denis Selyanin, "Researching Marvell Avastar Wi-Fi: From zero knowledge to over-the-air zero-touch RCE," in Zero Nights 2018, available at https://www.youtube.com/watch?v=Him_Lf5ZJ38

[P-16] Xiling Gong, Peter Pi, "QualPwn – Exploiting Qualcomm WLAN and Modem Over the Air," in Blackhat US 2019, available at `http://i.blackhat.com/USA-19/Thursday/us-19-Pi-Exploiting-Qualcomm-WLAN-And-Modem-Over-The-Air.pdf`

[P-17] Hugues Anguelkov, "Reverse-engineering Broadcom wireless chipsets," 2019, available at `https://blog.quarkslab.com/reverse-engineering-broadcom-wireless-chipsets.html`

[P-18] Charlie Miller, Collin Mulliner, "Fuzzing the Phone in Your Phone," in Blackhat US 2009, available at `https://www.blackhat.com/presentations/bh-usa-09/MILLER/BHUSA09-Miller-FuzzingPhone-SLIDES.pdf`

[P-19] Ralf-Philipp Weinmann, "Baseband Attacks: Remote Exploitation of Memory Corruptions in Cellular Protocol Stacks," in USENIX WOOT 2012, available at `https://www.usenix.org/system/files/conference/woot12/woot12-final24.pdf`

[P-20] Nico Golde, Daniel Komaromy, "Breaking Band: Reverse engineering and exploiting the shannon baseband," in recon 2016, available at `https://comsecuris.com/slides/recon2016-breaking_band.pdf`

[P-21] Gyorgy Miru, "Path of Least Resistance: Cellular Baseband to Application Processor Escalation on Mediatek Devices," in 2017, available at `https://comsecuris.com/blog/posts/path_of_least_resistance/`

[P-22] Amat Cama, "A walk with Shannon Walkthrough of a pwn2own baseband exploit," in 2018, available at `https://downloads.immunityinc.com/infiltrate2018-slidepacks/amat-cama-a-walk-with-shannon/presentation.pdf`

[P-23] Marco Grassi, Muqing Liu, Tianyi Xie, "Exploitation of a Modern Smartphone Baseband," in BlackHat US 2018, available at `http://i.blackhat.com/us-18/Thu-August-9/us-18-Grassi-Exploitation-of-a-Modern-Smartphone-Baseband.pdf`

[P-24] Jonathan Brossard, "Bypassing Pre-boot Authentication Passwords," in *DEFCON162008*, available at `www.defcon.org/images/defcon-16/dc16-presentations/brossard/defcon-16-brossard-wp.pdf`

[P-25] Charlie Miller, "Battery Firmware Hacking," in *BlackHat US 2011*, available at `https://media.blackhat.com/bh-us-11/Miller/BH_US_11_Miller_Battery_Firmware_Public_Slides.pdf`

[P-26] Alex Matrosov, Alexandre Gazet, "Breaking Through Another Side," in *Blackhat US 2019*, available at `http://i.blackhat.com/USA-19/Thursday/us-19-Matrosov-Breaking-Through-Another-Side-Bypassing-Firmware-Security-Boundaries-From-Embedded-Controller.pdf`

[P-27] Marc Witteman, "Secure Application Programming in the presence of Side Channel Attack," Riscure Whitepaper 2017, available at www.riscure.com/uploads/2018/11/201708_Riscure_Whitepaper_Side_Channel_Patterns.pdf

[P-28] Dag Arne Osvik, Adi Shamir, Eran Tromer, "Cache attacks and countermeasures: the case of AES," 2005, available at www.cs.tau.ac.il/~tromer/papers/cache.pdf.

[P-29] Eran Tromer, Dag Arne Osvik, Adi Shamir, "Efficient cache attacks in AES, and countermeasures," In *Journal of Cryptology 23, 2010*, available at www.cs.tau.ac.il/~tromer/papers/cache-joc-official.pdf

[P-30] Colin Pecival, "Cache missing for fun and profit," in Proceedings of BSDCan 2005, available at www.daemonology.net/papers/htt.pdf

[P-31] Yuval Yarom, Katrina Falkner, "FLUSH+RELOAD: a High Resolution, Low Noise, L3 Cache Side-Channel Attack," in *USENIX Security Symposium 2014*, available at https://eprint.iacr.org/2013/448.pdf

[P-32] Fangfei Liu, Yuval Yarom, Qian Ge, Gernot Heiser, Ruby B. Lee, "Last-level cache side-channel attacks are practical," in *IEEE Symposium on Security and Privacy 2015*, available at http://palms.ee.princeton.edu/system/files/SP_vfinal.pdf

[P-33] Fangfei Liu, Qian Ge, Yuval Yarom, Frank Mckeen, Carlos Rozas, Gernot Heiser, Ruby B. Lee, "CATalyst: Defeating Last-LevelCache Side Channel Attacks in Cloud Computing," 22nd IEEE Symposium onHigh Performance Computer Architecture, 2016, available at http://palms.ee.princeton.edu/system/files/CATalyst_vfinal_correct.pdf

[P-34] Zirak Allaf, Mo Adda, Alexander Gegov, "A Comparison Study on Flush+Reload and Prime+Probe Attacks on AES Using Machine Learning Approaches," in UKCI 2017, available at https://link.springer.com/content/pdf/10.1007%2F978-3-319-66939-7_17.pdf

[P-35] Paul Kocher, Jann Horn, Anders Fogh, Daniel Genkin, Daniel Gruss, Werner Haas, Mike Hamburg, Moritz Lipp, Stefan Mangard, Thomas Prescher, Michael Schwarz, Yuval Yarom, "Spectre Attacks: Exploiting Speculative Execution," 2018, available at https://spectreattack.com/spectre.pdf

[P-36] Moritz Lipp, Michael Schwarz, Daniel Gruss, Thomas Prescher, Werner Haas, Anders Fogh, Jann Horn, Stefan Mangard, Paul Kocher, Daniel Genkin, Yuval Yarom, Mike Hamburg, "Meltdown: Reading Kernel Memory from User Space," 2018, available at https://meltdownattack.com/meltdown.pdf

[P-37] Caroline Trippel, Daniel Lustig, Margaret Martonosi, "MeltdownPrime and SpectrePrime: Automatically-Synthesized Attacks Exploiting Invalidation-Based Coherence Protocols," 2018, available at `https://arxiv.org/pdf/1802.03802`

[P-38] Esmaeil Mohammadian Koruyeh, Khaled N. Khasawneh, Chengyu Song and Nael Abu-Ghazaleh, "Spectre Returns! Speculation Attacks using the Return Stack Buffer," in *USENIX 2018*, available at `www.usenix.org/system/files/conference/woot18/woot18-paper-koruyeh.pdf`

[P-39] Dmitry Evtyushkin, Ryan Riley, Nael Abu-Ghazaleh, Dmitry Ponomarev, "BranchScope : A New Side-Channel Attack on Directional Branch Predictor," in *ASPLOS 2018*, available at `www.cs.ucr.edu/~nael/pubs/asplos18.pdf`

[P-40] Jann Horn, "Reading Privileged Memory With Side-Channel," in *Project Zero 2018*, available at `https://googleprojectzero.blogspot.com/2018/01/reading-privileged-memory-with-side.html`

[P-41] Michael Schwarz, Moritz Lipp, Daniel Moghimi, Jo Van Bulck, Julian Stecklina, Thomas Prescher, Daniel Gruss, "ZombieLoad: Cross-Privilege-Boundary Data Sampling," in ACM Conference on Computer and Communications Security 2019, available at `https://zombieloadattack.com/zombieload.pdf`

[P-42] Jo Van Bulck, Marina Minkin, Ofir Weisse, Daniel Genkin, Baris Kasikci, Frank Piessens, Mark Silberstein, Thomas F. Wenisch, Yuval Yarom, Raoul Strackx, "FORESHADOW: Extracting the Keys to the Intel SGX Kingdom with Transient Out-of-Order Execution," in USENIX, available at `https://foreshadowattack.eu/foreshadow.pdf`

[P-43] Ofir Weisse, Jo Van Bulck, Marina Minkin, Daniel Genkin, Baris Kasikci, Frank Piessens, Mark Silberstein, Raoul Strackx, Thomas F. Wenisch, Yuval Yarom, "Foreshadow-NG: Breaking the Virtual Memory Abstraction with Transient Out-of-Order Execution," available at `https://foreshadowattack.eu/foreshadow-NG.pdf`

[P-44] Stephan van Schaik, Alyssa Milburn, Sebastian Osterlund, Pietro Frigo, Giorgi Maisuradze, Kaveh Razavi, Herbert Bos, Cristiano Giuffrida, "RIDL: Rogue In-Flight Data Load," in IEEE Symposium on Security and Privacy 2019, available at `https://mdsattacks.com/files/ridl.pdf`

[P-45] Claudio Canella, Daniel Genkin, Lukas Giner, Daniel Gruss, Moritz Lipp, Marina Minkin, Daniel Moghimi, Frank Piessens, Michael Schwarz, Berk Sunar, Jo Van Bulck, Yuval Yarom, "Fallout: Leaking Data on Meltdown-resistant CPUs," in ACM Conference on Computer and Communications Security 2019, available at `https://mdsattacks.com/files/fallout.pdf`

[P-46] Brett Giller, "Implementing Practical Electrical Glitching Attacks," in *Blackhat 2015*, available at `www.blackhat.com/docs/eu-15/materials/eu-15-Giller-Implementing-Electrical-Glitching-Attacks.pdf`

[P-47] Alyssa Milburn, Niek Timmers, "There will be Glitches," in *Blackat 2018*, available at `http://i.blackhat.com/us-18/Wed-August-8/us-18-Milburn-There-Will-Be-Glitches-Extracting-And-Analyzing-Automotive-Firmware-Efficiently.pdf`

[P-48] Claudio Bozzato, Riccardo Focardi and Francesco Palmarini, "Shaping the Glitch: Optimizing Voltage Fault Injection Attacks," in *IACR Transactions on Cryptographic Hardware and Embedded Systems*, *2019*(2), 199-224, available at `https://tches.iacr.org/index.php/TCHES/article/download/7390/6562/`

[P-49] Sergei Skorobogatov, "Fault attacks on secure chips: from glitch to flash," in *ECRYPT 2011*, available at `www.cl.cam.ac.uk/~sps32/ECRYPT2011_1.pdf`

[P-50] Yoongu Kim, Ross Daly, Jeremie Kim, Chris Fallin, Ji Hye Lee, Donghyuk Lee, Chris Wilkerson, Konrad Lai, Onur Mutlu, "Flipping Bits in Memory Without Accessing Them: An Experimental Study of DRAM Disturbance Errors," in *IEEE 2014*, available at `http://users.ece.cmu.edu/~yoonguk/papers/kim-isca14.pdf`

[P-51] Yoongu Kim, Ross Daly, Jeremie Kim, Chris Fallin, Ji Hye Lee, Donghyuk Lee, Chris Wilkerson, Konrad Lai, Onur Mutlu, "RowHammer: Reliability Analysis and Security Implications," 2015, available at `http://users.ece.cmu.edu/~omutlu/pub/rowhammer-summary.pdf`

[P-52] Adrian Tang, Simha Sethumadhavan, and Salvatore Stolfo, "CLKSCREW: Exposing the Perils of Security Oblivious Energy Management," in *USENIX 2017*, available at `www.usenix.org/system/files/conference/usenixsecurity17/sec17-tang.pdf`

[P-53] Tony Chen, "Guarding Against Physical Attacks: The Xbox One Story," in *Bluehat Seattle 2019*, `www.slideshare.net/MSbluehat/bluehat-seattle-2019-guarding-against-physical-attacks-the-xbox-one-story`

[P-54] Ang Cui, Rick Housley. "BADFET: Defeating modern secure boot using second-order pulsed electromagnetic fault injection," In USENIX, WOOT 2017, available at `www.usenix.org/system/files/conference/woot17/woot17-paper-cui.pdf`

[P-55] Daniel Genkin, Lev Pachmanov, Itamar Pipman, "ECDSA Key Extraction from Mobile Devices via Nonintrusive Physical Side Channels," 2016, available at `https://eprint.iacr.org/2016/230.pdf`

[P-56] Ryad Benadjila, Mathieu Renard, "Security offense and defense strategies: Video-game consoles architecture under microscope," in *Hack in Paris 2016*, available at `www.researchgate.net/publication/305154898_Security_offense_and_defense_strategies_Video-game_consoles_architecture_under_microscope`

[P-57] Daniel Gruss, "software based microarchitectural attacks," 2018, available at `https://gruss.cc/files/oecg_2018.pdf`

[P-58] Christopher Domas, "God Mode Unlocked Hardware Backdoors in X86 CPUs," in *BlackHat 2018*, available at `http://i.blackhat.com/us-18/Thu-August-9/us-18-Domas-God-Mode-Unlocked-Hardware-Backdoors-In-x86-CPUs.pdf`

[P-59] Thomas Wollinger, Jorge Guajardo, Christof Paar, "Security on FPGAs: State-of-the-Art Implementations and Attacks," in ACM transactions on embedded computing system 2003, `https://perso.univ-st-etienne.fr/bl16388h/salware/Bibliography_Salware/FPGA%20Bistream%20Security/Article/Wollinger2003.pdf`

[P-60] Jonathan Shimonovich, Glen Deskin, "Achilles: Small Chip, Big Peril," in Check Point 2020, `https://blog.checkpoint.com/2020/08/06/achilles-small-chip-big-peril/`, `https://www.brighttalk.com/webcast/16731/431234`

Specification and Guideline

[S-1] CMU SEI, "SEI CERT C Coding Standard," 2018 available at `https://wiki.sei.cmu.edu/confluence/display/c/SEI+CERT+C+Coding+Standard`

[S-2] MITRE, "The MITRE System Engineering Guide," 2014, available at `www.mitre.org/publications/technical-papers/the-mitre-systems-engineering-guide`

[S-3] OWASP org, "OWASP Secure Coding Practices – Quick Reference Guide," 2010, available at `www.owasp.org/index.php/OWASP_Secure_Coding_Practices_-_Quick_Reference_Guide`

Web

[W-1] OWASP, "How to write insecure code," `www.owasp.org/index.php/How_to_write_insecure_code`

[W-2] Microsoft, "What are the Microsoft SDL practices?," `www.microsoft.com/en-us/securityengineering/sdl/practices`

[W-3] Microsoft, "Security Development Lifecycle (SDL) Banned Function Calls," 2012, `https://msdn.microsoft.com/en-us/library/bb288454.aspx`

[W-4] David Wheeler, "Secure Programming for Linux and Unix HOWTO – Creating Secure Software," 2015, `www.dwheeler.com/secure-programs/`

[W-5] RedHat Secure Coding, `https://developers.redhat.com/topics/secure-coding/`

[W-6] Apple, "Secure Coding Guide," https://developer.apple.com/library/mac/documentation/Security/Conceptual/SecureCodingGuide/Introduction.html

[W-7] Mozilla, "Secure Development Guidelines," https://developer.mozilla.org/en-US/docs/Mozilla/Security/Secure_Development_Guidelines

[W-8] "Spectre and Meltdown," https://meltdownattack.com/

[W-9] "ZombieLoad," https://zombieloadattack.com/

[W-10] "Foreshadow," https://foreshadowattack.eu/

[W-11] "MDS: Microarchitectural Data Sampling," https://mdsattacks.com/

[W-12] Intel, "Host Firmware Speculative Execution Side Channel Mitigation," https://software.intel.com/security-software-guidance/insights/host-firmware-speculative-execution-side-channel-mitigation

[W-13] Intel, "Deep Dive: Intel Analysis of Microarchitectural Data Sampling," https://software.intel.com/security-software-guidance/insights/deep-dive-intel-analysis-microarchitectural-data-sampling

[W-14] Intel, "Deep Dive: Analyzing Potential Bounds Check Bypass Vulnerabilities," https://software.intel.com/security-software-guidance/insights/deep-dive-analyzing-potential-bounds-check-bypass-vulnerabilities

[W-15] Intel, "Deep Dive: Retpoline: A Branch Target Injection Mitigation," https://software.intel.com/security-software-guidance/insights/deep-dive-retpoline-branch-target-injection-mitigation

[W-16] Intel, "Security Best Practices for Side Channel Resistance," https://software.intel.com/security-software-guidance/insights/security-best-practices-side-channel-resistance

[W-17] Intel, "Guidelines for Mitigating Timing Side Channels Against Cryptographic Implementations," https://software.intel.com/security-software-guidance/insights/guidelines-mitigating-timing-side-channels-against-cryptographic-implementations

[W-18] AMD, "AMD Product Security," www.amd.com/en/corporate/product-security

[W-19] "AMD PSP: fTPM Remote Code Execution via crafted EK certificate," 2018, https://seclists.org/fulldisclosure/2018/Jan/12

[W-20] ARM, "ARM Security Updates," https://developer.arm.com/support/arm-security-updates

[W-21] ARM, "Cache Speculation Side-channels Whitepaper," https://developer.arm.com/support/arm-security-updates/speculative-processor-vulnerability/download-the-whitepaper

[W-22] Paul Turner, "Retpoline: a software construct for preventing branch-target-injection," available at https://support.google.com/faqs/answer/7625886

[W-23] Jonathan Corbet, "KAISER: hiding the kernel from user space," https://lwn.net/Articles/738975/

[W-24] Microsoft, "Protect your Windows devices against speculative execution side-channel attacks," https://support.microsoft.com/en-us/help/4073757/protect-windows-devices-from-speculative-execution-side-channel-attack

[W-25] Microsoft, "Windows Server guidance to protect against speculative execution side-channel vulnerabilities," https://support.microsoft.com/en-us/help/4072698/windows-server-speculative-execution-side-channel-vulnerabilities-prot

[W-26] Andrew Pardoe, "Spectre Mitigations in MSVC," https://devblogs.microsoft.com/cppblog/spectre-mitigations-in-msvc/

[W-27] Mehmet Iyigun, "Mitigating Spectre variant 2 with Retpoline on Windows," https://techcommunity.microsoft.com/t5/windows-kernel-internals/mitigating-spectre-variant-2-with-retpoline-on-windows/ba-p/295618#

[W-28] Terry Myerson, "Understanding the performance impact of Spectre and Meltdown mitigations on Windows Systems," www.microsoft.com/security/blog/2018/01/09/understanding-the-performance-impact-of-spectre-and-meltdown-mitigations-on-windows-systems/

[W-29] Dan Farmer, "IPMI: freight train to hell," at http://fish2.com/ipmi/

[W-30] OpenSSL heartbleed, https://heartbleed.com/

[W-31] LoRaDawn – Multiple LoRaWAN Security Vulnerabilities, https://blade.tencent.com/en/advisories/loradawn/

[W-32] UPnP CallStranger, http://callstranger.com/, https://kb.cert.org/vuls/id/339275

[W-33] ThinkPwn, http://blog.cr4.sh/2016/06/exploring-and-exploiting-lenovo.html

[W-34] 3 bulbs and 3 switches, www.geeksforgeeks.org/puzzle-7-3-bulbs-and-3-switches/

[W-35] USB FaceDancer, https://int3.cc/products/facedancer21

[W-36] PCI Leech, www.kitploit.com/2016/10/pcileech-direct-memory-access-dma.html

[W-37] Microblaze, https://github.com/Cr4sh/s6_pcie_microblaze

[W-38] Openssl POODLE, www.openssl.org/~bodo/ssl-poodle.pdf

[W-39] GRUB2 boothole, `https://eclypsium.com/wp-content/uploads/2020/07/Theres-a-Hole-in-the-Boot.pdf`

[W-40] ChipWhisperer, `https://wiki.newae.com/CW1173_ChipWhisperer-Lite`, `https://github.com/newaetech/chipwhisperer`

[W-41] SySS iCEstick Glitcher, `https://github.com/SySS-Research/icestick-glitcher`

CHAPTER 15

Compiler Defensive Technology

Today, most firmware implementations are written in the C language. At the same time, the C compiler provides rich compiler options to harden the software. Some of the compiler options can also be applied to the firmware. This chapter only focuses on the C language and C compiler. If the firmware is written in another language, such as Rust or Forth, we will discuss those details in Chapter 20.

There are two major types of compiler defensive methods – to eliminate the vulnerability and to thwart the exploit. To support eliminating the vulnerability, the compiler may provide a static analysis or a dynamic analysis capability, such as a static analyzer, address sanitizer, uninitialized data check, and arithmetic check. As such, the developer or test engineer may find issues at build time or debug the image at runtime. Then they can fix the issue before the production firmware is released. The compiler options are NOT used in the final production image for various reasons, such as not applicable, too much performance impact, or too much runtime memory consumed.

In contrast, to support thwarting the exploit, the compiler may inject some code into the final production image, such as stack checking, code protection (non-executable [NX] data), address space layout randomization, or control flow guard. Table 15-1 summarizes these compiler defensive technologies in the Microsoft Visual C++ (MSVC), GNU CC (GCC), and Clang compilers.

© Jiewen Yao and Vincent Zimmer 2020
J. Yao and V. Zimmer, *Building Secure Firmware*, https://doi.org/10.1007/978-1-4842-6106-4_15

Table 15-1. *Compiler Defensive Technology Summary*

Detection Method		MSVC	Clang/GCC
To break the exploit			
Stack check	Stack overflow	/GS	-fstack-protector
Code protection	Code injection	/NXCompat	LDLFAGS=-z noexecstack LDLFAGS=-z relro -z now
Address space layout randomization	Buffer overflow	/DynamicBase	-fPIE -fPIC LDLFAGS=-pie
Control flow (Software)	Control flow attack	/guard:cf	-fsanitize=cfi
Control flow (Hardware)	Control flow attack	/CETCompat	-fcf-protection=full (LDLFAGS=-z force-ibt -z shstk) -fcf-protection=branch -fsanitize=shadow-call-stack -mbranch-protection=pac-ret -mbranch-protection=bti
Side channel	Speculative execution attack	/Qspectre /Qspectre-load /Qspectre-load-cf	-mspeculative-load-hardening
To eliminate the vulnerability			
Static analysis	Coding error	/analyze (?)	Clang static analyzer
Dynamic analysis (address sanitizer)	Stack/heap overflow	/RTCs	-fsanitize=address
Dynamic analysis (uninitialized data)	Random data	/RTCu	-fsanitize=memory
Dynamic analysis (arithmetic check)	Information loss, integer overflow	/RTCc	-fsanitize=undefined -fsanitize=signed-integer-overflow -fsanitize=unsigned-integer-overflow

Break the Exploit

First, let's see how to leverage the compiler to generate code to resist the exploit at runtime.

Stack Check

The stack overflow attack is probably the first software attack. The famous Morris worm took advantage of this vulnerability. Modern compilers provide an option to insert a canary (GCC) or cookie (MSVC) value before the return function address on the stack. We use the term cookie in the following description. This cookie is checked before the return instruction. Therefore, if any stack overflow happens in the function and the return function address is modified, this attack can be detected because, in order to overwrite the return function address, the cookie value will be updated. See Figure 15-1.

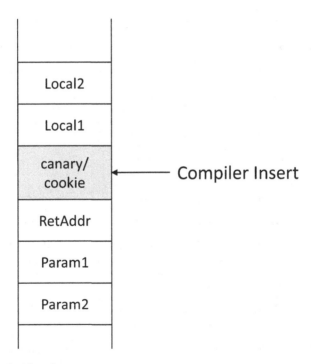

Figure 15-1. *Stack Check*

If the firmware uses this compiler option directly, a build will fail in the link phase. The reason is that the firmware usually does not link with the compiler's standard library, which provides the special function used by the compiler. In order to use this feature, we need to understand the code injected by the compiler in the target function and provide the corresponding canary.

Let's take MSVC 2019 as an example. If we compile the C code in Listing 15-1 with / GS, we will get the binary code in Listing 15-2.

Listing 15-1.

```
==========================
VOID
TestA (
  IN CHAR16    *Test
  )
{
  CHAR16   Buffer[10];

  StrCpy (Buffer, Test);
}
==========================
```

Listing 15-2.

```
==========================
TestA:
  0000000000000000: 48 89 4C 24 08     mov       qword ptr [rsp+8],rcx
  0000000000000005: 48 83 EC 48        sub       rsp,48h
  0000000000000009: 48 8B 05 00 00 00  mov       rax,qword ptr [__
                                                 security_cookie]
                    00
  0000000000000010: 48 33 C4           xor       rax,rsp
  0000000000000013: 48 89 44 24 38     mov       qword ptr [rsp+38h],rax
  0000000000000018: 48 8B 54 24 50     mov       rdx,qword ptr [rsp+50h]
  000000000000001D: 48 8D 4C 24 20     lea       rcx,[rsp+20h]
  0000000000000022: E8 00 00 00 00     call      StrCpy
  0000000000000027: 48 8B 4C 24 38     mov       rcx,qword ptr [rsp+38h]
```

```
000000000000002C: 48 33 CC            xor        rcx,rsp
000000000000002F: E8 00 00 00 00      call       __security_check_cookie
0000000000000034: 48 83 C4 48         add        rsp,48h
0000000000000038: C3                  ret
===========================
```

The new injected code requires two symbols – __security_cookie and __security_ check_cookie(). The first one is a global variable, and it will be XORed with the current stack pointer (RSP) and pushed on the stack. The second one is a checking function that is called before returning from the function to see if the cookie is modified. Listing 15-3 shows a sample implementation. __security_cookie is initialized as a random value in the module entry point. The __security_check_cookie() function checks the input value to see if it matches the global __security_cookie. If they are the same, that means the cookie on the stack is unmodified. The function can return normally. If they are different, then a stack overflow has occurred, and the function triggers a dead loop.

Listing 15-3.

```
===========================
UINTN __security_cookie = 0;

void __security_init_cookie(void)
{
  UINT64  Cookie;
  GetRandomNumber64(&Cookie);
  __security_cookie = (UINTN)Cookie;
}

RETURN_STATUS
EFIAPI
StackCheckLibConstructor(
  VOID
  )
{
  __security_init_cookie();
  return RETURN_SUCCESS;
}
```

```
__declspec(noreturn) void __cdecl __report_rangecheckfailure()
{
  DEBUG((EFI_D_ERROR, "\n!!! range check check failed in cookie
checker!!!\n"));
  ASSERT(FALSE);

  CpuDeadLoop();
}

void __fastcall __security_check_cookie(UINTN cookie)
{
  if (cookie == __security_cookie) {
    return;
  }

  __report_gsfailure(cookie);
  return ;
}
```

===========================

GCC "-fstack-protector" and "-fstack-protector-strong" use a similar mechanism but with different symbols. __stack_chk_guard is the global variable where the canary value is stored. Different from MSVC, GCC generates the code which checks the canary value and invokes the __stack_chk_fail() function if the check fails. The firmware needs to implement the _stack_chk_guard global variable and the __stack_chk_fail() function to report an error. Taking Listing 15-1 as an example, GCC will generate code in Listing 15-4.

Listing 15-4.

```
===========================
0000000000401586 <TestA>:
  401586:  55                     push  %rbp
  401587:  48 89 e5               mov   %rsp,%rbp
  40158a:  48 83 ec 50            sub   $0x50,%rsp
  40158e:  48 89 4d d8            mov   %rcx,-0x28(%rbp)
  401592:  48 8b 05 97 2e 00 00   mov   0x2e97(%rip),%rax
                                # 404430 <__fu0__stack_chk_guard>
  401599:  48 8b 08               mov   (%rax),%rcx
```

```
40159c:   48 89 4d f8            mov     %rcx,-0x8(%rbp)
4015a0:   31 c9                  xor     %ecx,%ecx
4015a2:   48 8b 55 d8            mov     -0x28(%rbp),%rdx
4015a6:   48 8d 45 e0            lea     -0x20(%rbp),%rax
4015aa:   48 89 c1              mov     %rax,%rcx
4015ad:   e8 9e ff ff ff         callq   401550 <StrCpy>
4015b2:   90                     nop
4015b3:   48 8b 05 76 2e 00 00   mov     0x2e76(%rip),%rax
                                   # 404430 <__fu0__stack_chk_guard>
4015ba:   48 8b 55 f8            mov     -0x8(%rbp),%rdx
4015be:   48 33 10              xor     (%rax),%rdx
4015c1:   74 06                  je      4015c9 <TestA+0x43>
4015c3:   e8 28 00 00 00         callq   4015f0 <__stack_chk_fail>
4015c8:   90                     nop
4015c9:   48 83 c4 50            add     $0x50,%rsp
4015cd:   5d                     pop     %rbp
4015ce:   c3                     retq
==========================
```

Code Protection

The code protection includes three aspects – data execution prevention (DEP), code integrity guard (CIG), and arbitrary code guard (ACG). To support DEP, the system kernel needs to mark code regions as write protected (WP) and mark data regions as non-executable (NX). Data regions include the image's data section, stack, and heap. CIG means any third-party code must be signed by an authorized owner. ACG means the code cannot be dynamically generated or modified. All those are efficient ways to prevent code injection. These methods can also be applied to the firmware. Figure 15-2 shows the memory layout with DEP/CIG/ACG in the UEFI firmware as an example.

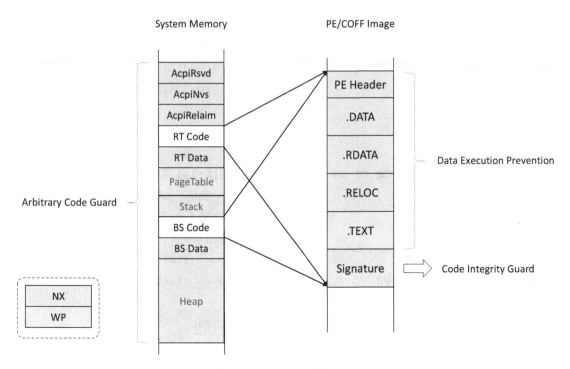

Figure 15-2. *Code Protection (DEP, CIG, ACG) in UEFI Firmware*

The code protection environment is set up by the kernel, such as UEFI firmware's DXE core. However, an executable image may require the code region write capability for some special purposes, for example, self-modified code, trampoline code, or arbitrary code. In order to support image compatibility, the compiler may have an option to inform the kernel of the capability. For example, MSVC provides the /NXCompact link option to indicate that an executable is compatible with the Windows data execution prevention (DEP) feature. GCC provides the "-z noexecstack" link option to indicate if this executable requires an executable stack or does not require it and "-z relro -z now" link option to indicate relocations are read-only (RELRO), which will set the relocation section to write protected.

The firmware kernel may use code protection, such as setting up non-executable data and write-protected code for data execution prevention (DEP), enabling the secure boot to enforce code integrity (CIG), and limiting arbitrary code generation (ACG). We will discuss the details of the code protection in the firmware kernel in Chapter 16.

Address Space Layout Randomization

Address space layout randomization (ASLR) is a technology to randomize the base address of an executable image or shared library, the program stack, and the program heap. ASLR makes it more difficult for an attacker to predict target addresses even if there is a vulnerability in the program. The randomization can be either shuffling or shifting. Figure 15-3 shows the memory layout with image shuffling and data shifting in the UEFI firmware as an example.

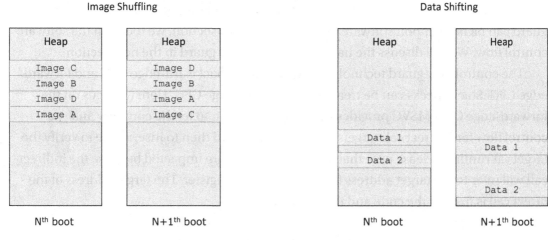

Figure 15-3. *ASLR in UEFI Firmware*

ASLR is enabled by the kernel or the software infrastructure. MSVC provides the / DynamicBase link option to indicate whether the application should be randomly rebased at load time. MSVC also enables virtual address allocation randomization, which affects the virtual memory location of heaps, stacks, and other operating system allocations. GCC provides "-pie" to request a dynamically linked Position-Independent Executable (PIE) which can be loaded at random positions.

The firmware kernel may apply ASLR to loaded images. We will discuss the details of ASLR in the firmware kernel in Chapter 16.

Control Flow Guard

A code module with execution privileges may contain small snippets of code sequences, known as gadgets, which include control transfer instructions, such as RET, CALL, and JMP. If the control transfer depends upon the data either in memory (stack, heap, or global data) or in a register, this gadget may be used for a return-oriented programming (ROP) attack or a call/jump-oriented programming (JOP/COP) attack. The control flow guard (CFG) or Control Flow Integrity (CFI) is the technology to defend against ROP- or JOP/COP-style control flow attacks. CFG is only useful when DEP is enabled. Otherwise, the attacker might just inject code to bypass the control flow guard. The control flow guard can be based upon software or hardware. In this section, we focus on the software control flow. We will discuss the hardware control flow guard in the next section.

The control flow guard technology is divided into backward-edge CFG and forward-edge CFG. Stack checks can be treated as backward-edge CFG. Here we focus on the forward-edge CFG. MSVC provides the /guard:cf option to let the compiler analyze control flow for indirect call targets at compile time and then to insert code to verify the targets at runtime. Please note that only indirect calls are impacted because the indirect call will refer to the target address from memory or a register. The target address of the direct call is fixed in the code and is read-only.

Let's take MSVC 2015 as an example. If we compile the C code in Listing 15-5 with /guard:cf, we will get the binary code in Listing 15-6.

Listing 15-5.

```
===========================
VOID
EFIAPI
CfgTest (
  VOID
  )
{
  EXTERNAL_FUNC Func;

  Func = (EXTERNAL_FUNC)((UINTN)ExternFunc);
  Func ();
}
===========================
```

Listing 15-6.

```
============================
CfgTest:
  0000000000000000: 48 83 EC 38          sub       rsp,38h
  0000000000000004: 48 8D 05 00 00 00    lea       rax,[ExternFunc]
                    00
  000000000000000B: 48 89 44 24 28       mov       qword ptr [rsp+28h],rax
  0000000000000010: 48 8B 44 24 28       mov       rax,qword ptr [rsp+28h]
  0000000000000015: 48 89 44 24 20       mov       qword ptr [rsp+20h],rax
  000000000000001A: 48 8B 4C 24 20       mov       rcx,qword ptr [rsp+20h]
  000000000000001F: FF 15 00 00 00 00    call      qword ptr [__guard_
                                                   check_icall_fptr]
  0000000000000025: FF 54 24 20          call      qword ptr [rsp+20h]
  0000000000000029: 48 83 C4 38          add       rsp,38h
  000000000000002D: C3                   ret
============================
```

The injected code calls the check function __guard_check_icall_fptr to check if the function address in [rsp+20h] is a valid function pointer. Similar to the stack check support described previously, we need to replace the compiler-provided checker function with our own checker function. See Listing 15-7.

Listing 15-7.

```
============================
extern void * __guard_check_icall_fptr;

void
__fastcall
_my_guard_check_icall (
    IN UINTN Target
    )
{
  ...
}
```

```
RETURN_STATUS
EFIAPI
CfgLibConstructor(
  VOID
  )
{
#ifdef WINNT
  DisableReadOnlyProtection (&__guard_check_icall_fptr, sizeof(__guard_
  check_icall_fptr));
#endif
  __guard_check_icall_fptr = (void *)_my_guard_check_icall;
#ifdef WINNT
  EnableReadOnlyProtection (&__guard_check_icall_fptr, sizeof(__guard_
  check_icall_fptr));
#endif

  return RETURN_SUCCESS;
}
============================
```

Then we need to check if the target function address is valid. Fortunately, the compiler generates that information in the Guard CF Function Table. See Listing 15-8 for the PE/COFF dump information.

Listing 15-8.

```
============================
  Section contains the following load config:

            00000094 size
                   0 time date stamp
                0.00 Version
                   0 GlobalFlags Clear
                   0 GlobalFlags Set
                   0 Critical Section Default Timeout
                   0 Decommit Free Block Threshold
                   0 Decommit Total Free Threshold
```

```
0000000000000000 Lock Prefix Table
               0 Maximum Allocation Size
               0 Virtual Memory Threshold
               0 Process Heap Flags
               0 Process Affinity Mask
               0 CSD Version
            0000 Dependent Load Flag
0000000000000000 Edit List
0000000000017090 Security Cookie
```
0000000000018000 Guard CF address of check-function pointer
0000000000018008 Guard CF address of dispatch-function pointer
0000000000015000 Guard CF function table
       13 Guard CF function count
```
        00013500 Guard Flags
                    CF Instrumented
                    FID table present
                    Protect delayload IAT
                    Delayload IAT in its own section
                    Long jump target table present
```

Guard CF Function Table

```
    Address
    --------
    0000000000011000  ExternFunc
    0000000000011010  _DriverUnloadHandler
    0000000000011050  _ModuleEntryPoint
    0000000000011140  DebugPrint
    00000000000113B0  DebugAssert
    0000000000011540  DebugAssertEnabled
    0000000000011550  DebugPrintEnabled
    0000000000011560  DebugPrintLevelEnabled
    00000000000117F0  CpuDeadLoop
    0000000000011F80  InitializeListHead
    0000000000011FC0  InsertTailList
    0000000000012040  RemoveEntryList
```

```
00000000000123D0  CfgLibDestructor
0000000000012430  GetCfgNode
00000000000124B0  _my_guard_check_icall
0000000000012790  UefiCfgLibConstructor
00000000000143C0  DisableReadOnlyProtection
0000000000014460  EnableReadOnlyProtection
0000000000014500  _guard_check_icall_nop
```

=============================

Therefore, what we can do is to get the Guard CF Function Table in the entry point and register the information in some sort of global CF function table (perhaps using an EFI protocol). Then the _my_guard_check_icall() function can get the function table and check if the target address is in the table. See Figure 15-4.

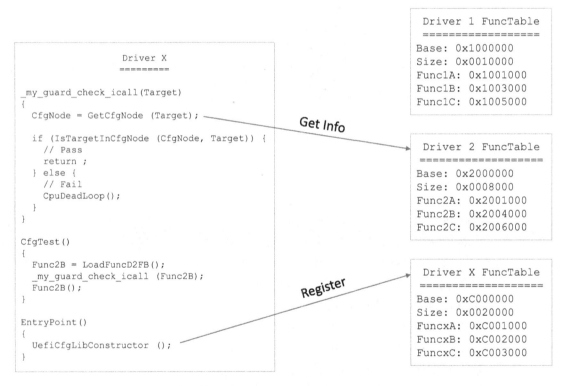

Figure 15-4. *Software CFG in UEFI Firmware*

Listing 15-9 shows the _my_guard_check_icall() function implementation.

Listing 15-9.

```
============================
void
__fastcall
_my_guard_check_icall (
    IN UINTN Target
    )
{
  UINTN        Index;
  UINTN        *Ptr;
  CFG_NODE     *CfgNode;
  CfgNode = GetCfgNode (Target);
  if (CfgNode != NULL) {
    for (Index = 0; Index < CfgNode->GuardCFFunctionCount; Index++) {
      if ((CfgNode->GuardCFFunctionTable[Index] + CfgNode->ImageBase) ==
      Target) {
        // found, pass
        return;
      }
    }
  }

  DEBUG ((DEBUG_ERROR, "\n!!! guard check fail !!!\n"));
  ASSERT (FALSE);

  CpuDeadLoop();
}
============================
```

However, with this solution, the final image links a big control flow check function provided by the compiler even if this function is not used by the firmware. This causes a big size impact for the final image.

Recently, MSVC added XFG as an extension to CFG, providing a finer granularity of control flow guard support including type signature checks. Basically, each function is assigned a type signature–based tag. For C functions, the tag is a hash of (type(return value), type(arg1), type(arg2), …). Besides checking the function address, the tag of the function is also checked in the runtime function call.

The Clang compiler provides "-fsanitize=cfi" for Control Flow Integrity (CFI) to abort the program upon detecting certain forms of undefined behavior that can potentially allow attackers to subvert the program's control flow. Taking Listing 15-5 as an example, Clang will generate code in Listing 15-10.

Listing 15-10.

```
============================
CfgTest:
00000000000007D0: 48 83 EC 28          sub         rsp,28h
00000000000007D4: 48 8D 0D 75 05 00    lea         rcx,[__typeid_?6AXXZ_
                                                    global_addr]
                  00
00000000000007DB: 48 89 4C 24 20       mov         qword ptr [rsp+20h],rcx
00000000000007E0: 48 8B 44 24 20       mov         rax,qword ptr [rsp+20h]
00000000000007E5: 48 89 C2             mov         rdx,rax
00000000000007E8: 48 29 CA             sub         rdx,rcx
00000000000007EB: 48 89 D1             mov         rcx,rdx
00000000000007EE: 48 C1 E9 03          shr         rcx,3
00000000000007F2: 48 C1 E2 3D          shl         rdx,3Dh
00000000000007F6: 48 09 D1             or          rcx,rdx
00000000000007F9: 48 83 F9 01          cmp         rcx,1
00000000000007FD: 76 07                jbe         0000000000000806
00000000000007FF: E8 6C 05 00 00       call        MyTrap
0000000000000804: 0F 0B                ud2
0000000000000806: FF D0                call        rax
0000000000000808: 48 83 C4 28          add         rsp,28h
000000000000080C: C3                   ret
...
__typeid_?6AXXZ_global_addr:
0000000000000D50: E9 CB F4 FF FF       jmp         ExternFunc
0000000000000D55: CC                   int         3
0000000000000D56: CC                   int         3
0000000000000D57: CC                   int         3
0000000000000D58: E9 C5 F4 FF FF       jmp         ExternFunc2
0000000000000D5D: CC                   int         3
0000000000000D5E: CC                   int         3
```

```
0000000000000D5F: CC                    int         3
0000000000000D60: 0F 0B                 ud2
===========================
```

The Clang compiler generates the __typeid_?6AXXZ_global_addr symbol and
puts the possible indirect call address there. If the address of an indirect call is not in
__typeid_?6AXXZ_global_addr, then this function will call a trap function specified by
"-ftrap-function flag," such as "-ftrap-function=MyTrap." The MyTrap() function can
dump some information. However, if the firmware has an implementation-specific
dynamic link, such as those found in UEFI Boot Services or in a UEFI protocol function
pointer, this solution does not work because the compiler does not have knowledge of
the address of the dynamic function pointer. For example, for Listing 15-11, the Clang
CFI will generate code in Listing 15-12. It always calls the trap function.

Listing 15-11.

```
===========================
EFI_STATUS
EFIAPI
CfgTestInitialize(
  IN EFI_HANDLE        ImageHandle,
  IN EFI_SYSTEM_TABLE  *SystemTable
  )
{
  EFI_STATUS  Status;
  EFI_HANDLE  Handle;

  Handle = NULL;
  Status = gBS->InstallProtocolInterface (
              &Handle,
              &gCfgTestProtocolGuid,
              EFI_NATIVE_INTERFACE,
              &mCfgTestProtocol
              );

  return EFI_SUCCESS;
}

===========================
```

Listing 15-12.

```
============================
CfgTestInitialize:
  0000000000007D0:  48 83 EC 48           sub      rsp,48h
  0000000000007D4:  45 31 C0              xor      r8d,r8d
  0000000000007D7:  48 89 54 24 40        mov      qword ptr [rsp+40h],rdx
  0000000000007DC:  48 89 4C 24 38        mov      qword ptr [rsp+38h],rcx
  0000000000007E1:  48 C7 44 24 28 00     mov      qword ptr [rsp+28h],0
                    00 00 00
  0000000000007EA:  48 8B 05 7F 0B 00     mov      rax,qword ptr [1370h]
                    00
  0000000000007F1:  48 8B 80 80 00 00     mov      rax,qword ptr [rax+80h]
                    00
  0000000000007F8:  41 F6 C0 01           test     r8b,1
  0000000000007FC:  75 07                 jne      0000000000000805
  0000000000007FE:  E8 FD 04 00 00        call     MyTrap
  000000000000803:  0F 0B                 ud2
  000000000000805:  4C 8D 0D 44 0B 00     lea      r9,[1350h]
                    00
  00000000000080C:  48 8D 4C 24 28        lea      rcx,[rsp+28h]
  000000000000811:  48 8D 15 28 0B 00     lea      rdx,[1340h]
                    00
  000000000000818:  45 31 C0              xor      r8d,r8d
  00000000000081B:  FF D0                 call     rax
  00000000000081D:  48 89 44 24 30        mov      qword ptr [rsp+30h],rax
  000000000000822:  48 83 C4 48           add      rsp,48h
  000000000000826:  C3                    ret
============================
```

Software control flow is a good feature. However, it is hard for it to handle dynamic function pointers. This limitation can be resolved by using hardware support for control flow guard.

Hardware-Based Control Flow Guard

Hardware-based control flow guard can simplify the software design for control flow guard. Both X86 and ARM introduced hardware-based backward-edge CFG and forward-edge CFG. See Table 15-2.

Table 15-2. *Hardware Control Flow Guard Summary*

Method	X86	ARM
Backward-edge	Shadow Stack	Pointer Authentication Code (PAC)
Forward-edge	Indirect Branch Tracking (ENDBR instruction)	Branch Target Identification (BTI instruction)

Intel Control Flow Enforcement Technology

Intel X86 architecture introduced the Control Flow Enforcement Technology (CET). It includes two parts: shadow stack (SS) and Indirect Branch Tracking (IBT).

Shadow stack (SS) is the backward-edge control flow guard technology.

When a program runs, it requires a data stack for C function calls. The return address of the calling function is pushed on the stack. Stack buffer overflow causes the return address to be overwritten. In order to catch a stack overflow, the system may set up a shadow stack for control transfer operations. If the shadow stack is enabled, the CALL instruction pushes the caller's return address to both the data stack and the shadow stack, and the RET instruction pops the caller return address from both the data stack and the shadow stack and then compares the two values. If they are the same, that means the return address is unmodified, and the function returns. If they are different, that means the return address is modified. The CPU triggers a control protection exception (#CP). See Figures 15-5 and 15-6 for the normal case and attack case.

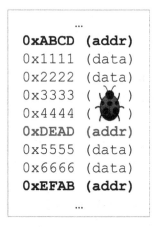

Data Stack

Shadow Stack

Figure 15-5. *CET-SS – Normal Case*

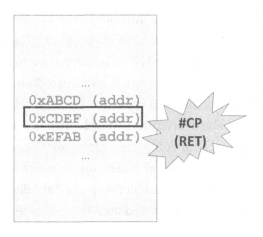

Data Stack

Shadow Stack

Figure 15-6. *CET-SS – Under Attack*

The shadow stack itself is set up by the kernel. The shadow stack is marked as read-only in the page table. As such, no software program can modify the contents of the shadow stack. Only a CPU internal instruction can update this memory via a push content to and pop content from the shadow stack.

MSVC provides the /CETCompat link option to indicate whether the executable image is compatible with Control Flow Enforcement Technology (CET) for shadow stack.

The firmware kernel may apply CET ShadowStack to support stack checking. We will discuss the details of the CET ShadowStack in the firmware kernel in Chapter 16.

Indirect Branch Tracking (IBT) is the forward-edge control flow guard technology.

Intel X86 architecture adds a new instruction – EndBranch (ENDBR32/ENDBR64) – to mark a valid jump target address of indirect calls and jumps in the program. Internally, the CPU implements a state machine to track the indirect calls or jump instructions. If these instructions are seen, the state machine is moved from IDLE state to WAIT_FOR_ENDBRANCH state. If the next instruction is EndBranch, the state machine is moved back to IDLE state. If the next instruction is NOT EndBranch, the CPU triggers a control protection exception (#CP). See Figures 15-7 and 15-8 for the normal case and attack case.

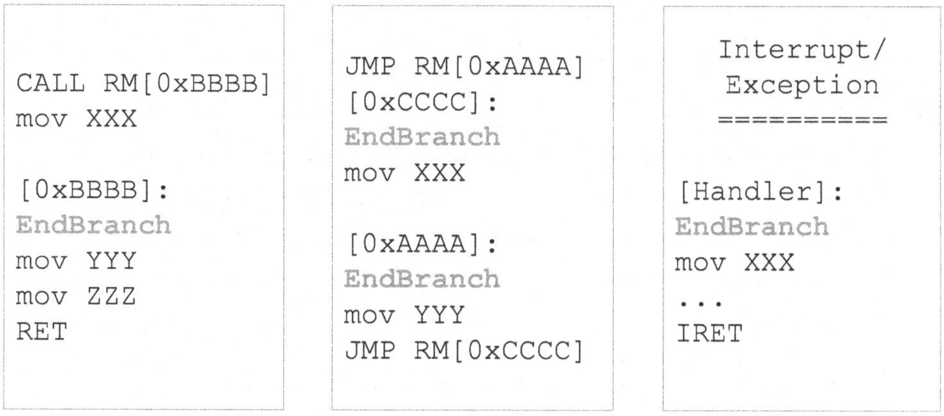

```
CALL RM[0xBBBB]        JMP RM[0xAAAA]          Interrupt/
mov XXX                [0xCCCC]:               Exception
                       EndBranch               ==========
                       mov XXX
[0xBBBB]:
EndBranch              [0xAAAA]:               [Handler]:
mov YYY                EndBranch               EndBranch
mov ZZZ                mov YYY                 mov XXX
RET                    JMP RM[0xCCCC]          ...
                                               IRET
```

Figure 15-7. *CET IBT – Normal Case*

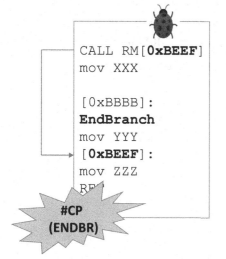

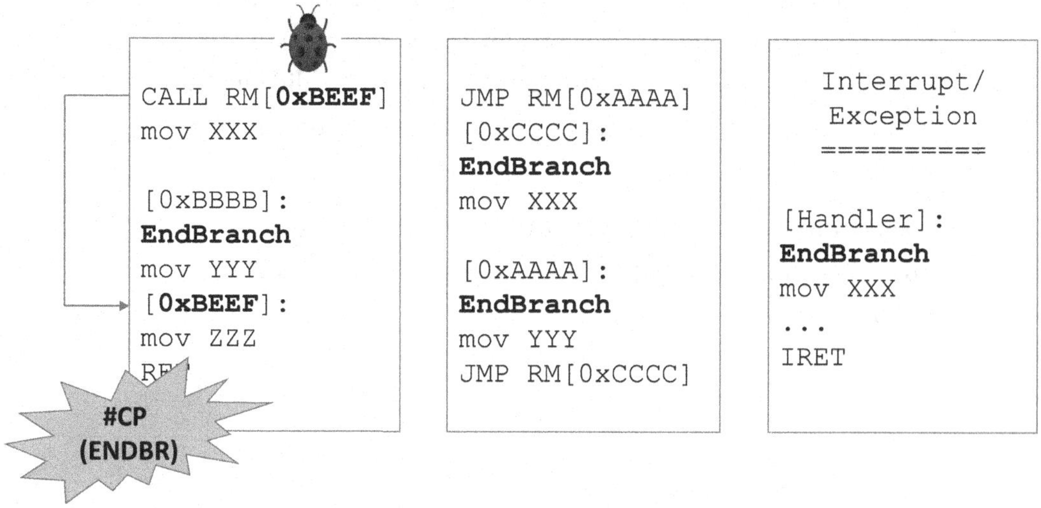

```
CALL RM[0xBEEF]        JMP RM[0xAAAA]          Interrupt/
mov XXX                [0xCCCC]:               Exception
                       EndBranch               ==========
                       mov XXX
[0xBBBB]:
EndBranch              [0xAAAA]:               [Handler]:
mov YYY                EndBranch               EndBranch
[0xBEEF]:              mov YYY                 mov XXX
mov ZZZ                JMP RM[0xCCCC]          ...
RET                                            IRET
```

#CP (ENDBR)

Figure 15-8. *CET IBT – Under Attack*

The CET IBT support relies on the compiler because only the compiler knows where to inject the EndBranch instruction at the beginning of a C function. GCC and Clang use the "-fcf-protection=branch" option to support the CET IBT feature.

The firmware kernel may use the CET IBT support also to support forward control flow guard. Most of the work is done by the compiler. The firmware must add EndBranch instructions explicitly in some assembly code, such as exception handlers. We will discuss the details of the CET IBT in the firmware kernel in Chapter 16.

ARM Pointer Authentication and Memory Access Control

ARMv8.3 introduces Pointer Authentication Code (PAC) as the backward-edge control flow guard technology.

ARM added new capabilities to enable the pointer authentication feature:

1) A set of instructions (PACxxx) to compute and insert a Pointer Authentication Code (PAC) for an instruction address or a data address using a specific key. The address is in a general-purpose register. The PAC value is in the upper bits of a register. These bits are extension bits that do not hold valid address bits. See Figure 15-9.

2) A set of instructions (AUTxxx) to extract the PAC from the register and authenticate the PAC value using a specific key. If the check passes, the instruction replaces PAC with the extension bits. If the check fails, the instruction replaces the PAC with the extension bits except that 2 bits of the extension are set to a fixed unique number. This action marks the address to be an invalid virtual address. Any reference to this address will cause a translation fault.

3) A set of instructions (XPACxxx) to strip the PAC value from an address and replace it with the extension bits without any verification.

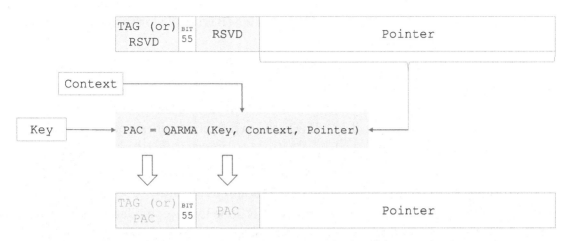

Figure 15-9. *ARM PAC*

The PAC support needs the compiler to inject instructions for PAC insertion and verification. GCC and Clang have the "-mbranch-protection=pac-ret" build option. Figure 15-10 shows a C function compiled with ARM PAC. In the function prologue, the compiler inserts PACIASP to add PAC for the Link Register (LR) with the stack pointer (SP) register as the context and then saves the value on the stack. In the epilogue, the compiler inserts AUTIASP to verify the LR with the SP register as the context, to ensure that the return address in LR loaded from the stack is unmodified. ARM PAC is different from Intel CET Shadow Stack because of the calling convention difference. In X86 calling convention, the return address is pushed on the stack, so that we need protect the stack. In ARM calling conversion, the return address is saved in the link register, so that we need protect the link register.

```
PACIASP // PACIA LR, SP
SUB sp, sp, #0x40
STP fp, lr, [sp, #0x30]
ADD fp, sp, #0x30

... // function body

LDP fp, lr, [sp, #0x30]
ADD sp, sp, #0x40
AUTIASP // AUTIA LR, SP
RET
```

Figure 15-10. *Function with ARM PAC*

ARMv8.5 introduced Branch Target Identification (BTI) as the forward-edge control flow guard technology.

ARM BTI is part of memory access control. It is similar to CET IBT. BTI instruction marks a valid jump target address of indirect calls and jumps in the program. If the program in a protected page tries to perform an indirect branch to an instruction other than the one that is marked BTI, the CPU will raise a branch target exception.

The ARM BTI support relies on the compiler to inject BTI instructions. GCC and Clang use "-mbranch-protection=bti" to support the ARM BTI feature.

The firmware kernel may apply both ARM PAC and BTI in order to support backward and forward control flow guard. Most of the work is done by the compiler. The firmware must add BTI instruction explicitly in some assembly code, such as exception handlers.

Speculative Load Hardening

Side channel attacks have generated a lot of attention these days. One type is the speculative execution side channel attack, known as Spectre variant 1. The compiler may help by inserting architecture-specific instructions as a speculative barrier.

X86 Load Fence (LFENCE)

The Intel X86 Load Fence (LFENCE) instruction can be a speculative barrier. MSVC compilers provide the /Qspectre option which causes the compiler to automatically insert the LFENCE instruction. Listing 15-13 shows the vulnerable code. MSVC will insert LFENCE to prevent speculation from going down the unsafe path, thus mitigating the issue. See Listing 15-14. The bold text shows the new instruction added with /Qspectre.

Listing 15-13.

```
============================
#define ARRAY1_NUM   256
#define ARRAY2_NUM   256

UINT8 Array1[ARRAY1_NUM];
UINT8 Array2[ARRAY2_NUM];

UINT8
TestA (
```

```
  IN UINTN   UntrustedIndex
  )
{
  UINT8   Value;
  UINT8   Value2 = 0;

  if (UntrustedIndex < ARRAY1_NUM) {
    Value = Array1[UntrustedIndex];
    Value2 = Array2[Value * 64];
  }
  return Value2;
}
===========================
```

Listing 15-14.

```
===========================
TestA:
  0000000000000000: 32 C0                 xor       al,al
  0000000000000002: 48 81 F9 00 01 00     cmp       rcx,100h
                    00
  0000000000000009: 73 1D                 jae       0000000000000028
  000000000000000B: 0F AE E8               lfence
  000000000000000E: 48 8D 15 00 00 00     lea       rdx,[__ImageBase]
                    00
  0000000000000015: 0F B6 84 11 00 00     movzx     eax,byte ptr
                                                    Array1[rcx+rdx]
                    00 00
  000000000000001D: 48 C1 E0 06           shl       rax,6
  0000000000000021: 8A 84 10 00 00 00     mov       al,byte ptr
                                                    Array2[rax+rdx]
                    00
  0000000000000028: C3                    ret
===========================
```

Please refer to "Intel Analysis of Speculative Execution Side Channels" for detailed information.

ARM Consumption of Speculative Data Barrier (CSDB)

The ARM architecture introduced the Consumption of Speculative Data Barrier (CSDB) instruction. This instruction can be inserted by the compiler as a speculative barrier.

Please refer to ARM's "Cache Speculation Side channels" for detailed information.

Software Speculative Hardening

The Clang compiler provides the "-mspeculative-load-hardening" flag with the same purpose. Instead of inserting a speculation barrier instruction, Clang uses a software mechanism to prevent speculative execution attacks. The bold text in Listing 15-15 is the new instruction added with this build option.

Listing 15-15.

```
============================
TestA:
  0000000000000810: 48 83 EC 10          sub       rsp,10h
  0000000000000814: 48 C7 C0 FF FF FF     mov       rax,0FFFFFFFFFFFFFFFFh
                    FF
  000000000000081B: 48 89 E2              mov       rdx,rsp
  000000000000081E: 48 C1 FA 3F           sar       rdx,3Fh
  0000000000000822: 48 89 4C 24 08        mov       qword ptr [rsp+8],rcx
  0000000000000827: C6 44 24 06 00        mov       byte ptr [rsp+6],0
  000000000000082C: 48 81 7C 24 08 00     cmp       qword ptr [rsp+8],100h
                    01 00 00
  0000000000000835: 73 02                 jae       0000000000000839
```
0000000000000837: EB 06   jmp   000000000000083F
0000000000000839: 48 0F 42 D0   cmovb   rdx,rax
000000000000083D: EB 37   jmp   0000000000000876
000000000000083F: 48 0F 43 D0   cmovae   rdx,rax
```
  0000000000000843: 48 8B 44 24 08        mov       rax,qword ptr [rsp+8]
  0000000000000848: 48 8D 0D F1 0B 00     lea       rcx,[1440h]
                    00
  000000000000084F: 8A 04 01              mov       al,byte ptr [rcx+rax]
  0000000000000852: 88 D1                 mov       cl,dl
```

```
0000000000000854: 08 C1                 or      cl,al
0000000000000856: 88 4C 24 07           mov     byte ptr [rsp+7],cl
000000000000085A: 0F B6 44 24 07        movzx   eax,byte ptr [rsp+7]
000000000000085F: C1 E0 06              shl     eax,6
0000000000000862: 48 98                 cdqe
0000000000000864: 48 8D 0D D5 0C 00     lea     rcx,[1540h]
                  00
000000000000086B: 8A 04 01              mov     al,byte ptr [rcx+rax]
000000000000086E: 88 D1                 mov     cl,dl
0000000000000870: 08 C1                 or      cl,al
0000000000000872: 88 4C 24 06           mov     byte ptr [rsp+6],cl
0000000000000876: 8A 44 24 06           mov     al,byte ptr [rsp+6]
000000000000087A: 48 C1 E2 2F           shl     rdx,2Fh
000000000000087E: 48 09 D4              or      rsp,rdx
0000000000000881: 48 83 C4 10           add     rsp,10h
0000000000000885: C3                    ret
============================
```

Please refer to "llvm document – Speculative Load Hardening" for detailed information.

Speculative execution attacks are for information leaks. We recommend that firmware engineers do a threat analysis first to see if such a threat exists and then perform the mitigation since not all firmware holds secrets.

Once the threat is identified, the firmware may choose to use those compiler options to prevent speculative attacks for the target modules. Either using hardware instructions or using software hardening is acceptable, as long as the speculative attack can be mitigated.

Care must be taken since the compiler might miss some mitigations in some cases or add too much code for the mitigation, impacting runtime performance. As such, a code review might still be needed for the impacted module. If the vulnerability is found, the developer can insert a speculative barrier function manually into the code to ensure the issue is mitigated.

Eliminate the Vulnerability

Besides generating code to resist an exploit at runtime, the compiler can help to eliminate the vulnerability at build time. The best way is to break the build. For example, "if (a = b)" is very suspicious and should lead to a broken build. There are some other ways, such as using a static analyzer or a sanitizer. Let's examine them in the next sections.

Static Analyzer

There are many commercial static analysis tools available, such as Klocwork's static code analysis tool, Coverity's static application security testing tool, Liverpool Data Research Associates' (LDRA) tool, and so on. Klocwork or Coverity can be used to scan the C code. The LDRA tool can be used to scan the assembly code. The open source LLVM/Clang project includes the Clang static analyzer (CSA) tool in the LLVM installation package. Each firmware project should make its own decision to choose the most appropriate static analysis tools.

Please be aware that running a static analysis tool is necessary for the firmware, but it is far from sufficient. It cannot be a replacement for secure coding practices and a security code review.

Address Sanitizer

The compiler may also support dynamic analysis. According to research results, about 70% of software security issues are related to memory safety. In system firmware, the percentage of memory safety security issues is about 50%. As such, compiler detection of out of bound accesses is a good mitigation.

MSVC supports /RTCs to detect overruns and underruns of local variables, such as arrays. Figure 15-11 shows the difference between /RTCs and /GS.

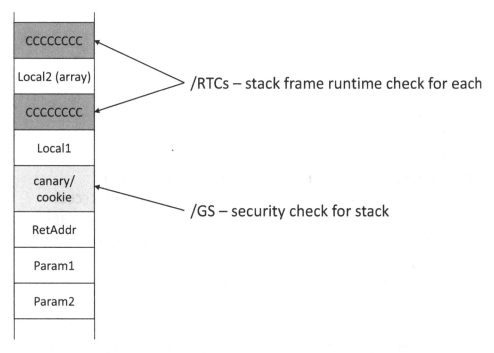

Figure 15-11. *Runtime Check for Stack*

Similar to /GS, the runtime check requires a special function provided by the compiler. In order to use this feature, we need to understand the code injected by the compiler in the target function and provide the corresponding symbols.

Let's take MSVC as an example. If we compile the C code in Listing 15-16 with /RTCs, we will get the binary code in Listing 15-17.

Listing 15-16.

```
===========================
VOID
TestA (
  UINTN Index
  )
{
  CHAR16    Buffer[10];

  Buffer[Index] = 1;
}
===========================
```

Listing 15-17.

```
============================
TestA:
  0000000000000000: 48 89 4C 24 08       mov      qword ptr [rsp+8],rcx
  0000000000000005: 57                    push     rdi
  0000000000000006: 48 83 EC 50           sub      rsp,50h
  000000000000000A: 48 8B FC              mov      rdi,rsp
  000000000000000D: B9 14 00 00 00        mov      ecx,14h
  0000000000000012: B8 CC CC CC CC        mov      eax,0CCCCCCCCh
  0000000000000017: F3 AB                 rep stos dword ptr [rdi]
  0000000000000019: 48 8B 4C 24 60        mov      rcx,qword ptr [rsp+60h]
  000000000000001E: B8 01 00 00 00        mov      eax,1
  0000000000000023: 48 8B 4C 24 60        mov      rcx,qword ptr [rsp+60h]
  0000000000000028: 66 89 44 4C 28        mov      word ptr
                                                   [rsp+rcx*2+28h],ax
  000000000000002D: 48 8B CC              mov      rcx,rsp
  0000000000000030: 48 8D 15 00 00 00     lea      rdx,[TestA$rtcFrameData]
                    00
  0000000000000037: E8 00 00 00 00        call     _RTC_CheckStackVars
  000000000000003C: 48 83 C4 50           add      rsp,50h
  0000000000000040: 5F                    pop      rdi
  0000000000000041: C3                    ret
============================
```

The new injected code requires one symbol – _RTC_CheckStackVars(). Listing 15-18 shows a sample implementation of the _RTC_CheckStackVars() function that checks the data before and after the local variable. If the data is not the cookie value 0xCCCCCCCC, that means the local variable was overwritten, and this function triggers a dead loop.

Listing 15-18.

```
============================
typedef struct _RTC_vardesc {
  int addr;
  int size;
```

```
  char *name;
} _RTC_vardesc;

typedef struct _RTC_framedesc {
  int varCount;
  _RTC_vardesc *variables;
} _RTC_framedesc;

#define RTC_STACK_CHECK_COOKIE  0xCCCCCCCC

static void _RTC_StackFailure (char *name)
{
  DEBUG ((EFI_D_ERROR, "\n!!! stack variable check failed in
  StackChecker!!!\n"));
  ASSERT (FALSE);

  CpuDeadLoop();
  return ;
}

void __fastcall _RTC_CheckStackVars (void *_Esp, _RTC_framedesc *_Fd)
{
  int   Index;
  UINT8 *Addr;

  for (Index = 0; Index < _Fd->varCount; Index++) {
    Addr = (UINT8 *)_Esp + _Fd->variables[Index].addr - sizeof(UINT32);
    if (*(int *)Addr != RTC_STACK_CHECK_COOKIE) {
      _RTC_StackFailure (_Fd->variables[Index].name);
    }

    Addr = (UINT8 *)_Esp + _Fd->variables[Index].addr + _Fd-
    >variables[Index].size;
    if (*(int *)Addr != RTC_STACK_CHECK_COOKIE) {
      _RTC_StackFailure (_Fd->variables[Index].name);
    }
  }
}
===========================
```

/RTCs can also help to initialize local variables to a non-zero value (0xCC), which can help to identify random corruption issues. Because this runtime check adds a cookie value around all local variables and initializes them with 0xCC, it introduces significant overhead compared to /GS. As such, this is only considered a debug feature and should be disabled in final production.

The Clang compiler provides the "-fsanitize=address" option for the address sanitizer (ASan), which can detect out of bound accesses to stack, heap, and global variables, use-after-free, use-after-return, use-after-scope, double-free, and invalid-free. Take Listing 15-16 as an example. Clang will generate code in Listing 15-19.

Listing 15-19.

```
=============================
TestA:
  0000000000000A70: 55                 push      rbp
  0000000000000A71: 53                 push      rbx
  0000000000000A72: 48 83 EC 28        sub       rsp,28h
  0000000000000A76: 48 8D 6C 24 20     lea       rbp,[rsp+20h]
  0000000000000A7B: 48 83 E4 E0        and       rsp,0FFFFFFFFFFFFFFE0h
  0000000000000A7F: 48 89 E3           mov       rbx,rsp
  0000000000000A82: 49 89 C8           mov       r8,rcx
  0000000000000A85: 4C 8B 0D EC 10 00  mov       r9,qword ptr
                                                 [__asan_shadow_
                                                 memory_dynamic_
                                                 address]
                    00
  0000000000000A8C: EB 00              jmp       0000000000000A8E
  0000000000000A8E: B8 60 00 00 00     mov       eax,60h
  0000000000000A93: 48 29 C4           sub       rsp,rax
  0000000000000A96: 49 89 E2           mov       r10,rsp
  0000000000000A99: 49 83 E2 E0        and       r10,0FFFFFFFFFFFFFFE0h
  0000000000000A9D: 4C 89 D4           mov       rsp,r10
  0000000000000AA0: 4C 89 53 18        mov       qword ptr [rbx+18h],r10
  0000000000000AA4: 4C 89 D1           mov       rcx,r10
  0000000000000AA7: 48 81 C1 20 00 00  add       rcx,20h
                    00
```

```
0000000000000AAE: 49 C7 02 B3 8A B5   mov      qword ptr
                                                [r10],41B58AB3h

                   41
0000000000000AB5: 48 8D 15 C4 06 00   lea      rdx,[1180h]
                   00
0000000000000ABC: 49 89 52 08         mov      qword ptr [r10+8],rdx
0000000000000AC0: 48 8D 15 A9 FF FF   lea      rdx,[0A70h]
                   FF
0000000000000AC7: 49 89 52 10         mov      qword ptr [r10+10h],rdx
0000000000000ACB: 4C 89 D2            mov      rdx,r10
0000000000000ACE: 48 C1 EA 03         shr      rdx,3
0000000000000AD2: 4C 01 CA            add      rdx,r9
0000000000000AD5: 48 B8 F1 F1 F1 F1   mov      rax,0F3F8F8F8F1F1F1F1h
                   F8 F8 F8 F3
0000000000000ADF: 48 89 02            mov      qword ptr [rdx],rax
0000000000000AE2: C7 42 08 F3 F3 F3   mov      dword ptr [rdx+8],
                                                0F3F3F3F3h

                   F3
0000000000000AE9: 4C 89 43 10         mov      qword ptr [rbx+10h],r8
0000000000000AED: 66 C7 42 04 00 00   mov      word ptr [rdx+4],0
0000000000000AF3: C6 42 06 04         mov      byte ptr [rdx+6],4
0000000000000AF7: 48 8B 43 10         mov      rax,qword ptr [rbx+10h]
0000000000000AFB: 48 C1 E0 01         shl      rax,1
0000000000000AFF: 48 01 C1            add      rcx,rax
0000000000000B02: 48 89 C8            mov      rax,rcx
0000000000000B05: 48 C1 E8 03         shr      rax,3
0000000000000B09: 4C 01 C8            add      rax,r9
0000000000000B0C: 44 8A 00            mov      r8b,byte ptr [rax]
0000000000000B0F: 41 80 F8 00         cmp      r8b,0
0000000000000B13: 74 23               je       0000000000000B38
0000000000000B15: 48 89 C8            mov      rax,rcx
0000000000000B18: 48 25 07 00 00 00   and      rax,7
0000000000000B1E: 48 05 01 00 00 00   add      rax,1
0000000000000B24: 44 38 C0            cmp      al,r8b
0000000000000B27: 7C 0F               jl       0000000000000B38
```

```
0000000000000B29: 48 83 EC 20          sub       rsp,20h
0000000000000B2D: E8 7E 00 00 00       call      __asan_report_store2
0000000000000B32: 48 83 C4 20          add       rsp,20h
0000000000000B36: 0F 0B               ud2
0000000000000B38: 66 C7 01 01 00       mov       word ptr [rcx],1
0000000000000B3D: 66 C7 42 04 F8 F8    mov       word ptr [rdx+4],0F8F8h
0000000000000B43: C6 42 06 F8          mov       byte ptr [rdx+6],0F8h
0000000000000B47: 49 C7 02 0E 36 E0    mov       qword ptr [r10],
                  45                              45E0360Eh

0000000000000B4E: 48 C7 02 00 00 00    mov       qword ptr [rdx],0
                  00
0000000000000B55: C7 42 08 00 00 00    mov       dword ptr [rdx+8],0
                  00
0000000000000B5C: 48 8D 65 08          lea       rsp,[rbp+8]
0000000000000B60: 5B                  pop       rbx
0000000000000B61: 5D                  pop       rbp
0000000000000B62: C3                  ret
============================
```

Only the instruction at 0000000000000B38 actually changes the 1 byte of the local variable. The rest of the code is to set up the buffer checking environment. The pseudo code is shown in Listing 15-20.

Listing 15-20.

```
============================
Address = &Buffer[Index];
ShadowAddress = (Address >> 3) + __asan_shadow_memory_dynamic_address;
if (ShadowIsPoisoned(ShadowAddress)) {
    __asan_report_store2 (Address);
}
*Address = 1;
============================
```

__asan_shadow_memory_dynamic_address is the shadow memory to record the buffer access in the memory sanitizer (MSan). Different from MSVC, Clang generates code to do the check before the real buffer access and invokes the __asan_report_store() function if the check fails. The firmware needs to allocate __asan_shadow_memory_dynamic_address for the shadow buffer and implement the __asan_report_store() function to report the error.

Clang ASan is also a debug feature because of its runtime performance impact. It should be disabled in the final production image.

The /RTCs and ASan are good for catching out of bound access to the stack. However, the firmware may have its own way to manage the heap instead of using the standard C language API – malloc/free. In order to detect heap overflow, we may add some special mechanisms for use by the firmware heap management functions. We will discuss the details in Chapter 16.

Hardware-Based Address Sanitizer

The software implementation of ASan needs an extra shadow buffer to hold the metadata information for the memory access. If the hardware has memory tagging capability, it may be used to assist the address sanitizer.

ARM Memory Tagging Extension

ARMv8.5 introduces the Memory Tagging Extension (MTE) to support runtime memory error detection to eliminate vulnerabilities arising from memory safety issues.

If a program allocates a buffer on the heap or stack, the 16-byte aligned buffer can be assigned a special 4-bit tag. The memory before or after the allocated buffer is assigned another tag. As such, the out of bound access can be detected because the tag is different. After the buffer is freed, the same buffer can be assigned with another tag. As such, use-after-free can also be detected. See Figure 15-12.

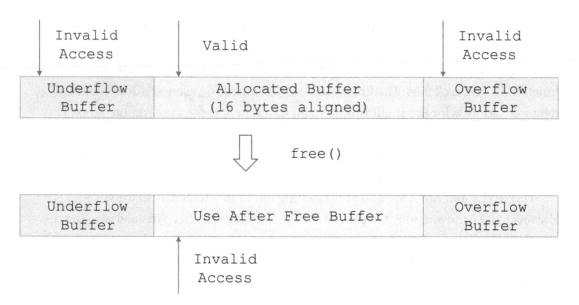

Figure 15-12. *MTE Capability*

In MTE, the tag is in the upper part of the 64-bit address. See Figure 15-13. ARM added a set of instructions to Insert Random Tag (IRG), Tag Mask Insert (GMI), Load Allocation Tag (LDG), Store Allocation Tag (STG), Store Allocation Tag and Zeroing (STZG), Store Allocation Tag and Pair (STGP), and so on. Figure 15-14 shows an example of how to add a tag for a function. First, the function calls IRG to copy SP to X0 and insert a random tag for X0. Then the function uses STGP to fill the data value on the stack and zero the rest of the 16 bytes. After SubFunc returns, the function uses STG to restore the default tag before exit.

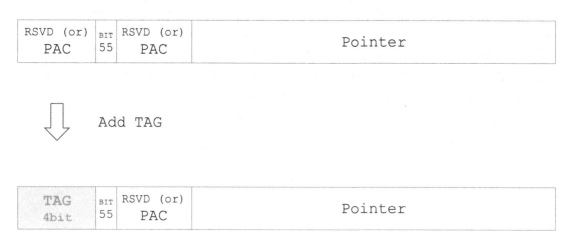

Figure 15-13. *MTE Tagging for Allocated Buffer*

```
VOID
Func ()
{
  UINTN Data = 1;
  SubFunc(&Data);
}
```

```
...
SUB   sp, sp, #16
IRG   x0, sp          // Insert Random Tag
MOV   x8, #1
STGP  x8, xzr, [x0]  // Store Allocation Tag and Pair
BL    SubFunc
STG   [sp], #16       // Store Allocation Tag
...
```

Figure 15-14. *Function with ARM MTE*

The Clang compiler provides "-fsanitize=hwaddress" for ARM to insert MTE instructions for stack, heap, and global variables. The firmware may enable this feature for the memory sanitizer if the hardware supports such a mechanism.

Intel Multi-key Total Memory Encryption

Intel Multi-key Total Memory Encryption (MKTME) uses the KeyID as the tag for the physical memory address. The concept of KeyID in the MKTME is similar to the tag in the ARM MTE. The difference is that the KeyID is always used along with the platform physical address instead of the virtual address. If the virtualization is not enabled, the KeyID is in the upper bits of the CPU page table. If the virtualization is enabled, the KeyID is in the upper bits of the virtual machine monitor (VMM) external page table (EPT). See Figure 15-15. The KeyID size can be determined by the IA32_TME_CAPABILITY MSR, such as 4 bits or 6 bits.

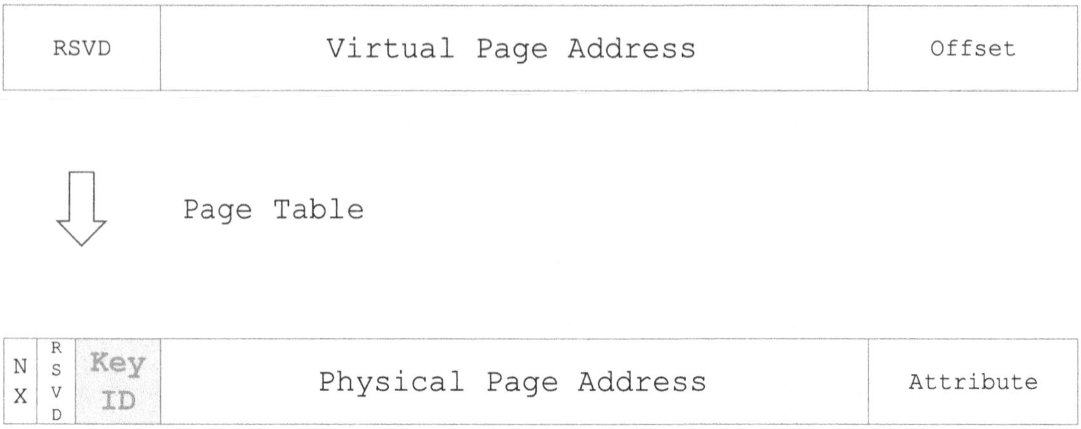

RSVD	Virtual Page Address	Offset

⇩   Page Table

N X	R S V D	Key ID	Physical Page Address	Attribute

Figure 15-15. *MKTME KeyID*

The firmware may leverage the hardware-based address sanitizer mechanism to catch a buffer overflow. There are two limitations:

1) The tag size: A system has only a limited number of tags. There might be a case in which the overflow happens, but the adjacent memory may have the same tag ID.

2) The tagged memory unit size" There might be a case in which the overflow is too small to be caught because it does not exceed the tagged memory unit size.

For the same reason that the firmware may have its own way to manage the heap instead of using standard C language API – malloc/free, we must update the firmware heap management function with such memory tagging support. We will discuss details in Chapter 16.

Uninitialized Data Check

Uninitialized data reads are a potential issue. The compilers support build-time detection and runtime error checking, such as MSVC or Clang. The firmware may use the compiler option. Similar to the address sanitizer, the runtime check requires a special function provided by the compiler. The firmware must implement these functions to use this feature.

MSVC reports warning /C4700 for uninitialized local variable, warning /C4701 for potentially uninitialized local variable, and warning /C4703 for potentially uninitialized local pointer variable. Sometimes, /C4701 and /C4703 are disabled because the uninitialized variable reported is only a potential issue and the compiler might generate a false-positive report. MSVC supports /RTCu to generate runtime error checks. If the variable is not initialized in the code path, a runtime error will occur. Take Listing 15-21 as an example, the MSVC will generate Listing 15-22.

Listing 15-21.

```
===========================
UINTN
TestA (
  UINTN Index
  )
{
  UINTN  Data;

  if (Index > 10) {
    Data = 0;
  }
  Data ++;
  return Data;
}
===========================
```

Listing 15-22.

```
===========================
TestA:
  0000000000000000: 48 89 4C 24 08       mov      qword ptr [rsp+8],rcx
  0000000000000005: 48 83 EC 38          sub      rsp,38h
  0000000000000009: C6 44 24 20 00       mov      byte ptr [rsp+20h],0
  000000000000000E: 48 83 7C 24 40 0A    cmp      qword ptr [rsp+40h],0Ah
  0000000000000014: 76 0E                jbe      0000000000000024
  0000000000000016: C6 44 24 20 01       mov      byte ptr [rsp+20h],1
  000000000000001B: 48 C7 44 24 28 00    mov      qword ptr [rsp+28h],0
                    00 00 00
```

```
0000000000000024: 80 7C 24 20 00        cmp         byte ptr [rsp+20h],0
0000000000000029: 75 0C                 jne         0000000000000037
000000000000002B: 48 8D 0D 00 00 00     lea         rcx,[TestA$rtcName$0]
                  00
0000000000000032: E8 00 00 00 00        call        _RTC_UninitUse
0000000000000037: 48 8B 44 24 28        mov         rax,qword ptr [rsp+28h]
000000000000003C: 48 FF C0              inc         rax
000000000000003F: C6 44 24 20 01        mov         byte ptr [rsp+20h],1
0000000000000044: 48 89 44 24 28        mov         qword ptr [rsp+28h],rax
0000000000000049: 80 7C 24 20 00        cmp         byte ptr [rsp+20h],0
000000000000004E: 75 0C                 jne         000000000000005C
0000000000000050: 48 8D 0D 00 00 00     lea         rcx,[TestA$rtcName$0]
                  00
0000000000000057: E8 00 00 00 00        call        _RTC_UninitUse
000000000000005C: 48 8B 44 24 28        mov         rax,qword ptr [rsp+28h]
0000000000000061: 48 83 C4 38           add         rsp,38h
0000000000000065: C3                    ret
============================
```

The generated code uses a flag to record if the local variable is initialized. This flag is checked before access. If the flag is not set, the code calls _RTC_UninitUse() to report the error, such as Listing 15-23.

Listing 15-23.

```
============================
VOID _RTC_UninitUse(CHAR *VarName)
{
  DEBUG ((EFI_D_ERROR, "\n!!! uninitialized var \"%a\" is used!!!\n",
  VarName));
  ASSERT (FALSE);

  CpuDeadLoop();
  return ;
}
============================
```

The Clang compiler provides "-fsanitize=memory" for memory sanitizer (MSan), which can detect uninitialized reads on the stack or heap. Taking Listing 15-16 as an example, Clang will generate code like Listing 15-24. The code checks if the data is initialized before read and calls __msan_warning_noreturn() if the check fails. The firmware needs to implement the __msan_warning_noreturn() function to report an error.

Unfortunately, the Windows targets are not supported by MSan. This feature can only be used for *nix platforms. Because EDK II firmware is using the *-unknown-windows target to generate the PE/COFF image, it cannot be used so far.

Listing 15-24.

```
==========================
0000000000496220 <TestA>:
  496220:  55                        push   %rbp
  496221:  48 89 e5                  mov    %rsp,%rbp
  496224:  48 83 ec 40               sub    $0x40,%rsp
  496228:  48 8b 05 b1 fd 22 00      mov    0x22fdb1(%rip),%rax      #
                                            6c5fe0 <_DYNAMIC+0x2b0>
  49622f:  64 48 8b 00               mov    %fs:(%rax),%rax
  496233:  48 b9 00 00 00 00 00      movabs $0x500000000000,%rcx
  49623a:  50 00 00
  49623d:  48 8d 55 f8               lea    -0x8(%rbp),%rdx
  496241:  48 31 ca                  xor    %rcx,%rdx
  496244:  48 c7 02 ff ff ff ff      movq   $0xffffffffffffffff,(%rdx)
  49624b:  48 8d 75 f0               lea    -0x10(%rbp),%rsi
  49624f:  48 31 ce                  xor    %rcx,%rsi
  496252:  48 c7 06 ff ff ff ff      movq   $0xffffffffffffffff,(%rsi)
  496259:  48 89 02                  mov    %rax,(%rdx)
  49625c:  48 89 7d f8               mov    %rdi,-0x8(%rbp)
  496260:  48 8b 45 f8               mov    -0x8(%rbp),%rax
  496264:  48 8b 0a                  mov    (%rdx),%rcx
  496267:  48 89 ca                  mov    %rcx,%rdx
  49626a:  48 f7 d2                  not    %rdx
  49626d:  48 89 c6                  mov    %rax,%rsi
  496270:  48 21 d6                  and    %rdx,%rsi
  496273:  48 83 ee 0a               sub    $0xa,%rsi
```

```
496277:    41 0f 92 c0              setb    %r8b
49627b:    48 89 c2                 mov     %rax,%rdx
49627e:    48 09 ca                 or      %rcx,%rdx
496281:    48 83 ea 0a              sub     $0xa,%rdx
496285:    41 0f 92 c1              setb    %r9b
496289:    45 88 c2                 mov     %r8b,%r10b
49628c:    45 30 ca                 xor     %r9b,%r10b
49628f:    48 83 e8 0a              sub     $0xa,%rax
496293:    41 0f 92 c3              setb    %r11b
496297:    45 28 c8                 sub     %r9b,%r8b
49629a:    44 88 55 ef              mov     %r10b,-0x11(%rbp)
49629e:    44 88 5d ee              mov     %r11b,-0x12(%rbp)
4962a2:    48 89 75 e0              mov     %rsi,-0x20(%rbp)
4962a6:    48 89 55 d8              mov     %rdx,-0x28(%rbp)
4962aa:    44 88 45 d7              mov     %r8b,-0x29(%rbp)
4962ae:    48 89 45 c8              mov     %rax,-0x38(%rbp)
4962b2:    0f 84 0a 00 00 00        je      4962c2 <TestA+0xa2>
4962b8:    e9 00 00 00 00           jmpq    4962bd <TestA+0x9d>
4962bd:    e8 ae 5c f8 ff           callq   41bf70 <__msan_warning_noreturn>
4962c2:    8a 45 ee                 mov     -0x12(%rbp),%al
4962c5:    a8 01                    test    $0x1,%al
4962c7:    0f 85 05 00 00 00        jne     4962d2 <TestA+0xb2>
4962cd:    e9 20 00 00 00           jmpq    4962f2 <TestA+0xd2>
4962d2:    48 b8 00 00 00 00 00     movabs  $0x500000000000,%rax
4962d9:    50 00 00
4962dc:    48 8d 4d f0              lea     -0x10(%rbp),%rcx
4962e0:    48 31 c1                 xor     %rax,%rcx
4962e3:    48 c7 01 00 00 00 00     movq    $0x0,(%rcx)
4962ea:    48 c7 45 f0 00 00 00     movq    $0x0,-0x10(%rbp)
4962f1:    00
4962f2:    48 8b 45 f0              mov     -0x10(%rbp),%rax
4962f6:    48 b9 00 00 00 00 00     movabs  $0x500000000000,%rcx
4962fd:    50 00 00
496300:    48 8d 55 f0              lea     -0x10(%rbp),%rdx
496304:    48 31 ca                 xor     %rcx,%rdx
496307:    48 83 c0 01              add     $0x1,%rax
```

```
49630b:    48 89 45 f0              mov      %rax,-0x10(%rbp)
49630f:    48 8b 45 f0              mov      -0x10(%rbp),%rax
496313:    48 8b 0a                 mov      (%rdx),%rcx
496316:    48 8b 15 93 fc 22 00     mov      0x22fc93(%rip),%rdx         #
6c5fb0 <_DYNAMIC+0x280>
49631d:    64 48 89 0a              mov      %rcx,%fs:(%rdx)
496321:    48 83 c4 40              add      $0x40,%rsp
496325:    5d                       pop      %rbp
496326:    c3                       retq
```
===========================

Similar to /RTCs and ASan, the /RTCu and MSan bring a performance penalty for the runtime check. As such, it is only a debug feature and should be disabled in the final production image.

Arithmetic Check

Arithmetic overflow is another potential issue. The compilers support build-time detection and runtime error checking. Similar to the address sanitizer, the runtime check requires a special function provided by the compiler. The firmware must implement these functions to use this feature.

MSVC supports /RTCs to detect errors when a value is assigned to a smaller data type that results in data loss. Listing 15-25 can be detected with warning /C4244: '=': conversion from 'UINTN' to 'UINT8', possible loss of data. As such, the developer may use a type cast for Data8 to pass the compilation in Listing 15-26. Then the compiler will generate code in Listing 15-27.

Listing 15-25.

```
===========================
UINT8
TestA (
  VOID
  )
{
  UINTN    Data = 0xFFFFFFFF;
  UINT8    Data8 = 0;
```

```
  Data8 = (Data >> 8);
  return Data8;
}
```

==========================

Listing 15-26.

==========================

```
UINT8
TestA (
  VOID
  )
{
  UINTN   Data = 0xFFFFFFFF;
  UINT8   Data8 = 0;

  Data8 = (CHAR8)(Data >> 8);
  return Data8;
}
```

==========================

Listing 15-27.

==========================

```
TestA:
  0000000000000000: 48 83 EC 38          sub      rsp,38h
  0000000000000004: B8 FF FF FF FF        mov      eax,0FFFFFFFFh
  0000000000000009: 48 89 44 24 28        mov      qword ptr [rsp+28h],rax
  000000000000000E: C6 44 24 20 00        mov      byte ptr [rsp+20h],0
  0000000000000013: 48 8B 44 24 28        mov      rax,qword ptr [rsp+28h]
  0000000000000018: 48 C1 E8 08           shr      rax,8
  000000000000001C: 48 8B C8              mov      rcx,rax
  000000000000001F: E8 00 00 00 00        call     _RTC_Check_8_to_1
  0000000000000024: 88 44 24 20           mov      byte ptr [rsp+20h],al
  0000000000000028: 8A 44 24 20           mov      al,byte ptr [rsp+20h]
  000000000000002C: 48 83 C4 38           add      rsp,38h
  0000000000000030: C3                    ret
```

==========================

The generated code calls _RTC_Check_8_to_1 () to check if the data is truncated. The firmware may implement a handler such as Listing 15-28 to do a similar check to detect such an error. In order to avoid this data loss check failure, the developer must use explicit data truncation, as shown in Listing 15-29.

Listing 15-28.

```
===========================
void _RTCc_Failure () {
  DEBUG ((EFI_D_ERROR, "\n!!! small type check failed!!!\n"));
  ASSERT (FALSE);

  CpuDeadLoop();
  return ;
}
char    __fastcall _RTC_Check_8_to_1(__int64 _Src)
{
  if ((_Src & 0xFFFFFFFFFFFFFF00) != 0) {
    _RTCc_Failure ();
  }
  return (char)(_Src & 0xFF);
}
===========================
```

Listing 15-29.

```
===========================
UINT8
TestA (
  VOID
  )
{
  UINTN    Data = 0xFFFFFFFF;
  UINT8    Data8 = 0;

  Data8 = (CHAR8)((Data >> 8) & 0xFF);
  return Data8;
}
===========================
```

The Clang compiler provides "-fsanitize=undefined" for the Undefined Behavior Sanitizer (UBSan), which can detect various undefined behaviors such as using misaligned data access, null pointers, and signed integer overflow. Taking Listing 15-30 as an example, Clang will generate the code in Listing 15-31.

Listing 15-30.

```
===========================
INT32
TestB (
  INT32  Test
  )
{
  INT32 Data = 0x7fffffff;
  Data += Test;
  return Data;
}
===========================
```

Listing 15-31.

```
===========================
TestB:
  00000000000009D0: 56                    push      rsi
  00000000000009D1: 48 83 EC 30           sub       rsp,30h
  00000000000009D5: C7 44 24 2C 03 00     mov       dword ptr [rsp+2Ch],3
                    00 00
  00000000000009DD: C7 44 24 28 FF FF     mov       dword ptr [rsp+28h],
  7FFFFFFFh
                    FF 7F
  00000000000009E5: 8B 44 24 2C           mov       eax,dword ptr [rsp+2Ch]
  00000000000009E9: 8B 54 24 28           mov       edx,dword ptr [rsp+28h]
  00000000000009ED: 89 D6                 mov       esi,edx
  00000000000009EF: 01 C6                 add       esi,eax
  00000000000009F1: 0F 90 C1              seto      cl
  00000000000009F4: 80 F1 FF              xor       cl,0FFh
  00000000000009F7: F6 C1 01              test      cl,1
```

```
0000000000009FA: 75 11                    jne      0000000000000A0D
0000000000009FC: 48 8D 0D DD 0D 00        lea      rcx,[17E0h]
                 00
0000000000000A03: 89 D2                   mov      edx,edx
0000000000000A05: 41 89 C0                mov      r8d,eax
0000000000000A08: E8 C3 04 00 00          call     __ubsan_handle_add_
                                                   overflow
0000000000000A0D: 89 74 24 28             mov      dword ptr [rsp+28h],esi
0000000000000A11: 48 83 C4 30             add      rsp,30h
0000000000000A15: 5E                      pop      rsi
0000000000000A16: C3                      ret
```

============================

Clang generates code to do the check for the overflow and invokes the __ubsan_handle_
add_overflow() function if the overflow flag is set. The firmware needs to implement the __
ubsan_handle_add_overflow() function to report the error. Listing 15-32 shows an example.

Listing 15-32.

```
============================
VOID
__ubsan_handle_add_overflow(
  struct overflow_data *data,
  UINTN lhs,
  UINTN rhs
  )
{
  DEBUG ((EFI_D_ERROR, "\n!!! __ubsan_handle_add_overflow - 0x%x,
0x%x!!!\n", lhs, rhs));
  ASSERT (FALSE);

  CpuDeadLoop();
  return ;
}
============================
```

/RTCc and UBSan also bring a performance penalty due to the runtime check. As
such, it is only a debug feature and should be disabled in the final production image.

Summary

In this chapter, we discussed the various compiler defensive technologies in MSVC and GCC/Clang. Some of these techniques can be included in final production images, such as stack checks and control flow. Some of them should only be debug features, such as the address sanitizer, uninitialized data check, and arithmetic check. In order to support these features, the firmware must provide the compiler's required symbols if the firmware does not use the compiler's standard library. In the next chapter, we will discuss how to harden the kernel by using similar technologies, such as code protection, address space layout randomization, and control flow guard.

References

Book

[B-1] Andrew S. Tanenbaum, Herbert Bos, *Modern Operating Systems, 4th edition*, Pearson, 2014

[B-2] Victor van der Veen, Nitish dutt-Sharma, Lorenzo Cavallaro, and Herbert Bos, *Memory Errors: the Past, the Present, and the Future*, Research in Attacks, Intrusions, and Defenses, Volume 7462 of the series Lecture Notes in Computer Science pp 86-106. Springer, 2012, available at `https://rd.springer.com/chapter/10.1007/978-3-642-33338-5_5`

[B-3] Mark E. Russinovich, David A. Solomon, Alex Ionescu, *Windows Internals, 6th edition*, Microsoft Press, 2012

Conference, Journal, and Paper

[P-1] Matt Miller, "Trends, Challenges, and Strategic Shifts in the Software Vulnerability Mitigation Landscape," in *BlueHat IL 2019*, available at `https://github.com/microsoft/MSRC-Security-Research/blob/master/presentations/2019_02_BlueHatIL/2019_01%20-%20BlueHatIL%20-%20Trends%2C%20challenge%2C%20and%20shifts%20in%20software%20vulnerability%20mitigation.pdf`

[P-2] David Weston, "Advancing Windows Security," in *Platform Security Summit 2019*, available at `www.platformsecuritysummit.com/2019/speaker/weston/`

[P-3] Periklis Akritidis, "Practical memory safety for C," *Technical Report – University of Cambridge. Computer Laboratory. University of Cambridge, Computer Laboratory 2017*, available at `www.cl.cam.ac.uk/techreports/UCAM-CL-TR-798.pdf`

[P-4] Kees Cook, "Security Feature Parity: GCC and Clang," in *Linux Plumbers Conference 2019*, `https://outflux.net/slides/2019/lpc/gcc-and-clang.pdf`

[P-5] Kees Cook, "Making-C-Less-Dangerous-3," in *Linux Security Summit 2018*, `https://events19.linuxfoundation.org/wp-content/uploads/2017/11/Making-C-Less-Dangerous-3.pdf`

[P-6] Jiewen Yao, Vincent Zimmer, "A Tour Beyond BIOS Security Enhancement to Mitigate Buffer Overflow in UEFI," *EDKII whitepaper 2018*, available at `www.gitbook.com/book/edk2-docs/a-tour-beyond-bios-mitigate-buffer-overflow-in-ue/details`

[P-7] Ken Johnson, Ma, Miller, "Exploit Mitigation Improvements in Windows 8," in *Blackhat US 2012*, available at `http://media.blackhat.com/bh-us-12/Briefings/M_Miller/BH_US_12_Miller_Exploit_Mitigation_Slides.pdf`

[P-8] Aleph, "Smashing The Stack For Fun And Profit," in *Phrack Magazine November 1996*, available at `http://phrack.org/issues/49/14.html`

[P-9] Crispan Cowan, Calton Pu, Dave Maier, Jonathan Walpole, Peat Bakke, Steve Beattie, Aaron Grier, Perry Wagle, Qian Zhang, "StackGuard: Automatic Adaptive Detection and Prevention of Buffer-Overflow Attacks," in *Proceedings of the 7th USENIX Security Symposium, January 1998*, available at `www.usenix.org/legacy/publications/library/proceedings/sec98/full_papers/cowan/cowan.pdf`

[P-10] Jonathan Afek, Adi Sharabani, "Dangling Pointer, Smashing the Pointer for Fun and Profit," in *Blackhat USA 2007*, available at `www.blackhat.com/presentations/bh-usa-07/Afek/Whitepaper/bh-usa-07-afek-WP.pdf`

[P-11] Mauro Conti, Stephen Crane, Tommaso Frassetto, Andrei Homescu, Georg Koppen, Per Larsen, Christopher Liebchen, Mike Perry, and Ahmad-Reza Sadeghi, "Selfrando: Securing the Tor Browser against De-anonymization Exploits," in *Proceedings on Privacy Enhancing Technologies 2016*, available at `www.ics.uci.edu/~perl/pets16_selfrando.pdf`

[P-12] Nergal, "The advanced return-into-lib(c) exploits: PaX case study," in *Phrack Magazine December 2001*, available at `http://phrack.org/issues/58/4.html`

[P-13] Martin Abadi, Mihai Budiu, Ulfar Erlingsson, Jay Ligatti, "Control-Flow Integrity – Principles, Implementations, and Applications," in *CCS05, ACM 2005*, available at `www.microsoft.com/en-us/research/wp-content/uploads/2005/11/ccs05.pdf`

[P-14] Hovav Shacham, "The geometry of innocent flesh on the bone: Returninto-libc without function calls (on the x86)," in *Proceedings of ACM Conference on Computer and Communications Security (CCS), 2007*, available at `https://hovav.net/ucsd/dist/geometry.pdf`

[P-15] FFRI, "Windows New Security Features – Control Flow Guard," FFRI report 2014, available at `www.ffri.jp/assets/files/monthly_research/MR201412_Control_Flow_Guard_ENG.pdf`

[P-16] Felix Schuster, Thomas Tendyck, Christopher Liebcheny, Lucas Daviy, Ahmad-Reza Sadeghiy, Thorsten Holz, "Counterfeit Object-oriented Programming," in *2015 IEEE Symposium on Security and Privacy*, available at `www.syssec.ruhr-uni-bochum.de/media/emma/veroeffentlichungen/2015/03/28/COOP-Oakland15.pdf`

[P-17] PaX Team, "RAP: RIP ROP," in *H2HC 2015*, available at `https://pax.grsecurity.net/docs/PaXTeam-H2HC15-RAP-RIP-ROP.pdf`

[P-18] Dean Sullivan, Orlando Arias, Ahmad-Reza Sadeghi, Lucas Davi, Yier Jin, "Policy-Agnostic-Control-Flow-Integrity-Implementation," in Blackhat 2016, `www.blackhat.com/docs/eu-16/materials/eu-16-Sullivan-Towards-A-Policy-Agnostic-Control-Flow-Integrity-Implementation.pdf`

[P-19] Joao Moreira, "Drop the Rop: Fine Grained Control Flow Integrity for the Linux Kernel," in *Blackhat Asia 2017*, available at `www.blackhat.com/docs/asia-17/materials/asia-17-Moreira-Drop-The-Rop-Fine-Grained-Control-Flow-Integrity-For-The-Linux-Kernel.pdf`

[P-20] Joe Bialek, "The Evolution of CFI Attacks and Defenses," in Offensive Con 2018, available at `https://github.com/Microsoft/MSRC-Security-Research/blob/master/presentations/2018_02_OffensiveCon/The%20Evolution%20of%20CFI%20Attacks%20and%20Defenses.pdf`

[P-21] Mark Rutland, "ARMv8.3 Pointer Authentication," in *Linux Security Summit 2017*, available at `https://events.static.linuxfound.org/sites/events/files/slides/slides_23.pdf`

[P-22] Qualcomm, "Pointer Authentication on ARMv8.3," Qualcomm Whitepaper 2017, `www.qualcomm.com/media/documents/files/whitepaper-pointer-authentication-on-armv8-3.pdf`

[P-23] Bing Sun, Jin Liu, Chong Xu, "How to Survive the Hardware Assisted Control Flow Integrity Enforcement," in *Blackhat Asia 2019*, `https://i.blackhat.com/asia-19/Thu-March-28/bh-asia-Sun-How-to-Survive-the-Hardware-Assisted-Control-Flow-Integrity-Enforcement.pdf`

[P-24] Intel, "Intel Analysis of Speculative Execution Side Channels," 2018, `https://newsroom.intel.com/wp-content/uploads/sites/11/2018/01/Intel-Analysis-of-Speculative-Execution-Side-Channels.pdf`

[P-25] ARM, "Cache Speculation Side-channels," 2018, `https://developer.arm.com/-/media/Files/pdf/Cache_Speculation_Side-channels.pdf?revision=966364ce-10aa-4580-8431-7e4ed42fb90b&la=en`

[P-26] Paul Kocher, Jann Horn, Anders Fogh, Daniel Genkin, Daniel Gruss, Werner Haas, Mike Hamburg, Moritz Lipp, Stefan Mangard, Thomas Prescher, Michael Schwarz, Yuval Yarom, "Spectre Attacks: Exploiting Speculative Execution," 2018, available at `https://spectreattack.com/spectre.pdf`

[P-27] Moritz Lipp, Michael Schwarz, Daniel Gruss, Thomas Prescher, Werner Haas, Anders Fogh, Jann Horn, Stefan Mangard, Paul Kocher, Daniel Genkin, Yuval Yarom, Mike Hamburg, "Meltdown: Reading Kernel Memory from User Space," 2018, available at `https://meltdownattack.com/meltdown.pdf`

[P-28] Kostya Serebryany, Evgenii Stepanov, Vlad Tsyrklevich, "Memory Tagging: how it improves C/C++ memory safety," LLVM 2018, available at `https://llvm.org/devmtg/2018-10/slides/Serebryany-Stepanov-Tsyrklevich-Memory-Tagging-Slides-LLVM-2018.pdf`

[P-29] Alexander Popov, "KASan in a Bare-Metal Hypervisor," LinuxCon Japan 2016, available at `www.slideshare.net/lfevents/kasan-in-a-baremetal-hypervisor`

Specification and Guideline

[S-1] Intel, "Intel 64 and IA-32 Architecture Software Developer Manuals," 2019, available at `https://software.intel.com/en-us/articles/intel-sdm`

[S-2] Intel, "Control Flow Enforcement Technology Specification," 2019, available at `https://software.intel.com/sites/default/files/managed/4d/2a/control-flow-enforcement-technology-preview.pdf`

[S-3] Intel, "Intel Architecture Memory Encryption Technologies Specification," 2019, available at `https://software.intel.com/sites/default/files/managed/a5/16/Multi-Key-Total-Memory-Encryption-Spec.pdf`

[S-4] ARM, "ARM Architecture Reference Manual," 2019, available at `https://static.docs.arm.com/ddi0487/ea/DDI0487E_a_armv8_arm.pdf`

[S-5] Microsoft, "Microsoft Portable Executable and Common Object File Format Specification," 2019, available at `https://docs.microsoft.com/en-us/windows/win32/debug/pe-format`

[S-6] Linux, "Tool Interface Standard (TIS) Executable and Linking Format (ELF) Specification," available at `https://refspecs.linuxfoundation.org/`

Web

[W-1] MSVC – Compiler Security Checks In Depth, `https://msdn.microsoft.com/library/aa290051.aspx`

[W-2] MSVC – /GS (Buffer Security Check), `https://msdn.microsoft.com/en-us/library/8dbf701c.aspx`

[W-3] MSVC – /RTC (Run-Time Error Checks), `https://msdn.microsoft.com/en-US/library/8wtf2dfz.aspx`

[W-4] MSVC – _fastfail, `https://msdn.microsoft.com/en-us/library/dn774154.aspx`

[W-5] MSCV – Control Flow Guard, `https://docs.microsoft.com/en-us/windows/win32/secbp/control-flow-guard?redirectedfrom=MSDN`

[W-6] Clang – Shadow Call Stack, `https://clang.llvm.org/docs/ShadowCallStack.html`

[W-7] Clang – Safe Stack, `http://clang.llvm.org/docs/SafeStack.html`

[W-8] Clang – Control Flow Integrity, `https://clang.llvm.org/docs/ControlFlowIntegrity.html`

[W-9] Clang – Control Flow Integrity Design, `https://clang.llvm.org/docs/ControlFlowIntegrityDesign.html`

[W-10] Clang – Speculative Load Hardening, `https://llvm.org/docs/SpeculativeLoadHardening.html`

[W-11] Clang – Address Sanitizer, `https://clang.llvm.org/docs/AddressSanitizer.html`

[W-12] Clang – Hardware Assisted Address Sanitizer, `https://clang.llvm.org/docs/HardwareAssistedAddressSanitizerDesign.html`

[W-13] Clang – Memory Sanitizer, `https://clang.llvm.org/docs/MemorySanitizer.html`

[W-14] Clang – Undefined Behavior Sanitizer, `https://clang.llvm.org/docs/UndefinedBehaviorSanitizer.html`

[W-15] GCC – Proposal to add a new stack-smashing-attack protection mechanism "-fstack-protector-strong," `https://docs.google.com/document/d/1xXBH6rRZue4f296vGt9YQcuLVQHeE516stHwt8M9xyU/edit`

[W-16] Address Sanitizer, `https://github.com/google/sanitizers/wiki/AddressSanitizer`

[W-17] Address Sanitizer Algorithm, `https://github.com/google/sanitizers/wiki/AddressSanitizerAlgorithm`

[W-18] Memory Sanitizer, `https://github.com/google/sanitizers/wiki/MemorySanitizer`

[W-19] Kernel Address Sanitizer, www.kernel.org/doc/html/latest/dev-tools/kasan.html

[W-20] Comparing GCC and Clang security features, https://lwn.net/Articles/798913/

[W-21] Raph Levien, With Undefined Behavior, Anything is Possible, https://raphlinus.github.io/programming/rust/2018/08/17/undefined-behavior.html

[W-22] Enhance Memory Protections in IE10, http://blogs.msdn.com/b/ie/archive/2012/03/12/enhanced-memory-protections-in-ie10.aspx

[W-23] Preventing the exploitation of user mode heap corruption vulnerabilities, 2009, https://blogs.technet.microsoft.com/srd/2009/08/04/preventing-the-exploitation-of-user-mode-heap-corruption-vulnerabilities/

[W-24] PaX Home Page, https://pax.grsecurity.net/

[W-25] Mitigating Arbitrary Native Code Execution, https://blogs.windows.com/msedgedev/2017/02/23/mitigating-arbitrary-native-code-execution/

[W-26] Hardening ELF binaries using relocation read-only, www.redhat.com/en/blog/hardening-elf-binaries-using-relocation-read-only-relro

[W-27] Position Independent Executable, https://access.redhat.com/blogs/766093/posts/1975793

[W-28] Spectre and meltdown, https://spectreattack.com/ or https://meltdownattack.com/

[W-29] Spectre mitigations in MSVC, https://devblogs.microsoft.com/cppblog/spectre-mitigations-in-msvc/

[W-30] EDKII Security Extension Package, https://github.com/jyao1/SecurityEx

[W-31] Klocwork static code analysis tool, www.perforce.com/products/klocwork

[W-32] Coverity static application security testing tool, www.synopsys.com/software-integrity/security-testing/static-analysis-sast.html

[W-33] LDRA tool, https://ldra.com/

CHAPTER 16

The Kernel

A firmware implementation is similar to an embedded operating system. It has a kernel to manage resources, such as the system memory, and the kernel is also responsible for the dispatching of tasks. The operating system can defend against software attacks in two ways – break the exploit and contain the damage. Similar to the list of compiler defensive technologies, the OS can break the exploitation by forcing the code protection, such as data execution prevention (DEP), code integrity guard (CIG), and arbitrary code guard (ACG). Address space layout randomization (ALSR) can make it harder for the attacker to predict the target address. The control flow guard (CFG) becomes more and more important today, because the control flow–based attack can bypass the fundamental hardening such as DEP.

If the kernel cannot break the exploitation, the kernel should contain the damage in a limited domain and prevent any persistent damage. Privilege isolation is one strategy for this containment. With the appropriate hardware support, we can use ring-based user mode/supervisor mode isolation and virtual machine monitor (VMM)–based isolation. Encrypted domain technology includes Intel Software Guard Extension (SGX), AMD Secure Encrypted Virtualization (SEV), and Intel Trust Domain Extensions (TDX). Domain isolation is another strategy too. A Trusted Execution Environment (TEE) is another good candidate, such as ARM TrustZone technology and Intel system management mode (SMM). If the hardware supports domain partitioning, a platform may run two or more systems independently. Table 16-1 lists the summary of kernel defensive technologies.

© Jiewen Yao and Vincent Zimmer 2020
J. Yao and V. Zimmer, *Building Secure Firmware*, https://doi.org/10.1007/978-1-4842-6106-4_16

Table 16-1. *Kernel Defensive Technology Summary*

Method	Detect/Prevent	Detail
To break the exploitation		
Code protection (code integrity guard)	Code injection	The kernel only allows signed executable image execution.
Code protection (data execution prevention)	Code injection	The kernel marks the code region to be read-only executable and the data region to be read-write non-executable. The execution environment, such as stack and heap, should also be non-executable.
Code protection (arbitrary code guard)	Code injection	The kernel marks memory regions to be non-executable by default, such as stack, heap, and freed memory. The executable memory cannot be allocated by other modules.
Address space layout randomization	Buffer overflow	The kernel allocates data from randomized locations in the heap and shifts the image load location.
Control flow guard	Control flow attack	The kernel sets up a control flow execution environment, such as shadow stack or branch target protection.
Address sanitizer (stack guard)	Stack overrun	The kernel sets up one guard page at the bottom of the stack to catch runtime stack overruns. Such overruns may be caused by too many recursive function invocations or the allocation of huge local variables.
Address sanitizer (heap guard)	Buffer overflow	The kernel sets up guard pages for the allocated memory in the heap to catch runtime buffer overflow.
Address sanitizer (memory tagging)	Buffer overflow	The kernel assigns a special tag for the allocated memory to catch runtime buffer overflows.

(*continued*)

Table 16-1. (*continued*)

Method	Detect/Prevent	Detail
To contain the damage		
Supervisor mode (Kernel Memory Protection)	Vulnerability in user mode	The kernel sets up ring-based privilege isolation to prevent the user mode code from accessing the kernel mode data.
Supervisor mode (User Memory Execution/ Access Prevention)	Vulnerability in user mode	The kernel sets up CPU-based protection to prevent the kernel from executing the user code and accessing the user data.
Supervisor mode (Kernel Address Isolation)	Vulnerability in user mode	The kernel sets up dual page tables to prevent side channel attacks from the user mode code.
Virtual machine monitor (Hypervisor-protected code integrity)	Vulnerability in the virtual machine	The kernel sets up hypervisor-based privilege isolation. The hypervisor verifies the integrity of the kernel code and sets up data execution prevention.
Virtual machine monitor (Kernel Data Protection, KDP)	Vulnerability in the virtual machine	The kernel sets up hypervisor-based privilege isolation. The hypervisor marks the critical kernel memory to be read-only.
Virtual machine monitor (sandbox)	Vulnerability in the virtual machine	The VM interpreter sets up a sandbox for the application code.
Trusted Execution Environment	Vulnerability in the non-trusted environment	The kernel sets up a TEE-based domain isolation.
System partitioning	Vulnerability in other partitions	The kernel sets up hardware-based domain isolation.

Break the Exploitation

First, let's see how the kernel can prevent the exploits at runtime.

Code Protection

The code protection techniques are used to prevent code injection attacks. Code protection includes three aspects – code integrity guard (CIG), data execution prevention (DEP), and arbitrary code guard (ACG). Figure 16-1 shows the memory layout with DEP/CIG/ACG in the UEFI firmware as an example.

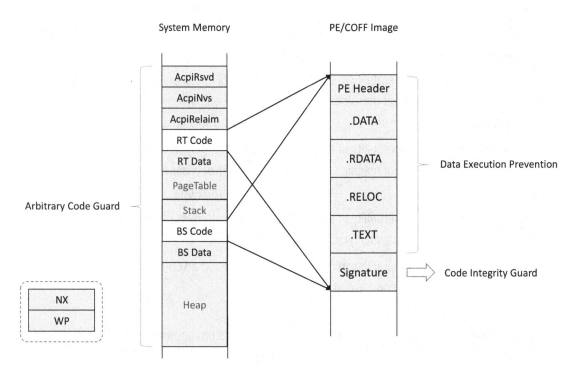

Figure 16-1. *Code Protection (DEP, CIG, ACG) in UEFI Firmware*

Code Integrity Guard

Code integrity guard means that the firmware can only load code that has been signed. If the code is not signed or the code is signed by an unknown entity, then the code will not be loaded.

In Chapters 4, 6, and 8, we have discussed different variants of a code integrity checker. Table 16-2 shows the summary of the verifier and the components to be verified. The final firmware solution may choose all of them or a partial subset of them based upon the threat model.

Table 16-2. *Code Integrity Guard Summary*

Technology	Verifier	Components to Be Verified
Cerberus, Titan	Platform Root-of-Trust	Entirety of host or non-host mutable firmware, including the platform OEM firmware, Baseboard Management Controller (BMC), and so on.
Intel Boot Guard	Silicon Authenticated Code Module	Host platform OEM firmware.
UEFI secure boot	Platform Original Equipment Manufacturer (OEM) firmware	Third-party firmware code, including PCI option ROMs and the operating system loader.
Linux Secure Boot Shim	Linux shim as loader	Linux OS loader, Linux kernel.
Windows CIG, Integrity Policy Enforcement (IPE)	Operating system	Windows executable, Linux executable.
SPDM, PCI Component Authentication	Host firmware and software, non-host or device initiator	Device firmware.

For example, if your platform trusts the non-host firmware but not the platform OEM firmware, then you can use either Cerberus or Titan as the platform Root-of-Trust or Intel Boot Guard as the silicon Authenticated Code Module to perform the verification. But if you want to verify the non-host firmware as well, then Intel Boot Guard is not a choice because it does not have such a capability.

If platform firmware needs to load the third-party components from other storage areas, such as the disk or a PCI host bus adapter card, then UEFI secure boot can be used to verify the integrity of the PCI option ROM or the OS loader. If the system is very specific in that it does not have the PCI card and the OS loader is integrated into system firmware, then UEFI secure boot is not required. You can choose a platform Root-of-Trust to verify the OEM firmware and the OS kernel and then depend upon the OS kernel to verify the drivers from disk.

Last of all, if a platform trusts all devices, then the device authentication process can be skipped. If you are designing a high-assurance platform and require verification of any hardware component, then you need a platform Root-of-Trust (PRoT) to verify the non-host firmware. These non-host firmware entities can include the baseboard management controller (BMC) and management engine (ME), also known as Server Platform Service (SPS), and so on. And these non-host firmware entities can have their device firmware accessed via the Secure Protocol and Data Model (SPDM) protocol via PCI data object exchange (DOE) or Management Component Transport Protocol (PMCI) on SMBus.

There are two typical ways for the code integrity verification to occur based upon if the image is readable:

1. Load the image and verify.

The verifier can hold an image hash as the verification policy. See Figure 16-2. The disadvantage of this technique is that whenever the image is updated, the image hash needs to be updated. The alternative is to use a digital signature for the image. The image can include a public key and the signature of the image. The verifier can carry the hash of the public key and use it to verify the public key of the image for use in the identification process. Then the verifier can use the public key itself to verify the signature for the authentication process. See Figure 16-3. This method is used when the verifier has the capability to load the image. Cerberus, Intel Boot Guard, and UEFI secure boot leverage this technique.

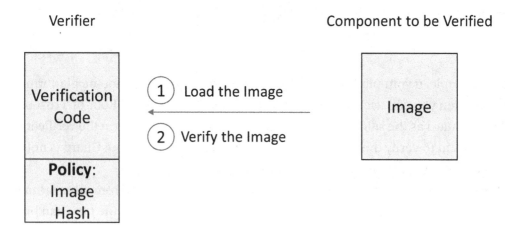

Figure 16-2. *Verification for Readable Firmware Image via Hash*

Figure 16-3. Verification for Readable Firmware Image via Digital Signature

2.   Read the key and challenge/response.

Sometimes the verifier does not have capability to read the image. For example, the host system firmware cannot access the device firmware. As such, we can rely on a device root-of-trust to verify the device firmware image and depend upon the device root-of-trust to provide verification evidence to the host system firmware. The host verifier can ask for a device public key and then send a challenge to the device with a random number. Then the host will verify the response based upon the signature of the random number signed with the private key by the device. See Figure 16-4. This technique is different from solution #1 to verify the image directly since herein we verify the identity of the device root-of-trust. Since it is a root-of-trust, we trust that it will verify the device firmware image. This protocol is defined in the Secure Protocol and Data Model (SPDM) specification and used for the device measurement, authentication, and session creation. It is also adopted by hardware device standards such as Peripheral Component Interconnection Express (PCIe), Compute Express Link (CXL), and Universal Serial Bus (USB).

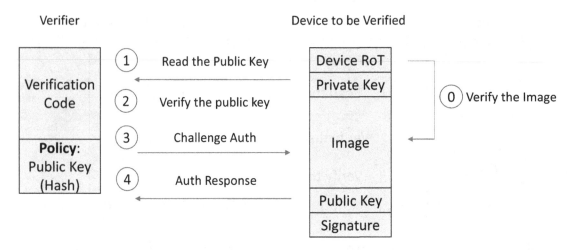

Figure 16-4. *Verification for Device Firmware Image via Challenge/Response*

Data Execution Prevention

Data execution prevention (DEP) means that the system kernel marks the code region to be write protected (WP) and marks the data region to be non-executable (NX). This rule could be applied to any executable images, such as the portable and executable (PE) common object file format (COFF) image or the executable and linkable format (ELF) image. It should also be applied to the execution environment, such as the stack or the heap. See Figure 16-5.

DEP is supported by the operating system directly. There are some firmware special enabling areas we need to take care of:

1) Most firmware has strict size requirements. As such, the link script might combine the code region to the data region and use minimal alignment settings, such as 32 bytes. The DEP technique cannot be applied to this configuration. The minimal requirement for DEP is to separate the code region from the data region and to use a minimal page size as alignment, such as 4K bytes.

2) Some firmware images may include self-modification code, especially mode switch code, because the segment location can only be determined at runtime. This is generally not recommended. The stack or global data region can be used to hold such information.

3) The execute in place (XIP) image on the flash region may be used in the early firmware boot phase before the permanent DRAM is initialized. The system may only have limited space for the page table. If we still need to apply the rule, we need to combine the multiple images into one big image. As such, we reduce the required entry numbers in the page table for the executable region.

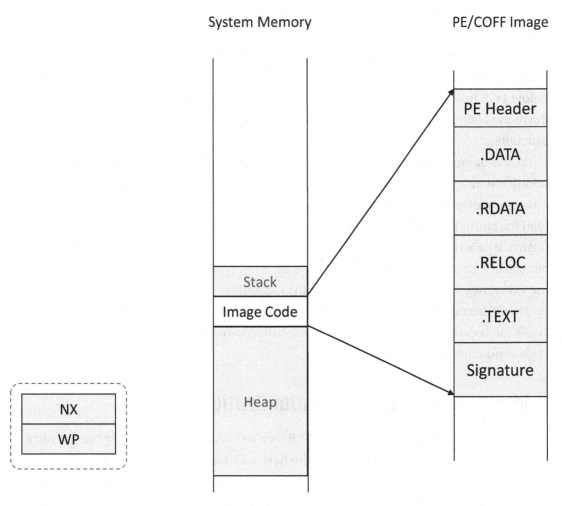

Figure 16-5. *Firmware DEP Environment*

Arbitrary Code Guard

The arbitrary code guard means that the system kernel marks all memory regions to be non-executable, including the stack, the heap, and any unused pages. The system kernel is the only entity that can allocate executable memory when it dispatches the images. Other modules cannot allocate the executable memory themselves.

The ACG technique is an extension of DEP. It blocks code injection because other modules cannot allocate code pages and all existing code pages are marked as read-only.

In practice, we do see some usages wherein a driver may allocate executable code. For example, a 64-bit mode UEFI code module may need to switch into 32-bit mode in order to call 32-bit Firmware Support Package (FSP) APIs. If this module detects itself to be located in above–4 GB memory, it will allocate an executable code region in memory below 4 GB in order to perform the mode switch. As such, a kernel can choose to lock down the code region allocation after it dispatches all modules to prevent arbitrary code executing.

A standalone firmware implementation can apply this rule easily because no additional images need to be loaded and no executable memory is required after all images are dispatched. However, things get complicated when the firmware needs to load the components from another domain, such as the operating system. Taking UEFI firmware as an example, after the UEFI kernel loads the OS loader, the OS loader can allocate the memory with the LoaderCode memory type for the OS kernel and jump to the OS kernel. The OS loader must have the capability to allocate executable memory for the OS kernel. The kernel needs to have knowledge of the new loaded modules and verify the code integrity before granting execution capability. Otherwise, the arbitrary code should not be executed.

Address Space Layout Randomization

Address space layout randomization (ASLR) is a technology to randomize the memory for the execution environment, such as the base address of an executable image or shared library, the program stack, and the program heap. ASLR makes it more difficult for an attacker to predict target addresses even if there is vulnerability in the program. The randomization technology can include shuffling, most likely for the image, or shifting, most likely for the data. Figure 16-6 shows the memory layout with image shuffling and data shifting in UEFI firmware as an example.

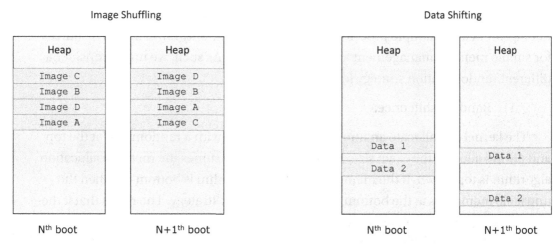

Figure 16-6. *ASLR in UEFI Firmware*

Data Shifting

Data shifting is for heap or stack randomization. The firmware kernel can reserve a large chunk of memory for the heap. When the kernel gets the request to allocate memory, the kernel allocate more memory and shifts the return address with a random number. The random number is measured as entropy. See Figure 16-7.

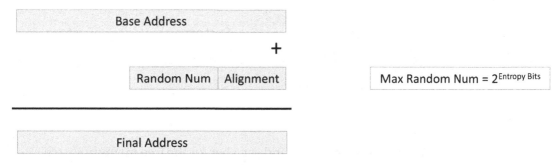

Figure 16-7. *ASLR in UEFI Firmware*

Let's see an example. We have page-level allocations, and the alignment is 4K. If we set the entropy to be 3 bits, then the maximum random number is 8. The random number has eight possibilities: 0, 1, 2, 3, 4, 5, 6, and 7. As such, the final address has eight possibilities: base address + 0, + 0x1000, + 0x2000, + 0x3000, + 0x4000, + 0x5000, + 0x6000, and + 0x7000. If the attacker wants to guess the address, they only have a one-eighth probability to get the right one.

In the OS, the entropy can be quite large because the OS uses virtual memory management and multiple processes. The firmware may only have limited resources for simple memory management and a single process. As such, we might consider a different randomization strategy for firmware.

1)   Random shift once.

The kernel can allocate an unused memory region with a random size at the top and always allocate the exact size. See Figure 16-8. It assumes the memory allocation algorithm is top-down. If the memory allocation algorithm is bottom-up, then the unusable memory is at the bottom. This is the simplest strategy. The risk is that if the attacker knows the delta, they can calculate the rest.

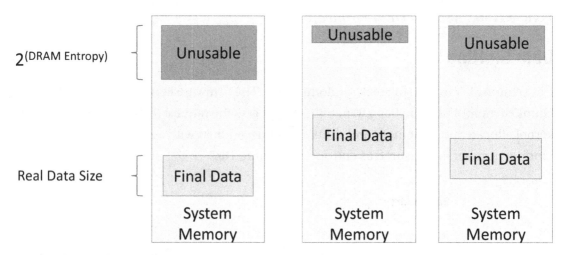

Figure 16-8. *ASLR – Random Shift Once*

2)   Set the randomized bar.

The kernel can shift with a random size and set a bar for the free memory search. Then the kernel allocates the exact size. See Figure 16-9. With this approach, the entropy must be a big number because a small number may cause the bar setting to be very close and to not bring too much randomness. However, there might be a case that the system has enough memory, but the bar is set too low to let the kernel find any freed memory there.

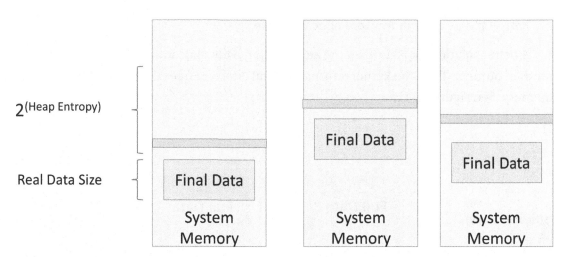

Figure 16-9. *ASLR – Set the Randomized Bar*

3)   Enlarge to a fixed allocation size.

The kernel can enlarge the allocation size based upon the entropy bit – the maximum random number. Then the kernel shifts a random size and returns the final data. See Figure 16-10. The good part of this approach is that the memory allocation is deterministic. The risk of this approach is that if the entropy is too large, then it may cause an out of resource condition for the larger memory allocations.

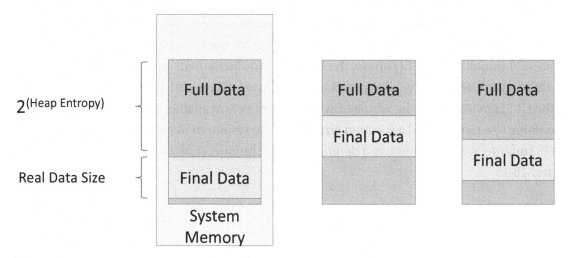

Figure 16-10. *ASLR – Enlarge to a Fixed Allocation Size*

   4)   Enlarge to a randomized allocation size.

A better solution for #3 is to let the kernel enlarge the allocation size based upon a random number. Then the kernel returns the final data and frees the rest of the allocated memory. See Figure 16-11.

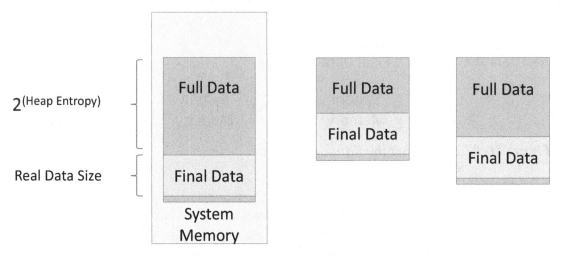

Figure 16-11. *ASLR – Enlarge to a Randomized Allocation Size*

Different firmware components may use different strategies. Take UEFI firmware as an example. The reserved memory, ACPI memory, and runtime memory cannot be randomized because we must maintain the same memory layout for the S4 resume process. As such, we need to pre-allocate a big bin for these usages at the top. In the pre-EFI Initialization (PEI) phase, the memory is quite limited, and the PEI core does not support the memory-free operation. As such, we may use #1 – random shift once. In the UEFI environment, the whole of system memory is available. Then we can use #4 – enlarge to a randomized allocation size. While the system management mode exists until OS runtime, we had better use a deterministic technique, such as #3. See Figures 16-12 and 16-13.

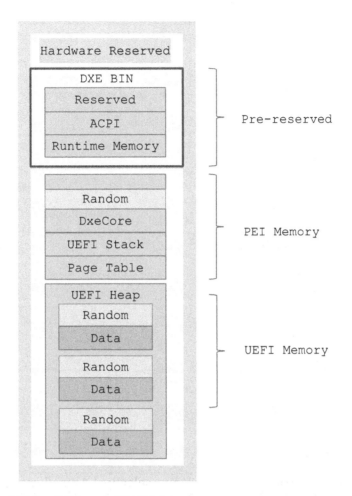

Figure 16-12. *ASLR – PEI and UEFI Memory*

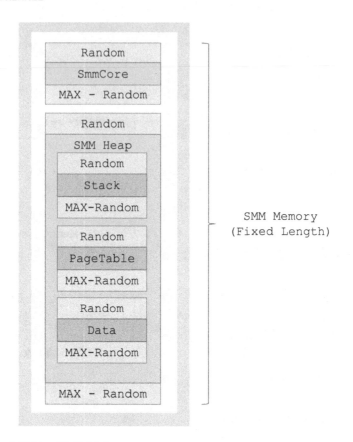

Figure 16-13. *ASLR – SMM Memory*

The biggest challenge of ALSR is the entropy selection. A small entropy number may result in a weakness in the protection. A small entropy number may also cause the address to be predictable within several system reboots. Taking the preceding example, the attacker can reboot the system eight times, and then they may get the right address once and attack the system successfully. However, a big entropy number may impact the stability of the system. The firmware usually runs in a resource-constrained environment. For example, X86 system management mode (SMM) only has 4~8 MB memory. A microcontroller may only have several kilobytes. A very aggressive randomization may waste the system memory too much and cause an out of resource condition in some special cases. It is also hard to debug these situations because of the randomness.

Data Shuffling

In order to achieve the randomization with limited resources, we can use data shuffling without shifting. This is a better solution because data shuffling can guarantee the memory reserved for the usage and eliminate the random out of resource problem. Figure 16-14 shows an example of a system employing image shuffling.

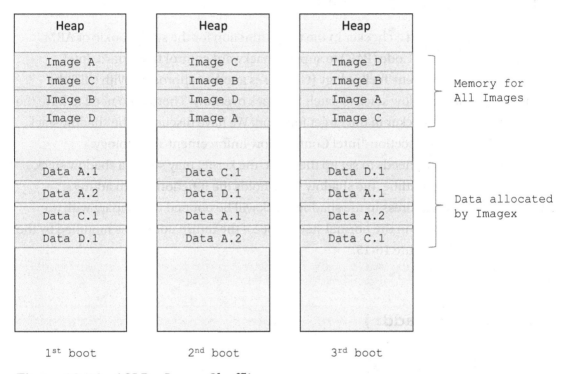

Figure 16-14. *ASLR – Image Shuffling*

The kernel may calculate the required space for all images and allocate a big chunk at one time. Then the kernel uses a random order to load the images one by one. Besides the image location being random, the kernel may choose a random order to execute the images. The benefit of this approach is that the data allocated by the image can also be shuffled automatically.

Control Flow Guard

Control flow guard can be enabled by compiler defensive technology, which has been discussed in Chapter 15. Here we discuss some control flow defenses that need to be set up by the kernel.

Backward-Edge Control Flow

The compiler may insert a checker in the target function for the stack cookie or ARM Pointer Authentication Code (PAC) to support backward control flow guard. Intel Control Flow Enforcement Technology (CET) uses another approach. With CET, the kernel can set up a shadow stack to catch the stack overflow. There is no need to have the compiler inject any checker in the target function. We have discussed the shadow stack concept in Chapter 15, section "Intel Control Flow Enforcement Technology."

Because the kernel needs to set up the stack, the kernel may set up a shadow stack at the same time. At runtime, the shadow stack holds the function return address. This function return address in the shadow stack will be popped to compare with the function return address in the normal stack to see if the return address is modified by the malicious code. See Figure 16-15.

Data Stack   Shadow Stack

Figure 16-15. *Intel CET – Shadow Stack*

A firmware implementation may implement a C standard library function – setjump() and longjump(). If so, the implementation must be updated to support the shadow stack. Besides saving the normal volatile registers (RBX, RSP, RBP, RDI, RSI, R12, R13, R14, R15, XMM6~XMM15, MXCSR) in the jump buffer context, the setjump() implementation must add the shadow stack pointer (SSP) into the jump buffer. As such, the longjump() can restore the original SSP to match the original stack pointer (RSP).

Because CET relies upon the page table, if a firmware implementation needs to disable paging, such as a mode switch from X64 long mode to IA32 protected mode, the CET feature must be disabled before the paging is disabled. And CET can be reenabled after the paging is reenabled.

When the firmware implements the CET shadow stack, it must ensure the shadow stack is implemented securely with adherence to the following listed guidelines:

1) The shadow stack must be in a read-only page, with the dirty (D) bit set in the page table entry. As such, the CPU knows this is a valid shadow stack memory location and writes the content into the shadow stack. At the same time, the kernel must clear the dirty (D) bit for the normal read-only page to prevent the CPU writing any data to the normal read-only page by mistake.

2) The shadow stack contains both the segment value and return address. The valid segment value in X86 is 16 bits. As such, the kernel needs to ensure that the first 64K-byte memory is non-executable to prevent the CPU from popping the segment value as the return address and executing the code there.

3) Although CET supports the shadow stack write instruction, it is highly recommended to disable this write-shadow-stack (WRSS) feature.

Forward-Edge Control Flow

The compiler also supports the ability to insert a checker for the forward-edge control flow, such as the Clang Control Flow Integrity (CFI) and Microsoft Visual Studio Control Flow Guard (CFG). The compiler also supports the hardware-based control flow, such as Intel CET Indirect Branch Tracking (IBT) and ARM Branch Target Identification (BTI).

We have discussed those features in Chapter 15, sections "Intel Control Flow Enforcement Technology" and "ARM Pointer Authentication and Memory Access Control."

Besides the compiler inserting the ENDBRANCH or BTI instruction at the target function, the kernel implementation needs to explicitly add the ENDBRANCH or BTI instruction to the assembly code which might be used for an indirect branch. See Figure 16-16. One example is the exception handler, and the other example is the mode switch code. Both of them are implemented in assembly code usually.

```
CALL RM[0xBBBB]
mov XXX

[0xBBBB]:
EndBranch
mov YYY
mov ZZZ
RET
```

```
JMP RM[0xAAAA]
[0xCCCC]:
EndBranch
mov XXX

[0xAAAA]:
EndBranch
mov YYY
JMP RM[0xCCCC]
```

```
Interrupt/
Exception
==========

[Handler]:
EndBranch
mov XXX
...
IRET
```

Figure 16-16. *Intel CET – Indirect Branch Tracking*

Address Sanitizer

The address sanitizer is supported in the Clang compiler to detect buffer overflows. But the compiler needs to insert a checker to each function, which will increase the firmware code size. This might be a problem in firmware, because the firmware may load third-party binary modules. Similarly, the kernel can support the address sanitizer at some level which is independent of the compiler feature. The advantage of this approach is that only the kernel needs to be updated and other drivers can work as is.

Page Table–Based Heap Guard

The basic idea to detect the buffer overflow in a heap is to add a tag before and after the target buffer. Most memory management libraries already have such a tag, but the tag is only checked when the buffer is freed. We hope to do more to detect the buffer overflow at runtime, instead of just at the time of freeing the buffer. The compiler sanitizer inserts the checker for the tag when the buffer is accessed. This cannot be applied for the kernel because the kernel cannot modify the module code. What the kernel can do, though, is to leverage the hardware capability to mark the tag region to be not accessible. The page table is one option. The tag can be a not-present page. It is also called a guard page. See Figure 16-17.

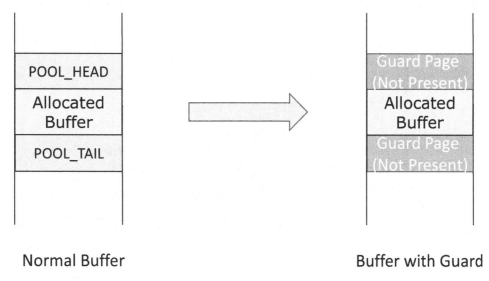

Normal Buffer   Buffer with Guard

Figure 16-17. *Guard Page*

Page table–based heap guard is to add a not-present page before and after an allocated buffer. Whenever the kernel memory management module gets the buffer allocation request, it allocates more memory for the guard pages, updates the page table to mark the two guard pages to be not present, and returns the allocated buffer in the middle. If the buffer overflow happens and the guard page is accessed, the CPU will generate a page fault exception because the guard page is marked as not-present memory.

In practice, the buffer allocation can be page-level allocation or pool-level allocation. For the page-level allocation, the guard page can be just before and after the allocated pages. See Figure 16-18. One special feature for the page-level allocation is that the allocated page can be partially freed. Figure 16-19 shows an example. There are three pages allocated at the beginning. Then the caller frees the second page in the middle and leaves a hole. In order to support the heap guard capability, the kernel memory management module needs to put the guard page in the middle to ensure the first and third pages are still guarded.

For the pool-level allocation, the guard page design is a little different. One problem with the pool-level allocation is that the allocated buffer size might not be a multiple of the page size. As such, the guard page could not catch the buffer overflow and underflow at the same time. The kernel memory management module may choose to add a guard page after the buffer to catch overflow or add a guard page before the buffer to catch underflow. See Figure 16-20. In most cases, we have seen the issues are caused by buffer overflow. As such, the guard page after the buffer can catch more issues.

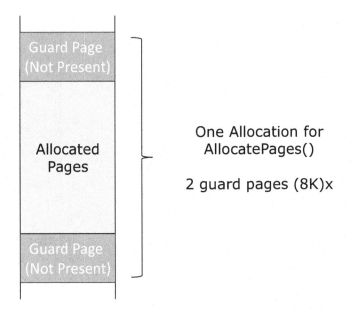

Figure 16-18. *Guard Page for Page-Level Allocation*

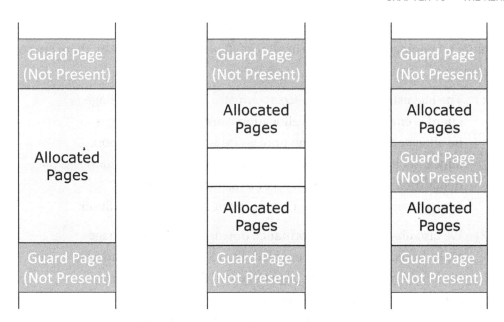

Figure 16-19. *Guard Page for Page-Level Allocation with Partial Free*

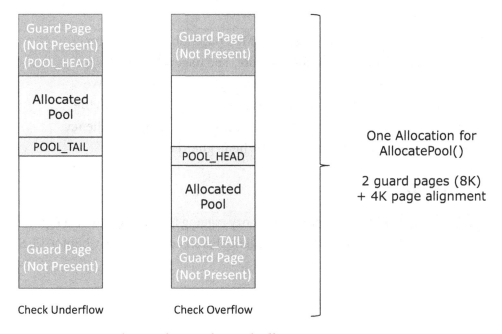

Figure 16-20. *Guard Page for Pool-Level Allocation*

The heap guard solution is a simple way to catch the buffer overflows. The page table is a mature technology and available in almost all processors. However, there are some limitations:

1) The biggest problem is the size overhead. When the heap page guard is enabled, any page allocation causes two more pages to be allocated. When the heap pool guard is enabled, each pool allocation becomes a page allocation. Even a 1-byte allocation needs three pages of memory. For a resource-constrained environment, it may cause a memory out of resource condition.

2) We also observed the performance downgrade when the page table–based heap guard is enabled. For each allocation and free, the kernel must reload the page table and flush the page table catch – Translation Lookaside Buffer (TLB). In a multiprocessor environment, the kernel must synchronize the page tables and flush the TLB for all processors to make sure the buffer overflow can be caught in all CPU environments.

3) Some firmware solutions use a ROMed page table, such as the early initial phase of an X86 firmware. The page table itself is on the flash memory mapped I/O space, and it is not writable. We also observed that there are firmware solutions to lock down the page table at some level, such as the Intel BIOS runtime resiliency feature. As such, we cannot use the heap guard feature.

Memory Tagging

Compared to page-level protection, the memory tagging technique can be a lightweight choice. We have discussed ARM Memory Tagging Extension (MTE) in Chapter 15. See Figure 16-21.

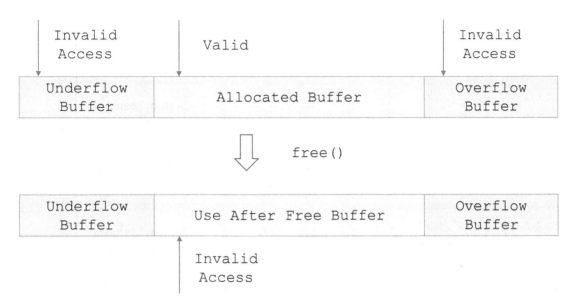

Figure 16-21. *Memory Tagging*

When the kernel gets the memory allocation request, the kernel assigns a new tag for the allocated buffer and returns to the requester. The memory before or after the allocated buffer is assigned with other tags. As such, if the out of bound access occurs, it can be detected because the tag is different. After the buffer is freed, the same buffer can be assigned with another tag. As such, the use-after-free can also be detected.

The tag is actually the high bits in the memory address. From the processor perspective, the address space is expanded. Figure 16-22 shows an example that a system has 2 bits for the tag and four tags totally.

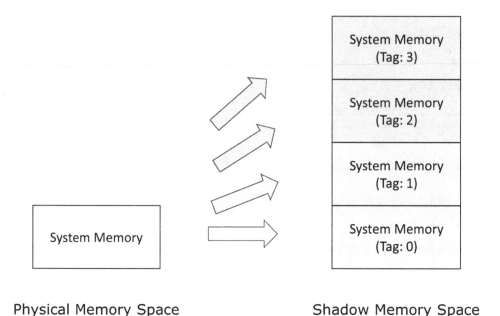

Physical Memory Space   Shadow Memory Space

Figure 16-22. *Shadow Memory Space with Tagging*

Figure 16-23 shows a buffer allocation case. For example, a requester invokes a service to allocate 0x60 bytes of memory. The kernel finds a free memory chunk at the address 0x8765_0080 ~ 0x8765_0100. The memory after this buffer (0x8765_0100 ~ 0x8765_0200) is marked as tag 2; then the final address after the buffer is 0x0200_0000_8765_0100 ~ 0x0200_0000_8765_0200. The memory before this buffer (0x8765_00040 ~ 0x8765_0080) is marked as tag 3; then the final address before the buffer is 0x0300_0000_8765_0080 ~ 0x0300_0000_8765_0040. The kernel chooses tag 1 for this buffer and returns 0x0100_0000_8765_0100 ~ 0x0100_0000_8765_0080. If the program has an overflow access to the memory after the buffer, then the pointer will be between 0x0100_0000_8765_0100 and 0x0100_0000_8765_0200. Because the tag of this address range is different from the valid one 0x0300_0000_8765_0100 ~ 0x0300_0000_8765_0200, the access is blocked by the CPU, and an exception is generated.

After the memory is used, the kernel needs to free the memory. The kernel changes the memory to tag 0. The valid address is switched to 0x0000_0000_8765_0100 ~ 0x0000_0000_8765_0080. Then if the program has a use-after-free issue and still accesses this region with address between 0x0100_0000_8765_0100 and 0x0100_0000_8765_0080, then the tag mismatch can be caught again.

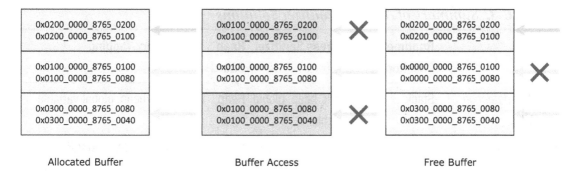

Figure 16-23. *Buffer Overflow Detection with Memory Tagging*

One special advantage of memory tagging is that it can support cross-object detection if the two objects are using different tags. Similar to page table–based heap guard, the memory tagging also has some limitations:

1) The tagged memory size has the processor-specific alignment requirement. For example, the ARM MTE requests 16-byte aligned tagged memory. A small-sized overflow or underflow might not be detected.

2) The memory tag numbers are limited. Take ARM MTE as the example. The tag field only has 4 bits. That means there are 16 different tags available totally. The memory allocation algorithm needs to guarantee that two adjacent memory regions have different tags. In some rare cases, if the overflow happens in two address regions with the same tag, then the overflow cannot be detected.

Table 16-3 shows the summary of the address sanitizer solutions.

Table 16-3. *Summary of Address Sanitizer Solutions*

	Runtime Checker	Address Sanitizer	Heap Guard	Memory Tagging
Overflow detection capability	Stack	Stack, heap, global variable	Heap	Stack, heap, global variable
Hardware dependency	NO	NO	Paging	Hardware tagging (ARM MTE)
Compiler dependency	MSVC	Clang, GCC	NO	NO for heap, YES for stack and global variable
Alignment	4 bytes	8 bytes	Page	Processor specific (16 bytes for ARM)
Cross-object detection	NO	NO	NO	YES
Production build	NO	NO	NO	YES

Stack Guard

The firmware kernel usually sets up the stack and heap for other drivers and applications. For the resource-constrained environment, we need to calculate the required stack size and required heap size precisely. One potential risk is stack overrun. If the allocated stack is too small, the stack may overlap with the heap memory which causes heap corruption. See the left-hand side of Figure 16-24.

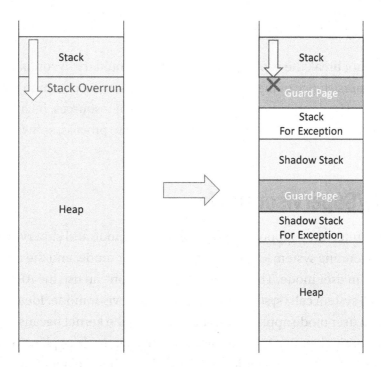

Figure 16-24. *Stack Without Guard and with Guard*

In order to detect a stack overrun, we can allocate a guard page – a not-present page in the page table – at the bottom of the stack. As such, when the stack overrun occurs, the CPU generates the page fault exception because of a not-present page access. Besides the guard page, we also need to allocate a known good page as the stack for the exception handler because we don't have any space in the normal stack. The stack switch is processor specific. For example, an IA32 processor needs to set up a task and use task switching for the exception. An X64 processor can use the stack switch directly as indicated in the exception handler. If we enable the shadow stack feature, then we can use the same mechanism for shadow stack as well. This is for the potential case wherein the shadow stack overrun occurs at the same time as for the normal stack. The final memory layout of the stack guard capability is shown in the right-hand side of Figure 16-24.

Contain the Damage

If the kernel cannot break the exploit, then the kernel should try to contain the damage and prevent the persistence of the attack. Domain isolation is a common way to achieve this containment. The domain here means a collection of resources, including physical memory, hardware devices, device input/output, software process, software services, and so on.

User Mode/Supervisor Mode

Modern CPU architectures support the concept of user mode and supervisor mode isolation. The operating system kernel runs in supervisor mode, and the normal application runs in user mode. The user mode application can use the ARM supervisor call (SVC) or X86 system call (sysCall) to enter into supervisor mode. Ideally, a vulnerability in a user mode application cannot impact the kernel because the kernel has its own execution domain. A vulnerability in one user mode application cannot impact the other user mode applications because the kernel provides different execution domains for different applications.

There are two basic designs for the operating system architecture – the monolithic kernel and the microkernel. See Figure 16-25.

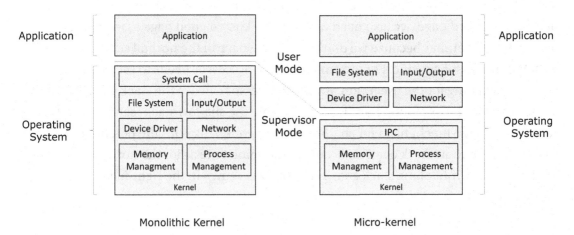

Figure 16-25. *Operating System Architecture*

With the monolithic kernel, all operating system components are in supervisor mode, such as the memory management, process management, device driver, network driver, input/output driver, file system driver, and so on. The application uses the system call interface to communicate with the kernel. Typical monolithic kernels include MS-DOS, Unix, and the Linux operating system. The application uses system calls to communicate with the kernel.

With the evolution of the operating system moving forward, people reduced the number of components in the kernel. The monolithic kernel thus evolved into a microkernel. Only the necessary components are still in supervisor mode, such as the memory management and process management. The other operating system components are deprivileged into user mode and use inter-process communication (IPC) to communicate with each other. With a minimal number of components in the kernel, the operating system can be more secure. A vulnerability in a device driver won't impact the kernel. However, when this was implemented, people also realized that the microkernel brings a performance penalty because the user mode/supervisor mode switch becomes much more frequent than the ones required in a monolithic kernel model.

In practice, the microkernel is much smaller than the monolithic kernel. A typical microkernel includes MINIX, L3, and L4. One important property of the microkernel is security. Recently, people have focused on formal specifications of the microkernel API, including formal proofs of the API's security properties and the correctness of the implementation. The third-generation microkernel seL4 is claimed to be a high-assurance, high-performance operating system microkernel. It is unique because of its comprehensive formal verification, without compromising performance. Other microkernels include the QNX Neutrino and the Google Fuchsia Zircon kernel.

Today, operating systems use a hybrid model to balance the modular design in the microkernel and the performance benefit from the monolithic kernel. It runs a microkernel and other operating system components, and the components are in supervisor mode, for example, the Windows NT kernel and hybrid Mach kernel underneath macOS.

Most system firmware today is using a monolithic kernel, such as the TianoCore EDK II or coreboot. Because the majority of the tasks of the system firmware is to initialize the silicon, the supervisor privilege is required to access the devices, such as memory mapped I/O (MMIO), I/O, CPU model-specific register (MSR), and so on.

In the UEFI environment, it is possible to enable ring 3 user mode execution for the PCIe option ROM (OROM). Apple Mac system deprivileged the OROM and made it run in ring 3 user mode and uses OROM sandbox to monitor the behavior of the OROM. The OROMs can only call and only install a limited subset of expected UEFI interfaces, such as read and write to disk blocks or draw to graphics. Also the OROM can only talk to the assigned device. Each OROM is isolated, so that they cannot attack each other. As such, the damage in one OROM won't impact the system and other components. See Figure 16-26.

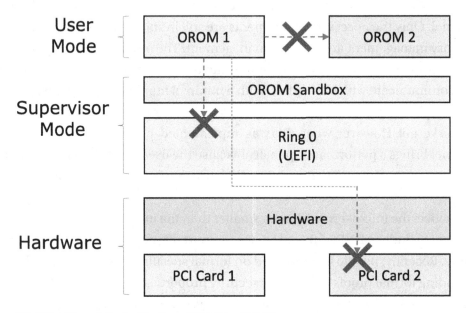

Figure 16-26. *User Mode Option ROM in UEFI*

Some special non-host firmware may implement the user mode/supervisor mode isolation, such as the Management Engine (ME) or Baseboard Management Controller (BMC). An embedded OS may be used for this type of firmware, such as ThreadX, FreeRTOS, Zephyr, or Yocto.

Kernel Memory Protection

If the supervisor mode is enabled, the kernel needs to protect itself to resist any attacks from user mode. The CPU provides the capability to prevent the user code from accessing kernel mode code or kernel data. However, the opposite is not true. The kernel is usually mapped into the address space of each process to achieve the best performance. See Figure 16-27.

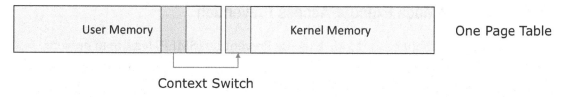

Context Switch

Figure 16-27. *One Page Table*

The risk of this approach is the classic return-to-user (ret2usr) attack. The attack can be achieved by overwriting the kernel-controlled data, such as return address, jump table, function table, and so on, with a user space address. Figure 16-28 shows two patterns of ret2usr attacks. The kernel code may take a user function pointer and execute the user code, or the kernel code may refer to a data structure that points to a user data structure and execute a function there. One old example is the NULL pointer access. The user mode code can prepare a carefully chosen set of parameters to trigger a NULL pointer dereference in the kernel and build a program with arbitrary code mapped to address zero. Then the kernel may invoke the user-provided function directly.

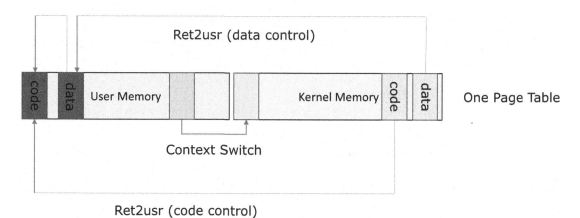

Figure 16-28. *Return-to-User Attack*

User Memory Execution/Access Prevention

Because the pattern of this attack is that the user mode code is executed with the kernel privilege or the user mode data is accessed in the kernel code, one simple mitigation is to prevent the user mode code from being executed with kernel privilege and to prevent user mode data from being accessed, with the hardware support.

Intel Supervisor Mode Execute/Access Prevention

Intel introduced the Supervisor Mode Execute Prevention (SMEP) feature to prevent the execution of the arbitrary user mode code by the kernel. Intel also introduced the Supervisor Mode Access Prevention (SMAP) feature to prevent the access of arbitrary user data by the kernel.

ARM Privileged Execute/Access Never

ARM introduced the Privileged Execute-Never (PXN) feature, which is similar to SMEP, and the Privileged Access-Never (PAN) feature, which is similar to SMAP. With those features enabled, the two patterns of ret2usr attacks, code control and data control, can be blocked. See Figure 16-29.

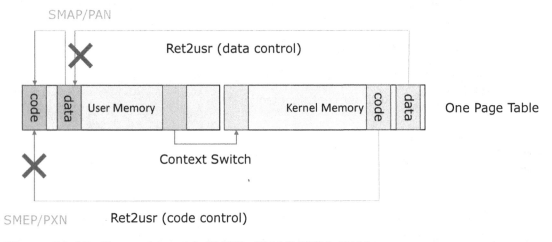

Figure 16-29. *Protection with SMEP+SMAP/PXN+PAN*

Unfortunately, there are still attacks to bypass the SMEP+SMAP/ PXN+PAN. Meltdown is a side channel attack that takes advantage of the out-of-order execution. In the attack, the user mode code may try to access a kernel data structure. Although the access will cause an exception because of the privilege violation, the CPU still executes the instruction out of order to get the kernel data and load it into the CPU cache. Although the final result is not committed when the instruction is retired, the data in the CPU cache is not cleaned up. From a memory and register perspective, there is no way to get the kernel data. However, the data is in the cache. It is not invisible. Later, the user mode code discerns the data in the cache based upon the time difference between cache access and memory access. That is a typical time-based side channel attack.

Kernel Address Isolation

One reason that the Meltdown attack can succeed is that the user mode and the kernel mode code share the same page table. As such, the out-of-order code can be executed to bypass the privilege mode isolation. In order to mitigate the Meltdown attacks, one technique is to separate the kernel mode page table from the user mode page table. The user page table only maps the user memory and minimal kernel memory required for a context switch. The rest of the kernel memory should be not present. The kernel page table maps the kernel memory. The user memory should be not present or be isolated by SMAP+SMEP/PXN+PAN. See Figure 16-30.

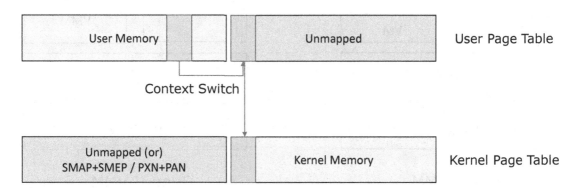

Figure 16-30. *Kernel Address Isolation*

Linux implements KAISER also known as kernel page table isolation (KPTI) to support Kernel Address Isolation. KAISER chooses SMAP+SMEP as a practical way instead of unmapped user memory, also known as strong kernel isolation, because the strong kernel isolation requires an effort to rewrite large parts of today's kernels.

The firmware may implement user mode/supervisor mode isolation. As such, a vulnerability in the user mode code will not impact the kernel. If this is implemented, the firmware should adopt current best practices. For example, the SMAP+SMEP/PXN+PAN should be enabled to prevent user mode code from being executed or accessed by the kernel. The Kernel Address Isolation should be enabled to resist the Meltdown attack.

Virtual Machine Monitor

The virtual machine monitor (VMM) is a concept introduced long time ago. It can work as a reference monitor to monitor the system behavior. One important usage of the virtual machine monitor is to isolate the untrusted application in one virtual machine domain.

There are two fundamental types of VMMs. A type I VMM runs directly on the machine hardware. It can be part of the operating system kernel. It must perform scheduling and resource allocation for all virtual machines in the system and requires drivers for hardware peripherals. A type II VMM runs as an application on a host operating system and relies on the host system for memory management, processor scheduling, resource allocation, and hardware drivers. See Figure 16-31.

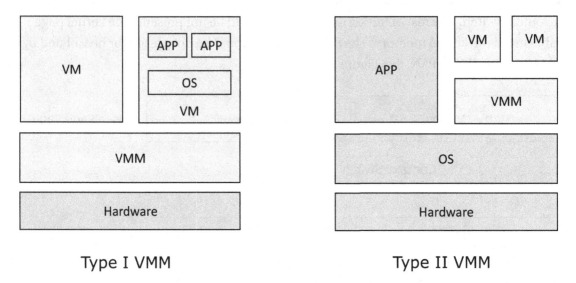

Figure 16-31. *Two Types of VMM*

Although most of the CPUs have instruction-level support for supervisor mode and user mode isolation, the instruction set in the supervisor mode cannot meet the VMM type I requirement defined by Popek and Goldberg. For example, Robin and Irvine summarized Intel Pentium's ability to support a secure VMM. Today most CPUs add VMM support with a set of new instructions and a new execution mode, such as the ROOT mode in Intel X86 CPU and the HYP mode or exception level 2 (EL2) in ARM CPU. The hypervisor mode can be entered with ARM hypervisor call (HVC) or X86 VM call (VmCall).

Virtualization-Based Security (VBS)

Today, we have Microsoft Hyper-V for Windows systems and Linux Kernel-Based Virtual Machine (KVM) for Linux systems. This type of virtual machine monitor can be used to secure the system. Taking Microsoft as an example, the basic OS hardening happened in the Windows operating system, such as code integrity guard (CIG), data execution prevention (DEP), arbitrary code guard (ACG), address space layout randomization (ASLR), and control flow guard (CFG). This OS hardening requires that the UEFI secure boot feature and TCG trusted boot be enabled in the platform.

On top of that, Microsoft added virtualization-based security (VBS). The VBS capability can enhance Windows system security by creating an isolated and hypervisor-restricted subsystem. It can isolate some sensitive information in places which are not accessible by the normal OS, such as credentials. VBS requires a set of features, such as the UEFI memory attribute table, TCG MOR2, I/O memory management unit (IOMMU) such as Intel Virtualization Technology for Directed I/O (VT-d) or AMD IOMMU, virtualization second-level address translation (SLAT) such as Intel Extended Page Table (EPT) or AMD Rapid Virtualization Indexing (RVI) also known as Nested Page Table (NPT), and hypervisor-protected code integrity (HVCI).

Recently, Microsoft announced the secure core PC. It includes new features, such as secure launch of a trusted virtual machine monitor with hardware-based dynamic root-of-trust, such as Intel Trusted Execution Technology (TXT) or AMD Secure Virtual Machine (SVM), SMM paging protection and attestation, and the Kernel Data Protection (KDP).

Hypervisor-Protected Code Integrity (HVCI)

The hypervisor-protected code integrity (HVCI) is a feature to maintain the integrity of code that runs in the Windows kernel. HVCI itself runs in an isolated execution environment. As such, it cannot be tampered with by other code running in the kernel. The HVCI feature verifies the integrity of the kernel code according to the kernel singing policy. HVCI also maintains a blacklist of drivers and blocks them from loading. This is the kernel version of a code integrity guard (CIG).

HVCI can also make sure the kernel memory pages are never simultaneously writable and executable in order to prevent the code injection attack. This is the kernel version of data execution prevention (DEP). See Figure 16-32.

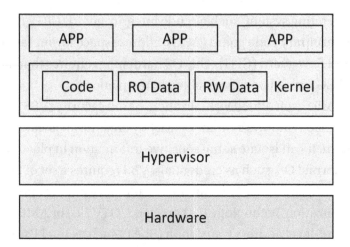

Figure 16-32. *Hypervisor-Based Protection*

Kernel Data Protection (KDP)

Kernel Data Protection (KDP) provides software running in the OS kernel with the ability to mark some kernel memory to be read-only protected. Many kernel components set the data only once during boot, and the setting remains unchanged for the rest of the boot cycle. That is a good candidate for the protection. The hypervisor uses the second-level address translation (SLAT) tables to protect the kernel data. As such, it cannot be tampered with by other code running in the kernel. See Figure 16-31.

The fundamental idea of the virtualization-based security is that the kernel protects the application and tries to protect itself. The hypervisor enforces the kernel protection policy, protects the kernel, and protects itself.

As we discussed in the previous section, most firmware just uses the supervisor mode to run all code. If it is hard to deprivilege the existing applications to user mode, the firmware may enable a type I bare metal hypervisor to protect the kernel. The bare metal hypervisor could be very simple, and it is unnecessary to include an operating system. This bare metal one is also called type 0 hypervisor. Today we have seen the hypervisor running in the UEFI firmware environment, such as Firmware Reference Monitor (FRM), Bareflank Hypervisor Software Development Kit (SDK), and MiniVisor.

Sandbox

A language-specific interpreter is a typical type II virtual machine embodiment. Examples of such an interpreter include the Java virtual machine (JVM), .NET Common

Language Runtime (CLR), and WebAssembly (wasm) virtual machine (WAVM). This type of virtual machine monitor can be used as a sandbox to provide an isolated execution environment. See Figure 16-33.

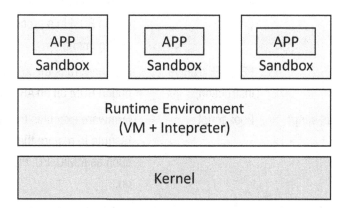

Figure 16-33. *Sandbox-Based Protection*

The firmware may enable a language-based interpreter as the type II virtual machine. One typical example is the EFI Byte Code (EBC) virtual machine defined in the UEFI specification. The original purpose of inventing EBC is to provide platform- and processor-independent mechanisms for loading and executing EFI device drivers, especially for the PCI option ROM. However, we noticed that the EBC VM can also be used as a sandbox to evaluate the behavior of the UEFI device driver to ensure it does not harm the system. EBC is a good architectural approach. However, most PCI cards still use X64 as the default architecture for their option ROMs. In order to run these option ROMs, we can use a PE/COFF emulator. As such, we can run the X64 PCI ROM on an ARM 64-bit platform.

The UEFI PI specification also defines the boot script. This is a lightweight language definition to program the system registers in the S3 resume phase. It includes the write and modify the memory mapped I/O (MMIO) register, I/O register, PCI register, SMBus register, stall, and external function call.

The ACPI specification defines an ACPI machine language (AML) to allow the operating system to control the platform device and query the device information at the OS runtime. AML is a byte stream, and it is parsed by an ACPI interpreter.

Other examples, including embedded Java, .NET Micro Framework, and WebAssembly micro runtime, can also run on top of the firmware environment to provide a sandbox execution environment. Table 16-4 lists different sandbox VMs that can run on the firmware or embedded system.

Table 16-4. *Sandbox Solution Example*

Technology	Source Code	Binary Format	Usage
EFI Byte Code (EBC)	C	PE/COFF (EFI Byte Code)	Firmware runs the EBC version PCI option ROM in a processor-independent environment.
PE/COFF emulator	C	PE/COFF (Native Instruction)	Firmware runs the X64 version PCI option ROM on an ARM system.
UEFI PI Boot Script	Boot script	Boot script	Firmware executes the boot script in S3 resume to restore the silicon register, such as MMIO, I/O, PCI, SMBus, and so on.
ACPI control method	ACPI Source Language (ASL)	ACPI machine language (AML)	The operating system ACPI module runs the AML code to configure the device or get the device information in OS runtime.
Embedded Java	Java	Java Bytecode	Run Java program on an embedded system.
.NET Micro Framework	C#	Common Intermediate Language (CIL)	Run .NET program on an embedded system.
WebAssembly	C/C++	WebAssembly (wasm)	Run C/C++ program on an embedded system.

There are lots of books introducing the security of Java and .NET Common Language Runtime (CLR), so we will not discuss those languages. Instead, we will focus on the new technology – WebAssembly.

WebAssembly (wasm) is a binary instruction format for a stack-based virtual machine. It is designed to be encoded in a size- and load-time–efficient binary format. WebAssembly describes a memory-safe, sandboxed execution environment. Originally, WebAssembly is designed to improve the portability, performance, and security of JavaScript used in the web browser. Since it is another type of virtual machine, it can also be used in other areas, such as embedded systems. The modular system interface is defined by the WebAssembly System Interface (WASI).

Memory Safety

The traditional C programming language has memory safety issues. Two major categories of memory safety issues are spatial safety issues, such as buffer overflow, and temporal safety issues, such as use-after-free.

In wasm, each function has a fixed, pre-declared number of local variables which occupy a single index space local to the function. Each local variable has a value type. Parameters are addressed as local variables. A global variable stores a single value of a fixed value type. Global variables are accessed via an integer index into the module-defined global index space. Both local variables and global variables are represented as fixed-type values stored by index instead of the linear memory address. References to these memory regions can be detected to avoid out of bound accesses. Listing 16-1 shows a simple C function – add(). Listing 16-2 shows the wasm bytecode of the add() function. "local.set <index>," "local.get <index>," "global.set <index>," and "global.get <index>" are the syntax to access a local variable or global variable via index.

Listing 16-1.

```
===========================
int add (int a, int b)
{
  return a + b;
}
===========================
```

Listing 16-2.

```
===========================
(module
  (type (;0;) (func (param i32 i32) (result i32)))
  (import "env" "__linear_memory" (memory (;0;) 0))
  (import "env" "__indirect_function_table" (table (;0;) 0 funcref))
  (import "env" "__stack_pointer" (global (;0;) (mut i32)))
  (func $add (type 0) (param i32 i32) (result i32)
    (local i32 i32 i32 i32 i32 i32)
    global.get 0
```

```
        local.set 2
        i32.const 16
        local.set 3
        local.get 2
        local.get 3
        i32.sub
        local.set 4
        local.get 4
        local.get 0
        i32.store offset=12
        local.get 4
        local.get 1
        i32.store offset=8
        local.get 4
        i32.load offset=12
        local.set 5
        local.get 4
        i32.load offset=8
        local.set 6
        local.get 5
        local.get 6
        i32.add
        local.set 7
        local.get 7
return))
```

============================

However, the heap is not managed by the wasm. It is implemented as a runtime environment–specific behavior. For example, a wasm runtime needs to implement a platform-specific C standard library for common C programs, including malloc() and free(). At the same time, the wasm runtime may implement other non-standard functions for the firmware environment, such as UEFI AllocatePages(), C11 aligned_alloc(), Windows _aligned_malloc(), or posix_memalign(). The memory safety of the heap is not guaranteed by the wasm architecture.

Control Flow Integrity

In wasm, each function is represented as a function section index, and the wasm maintains a protected call stack. As such, the Control Flow Integrity of the direction function call and the function return can be guaranteed by wasm. For the indirect function, the type signature of the function is also checked by wasm at runtime. Listing 16-3 shows a simple C function – ext_test() – to call an external function. Listing 16-4 shows the wasm bytecode of the ext_test module. It declares a function named "ext_func" and its function type signature. The function is called via "call <index>" in the code.

Listing 16-3.

```
============================
int ext_func(int a);

int ext_test(int a)
{
  return ext_func(a);
}
============================
```

Listing 16-4.

```
============================
(module
  (type (;0;) (func (param i32) (result i32)))
  (import "env" "__linear_memory" (memory (;0;) 0))
  (import "env" "__indirect_function_table" (table (;0;) 0 funcref))
  (import "env" "__stack_pointer" (global (;0;) (mut i32)))
  (import "env" "ext_func" (func (;0;) (type 0)))
  (func $ext_test (type 0) (param i32) (result i32)
    (local i32 i32 i32 i32 i32 i32 i32)
    global.get 0
    local.set 1
    i32.const 16
    local.set 2
    local.get 1
    local.get 2
```

```
i32.sub
local.set 3
local.get 3
global.set 0
local.get 3
local.get 0
i32.store offset=12
local.get 3
i32.load offset=12
local.set 4
local.get 4
call 0
local.set 5
i32.const 16
local.set 6
local.get 3
local.get 6
i32.add
local.set 7
local.get 7
global.set 0
local.get 5
return))
```

============================

The wasm may be used in the firmware environment, as long as the firmware includes a wasm interpreter. For example, WebAssembly Micro Runtime (WAMR) is a standalone WebAssembly (WASM) runtime with a small footprint. It can be enabled in vxworkd, zephyr or even UEFI/EDK II environment.

Resource Access Control

Sandbox solutions may include a resource access control mechanism to precisely control which subject can access which object. Depending upon the different security models, the access control policy can be an access control list (ACL), capability, or security label (SL) enforced by the platform. Figure 16-34 shows an example of the policy for two subjects and two objects. The firmware may have a security manager to control all access policies.

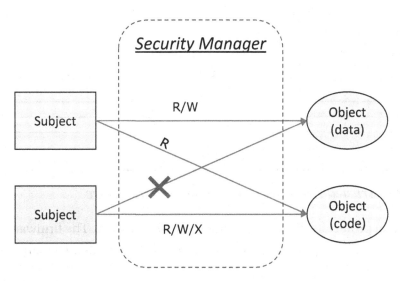

Figure 16-34. *Sandbox-Based Access Control*

Trusted Execution Environment

A trusted execution environment is independent of the normal execution environment. ARM TrustZone is one example. It runs in the secure world, which is independent of the normal world. The secure world is entered when the system receives a secure monitor call (SMC). The system management mode (SMM) in X86 architecture can also be an example. The system management interrupt (SMI) brings the system into SMM code and runs the code in system management RAM (SMRAM). Figure 16-35 shows a full picture of the rich execution environment (REE), also known as the normal world, and the trusted execution environment (TEE), also known as the secure world.

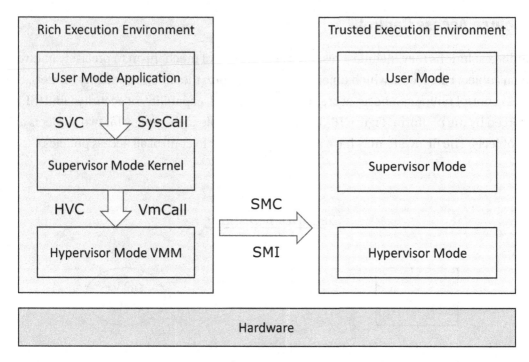

Figure 16-35. *Trusted Execution Environment Architecture*

The TEE can protect itself from being tampered by the REE. The firmware may use the TEE for security storage and secure processing, such as credential management or signature verification.

Please note that the trusted execution environment is a concept. There might be other implementations, such as Intel Software Guard Extension (SGX), RISC-V HEX Five MultiZone TEE, and RISC-V Keystone TEE. The GlobalPlatform organization has created a TEE committee to define an open security architecture for consumer and connected devices. Recently researchers invented the Capability Hardware Enhanced RISC Instructions (CHERI) which extend conventional hardware Instruction-Set Architectures (ISAs) with new architectural features to enable fine-grained memory protection and highly scalable software compartmentalization. CHERI supports ARM and RISC-V. We will discuss the details of TEEs in Chapter 17.

System Partitioning

The last option to contain the damage is partitioning. With partitioning,, we can run multiple logical systems on one physical system. On one motherboard, we can put multiple CPU sockets, multiple DIMM sockets, multiple flash sockets, multiple PCI device sockets, multiple interrupt controllers, and so on. Some of the devices and sockets are assigned to one system, and the rest are assigned to the other system. The two systems can communicate with each other via an internal bus, link, or network. See Figure 16-36.

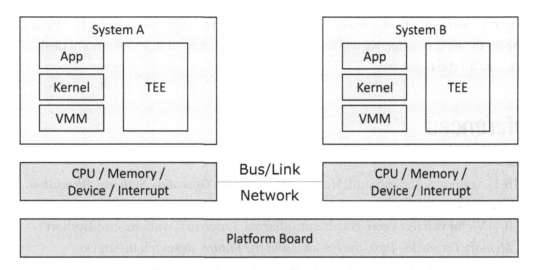

Figure 16-36. *System Partitioning*

One current example is the Baseboard Management Controller (BMC), Embedded Controller (EC), Intel Management Engine (ME), or AMD Platform Secure Processor (PSP). It is a standalone execution environment and has its own processor, memory, flash, and execution environment. The host system communicates with the ME via the Host Embedded Controller Interface (HECI) and communicates with the BMC via the Intelligent Platform Management Interface (IPMI) or RedFish interface. With this design approach, any damage in the host system firmware will not impact the BMC, ME, or PSP firmware.

Care must be taken that an isolated system does not mean a secure system. We have seen examples that a vulnerability in the BMC, EC, ME, or PSP causes the security properties to be broken. All secure design principles should also be applied to the isolated system. For example, the untrusted external input should be verified, all unnecessary external APIs should be removed, and the TCB should be kept as smaller as possible.

Summary

In this chapter, we discussed the design of the firmware kernel. The kernel can use code protection, address space layout randomization, and control flow guard to break exploits. The kernel may choose to implement the supervisor mode, hypervisor, trusted execution environment, or even system partitioning to contain the damage to a limited scope. In the next chapter, we will focus on the trusted execution environment design and usage for the firmware.

References

Book

[B-1] Andrew S. Tanenbaum, Herbert Bos, *Modern Operating Systems, 4th edition*, Pearson, 2014

[B-2] Victor van der Veen, Nitish dutt-Sharma, Lorenzo Cavallaro, and Herbert Bos, *Memory Errors: the Past, the Present, and the Future*, Research in Attacks, Intrusions, and Defenses, Volume 7462 of the series Lecture Notes in Computer Science pp 86-106. Springer, 2012, available at `https://rd.springer.com/chapter/10.1007/978-3-642-33338-5_5`

[B-3] Mark E. Russinovich, David A. Solomon, Alex Ionescu, *Windows Internals, 6th edition*, Microsoft Press, 2012

[B-4] Jim Smith, Ravi Nair, *Virtual Machines: Versatile Platforms for Systems and Processes*, Morgan Kaufmann, 2005

[B-5] Xiaoyu Ruan, *Platform Embedded Security Technology Revealed: Safeguarding the Future of Computing with Intel Embedded Security and Management Engine*, Apress, 2014

Conference, Journal, and Paper

[P-1] Matt Miller, "Trends, Challenges, and Strategic Shifts in the Software Vulnerability Mitigation Landscape," in *BlueHat IL 2019*, available at `https://github.com/microsoft/MSRC-Security-Research/blob/master/presentations/2019_02_BlueHatIL/2019_01%20-%20BlueHatIL%20-%20Trends%2C%20challenge%2C%20and%20shifts%20in%20software%20vulnerability%20mitigation.pdf`

[P-2] David Weston, "Advancing Windows Security," in *Platform Security Summit 2019*, available at `www.platformsecuritysummit.com/2019/speaker/weston/`

[P-3] Yunhai Zhang, "Liar Game: The Secret of Mitigation Bypass Techniques," in *Bluehat Shanghai 2019*, available at `www.microsoft.com/china/bluehatshanghai/2019/`

[P-4] Ken Johnson, Ma, Miller, "Exploit Mitigation Improvements in Windows 8," in *Blackhat US 2012*, available at `http://media.blackhat.com/bh-us-12/Briefings/M_Miller/BH_US_12_Miller_Exploit_Mitigation_Slides.pdf`

[P-5] Theo de Raadt, "Exploit Mitigation Techniques in OpenBSD," in *Tokyo PC Users Group, 2006*, available at `www.openbsd.org/papers/ven05-deraadt`

[P-6] Brad Spengler, "PaX presentation," `https://grsecurity.net/PaX-presentation.ppt`

[P-7] Dan Rosenberg, Jon Oberheide, "Stackjacking Your Way to grsecurity/PaX Bypass," in *Infiltrate 2011*, available at `https://jon.oberheide.org/files/stackjacking-hes11.pdf`

[P-8] Jiewen Yao, Vincent Zimmer, "A Tour Beyond BIOS Memory Map And Practices in UEFI BIOS," *EDKII whitepaper 2016*, available at `https://github.com/tianocoredocs/Docs/raw/master/White_Papers/A_Tour_Beyond_BIOS_Memory_Map_And_Practices_in_UEFI_BIOS_V2.pdf`

[P-9] Jiewen Yao, Vincent Zimmer, "A Tour Beyond BIOS- Memory Protection in UEFI BIOS," *EDKII whitepaper 2017*, available at `www.gitbook.com/book/edk2-docs/a-tour-beyond-bios-memory-protection-in-uefi-bios/details`

[P-10] Jiewen Yao, Vincent Zimmer, "A Tour Beyond BIOS Security Enhancement to Mitigate Buffer Overflow in UEFI," *EDKII whitepaper 2018*, available at `www.gitbook.com/book/edk2-docs/a-tour-beyond-bios-mitigate-buffer-overflow-in-ue/details`

[P-11] Tyler Durden, "Bypassing PaX ASLR Protection," in *Phrack Magazine July 2002*, available at `http://phrack.org/issues/59/9.html`

[P-12] Kurt Miller, "OpenBSD's Position Independent Executable (PIE) Implementation," in *DCBSDCon 2009*, available at `www.openbsd.org/papers/nycbsdcon08-pie/`

[P-13] Nergal, "The advanced return-into-lib(c) exploits: PaX case study," in *Phrack Magazine December 2001*, available at `http://phrack.org/issues/58/4.html`

[P-14] Martin Abadi, Mihai Budiu, Ulfar Erlingsson, Jay Ligatti, "Control-Flow Integrity – Principles, Implementations, and Applications," in *CCS05, ACM 2005*, available at `www.microsoft.com/en-us/research/wp-content/uploads/2005/11/ccs05.pdf`

[P-15] Shacham Hovav, "The geometry of innocent flesh on the bone: Returninto-libc without function calls (on the x86)," in *Proceedings of ACM Conference on Computer and Communications Security (CCS), 2007*, available at `https://hovav.net/ucsd/dist/geometry.pdf`

[P-16] FFRI, "Windows New Security Features – Control Flow Guard," FFRI report 2014, available at `www.ffri.jp/assets/files/monthly_research/MR201412_Control_Flow_Guard_ENG.pdf`

[P-17] PaX Team, "RAP: RIP ROP," in *H2HC 2015*, available at `https://pax.grsecurity.net/docs/PaXTeam-H2HC15-RAP-RIP-ROP.pdf`

[P-18] Dean Sullivan, Orlando Arias, Ahmad-Reza Sadeghi, Lucas Davi, Yier Jin, "Policy-Agnostic-Control-Flow-Integrity-Implementation," in Blackhat 2016, `www.blackhat.com/docs/eu-16/materials/eu-16-Sullivan-Towards-A-Policy-Agnostic-Control-Flow-Integrity-Implementation.pdf`

[P-19] Joao Moreira, "Drop the Rop: Fine Grained Control Flow Integrity for the Linux Kernel," in *Blackhat Asia 2017*, available at `www.blackhat.com/docs/asia-17/materials/asia-17-Moreira-Drop-The-Rop-Fine-Grained-Control-Flow-Integrity-For-The-Linux-Kernel.pdf`

[P-20] Jack Tang, "Exploring Control Flow Guard in Windows 10," `https://documents.trendmicro.com/assets/wp/exploring-control-flow-guard-in-windows10.pdf`

[P-21] Alexander Anisimov, "Defeating Microsoft Windows XP SP2 Heap protection and DEP bypass," 2004, available at `www.ptsecurity.com/ww-en/download/defeating-xpsp2-heap-protection.pdf`

[P-22] Ben Hawkes, "Attacking the Vista Heap," in *Blackhat US 2008*, available at `www.blackhat.com/presentations/bh-usa-08/Hawkes/BH_US_08_Hawkes_Attacking_Vista_Heap.pdf`

[P-23] John McDonald, Christopher Valasek, "Practical Windows XPSP3/2003 Heap Exploitation," in *Blackhat US 2009*, available at `www.blackhat.com/presentations/bh-usa-09/MCDONALD/BHUSA09-McDonald-WindowsHeap-PAPER.pdf`

[P-24] Paul Kocher, Jann Horn, Anders Fogh, Daniel Genkin, Daniel Gruss, Werner Haas, Mike Hamburg, Moritz Lipp, Stefan Mangard, Thomas Prescher, Michael Schwarz, Yuval Yarom, "Spectre Attacks: Exploiting Speculative Execution," 2018, available at `https://spectreattack.com/spectre.pdf`

[P-25] Moritz Lipp, Michael Schwarz, Daniel Gruss, Thomas Prescher, Werner Haas, Anders Fogh, Jann Horn, Stefan Mangard, Paul Kocher, Daniel Genkin, Yuval Yarom, Mike Hamburg, "Meltdown: Reading Kernel Memory from User Space," 2018, available at `https://meltdownattack.com/meltdown.pdf`

[P-26] Daniel Gruss, Moritz Lipp, Michael Schwarz, Richard Fellner, Clementine Maurice, Stefan Mangard, "KASLR is Dead: Long Live KASLR," in *ESSoS 2017*, `https://gruss.cc/files/kaiser.pdf`

[P-27] Vasileios P. Kemerlis, Michalis Polychronakis, Angelos D. Keromytis, "ret2dir: Rethinking kernel isolation," in *USENIX Security Symposium 2014*, available at `www.usenix.org/system/files/conference/usenixsecurity14/sec14-paper-kemerlis.pdf`

[P-28] Vasileios P. Kemerlis, Georgios Portokalidis, Angelos D. Keromytis, "kGuard: Lightweight Kernel Protection against Return-to-user Attacks," in *Proc. of USENIX Sec, 2012*, available at `www.usenix.org/system/files/conference/usenixsecurity12/sec12-final143.pdf`

[P-29] Andrew S. Tanenbaum, "Lessons Learned from 30 Years of MINIX," in *Communications of the ACM 2016*, available at `https://cacm.acm.org/magazines/2016/3/198874-lessons-learned-from-30-years-of-minix/fulltext`

[P-30] Ronald Aigner, "Communication in Microkernel-Based Operating Systems," 2010, available at `https://pdfs.semanticscholar.org/1cd7/edefcdd4cec5babb6b5b2d9e6572aa27a046.pdf`

[P-31] Hermann Hartig, Jork Loser, Frank Mehnert, Lars Reuther, Martin Pohlack, Alexander Warg, "An I/O Architecture for Microkernel-Based Operating Systems," 2003, available at `https://pdfs.semanticscholar.org/8559/e6c101b14511002dd5178097f7d2d2acb247.pdf`

[P-32] Kevin Elphinstone, Gernot Heiser, "From L3 to seL4: What Have We Learnt in 20 Years of L4 Microkernels?" in SOSP '13 Proceedings of the Twenty-Fourth ACM Symposium on Operating Systems Principles, 2013, available at `http://sigops.org/s/conferences/sosp/2013/papers/p133-elphinstone.pdf`

[P-33] Gernot Heiser, Kevin Elphinstone, "L4 Microkernels: The Lessons from 20 Years of Research and Deployment," in *ACM Transactions on Computer Systems, 2016*, available at `https://dl.acm.org/doi/pdf/10.1145/2893177`

[P-34] Geoffrey Lee, Charles Gray, "L4/Darwin: Evolving UNIX," 2016, `https://ts.data61.csiro.au/publications/papers/Lee_Gray_06.pdf`

[P-35] Ivan Krstic, "Behind the scenes of iOS and Mac Security," in *Blackhat US 2019*, available at `https://i.blackhat.com/USA-19/Thursday/us-19-Krstic-Behind-The-Scenes-Of-IOS-And-Mas-Security.pdf`

[P-36] Chia-Che Tsai, "Library OS is the New Container," the Linux foundation open source summit 2017, `https://events19.linuxfoundation.org/wp-content/uploads/2017/12/Library-OS-is-the-New-Container-Why-is-Library-OS-A-Better-Option-for-Compatibility-and-Sandboxing-Chia-Che-Tsai-UC-Berkeley.pdf`

[P-37] J. P. Anderson, "Computer security technology planning study," in *Technical Report ESD-TR-73-51, vols I & II, AD-758 206, USAF Electronic Systems Division, 1972*

[P-38] Gerald J. Popek, Robert P. Goldberg, "Formal Requirements for Virtualizable Third Generation Architectures," in *ACM SIGOPS Operating Systems Review 17:412-421, January 1974*

[P-39] John Scott Robin, Cynthia E. Irvine, "Analysis of the Intel Pentium's Ability to Support a Secure Virtual Machine Monitor," in *Proc. 9th USENIX Security Symposium 2000*, available at `www.usenix.org/legacy/events/sec2000/full_papers/robin/robin.pdf`

[P-40] Jiewen Yao, Vincent Zimmer, "A Tour Beyond BIOS – Launching a VMM in EDK II," Intel Whitepaper 2015,
`https://software.intel.com/sites/default/files/managed/7a/3c/a_tour_beyond_bios_launching_vmm_in_efi_developer_kit_ii_0.pdf`

[P-41] Craig Disselkoen, John Renner, Conrad Watt, Tal Garfnkel, Amit Levy, Deian Stefan, "Progressive Memory Safety for WebAssembly," in Association for Computing Machinery, 2019, available at `https://dl.acm.org/doi/pdf/10.1145/3337167.3337171`

[P-42] Dayeol Lee, David Kohlbrenner, Shweta Shinde, Krste Asanovic, Dawn Song, "Keystone: An Open Framework for Architecting TEEs," in *OSEW 2019*, available at `https://arxiv.org/pdf/1907.10119.pdf`, `https://keystone-enclave.org/open-source-enclaves-workshop/slides/OSEW19_DayeolLee_UCBerkeley.pdf`

[P-43] Cesare Garlati, "Multi Zone Trusted Execution Environment Free And Open API," in *RISC-V Workshop, 2019*, available at `https://content.riscv.org/wp-content/uploads/2019/06/15.20-An-open-source-API-proposal-for-a-multi-domain-RISC-V-TEE-Cesare-Garlati-Hex-Five-12-JUN-19.pdf`

[P-44] Robert N. M. Watson, Jonathan Woodruff, Peter G. Neumann, Simon W. Moore, Jonathan Anderson, David Chisnall, Nirav Dave, Brooks Davis, Khilan Gudka, Ben Laurie, Steven J. Murdoch, Robert Norton, Michael Roe, Stacey Son, Munraj Vadera, "CHERI: A Hybrid Capability-System Architecture for Scalable Software Compartmentalization," in *IEEE Symposium on Security and Privacy SP, 2015*, available at `www.cl.cam.ac.uk/research/security/ctsrd/pdfs/201505-oakland2015-cheri-compartmentalization.pdf`

[P-45] Shai Hasarfaty, Yanai Moyal, "Behind the Scenes of Intel Security and Manageability Engine," in *BlackHat US 2019*, `http://i.blackhat.com/USA-19/Wednesday/us-19-Hasarfaty-Behind-The-Scenes-Of-Intel-Security-And-Manageability-Engine.pdf`

[P-46] Dmitriy Evdokimov, Alexander Ermolov, Maksim Malyutin, "Intel AMT Stealth Breakthrough," in *BlackHat 2017*, available at `www.blackhat.com/docs/us-17/thursday/us-17-Evdokimov-Intel-AMT-Stealth-Breakthrough.pdf`

[P-47] Fabien Périgaud, Alexandre Gazet, Joffrey Czarny, "Backdooring your server through its BMC," in *SSTIC 2018*, available at `www.sstic.org/media/SSTIC2018/SSTIC-actes/subverting_your_server_through_its_bmc_the_hpe_ilo/SSTIC2018-Slides-subverting_your_server_through_its_bmc_the_hpe_ilo4_case-gazet_perigaud_czarny.pdf`

[P-48] Nico Waisman, Matias Sebastian Soler, "The Unbearable Lightness of BMCs," in *BlackHat US 2018*, available at `http://i.blackhat.com/us-18/Wed-August-8/us-18-Waisman-Soler-The-Unbearable-Lightness-of-BMC.pdf`

[P-49] Fabien Perigaud, Alexandre Gazet, Joffrey Czarny, "Turning your BMC into a revolving door," in ZeroNight 2018, `https://airbus-seclab.github.io/ilo/ZERONIGHTS2018-Slides-EN-Turning_your_BMC_into_a_revolving_door-perigaud-gazet-czarny.pdf`

[P-50] Ralf-Philipp Weinmann , "The hidden nemesis," in *27th Chaos Communication Congress (27C3) 2010*, available at `https://comsecuris.com/slides/rpw-27c3-thmbec.pdf`

[P-51] Alex Matrosov, Alexandre Gazet, "Breaking Through Another Side," in *Blackhat US 2019*, available at `http://i.blackhat.com/USA-19/Thursday/us-19-Matrosov-Breaking-Through-Another-Side-Bypassing-Firmware-Security-Boundaries-From-Embedded-Controller.pdf`

[P-52] Sheila Ayelen Berta , "Backdooring Hardware Devices by Injecting Malicious Payloads on Microcontrollers," in Blackhat US 2019, available at `http://i.blackhat.com/USA-19/Thursday/us-19-Berta-Backdooring-Hardware-Devices-By-Injecting-Malicious-Payloads-On-Microcontrollers.pdf`

Specification and Guideline

[S-1] Intel, "Control Flow Enforcement Technology Specification," 2019, available at `https://software.intel.com/sites/default/files/managed/4d/2a/control-flow-enforcement-technology-preview.pdf`

[S-2] Intel, "Intel 64 and IA-32 Architecture Software Developer Manuals," 2019, available at `https://software.intel.com/en-us/articles/intel-sdm`

[S-3] AMD, "AMD Architecture Programmer's Manual," 2019, available at `www.amd.com/en/support/tech-docs`

[S-4] GlobalPlatform, "TEE System Architecture," 2018, available at `https://globalplatform.org/specs-library/?filter-committee=tee`

[S-5] Intel, "IPMI Specification," 2013, available at `www.intel.com/content/www/us/en/products/docs/servers/ipmi/ipmi-second-gen-interface-spec-v2-rev1-1.html`

[S-6] DMTF, "RedFish Specification," 2019, available at `www.dmtf.org/standards/redfish`

Web

[W-1] Secured-core PCs: A brief showcase of chip-to-cloud security against kernel attacks, `www.microsoft.com/security/blog/2020/03/17/secured-core-pcs-a-brief-showcase-of-chip-to-cloud-security-against-kernel-attacks/`

[W-2] Enhance Memory Protections in IE10, `http://blogs.msdn.com/b/ie/archive/2012/03/12/enhanced-memory-protections-in-ie10.aspx`

[W-3] Microsoft Integrity Policy Enforcement, `https://microsoft.github.io/ipe/`, `https://github.com/microsoft/ipe`

[W-4] Preventing the exploitation of user mode heap corruption vulnerabilities, 2009, `https://blogs.technet.microsoft.com/srd/2009/08/04/preventing-the-exploitation-of-user-mode-heap-corruption-vulnerabilities/`

[W-5] Mitigating Arbitrary Native Code Execution, `https://blogs.windows.com/msedgedev/2017/02/23/mitigating-arbitrary-native-code-execution/`

[W-6] PaX Home Page, `https://pax.grsecurity.net/`

[W-7] EDKII Security Extension Package, `https://github.com/jyao1/SecurityEx`

[W-8] seL4, `https://sel4.systems/`

[W-9] Microsoft Singularity OS, `www.microsoft.com/en-us/research/project/singularity/`

[W-10] Mirage OS, `https://mirage.io/`

[W-11] TianoCore EDK II, `https://github.com/tianocore`

[W-12] coreboot, `www.coreboot.org/`

[W-13] ThreadX, `https://github.com/azure-rtos/threadx`

[W-14] FreeRTOS, `https://github.com/aws/amazon-freertos`

[W-15] Zephyr, `www.zephyrproject.org/`

[W-16] Yocto, `www.yoctoproject.org/`

[W-17] OpenBmc, `www.openbmc.org/`

[W-18] Chromium EC, `https://chromium.googlesource.com/chromiumos/platform/ec/+/master/README.md`

[W-19] ACRN, `https://projectacrn.org/`

[W-20] STM and FRM, `https://github.com/jyao1/STM`

[W-21] Bareflank, `https://github.com/Bareflank/hypervisor`

[W-22] MiniVisor, https://github.com/tandasat/MiniVisorPkg

[W-23] ACPICA, www.acpica.org/

[W-24] x86 emulator, https://github.com/ardbiesheuvel/X86EmulatorPkg

[W-25] embedded java, www.oracle.com/java/technologies/java-embedded.html

[W-26] .Net Micro Framework, http://informatix.miloush.net/microframework/

[W-27] WebAssembly, https://webassembly.org/

[W-28] WebAssembly System Interface, https://wasi.dev/

[W-29] WebAssembly Security, https://webassembly.org/docs/security/

[W-30] wasm micro runtime, https://github.com/bytecodealliance/
wasm-micro-runtime

[W-31] wasm micro runtime in UEFI/EDKII, https://github.com/jyao1/
EfiSandbox

[W-32] ARM TrustZone, https://developer.arm.com/ip-products/
security-ip/trustzone

[W-33] Global Platform TEE, https://globalplatform.org/technical-
committees/trusted-execution-environment-tee-committee/

[W-34] Keystone Enclave, https://keystone-enclave.org/

[W-35] HEX Five, https://hex-five.com/

[W-36] CHERI, www.cl.cam.ac.uk/research/security/ctsrd/cheri/

CHAPTER 17

Trusted Execution Environment

A trusted execution environment (TEE) means a secure area which can guarantee the confidentiality and integrity of the code and data inside of this area. Usually a TEE is an isolated execution environment. It may be implemented as a special secure mode of the main processor, or a TEE could be maintained by a secure coprocessor.

CPU-Based TEE

First, let's take a look at the CPU-based TEE.

X86 SMM

Dating back to 1990, system management mode (SMM) was introduced in the Intel 386SL processor. Just like its name, SMM is designed for system management, such as system event handling, deeper sleep power management, voltage regulator management, and special wakeup support. Later, people found this isolated environment to be useful for security features, such as flash lock, UEFI secure boot authenticated variables, and TCG MOR2.

© Jiewen Yao and Vincent Zimmer 2020
J. Yao and V. Zimmer, *Building Secure Firmware*, https://doi.org/10.1007/978-1-4842-6106-4_17

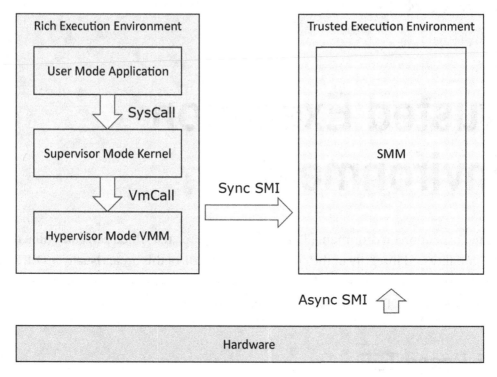

Figure 17-1. *SMM TEE*

Figure 17-1 shows the SMM TEE. The SMM execution environment is in a special portion of memory known as system management RAM (SMRAM). When the CPU receives a system management interrupt (SMI), it switches from the normal execution mode to the SMM. The normal world can trigger a synchronous SMI. For example, writing a value to the I/O port 0xB2 can trigger a synchronous SMI, also called a software SMI. Similarly, writing a value to the power control register can trigger a sleep control SMI when entering the S1, S3, S4, or S5 sleep state. The hardware can generate asynchronous SMIs based upon system events. For example, a general-purpose input (GPI) can be configured as a source of an SMI. In a normal operating system, when a user presses the power button, it triggers an ACPI System Control Interrupt (SCI) and is handled by the operating system ACPI power management subsystem. However, in the pre-OS boot phase, the ACPI SCI has not been enabled yet. In this phase, the power button event is configured as an SMI event. When a user presses the power button while booting the firmware, the event is delivered to SMM, and the handler for that event will shut down the machine.

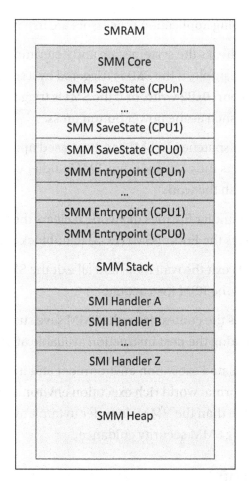

Figure 17-2. *SMM Memory Layout*

Figure 17-2 shows a typical memory layout. Each CPU has its own SMM entry point code and SMM save state inside of SMRAM.

The general flow for an SMI is shown here:

1) When the CPU receives an SMI, it saves the current context into the SMM SaveState buffer, such as RAX, RBX, RCD, RDX, RSP (stack pointer), RIP (instruction pointer), CS (code segment), GDT, IDT, and so on.

2) The CPU switches to the SMM entry point.

3) All CPUs rendezvous, and only a single processor is selected to continue.

4) The selected processor enters the SMM core.

5) All of the remaining application processors are in a wait loop.

6) The SMM core checks the system state and determines the source of the SMI, for example, if the SMI is triggered by a software SMI, such as the I/O port 0xB2 write, or if the SMI is triggered by a hardware event such as the power button press.

7) The SMM core dispatches an SMI handler based upon the source of the SMI and lets the corresponding SMI handler commence execution to finish the work.

8) When the SMI handler finishes the work, it clears the SMI source indicator and sets the End-of-SMI (EOS) to unblock the next SMI.

9) All waiting CPUs exit the wait loop, and all exit the SMM environment via the RSM instruction.

10) The CPU restores the context from the SMM save state buffer and continues executing the next instruction available after the SMI.

Because SMM is an isolated execution environment and it can touch all system resources, including the normal world rich execution environment, people usually think SMM has a higher privilege than the VMM. In order to implement SMM correctly, we need to follow the following SMM security guidance.

Secure World Isolation

The SMM environment must be isolated from the non-SMM environment.

Memory Isolation

The SMM environment execution occurs in a special memory location named system management RAM (SMRAM). The SMRAM region is part of normal DRAM. In X86 systems, there are two regions that can be used as SMRAM. One is at the 0xA0000 – 0xBFFFF low memory region, which is called the compatibility segment (CSEG). The other is at the top of the DRAM via memory sequestered from OS or normal world usage, which is called the top segment (TSEG). The memory controller has a SMRAM base register and SMRAM control register. Once SMRAM is closed, the SMRAM can only be accessed while in the CPU SMM. If the CPU is in normal mode, the memory controller will ignore SMRAM write requests and always return all one's for SMRAM read requests. Figure 17-3 shows the SMRAM TSEG and CSEG location in the system memory map.

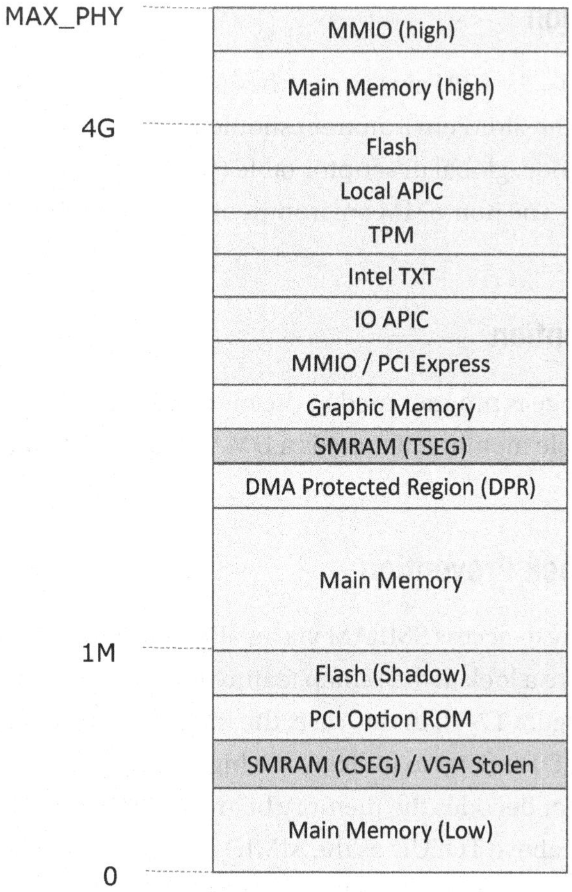

Figure 17-3. *SMRAM in the System Memory Layout*

Configuration Lockdown

In the memory controller, the SMRAM configuration can be locked so that it cannot be changed until the next reset.

In former days, some firmware code forgot to lock the SMRAM region. As such, the attacker could open the SMRAM region, inject malicious code into SMRAM, and then close it. This vulnerability can be mitigated by forcing a SMRAM lock to occur before the firmware releases control to any third-party code, including the operating system. It is easy to discover such an issue by using a vulnerability scanning tool. We will discuss more details in Chapter 18.

CPU State Protection

When an SMI happens, the CPU always switches to an entry point defined by the SMM environment setup. The SMM environment should be set up by the SMM code, such as the CPU execution mode, global descriptor table (GDT), interrupt descriptor table (IDT), page table, and so on. The non-SMM environment cannot set the SMM entry point or any SMM context.

DMA Attack Prevention

Once the SMRAM range is programmed in the memory controller, the SMRAM DRAM is no longer DMA capable memory. If there is a DMA read or write request sent to SMRAM, it will be blocked.

Address Alias Attack Prevention

If the system has a way to access SMRAM via an alias address, it is a potential vulnerability. Let's take a look at the remap feature found in some memory controllers as an example (see Figure 17-4). In this case, the memory controller has a Top of Low Usable DRAM (TOLUD) register to indicate the highest address for DRAM below 4GB. The memory controller decodes the memory below TOLUD as usable DRAM and decodes the memory above TOLUD as the MMIO resource range, such as the flash device, local Advanced Programmable Interrupt Controller (APIC), Trusted Platform Module (TPM), Intel Trusted Execution Technology (TXT), I/O ACPI, and PCI express configuration region.

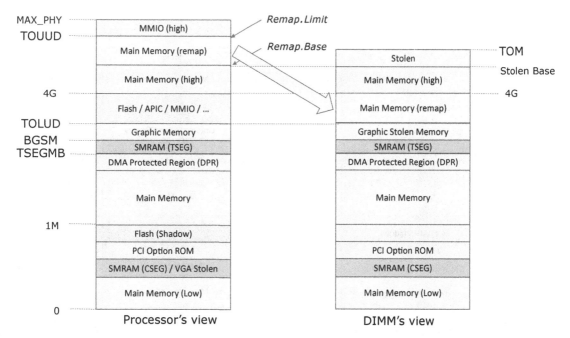

Figure 17-4. *Memory Remap*

Now the problem is as follows: if a system has more memory above the TOLUD, how can the CPU access that memory? The memory controller has registers to define a remap region (REMAP_BASE, REMAP_LIMIT) above 4GB. The memory above the TOLUD is mapped to the remap region. The right-hand side of Figure 17-4 shows the memory layout from the DIMM's view, and the left-hand side of Figure 17-4 shows the memory layout from the processor's view. With the remap register enabled, the system can access the memory between TOLUD and the 4GB limit via the memory addresses between REMAP.BASE and REMAP.LIMIT.

This memory address aliasing may be used to attack SMM. The attacker may purposely set up the remap region to reference SMRAM on the DIMM. Now the act of accessing the memory addresses between REMAP.BASE and REMAP.LIMIT will resolve into an access to the SMRAM region bypassing the SMRAM protection. See Figure 17-5. As mitigation, the silicon configuration register must be locked down to prevent the reconfiguration.

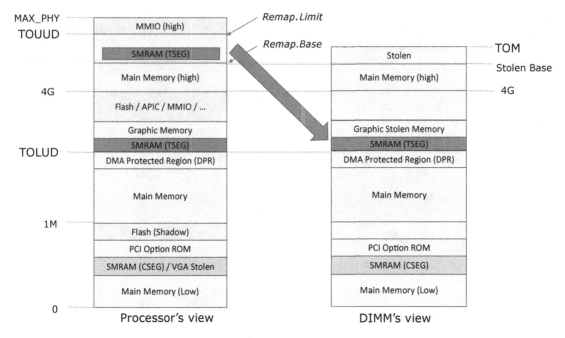

Figure 17-5. *Memory Remap Attack*

Cache Poisoning Attack Prevention

In the old days, the SMM environment and normal world shared the same memory cache setting registers, namely, the Memory Type Range Registers (MTRRs). This design is vulnerable to the cache poisoning attack. See Figure 17-6.

The steps to attack a platform with just MTRRs are as follows:

1) The attacker sets up the MTRRs to mark the SMRAM region to be of write-back cache type.

2) The attacker writes malicious SMM code to the SMRAM address. Because the address range is write-back cacheable, the code is written into the cache. NOTE: The memory controller only controls data writes to SMRAM in the DRAM, but the memory controller cannot control data writes into the cache because the cache is managed by the CPU.

3) The attacker triggers an SMI immediately. Now the CPU needs to execute the code in SMRAM. The CPU finds the data in the cache and just executes the data in the cache. Thus, the SMRAM protection is bypassed.

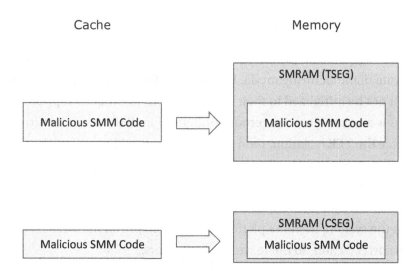

Figure 17-6. *SMRAM Cache Poisoning Attack*

In order to mitigate this attack, the hardware introduced a new SMRAM range register (SMRR) for SMRAM. This SMRR can only be accessed from inside of SMRAM. The cache ability of SMRAM is managed by the SMRR instead of the MTRR. If the system is in non-SMM, no matter what the MTRR value is, the SMRAM is always treated as not cacheable. During the firmware boot, the SMM code must set up the SMRR to cover the whole TSEG region. Care must be taken to ensure that the SMRR is similar to MTRR and uses the same base and mask for the memory range. That means the SMRAM size must be a power of two and the SMRAM base address must be a power of two aligned. Each CPU only has one SMRR, and this SMRR covers the TSEG region. As such, the CSEG region must not be used for SMRAM because it is vulnerable to a cache poisoning attack.

Debugger Attack Prevention

The non-SMM environment may set up debug registers, performance monitoring, branch profiling, processor trace (PT), and so on. All those advanced feature registers will be disabled at the entry point of SMM. If a special SMI handler wants to use these registers, it should save the current OS context, use the resource in the SMM context, and then restore the original OS context prior to exiting SMM.

Care must be taken when using these advanced features to avoid information leaks or integrity tampering issues in SMM. We will discuss more in a future section.

Non-production Mode Prevention

The systems are shipped with production mode. However, in some cases, the system allows to activate manufacturing mode. In this manufacturing mode, some special lock registers might not be initialized to their secure settings in order to support the system provision. This is an extremely dangerous configuration. If the manufacturing mode does not enforce the TEE isolation, then the platform should not allow the user to trigger booting in manufacturing mode. Otherwise, the attacker could perform a physical attack to activate the manufacturing mode and break the system.

If the system really wants to support the manufacturing mode to recover the system or to maintain the system, then the platform should ensure all hardware security settings are still set up correctly and do not leave any backdoors.

Secure World Enabling Enforcement

The SMI can be configured to be enabled or disabled. There is a global SMI enable (GBL_SMI_EN) control in some chipsets. The attacker may disable GBL_SMI_EN to disable the ability to generate SMIs and therefore remove access to features that take advantage of SMM-based protection, such as flash lock protection. As such, the BIOS needs to set the SMI lock (SMI_LOCK) in the chipset to prevent modification of GBL_SMI_EN in order to prevent such an SMI disable attack.

Hot Plug Consideration

The SMM implementation needs to support hot plug features. We have discussed the details of CPU and memory hot plug support in Chapter 8. To maintain the integrity of SMM, the newly added CPU should never execute any code from the untrusted world.

Side Channel Attack Prevention

Side channel attacks in SMRAM are also possible. For example, if an SMI handler contains the code pattern (index-based array size validation) from the Spectre variant 1, the speculative cache load can be exploited to read secrets from SMRAM. The software in SMM must follow the generic side channel mitigation guidelines to prevent the attacks, such as Spectre and Meltdown. Last but not least, the SMM implementation should stuff the Return Stack Buffer (RSB) before returning from SMM.

Secure Normal World Interaction

The SMM environment needs to interact with the non-SMM environment.

Normal World Code Execution Prevention

The SMM code must never call into the non-SMM code after the SMRAM environment is locked. Otherwise, the attacker can prepare code in the non-SMM environment that the SMM code calls and then trigger the SMI handler to escalate the privilege for that code. In older days, we relied upon each SMI handler to follow the rule of "no callout," but we kept observing the appearance of vulnerable SMI handlers. For example, invisiblethingslab demonstrated how to use an SMI to attack the hypervisor in 2019. The ThinkPwn attack demonstrated how to use SMI to burn a new flash image in 2016.

A good mitigation for code injection attacks against SMM is to use the SMM page table to mark the non-SMM region as non-executable. As such, an SMM callout will trigger the page fault exception. The page table management might be complicated. Today, newer CPUs have the SMM_CODE_CHECK feature. The SMM environment just needs to set a CPU model-specific register (MSR) to enable the SMM_CODE_CHECK capability. The CPU can determine the boundaries of the SMM region by the SMRR, and the SMM callout will trigger the machine check exception by the CPU. This is similar to the Supervisor Mode Execute Prevention (SMEP) or Privileged Execute-Never (PXN) feature – the higher privilege code should not execute the code in the lower-privilege region.

Normal World Data Access Prevention

The SMM environment has the capability to access any memory region by default. That means that a vulnerable SMI handler may access any OS memory or hypervisor memory during runtime, including that which contains secrets. In order to mitigate such risks, the SMM kernel should set the OS or hypervisor memory to be non-present in the SMM page table. This is similar to the Supervisor Mode Access Prevention (SMAP) or Privileged Access-Never (PAN) feature.

Normal World Communication Verification

A software SMI handler needs to exchange data with the non-SMM environment. The software SMI is similar to a system call (from a user application into the OS kernel) or a hyper call (from the OS into the hypervisor). The parameters of the software SMI can be in a global SMM communication area, a general-purpose register (GPR), or a scratch silicon register. Because this data is from an untrusted source, the SMI handler must verify the data before using it. For example, the SMI handler must verify the data length to prevent a buffer overflow. The SMI handler must verify the data location to prevent a confused deputy attack. We will discuss more details in the next section.

Normal World System Resource Access Check

The SMI handler may also need to access system resources, including but not limited to memory mapped I/O (MMIO), I/O, PCI configuration space, and CPU model-specific registers (MSRs).

Figure 17-7 shows the SMM page table setup for the non-SMM memory.

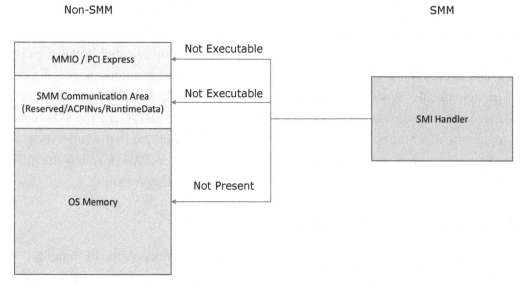

Figure 17-7. *SMM Page Table Setup for non-SMM*

Confused Deputy Attack Prevention

In the context of computer security, a confused deputy means the more privileged program is tricked by another program into misusing its authority on the system. Because of the high privilege of the SMM environment, an SMI handler might be a confused deputy. An attacker may take advantage of an SMI vulnerability to escalate the attacker's privilege.

Pointer in the Communication Buffer

The communication buffer is used for the parameter passing between the SMI handler and the OS agent. According to Figure 17-8, the valid SMM communication buffer should be in the global SMM communication area. This area should only be in OS reserved memory, ACPI non-volatile storage (NVS) memory, or UEFI runtime memory. For a given SMI handler, the data structure of the SMM communication buffer is predefined. Usually it contains a Globally Unique Identifier (GUID) to identify the buffer owner, a buffer length, a function identifier (ID), a return status, and a payload. There might be a case that the payload contains a buffer pointer or an offset to indicate the location of the next-level data structure. Ideally, the next-level communication buffer should also be in the global SMM communication area. See Figure 17-8.

SMM Communication

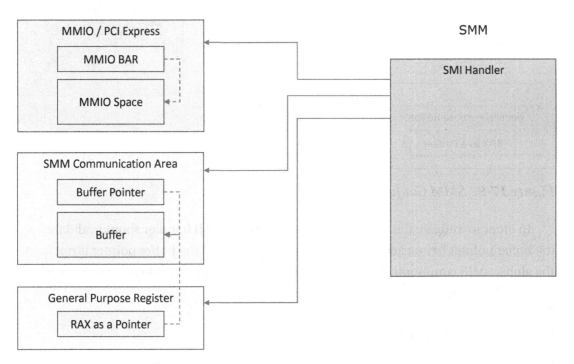

Figure 17-8.   *Normal SMM Communication*

However, because the communication buffer is controlled by the non-SMM environment, the attacker may conduct a confused deputy attack by creating a buffer pointer to point to a target SMRAM. See Figure 17-9. If the buffer is used to hold the

returned data from the SMM, the SMM needs to write the data to the location pointed –
that is, the target SMRAM. The OS agent in the non-SMM environment cannot write the
target SMRAM, but the SMI handler can. This SMI handler acts like a confused deputy.

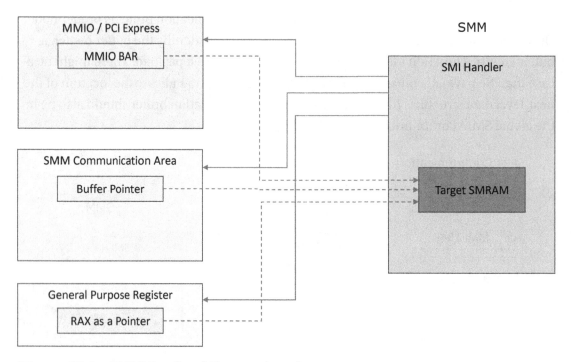

Figure 17-9. *SMM Confused Deputy Attack*

In order to mitigate the confused deputy attack, the SMI handler should validate
the buffer pointer before accessing the data in the buffer. If the buffer pointer is not in
the global SMM communication area, such as OS memory or the MMIO space, the SMI
handler should return with an error status immediately.

General-Purpose Register

Sometimes the communication buffer pointer is indicated by a general-purpose register
(GPR), such as RAX or RDX. The SMM confused deputy attack can also be applied in this
case. The SMI handler should perform the same check for the GPR before accessing the
data indicated by the GPR and return an error if the buffer pointer is not in the global
SMM communication area. Figures 17-8 and 17-9 also show the concept.

MMIO Base Address Register

Besides the pointer in the communication buffer and the general-purpose register technique, the memory mapped I/O (MMIO) base address registers (BARs) can also be used for the confused deputy attack. For example, the flash update SMI handler may need to access the Serial Peripheral Interface (SPI) BAR to unlock and lock the flash region access. The attacker may modify the SPI BAR to target SMRAM and trigger a flash write request, such as the UEFI variable write. Then the flash update SMI handler will write the SPI configuration to target SMRAM instead of the MMIO of the flash part. The mitigation should be to check if the MMIO BAR is a valid MMIO address. If it is not, then this request should be aborted. Figures 17-8 and 17-9 also show the concept.

Critical Resource Protection

In the preceding example, the attack target is the SMRAM region because the OS agent cannot normally access it. Another attack target is critical MMIO regions, such as the Intel Virtualization Technology for Directed I/O (VT-d) configuration space. Usually, VT-d is set up by the OS kernel or the hypervisor to resist DMA attacks. As such, the VT-d region is protected. The malicious OS agent may modify the SPI BAR to let it point to the VT-d configuration space to perform the confused deputy attack. See Figure 17-10.

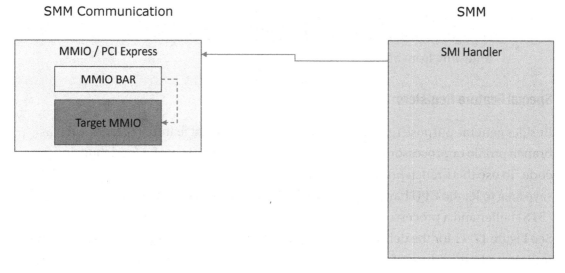

Figure 17-10. *SMM Confused Deputy Attack for MMIO*

In order to mitigate such an attack, the SMI handler must have knowledge regarding the ownership of the MMIO or PCI express configuration space:

1) SMM-owned configuration space: For this case, the configuration space should only be accessed in SMM. The SMM environment may choose to lock the MMIO space to prevent the attack from the OS. The possible mitigation includes to lock the SMM access control policy, lock the BIOS flash access, and lock the TOLUD register and remap register.

2) OS-owned configuration space: For this case, the configuration space should not be accessed in SMM to prevent a confused deputy attack. The SMI handler needs to perform the check for every configuration access to make sure it does not overlap with OS-owned configuration space. For example, the VT-d configuration space should be owned by the OS. When the SMM environment accesses any MMIO region, it needs to ensure that the MMIO region does not overlap with the VT-d configuration space.

3) Shared configuration space: For this case, the configuration space can be accessed by both SMM and the OS. There is no security risk, but there is functionality risk. The SMM should ensure that configuration updates from SMM will not impact the OS after returning from SMM.

Special Feature Registers

Besides general-purpose registers, the CPU includes special feature registers, such as branch profile or processor trace. A trace of taken branches is useful for debugging the code. To use this branch profile feature, the software needs to set up a debug store (DS) save area to let the CPU hardware collect the branch records in a branch trace store (BTS) buffer and a processor event-based sampling (PEBS) record in a PEBS buffer. See Figure 17-11 for the debug store save area layout. The IA32_DS_AREA MSR register indicates a base address of a DS save area. The DS save area includes address pointers to the BTS buffer and the PEBS buffer. The SMM environment may set up the DS save area for profiling and debugging purposes. Because the BTS buffer and PEBS buffer need to be large enough to hold all useful information, SMM may use non-SMRAM memory for this storage. However, if the DS area is in non-SMRAM, the attacker may change the BTS buffer base and PEBS buffer base to point to SMRAM as a confused deputy attack. If the BTS buffer or PEBS buffer is in non-SMRAM, the attacker may collect branch information regarding SMM execution which might lead to an information leak.

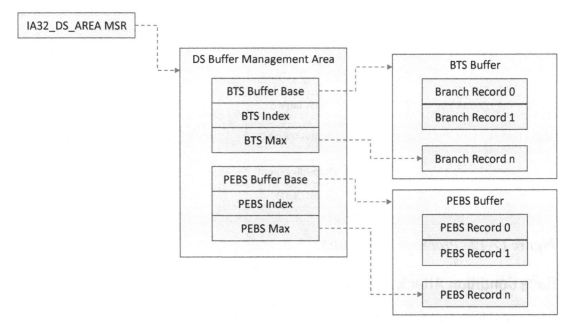

Figure 17-11. *Debug Store Save Area*

Processor trace (PT) is an advanced feature to trace the program flow information, such as branch targets and branch taken/not taken indications, and the program-induced mode-related information, such as CR3 changes. PT uses physical address directly, and the trace output stores bypass the caches and the TLBs to minimize the performance impact. See Figure 17-12 for the process trace required memory layout. The IA32_RTIT_OUTPUT_BASE MSR indicates the base address of the Table of Physical Addresses (ToPA). The ToPA entry indicates a set of output regions used by the CPU hardware to collect the trace information. The ToPA is a linked list. The last entry of the ToPA is the base address of the next ToPA. Similar to BTS, the SMM environment may also use PT for tracing or debugging purposes. The ToPA and the output region should be set up correctly to prevent a confused deputy attack or information leak.

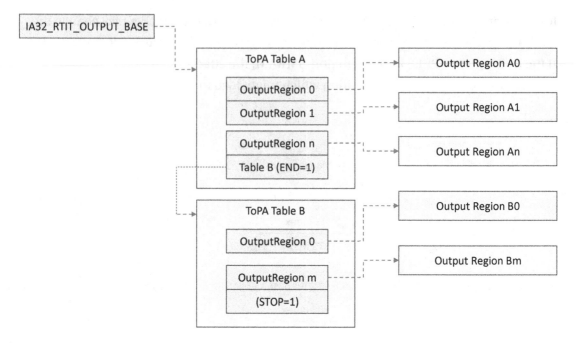

Figure 17-12. *Processor Trace ToPA*

Race Condition Attack Prevention

Race conditions are another type of common attack on SMM communication.

Communication Buffer Process

Because the communication buffer is provided by an untrusted OS agent, the SMI
handler needs to perform a sanity check before processing the communication buffer
contents. For example, if the communication buffer contains a new BIOS image and the
OS agent requests the SMI handler to update the BIOS, the SMI handler must verify the
digital signature of the BIOS image before it updates the BIOS flash.

When an SMI handler processes the communication buffer, the Time-of-Check/
Time-of-Use (TOC/TOU) attack should be considered. See Figure 17-13. The SMI
handler checks the communication buffer and uses the communication buffer. Between
those two steps, a malicious OS agent or a DMA agent may modify the communication
buffer because it is visible to the normal world. As such, the contents used may be
different from the contents checked by the SMI handler.

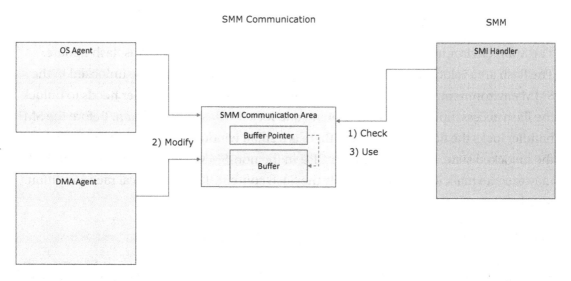

Figure 17-13. *SMM Communication TOC/TOU*

As a mitigation, the SMI handler should copy all the communication buffer contents from the SMM communication area to the SMRAM region, perform the check, use the data inside of the SMRAM immediately, and then copy the results back to the SMM communication area. The gist is that the check and use action happens in one SMI and the content that is both checked and used resides inside of SMRAM. As such, the OS agent and DMA agent cannot modify the SMRAM variant of the buffer. If the communication buffer includes a pointer, the pointed data should be copied into SMRAM too. See Figure 17-14.

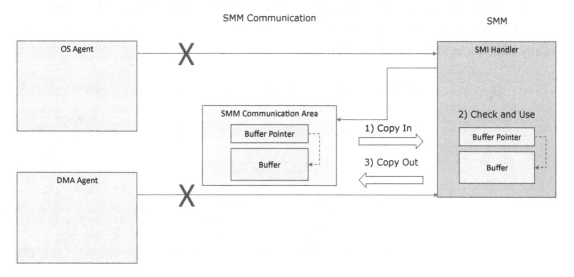

Figure 17-14. *SMM Communication Process*

Register Unlock Process

The SMM environment can be used to perform a secure action, such as flash update. The flash area is locked in the non-SMM environment and can only be unlocked in the SMM environment. In order to update the flash region, the SMI handler needs to unlock the flash access, update the flash content, and lock the flash access again. Before the SMI handler locks the flash access again, there is a small window that the flash device is in the unlocked state. If there is another CPU in the non-SMM environment, then this CPU may execute malicious code to modify the flash content. This is a typical race condition attack. See Figure 17-15.

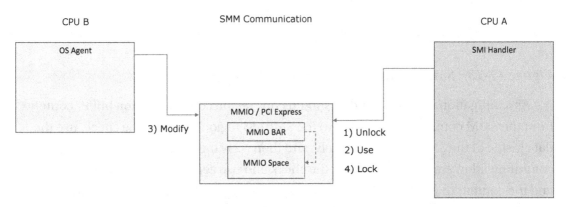

Figure 17-15. *SMM Register Unlock Race Condition*

In order to mitigate this attack, the SMM kernel should try to pull all CPUs into the SMM environment before the SMI handler process that performs the unlock action. Also, the SMI handler should check if all CPUs are in SMM and abort the unlock action if there is any CPU not in SMM. See Figure 17-16.

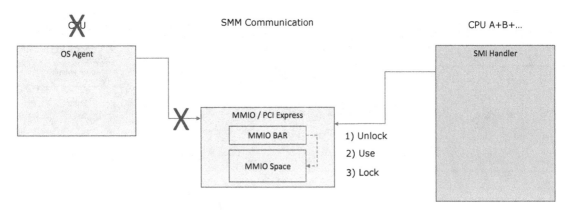

Figure 17-16. *SMM Register Unlock Process*

Information Leak Prevention

As a TEE, the SMM environment should prevent any information leaks. Besides side channels, the potential information leak may have two sources:

1) Software-based information leaks: The SMI handler should not copy arbitrary SMRAM content to regions outside of SMM. The SMI handler should not expose any SMM address information to agents outside of SMM, including the address of a global variable, the address of a critical data structure in the heap, and the address of a function pointer. This profiling information may be used for debug purposes in the development phase, but this should be removed in the final production image.

2) Hardware-based information leaks: If an SMI handler needs to collect the profile information, then this information should be kept inside of SMRAM by default. If the SMM environment needs to use non-SMRAM for the profile information storage temporarily, the SMM environment should ensure that the profile information is cleared before SMM exits.

Secure World Kernel Protection

Current SMM implementations run all code in the supervisor mode of the CPU. All kernel protection techniques we discussed in Chapter 16, Table 16-1, could be applied to the SMM kernel.

Kernel Load-Time Protection

During boot, the boot firmware needs to load the image into SMRAM to construct the SMM environment.

Code Integrity Guard

The SMM code should be signed and verified before launch. Because the SMM code is provided by the OEM, the OEM may choose to combine SMM code with normal BIOS boot code and sign them together. The existing system firmware secure boot can be used to verify the integrity of the SMM code, such as that provided by Intel Boot Guard. After the system exits the OEM phase (EndOfDxe event), when third-party code might be executed, the services to load an SMM image should be closed.

Rollback Prevention

Care must be taken that the version check should also be included in addition to signature verification. Otherwise, the attacker may perform a rollback attack to update the image to an old one containing known vulnerabilities. A secure version number (SVN) or lowest support version (LSV) should always be checked when a system performs the SMM image update.

Kernel Runtime Protection

The SMM kernel should implement various protections. To begin with, data execution prevention (DEP) protection should be applied, including a non-executable SMM image data region, read-only SMM image code region, non-executable SMM save state, and read-only SMM entry point. In addition to DEP, guards should be applied, including the arbitrary code guards (ACGs) (such as a non-executable stack and heap) and control flow guards (CFGs) (such as shadow stack, address space layout randomization (ALSR), and stack cookies) to break the potential exploitation. See Figure 17-17 for SMM kernel protection.

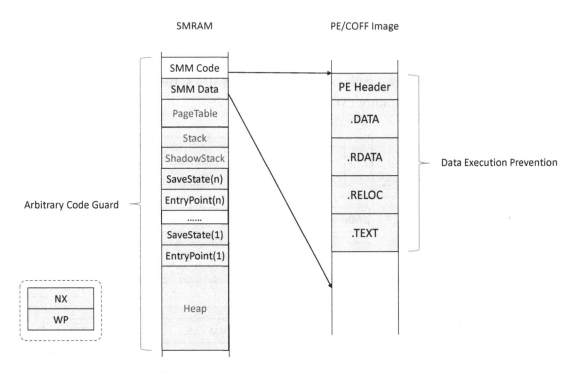

Figure 17-17. *SMM Kernel Protection*

To limit the damage, the SMM kernel may choose to deprivilege the SMI handler to ring 3 and set up the page table to only allow ring 3 handlers to access limited resources. For example, Intel Hardware Shield component and AMD SMM protection component run itself in supervisor mode and run SMI handler in user mode. Figure 17-18 shows the concept.

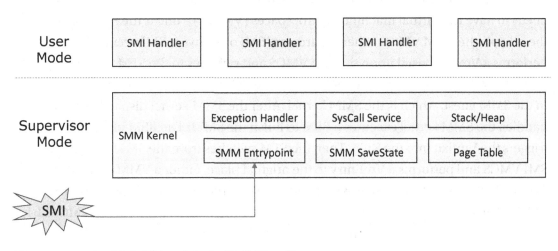

Figure 17-18. *SMM User Mode SMI Handler*

SMI Transfer Monitor

As another implementation choice, a hypervisor may be implemented inside of SMM to deprivilege the SMI handler together with the existing SMM kernel. This hypervisor is named the SMI Transfer Monitor (STM). See Figure 17-19.

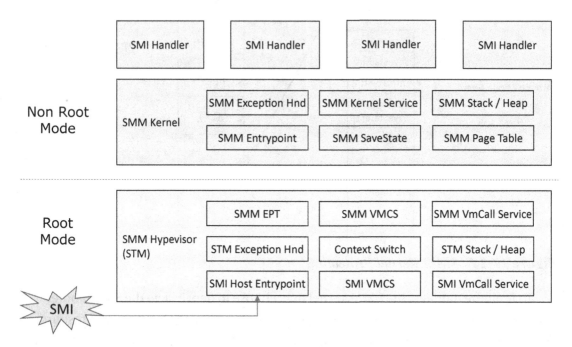

Figure 17-19. *SMM Non-Root Mode SMI Handler*

The STM works as a hypervisor. Different from the normal hypervisor, the STM needs to have two virtual machine control spaces (VMCSs) – one is the SMI VMCS and the other is the SMM VMCS. When a hardware SMI or software SMI occurs, the CPU performs a VmExit based upon the SMI VMCS and switches to the STM SMI entry point. Then the STM switches from the SMI VMCS to the SMM VMCS and performs a VmEntry to the SMM guest, which is the SMM kernel. After the SMM kernel dispatches the SMI handler, the SMM kernel executes a RSM to finish the SMM. The RSM instruction triggers the VmExit into the STM. Then the STM switches from the SMM VMCS to the SMI VMCS and performs a VmEntry to the original place, either a VMM or a VMM guest. Figure 17-20 shows the SMI flow with a STM. Besides the SMI, the VMM can invoke the VMCALL instruction in root mode to enter the STM. This special root mode VMCALL is a way to let two hypervisors communicate with each other.

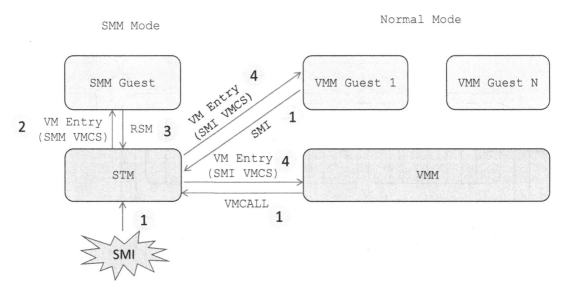

Figure 17-20. *STM-Involved SMI Flow*

The STM can have several capabilities:

1) STM should prevent the STM from being attacked by the SMM guest, VMM, or VMM guest.

2) STM should prevent the SMM kernel from being attacked by the SMI handler.

3) STM should prevent the VMM from being attacked by the SMI handler.

Figure 17-21 shows the STM as a monitor. During the system boot, the VMM can use root-VMCALL to communicate with the STM to let STM perform the protection for the VMM-owned memory and I/O/ MMIO/ PCI express configuration. The STM can set up the extended page tables (EPTs) to protect the memory, MMIO, and PCI express configuration and set up the I/O Bitmap to protect the I/O configuration for the different domains. The VMM can also set up a trusted region for the SMI source. Only a limited memory region can issue an SMI command. As such, the malicious VM code cannot send the SMI command.

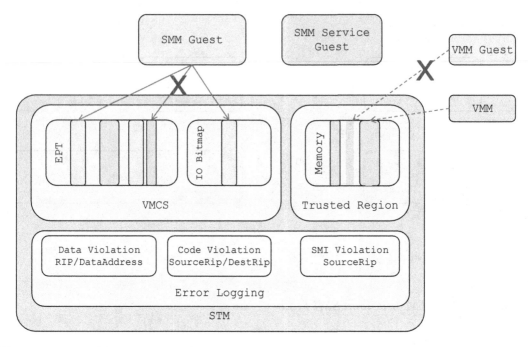

Figure 17-21. *STM as a Monitor*

Because the STM is a hypervisor, the STM has the capability to launch multiple
SMM guests. For example, one SMM guest can be created to handle the SMI request and
another SMM service guest to monitor the VMM state periodically.

Figure 17-22 shows the overall system resource and components.

1) The SMM domain owns the SMRAM- and SMM-owned
   configuration. The memory should be invisible to the OS/
   hypervisor, and the configuration should be locked. This is
   designed to maintain the integrity and confidentiality of SMM.

2) The OS/hypervisor owns the OS/hypervisor memory. The
   SMM should not touch the OS memory or configuration. This is
   designed to maintain the integrity of the OS/hypervisor to prevent
   a confused deputy attack.

3) The SMM communication buffer and shared configuration space
   can be accessed by both SMM and the OS/hypervisor. This is
   designed to provide a means of communication between two
   domains.

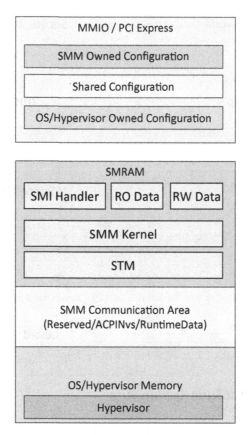

Figure 17-22. *System Resource and Components with STM*

ARM TrustZone

SMM is a good design for the isolated execution environment. However, the biggest problem is that it is controlled by the Original Equipment Manufacturer (OEM). The SMM environment is invisible to most software developers, and the normal software developer cannot load any code into SMM.

ARM announced TrustZone technology in 2005. It is similar to X86 SMM, but TrustZone defines the concept of the secure world officially and extends the environment for user extension. Figure 17-23 shows a typical TrustZone architecture. In the normal world, we have user mode applications and a supervisor mode operating system. The secure world is an isolated environment. It includes a small trusted firmware component in the monitor mode, a trusted kernel running in the supervisor mode, and user mode applications known as trustlets. The normal world can use the secure monitor call (SMC) to switch to the secure world.

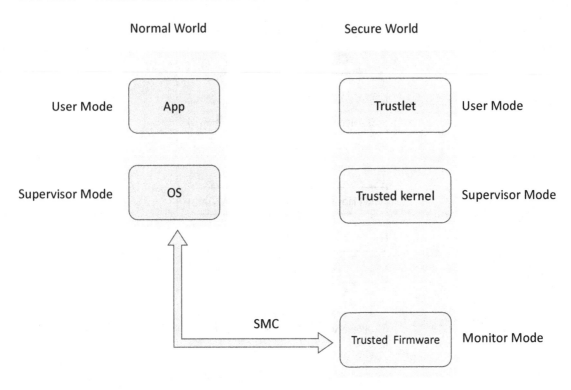

Figure 17-23. *ARM TrustZone Architecture*

Besides the ARM A-profile, ARMv8 M-profile also adopted the TrustZone as an optional security extension. Because the M-profile describes a resource-constrained environment, the secure world may use a monolithic kernel or application. Table 17-1 shows the TrustZone features for ARMv8 A-profile and M-profile.

Table 17-1. *TrustZone Features for ARMv8 A-Profile and M-Profile*

Feature	A-Profile	M-Profile
Additional security states	SEL0 – Trusted apps SEL1 – Trusted OS EL3 – Trusted-Firmware-A	Secure thread – trusted code/data Secure handler – trusted device drivers, real-time OS (RTOS)
Secure interrupt	Yes	Yes (fast)
State transition (boundary crossing)	Software transition	Hardware transition (fast)
Memory management	Virtual memory – memory management unit (MMU) with secure attributes	Secure Attribution Unit (SAU) and Memory Protection Unit (MPU) memory partitions
System interconnect security	Yes	Yes
Secure code, data, and memory	Yes	Yes
Trusted boot	Yes	Yes
Software	Trusted-Firmware-A (and third-party TEEs)	Arm Keil Microcontroller Development Kit (MDK), Cortex Microcontroller Software Interface Standard (CMSIS), Arm Mbed OS, Trusted-Firmware-M, and third-party software

Currently TrustZone is not only used in a standalone ARM processor solution, but TrustZone is also used as a secure coprocessor. For example, Microsoft used TrustZone to implement the firmware Trusted Platform Module (fTPM). AMD used TrustZone to implement the Platform Secure Processor (PSP).

Similar to X86 SMM, the security of ARM TrustZone relies on the proper implementation of the software in the TrustZone area. Lots of attack methods against X86 SMM can be applied to attack ARM TrustZone. As such, the security guidelines for X86 SMM can be applied to harden the ARM TrustZone implementation.

Secure World Isolation

The fundamental requirement for TrustZone is to partition the memory into a secure world memory and non-secure world memory. This includes the system firmware, system DRAM, system SRAM, device memory, and so on. The DMA attack and cache poisoning attack should also be prevented.

Side Channel Attack

Unfortunately, side channel attacks in TrustZone are possible. For example, the TrustZone kernel should implement the Kernel Address Isolation to resist a Meltdown-style attack. The TrustZone firmware, kernel, and applications must follow the generic side channel mitigation guidelines to prevent the attack, such as bounds check bypass and branch target injection. Last but not least, the secure world should flush the shared microarchitectural structures when switching to the non-secure world.

Secure Normal World Interaction

The secure world needs to interact with the non-secure world. This communication is a perfect attack surface. Similar to SMM, the majority of TrustZone attacks target the TrustZone communication infrastructure.

In the normal world, the user mode application can set up a trustlet communication area to communicate with the trustlet in the secure world. The operating system can set up the kernel communication area to communicate with the trusted kernel. Once the communication buffer is set up, the normal world uses a secure monitor call (SMC) to switch to the secure world. Then the trusted kernel or the trustlet can check the command identifier in the communication buffer and do the corresponding work. See Figure 17-24.

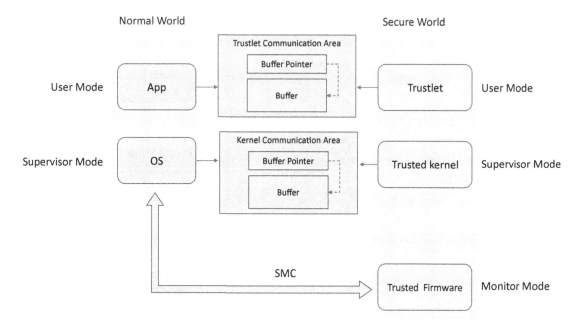

Figure 17-24. *ARM TrustZone Communication*

Normal World Communication Verification

Because the content in the communication buffer is from the non-secure world, the secure world SMC handler must verify the length of the communication buffer to prevent an input or output buffer overflow attack.

Confused Deputy Attack Prevention

The malicious normal world application or kernel can prepare a modified communication buffer and let it point to the secure world memory. If the code in the secure world does not check the buffer location, then the attacker may use this confused deputy attack to modify the target memory in the secure world or even inject shellcode into the secure world. Figure 17-25 shows how the normal world program modifies the target memory in the secure world. The kernel communication buffer can be used to attack the trusted kernel directly. The trustlet communication buffer attack is also useful because the attacker may use the trustlet to attack the trusted kernel as the next step such as ret2libc.

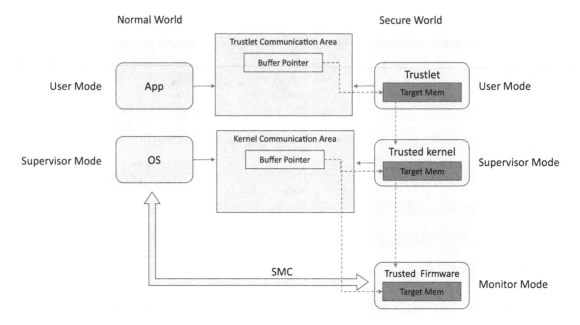

Figure 17-25. *ARM TrustZone Confused Deputy Attack*

Here the communication area is a general term. It could be a DRAM communication buffer, a general-purpose register as a pointer, a memory mapped I/O (MMIO) area, and even a debug or trace buffer. In order to mitigate such attacks, the SMC handler in the secure world must check the buffer pointer inside of the communication area.

Race Condition Attack Prevention

A race condition attack on the communication buffer is also possible if the secure world allows some CPUs into the secure world and leaves other CPUs in the non-secure world. As a mitigation, the communication buffer check actions must be done on the buffer inside of the trusted world.

Secure World Kernel Protection

The secure world software infrastructure is similar to the general software infrastructure – OS and application. All kernel protection techniques we discussed in Chapter 16, Table 16-1, should be applied to the TrustZone kernel.

Kernel Load-Time Protection

During the boot, the system starts in the secure world. The trusted firmware loads the trusted kernel, and the kernel loads the trustlet. A secure boot mechanism should be enabled to check the integrity of the code. The rollback protection should also be considered to prevent loading an old image with a known vulnerability.

Kernel Runtime Protection

At runtime, the trusted kernel should implement data execution prevention (DEP), such as non-executable data region and read-only code region, arbitrary code guard (ACG) such as non-executable stack and heap, and control flow guard (CFG) such as shadow stack, address space layout randomization (ALSR), and stack cookies to break the potential exploitation.

TrustZone Secure Partition Manager

The challenge for the ARM TrustZone deployment is the integration of trusted code from different vendors. A trusted OS needs to access trusted hardware resources to provide its services. In some cases, a silicon vendor provides a driver to access the trusted resource. In other cases, the silicon vendor provides its own trusted OS. Besides the security services, the silicon vendor also provides the platform services, such as Power State Coordination Interface (PSCI), which need to be integrated into the trusted firmware. Figure 17-26 shows the components integrated in different areas.

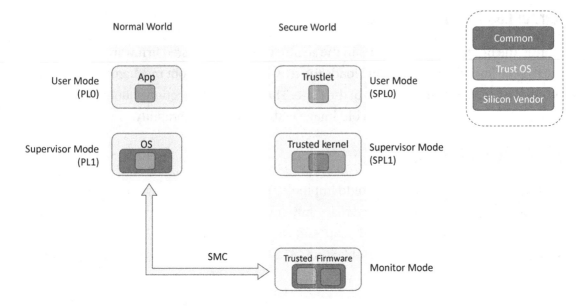

Figure 17-26. *ARM TrustZone Component Integration*

This design brings difficulty for the OS to integrate the features. It also violates the least privilege design principle because there is no hardware isolation between supervisor mode and monitor mode and there is no isolation between different components.

ARMv8.4 adds hypervisor mode in the secure world and changes the original privilege level (PL) to exception level (EL). The trusted firmware still runs in the monitor mode – EL3. A new Secure Partition Manager (SPM) runs in the hypervisor mode – secure EL2 (SEL2). The trusted OS kernel runs in the supervisor mode – secure EL1 (SLE1). Besides the trusted OS, the SPM enables another secure partition runtime (SPRT) to run the silicon vendor services at the supervisor mode privilege – secure EL1 (SEL1). See Figure 17-27.

With this new architecture, the SPM enables

1) The isolation of SEL3 software from SEL1 software

2) The isolation of normal world software from SEL1 software

3) The isolation of distinct SEL1 software components from each other

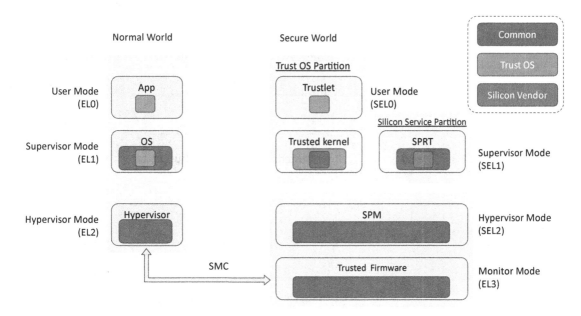

Figure 17-27. *ARM TrustZone Component Integration with SPM*

The ARM platform security architecture (PSA) defines multiple levels of isolation:

- Level 1: ARM TrustZone can provide the isolation between the secure world and normal world.

- Level 2: The Secure Partition Manager (SPM) is designed to provide isolation between PSA Root-of-Trust (PSA-RoT) and Application Root-of-Trust (ARoT). This can be achieved by the exception-level (EL) isolation.

- Level 3: The SPM may also provide additional isolation for different Security Partitions in ARoT. A virtual machine monitor may be needed to support this. See Figure 17-28.

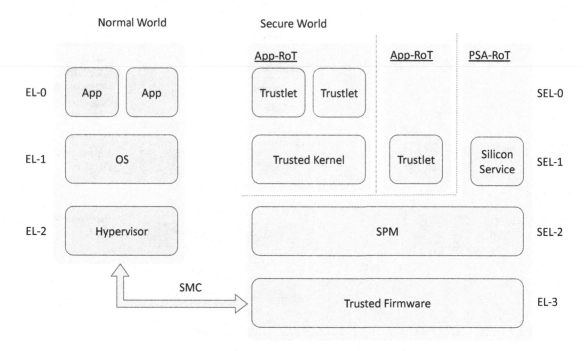

Figure 17-28. *ARM TrustZone Component Isolation with SPM*

The Secure Partition Manager concept can be applied to both the ARM A-profile and M-profile. For a high-assurance platform, the level 3 isolation should be implemented. In case any trustlet is tampered with, the SPM can ensure the damage is contained in this specific ARoT domain and that such damage won't impact any other RoT domain.

Please refer to the ARM TrustZone technology whitepaper for more detailed information.

Intel SGX

Intel defined Software Guard Extension (SGX) as an official solution for a trusted execution environment. Different from SMM or TrustZone, an SGX enclave can only run in user mode. No supervisor mode or hypervisor mode code is allowed to run inside of the SGX enclave. See Figure 17-29.

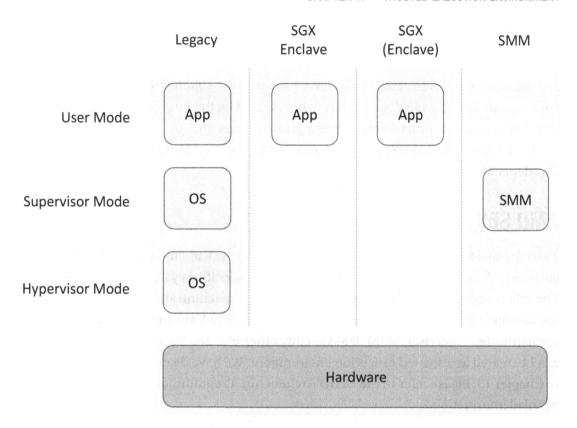

Figure 17-29. *Intel SGX Component Isolation*

Secure World Isolation

The SGX enclave is protected by the CPU hardware. As such, non-enclave code, such as the OS kernel, hypervisor, SMM, or DMA, cannot access the contents in the SGX enclave. Because the contents inside of SGX are encrypted by the CPU, even a simple hardware attack cannot compromise SGX. The SGX enclaves are also isolated from each other, since each enclave has its own specific encryption key.

Side Channel Attack

Similar to any other TEE, a side channel attack against an SGX enclave is possible. For example, the attacker relies on the use of a shared resource to discover information about processing occurring in some other privileged domain to which it does not have direct access. The enclave developer should follow the side channel developer's guidance carefully to maintain the confidentiality of the enclave.

Secure World Kernel Protection

The enclave itself is still software. The memory safety issues, such as buffer overflows, are still a concern inside of the enclave. We have seen the solution to use a type-safe language, such as Rust, to develop the enclave, including the Rust-SGX-SDK. We will discuss the details of programming languages in Chapter 20.

For more details on SGX, please refer to the "Intel 64 and IA-32 Architecture Software Developer Manuals."

AMD SEV

AMD defined Secure Encrypted Virtualization (SEV). SEV is similar to Intel SGX in that each virtual machine (VM) is encrypted with a VM-specific key by the CPU hardware. The difference is that the SEV VM is a normal virtual machine and can run both user mode applications and supervisor mode OS kernels. The VM can resist attacks from the hardware, hypervisor, SMM, DMA, or any other VM. See Figure 17-30. Each VM can be treated as a trusted execution environment. We have discussed the AMD SEV in Chapter 13. Please refer to the "AMD Architecture Programmer's Manual" for more detailed information.

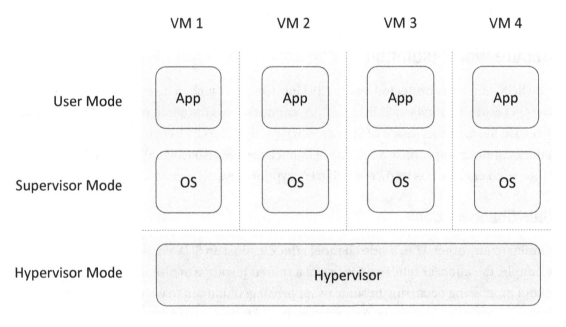

Figure 17-30. *VM-Based Component Isolation*

Intel TDX

Intel extended the SGX enclave concept from a single user mode application to the virtual machine domain by the Trust Domain Extensions (TDX) capability. Similar to AMD SEV, Intel TDX can be enabled by a hypervisor and achieve virtual machine domain–level isolation. Figure 17-30 can be applied to Intel TDX. We have discussed the Intel TDX in Chapter 13.

IBM Z

IBM announced secure execution on IBM Z. Secure execution is an IBM LinuxONE and Linux on IBM Z exclusive trusted execution environment (TEE) technology that is designed to protect and isolate workloads from both internal and external threats.

The secure execution on IBM Z provides a Linux Kernel-Based Virtual Machine (KVM) that is fully isolated and protected from the hypervisor, with encryption keys that are only accessed by the IBM Z hardware and firmware. Figure 17-30 can also be applied to the IBM Z secure execution TEE.

RISC-V Keystone

Keystone is an open source project for building trusted execution environments (TEEs) with secure hardware enclaves, based on the RISC-V architecture. Keystone is based upon the RISC-V physical memory protection (PMP) – a primitive which allows a machine mode security monitor (SM) underneath the OS to specify arbitrary protections on physical memory regions. See Figure 17-31.

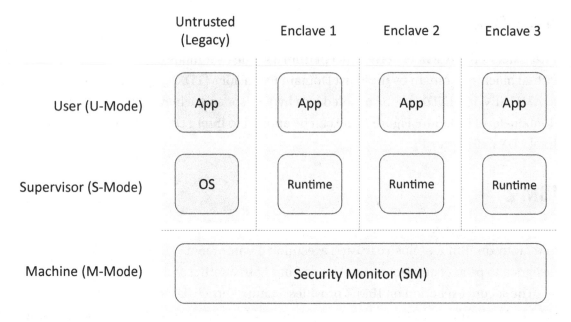

Figure 17-31. *Keystone Component Isolation*

Keystone can launch multiple enclaves. Each enclave operates in its own isolated physical memory region and has its own runtime (RT) component which executes in supervisor mode and manages the virtual memory of the enclave. In case there is a vulnerability in one enclave, the damage is contained to this enclave only. Hypervisor mode is not needed in the Keystone solution.

RISC-V/ARM-M MultiZone

The ARM TrustZone design only defines one secure world. The concept can be extended to multiple secure worlds – that is named as MultiZone. HEX Five defines the hardware-enforced, software-defined separation of multiple, equally secure, functional domains. A MultiZone kernel starts up the system and sets up the multiple domains. Figure 17-32 shows the MultiZone-based component isolation.

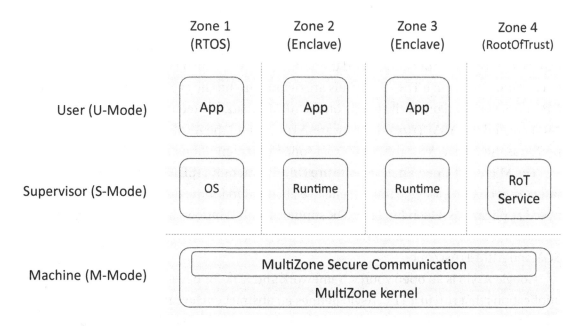

Figure 17-32. *MultiZone Component Isolation*

MultiZone can be implemented on a RISC-V and ARM M-profile microcontroller unit (MCU). The resource-constrained MCUs typically have simplified versions of the memory management unit (MMU), such as Memory Protection Unit (MPU), Secure Attribute Unit (SAU), or an implementation-defined attribute unit (IDAU). The MPU/SAU/IDAU uses a set of range registers to define the address of each zone and the access attributes of each zone. As such, the whole memory region can be partitioned into multiple zones.

With the MultiZone architecture, no single zone can have access to all system resources and compromise the CIA – confidentiality, integrity, and availability – of the whole system.

Standards, Frameworks, and SDKs

Currently, there are different hardware TEE implementations. In order to run software in the TEE, we need to standardize the application program interface (API). Currently, the GlobalPlatform (GP) organization has developed a set of specifications so that the digital services and devices can be trusted and managed securely, including the secure element (SE), trusted execution environment (TEE), and trusted platform services (TPSs).

The Open Portable TEE (OP-TEE) is an open source project compliant with GlobalPlatform. OP-TEE implements the TEE Internal Core API, which is the API exposed to trusted applications, and the TEE Client API, which is the API describing how to communicate with a TEE. Both APIs are defined in the GlobalPlatform specification. OP-TEE is designed primarily to rely on the ARM TrustZone technology. Below OP-TEE, ARM created the ARM Trusted-Firmware-A profile and the ARM Trusted-Firmware-M profile as the full stack for the ARM TrustZone implementations.

The Microsoft Open Enclave Software Development Kit (SDK) is an open source SDK targeted at creating a single unified enclave abstraction for the developer to build TEE-based applications. Open Enclave SDK supports both Windows and Linux, and Open Enclave allows for the development of code that is portable between TEEs, such as Intel SGX and ARM TrustZone.

Google Asylo is an open source framework and SDK for developing enclave applications that run in a TEE. Asylo defines an abstract enclave model that can be mapped transparently onto a variety of TEE technologies, such as Intel SGX and ARM TrustZone. Asylo applications do not need to be aware of the intricacies of specific TEE implementations. The apps can run on a laptop, a workstation, a virtual machine in an on-premises server, or an instance in the cloud.

Red Hat announced Enarx, an open source project, which is an application deployment framework enabling applications to run within TEEs without rewriting for particular platforms or SDKs. It handles attestation and delivery in a runtime "Keep" based on WebAssembly. Enarx is a CPU architecture-independent solution. Current work is on AMD SEV and Intel SGX.

Baidu embraced the Rust language and provided Rust-SGX-SDK. This is a great example of how to support a type-safe language in the TEE.

IETF created Trusted Execution Environment Provisioning (TEEP) working group to develop a protocol providing TEEs with lifecycle management and security domain management for trusted applications.

Summary

As summary, Table 17-2 lists the different TEE solutions.

Table 17-2. *Different TEE Solutions*

Feature	X86 SMM	ARM TrustZone	Intel SGX	AMD SEV, Intel TDX, IBM Z TEE	RISC-V Keystone, RISC-V/ARM-M MultiZone
Protection	CPU mode – SMM	CPU mode – secure world	Enclave encryption	Domain encryption	Memory isolation – PMP, MPU
TEE number	1	1 without SPM, multiple with SPM	Multiple	Multiple	Multiple
TEE highest privilege	Hypervisor (STM)	Hypervisor (SPM)	User app	Supervisor (OS in VM)	Supervisor (OS)
Protection mechanism	CPU mode – SMM	CPU mode – secure world	Enclave encryption	Key encryption	Memory isolation – PMP, MPU/SAU
Loader	Boot firmware	Trusted firmware	OS kernel driver	Hypervisor VMM	Machine mode kernel, secure monitor

Coprocessor-Based TEE

The TEE can also be implemented in a coprocessor. Figure 17-33 shows three different types of TEE locations. The first is the CPU-based TEE, which we have introduced in the previous section, such as Intel SGX, ARM TrustZone, or RISC-V Keystone. The second one is the coprocessor-based TEE in one system on a chip (SOC), such as the Apple secure enclave processor (SEP), AMD Platform Secure Processor (PSP), or Intel Converged Security and Management Engine (CSME). The third one is the coprocessor-based TEE in an external SOC, such as Google Titan, Microsoft Cerberus, or a Trusted Platform Module (TPM).

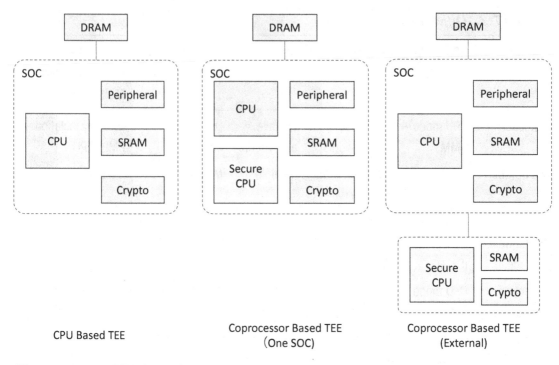

Figure 17-33. *TEE Location*

Intel Converged Security and Management Engine (CSME)

Intel Active Management Technology (AMT) relied on the Intel Management Engine (ME), which is a coprocessor in the Platform Control Hub (PCH). Later people added security features into ME and made it to be Intel Converged Security and Management Engine (CSME). It is also named as Trusted Execution Engine (TXE) in the small core system or Server Platform Services (SPS) in the server system.

Intel CSME includes a crypto engine and implements a firmware Trusted Platform Module (fTPM), which has the same functions as a discrete TPM attached to the motherboard. The TPM is defined by the Trusted Computing Group (TCG). We have discussed the details of TPMs in Chapter 7.

Intel CSME also implements Enhanced Privacy ID (EPID). EPID is a procedure for remote attestation of trusted systems that allows identifying individual computers while preserving privacy. Intel EPID addresses two device-level security issues: anonymity and membership revocation. The Intel EPID scheme works with three types of keys: the group public key, the group private key, and the member EPID private key. The issuer generates the group public/private key pair, publishes the group public key, and keeps the group private key in local. Based upon the request, the issuer creates the member EPID private key and deploys the member EPID private key to the device. Later, the verifier gets the group public key and verifies the member device and then uses a challenge/response to verify the signature generated by the member device with the member EPID key. The verifier only knows the member device belongs to a group but does not know which specific device it is. Figure 17-34 shows the Intel EPID solution in CSME.

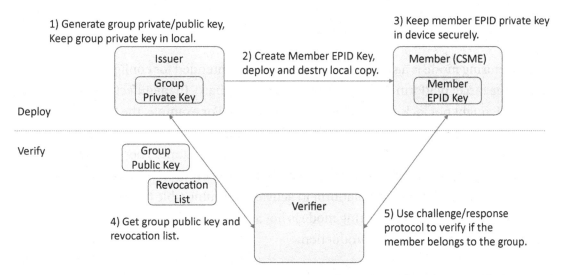

Figure 17-34. *Intel EPID Solution*

Secure World Isolation

Intel CSME runs on a different processor, and it is fully isolated from the software perspective. However, other hardware may still have a way to communicate with the CSME.

DMA Attack Prevention

Intel CSME has an isolated SRAM. A minute system agent allows the CPU to securely access the SRAM and enforce access control to the SRAM from internal/external devices by using IOMMU. In order to prevent the attack from other devices, the IOMMU should be set up and enabled by default.

Debugger Attack Prevention

Intel CSME can be accessed by attaching an Intel Direct Connect Interface (DCI) USB device. The DCI USB works as a JTAG device. The attacker may use it to trace the internal logic for debug purposes. A production CSME should keep all security enforcement even if a debugger is attached. A JTAG password is required to fully access the CSME internal state. This JTAG password must be kept as a secret for the platform.

Non-production Mode Prevention

Manufacturing mode is a special boot mode which is intended for configuring and testing the target platform during the manufacturing phase. In manufacturing mode, the CSME might not lock down all of its configuration. For example, the CSME firmware region in the SPI flash is not fully locked, and the BIOS can send Host ME Region Flash Protection Override (HMR FPO) commands to CSME at any time. Then the attacker can flash a vulnerable CSME image and send another HECI command to reset the CSME only without resetting the host platform to activate the vulnerable CSME image.

Since the CSME manufacturing mode is not a proper production mode, it should always be disabled in the final production.

Secure Normal World Interaction

The host CPU has a couple of ways to communicate with the CSME, such as the host-embedded communication interface (HECI), network packets, and the firmware SPI flash. Any untrusted external data must be verified carefully before use to avoid the buffer overflows, integer overflows, and so on.

Secure World Kernel Protection

The CSME is part of the firmware on the flash part. The flash part must be locked correctly. The CSME update must perform the signature check and rollback check. The CSME kernel is still software. All general kernel protection techniques should be applied such as firmware boot verification, kernel supervisor mode protection, data execution prevention, stack cookie, and so on.

Apple Secure Enclave Processor (SEP)

The Apple secure enclave processor (SEP) is a secure coprocessor that includes a hardware-based key manager. The key data is encrypted in the secure enclave SOC, which includes a random number generator.

The secure enclave also maintains the integrity of its cryptographic operations, even if the device kernel has been compromised. Figure 17-35 shows the usage of the secure enclave processor.

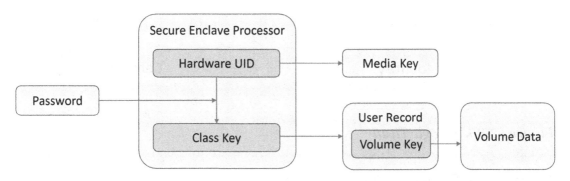

Figure 17-35. *Apple SEP*

The secure enclave is also used in Touch ID – a fingerprint sensing system. The fingerprint data is encrypted, stored on the device, and protected with a key available only to the secure enclave. When the fingerprint sensor detects the touch of a finger, it triggers the advanced imaging array to scan the finger and sends the scan to the secure enclave for the verification.

Google Titan

The Google Titan design is a Platform Root-of-Trust. Besides the verified boot and the first instruction integrity, Titan can also work as a secure enclave to provide the trusted identity and the physical tamper-resistant security capabilities.

The Titan chip manufacturing process generates a unique identity for each chip. The identity is derived from secrets delivered by different silicon technologies and the firmware. The benefit of adding the firmware is to ensure that only a patched Titan chip gets the certificate. The identity is exported to a registry via a secure channel and signed by a Titan Certification Authority (CA). Individual Titan chips can generate certificate signing requests (CSRs) directed at the Titan CA and get the certificate for installation and attestation later. The identity is generated in the secure enclave environment and cannot be tampered with by any other device. Figure 17-36 shows the trusted identity of the Titan chip.

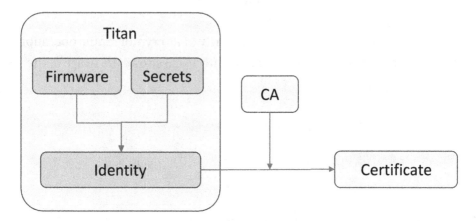

Figure 17-36. *Google Titan*

Microsoft Azure Sphere: Pluton

Microsoft Azure Sphere is a secured, high-level application platform with built-in communication and security features for Internet-connected devices. Azure Sphere includes an ARM Context-A–based high-level application core. The user application runs in the normal world, and a Microsoft security monitor runs in the secure world.

The Azure Sphere microcontroller unit also includes an isolated security subsystem – known as Pluton. Pluton includes a true random number generator and cryptographic helpers. Besides secure boot, Pluton implements the measured boot and remote attestation in silicon. Pluton generates its own elliptic curve cryptography (ECC) key pairs in silicon during the manufacturing process. The private keys are never visible to software. Even the most trusted firmware on the device does not have access to the private keys. The chips' public keys are sent to Microsoft from the silicon manufacturer, which means Microsoft knows about and establishes a trust relationship with every Azure Sphere chip from the point the chip is manufactured. If remote attestation is required, Pluton can sign the boot measurement with the Pluton's private ECC attestation key and send it back to Azure Sphere Security Service (AS3). AS3 already has the device's public ECC attestation key and can therefore determine whether the device is authentic and was booted with genuine software and if the genuine software is trusted.

Azure Sphere uses hardware firewalls as the silicon countermeasures to provide "sandbox" protection to ensure that I/O peripherals are accessible only to the core to which they are mapped. The firewalls impose compartmentalization, thus preventing a security threat in one core from affecting the other cores. Figure 17-37 shows the Microsoft Azure Sphere MCU components.

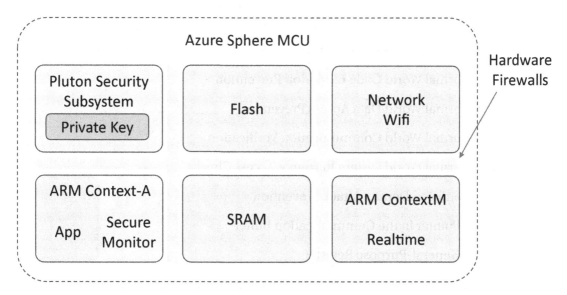

Figure 17-37. *Microsoft Azure Sphere*

Summary

In this chapter, we discussed the different TEE implementations, including the CPU-based TEEs, such as X86 SMM, ARM TrustZone, Intel SGX, AMD SEV, RISC-V Keystone, and so on, and the coprocessor-based TEEs, such as Intel CSME, Apple SEP, Google Titan, and Microsoft Azure Sphere Pluton. The following is the summary of the secure implementation guide for the TEE:

     1. Secure World Isolation

     1.1 Memory Isolation

     1.2 Configuration Lockdown

     1.3. CPU State Protection

     1.4. DMA Attack Prevention

     1.5. Address Alias Attack Prevention

1.6. Cache Poisoning Attack Prevention

1.7. Debugger Attack Prevention

1.8. Non-production Mode Prevention

1.9. Hot Plug Consideration

1.10. Side Channel Attack Prevention

2. Secure Normal World Interaction

2.1. Normal World Code Execution Prevention

2.2. Normal World Data Access Prevention

2.3. Normal World Communication Verification

2.4. Normal World System Resource Access Check

2.5. Confused Deputy Attack Prevention

2.5.1. Pointer in the Communication Buffer

2.5.2. General-Purpose Register

2.5.3. MMIO Base Address Register

2.5.4. Critical Resource Protection

2.5.5. Special Feature Registers

2.6. Race Condition Attack Prevention

2.6.1. Communication Buffer Process

2.6.2. Register Unlock Process

2.7. Information Leak Prevention

3. Secure World Kernel Protection

3.1. Secure Boot and Secure Update

3.1.1. Code Integrity Guard

3.1.2. Rollback Prevention

3.2. Kernel Runtime Protection

3.2.1. Data Execution Prevention

3.2.2. Address Space Layout Randomization

3.2.3. Control Flow Guard

3.2.4. Stack Cookie

3.3. Domain Isolation

3.3.1. User Memory Execution/Access Prevention

3.3.2. Kernel Address Isolation

3.3.3. Hardware Domain Isolation or Software Secure Partition Manager

From our observation, the majority of TEE attacks focus on the normal world communication attacks for integrity and side channel attacks for confidentiality. Care must be taken for those areas where the TEE is implemented in order to prevent vulnerabilities, especially those that can lead to a confused deputy attack. The coprocessor-based TEE is a fully isolated system, and it may be vulnerable to DMA attacks, debugger attacks, or manufacturing mode attacks. All firmware resiliency protection should be applied, such as secure boot and secure update. The TEE kernel should enable existing mature technologies to mitigate attacks, such as data execution prevention, user memory execution/access prevention, address space layout randomization, stack cookies, and so on. As always, domain isolation is the best choice to limit the damage.

The Azure Sphere team has summarized seven properties of highly secured devices:

1. Hardware-based root-of-trust: A hardware-based root-of-trust ensures that the device and its identity cannot be separated, thus preventing device forgery or spoofing. Every secured device should be identified by an unforgeable cryptographic key that is generated and protected by the hardware. This ensures a tamper-resistant, secured hardware root-of-trust from factory to end user.

2. Small trusted computing base: Most of the device's software remains outside the trusted computing base, thus reducing the surface area for attacks. Only the secured security monitor runs on the trusted computing base.

3. Defense in depth: Defense in depth provides for multiple layers of security and thus multiple mitigations against each threat. Each layer of software verifies that the layer above it is secured.

4. Compartmentalization: Compartmentalization limits the reach of any single failure. The secured device should contain silicon countermeasures, including hardware firewalls, to prevent a security breach in one component from propagating to other components. A constrained, "sandboxed" runtime environment prevents applications from corrupting secured code or data.

5. Certificate-based authentication: The use of signed certificates, validated by an unforgeable cryptographic key, provides much stronger authentication than passwords. Every software element should be signed. Device-to-cloud and cloud-to-device communications require further certificate-based authentication.

6. Renewable security: The device software is automatically updated to correct known vulnerabilities or security breaches, requiring no intervention from the product manufacturer or the end user.

7. Failure reporting: Failures in device software or hardware are typical in emerging security attacks; device failure by itself constitutes a denial-of-service attack. Device-to-cloud communication provides early warning of potential failures. The secured device should have capability to automatically report operational data and failures to a cloud-based analysis system, and updates and servicing can be performed remotely.

In the next chapter, we will discuss the silicon secure configuration.

References

Conference, Journal, and Paper

[P-1] Jiewen Yao, "SMM Protection in EDK II," in *UEFI Plugfest 2017*, www.uefi.org/sites/default/files/resources/Jiewen%20Yao%20-%20SMM%20Protection%20in%20%20EDKII_Intel.pdf

[P-2] Jiewen Yao, Vincent Zimmer, Star Zeng, "A Tour Beyond BIOS Secure SMM Communication," *Intel Whitepaper 2016*, https://github.com/tianocore-docs/Docs/raw/master/White_Papers/A_Tour_Beyond_BIOS_Secure_SMM_Communication.pdf

[P-3] Jiewen Yao, Vincent Zimmer, "A Tour Beyond BIOS – Launching STM to Monitor SMM in EDK II," Intel Whitepaper 2015, `https://software.intel.com/sites/default/files/managed/f0/46/a_tour_beyond_bios_launching_stm_to_monitor_smm_in_efi_developer_kit_ii.pdf`

[P-4] Jiewen Yao, Vincent Zimmer, "A Tour Beyond BIOS – Supporting SMM Resource Monitor using EDK II," Intel Whitepaper 2015,
`https://software.intel.com/sites/default/files/managed/85/7d/a_tour_beyond_bios_supporting_smm_resource_monitor_using_the_efi_developer_kit_ii.pdf`

[P-5] Justin Johnson, "Dell Firmware Security," in Platform Security Summit 2018, `www.platformsecuritysummit.com/2018/speaker/johnson/PSEC2018-Dell-Firmware-Security-Justin-Johnson.pdf`

[P-6] Loic Duflot, Daniel Etiemble, Olivier Grumelard, "Using CPU system management mode to Circumvent Operating System Security Function," 2006, available at `https://pdfs.semanticscholar.org/62be/ba49b7a9eb50c0a860547cceb2863e994aa2.pdf`

[P-7] Joanna Rutkowska, Rafal Wojtczuk, "Preventing and Detecting Xen Hypervisor Subversions," in *BlackHat US 2008*, available at `https://invisiblethingslab.com/resources/bh08/part2-full.pdf`

[P-8] Rafal Wojtczuk, Joanna Rutkowska, "Attack Intel TXT," in *BlackHat DC 2009*, available at `www.blackhat.com/presentations/bh-dc-09/Wojtczuk_Rutkowska/BlackHat-DC-09-Rutkowska-Attacking-Intel-TXT-slides.pdf`

[P-9] Loic Duflot, Olivier Levillain, Benjamin Morin, Olivier Grumelard, "Getting into the SMRAM: SMM Reloaded," in CanSecWest 2009, available at `https://cansecwest.com/csw09/csw09-duflot.pdf`

[P-10] Rafal Wojtczuk, Joanna Rutkowska, "Attacking SMM Memory via Intel® CPU Cache Poisoning," in invisiblethingslab 2009, available at `http://invisiblethingslab.com/resources/misc09/smm_cache_fun.pdf`

[P-11] Joanna Rutkowska, "Quest to the Core," in Intel Security Summit 2009, available at `http://invisiblethingslab.com/resources/misc09/Quest%20To%20The%20Core%20(public).pdf`

[P-12] Oleksandr Bazhaniuk, Yuriy Bulygin, Andrew Furtak, Mikhail Gorobets, John Loucaides, Alexander Matrosov, Mickey Shkatov, "A New Class of Vulnerability in SMI handlers," CanSecWest 2015, `www.c7zero.info/stuff/ANewClassOfVulnInSMIHandlers_csw2015.pdf`

[P-13] Mikhail Gorobets, Oleksandr Bazhaniuk, Alex Matrosov, Andrew Furtak, Yuriy Bulygin, "Attacking Hypervisors Through Firmware and Hardware," in BlackHat US 2015, available at `www.c7zero.info/stuff/AttackingHypervisorsViaFirmware_bhusa15_dc23.pdf`

[P-14] Exploring Lenovo, `http://blog.cr4.sh/2016/06/exploring-and-exploiting-lenovo.html`

[P-15] Yuriy Bulygin, Oleksandr Bazhaniuk, "BARing the system: New vulnerabilities in SMM of Coreboot and UEFI based systems," RECon 2017, available at `www.c7zero.info/stuff/REConBrussels2017_BARing_the_system.pdf`

[P-16] Oleksandr Bazhaniuk, Mikhail Gorobets, Andrew Furtak, Yuriy Bulygin, "Exploring your system deeper is not naughty," CanSecWest 2017, available at `www.c7zero.info/stuff/csw2017_ExploringYourSystemDeeper_updated.pdf`

[P-17] Ryan P Nakamoto, "Secure Boot and Image Authentication Technical Overview," Qualcomm Whitepaper, 2016, `www.qualcomm.com/media/documents/files/secure-boot-and-image-authentication-technical-overview-v1-0.pdf`

[P-18] Thomas Rothm, "Next Generation Mobile Rootkits," in Blackhat EU 2013, `https://media.blackhat.com/eu-13/videos/eu-13-Roth-mobile-rootkits.mp4`

[P-19] Dan Rosenberg, "Unlocking the Motorola Bootloader," 2013, `http://blog.azimuthsecurity.com/2013/04/unlocking-motorola-bootloader.html`

[P-20] Dan Rosenberg, "Reflections on Trusting TrustZone," in *BlackHat US 2014*, `www.blackhat.com/docs/us-14/materials/us-14-Rosenberg-Reflections-on-Trusting-TrustZone.pdf`

[P-21] laginimaineb, "Exploring Qualcomm's TrustZone implementation," 2015, `http://bits-please.blogspot.com/2015/03/getting-arbitrary-code-execution-in.html`, `http://bits-please.blogspot.com/2015/08/exploring-qualcomms-trustzone.html`

[P-22] Di Shen, "Attacking your Trusted Core – Exploiting Trustzone on Android," in *BlackHat US 2015*, `www.blackhat.com/docs/us-15/materials/us-15-Shen-Attacking-Your-Trusted-Core-Exploiting-Trustzone-On-Android.pdf`

[P-23] Moritz Lipp, Daniel Gruss, Raphael Spreitzer, Clémentine Maurice, Stefan Mangard. "Armageddon: Cache attacks on mobile devices," in *25th USENIX Security Symposium 2016*, `www.usenix.org/system/files/conference/usenixsecurity16/sec16_paper_lipp.pdf`

[P-24] Ning Zhang, Kun Sun, Deborah Shands, Wenjing Lou, and Y Thomas Hou,s "TruSpy: Cache sidechannel information leakage from the secure world on ARM devices," 2016, `https://eprint.iacr.org/2016/980.pdf`

[P-25] Adrian Tang, Simha Sethumadhavan, and Salvatore Stolfo. "CLKSCREW: Exposing the perils of security-oblivious energy management," in *26th USENIX Security Symposium 2017*, `www.usenix.org/system/files/conference/usenixsecurity17/sec17-tang.pdf`

[P-26] Oleksandr Bazhaniuk, Yuriy Bulygin, "Blue Pill for Your Phone," in BlackHat 2017, available at `www.blackhat.com/docs/us-17/wednesday/us-17-Bazhaniuk-BluePill-For-Your-Phone.pdf`

[P-27] Gal Beniamini, "Trust Issues: Exploiting TrustZone TEEs," 2017, `https://googleprojectzero.blogspot.com/2017/07/trust-issues-exploiting-trustzone-tees.html`

[P-28] Fernand Lone Sang, "Reverse Engineering Samsung S6 SBOOT," 2017, `https://blog.quarkslab.com/reverse-engineering-samsung-s6-sboot-part-i.html`, `https://blog.quarkslab.com/reverse-engineering-samsung-s6-sboot-part-ii.html`

[P-29] Daniel Komaromy, "Unbox Your Phone – Exploring and Breaking Samsung's TrustZone Sandboxes," in EKOPARTY 2017, `www.youtube.com/watch?v=L2Mo8WcmmZo`

[P-30] Joffrey Guilbon, "Attacking the ARM's TrustZone," 2018, `https://blog.quarkslab.com/attacking-the-arms-trustzone.html`

[P-31] Maxime Peterlin, Alexandre Adamski, Joffrey Guilbon, "Breaking Samsung's ARM TrustZone," in Blackhat US 2019, `http://i.blackhat.com/USA-19/Thursday/us-19-Peterlin-Breaking-Samsungs-ARM-TrustZone.pdf`

[P-32] Keegan Ryan, "Hardware-Backed Heist: Extracting ECDSA Keys from Qualcomm's TrustZone," NCC Group Whitepaper, 2019, `www.nccgroup.trust/globalassets/our-research/us/whitepapers/2019/hardwarebackedhesit.pdf`

[P-33] Yogesh Prem Swami, "SGX Remote Attestation is not sufficient," in *Blackhat US 2017*, `www.blackhat.com/docs/us-17/thursday/us-17-Swami-SGX-Remote-Attestation-Is-Not-Sufficient.pdf`

[P-34] Ahmad Moghimi, Gorka Irazoqui, Thomas Eisenbarth, "Cachezoom: How SGX amplifies the power of cache attacks," in *International Conference on Cryptographic Hardware and Embedded Systems, 2017*, `https://eprint.iacr.org/2017/618.pdf`

[P-35] Jo Van Bulck, Frank Piessens, Raoul Strackx, "Nemesis: Studying microarchitectural timing leaks in rudimentary CPU interrupt logic," in *Proceedings of the 2018 ACM SIGSAC Conference on Computer and Communications Security*, `https://people.cs.kuleuven.be/~jo.vanbulck/ccs18.pdf`

[P-36] ARM, "Arm Platform Security Architecture Overview," whitepaper 2018, `https://pages.arm.com/rs/312-SAX-488/images/Arm_Platform_Security_Architecture_Overview_WhitePaper.pdf`

[P-37] ARM, "Isolation using virtualization in the Secure World," whitepaper 2018, https://armkeil.blob.core.windows.net/developer/Files/pdf/Isolation%20 using%20virtualization%20in%20the%20Secure%20World_Whitepaper.pdf

[P-38] Sandrine Bailleux, "Trusted Firmware-A Secure Partitions," in OSFC 2018, https://2018.osfc.io/uploads/talk/paper/18/osfc_secure_partitions.pdf

[P-39] Miklos Balint, Ken Liu, "Compartmentalization in IoT Trusted Firmware M Secure Partitioning," in OpenIoT Summit Europe 2018, https://elinux. org/images/4/4b/Trusted-Firmware-M-Secure-Partitioning-%E2%80%93- Compartmentalization-in-IoT-Miklos-Balint-Ken-Liu-Arm.pdf

[P-40] Dayeol Lee, David Kohlbrenner, Shweta Shinde, Krste Asanovic, Dawn Song, "Keystone: An Open Framework for Architecting TEEs," in *OSEW 2019*, available at https://arxiv.org/pdf/1907.10119.pdf, https://keystone-enclave.org/open- source-enclaves-workshop/slides/OSEW19_DayeolLee_UCBerkeley.pdf

[P-41] Cesare Garlati, "Multi Zone Trusted Execution Environment Free And Open API," in *RISC-V Workshop, 2019*, available at https://content.riscv.org/wp-content/ uploads/2019/06/15.20-An-open-source-API-proposal-for-a-multi-domain-RISC- V-TEE-Cesare-Garlati-Hex-Five-12-JUN-19.pdf

[P-42] Robert N. M. Watson, Jonathan Woodruff, Peter G. Neumann, Simon W. Moore, Jonathan Anderson, David Chisnall, Nirav Dave, Brooks Davis, Khilan Gudka, Ben Laurie, Steven J. Murdoch, Robert Norton, Michael Roe, Stacey Son, Munraj Vadera, "CHERI: A Hybrid Capability-System Architecture for Scalable Software Compartmentalization," in *IEEE Symposium on Security and Privacy SP, 2015*, available at www.cl.cam.ac.uk/research/security/ctsrd/pdfs/201505-oakland2015-cheri- compartmentalization.pdf

[P-43] Intel, "Intel Software Guard Extensions," 2015, https://software.intel.com/ sites/default/files/332680-001.pdf

[P-44] Chia-Che Tsai, "Library OS is the New Container," the Linux foundation open source summit 2017, https://events19.linuxfoundation.org/wp-content/ uploads/2017/12/Library-OS-is-the-New-Container-Why-is-Library-OS-A-Better- Option-for-Compatibility-and-Sandboxing-Chia-Che-Tsai-UC-Berkeley.pdf

[P-45] Marcela S. Melara, Michael J. Freedman, Mic Bowman, "EnclaveDom: Privilege Separation for Large-TCB Applications in Trusted Execution Environments," https://arxiv.org/pdf/1907.13245.pdf

[P-46] Sangho Lee, Ming-Wei Shih, Prasun Gera, Taesoo Kim, Hyesoon Kim, and Marcus Peinado, "Inferring fine-grained control flow inside SGX enclaves with branch shadowing," in *26th USENIX Security Symposium 2017*, `www.usenix.org/system/files/conference/usenixsecurity17/sec17-lee-sangho.pdf`

[P-47] Jo Van Bulck, Marina Minkin, Ofir Weisse, Daniel Genkin, and Baris Kasikci, Frank Piessens, Mark Silberstein, Thomas F. Wenisch, Yuval Yarom, Raoul Strackx, "Foreshadow: Extracting the Keys to the Intel SGX Kingdom with Transient Out-of-Order Execution," in *27th USENIX Security Symposium 2018*, available at `www.usenix.org/system/files/conference/usenixsecurity18/sec18-van_bulck.pdf`

[P-48] Ofir Weisse, Jo Van Bulck, Marina Minkin, Daniel Genkin, Baris Kasikci, Frank Piessens, Mark Silberstein, Raoul Strackx, Thomas F. Wenisch, Yuval Yarom, "Foreshadow-NG: Breaking the Virtual Memory Abstraction with Transient Out-of-Order Execution," 2018 `https://foreshadowattack.eu/foreshadow-NG.pdf`

[P-49] Michael Schwarz, Moritz Lipp, Daniel Moghimi, Jo Van Bulck, Julian Stecklina, Thomas Prescher, Daniel Gruss, "ZombieLoad: Cross-Privilege-Boundary Data Sampling," 2019, `https://zombieloadattack.com/zombieload.pdf`

[P-50] Kit Murdock, David Oswald, Flavio D. Garcia, Jo Van Bulck, Daniel Gruss, Frank Piessens "Plundervolt: Software-based Fault Injection Attacks against Intel SGX," 2019, `https://plundervolt.com/doc/plundervolt.pdf`

[P-51] Rodrigo Branco, Shay Gueron, "Blinded random corruption attacks," in *IEEE International Symposium on Hardware Oriented Security and Trust (HOST)*, 2016

[P-52] Mathias Morbitzer, Manuel Huber, Julian Horsch, Sascha Wessel, "SEVered: Subverting AMD's Virtual Machine Encryption," in Proceedings of the 11th European Workshop on Systems Security 2018, `https://arxiv.org/pdf/1805.09604`

[P-53] "AMD-SEV: Platform DH key recovery via invalid curve attack," 2019, available at `https://seclists.org/fulldisclosure/2019/Jun/46`

[P-54] Mengyuan Li, Yinqian Zhang, Zhiqiang Lin, Yan Solihin, "Exploiting Unprotected I/O Operations in AMD's Secure Encrypted Virtualization," in *Proceedings of the 28th USENIX Security Symposium 2019*, `www.usenix.org/system/files/sec19-li-mengyuan_0.pdf`

[P-55] "AMD PSP: fTPM Remote Code Execution via crafted EK certificate," 2018, `https://seclists.org/fulldisclosure/2018/Jan/12`

[P-56] CTS Labs, "Severe Security Advisory on AMD Processors," *CTS whitepaper 2018*, available at `https://safefirmware.com/amdflaws_whitepaper.pdf`

[P-57] P. Stewin and I. Bystrov, "Understanding DMA Malware," in *Detection of Intrusions and Malware, and Vulnerability Assessment (DIMVA'12), 2012*, available at `https://pdfs.semanticscholar.org/88ad/913424405ac32657a8557f74003b22e9be3c.pdf`.

[P-58] Hervé Sibert, "Le TEE, nouvelle ligne de défense dans les mobiles," in *SSTIC 2013*, available at `www.sstic.org/media/SSTIC2013/SSTIC-actes/conf_invit1_j3_2013/SSTIC2013-Slides-conf_invit1_j3_2013-sibert.pdf`

[P-59] Shai Hasarfaty, Yanai Moyal, "Behind the Scenes of Intel Security and Manageability Engine," in *BlackHat US 2019*, `http://i.blackhat.com/USA-19/Wednesday/us-19-Hasarfaty-Behind-The-Scenes-Of-Intel-Security-And-Manageability-Engine.pdf`

[P-60] Tarjei Mandt, Mathew Solnik, David Wang, "Demystifying the Secure Enclave Processor," in *Blackhat US 2016*, available at `www.blackhat.com/docs/us-16/materials/us-16-Mandt-Demystifying-The-Secure-Enclave-Processor.pdf`

[P-61] Mikhail Davidov, Jeremy Erickson, "Inside the Apple T2," in *Blackhat US 2019*, available at `http://i.blackhat.com/USA-19/Thursday/us-19-Davidov-Inside-The-Apple-T2.pdf`

[P-62] Alexander Tereshkin, Rafal Wojtczuk, "A Ring -3 Rootkits," in *BlackHat US 2009*, available at `https://invisiblethingslab.com/resources/bh09usa/Ring%20-3%20Rootkits.pdf`

[P-63] Vassilios Ververis, "Security Evaluation of Intel's Active Management Technology," in *TRITA-ICT-EX 2010*, `https://people.kth.se/~maguire/DEGREE-PROJECT-REPORTS/100402-Vassilios_Ververis-with-cover.pdf`

[P-64] Igor Skochinsky, "Intel ME Secrets," in *RECON 2014*, `https://recon.cx/2014/slides/Recon%202014%20Skochinsky.pdf`

[P-65] Maxim Goryachy, Mark Ermalov, "Tapping into the Core," in *33C3 2016*, `www.slideshare.net/phdays/tapping-into-the-core`

[P-66] Maxim Goryachy, Mark Ermalov, "Intel DCI," in *hibseconf 2017*, `https://conference.hitb.org/hitbsecconf2017ams/materials/D2T4%20-%20Maxim%20Goryachy%20and%20Mark%20Ermalov%20-%20Intel%20DCI%20Secrets.pdf`

[P-67] Maxim Goryachy, Mark Ermolov, "Intel ME: The Way of the. Static Analysis," in *troopers 2017*, `www.troopers.de/downloads/troopers17/TR17_ME11_Static.pdf`

[P-68] Dmitry Sklyarov, "Intel ME: Flash File System Explained," in *BlackHat EU 2017*, available at `www.blackhat.com/docs/eu-17/materials/eu-17-Sklyarov-Intel-ME-Flash-File-System-Explained.pdf`

[P-69] Dmitriy Evdokimov, Alexander Ermolov, Maksim Malyutin, "Intel AMT Stealth Breakthrough," in *BlackHat US 2017*, available at `www.blackhat.com/docs/us-17/thursday/us-17-Evdokimov-Intel-AMT-Stealth-Breakthrough.pdf`

[P-70] Mark Ermolov, Maxim Goryachy, "How to Hack a Turned-Off Computer, or Running Unsigned Code in Intel Management Engine," in *BlackHat EU 2017*, `www.blackhat.com/docs/eu-17/materials/eu-17-Goryachy-How-To-Hack-A-Turned-Off-Computer-Or-Running-Unsigned-Code-In-Intel-Management-Engine.pdf` .

[P-71] Mark Ermolov, Maxim Goryachy, "Inside Intel Management Engine," in 34c3 2017, `www.youtube.com/watch?v=JMEJCLX2dtw`

[P-72] Maxim Goryachy, Mark Ermolov, "Intel ME Manufacturing Mode: obscured dangers and their relationship to Apple MacBook," 2018, `http://blog.ptsecurity.com/2018/10/intel-me-manufacturing-mode-macbook.html`

[P-73] Dmitry Sklyarov, Maxim Goryachy, "Intel ME Security keys Genealogy, Obfuscation and other Magic," in *CONFidence 2018*, `https://github.com/ptresearch/IntelME-Crypto/blob/master/Intel%20ME%20Security%20keys%20Genealogy%2C%20Obfuscation%20and%20other%20Magic.pdf`

[P-74] Mark Ermolov, Maxim Goryachy, "Intel VISA: Through the Rabbit Hole," in *BlackHat Asia 2019*, available at `https://i.blackhat.com/asia-19/Thu-March-28/bh-asia-Goryachy-Ermolov-Intel-Visa-Through-the-Rabbit-Hole.pdf`

[P-75] Shai Hasarfaty, Yanai Moyal, "Behind the Scenes of Intel Security and Manageability Engine," in *Blackhat US 2019*, available at `https://i.blackhat.com/USA-19/Wednesday/us-19-Hasarfaty-Behind-The-Scenes-Of-Intel-Security-And-Manageability-Engine.pdf`

[P-76] Mark Ermolov, "Intel x86 Root of Trust: loss of trust," in 2020, available at in hi`https://blog.ptsecurity.com/2020/03/intelx86-root-of-trust-loss-of-trust.html`

[P-77] Intel, "The Intel Converged Security and Management Engine IOMMU Hardware Issue – CVE-2019-0090," 2020, `www.intel.com/content/dam/www/public/us/en/security-advisory/documents/cve-2019-0090-whitepaper.pdf`

[P-78] Scott Johnson, "Titan silicon root of trust for Google Cloud," in *Secure Enclaves Workshop 2018*, available at `https://keystone-enclave.org/workshop-website-2018/slides/Scott_Google_Titan.pdf`

[P-79] Doug Stiles, "The Hardware Security Platform Behind Azure Sphere," in HC30, `www.hotchips.org/hc30/1conf/1.13_Microsoft_Hardware_Security_Platform_Behind_Azure_Sphere.pdf`

[P-80] Galen Hunt, George Letey, Edmund B. Nightingale, "The Seven Properties of Highly Secure Devices," Microsoft Whitepaper 2017, `www.microsoft.com/en-us/research/wp-content/uploads/2017/03/SevenPropertiesofHighlySecureDevices.pdf`

[P-81] Fengwei Zhang and Hongwei Zhang, "SoK: A Study of Using Hardware Assisted Isolated Execution," in *Proceedings of the Hardware and Architectural Support for Security and Privacy 2016*, `https://pdfs.semanticscholar.org/9e44/9c2fa294112 2fd3b93fc9c7ef28ec588829f.pdf`

`https://caslab.csl.yale.edu/workshops/hasp2016/HASP16-09_slides.pdf`

[P-82] "seTPM: Towards Flexible Trusted Computing on Mobile Devices Based on GlobalPlatform Secure Elements," `https://rd.springer.com/chapter/10.1007/978-3-319-31271-2_4`

[P-83] Jeremy Boone, "TPM Genie," in *CanSecWest 2018*, available at `https://github.com/nccgroup/TPMGenie/blob/master/docs/CanSecWest_2018_-_TPM_Genie_-_Jeremy_Boone.pdf`

[P-84] Daniel Moghimi, Berk Sunar, Thomas Eisenbarth, Nadia Heninger, "TPM fail: TPM meets Timing and Lattice Attacks," `https://tpm.fail/tpmfail.pdf`

[P-85] Nemec, Matus; Sys, Marek; Svenda, Petr; Klinec, Dusan; Matyas, Vashek, "The Return of Coppersmith's Attack: Practical Factorization of Widely Used RSA Moduli," in *Proceedings of the 2017 ACM SIGSAC Conference on Computer and Communications Security.* `https://crocs.fi.muni.cz/_media/public/papers/nemec_roca_ccs17_preprint.pdf`

[P-86] Ang Cui, Rick Housley "BADFET: Defeating modern secure boot using second-order pulsed electromagnetic fault injection," n *USENIX, WOOT 2017*, available at `www.usenix.org/system/files/conference/woot17/woot17-paper-cui.pdf`

Specification and Guideline

[S-1] AMD, "AMD Architecture Programmer's Manual," 2019, available at `www.amd.com/en/support/tech-docs`

[S-2] AMD, "Secure Encrypted Virtualization API," 2019, available at `https://developer.amd.com/wp-content/resources/55766.PDF`

[S-3] ARM, "ARM Architecture Reference Manual," 2019, available at `https://static.docs.arm.com/ddi0487/ea/DDI0487E_a_armv8_arm.pdf`

[S-4] ARM, "Armv8-M Architecture Reference Manual," 2019, available at `https://static.docs.arm.com/ddi0553/bi/DDI0553B_i_armv8m_arm.pdf`

[S-5] ARM, "ARM Security Technology – Building a Secure System using TrustZone Technology," 2009, available at `http://infocenter.arm.com/help/topic/com.arm.doc.prd29-genc-009492c/PRD29-GENC-009492C_trustzone_security_whitepaper.pdf`

[S-6] ARM, "ARM Security Technology – Building a Secure System using TrustZone Technology," 2009, available at `http://infocenter.arm.com/help/topic/com.arm.doc.prd29-genc-009492c/PRD29-GENC-009492C_trustzone_security_whitepaper.pdf`

[S-7] ARM, "Memory Protection Unit (MPU)," 2016, available at `https://static.docs.arm.com/100699/0100/armv8m_architecture_memory_protection_unit_100699_0100_00_en.pdf`

[S-8] ARM, "TrustZone technology for the ARMv8-M architecture," 2017, available at `https://static.docs.arm.com/100690/0200/armv8m_trustzone_technology_100690_0200.pdf`

[S-9] ARM, "Arm Platform Security Architecture Firmware Framework," 2019, available at `https://armkeil.blob.core.windows.net/developer/Files/pdf/PlatformSecurityArchitecture/Architect/DEN0063-PSA_Firmware_Framework-1.0.0-2.pdf`

[S-10] ARM, "Arm Platform Security Architecture Trusted Boot and Firmware Update," 2018, available at `https://pages.arm.com/rs/312-SAX-488/images/DEN0072-PSA_TBFU_1.0-bet1.pdf`

[S-11] ARM, "Arm Platform Security Architecture Security Model," 2019, available at `https://armkeil.blob.core.windows.net/developer/Files/pdf/PlatformSecurityArchitecture/Architect/DEN0079-PSA_SM_ALPHA-02.pdf`

[S-12] ARM, "Arm® Platform Security Architecture Trusted Base System Architecture for Arm®v6-M, Arm®v7-M and Arm®v8-M," 2019, available at `https://pages.arm.com/psa-resources-tbsa-m.html`

[S-13] Intel, "Intel 64 and IA-32 Architecture Software Developer Manuals," 2019, available at `https://software.intel.com/en-us/articles/intel-sdm`

[S-14] Intel, "Intel Architecture Memory Encryption Technologies Specification," 2019, available at `https://software.intel.com/sites/default/files/managed/a5/16/Multi-Key-Total-Memory-Encryption-Spec.pdf`

[S-15] Intel, "STM User Guide," 2015, `https://software.intel.com/sites/default/files/managed/0c/92/STM_User_Guide-001.pdf`

[S-16] RISC-V, "The RISC-V Instruction Set Manual," 2017, `https://riscv.org/specifications/`

[S-17] Global Platform, "TEE System Architecture," 2018, available at `https://globalplatform.org/specs-library/`

[S-18] IETF, "TEEP: Trusted Execution Environment Provisioning (TEEP) Architecture," 2020, `https://datatracker.ietf.org/doc/draft-ietf-teep-architecture/`

Web

[W-1] STM source, `https://software.intel.com/en-us/articles/smi-transfer-monitor-stm`

[W-2] STM sample implementation, `https://github.com/jyao1/stm`

[W-3] ThinkPwn, `https://github.com/Cr4sh/ThinkPwn`

[W-4] eclypsium, SMM speculative execution attacks, `https://eclypsium.com/2018/05/17/system-management-mode-speculative-execution-attacks/`

[W-5] ARM TrustZone, `https://developer.arm.com/ip-products/security-ip/trustzone`

[W-6] Keystone, `https://keystone-enclave.org/`

[W-7] Hex-five, `https://hex-five.com/`

[W-8] Joakim Bech, Joakim Bech, Ard Biesheuvel, Mark Brown, Daniel Thompson, "Implications of Meltdown and Spectre," `www.linaro.org/blog/meltdown-spectre/`, `www.linaro.org/blog/meltdown-spectre-2/`

[W-9] SERECA: Hardware-Assisted Cloud Security, `https://lsds.doc.ic.ac.uk/projects/sereca`

[W-10] Global Platform, `https://globalplatform.org/`

[W-11] op-tee, `www.op-tee.org/`

[W-12] op-tee, `www.linaro.org/blog/op-tee-open-source-security-mass-market/`

[W-13] openenclave, `https://github.com/openenclave/openenclave`

[W-14] Google asylo, `https://github.com/google/asylo`

[W-15] Google asylo, `https://cloud.google.com/blog/products/gcp/introducing-asylo-an-open-source-framework-for-confidential-computing`

[W-16] Intel SGX SDK, `https://software.intel.com/en-us/sgx/sdk`

[W-17] Remote Attestation, Overall View of Intel SGX Infrastructure Services, `www.sgx101.com/portfolio/remote_attestation/`

[W-18] Spectre attack SGX, `https://github.com/lsds/spectre-attack-sgx`

[W-19] rust sgx sdk, `https://github.com/apache/incubator-teaclave-sgx-sdk`

[W-20] Graphene, `https://grapheneproject.io/`, `https://github.com/oscarlab/graphene`

[W-21] enarx, `https://github.com/enarx/enarx`

[W-22] `https://courses.cs.ut.ee/MTAT.07.022/2017_spring/uploads/Main/hiie-report-s16-17.pdf`

[W-23] Architecting more secure world with isolation and virtualization, `https://community.arm.com/developer/ip-products/processors/b/processors-ip-blog/posts/architecting-more-secure-world-with-isolation-and-virtualization`

[W-24] IBM, technical overview of secure execution for Linux on IBM Z, `https://developer.ibm.com/blogs/technical-overview-of-secure-execution-for-linux-on-ibm-z/`

[W-25] Digital Security by Design, `www.arm.com/blogs/blueprint/digital-security-by-design`

[W-26] Matt Chandler, "Intel Enhanced Privacy ID (EPID) Security Technology," 2017, `https://software.intel.com/en-us/articles/intel-enhanced-privacy-id-epid-security-technology`

[W-27] Dynamic Application Loader (DAL), `https://software.intel.com/en-us/dal-developer-guide`

[W-28] Titan in depth security in plaintext, available at `https://cloud.google.com/blog/products/gcp/titan-in-depth-security-in-plaintext`

[W-29] Google, "OpenTitan: Open source silicon root of trust (RoT)," `https://opentitan.org/`

[W-30] Apple T2 Security Chip Overview, available at `www.apple.com/mac/docs/Apple_T2_Security_Chip_Overview.pdf`

[W-31] Apple Secure Enclave Overview, `https://support.apple.com/guide/security/secure-enclave-overview-sec59b0b31ff/web`

[W-32] About Touch ID advanced security technology, `https://support.apple.com/en-us/HT204587`

[W-33] MS TPM 2.0 Reference Implementation, `https://github.com/microsoft/ms-tpm-20-ref`

[W-34] What is Azure Sphere, `https://docs.microsoft.com/en-us/azure-sphere/product-overview/what-is-azure-sphere`

[W-35] Microsoft, Anatomy of a secure MCU, `https://azure.microsoft.com/en-us/blog/anatomy-of-a-secured-mcu`

[W-36] Microsoft, Force firmware code to be measured and attested by Secure Launch on Windows 10, `https://www.microsoft.com/security/blog/2020/09/01/force-firmware-code-to-be-measured-and-attested-by-secure-launch-on-windows-10/`

CHAPTER 18

Silicon Secure Configuration

The role and responsibility of the system firmware is to initialize the silicon and boot the operating system. One important task in the silicon initialization is to configure the system registers into a secure state. We cannot touch all possible silicon security lock registers in this chapter. As such, we will only discuss some of the more important register settings as examples.

Flash Lock

The system firmware is located on the flash part. It should be locked and only have the firmware allowed to perform the secure unlock and update.

BIOS Write Protection

Silicon may define a set of registers to lock the firmware. Figure 18-1 shows the BIOS lock–related registers in the Intel Platform Controller Hub (PCH).

© Jiewen Yao and Vincent Zimmer 2020
J. Yao and V. Zimmer, *Building Secure Firmware*, https://doi.org/10.1007/978-1-4842-6106-4_18

BIOS_CNTL—BIOS Control Register (LPC I/F—D31:F0)

Offset Address:	DCh	Attribute:	R/WLO, R/W, RO
Default Value:	20h	Size:	8 bits
Lockable:	No	Power Well:	Core

Bit	Description
7:6	Reserved
5	**SMM BIOS Write Protect Disable (SMM_BWP)**—R/WL. This bit set defines when the BIOS region can be written by the host. 0 = BIOS region SMM protection is disabled. The BIOS Region is writable regardless if processors are in SMM or not. (Set this field to 0 for legacy behavior). 1 = BIOS region SMM protection is enabled. The BIOS Region is not writable unless all processors are in SMM and BIOS Write Enable (BIOSWE) is set to '1'.
4	**Top Swap Status (TSS)**—RO. This bit provides a read-only path to view the state of the Top Swap bit that is at offset 3414h, bit 0.
1	**BIOS Lock Enable (BLE)**—R/WLO. 0 = Transition of BIOSWE from '0' to '1' will not cause an SMI to be asserted. 1 = Enables setting the BIOSWE bit to cause SMIs and locks SMM_BWP. Once set, this bit can only be cleared by a PLTRST#.
0	**BIOS Write Enable (BIOSWE)**—R/W. 0 = Only read cycles result in Firmware Hub or SPI I/F cycles. 1 = Access to the BIOS space is enabled for both read and write cycles. When this bit is written from a 0 to a 1 and BIOS Lock Enable (BLE) is also set, an SMI# is generated. This ensures that only SMI code can update BIOS.

Figure 18-1. BIOS Control Registers (Source: 9-series-chipset-pch-datasheet)

The BIOS image includes both code and data. Sometimes, we may want to update the data, but we don't want to update the code. As such, the update must happen in an isolated and privileged environment, such as system management mode (SMM). The silicon provides a way to lock the BIOS region in non-SMM and requires that an unlock of the BIOS region occurs only in SMM. This work is done by the SMM BIOS Write Protect Disable (SMM_BWP), BIOS Write Enable (BIOSWE), and BIOS Lock Enable (BLE) register bits.

In a normal boot environment, the SMM_BWP is 1, BLE is 1, and BIOSWE is 0. Because the Write Enable is clear, the BIOS space cannot be written. If a non-SMM malicious program wants to set BIOSWE from 0 to 1, an SMI will be generated, and the SMI handler may clear this BIOSWE bit.

If an SMM program wants to provide updates to the BIOS, it may take the following steps:

1. The SMM program sets BIOSWE from 0 to 1. Since the system is already in SMM, this bit can be set successfully.

2. The SMM program starts modifying the BIOS region.

3. Once the SMM program finishes the update, it clears BIOSWE to protect the BIOS region again.

Since the lock highly depends upon the SMM implementation, the SMM_BWP is introduced to make sure the BIOS region is not writeable unless all the processors are in SMM.

BIOS Region Selection

The BIOS region selection is a feature to decode from where to boot. Figure 18-2 shows the BIOS region selection–related registers.

GCS—General Control and Status Register

Offset Address: 3410–3413h   Attribute: R/W, R/WLO
Default Value: 00000yy0h (yy = xx0000x0b)   Size: 32-bit

Bit	Description
31:12	Reserved
11:10	**Boot BIOS Straps (BBS)**—R/W. This field determines the destination of accesses to the BIOS memory range. The default values for these bits represent the strap values of GPIO51 (bit 11) at the rising edge of PWROK and SATA1GP/GPIO19 (bit 10) at the rising edge of PWROK. **Bits 11:10** **Description** 00b LPC 01b Reserved 10b Reserved 11b SPI When SPI or LPC is selected, the range that is decoded is further qualified by other configuration bits described in the respective sections. The value in this field can be overwritten by software as long as the BIOS Interface Lock-Down (bit 0) is not set. Boot BIOS Destination Select to LPC by functional strap or using Boot BIOS Destination Bit will not affect SPI accesses initiated by Intel Management Engine or Integrated GbE LAN.
0	**BIOS Interface Lock-Down (BILD)**—R/WLO. 0 = Disabled. 1 = Prevents BUC.TS (offset 3414, bit 0) and GCS.BBS (offset 3410h, bits 11:10) from being changed. This bit can only be written from 0 to 1 once.

Figure 18-2(A). *BIOS Region Selection Registers (Source: 9-series-chipset-pch-datasheet)*

BUC—Backed Up Control Register

Offset Address: 3414h   Attribute: R/W
Default Value: 0000000xb   Size: 8-bit

All bits in this register are in the RTC well and only cleared by RTCRST#.

Bit	Description
0	**Top Swap (TS)**—R/W. 0 = PCH will not allow invert the boot block. 1 = PCH will allow boot block invert, for cycles going to the BIOS space. ***Note:*** If Top Swap is enabled (TS = 1b): 1. If booting from SPI, then the BIOS boot block size (BOOT_BLOCK_SIZE) **soft strap** determines if A16, A17, A18, A19 or A20 should be inverted. 2. If booting from LPC (FWH), then the boot-block size is hard-set to 64 KB and only A16 is inverted (soft strap is ignored in this case). 3. If PCH is strapped for Top Swap (GPIO55 is low at rising edge of PWROK), then this bit **cannot** be cleared by software. The strap jumper should be removed and the system rebooted.

Figure 18-2(B).   *BIOS Region Selection Registers (Source: 9-series-chipset-pch-datasheet)*

Top Swap (TS) is a feature to swap the top block of the Firmware Hub or Serial Peripheral Interface (SPI) flash (also known as boot block) with another location. This is designed for a safe update of the boot block. When it is enabled, the PCH will invert the address for cycles going to the two top blocks of the flash. For example, if the block size is 64 K, accessing the FFFF_0000h–FFFF_FFFFh MMIO address becomes an access to the FFFE_0000h–FFFE_FFFFh flash address and vice versa.

The secure boot block update can be used as described in the following:

1. The firmware backs up the top block to the block below the top (the swap block).

2. The firmware enables the Top Swap feature. This will invert the appropriate address bits for the cycles going to the FWH or SPI. This bit is stored in the RTC well.

3. The firmware erases the top block and writes the new top block.

4. The firmware disables the Top Swap feature.

If there is any power failure reset happening in step 3, the system will boot from the boot block backed up in step 1 and perform the recovery.

The Boot BIOS Strap (BBS) is a feature to select the region from where the BIOS boots. It could be from the LPC bus or SPI bus. Previous generations even had the capability to boot the BIOS from a plug-in PCI card to support system recovery, but now the feature is removed.

Both TS and BBS shall be locked by the BIOS Interface Lock Down (BILD) register.

SPI Region Lock

Besides the BIOS lock register, an SPI control may have additional locking capability. Figure 18-3 shows a set of protected region registers to control the read and write access for a specific region.

PR0—Protected Range 0 Register (SPI Memory Mapped Configuration Registers)

Memory Address: SPIBAR + 74h   Attribute: R/W
Default Value: 00000000h   Size: 32 bits

This register can not be written when the FLOCKDN bit is set to 1.

Bit	Description
31	**Write Protection Enable**—R/W. When set, this bit indicates that the Base and Limit fields in this register are valid and that writes and erases directed to addresses between them (inclusive) must be blocked by hardware. The base and limit fields are ignored when this bit is cleared.
30:29	Reserved
28:16	**Protected Range Limit**—R/W. This field corresponds to FLA address bits 24:12 and specifies the upper limit of the protected range. Address bits 11:0 are assumed to be FFFh for the limit comparison. Any address greater than the value programmed in this field is unaffected by this protected range.
15	**Read Protection Enable**—R/W. When set, this bit indicates that the Base and Limit fields in this register are valid and that read directed to addresses between them (inclusive) must be blocked by hardware. The base and limit fields are ignored when this bit is cleared.
14:13	Reserved
12:0	**Protected Range Base**—R/W. This field corresponds to FLA address bits 24:12 and specifies the lower base of the protected range. Address bits 11:0 are assumed to be 000h for the base comparison. Any address less than the value programmed in this field is unaffected by this protected range.

Figure 18-3(A). *SPI Region Registers (Source: 9-series-chipset-pch-datasheet)*

HSFS—Hardware Sequencing Flash Status Register (SPI Memory Mapped Configuration Registers)

Memory Address: SPIBAR + 04h   Attribute: RO, R/WC, R/W
Default Value: 0000h   Size: 16 bits

Bit	Description
15	**Flash Configuration Lock-Down (FLOCKDN)**—R/W/L. When set to 1, those Flash Program Registers that are locked down by this FLOCKDN bit cannot be written. Once set to 1, this bit can only be cleared by a hardware reset due to a global reset or host partition reset in an Intel ME enabled system.

Figure 18-3(B).   *SPI Region Registers (Source: 9-series-chipset-pch-datasheet)*

The PCH SPI controller provides a set of protected range (PR) registers. The benefit of the PR register is to decouple the flash protection from the SMM environment. During boot, the firmware may set the code region to be protected by the PR and lock it with the Flash Configuration Lock Down (FLOCKDN) capability. As such, even if the SMM environment is compromised, the BIOS code region can still be protected.

SPI Region Access Control

The SPI region may be separated to different masters, such as BIOS or Management Engine (ME). As such, we might need fine-grained access control to not allow a BIOS master to access the ME region and correspondingly not allow the ME master to access the BIOS region. Figure 18-4 shows the flash region access permission (FRAP) register provided in the PCH.

FRAP—Flash Regions Access Permissions Register (SPI Memory Mapped Configuration Registers)

Memory Address: SPIBAR + 50h   Attribute: RO, R/W
Default Value: 00000202h   Size: 32 bits

This register is only applicable when SPI device is in descriptor mode.

Bit	Description
31:24	**BIOS Master Write Access Grant (BMWAG)**—R/W. Each bit [31:24] corresponds to Master[7:0]. BIOS can grant one or more masters write access to the BIOS region 1 overriding the permissions in the Flash Descriptor. Master[1] is Host processor/BIOS, Master[2] is Intel Management Engine, Master[3] is Host processor/GbE. Master[0] and Master[7:4] are reserved. The contents of this register field are locked by the FLOCKDN bit.
23:16	**BIOS Master Read Access Grant (BMRAG)**—R/W. Each bit [23:16] corresponds to Master[7:0]. BIOS can grant one or more masters read access to the BIOS region 1 overriding the read permissions in the Flash Descriptor. Master[1] is Host processor/BIOS, Master[2] is Intel Management Engine, Master[3] is Host processor/GbE. Master[0] and Master[7:4] are reserved. The contents of this register field are locked by the FLOCKDN bit
15:8	**BIOS Region Write Access (BRWA)**—RO. Each bit [15:8] corresponds to Regions [7:0]. If the bit is set, this master can erase and write that particular region through register accesses. The contents of this register field are that of the Flash Descriptor. Flash Master 1 Master Region Write Access OR a particular master has granted BIOS write permissions in their Master Write Access Grant register or the Flash Descriptor Security Override strap is set.
7:0	**BIOS Region Read Access (BRRA)**—RO. Each bit [7:0] corresponds to Regions [7:0]. If the bit is set, this master can read that particular region through register accesses. The contents of this register field are that of the Flash Descriptor.Flash Master 1.Master Region Write Access OR a particular master has granted BIOS read permissions in their Master Read Access Grant register or the Flash Descriptor Security Override strap is set.

Figure 18-4. *SPI Flash Region Access Permission Register (Source: 9-series-chipset-pch-datasheet)*

SMM Lock

The system management mode (SMM) lock is as important as the flash lock because the SMM environment has higher execution privilege than the operating system kernel and even the hypervisor.

SMRAM Access Lock

The system management RAM (SMRAM) is controlled by the memory controller. Figure 18-5 shows the SMRAM control (SMRAMC) register in the Intel memory controller hub (MCH).

System Management RAM Control (SMRAMC)—Offset 88h

The SMRAMC register controls how accesses to Compatible SMRAM spaces are treated. The Open, Close and Lock bits function only when G_SMRAME bit is set to 1. Also, the Open bit must be reset before the Lock bit is set.

Access Method

Type: CFG   **Offset:** [B:0, D:0, F:0] + 88h

Bit Range	Default & Access	Field Name (ID): Description
7	0h RO	**Reserved (RSVD):** Reserved.
6	0h RW_LV	**D_OPEN:** When D_OPEN = 1 and D_LCK = 0, the SMM DRAM space is made visible even when SMM decode is not active. This is intended to help BIOS initialize SMM space. Software should ensure that D_OPEN = 1 and D_CLS = 1 are not set at the same time.
5	0h RW_L	**D_CLS:** When D_CLS = 1, SMM DRAM space is not accessible to data references, even if SMM decode is active. Code references may still access SMM DRAM space. This will allow SMM software to reference through SMM space to update the display even when SMM is mapped over the VGA range. Software should ensure that D_OPEN = 1 and D_CLS = 1 are not set at the same time.
4	0h RW_KL	**D_LCK:** When D_LCK=1, then D_OPEN is reset to 0 and all writeable fields in this register are locked (become RO). D_LCK can be set to 1 via a normal configuration space write but can only be cleared by a Full Reset. The combination of D_LCK and D_OPEN provide convenience with security. The BIOS can use the D_OPEN function to initialize SMM space and then use D_LCK to "lock down" SMM space in the future so that no application software (or even BIOS itself) can violate the integrity of SMM space, even if the program has knowledge of the D_OPEN function.
3	0h RW_L	**G_SMRAME:** If set to '1', then Compatible SMRAM functions are enabled, providing 128KB of DRAM accessible at the A_0000h address while in SMM. Once D_LCK is set, this bit becomes RO.
2:0	2h RO	**C_BASE_SEG:** This field indicates the location of SMM space. SMM DRAM is not remapped. It is simply made visible if the conditions are right to access SMM space, otherwise the access is forwarded to DMI. Only SMM space bewteen A_0000h and B_FFFFh is supported, so this field is hardwired to 010b.

Figure 18-5. *SMRAM Control Register (Source: desktop-6th-gen-core-family-datasheet)*

When the D_OPEN is set, the SMRAM is visible to the normal execution mode. In this state, the BIOS can initialize the contents within SMRAM. Once the BIOS finishes the SMRAM content update, the BIOS should set the D_CLS bit to close the SMRAM region and set the D_LCK bit to lock the configuration in order to prevent malicious code from tampering with the contents of SMRAM.

SMRAM Location Lock

The system management RAM (SMRAM) location is also defined by the memory controller. Figure 18-6 shows the TSEG Memory Base (TSEGMB) register and the Base of Graphic Translation Table (GTT) stolen memory (BGSM) register in the Intel memory controller hub (MCH).

TSEG Memory Base (TSEGMB)—Offset B8h

This register contains the base address of TSEG DRAM memory. BIOS determines the base of TSEG memory which must be at or below Graphics Base of GTT Stolen Memory (PCI Device 0 Offset B4 bits 31:20).

Access Method

Type: CFG   **Offset:** [B:0, D:0, F:0] + B8h

Bit Range	Default & Access	Field Name (ID): Description
31:20	0h RW_L	**TSEGMB:** This register contains the base address of TSEG DRAM memory. BIOS determines the base of TSEG memory which must be at or below Graphics Base of GTT Stolen Memory (PCI Device 0 Offset B4 bits 31:20). BIOS must program the value of TSEGMB to be the same as BGSM when TSEG is disabled.
19:1	0h RO	**Reserved (RSVD):** Reserved.
0	0h RW_KL	**LOCK:** This bit will lock all writeable settings in this register, including itself.

Figure 18-6(A). *TSEG Memory Base Register (Source: desktop-6th-gen-core-family-datasheet)*

Base of GTT stolen Memory (BGSM)—Offset B4h

This register contains the base address of stolen DRAM memory for the GTT. BIOS determines the base of GTT stolen memory by subtracting the GTT graphics stolen memory size (PCI Device 0 offset 52 bits 9:8) from the Graphics Base of Data Stolen Memory (PCI Device 0 offset B0 bits 31:20).

Access Method

Type: CFG   **Offset:** [B:0, D:0, F:0] + B4h

Bit Range	Default & Access	Field Name (ID): Description
31:20	1h RW_L	**BGSM:** This register contains the base address of stolen DRAM memory for the GTT. BIOS determines the base of GTT stolen memory by subtracting the GTT graphics stolen memory size (PCI Device 0 offset 50 bits 7:6) from the Graphics Base of Data Stolen Memory (PCI Device 0 offset B0 bits 31:20).
19:1	0h RO	**Reserved (RSVD):** Reserved.
0	0h RW_KL	**LOCK:** This bit will lock all writeable settings in this register, including itself.

Figure 18-6(B).   *Base of GTT Stolen Memory Register (Source: desktop-6th-gen-core-family-datasheet)*

The memory between the TSEGMB and BGSM range is SMRAM. As such, the BIOS should lock the TSEGMB and BGSM during the BIOS boot.

SMRAM Address Alias Lock

In Chapter 16, we have discussed the address alias attack to SMM by using the hardware remapping mechanism.

The mitigation is that the BIOS should always lock down the system memory layout registers. Figure 18-7 shows a set of memory layout registers defined in the Intel memory controller hub (MCH), including Remap Base Address (REMAPBASE), Remap Limit Address (REMAPLMIT), Top of Memory (TOM), Top of Upper Usable DRAM (TOUUD), and Top of Low Usable DRAM (TOLUD). The details of the memory layout have been shown in Chapter 16, Figure 16-4.

The BIOS should lock all those memory layout configuration registers during boot. Otherwise, the attacker can perform address alias exploit by changing the layout of memory mapping and causing a memory overlap.

Remap Base Address Register (REMAPBASE)—Offset 90h

Access Method

Type: CFG   **Offset:** [B:0, D:0, F:0] + 90h

Bit Range	Default & Access	Field Name (ID): Description
63:39	0h RO	**Reserved (RSVD):** Reserved.
38:20	7FFFFh RW_L	**REMAPBASE:** The value in this register defines the lower boundary of the Remap window. The Remap window is inclusive of this address. In the decoder A[19:0] of the Remap Base Address are assumed to be 0's. Thus the bottom of the defined memory range will be aligned to a 1MB boundary. When the value in this register is greater than the value programmed into the Remap Limit register, the Remap window is disabled. These bits are Intel TXT lockable.
19:1	0h RO	**Reserved (RSVD):** Reserved.
0	0h RW_KL	**LOCK:** This bit will lock all writeable settings in this register, including itself.

Figure 18-7(A). *Remap Base Address Register (Source: desktop-6th-gen-core-family-datasheet)*

Remap Limit Address Register (REMAPLIMIT)—Offset 98h

Access Method

Type: CFG   **Offset:** [B:0, D:0, F:0] + 98h

Bit Range	Default & Access	Field Name (ID): Description
63:39	0h RO	**Reserved (RSVD):** Reserved.
38:20	0h RW_L	**REMAPLMT:** The value in this register defines the upper boundary of the Remap window. The Remap window is inclusive of this address. In the decoder A[19:0] of the remap limit address are assumed to be F's. Thus the top of the defined range will be one byte less than a 1MB boundary. When the value in this register is less than the value programmed into the Remap Base register, the Remap window is disabled. These Bits are Intel TXT lockable.
19:1	0h RO	**Reserved (RSVD):** Reserved.
0	0h RW_KL	**LOCK:** This bit will lock all writeable settings in this register, including itself.

Figure 18-7(B). *Remap Limit Address Register (Source: desktop-6th-gen-core-family-datasheet)*

Top of Memory (TOM)—Offset A0h

This Register contains the size of physical memory. BIOS determines the memory size reported to the OS using this Register.

Access Method

Type: CFG   **Offset:** [B:0, D:0, F:0] + A0h

Bit Range	Default & Access	Field Name (ID): Description
63:39	0h RO	**Reserved (RSVD):** Reserved.
38:20	7FFFFh RW_L	**TOM:** This register reflects the total amount of populated physical memory. This is NOT necessarily the highest main memory address (holes may exist in main memory address map due to addresses allocated for memory mapped IO). These bits correspond to address bits 38:20 (1MB granularity). Bits 19:0 are assumed to be 0. All the bits in this register are locked in Intel TXT mode.
19:1	0h RO	**Reserved (RSVD):** Reserved.
0	0h RW_KL	**LOCK:** This bit will lock all writeable settings in this register, including itself.

Figure 18-7(C). *Top of Memory Register (Source: desktop-6th-gen-core-family-datasheet)*

Top of Upper Usable DRAM (TOUUD)—Offset A8h

This 64 bit register defines the Top of Upper Usable DRAM.
Configuration software must set this value to TOM minus all ME stolen memory if
reclaim is disabled. If reclaim is enabled, this value must be set to reclaim limit +
1byte, 1MB aligned, since reclaim limit is 1MB aligned. Address bits 19:0 are assumed
to be 000_0000h for the purposes of address comparison. The Host interface
positively decodes an address towards DRAM if the incoming address is less than the
value programmed in this register and greater than or equal to 4GB.
BIOS Restriction: Minimum value for TOUUD is 4GB.
These bits are Intel TXT lockable.

Access Method

Type: CFG   **Offset:** [B:0, D:0, F:0] + A8h

Bit Range	Default & Access	Field Name (ID): Description
63:39	0h RO	**Reserved (RSVD):** Reserved.
38:20	0h RW_L	**TOUUD:** This register contains bits 38 to 20 of an address one byte above the maximum DRAM memory above 4G that is usable by the operating system. Configuration software must set this value to TOM minus all ME stolen memory if reclaim is disabled. If reclaim is enabled, this value must be set to reclaim limit 1MB aligned since reclaim limit + 1byte is 1MB aligned. Address bits 19:0 are assumed to be 000_0000h for the purposes of address comparison. The Host interface positively decodes an address towards DRAM if the incoming address is less than the value programmed in this register and greater than 4GB. All the bits in this register are locked in Intel TXT mode.
19:1	0h RO	**Reserved (RSVD):** Reserved.
0	0h RW_KL	**LOCK:** This bit will lock all writeable settings in this register, including itself.

Figure 18-7(D). *Top of Upper Usable DRAM Register (Source: desktop-6th-gen-core-family-datasheet)*

Top of Low Usable DRAM (TOLUD)—Offset BCh

This 32 bit register defines the Top of Low Usable DRAM. TSEG, GTT Graphics memory and Graphics Stolen Memory are within the DRAM space defined. From the top, the Host optionally claims 1 to 64MBs of DRAM for internal graphics if enabled, 1or 2MB of DRAM for GTT Graphics Stolen Memory (if enabled) and 1, 2, or 8 MB of DRAM for TSEG if enabled.

> Programming Example:
> C1DRB3 is set to 4GB
> TSEG is enabled and TSEG size is set to 1MB
> Internal Graphics is enabled, and Graphics Mode Select is set to 32MB
> GTT Graphics Stolen Memory Size set to 2MB
> BIOS knows the OS requires 1G of PCI space.

BIOS also knows the range from 0_FEC0_0000h to 0_FFFF_FFFFh is not usable by the system. This 20MB range at the very top of addressable memory space is lost to APIC and Intel TXT.

> According to the above equation, TOLUD is originally calculated to: 4GB = 1_0000_0000h

> The system memory requirements are: 4GB (max addressable space) - 1GB (pci space) - 35MB (lost memory) = 3GB - 35MB (minimum granularity) = 0_ECB0_0000h

> Since 0_ECB0_0000h (PCI and other system requirements) is less than 1_0000_0000h, TOLUD should be programmed to ECBh.

These bits are Intel TXT lockable.

Access Method

Type: CFG		Offset: [B:0, D:0, F:0] + BCh

Bit Range	Default & Access	Field Name (ID): Description
31:20	1h RW_L	**TOLUD:** This register contains bits 31 to 20 of an address one byte above the maximum DRAM memory below 4G that is usable by the operating system. Address bits 31 down to 20 programmed to 01h implies a minimum memory size of 1MB. Configuration software must set this value to the smaller of the following 2 choices: maximum amount memory in the system minus ME stolen memory plus one byte or the minimum address allocated for PCI memory. Address bits 19:0 are assumed to be 0_0000h for the purposes of address comparison. The Host interface positively decodes an address towards DRAM if the incoming address is less than the value programmed in this register. The Top of Low Usable DRAM is the lowest address above both Graphics Stolen memory and Tseg. BIOS determines the base of Graphics Stolen Memory by subtracting the Graphics Stolen Memory Size from TOLUD and further decrements by Tseg size to determine base of Tseg. All the Bits in this register are locked in Intel TXT mode. This register must be 1MB aligned when reclaim is enabled.
19:1	0h RO	**Reserved (RSVD):** Reserved.
0	0h RW_KL	**LOCK:** This bit will lock all writeable settings in this register, including itself.

Figure 18-7(E). *Top of Low Usable DRAM Register (Source: desktop-6th-gen-core-family-datasheet)*

SMRR

We have discussed in Chapter 17 that Intel CPU introduced the SMRAM range register (SMRR) to resist the cache poisoning attack. Figure 18-8 shows the SMRR in the "Intel 64 and IA-32 Architecture Software Developer Manuals."

Register Address		Architectural MSR Name / Bit Fields (Former MSR Name)	MSR/Bit Description	Comment
Hex	Decimal			
1F2H	498	IA32_SMRR_PHYSBASE	SMRR Base Address (Writeable only in SMM) Base address of SMM memory range.	If IA32_MTRRCAP.SMRR[11] = 1
		7:0	Type. Specifies memory type of the range.	
		11:8	Reserved	
		31:12	PhysBase SMRR physical Base Address.	
		63:32	Reserved	
1F3H	499	IA32_SMRR_PHYSMASK	SMRR Range Mask (Writeable only in SMM) Range Mask of SMM memory range.	If IA32_MTRRCAP[SMRR] = 1
		10:0	Reserved	
		11	Valid Enable range mask.	
		31:12	PhysMask SMRR address range mask.	
		63:32	Reserved	

Figure 18-8. *SMRR (Source: Intel 64 and IA-32 Architecture Software Developer Manuals)*

The SMRR physical base and physical mask pair define the cacheability of the SMRAM region inside of SMM. If the system is in non-SMM code, the SMRAM is always treated as non-cacheable. The BIOS should always initialize the SMRR to protect the SMRAM from the cache attack. Care must be taken that the SMRR setting should be identical to the SMRAM setting in the memory controller hub.

SMM Code Access Check

Because SMM has such high privilege, one possible SMM attack is to let SMM code execute non-SMM code. This is similar to the return-to-user attack. Intel CPUs introduced the SMM code access check to generate a machine check exception (MCE) if the SMM code calls out of SMRAM. This solution uses a similar idea to the Supervisor Mode Execute Prevention (SMEP). See Figure 18-9.

Register Address		Register Name / Bit Fields	Scope	Bit Description
Hex	Dec			
4E0H	1248	MSR_SMM_FEATURE_CONTROL	Package	Enhanced SMM Feature Control (SMM-RW)
				Reports SMM capability Enhancement. Accessible only while in SMM.
		0		Lock (SMM-RWO)
				When set to '1' locks this register from further changes.
		1		Reserved
		2		SMM_Code_Chk_En (SMM-RW)
				This control bit is available only if MSR_SMM_MCA_CAP[58] == 1. When set to '0' (default) none of the logical processors are prevented from executing SMM code outside the ranges defined by the SMRR.
				When set to '1' any logical processor in the package that attempts to execute SMM code not within the ranges defined by the SMRR will assert an unrecoverable MCE.
		63:3		Reserved

Figure 18-9. *SMM Code Access Check (Source: Intel 64 and IA-32 Architecture Software Developer Manuals)*

Global SMI Lock

Some BIOS protections, such as flash protection, rely upon SMM. If the attacker wants to perform an unlock, then an SMI is triggered. The SMI handler can lock the configuration again. However, the SMI can be enabled or disabled in the PCH register. If the attacker disables the SMI, then the SMM-based protection can be bypassed.

Figure 18-10 shows the SMI enable register and the SMI lock register in the Intel Platform Controller Hub (PCH). A global SMI enable (GBL_SMI_EN) bit in the SMI_EN register indicates if the SMI can be generated based upon the enabled event. This bit can be locked by the SMI lock (SMI_LOCK) bit in the general PM configuration (GEN_PMCON) register. The BIOS should set SMI_LOCK in PCH to lock the GBL_SMI_EN to prevent such an SMI disable attack.

SMI_EN—SMI Control and Enable Register

I/O Address:	PMBASE + 30h	Attribute:	R/W, R/WO, WO
Default Value:	00000002h	Size:	32 bit
Lockable:	No	Usage:	ACPI or Legacy
Power Well:	Core		

Bit	Description
1	**End of SMI (EOS)—**R/W (special). This bit controls the arbitration of the SMI signal to the processor. This bit must be set for the PCH to assert SMI# low to the processor after SMI# has been asserted previously. 0 = Once the PCH asserts SMI# low, the EOS bit is automatically cleared. 1 = When this bit is set to 1, SMI# signal will be de-asserted for 4 PCI clocks before its assertion. In the SMI handler, the processor should clear all pending SMIs (by servicing them and then clearing their respective status bits), set the EOS bit, and exit SMM. This will allow the SMI arbiter to re-assert SMI upon detection of an SMI event and the setting of a SMI status bit. **Note:** The PCH is able to generate 1st SMI after reset even though EOS bit is not set. Subsequent SMI require EOS bit is set.
0	**GBL_SMI_EN—**R/W. 0 = No SMI# will be generated by PCH. This bit is reset by a PCI reset event. 1 = Enables the generation of SMI# in the system upon any enabled SMI event. › **Note:** When the SMI_LOCK bit is set, this bit cannot be changed.

Figure 18-10(A). *Global SMI Enable Register (Source: 9-series-chipset-pch-datasheet)*

GEN_PMCON_1—General PM Configuration 1 Register (PM—D31:F0)

Offset Address:	A0–A1h	Attribute:	R/W, RO, R/WLO
Default Value:	0000h	Size:	16 bits
Lockable:	No	Usage:	ACPI, Legacy
		Power Well:	Core

Bit	Description
4	**SMI_LOCK—**R/WLO. When this bit is set, writes to the GLB_SMI_EN bit (PMBASE + 30h, bit 0) will have no effect. Once the SMI_LOCK bit is set, writes of 0 to SMI_LOCK bit will have no effect (that is, once set, this bit can only be cleared by PLTRST#).

Figure 18-10(B). *SMI Lock Register (Source: 9-series-chipset-pch-datasheet)*

IOMMU

We have discussed the device security in Chapter 8. One threat from devices is the Direct Memory Access (DMA) attack. In order to mitigate this threat, the firmware should set up the I/O memory management unit (IOMMU) to prevent the DMA from the external device or even from an internal device if the internal device is also considered as untrusted. As an implementation choice, the firmware may setup a DMA translation table to provide fine-grained control or a set of DMA-protected memory regions for coarse-grained control.

IOMMU Protection for DRAM

The time to set up the IOMMU is important. Usually, the external Peripheral Component Interconnect (PCI) device has the Bus Master Enable (BME) control in the PCI configuration space, and the BME bit is disabled by default. However, some internal devices can always perform as a bus master. And there is no way to disable the bus master, or the BME is enabled by default. Also, a rogue PCI device, such as an attack FPGA, could claim to support BME but in fact not honor the control. As such, the BIOS should set up the IOMMU to protect the dynamic RAM (DRAM) before the DRAM is initialized by the memory controller in order to prevent the DMA attack from the internal devices.

IOMMU Protection for SRAM

The internal device may also perform DMA to the static RAM (SRAM). For example, the IOMMU mechanisms of Minute IA System Agent (MISA) provides access to SRAM of the Intel Converged Security and Management Engine (CSME) for external DMA agents. The hardware should enable the IOMMU by default to prevent DMA attack to the SRAM. Afterward, the firmware can grant the DMA access rights to some devices per request.

Silicon Support for DMA Prevention

Different hardware may support different ways to enable/disable the DMA capability. For example, a standard PCI device includes a Bus Master Enable (BME) bit in the command register. If the host software enables the BME on a specific PCI device, then the PCI device has the capability to generate DMA to the host memory.

The host system may use different ways to set up DMA capable memory or the DMA non-capable memory. We have discussed some techniques in Chapter 8, such as the I/O memory management unit (IOMMU) translation table, Intel VT-d Protected Memory Region (PMR), Intel DMA Protected Region (DPA), and Intel Generic Protected Memory Range (GENPROTRANGE).

Intel Quark X1000 SOC contains a set of range registers called Isolated Memory Region (IMR). IMR can be used to protect memory from unwanted access by specific system agents. For example, some I/O peripheral devices may attempt to write to a portion of memory that contains execution code and that should only be accessible to the host core, such as DMA access. There are three types of IMR in a system: generic IMR for the system DRAM, host memory I/O Boundary IMR for the system MMIO, and SMM IMR for the SMRAM. The IMR setting can be temporary if it is not locked, or the IMR setting can be permanent after it is locked. This is similar to the ARM Memory Protection Unit (MPU) and the SPI flash region access permission (FRAP) register. Figure 18-11 shows the IMR region and access control registers.

Isolated Memory Region 0 Low Address (IMR0L)—Offset 40h

Access Method

Type: Message Bus Register
(Size: 32 bits)

IMR0L: [Port: 0x05] + 40h

Bit Range	Default & Access	Description
31	0b RW/O	**IMR Lock (IMR_LOCK):** Setting this bit to "1" locks the IMRX registers, preventing further updates.
30:24	00h RO	**Reserved (RSV1):** Reserved.
23:2	000000h RW/L	**IMR Low Address (IMRL):** These bits are compared with bits 31:10 of the incoming address to determine the lower 1KB aligned value of the protected range
1:0	00h RO	**Reserved (RSV0):** Reserved.

Figure 18-11(A). *IMR Low Address Register (Source: Quark X1000 Datasheet)*

Isolated Memory Region 0 High Address (IMR0H)—Offset 41h

Access Method

Type: Message Bus Register
(Size: 32 bits)

IMR0H: [Port: 0x05] + 41h

Bit Range	Default & Access	Description
31:24	00h RO	**Reserved (RSV1):** Reserved.
23:2	000000h RW/L	**IMR High Address (IMRH):** These bits are compared with bits 31:10 of the incoming address to determine the upper 1KB aligned value of the protected range
1:0	0h RO	**Reserved (RSV0):** Reserved.

Figure 18-11(B). *IMR High Address Register (Source: Quark X1000 Datasheet)*

Isolated Memory Region 0 Read Mask (IMR0RM)—Offset 42h

Access Method

Type: Message Bus Register
(Size: 32 bits)

IMR0RM: [Port: 0x05] + 42h

Bit Range	Default & Access	Description
31	1b RW/L	**eSRAM Flush/Init (ESRAM_FLUSH_INIT):** eSRAM Flush/Init Read Access Allowed to memory delineated by IMRxL and IMRxH
29	1b RW/L	**Remote Management Unit (PUNIT):** Remote Management Unit Read Access Allowed to memory delineated by IMRxL and IMRxH
15	1b RW/L	**Host Bridge Arbiter VC1 Sub-Channel 3 (VC1_SAI_ID3):** Host Bridge Arbiter VC1 Sub-Channel 3 Read Accesses Allowed to memory delineated by IMRxL and IMRxH.
14	1b RW/L	**Host Bridge Arbiter VC1 Sub-Channel 2 (VC1_SAI_ID2):** Host Bridge Arbiter VC1 Sub-Channel 2 Read Accesses Allowed to memory delineated by IMRxL and IMRxH.
13	1b RW/L	**Host Bridge Arbiter VC1 Sub-Channel 1 (VC1_SAI_ID1):** Host Bridge Arbiter VC1 Sub-Channel 1 Read Accesses Allowed to memory delineated by IMRxL and IMRxH.
12	1b RW/L	**Host Bridge Arbiter VC1 Sub-Channel 0 (VC1_SAI_ID0):** Host Bridge Arbiter VC1 Sub-Channel 0 Read Accesses Allowed to memory delineated by IMRxL and IMRxH.
11	1b RW/L	**Host Bridge Arbiter VC0 Sub-Channel 3 (VC0_SAI_ID3):** Host Bridge Arbiter VC0 Sub-Channel 3 Read Accesses Allowed to memory delineated by IMRxL and IMRxH.
10	1b RW/L	**Host Bridge Arbiter VC0 Sub-Channel 2 (VC0_SAI_ID2):** Host Bridge Arbiter VC0 Sub-Channel 2 Read Accesses Allowed to memory delineated by IMRxL and IMRxH.
9	1b RW/L	**Host Bridge Arbiter VC0 Sub-Channel 1 (VC0_SAI_ID1):** Host Bridge Arbiter VC0 Sub-Channel 1 Read Accesses Allowed to memory delineated by IMRxL and IMRxH.
8	1b RW/L	**Host Bridge Arbiter VC0 Sub-Channel 0 (VC0_SAI_ID0):** Host Bridge Arbiter VC0 Sub-Channel 0 Read Accesses Allowed to memory delineated by IMRxL and IMRxH.
1	1b RW/L	**CPU (CPU_0):** CPU Read Access Allowed to memory region delineated by IMRxL and IMRxH. Note: Bit[0] and bit [1] of the IMR Read Mask register must always be programmed to the same value
0	1b RW/L	**CPU (CPU0):** CPU Read Access Allowed to memory region delineated by IMRxL and IMRxH. Note: Bit[0] and bit [1] of the IMR Read Mask register must always be programmed to the same value

Figure 18-11(C). *IMR Read Mask Register (Source: Quark X1000 Datasheet)*

Summary

In this chapter, we discussed a couple of silicon secure configuration mechanisms, including flash lock, SMM lock, and IOMMU enabling. In the next chapter, we will discuss the cryptography used in the firmware.

References

Conference, Journal, and Paper

[P-1] Bing Sun, "BIOS Boot Hijacking," in *Power of Community 2007*, available at `http://powerofcommunity.net/poc2007/sunbing.pdf`

[P-2] Rafal Wojtczuk, Joanna Rutkowska, Alexander Tereshkin, "Another Way to Circumvent Intel® Trusted Execution Technology," in *invisiblethingslab whitepaper 2009*, available at `https://invisiblethingslab.com/resources/misc09/Another%20TXT%20Attack.pdf`

[P-3] Joanna Rutkowska, Rafal Wojtczuk, "Preventing and Detecting Xen Hypervisor Subversions," in *BlackHat US 2008*, available at `https://invisiblethingslab.com/resources/bh08/part2-full.pdf`

[P-4] Shai Hasarfaty, Yanai Moyal, "Behind the Scenes of Intel Security and Manageability Engine," in *Blackhat US 2019*, `https://i.blackhat.com/USA-19/Wednesday/us-19-Hasarfaty-Behind-The-Scenes-Of-Intel-Security-And-Manageability-Engine.pdf`

[P-5] Mark Ermolov, "Intel x86 Root of Trust: loss of trust," in 2020, `https://blog.ptsecurity.com/2020/03/intelx86-root-of-trust-loss-of-trust.html`

[P-6] Cuauhtemoc Chavez-Corona, Jorge Gonzalez-Diaz, Rene Henriquez-Garcia, Laura Fuentes-Castaneda, Jan Seidl, "Abusing CPU Hot-Add weaknesses to escalate privileges in Server Datacenters," in *CanSecWest 2017*, available at `https://cansecwest.com/slides/2017/CSW2017_Cuauhtemoc-Rene_CPU_Hot-Add_flow.pdf`

[P-7] Intel, "The Intel Converged Security and Management Engine IOMMU Hardware Issue – CVE-2019-0090," 2020, `www.intel.com/content/dam/www/public/us/en/security-advisory/documents/cve-2019-0090-whitepaper.pdf`

Specification and Guideline

[S-1] Intel, "Intel 64 and IA-32 Architecture Software Developer Manuals," 2019, available at `https://software.intel.com/en-us/articles/intel-sdm`

[S-2] Intel, "6th Generation Intel® Processor Datasheet for S-Platforms," 2016, `www.intel.com/content/dam/www/public/us/en/documents/datasheets/desktop-6th-gen-core-family-datasheet-vol-1.pdf`, `www.intel.com/content/dam/www/public/us/en/documents/datasheets/desktop-6th-gen-core-family-datasheet-vol-2.pdf`

[S-3] Intel, "Intel 9 Series Chipset Family Platform Controller Hub," 2015, `www.intel.com/content/dam/www/public/us/en/documents/datasheets/9-series-chipset-pch-datasheet.pdf`

[S-4] Intel, "Intel® Quark SoC X1000 Data Sheet," 2015, www.intel.com/content/www/us/en/embedded/products/quark/quark-x1000-datasheet.html

[S-5] Intel, "Intel® Quark SoC X1000 Secure Boot – Programmer's Reference Manual (PRM)," 2014, www.intel.com/content/dam/support/us/en/documents/processors/quark/sb/quark_securebootprm_330234_001.pdf

[S-6] Microsoft, "Hardware Security Testability Specification," 2018, https://docs.microsoft.com/en-us/windows-hardware/test/hlk/testref/hardware-security-testability-specification

CHAPTER 19

Cryptography

When we implement the firmware and add security features, such as firmware image verification and firmware attestation, we need to use cryptography to protect our system. Classic cryptography can be traced back to the Roman empire when people used the Caesar cipher. It ended at World War II when the Germans used the Enigma machine to encrypt the message, and the Enigma was cracked finally by Bombe – an electromechanical device used by the British cryptologists. The two types of classic ciphers are substitution and transposition. However, most classic ciphers can be computed by hand and broken with the modern computer and modem technologies. We moved into the modern cryptography age in the 1970s.

In 1972, the US National Bureau of Standards (NBS) called for the proposal of a standardized cipher which could be used for message encryption. Finally, the NBS released the Data Encryption Standard (DES) in 1977. This was a big revolution because it was the first time that a cryptographic algorithm was standardized. Today, NBS has become the National Institute of Standards and Technology (NIST). DES is no longer secure. It is replaced by the Advanced Encryption Standard (AES). There are lots of cryptography books introducing these standardized cryptographic algorithms and the mathematical principles behind. In this chapter, we will not discuss the details of cryptographic algorithms. Instead, we will focus on how to use these standardized cryptographic algorithms to harden our system.

Modern Cryptography

Modern cryptography includes two major domains: symmetric algorithms and asymmetric algorithms. The symmetric algorithm has been around since classic cryptography. In a symmetric algorithm, the sender and the receiver use the same key to encrypt and decrypt the data. See Figure 19-1.

© Jiewen Yao and Vincent Zimmer 2020

J. Yao and V. Zimmer, *Building Secure Firmware*, https://doi.org/10.1007/978-1-4842-6106-4_19

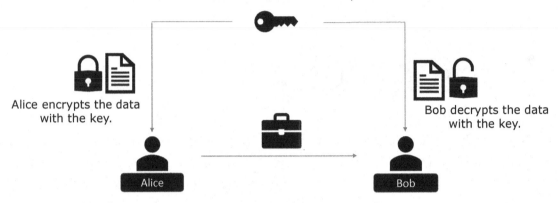

Figure 19-1. *Symmetric Cryptography*

For a long time, this was considered as the only way for encryption and decryption. The breakthrough was in 1976 when Whitfield Diffie and Martin Hellman published "New Directions in Cryptography" and proposed the public key cryptography, also known as asymmetric cryptography. With asymmetric cryptography, we can achieve more capabilities besides data encryption, such as the digital signatures and key establishments. See Figures 19-2, 19-3, and 19-4.

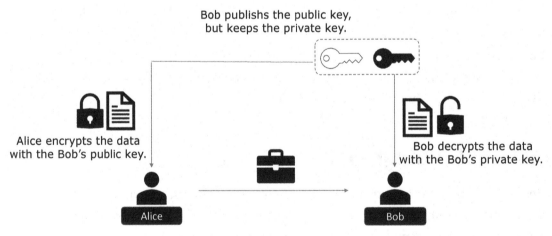

Figure 19-2. *Asymmetric Cryptography – Data Encryption*

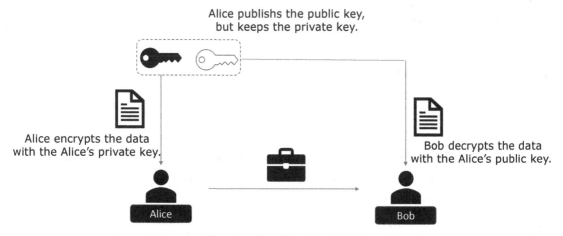

Alice publishs the public key,
but keeps the private key.

Alice encrypts the data
with the Alice's private key.

Bob decrypts the data
with the Alice's public key.

Alice

Bob

Alice transfers the data to Bob.

Everybody can see the data.
But the data can only be from Alice.

Figure 19-3. *Asymmetric Cryptography – Digital Signature*

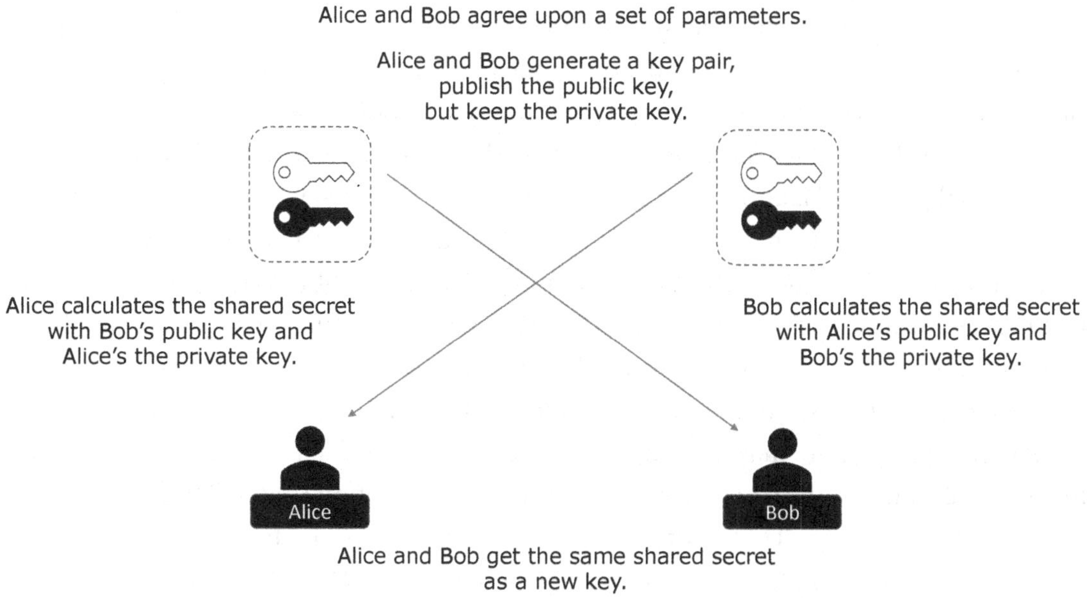

Alice and Bob agree upon a set of parameters.

Alice and Bob generate a key pair,
publish the public key,
but keep the private key.

Alice calculates the shared secret
with Bob's public key and
Alice's the private key.

Bob calculates the shared secret
with Alice's public key and
Bob's the private key.

Alice

Bob

Alice and Bob get the same shared secret
as a new key.

Figure 19-4. *Asymmetric Cryptography – Key Establishment*

Cryptography Usage in the Firmware

The firmware may include both symmetric algorithms and asymmetric algorithms. Table 19-1 shows the cryptographic algorithm usage in the firmware. From the table, we can see the most popular usage is the digital signature verification, including the hash. Digital signatures are a way to verify the integrity and authenticity of the firmware image or data. In Chapters 3, 4, and 5, we have discussed the secure boot, firmware update, and firmware recovery. Those features require the signature verification. The image encryption is not a mandatory requirement for the integrity consideration, but it is a good way for the confidentiality consideration to protect the intelligent property (IP) and raises the bar for the attack. In Chapter 7, we have discussed the trusted boot feature. It does not verify the digital signature but extends the hash of the image or data as the measurement to a tamper-proof space, such as Trusted Platform Module (TPM), for later local or remote attestation.

In Chapter 8, we have discussed the host-device firmware interaction with the Secure Protocol and Data Model (SPDM). SPDM 1.0 measurement and authentication requires the hash function and digital signature verification. SPDM 1.1 includes the key exchange capability with the message authentication code (MAC) to create a session. Then both sides can use the block cipher to encrypt the communication data.

In Chapter 10, we have discussed the user authentication feature and hard disk drive (HDD) password feature. In order to support the password verification, we need to save the hash value with the salt data into a UEFI variable. In Chapter 11, we have discussed the configuration protection and used the UEFI variable as an example. UEFI authentication variable update requires the signature verification to maintain the integrity of the variable region. UEFI variables can also use a block cipher to encrypt the data and use the message authentication code (MAC) to prevent a rollback attack.

Finally, the firmware may include a network stack. The iSCSI boot mechanism uses the hash algorithm in the Challenge-Handshake Authentication Protocol (CHAP). The HTTPs boot requires the Transport Layer Security (TLS) support. The TLS handshake includes the digital signature verification, key exchange, and MAC. Once the session key is created, the TLS driver uses the block cipher or stream cipher to encrypt the communication.

Table 19-1. *Cryptographic Algorithm Usage in Firmware*

Function	Symmetric Algorithm				Asymmetric Algorithm		
	Block Cipher	Stream Cipher	Hash	Message Authentication Code	Digital Signing	Digital Signature Verification	Key Exchange
Secure boot (image verification)			V			V	
Firmware update			V			V	
Firmware recovery			V			V	
Image encryption	V						
Trusted boot (measurement)			V				
SPDM	V		V	V	(V)	V	V
User authentication			V				
HDD password			V				
Authenticated Variable update			V			V	
Variable encryption and rollback prevention	V			V			
iSCSI boot			V				
HTTPs boot	V		V	V	(V)	V	V

Algorithm Recommendation

The cryptographic algorithm can be from different sources, including the Internet Engineering Task Force (IETF), International Organization for Standardization (ISO), and National Institute of Standards and Technology (NIST) Federal Information Processing Standards (FIPS). The NIST also publishes the SP800 serial document to provide the recommendation or guidance for the cryptographic algorithm usage. The National Security Agency (NSA) published the Commercial National Security Algorithm (CNSA) suite for the recommended algorithm to protect the top-secret information. See Table 19-2.

Table 19-2. *Cryptographic Algorithm Recommendation*

Function		Algorithm	NIST Recommendation (NIST SP800-131A)	NSA Recommendation (NSA CNSA)
Symmetric algorithm	Block cipher	AES	AES-128	AES-256
	Hash	SHA	SHA256	SHA384
Asymmetric algorithm	Digital signature	RSA	RSA-2048	RSA-3072
		ECDSA	P-256	P-384
	Key establishment	RSA	RSA-2048	RSA-3072
		DH	DH 2048bit	DH 3072bit
		EC-DH	P-256	P-384

Some Concepts

Besides choosing the right algorithm, we also need to understand some basic concepts in cryptography to design a proper solution for production.

Kerckhoffs's Principle

In 1883, Kerckhoffs published a paper and stated the security of a system should be based upon the key instead of the algorithm. The algorithm should be public. The key should be the only secret.

Today, most cryptographers agree with Kerckhoffs's principle. They believe that we should publish the algorithm and open source the implementation so that more people can have the chance to review and find the vulnerability earlier.

On the other hand, hiding the algorithm may have some advantages. Because the enemy does not know the design, they need to spend more time and more resources to break the system.

Taking firmware as an example, most of the firmware binaries are write protected but not encrypted. Once the attacker dumps the binary, they can do reverse engineering. We also observed some firmware binaries are encrypted. Even if an attacker gets the binary, the binary analysis is not feasible. Maybe this is valuable for intellectual property protection, but it also raises the bar of attacking the system.

Random Number and One-Time Pad

A random number may be required in the firmware, such as a salt for the password hash or a random number in the TLS handshake. Fundamentally, there are two ways to generate a random number:

1) To generate a random number based upon an unpredictable physical source, such as noise: This is named as a non-deterministic random number generator (NDRNG) or true random number generator (TRNG).

2) To generate a random number based upon a predefined algorithm: This is called a deterministic random number generator (DRNG) or pseudo random number generator (PRNG).

Because the TRNG is slow while the PRNG is comparatively fast, a typical implementation combines them together. As John von Neumann quipped, "Anyone who considers arithmetical methods of producing random digits is, of course, in a state of sin." As such, the TRNG is used to generate the first random number as a seed. Then the PRNG is used to create the rest of the random numbers. See Figure 19-5.

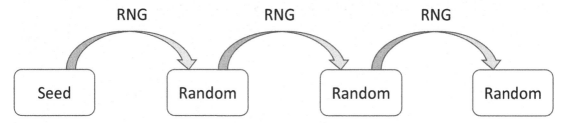

Figure 19-5. *Random Number Generator*

The random number generator can be supported by software or hardware. NIST SP800-90 provides the detailed requirements on the random number generation. The software implementation for the pseudo random generation shall follow NIST SP800-90 recommendations, such as hash-based PRNG, HMAC-based PRNG, or block cipher counter (CTR) mode–based RRNG. Currently the Intel X86 architecture defines two random number instructions: RDSEED and RDRNG. RDSEED returns random numbers that are supplied by a cryptographically secure, enhanced non-deterministic random bit generator (NDRBG). RDRAND returns random numbers that are supplied by a cryptographically secure, deterministic random bit generator (DRBG). ARMv8.5 also defines the RNDR and RNDRRS instruction. If possible, the software needs to use the hardware instructions as the TRNG.

The random number may be used in a one-time pad (OTP). The one-time pad is an example of perfect security or unconditional security. It cannot be broken if it is implemented correctly. The gist of OTP is 1) the key is generated with TRNG, 2) the key is only known by the sender and receiver, 3) the key must be only used once, and 4) the key must be as long as the message.

However, it is impractical in most situations because of those hard requirements. The one-time key distribution and storage is a big problem for the firmware usage.

Block Cipher and Modes of Operation

Block cipher may be used in firmware to encrypt and decrypt the messages between two entities. It is required in secure communication protocols such as Transport Layer Security (TLS) in the network stack or Secure Protocol and Data Model (SPDM) in device communication.

Currently, the Advanced Encryption Standard (AES) defined in NIST FIPS-197 is the recommended block cipher algorithm. The block cipher has different modes of operation. You should choose the correct modes of operation for the data encryption. Otherwise, the solution might be vulnerable. Let's take a look at them in Table 19-3.

Table 19-3. *Block Cipher Modes of Operation*

Mode of Operation	Description	Attribute
Deterministic encryption		
Electronic Code Book (ECB) mode	Each block is encrypted separately. Those identical plain text blocks result in identical ciphertext blocks.	It can be parallelized. No error propagation.
Probabilistic encryption		
Cipher Block Chaining (CBC) mode	The encryption of all blocks is chained together. The encryption is randomized by using an initialization vector (IV).	It supports parallelized decryption. Error propagation.
Cipher Feedback (CFB) mode	It is used to build a stream cipher encryption scheme.	It supports parallelized decryption. Error propagation.
Output Feedback (OFB) mode	It is used to build a stream cipher encryption scheme.	It cannot be parallelized. No error propagation.
Counter (CTR) mode	It is used to build a stream cipher encryption scheme. IV + counter as the initialized input.	It can be parallelized. No error propagation.
Authenticated Encryption with Associated Data (AEAD)		
Galois Counter Mode (GCM)	It provides the confidentiality and authenticity of data. IV and additional associated data (ADD) as input.	-
Counter with CBC-MAC (CCM)	It provides the confidentiality and authenticity of data. Nonce and additional associated data (ADD) as input.	-

NIST SP800-38 provides the detailed recommendations for each mode. The deterministic encryption has a weakness that the identical plain text results in identical ciphertext block. Also, the reordering of a valid plain text cannot be detected.

In general, if there is only a confidentiality requirement, a probabilistic encryption method should be used. The randomness in the probabilistic encryption is based upon the initialization vector (IV). They must be random at each encryption.

If there is a requirement for both data confidentiality and data authenticity, we need to include both encryption and message authentication code (MAC). Because we have seen issues in Encrypt-and-MAC (E&M), Encrypt-then-MAC (EtM), and MAC-then-Encrypt (MtE), the general recommendation is to use the existing standard Authenticated Encryption with Associated Data (AEAD) algorithm, such as GCM or ChaCha20Poly1305.

The different modes may require different input. The IV, which stands for initialization vector, must be uniformly generated in a random fashion. The nonce, which means "number used once," must be unrepeatable and unpredictable. The counter is incremented in each message, and it is predictable. Semantically, an IV is different from a nonce. If an IV is not uniformly random, the solution may have a vulnerability.

Digital Signature and Signature Scheme

The digital signature is probably the most popular usage of cryptography in the firmware. The NIST SP800-193 standard requires firmware resiliency. Both update protection and detection rely upon the digital signature.

NIST FIPS-186 describes the approved digital signature standards, including RSA (Rivest-Shamir-Adleman), Elliptic Curve Digital Signature Algorithm (ECDSA), and Edwards-Curve Digital Signature Algorithm (EdDSA).

Similar to the block cipher encryption, the digital signature can be deterministic or probabilistic. Table 19-4 shows the three examples – RSA, ECDSA, and EdDSA.

Table 19-4. *Digital Signature Scheme*

Signature Scheme	Description	Attribute
Deterministic signature		
RSASSA-PKCS1-v1_5	The signature is the encoding message with hash and algorithm ID.	Fast.
Deterministic ECDSA	Weierstrass Curve. The per-message secret number (k) is derived from the message to be signed and the private key. k is involved in the signature generation.	Small key size.
EdDSA	Twisted Edwards curve. A different model. A unique value computed from the hash of the private key and the message is used in the signature generation process.	Simpler and faster than ECDSA.
Probabilistic signature		
RSASSA Probabilistic Signature Scheme (RSASSA-PSS)	A random salt is involved. The signature is the encoding message with hash and salt.	Fast.
ECDSA	Weierstrass Curve. The per-message secret number (k) is random. k is involved in the signature generation.	Small key size.

In general, the RSA signature method is faster than the ECDSA. For RSA, the signing scheme includes a padding for the message. With the padding, the final signature might be deterministic or non-deterministic. The RSASSA-PKCS1-v1_5 is deterministic, where the identical plain text results in the identical signature. The RSASSA Probabilistic Signature Scheme (RSASSA-PSS) adds a random salt value in the signature. As such, the identical plain text results in a different signature. Currently RSASSA-PSS is recommended. In RSASSA-PSS, the salt length is between 0 and the hash length. In practice, the salt length should be same as the hash length.

The ECDSA is used by the device usually because the key size is smaller. If the device has the capability to generate the random numbers for the per-message secret number, the ECDSA should be used. The use of deterministic ECDSA may be desirable for devices that do not have a good source of the random numbers. The per-message secret number is derived from the message and private key. As such, the final signature result is deterministic.

The Edwards curves offer high performance for elliptic curve calculations and protection against side channel attacks, because it is easier to write branch-free, constant time code to implement Edwards curves. However, care must be taken to implement the deterministic signatures. The secrecy of the private key in the EdDSA calculation is critical.

The RSA can also be used for encryption with a receiver's public key. Table 19-5 shows the encryption scheme.

Table 19-5. *Asymmetric Encryption Scheme*

Encryption Scheme	Description	Attribute
Probabilistic Scheme		
RSAES-PKCS1-v1_5	Random octets are included in the encrypted message.	Known weakness.
RSAES Optimal Asymmetric Encryption Padding (RSAES-OAEP)	Random octets are involved in the encrypted message. An optional label (L) is associated, which is required for both encryption and decryption.	Recommended.

Similar to symmetric authenticated encryption, some solution may require asymmetric encryption and signing. A naïve asymmetric sign-and-encrypt has different security properties from symmetric encryption. From the sender perspective, they are the same. The sender is sure that 1) the recipient knows who wrote the message and 2) only the recipient can decrypt the message. From the recipient perspective, they are different. The recipient of the symmetric encrypted message knows who sent it to them. The recipient of the naïve asymmetric signed-and-encrypted message only knows who wrote the message but does not know who encrypted it. This naïve sign-and-encrypt vulnerability is known as "surreptitious forwarding." The solution for this problem includes 1) adding the sender and/or recipient name, 2) using sign-encrypt-sign, and 3) using encrypt-sign-encrypt.

RFC 8017 defines the encryption scheme (RSAES-OAEP and RSAES-PKCS1-v1_5) and signature scheme (RSASSA-PSS and RSASSA-PKCS1-v1_5).

Key Establishment and Forward Secrecy

Key exchange may be used in firmware to exchange a pre-master key or shared secret between two entities. It is required in the secure communication handshake, such as Transport Layer Security (TLS) in the network stack or Secure Protocol and Data Model (SPDM) in the device communication.

From the cryptography perspective, the key establishment can use the symmetric algorithm. For example, a trusted key distribution center (KDC) can be set up to share the secret key with each user. The key is named as the key encryption key (KEK) and used to encrypt the session key. In practice, there are lots of problems in the solution, such as establishing a secure channel during initialization, a single point of failure, and no forward security. As such, the practical key establishment usages employ the asymmetric algorithm.

NIST SP800-56 provides the recommendations for the discrete logarithm-based key establishment, such as Diffie-Hellman (DH), Elliptic Curve Diffie-Hellman (ECDH), and so on, and integer factorization–based key establishment such as RSA.

One important security assurance in key establishment is forward secrecy (FS). Forward secrecy means even if the long-term private keys of one or two parties are compromised in the future, the session key derived from these long-term public/private key pairs before will not be compromised. Think of failures such as the OpenSSL heartbleed security bug. If the forward secrecy is used, the data in the previous session is still secure and cannot be decrypted. Forward secrecy only provides for confidentiality protection, but not integrity. Also forward secrecy can only protect the established session key, but not the private keys themselves. Table 19-6 shows key establishment examples with and without forward secrecy.

Table 19-6. *Key Establishment*

Key Establishment	Description	Attribute
Without forward secrecy		
RSA	Client generates random (S) and encrypts it with server public key as C. Server decrypts the C with server private key. Both client and server get S as secret.	Very fast.
With forward secrecy		
DH Ephemeral (DHE)	Client generates random (a) and server generates random (b) as a and b are used as exponents to generate A and B. A and B are published. Client generates secret (S) based upon a and B, and server generates same secret (S) based upon b and A.	Slow.
ECDH Ephemeral (ECDHE)	Similar to DHE, the only difference is that the random a and b are used for elliptic curve calculation.	Faster than DHE.

If a long-term public/private key pair is involved in the pre-master secret generation, this is not a forward secrecy solution because once the long-term key is compromised, the attacker can calculate the secret (S).

In forward secrecy, an ephemeral key (EK) pair is generated as a random number, and the only usage of this ephemeral key pair is to establish a secret (S). The long-term public/private key pairs should never be involved in the secret calculation.

The client/server long-term public/private key pairs are still important for user identity and authentication purposes. Without the authentication step, the communication channel may be vulnerable to a man-in-the-middle attack.

If forward secrecy is required, please make sure you choose the right cipher suites to support generation of the ephemeral key. The ECDHE is much faster than DHE. But just in case the elliptic curve cryptography (ECC) is not well supported on the other side, then DHE can be used instead.

Hash, Message Authentication Code, and Key Deviation

Hash is another popular usage in the firmware. The trusted boot process needs to measure the hash of a firmware image and data into the Trusted Platform Module (TPM) Platform Configuration Register (PCR) to establish the static root-of-trust for measurement (SRTM).

A hash function translates an arbitrary-length message to a fixed-length digest. The three important properties of a hash function are as follows:

1) Preimage resistance (or one-wayness): Given X, it is easy to calculate Hash(X). But given Hash(X), it is hard to calculate X.

2) Second preimage resistance (or weak collision resistance): Given Hash(X), it is hard to find Y, where Hash(Y) == Hash(X).

3) Collision resistance (or strong collision resistance): It is hard to find both X and Y, where Hash(X) == Hash(Y).

The NIST defines the SHA2 family in NIST FIPS-184 and the SHA3 family in FIPS-202 document. See Table 19-7.

Table 19-7. *Hash Function*

Hash Function	Description	Attribute
SHA2 family		
SHA224, SHA256	512-bit block size, 32-bit word size	Used today
SHA384, SHA512	1024-bit block size, 64-bit word size	More security strength
SHA3 family		
SHA3224, SHA3256, SHA3384, SHA3512	Based upon the KECCAK algorithm	-
SHAKE128, SHAKE256	Extendable-output function (XOF)	-

SHA2 is the classic hash algorithm and widely used today. The core of the SHA3 family is the new KECCAK algorithm. The SHA3 also supports the extendable-output function (XOF), which means the hash output can be extended to any desired length. For the XOF function, the suffix 128 or 256 means the security strengths, instead of digest length.

Two typical usages of the hash function are digital signature and message authentication code. The message authentication code (MAC) is also known as a cryptography checksum. Similar to the hash, the MAC function accepts an arbitrary-length message and creates a fixed-length authentication tag. MAC can provide the message integrity and authentication. The fundamental difference between MAC and digital signature is that MAC does not provide non-repudiation. The reason is that the key used in the MAC function is a symmetric key shared between two entities, whereas the key used in the digital signing function is a private key and only known by the sender.

The MAC may be based upon hash or block ciphers. See Table 19-8.

Table 19-8. *Message Authentication Code*

MAC Function	Description	Attribute
Hash-based MAC		
Hash-based MAC (HMAC)	It is based upon approved hash.	Fast.
KECCAK MAC (KMAC)	It is based upon SHA3 KECCAK.	-
Block cipher–based MAC		
Cipher Block Chaining MAC (CBC-MAC)	It is based upon approved block cipher.	Known deficiency.
CMAC	It is the enhancement of CBC-MAC. It is one-key CBC-MAC1 (OMAC1).	Replaces CBC-MAC.
Galois Counter MAC (GMAC)	It is a variant of the Galois Counter Mode (GCM), where the input data is not encrypted.	-

NIST FIPS-198 defines the HMAC, and NIST SP800-38B and SP800-38D provide recommendations for CMAC and GMAC.

If there is a requirement for an authentication code, we need to use the MAC function. Because we have seen issues in secret-prefix MAC or secret-suffix MAC, the general recommendation is to use the existing standard MAC function, such as HMAC, KMAC, or CMAC.

Beyond message integrity and authentication, one important usage of HMAC is to help derive the key. This might be a use case in the firmware. The firmware may include the user authentication with the password and use the password to derive the key to protect the user data. Or the firmware may get a master secret from a hardware engine and derive the key to protect the platform data.

RFC 8018 PKCS#5 defines the password-based key derivation functions (PBKDFs). Usually the password is chosen from a relatively small space. It cannot be used directly as a key for encryption. We need a key derivation function to convert the password into a key. First, we need to add a random salt to resist the password rainbow table attack. As such, the pre-build hash table by the attacker is useless. The length of the salt should be the same as the digest length chosen in the KDF. Second, we need to include an iteration count of processing to increase time of brute force attack. The minimal iteration count is 1000.

RFC 5869 defines a HMAC-Based Extract-and-Expand Key Derivation Function (HKDF). The typical usage of HKDF is to derive a session key from a master shared secret from the key establishment or derive a subkey from a root key. HKDF includes two phases: HKDF_Extract and HKDF_Expand. HKDF_Extract adds a random salt to derive a pseudorandom key (PRK). HKDF_Expand adds a fixed context info to derive the final output key. A solution may choose to include both phases or only include the HKDF_Expand to derive a key deterministically.

The HKDF must not be used to derive a key from a user password because the HKDF does not include the iteration count. For passwords, the PBKDF should be used to slow down the dictionary attack by adding iteration counts. See Table 19-9 for the key derivation function.

Table 19-9. *Key Derivation Function*

Key Derivation Function	Description	Attribute
PKCS5 Password-Based Key Derivation Function 2 (PBKDF2)	Input: password, a random salt, iteration count Output: key	Includes iteration count. Slow.
HMAC-Based Extract-and-Expand Key Derivation Function (HKDF)	Two phases: 1) HKDF_Extract Input: input key material (IKM), random salt Output: pseudorandom key (PRK) 2) HKDF_Expand Input: PRK, context info Output: output key material (OKM)	No iteration. Fast.

Digital Certificate and Certificate Chain

In the previous section, we introduced the digital signature. An entity may generate a public and private key pair, sign the message with the private key, and publish the public key to let other entities verify the signature. In practice, a single public key is not enough to describe the identity of the entity. We need more information such as the key owner's information. To combine the information together, we can generate a certificate.

A certificate should include the validity period; the information of the subject such as country, organization, name, and so on; and the public key of the subject. Similar to a driver's license or a passport, there must be a trusted authority to issue the certificate. This issuer is called Certificate Authority (CA). The subject needs to create a certificate signing request including all of the preceding information and send it to the CA. Then the CA adds the issuer information, signs the certificate with the CA's private key as the signing key, and appends the key ID and the signature. That becomes the final valid certificate for the subject. The format of the public certificate is defined in the X.509 standard. Figure 19-6 shows the flow on how to create a certificate from a public/private key pair.

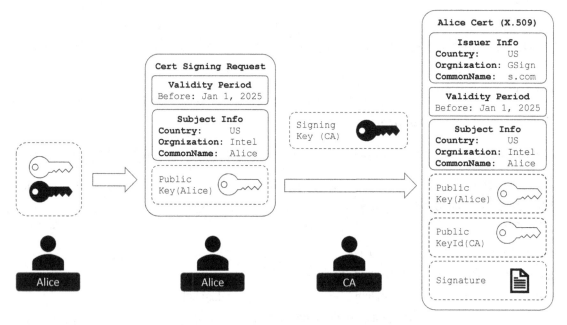

Figure 19-6. *X.509 Certificate Generation*

In order to verify if a certificate of the subject is valid, the verifier can check the digital signature of the certificate with the CA's public certificate. Because the CA itself is always trusted, the certificate of the CA is a self-signed certificate. The subject and issuer are the same. This is called root CA. In practice, we cannot have a root CA to sign every certificate. The root CA can sign an intermediate CA and let the intermediate CA to do the rest of the signing work. Now we create a certificate chain. See Figure 19-7.

Once the certificate chain is created, the verification process needs additional steps. The verifier needs to discover the issuer of the certificate – the intermediate CA – and verify if the certificate of the subject is valid based upon the certificate of the intermediate CA. Then the verifier needs to find out the issuer of the intermediate CA's certificate – the root CA – and verify if the certificate of the intermediate CA is valid based upon the certificate of the root CA.

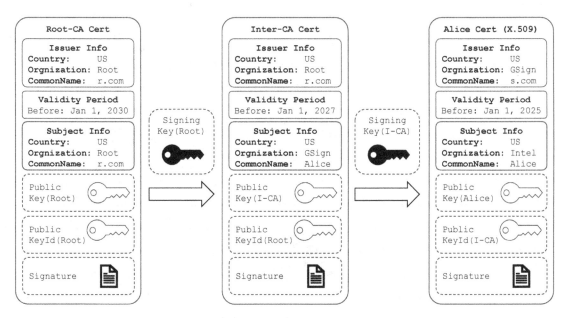

Figure 19-7. *X.509 Certificate Chain*

We have created the subject certificate and the certificate chain. Now we can sign the data with the private key. The RFC2315 PKCS#7 defines cryptographic message syntax for the digital signature and digital envelopes. The signer needs to add certificates in the certificate chain and use the private key as the signing key to generate the digital signature. The final PKCS#7 signed data may include the original data as the content information, the certificates and the signer information such as the issuer info, the

signing time, and the signature. See Figure 19-8. The final PKCS#7 signature can be sent
to the receiver for verification. Please be aware that the PKCS#7 signature might be a
detached one if the data is excluded and sent to a receiver in another way.

Once the receiver gets the data and the PKCS#7 signature, they can use the root CA
certificate to verify the whole PKCS#7 signature. The root CA certificate is used to verify
the certificate chain. The signer's certificate is used to verify the data. See Figure 19-9.

Today the X.509 public certificate format is widely used in the industry, such as by
network Transport Layer Security (TLS). PKCS#7 is also widely used as the cryptographic
message syntax for the signature, such as the executable image signing. But they are
not the only one. For example, in the Internet of Things (IoT) environment, people are
considering using Concise Binary Object Representation (CBOR) Object Signing and
Encryption (COSE) syntax to replace the complicated ASN.1 format used in X.509 and
PKCS#7.

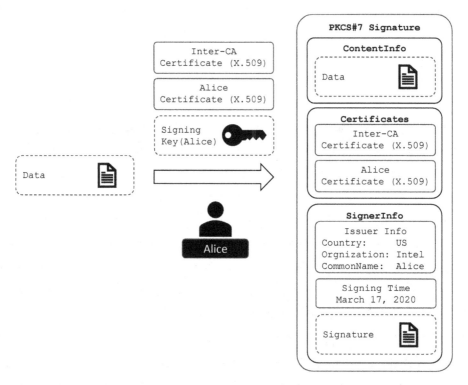

Figure 19-8. *PKCS#7 Digital Signature Generation*

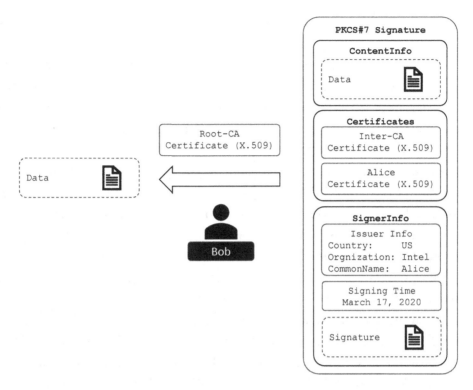

Figure 19-9. *PKCS#7 Digital Signature Verification*

Challenge in the Firmware

Now let's see what the challenges are that we may have to implement the cryptography algorithms in the firmware.

Certificate Management

Saving a public certificate in the firmware requires the non-volatile (NV) storage. The typical firmware only has limited NV storage, such as an 8M-byte Serial Peripheral Interface (SPI) NOR flash. The NAND flash Replay Protected Memory Block (RPMB) area is bigger, but not all platforms include the RPMB flash. System partition of an operating system (OS) disk is another option available for non-volatile storage for the firmware. Unfortunately, it is unprotected. The attack may update the content there directly.

The certificate revocation is also a challenge. For the OS that has network capability, the Online Certificate Status Protocol (OCSP) can be used. However, it is not practical for the standalone firmware solution if the firmware does not have network support. The firmware may expose an interface to update the certificate with the help of another authorized entity. The UEFI specification defines UEFI authenticated variables as the UEFI image signature database. Any user may read it, but only an authenticated user can write it. The OS can update the allowed certificate or add the revoked certificate to the forbidden signature database if it has an entry in the KEK. The Cerberus specification defines a set of root-of-trust (RoT) commands to update the platform manifest and the component manifest. Some of them became part of the Secure Protocol and Data Model (SPDM) specification for the device management.

One reminder is that when the final production image is generated, the pre-production certificate or test certificate must be removed from the production image. Otherwise, any developer can generate a new signed image. The firmware may implement a built-in self-detection mechanism. We can standardize the pre-production certificate and test certificate and let firmware display a warning message to tell people that this firmware is only for test purpose and should not be released, in hopes that the validation engineers will report issues in case that they see this message.

Not all firmware has confidentiality support. In that case, the firmware may not include a private certificate for the data signing purpose. This might become a limitation for the mutual authentication use case, such as the handshake phase of the Transport Layer Security (TLS) or Secure Protocol and Data Model (SPDM). In order to achieve that, we can use some other mechanisms. For example, we can let the firmware get the private certificate from another security coprocessor such as the management engine (ME) and use it once and discard it afterward. With this solution, the security coprocessor should implement an interface to lock down the private certificate retrieving. Another solution is to leverage the hardware to generate the certificate such as Software Guard Extension (SGX).

Cryptographic Algorithm Agility

There are lots of cryptographic algorithms in the world, and there is no need to support all of them in a single firmware. Taking the Trusted Platform Module (TPM) as an example, a TPM chip may support three different hash algorithms – SHA1 for the legacy system, SHA256 for the current system, and SM3 for the Chinese market. The final platform may just choose one of them. On the one hand, the system firmware should only enable one hash algorithm for the firmware hash calculation to save the system boot time. On the other hand, the system firmware should be designed with multiple hash capabilities. This is important because it will help to migrate from one hash algorithm to the other. For example, SHA1 was used in the old system. After it has been proved to be insecure, we can migrate to SHA256. The current system configurations use the RSA2048 and SHA256. NSA gives the recommendation that we should move to RSA3072 and SHA384 for future production.

Besides upgrade requirements, different markets or governments may have different requirements. Table 19-10 lists the Chinese cryptographic algorithms.

Table 19-10. *Chinese Cryptographic Algorithms*

Function		Algorithm	Parameter
Symmetric algorithm	**Block cipher**	SM4	128 bits
	Stream cipher	ZUC	-
	Hash	SM3	256 bits
Asymmetric algorithm	**Digital signature**	SM2	256-bit ECC
	Key establishment	SM2	256-bit ECC

Performance and Size

Most cryptographic algorithms might be complicated and need lots of calculation. It may bring firmware code size impacts and runtime performance impacts. For example, the OpenSSL is a good choice for the cryptographic algorithm implementation, but it is big because it is designed for OS applications. For the embedded system, we need to find a smaller one, such as mbed TLS or wolfSSL.

The hardware may also add instructions to support the algorithms. Besides true random number generation, the Intel X86 architecture defines Advanced Encryption Standard new instructions (AES-NIs) such as AESENC, AESDEC, AESIMC, AESKEYGEN, and so on and SHA extensions such as SHA256MSG1, SHA256MSG2, and so on. The ARMv8.0 architecture also defines cryptographic extension for AES such as AESD, AESE, AESIMC, AESMC, and so on and SHA such as SHA256H, SHA256H2, and so on. The firmware may leverage these hardware capabilities.

A Hardware Security Module (HSM) is another possible implementation for the cryptographic algorithms. It might be hard for the firmware to leverage because it is a vendor-specific solution.

Attack and Mitigation

The attacks against the cryptographic algorithms can be separated into two parts: cryptanalysis and implementation attack.

Cryptanalysis

Most likely, cryptanalysis is done by the cryptography expert. What we need to pay attention to is

1) To keep the product aligned with the latest approved, recommended algorithm and its parameters. The deprecated algorithms must not be used, such as SHA1 or MD5.

2) To ensure that the algorithm is used in the right place. For example, using HKDF on the user password is a bad choice. Instead, the PBKDF should be used.

3) To follow the industry best practice. For example, the ephemeral key (EK) should be used in the key exchange for the forward secrecy consideration.

Last but not least of importance, please do not try to invent a cryptographic algorithm or protocol without a review with a cryptography expert. For example, if there is encryption and authentication requirement, the standard AEAD should be used instead of a customized E&M, EtM, or MtE.

Implementation Attack

Implementation attack means there is no problem with the cryptographic algorithm and the usage, but a coding error caused the security claims to be broken.

Untrusted External Input

Untrusted external input is still the most potent attack in practice because of the memory safety issue in the software. Take OpenSSL heartbleed as an example, wherein an unchecked memcpy() exposes the memory which may contain the secret. A similar case can be found in the AMD PSP fTPM wherein a stack overflow in EkCheckCurrentCert may cause remote code execution. Any external input must be validated.

Data Used Before Verified

The cryptographic algorithm may be used for data verification. In such case, the data cannot be used before it is verified. Violations may cause a security issue. Take FPGA starbleed as an example. The Xilinx FPGA bitstream is interpreted before HMAC validation, so it causes the whole decrypted bitstream data being exposed.

Key Included in Data

The second issue of FPGA starbleed is that the HMAC key is stored inside of the bitstream data. Once the bitstream data is exposed, the key is exposed as well. Then the attacker may construct a valid bitstream to pass the HMAC verification.

Downgrade Attack

The industry standards are moving forward. An old implementation might be insecure and deprecated. However, an implementation may support the ability to download an old version for the compatibility considerations. Take SSL Padding Oracle on Downgraded Legacy Encryption (POODLE) as an example. If the solution supports to downgrade from TLS1.0 to SSL3.0, then the POODLE attack may steal "secure" HTTP cookies. Qualcomm DSP Achilles is another example of downgrade vulnerability. The signature of binary is verified but not the version of the binary. The insecure downgrade must be prohibited.

Technologies such as security version numbers (SVNs) or lowest support version number (LSN) can be used to note which successive versions are security related so that we can create "fences" that allow downgrades of versions without security fixes but prohibit a downgrade that crosses an SVN or LSN.

Security Policy

Security policy is the enforcement to ensure that the security check must happen and includes all necessary steps, such as public key comparison, version comparison, and signature comparison. We have seen that UEFI secure boot is bypassed because of bad policy control. Another example is the HP iLO BMC secure boot. It is broken because the attacker finds a path to bypass the signature check by triggering a failure on load_legacy_key(). If the verifier fails to get enough information or policy such as public key or hash for the verification, the result must be failure instead of success.

Quantum Safe Cryptography

Today's computers are built based upon classical physics. However, at the nanoscopic level, everything follows quantum physics instead of classical physics. More and more researchers have figured out it is possible to build a machine based upon quantum mechanics, which is known as the quantum computer.

In classical computing, the fundamental unit of information storage is the bit. A bit can be either 0 or 1, and it can only be 0 or 1. However, in quantum computing, the fundamental unit can hold both 0 and 1 at the same time. This unit is called "qubit." The state is named as "superposition." Once we measure the qubit state, the action will disturb the superposition and cause the qubit to collapse into either 0 or 1. These characteristics of the qubit change the way of computing. Multiple dimensions of processing can occur in 1 qubit. The computing power can grow exponentially.

Recently, more and more companies have started building quantum computers. For supercomputing, D-Wave released the D-Wave 2000Q computer with 2048 qubits in 2017 and announced a next-generation Pegasus which will have 5640 qubits. For smaller computers, IBM prototyped a 50-qubit system. Intel delivered the Tangle Lake prototype in 2018, which has 49 qubits. Google announced a 72-qubit system Bristlecone in 2018.

Security Challenge

According to Shannon's theory, there are different kinds of security:

> Unconditional security: It means that the cryptosystem cannot be broken, even if the attacker has unlimited computational resources. This is the strongest cryptographic algorithm. One example is the one-time pad (OTP) cipher, also known as Vernam's cipher.

> Computational security: It means that the cryptosystem can be broken with a fixed number of operations. However, because the number is very large, this cannot be achieved with current computational resources. For example, the brute force attack may take a long time. In reality, it is hard to prove that we only need a fixed number of operations to break the system. Maybe it is not broken just because we have not figured out a good algorithm.

Provable security: It means that the cryptosystem is built based upon well-studied hard mathematical problems, such as large integer factorization, discrete logarithm, elliptic curve discrete logarithm, and so on. Again, if someone can figure out a way to resolve the mathematical problem, then this cryptosystem can be broken. Today, most pervasive asymmetric cryptographies are built upon this, such as Rivest-Shamir-Adleman (RSA), elliptic curve cryptography (ECC), and Diffie-Hellman (DH).

Now let's see how the quantum algorithm can break the security.

Shor's Algorithm

In 1994, Shor published the paper "Algorithms for quantum computation: Discrete logarithms and factoring." It described a polynomial-time quantum computer algorithm for the integer factorization problem and discrete logarithm problem. With Shor's algorithm, the Rivest-Shamir-Adleman (RSA), elliptic curve cryptography (ECC), and Diffie-Hellman (DH) become vulnerable in the quantum computing world because the attacker can use Shor's algorithm to resolve the hard mathematical problem in polynomial time and reconstruct the private key easily. See Table 19-11.

Table 19-11. *Cryptographic Algorithm Impacted by Shor's Algorithm*

Function	Algorithm	Hard Problem
Digital signature	RSA	Integer factorization
	DSA	Finite field cryptography
	ECDSA	Elliptic curve discrete logarithm
Key establishment	RSA	Integer factorization
	DH	Discrete logarithm
	ECDH	Elliptic curve discrete logarithm

Grover's Algorithm

In 1996, Grover published the paper "A fast quantum mechanical algorithm for database search." It described a quantum algorithm that finds with high probability the unique input to a function that produces a particular output value. Grover's algorithm helps the brute attack for key searching by reducing the effective key strength to half. See Table 19-12.

Table 19-12. *Cryptographic Algorithm Impacted by Grover's Algorithm*

Function	Algorithm	Effective Key Strength (Current)	Effective Key Strength (Quantum Computing)
Block cipher	AES-128	128	64
	AES-256	256	128
Hash	SHA256	256	128
	SHA3256	256	128

Quantum Safe Algorithm

With quantum computing, some cryptographic algorithms are proved to be vulnerable. Some other algorithms are believed to be quantum safe because we have not figured out a way to attack based upon current knowledge. These algorithms are presumed to be quantum safe at this moment.

Please be aware that a quantum safe algorithm today might be vulnerable tomorrow if we can find a new algorithm to break the cryptographic primitive. The only unimpacted algorithm is the one-time pad (OTP), which is proved to be unconditionally secure.

Symmetric Algorithm

The symmetric cryptography is not impacted too much. AES is presumed to be quantum safe because Grover's algorithm just aids the brute force search. What we need to do is to double the key size from AES-128 to AES-256.

Asymmetric Algorithm

The asymmetric cryptography is heavily impacted, though. RSA/ECC/DH and their derivatives are not quantum safe because of Shor's algorithm. As such, we have to figure out the replacement. Fortunately, there are some other asymmetric algorithms that are presumed to be quantum safe, such as hash-based digital signature, lattice-based cryptography, code-based cryptography, Multivariate Public Key Cryptography, and so on. Before a new asymmetric algorithm is used, the RSA and DH are preferred than the ECDSA and ECDH, because the ECC uses a smaller key size and is considered to be an easier target for quantum computers.

Because the majority of cryptographic algorithm usage in firmware is the digital signature, it is important to know the basic principle of the quantum safe algorithms. In the following sections, we will give a brief introduction to the hash-based signature.

Hash-Based Signature

In 1979, Lamport published "Constructing digital signatures from a one-way function" and invented the hash-based signature. The gist of the digital signature is to provide evidence that the message data is created by the known sender and the message is not modified in transit. Because the hash is a one-way function, we can create the digital signature only with the hash function. The security of the hash-based signature is based upon the collision resistance of the hash function.

Lamport One-Time Signature Scheme

Let's see how to sign a 256-bit message in Lamport's paper in Figure 19-10.

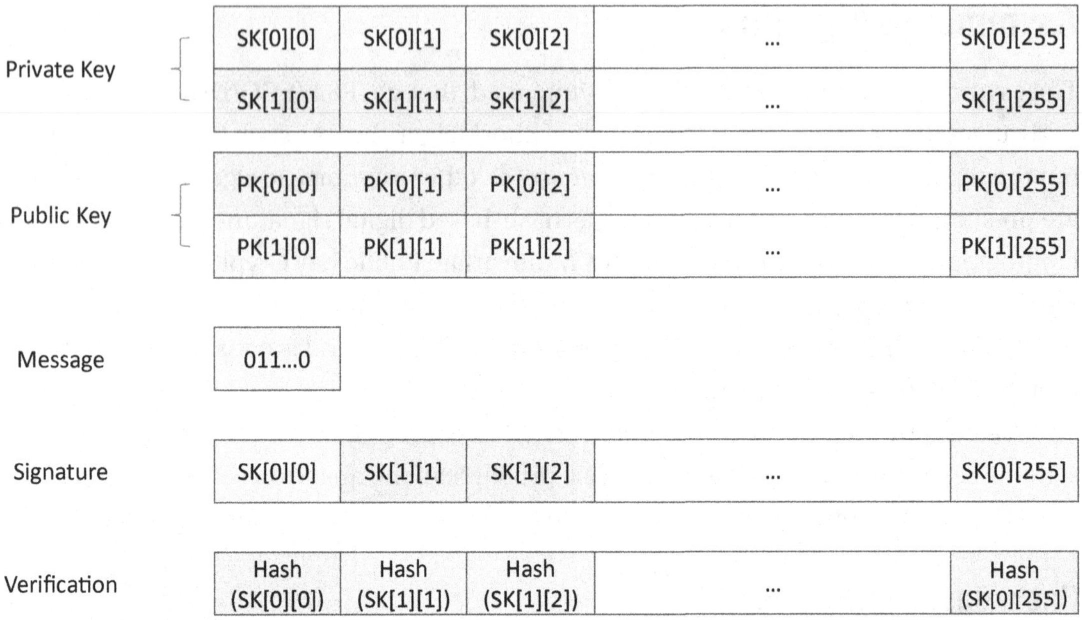

SK[0][0]	SK[0][1]	SK[0][2]	...		SK[0][255]
SK[1][0]	SK[1][1]	SK[1][2]	...		SK[1][255]

Private Key

PK[0][0]	PK[0][1]	PK[0][2]	...		PK[0][255]
PK[1][0]	PK[1][1]	PK[1][2]	...		PK[1][255]

Public Key

Message

011...0

Signature

SK[0][0]	SK[1][1]	SK[1][2]	...	SK[0][255]

Verification

Hash (SK[0][0])	Hash (SK[1][1])	Hash (SK[1][2])	...	Hash (SK[0][255])

Figure 19-10. *Lamport One-Time Signature Scheme*

1)   First, we need to generate the key. In order to sign the 256-bit message, we need to generate 512 bit strings. Each bit string has 256 bits. The private key is SK where

```
SK = SK[0] || SK[1]
SK[0] = SK[0][0] || SK[0][1] || SK[0][2] || ... || SK[0][255]
SK[1] = SK[1][0] || SK[0][1] || SK[0][2] || ... || SK[0][255]
SK[x][y] = Random, (x=0,1; y=0,1,2,...,255)
```

Each SK[x][y] is a 256-bit random data. The total private key length is 512*256 bits =128K bits = 16K bytes.

The public key is PK where

```
PK = PK[0] || PK[1]
PK[0] = PK[0][0] || PK[0][1] || PK[0][2] || ... || PK[0][255]
PK[1] = PK[1][0] || PK[0][1] || PK[0][2] || ... || PK[0][255]
PK[x][y] = HASH (SK[x][y]), (x=0,1; y=0,1,2,...,255)
```

Each PK[x][y] is the hash of the SK[x][y]. Assuming we are using SHA256 as the hash function, then each PK[x][y] is 256 bits. The total public key size is also 16K bytes.

2) Second, we need to sign the message. Assuming the 256-bit message is M where

```
M=m[0] || m[1] || m[2] || ... || m[255]
m[i] (i=0,1,2,...,255) = 0 or 1.
```

then the message signature is Sig(M) where

```
Sig(M) = s[0] || s[1] || s[2] || ... || s[255]
s[i] = SK[m[i]][i], (i=0,1,2,...,255)
```

Each s[i] is SK[0][i] or SK[1][i] based upon the m[i] value 0 or 1. As such, the total signature length is 256 * 256 bits = 64K bits = 8K bytes.

Now, the sender transmits the message M, with the signature Sig(M). How does the receiver verify the message?

1) First, the receiver needs to generate the verification data Ver(M) with the message Sig(M):

```
Sig(M) = s[0] || s[1] || s[2] || ... || s[255]
Ver(M) = v[0] || v[1] || v[2] || ... || v[255]
v[i] = HASH(s[i]), (i=0,1,2,...,255)
```

Each v[i] is the hash of the s[i]. The verification data is also 256 * 256 bits = 8K bytes.

2) Second, the receiver can verify the message M with PK:

```
M=m[0] || m[1] || m[2] || ... || m[255]
PK = PK[0] || PK[1]
PK[0] = PK[0][0] || PK[0][1] || PK[0][2] || ... || PK[0][255]
PK[1] = PK[1][0] || PK[0][1] || PK[0][2] || ... || PK[0][255]
VerificationResult = (v[i] == PK[m[i]][i]), (i=0,1,2,...,255)
```

Each v[i] should be checked with PK[0][i] or PK[1][i] based upon the m[i] value 0 or 1. If all v[i] are the same as the corresponding PK[][i] value, then the verification passes. Otherwise, the verification fails.

The security of this hash-based signature is based upon the hash function. Because of preimage resistance and collision resistance properties, the attacker cannot calculate the SK and cannot calculate the Sig(M).

The Lamport OTS scheme is simple and beautiful. There are two limitations:

1) The key size and signature size are big. In the preceding example, the private key and public key size are 16K bytes. The signature is 8K bytes. Comparing to RSA2048, the signature is 2048 bits = 256 bytes.

2) The signature can only be used once. Once you sign a message, you expose half of the private key. If you sign the second message, you may expose the other half of the private key based upon how many bits are the same as the first message. In the worst case, if the bits in the two messages are totally different, then you expose the whole private key.

Winternitz One-Time Signature Scheme

In order to resolve the Lamport OTS limitation on large signature sizes, Winternitz proposed an idea based upon time-space trade-off. The signature size can be reduced at the cost of more hash operations. The gist of the Winternitz one-time signature (WOTS) scheme is to sign multiple bits at one time, instead of 1 bit at one time. This number of bits that can be signed at one time is named as the Winternitz parameter (w).

Let's see how to sign a 256-bit message with w being 4 in Figure 19-11.

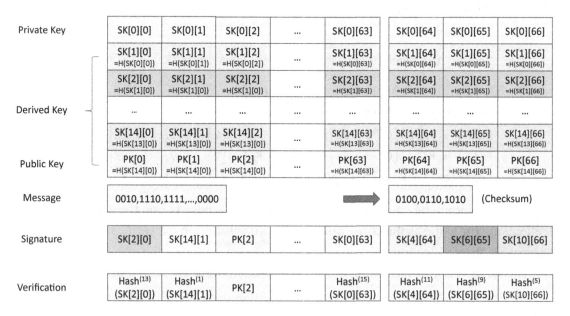

Figure 19-11. *Winternitz One-Time Signature Scheme*

1) First, we need to generate the key. If we divide the 256-bit message
    by 4 bits, we can get 64 chunk messages. In order to sign the 64
    chunk messages, we need to generate 64 bit strings. Each bit string
    has 256 bits. The private key is SK where

```
SK = SK[0]
SK[0] = SK[0][0] || SK[0][1] || SK[0][2] || ... || SK[0][63]
SK[0][y] = Random, (y=0,1,2,...,63)
```

Each SK[0][y] is a 256-bit random data. The total key size is
reduced to 64*256 bits =16K bits = 2K bytes.

Because each chunk message is 4 bits, we need 2^4 = 16 possible
signing keys. Instead of generating other random bit strings, we
can hash the SK[0] and use the result as SK[1]. Then we can hash
the SK[1] and use the result as SK[2]. Finally we can hash SK[14]
and use the result as SK[15]. The public key PK is SK[15]:

```
SK[x] = SK[x][0] || SK[x][1] || SK[x][2] || ... || SK[x][63],
(x=1,2,...,15)
SK[x][y] = HASH (SK[x-1][y]), (x=1,2,...,15; y=0,1,2,...,63)
PK = SK[15]
PK[y] = SK[15][y], (y=0,1,2,...,63)
```

With this method, all the signing keys can be derived from the
original SK.

2) Second, we need to sign the message. Assuming the 256-bit
    message is M where

```
M=m[0] || m[1] || m[2] || ... || m[63]
m[i] (i=0,1,2,...,63) = 0,1,2,...15.
```

then the message signature is Sig(M) where

```
Sig(M) = s[0] || s[1] || s[2] || ... || s[63]
s[i] = SK[m[i]][i], (i=0,1,2,...,63)
```

Each s[i] is SK[x][i] based upon the m[i] value. As such, the total signature length is
2K bytes.

Now, the sender transmits the message M, with the signature Sig(M). How does the receiver verify the message?

1) First, the receiver needs to generate the verification data Ver(M) with the message Sig(M):

```
M=m[0] || m[1] || m[2] || ... || m[63]
Sig(M) = s[0] || s[1] || s[2] || ... || s[63]
Ver(M) = v[0] || v[1] || v[2] || ... || v[63]
v[i] = HASH (2^w - 1 - m[i], s[i]), (i=0,1,2,...,63)
```

Each v[i] is the hash of the s[i]. Given a message chunk m[i], the hash operation should be repeated with (2^w - 1 - m[i]) times. For example, if m[i] is 1, then we need to call the hash function 14 times. If the m[i] is 10, then we need to call the hash function 5 times. If m[i] is 15, then we don't need to call the hash function because the SK[15] is PK itself.

2) Second, the receiver can verify the message M with PK:

```
PK = PK[0] || PK[1] || PK[2] || ... || PK[63]
VerificationResult = (v[i] == PK[i]), (i=0,1,2,...,63)
```

Each v[i] should be checked with PK[i]. If all v[i] are the same as the corresponding PK[][i] value, then the verification passes. Otherwise, the verification fails.

The preceding method looks like a good way to reduce the key size and signature size. However, there is a vulnerability. An attacker may change the message chunk to a bigger value and calculate the next derived key SK with the hash function. In order to detect such a modification, we need to calculate the checksum of the original message and append the signature for the checksum as additional verification data. The checksum is C where

```
C = (16 - m[0]) + (16 - m[1]) + (16 - m[2]) + ... + (16 - m[63])
```

Then we need to add an additional SK for the checksum – SK[64], SK[65], SK[66]. In the verification phase, the receiver needs to reconstruct the checksum and verify the signature of the checksum. The right side of Figure 19-6 shows the checksum signing and verification. Even with the additional signing key for the checksum, the final key size in Winternitz OTS is still much smaller than the key size in Lamport OTS.

Merkle Signature Scheme

The second limitation of Lamport OTS is the one-time usage. This is an even bigger problem because of the key management requirements. Exchanging a public key is complicated. If a new public key is always required for a new signature, the OTS scheme is hard to be used in practice. In order to make OTS feasible, Merkle introduced the Merkle Signature Scheme (MSS). With MSS, one public key can be used to verify many messages signed by the private key. The user may choose a height value h, and the MSS can help to generate the private key to sign N = 2^h messages.

Let's see how to sign a 256-bit message with h being 3.

   1) First, we need to generate the keys – a Merkle tree. See Figure 19-12.

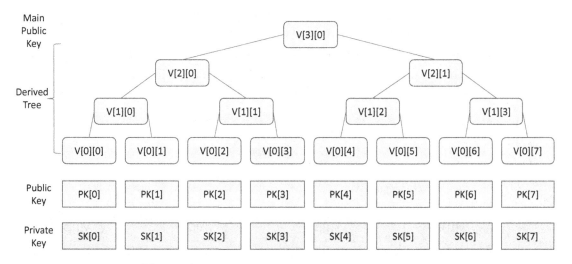

Figure 19-12. *Merkle Hash Tree*

In order to generate the main public key, we need to generate 2^h private/public key pairs. Here h is 3, so we need to generate eight key pairs where

```
SK[0], SK[1], ..., SK[7]
PK[0], PK[1], ..., PK[7]
```

Then we start building the leaf nodes of a Merkle tree based upon the PK:

```
v[0][0], v[0][1], ..., v[0][7]
v[0][i] = HASH (PK[i])
```

Then we calculate the non-root node at level h based upon the node at level h-1. The parent node is the hash of the concatenation of its left child and right child. The root node of the tree hash is the main public key:

```
v[h][i] = HASH (v[h - 1][2 * i] || v[h - 1][2 * j + 1])
RootNode = v[3][0]
```

The main public key is the only public key which needs to be published. The SK/PK pairs and the other parts of the Merkle tree do not need to be published. This single main public key can be used to verify the $N = 2^h$ messages in MSS:

2)   Second, we need to sign the message. We choose the SK[s] to sign the message M and generate Sig(M). This is same as OTS. Then we need to calculate a Path(s), which is the sequence of nodes in the Merkle tree, from the leaf node to the root node. From the Path(s) we can get an authentication path – AuthPath(s) – which is the sequence of nodes in the Merkle tree to help the node in Path(s) to create the main public key.

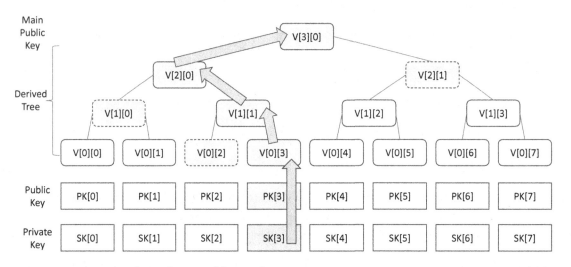

Figure 19-13.   *Path in the Merkle Hash Tree*

See Figure 19-13. The s is 3. We choose SK[3] and PK[3] as the signing key and verification key. The arrow indicates the Path[3] - (v[0][3], v[1][1], v[2][0]). The dashed node denotes the AuthPath[3] - (v[0][2], v[1][0], v[2][1]).

The final signature is SigMerkle (M, s) = (s, Sig(M), PK[s], AuthPath[s]). AuthPath adds the additional size of the final signature, and it highly depends upon the h value. Here the h is 3, and then the AuthPath size is 3 * 256 bits = 768 bits. In practice, the h will be much bigger to support signing more messages with one main public key.

Now, the sender transmits the message M, with the signature SigMerkle (M). How does the receiver verify the message?

1) First, the receiver uses PK[s] in the SigMerkle to verify the Sig(M). This step is the same as OTS.

2) Second, the receiver needs to verify the PK[s] with the main public key. This can be achieved to reconstruct the Path[s] with the help of AuthPath[s]. Here, the verifier needs to calculate the following:

```
v[0][3] = HASH(PK[3])
v[1][1] = HASH(v[0][2] || v[0][3]), where v[0][2] is from AuthPath[3]
v[2][0] = HASH(v[1][0] || v[1][1]), where v[1][0] is from AuthPath[3]
v[3][0] = HASH(v[2][0] || v[2][1]), where v[2][1] is from AuthPath[3]
```

If the final calculated v[3][0] is same as the published main public key, then the verification passes. Otherwise, the verification fails.

Once s = 3 is selected, then Path[3] cannot be used anymore. In the next time, we need to choose another path.

Current Status

The key concept of hash-based signature (HBS) schemes is based upon the one-time signature and hash tree scheme in Figure 19-14. The OTS is used to sign the message, and the hash tree is used to create the main public key. The authentication path is included in the final signature to help the verification. Because those schemes need to record the state of the private keys, they are called stateful hash-based signature schemes.

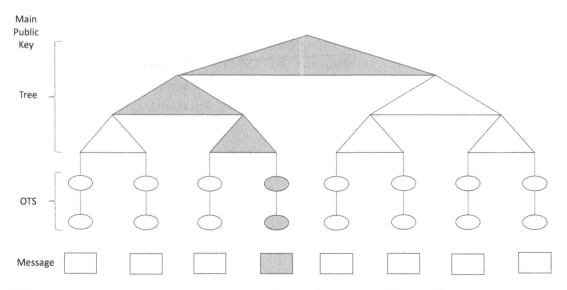

Figure 19-14. *Hash-Based Signature Scheme (OTS + Merkle Tree)*

Today, we have other OTS variants, such as Winternitz OTS+ (WOTS+), Hash to Obtain Random Subset (HORS), Forest of Random Subsets (FORS), and so on, with the purpose to shorten the signature size and accelerate signing and verification. Some of them can be used for more than one time. They are called few-times signature (FTS) schemes. People build other hash-based signature (HBS) schemes, such eXtended Merkle Signature Scheme (XMSS)/Multi-tree XMSS (XMSS-MT) and Leighton-Micali Signatures (LMS). Take XMSS as an example. The big difference is the leaf node. It is not a hash of the OTS public key, but the root node of another tree called L-tree. The L-tree is similar to the Merkle tree. The WOTS+ public key is stored in the leaf node of the L-tree.

Unfortunately, stateful HBS schemes are easy to be misused. Because they are one-time signatures, any private key cannot be used on two or more messages. The implementation must maintain the state to keep track of the one-time private key usage in order to prevent the reuse. The stateful HBS may be used for image signing in the firmware security area. Assuming we choose h to be 10 in a Merkle tree, we can sign 1024 images with one main public key. If the firmware image is released every month, this main public key will cover 85 years.

At the same time, the stateless hash-based signature (HBS) scheme is also created. Take SPHINCS+ as an example. It creates a hyper tree structure in Figure 19-15. Each layer of SPHINCS+ uses a XMSS WOTS+ L-tree as a node. This WOTS+ L-tree is used to sign to its children WOTS+ L-tree in the next level. The leaf node of the SPHINCS+ uses the Forest of Random Subsets (FORS) tree to sign the message.

The benefit of stateless HBS is to eliminate the state maintenance requirement. Since it is also hash based, the security is based upon the hash algorithm. However, the disadvantage of SPHINCS+ is the signature size and speed, because it eliminates the state by using the components from XMSS and working with larger keys and signatures.

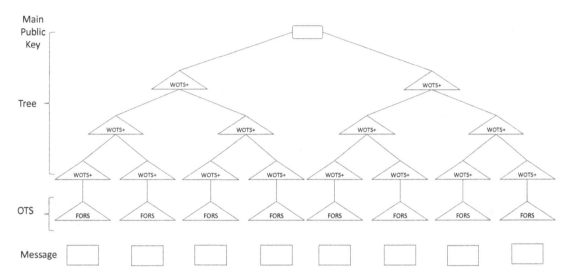

Figure 19-15. *SPHINCS+ Hyper Tree*

For more details of XMSS, LMS, and SPHINCS+, please refer to the RFC 8391, RFC 8554, and the SPHINCS specifications.

Quantum Cryptography

In the previous section, we introduced some cryptographic algorithms which are presumed to be quantum safe. But they are still modern cryptographic algorithms and do not use any quantum mechanism. In this section, we will introduce some cryptographic algorithms which use quantum mechanics as a cryptographic solution.

Quantum Key Distribution (QKD)

Quantum key distribution (QKD) is an advanced secure communication method for key exchange. With QKD, two parties can produce and share a common secret for encryption and decryption. QKD is tamper-proof naturally because it is based upon the properties of quantum mechanics. If there is a third party trying to eavesdrop upon the communication, this action will disturb the system. If the modification is detected, then the key distribution can be aborted.

In 1984, Bennet and Brassard published "Quantum cryptography: Public key distribution and coin tossing" to describe a quantum key distribution mechanism. This is the first quantum cryptography protocol, and it is provably secure based upon the quantum property. It is also named as the BB84 protocol.

Let's take a look at how BB84 works. Alice wants to negotiate a secret with Bob. They need to set up two communication channels. One is the quantum channel which is used to transmit photons. The other is the classic channel which is used to transmit digital information. In order to transmit photons in the quantum channel, Alice needs two digital polarizers, and Bob needs two digital beam splitters. We name the rectilinear polarizer/ beam splitter to be R and the diagonal polarizer/ beam splitter to be D. See Figure 19-16.

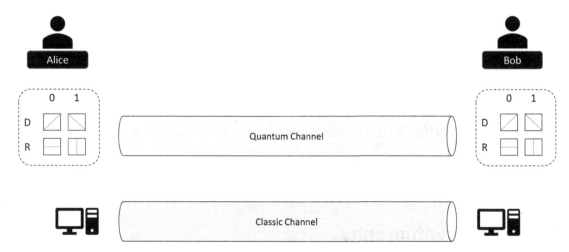

Figure 19-16. *BB84 Communication Channel*

Alice can send photon from either the R or D polarizer. The photon sent from R could be vertical (bit 1) or horizontal (bit 0). The photon sent from D could be 135 degrees (bit 1) or 45 degrees (bit 0). Bob can choose either the R or D beam splitter and check the photon detector. If Bob chooses the same R or D with Alice, the final result will be correct. If Bob choses the different R or D with Alice, the result is unknown – 50% correct and 50% wrong. Realistically, some photons may be lost in transition because of the limitation of the detector.

Now Alice and Bob can start negotiating the secret. See Figure 19-17.

Step 1: Quantum qommunication phase

1) Alice generates a random bit string.

2) Alice chooses a random sequence of sending base – D or R.

3) Alice encodes each bit 0 or 1 in the bit string and sends the photons in the quantum channel. There are four types of photons in the quantum channel.

4) Bob chooses a random sequence of receiving base – D or R.

5) Bob receives the photon sent from Alice and decodes it to 0 or 1. Because some photons might be lost in transition, some bits might be missing in the final result. Because Bob may choose a different receiving base, some bits might be incorrect.

Step 2: Classic communication phase

6) Bob reports the sequence of bases which receive the bit. This step filters the bits lost in transition.

7) Alice checks the sequence and tells Bob which one is correct. This step filters the bits which are decoded with a different base D or R. At this time, both Alice and Bob know the correct bits. This correct bit sequence can be treated as a presumably shared secret if there is eavesdropping on the quantum channel. We call it pre-shared secret.

8) Bob reveals some random bits in the pre-shared secret and sends to Alice. This step is to test for eavesdrops. If it happens, the photon state will be disturbed. The bit value might be incorrect.

9) Alice checks the random bits from Bob by comparing them with the original random bits generated. If they are different, that means eavesdrops happened and the communication must be aborted. If they are the same, Alice sends the confirmation to Bob.

Step 3: Shared secret generation phase

10) Alice and Bob remove the revealed bits from the pre-shared secret and use the rest of the bits as the shared secret. Now Alice and Bob finish the negotiation and have a common secret.

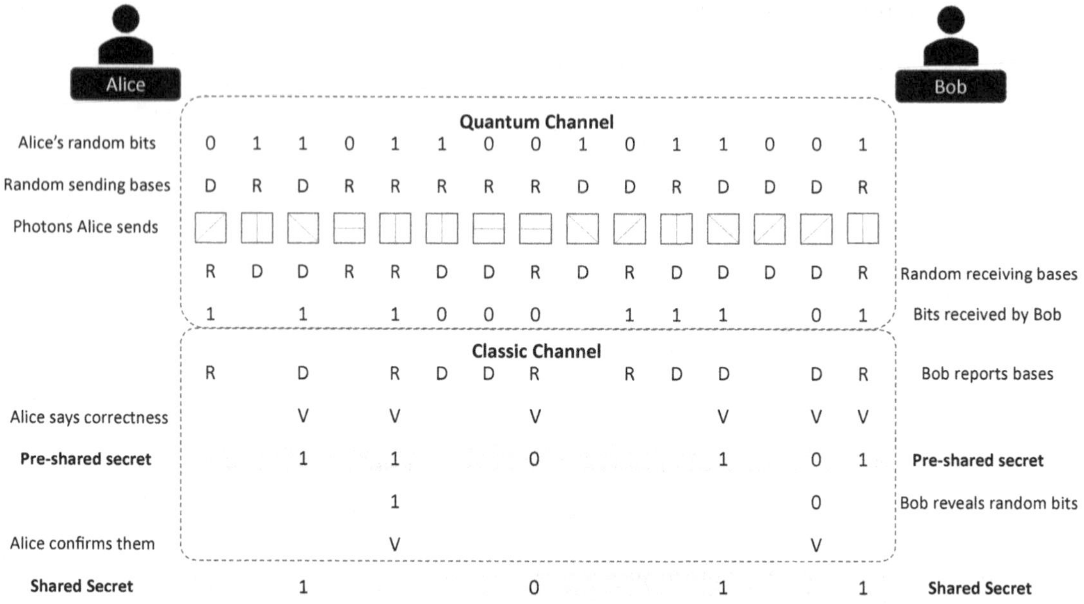

Quantum Channel

Alice's random bits	0	1	1	0	1	1	0	0	1	0	1	1	0	0	1
Random sending bases	D	R	D	R	R	R	R	R	D	D	R	D	D	D	R
Photons Alice sends															
Random receiving bases	R	D	D	R	R	D	D	R	D	R	D	D	D	D	R
Bits received by Bob	1		1		1	0	0	0		1	1	1		0	1

Classic Channel

Bob reports bases	R		D		R	D	D	R			R	D	D		D	R
Alice says correctness			V		V			V				V	V		V
Pre-shared secret			1		1			0				1			0	1
			1												
Alice confirms them			V												
Shared Secret			1					0				1			1

Bob reports bases / Alice says correctness / Pre-shared secret / Bob reveals random bits / Alice confirms them / Shared Secret

Figure 19-17. *BB84 Communication Protocol*

The QKD process can help to generate the one-time pad (OTP) password. It must be used one time, and its length must be as long as the message itself.

Quantum Random Number Generation (QRNG)

The quantum mechanism can be used to produce a random number. Figure 19-18 uses a Bloch sphere to show the concept. The north pole of the Bloch sphere presents the classic value 0, and the south pole presents the classic value 1. Any other point on the Bloch sphere presents the superposition. The closer point to a pole means the higher probability when the qubit collapses into the classical value. We can use the following steps to get a random bit:

1) We initialize the qubit to state 0.

2) We put the qubit in the superposition in which the probabilities for 0 and 1 are the same.

3) We measure the value and record the output. Because the output is random – 50% 0 and 50% 1 – we get a random bit.

4) We can repeat steps 1–3 and get a random bit stream.

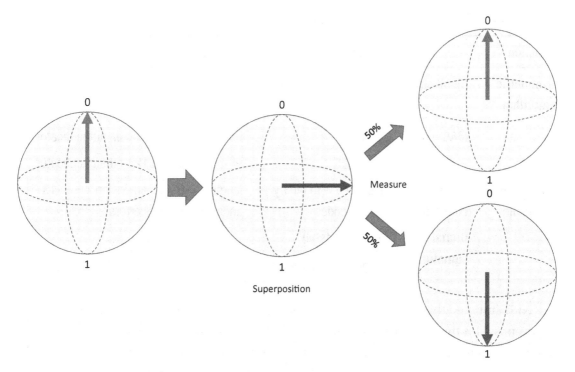

Figure 19-18. *Quantum Random Bit Generation*

Algorithm Recommendation

Similar to modern cryptography, different organizations have started giving recommendations for the quantum safe cryptographic algorithms, also known as post-quantum cryptographic algorithms.

In 2015, PQCRYPTO published the initial recommendation in Table 19-13.

Table 19-13. *PQCRYPTO Initial Recommendation*

Function		Algorithm	Parameter
Symmetric algorithm	**Block cipher**	AES-256	256-bit key
		Salsa20	256-bit key
	MAC	GCM	96-bit nonce and 128-bit authenticator
		Poly1305	96-bit nonce and 128-bit authenticator
Asymmetric algorithm	**Public key encryption**	McEliece with binary Goppa codes	length n = 6960, dimension k = 5413 andadding t = 119 errors
	Digital signature	XMSS (stateful)	
		SPHINCS-256 (stateless)	

NIST initiated the post-quantum cryptography project in 2016 and started the call for proposal for the quantum safe algorithms. The focus is on public key encryption/ key establishment algorithms and digital signature algorithms. Table 19-14 shows a list of post-quantum algorithm candidates. Most of them are hash-based digital signature, lattice-based cryptography, code-based cryptography, and Multivariate Public Key Cryptography. They are probably secure.

Table 19-14. *NIST Post-Quantum Algorithm Candidates*

Usage	Algorithm	Hard Problem
Public key encryption and key establishment	BIKE, Classic McEliece, HQC, LEDAcrypt, NTS-KEM, ROLLO, RQC	Code
	CRYSTALS-KYBER, FrodoKEM, LAC, NewHope, NTRU, NTRU Prime, Round5, SABER	Lattice
	SIKE	Isogeny
	Three Bears	Integer ring
Digital signature	SPHINCS+, Picnic	Hash
	CRYSTALS-DILITHIUM, FALCON, qTESLA	Lattice
	GeMSS, LUOV, MQDSS, Rainbow	Multivariate

In 2019, NIST drafted the recommendation for two stateful hash-based signature schemes – Leighton-Micali Signatures (LMS) described in RFC 8554 and eXtended Merkle Signature Scheme (XMSS) described in RFC 8391. Table 19-15 shows the LMS and XMSS parameters.

Table 19-15. *NIST Recommendation for Stateful Hash-Based Signatures*

Function		Algorithm	Parameter
Asymmetric algorithm	**Digital signature**	LMS	LMOTS_[SHA256ISHAKE]_[N32IN24]_[W1IW2IW4IW8]
			LMS_[SHA256ISHAKE]_[M32IM24]_[H5IH10IH15IH20IH25]
		XMSS	WOTPS-[SHA2ISHAKE256]_[256I192]
			XMSS-[SHA2ISHAKE256]_[10I16I20]_[256I192]
			XMSSMT-[SHA2ISHAKE256]_ [20/2I20/4I40/2I40/4I40/8I60/3I60/6I60/12]_[256I192]

As we mentioned in the previous section, the stateful hash-based signature has limited use cases, such as image signing, because of the state management requirement. The stateless hash-based signature and other algorithms are still under evaluation.

Image signing is an important use case in the firmware, such as UEFI secure boot feature. Fortunately, the PKCS#7 standards allow for multiple signatures in a SignedData content type. An image may consider including dual signatures. One signature uses the existing asymmetric cryptographic algorithm such as RSA or ECDSA. The other uses the quantum safe algorithm such as XMSS or LMS. The existing system can verify the RSA or ECDSA signature, while the HBS capable system can verify the XMSS or LMS signature.

For the key establishment, using quantum safe modern cryptography could still be the first choice, such as McEliece and other candidates, unless they are proven to be insecure. Quantum cryptography such as QKD might be still a long way from broad usage.

Preparation for the Future

Since we know the quantum computers and quantum computing age are coming, is there anything we need to worry about now?

Mosca's Theorem

Mosca's theorem tells us that it depends on the three variables – X, Y, and Z, where

X = the number of years you need your public key cryptography to remain unbroken.

Y = the number of years it will take to replace the current system with one that is quantum safe.

Z = the number of years it will take to break the current tools, using quantum computers or other means.

See Figure 19-19. If X+Y>Z, then we have a problem because the secret will be exposed between [Z, X+Y].

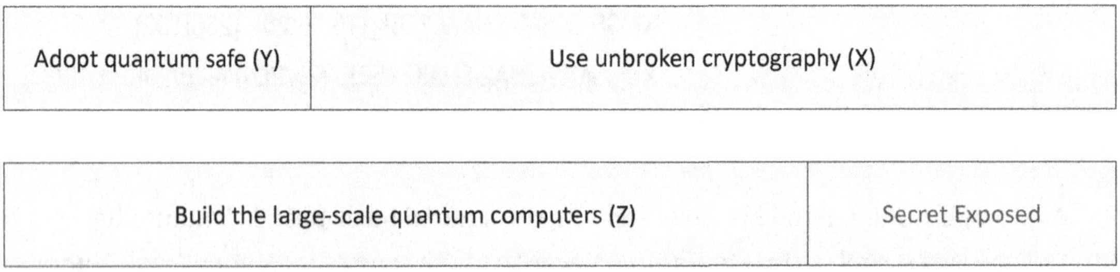

Adopt quantum safe (Y)	Use unbroken cryptography (X)

Build the large-scale quantum computers (Z)	Secret Exposed

Figure 19-19. *Mosca's Theorem*

The X factor is determined by the product in the organization. The organization needs to decide the update plan and the end-of-life plan for the product carefully. If X is much small, such as two years, that means your product will have its end of life before the quantum age. Then you don't need to worry. But if the X is big in the Internet of Things (IoT) environment, such as ten years from now, then you probably need think about the transition plan.

The Y factor is the migration time from the existing infrastructure to the quantum safe infrastructure. It is determined by the readiness of the industry development environment. Currently, there are lots of activities on Y. For example, NIST started the call for proposal for the post-quantum algorithm and hopefully will provide recommendations after two or three years.

The Z factor is determined by the companies which are building the quantum computers. According to research, the large-scale quantum computers that can break 2000-bit RSA are likely to be built in 2030.

Post-Quantum Cryptography Project

Currently, there is an open quantum safe (OQS) project created on GitHub. The goal is to provide an open source library for the quantum safe cryptographic algorithms. It includes a set of key establishment algorithms and digital signature algorithms. liboqs is the open source version quantum safe API. Open quantum safe OpenSSL (OQS-OpenSSL) is a fork of the OpenSSL and adds quantum safe key exchange and authentication algorithms using liboqs for the network Transport Layer Security (TLS) protocol. This prototype can help people understand the quantum safe cryptography and prepare for the migration.

Care must be taken when we include a quantum safe algorithm implementation in the firmware. Most firmware only has limited stack and heap, while we observed that some quantum safe implementations use a large stack during runtime, which may cause the program crash. It is recommended to enable the stack guard feature to detect such stack overrun issue.

Quantum Cryptography Project

At the same time, the industry companies are creating quantum programming projects. For example, Microsoft introduced a Q# programming language and Microsoft Quantum Development Kit. People can write quantum programming code and run on a quantum platform simulation, such as quantum random number generation, BB84 protocol, Grover search, and so on. ProjectQ is an open source software framework for quantum computing with the Python language. It includes examples such as Shor's algorithm, Grover's algorithm, and so on. Qiskit is a rich open source framework for working with noisy quantum computers at the level of pulses, circuits, and algorithms. It includes four elements: Aer, a high-performance simulator for quantum circuit with noise; Terra, a set of tools to compose a quantum program at the level of circuits and pulses; Ignis, a framework to understand and mitigate noise in quantum circuits and systems; and Aqua, quantum algorithms and applications.

Summary

In this chapter, we introduced some important concepts in modern cryptography, such as the random number, mode of operation, signature scheme, forward security, and certificate chain, as well as the challenges in the firmware implementation. In the second half, we introduced the advances in quantum safe cryptography, with the hash-based signature (HBS) and quantum key distribution (QKD) as examples, and how we should prepare for the future according to Mosca's theorem. Figure 19-20 shows the overall progress in cryptography. In the next chapter, we will discuss the language choice in the firmware development.

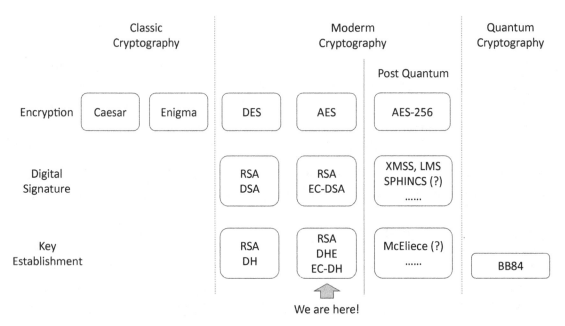

Figure 19-20. *Progress in Cryptography*

References

Book

[B-1] Ross J. Anderson, *Security Engineering: A Guide to Building Dependable Distributed Systems, 2nd edition*, Wiley, 2008

[B-2] Bruce Schneier, *Applied Cryptography: Protocols, Algorithms and Source Code in C, 2nd edition*, Wiley, 1996

[B-3] Bruce Schneier, *Secrets and Lies: Digital Security in a Networked World*, Wiley, 2004

[B-4] Niels Ferguson, Bruce Schneier, Tadayoshi Kohno, *Cryptography Engineering: Design Principles and Practical Applications*, Wiley 2010

[B-5] Oded Goldreich, *Foundations of Cryptography, volume I & volume II*, Cambridge University Press, 2001

[B-6] Jean-Philippe Aumasson, *Serious Cryptography: A Practical Introduction to Modern Encryption*, No Starch Press, 2017

[B-7] David Johnston, *Random Number Generators – Principles and Practices*, DeG Press, 2018

[B-8] David Kleidermacher, *Embedded System Security – Practical Methods for Safe and Secure Software and Systems Development*, Newnes, 2012.

[B-9] Daniel J. Bernstein, Johannes Buchmann, Erik Dahmen, *Post-Quantum Cryptography*, Springer, 2009

[B-10] Michael A. Nielsen, Isaac L. Chuang, *Quantum Computation and Quantum Information*, Cambridge University Press, 2011

[B-11] Scott Aaronson, *Quantum Computing since Democritus*, Cambridge University Press, 2013

[B-12] Eleanor G. Rieffel, Wolfgang Polak, *Quantum Computing: A Gentle Introduction*, MIT Press, 2014

Conference, Journal, and Paper

[P-1] Auguste Kerckhoffs, "La cryptographie militaire," Journal des sciences militaires, vol. IX, 1883, `www.petitcolas.net/kerckhoffs/index.html`

[P-2] Claude Shannon. "Communication Theory of Secrecy Systems," Bell System Technical Journal, 1949. `http://netlab.cs.ucla.edu/wiki/files/shannon1949.pdf`

[P-3] Whitfield Diffie, Martin E Hellman, "New Directions in Cryptography," in IEEE Transactions on Information Theory, 1976, available at `https://ee.stanford.edu/~hellman/publications/24.pdf`

[P-5] Mihir Bellare, Chanathip Namprempre, "Authenticated Encryption: Relations among notions and analysis of the generic composition paradigm," in *Extended Abstract in Advances in Cryptology: Asiacrypt 2007 Proceedings*, `http://cseweb.ucsd.edu/~mihir/papers/oem.pdf`

[P-6] Hugo Krawczyk, "The Order of Encryption and Authentication for Protecting Communications (Or: How Secure is SSL?)," in Crypto 2001, available at `www.iacr.org/archive/crypto2001/21390309.pdf`

[P-7] Don Davis, "Defective Sign & Encrypt in S/MIME, PKCS#7, MOSS, PEM, PGP, and XML," 2001 `http://world.std.com/~dtd/sign_encrypt/sign_encrypt7.html`

[P-8] Phillip Rogaway, "Evaluation of Some Blockcipher Modes of Operation," in *Cryptography Research and Evaluation Committees (CRYPTREC)*, 2011, available at `https://web.cs.ucdavis.edu/~rogaway/papers/modes.pdf`

[P-9] Chanathip Namprempre, Phillip Rogaway, Thomas Shrimpton, "Reconsidering Generic Composition," in *EUROCRYPT 2014*, available at https://eprint.iacr.org/2014/206.pdf

[P-10] Pierre L'Ecuyer, "Random Number Generators: Design Principles and Statistical Testing," Mixmax Workshop CERN, 2016, available at www.iro.umontreal.ca/~lecuyer/myftp/slides/mixmax-cern16.pdf

[P-11] FailOverflow, "Console Hacking – PS3 Epic Fail," in *27C3 2010*, available at www.cs.cmu.edu/~dst/GeoHot/1780_27c3_console_hacking_2010.pdf

[P-12] Bodo Möller, Thai Duong, Krzysztof Kotowicz, "This POODLE Bites: Exploiting The SSL 3.0 Fallback," google 2014, www.openssl.org/~bodo/ssl-poodle.pdf

[P-13] David Adrian, Karthikeyan Bhargavan, Zakir Durumeric, Pierrick Gaudry, Matthew Green, J. Alex Halderman, Nadia Heninger, Drew Springall, Emmanuel Thomé, Luke Valenta, Benjamin VanderSloot, Eric Wustrow, Santiago Zanella-Béguelin, and Paul Zimmermann, "Imperfect Forward Secrecy: How Diffie-Hellman Fails in Practice," in *22nd ACM Conference on Computer and Communications Security (CCS '15)*, https://weakdh.org/imperfect-forward-secrecy-ccs15.pdf

[P-14] Fabien Perigaud, Alexandre Gazet, Joffrey Czarny, "Turning your BMC into a revolving door," in ZeroNight 2018, https://airbus-seclab.github.io/ilo/ZERONIGHTS2018-Slides-EN-Turning_your_BMC_into_a_revolving_door-perigaud-gazet-czarny.pdf

[P-15] Maik Ender, Amir Moradi, Christof Paar, "The Unpatchable Silicon: A Full Break of the Bitstream Encryption of Xilinx 7-Series FPGAs," in USENIX 2020, available at www.usenix.org/system/files/sec20fall_ender_prepub.pdf, https://bit.ly/Starbleed

[P-16] Vincent Lee, "Dealing With Encrypted Router Firmware," 2020, www.thezdi.com/blog/2020/2/6/mindshare-dealing-with-encrypted-router-firmware

[P-17] "AMD PSP: fTPM Remote Code Execution via crafted EK certificate," 2018, https://seclists.org/fulldisclosure/2018/Jan/12

[P-18] "AMD-SEV: Platform DH key recovery via invalid curve attack," 2019, https://seclists.org/fulldisclosure/2019/Jun/46

[P-19] Daniel Moghimi, Berk Sunar, Thomas Eisenbarth, Nadia Heninger, "TPM-FAIL: TPM meets Timing and Lattice Attacks," in 29th USENIX Security Symposium 2020, available at https://arxiv.org/abs/1911.05673

[P-20] Matus Nemec, Marek Sys, Petr Svenda, Dusan Klinec, Vashek Matyas, "The Return of Coppersmith's Attack: Practical Factorization of Widely Used RSA Moduli," in ACM CCS 2017, available at `https://crocs.fi.muni.cz/_media/public/papers/nemec_roca_ccs17_preprint.pdf`, `https://crocs.fi.muni.cz/_media/public/papers/ccs-nemec-handout.pdf`

[P-21] Leslie B. Lamport, "Constructing digital signatures from a one-way function," in *Technical Report SRI-CSL-98, SRI International Computer Science Laboratory*, 1979. available at `www.microsoft.com/en-us/research/uploads/prod/2016/12/Constructing-Digital-Signatures-from-a-One-Way-Function.pdf`

[P-22] Charles H. Bennett and Gilles Brassard, "Quantum cryptography: Public key distribution and coin tossing," in *Proceedings of IEEE International Conference on Computers, Systems and Signal Processing*, 1984, available at `http://researcher.watson.ibm.com/researcher/files/us-bennetc/BB84highest.pdf`

[P-23] Ralph C. Merkle, "A Digital Signature Based on a Conventional Encryption Function," in *Proceeding of CRYPTO '87*, 1987, available at `https://people.eecs.berkeley.edu/~raluca/cs261-f15/readings/merkle.pdf`

[P-24] Peter W. Shor, "Algorithms for quantum computation: discrete logarithms and factoring," in *Proceedings 35th Annual Symposium on Foundations of Computer Science*, 1994, available at `https://pdfs.semanticscholar.org/6902/cb196ec032852ff31cc178ca822a5f67b2f2.pdf`

[P-25] Peter. W. Shor, "Polynomial-time algorithms for prime factorization and discrete logarithms on a quantum computer," in SIAM Journal of Computing 1997, available at `https://arxiv.org/pdf/quant-ph/9508027`

[P-26] Lov K. Grover, "A fast quantum mechanical algorithm for database search," in *Proceedings 28th Annual ACM Symposium on the Theory of Computing*, 1996, available at `https://arxiv.org/pdf/quant-ph/9605043.pdf`

[P-27] John Proos, Christof Zalka, "Shor's discrete logarithm quantum algorithm for elliptic curves," in *Quantum Information & Computation 2003*, available at `https://arxiv.org/pdf/quant-ph/0301141.pdf`

[P-28] Martin Roetteler, Michael Naehrig, Krysta M. Svore, Kristin Lauter, "Quantum resource estimates for computing elliptic curve discrete logarithms," in *ASIACRYPT 2017*, available at `https://arxiv.org/pdf/1706.06752`

[P-29] Georg Becker, "Merkle Signature Schemes, Merkle Trees and Their Cryptanalysis," Seminararbeit Ruhr-Universität Bochum, 2008, available at `www.emsec.ruhr-uni-bochum.de/media/crypto/attachments/files/2011/04/becker_1.pdf`

[P-30] Mosca M, "Setting the Scene for the ETSI Quantum-safe Cryptography Workshop," in *e-proceedings of 1st Quantum-Safe-Crypto Workshop*, 2013, available at `http://docbox.etsi.org/Workshop/2013/201309_CRYPTO/e-proceedings_Crypto_2013.pdf`

[P-31] European Telecommunications Standards Institute, "Quantum Safe Cryptography and Security: An Introduction, Benefits, Enablers and Challenges," ETSI Whitepaper 2015, available at `https://portal.etsi.org/Portals/0/TBpages/QSC/Docs/Quantum_Safe_Whitepaper_1_0_0.pdf`

[P-32] NIST NISTIR-8105, "Report on Post-Quantum Cryptography," 2016, available at `https://csrc.nist.gov/publications/nistir`

[P-33] Daniel J. Bernstein, Tanja Lange, "Post-quantum cryptography – dealing with the fallout of physics success," in *Nature 2017*, available at `https://cr.yp.to/papers/fallout-20170409.pdf`

[P-34] Konstantinos Karagiannis, "Quantum Computing Is Here, Powered by Open Source," 2018, `www.rsaconference.com/industry-topics/presentation/quantum-computing-is-here-powered-by-open-source`

[P-35] Panos Kampanakis, Dimitrios Sikeridis, "Two Post-Quantum Signature Use-cases: Non-issues, Challenges and Potential Solutions," in 7th ETSI/IQC Quantum Safe Cryptography Workshop, 2019, available at `https://eprint.iacr.org/2019/1276.pdf`

[P-36] Leon Groot Bruinderink, Andreas Hulsing, "Oops, I did it again – Security of One-Time Signatures under Two-Message Attacks," in *Selected Areas in Cryptography – SAC 2017*, `https://leongb.nl/wp-content/uploads/2016/03/SAC2017.pdf`

Specification and Guideline

[S-1] IETF, "RFC 8708 – Use of the HSS/LMS Hash-Based Signature Algorithm in the Cryptographic Message Syntax (CMS)," 2020, available at `https://tools.ietf.org/html/rfc8708`

[S-2] IETF, "RFC 8554 – Leighton-Micali Hash-Based Signatures," 2019, available at `https://tools.ietf.org/html/rfc8554`

[S-3] IETF, "RFC 8512 – CBOR Object Signing and Encryption (COSE)," 2017, available at `https://tools.ietf.org/html/rfc8512`

[S-4] IETF, "RFC 8439 – ChaCha20 and Poly1305 for IETF Protocols," 2018, available at `https://tools.ietf.org/html/rfc8439`

[S-5] IETF, "RFC 8422 – Elliptic Curve Cryptography (ECC) Cipher Suites for Transport Layer Security (TLS) Versions 1.2 and Earlier," 2018, available at `https://tools.ietf.org/html/rfc8422`

[S-6] IETF, "RFC 8391 – XMSS eXtended Merkle Signature Scheme," 2018, available at https://tools.ietf.org/html/rfc8391

[S-7] IETF, "RFC 8018: PKCS #5: Password-Based Cryptography Specification Version 2.1," 2017, available at https://tools.ietf.org/html/rfc8018

[S-8] IETF, "RFC 8017 – PKCS #1: RSA Cryptography Specifications Version 2.2," 2016, available at https://tools.ietf.org/html/rfc8017

[S-9] IETF, "RFC 7919 – Negotiated Finite Field Diffie-Hellman Ephemeral (FFDHE) Parameters for Transport Layer Security (TLS)," 2016, available at https://tools.ietf.org/html/rfc7919

[S-10] IETF, "RFC 7049 – Concise Binary Object Representation (CBOR)," 2013, available at https://tools.ietf.org/html/rfc7049

[S-11] IETF, "RFC 6979: Deterministic Usage of the Digital Signature Algorithm (DSA) and Elliptic Curve Digital Signature Algorithm (ECDSA)," 2013, available at https://tools.ietf.org/html/rfc6979

[S-12] IETF, "RFC 5869: HMAC-based Extract-and-Expand Key Derivation Function (HKDF)," 2010, available at https://tools.ietf.org/html/rfc5869

[S-13] IETF, "RFC 5116 – An Interface and Algorithms for Authenticated Encryption," 2008, available at https://tools.ietf.org/html/rfc5116

[S-14] IETF, "RFC 3526 – More Modular Exponential (MODP) Diffie-Hellman groups for Internet Key Exchange (IKE)," 2003, available at https://tools.ietf.org/html/rfc3526

[S-15] IETF, "RFC 2315 – PKCS #7: Cryptographic Message Syntax Version 1.5," 1998, available at https://tools.ietf.org/html/rfc2315

[S-16] ITU, "X.509 : Information technology – Open Systems Interconnection – The Directory: Public-key and attribute certificate frameworks," 2019, www.itu.int/rec/T-REC-X.509

[S-17] ITU, "X.680 : Information technology – Abstract Syntax Notation One (ASN.1): Specification of basic notation," 2015, www.itu.int/rec/T-REC-X.680-201508-I/

[S-18] NIST SP800-208, "Recommendation for Stateful Hash-Based Signature Schemes," 2015, available at https://csrc.nist.gov/publications/sp800

[S-19] NIST SP800-186, "Recommendations for Discrete Logarithm-Based Cryptography: Elliptic Curve Domain Parameters," 2019, available at https://csrc.nist.gov/publications/sp800

[S-20] NIST SP800-185, "SHA-3 Derived Functions: cSHAKE, KMAC, TupleHash, and ParallelHash," 2016, available at https://csrc.nist.gov/publications/sp800

[S-21] NIST SP800-132, "Recommendation for Password-Based Key Derivation," 2010, available at `https://csrc.nist.gov/publications/sp800`

[S-22] NIST SP800-131A, "Transitioning the Use of Cryptographic Algorithms and Key Lengths," 2019, available at `https://csrc.nist.gov/publications/sp800`

[S-23] NIST SP800-108, "Recommendation for Key Derivation Using Pseudorandom Functions," 2009, available at `https://csrc.nist.gov/publications/sp800`

[S-24] NIST SP800-90C, "Recommendation for Random Bit Generator (RBG) Constructions," 2016, available at `https://csrc.nist.gov/publications/sp800`

[S-25] NIST SP800-90B, "Recommendation for the Entropy Sources Used for Random Bit Generation," 2018, available at `https://csrc.nist.gov/publications/sp800`

[S-26] NIST SP800-90A, "Recommendation for Random Number Generation Using Deterministic Random Bit Generators," 2015, available at `https://csrc.nist.gov/publications/sp800`

[S-27] NIST SP800-67, "Recommendation for the Triple Data Encryption Algorithm (TDEA) Block Cipher," 2017, available at `https://csrc.nist.gov/publications/sp800`

[S-28] NIST SP800-56C, "Recommendation for Key-Derivation Methods in Key-Establishment Schemes," 2018, available at `https://csrc.nist.gov/publications/sp800`

[S-29] NIST SP800-56B, "Recommendation for Pair-Wise Key-Establishment Using Integer Factorization Cryptography," 2019, available at `https://csrc.nist.gov/publications/sp800`

[S-30] NIST SP800-56A, "Recommendation for Pair-Wise Key-Establishment Schemes Using Discrete Logarithm Cryptography," 2018, available at `https://csrc.nist.gov/publications/sp800`

[S-31] NIST SP800-38G, "Recommendation for Block Cipher Modes of Operation: Methods for Format-Preserving Encryption," 2016, available at `https://csrc.nist.gov/publications/sp800`

[S-32] NIST SP800-38F, "Recommendation for Block Cipher Modes of Operation: Methods for Key Wrapping," 2012, available at `https://csrc.nist.gov/publications/sp800`

[S-33] NIST SP800-38E, "Recommendation for Block Cipher Modes of Operation: the XTS-AES Mode for Confidentiality on Storage Devices," 2010, available at `https://csrc.nist.gov/publications/sp800`

[S-34] NIST SP800-38D, "Cipher Modes of Operation: Galois / Counter Mode (GCM) and GMAC," 2007, available at `https://csrc.nist.gov/publications/sp800`

[S-35] NIST SP800-38C, "Cipher Modes of Operation: The CCM Mode for Authentication and Confidentiality," 2007, available at `https://csrc.nist.gov/publications/sp800`

[S-36] NIST SP800-38B, "Recommendation for Block Cipher Modes of Operation: the CMAC Mode for Authentication," 2016, available at `https://csrc.nist.gov/publications/sp800`

[S-37] NIST SP800-38A Addendum, "Recommendation for Block Cipher Modes of Operation: Three Variants of Ciphertext Stealing for CBC Mode," 2010, available at `https://csrc.nist.gov/publications/sp800`

[S-38] NIST SP800-38A, "Recommendation for Block Cipher Modes of Operation: Methods and Techniques," 2001, available at `https://csrc.nist.gov/publications/sp800`

[S-39] NIST FIPS 202, "SHA-3 Standard: Permutation-Based Hash and Extendable-Output Functions," 2015, `https://csrc.nist.gov/publications/fips`

[S-40] NIST FIPS 198-1, "The Keyed-Hash Message Authentication Code (HMAC)," 2008, `https://csrc.nist.gov/publications/fips`

[S-41] NIST FIPS 197, "Advanced Encryption Standard (AES)," 2001, `https://csrc.nist.gov/publications/fips`

[S-42] NIST FIPS 186-5, "Digital Signature Standard (DSS)," 2019, `https://csrc.nist.gov/publications/fips`

[S-43] NIST FIPS 180-4, "Secure Hash Standard (SHS)," 2015, `https://csrc.nist.gov/publications/fips`

[S-44] NIST FIPS 140-3, "Security Requirements for Cryptographic Modules," 2019, `https://csrc.nist.gov/publications/fips`

[S-45] SPHINCS org, "SPHINCS+ specification," 2019, available at `https://sphincs.org/resources.html`

[S-46] GB/T 35276, "SM2 cryptographic algorithm usage specification," 2017, available at `http://openstd.samr.gov.cn`

[S-47] GB/T 35275, "SM2 cryptographic algorithm encrypted signature message syntax specification," 2017, available at `http://openstd.samr.gov.cn`

[S-48] GB/T 33133, "ZUC stream cipher algorithm," 2016, available at `http://openstd.samr.gov.cn`

[S-49] GB/T 32918, "Public key cryptographic algorithm SM2 based on elliptic curves," 2016, available at `http://openstd.samr.gov.cn`

[S-50] GB/T 32907, "SM4 block cipher algorithm," 2016, available at `http://openstd.samr.gov.cn`

[S-51] GB/T 32905, "SM3 cryptographic hash algorithm," 2016, available at `http://openstd.samr.gov.cn`

[S-52] Intel, "Intel 64 and IA-32 Architecture Software Developer Manuals," 2019, available at `https://software.intel.com/en-us/articles/intel-sdm`

[S-53] ARM, "ARM TrustZone True Random Number Generator Technical Reference Manual," 2017, available at `http://infocenter.arm.com/help/topic/com.arm.doc.100976_0000_00_en/trustzone_true_random_number_generator_technical_reference_manual_100976_0000_00_en.pdf`

Web

[W-1] NSA Commercial National Security Algorithm Suite, `https://apps.nsa.gov/iaarchive/programs/iad-initiatives/cnsa-suite.cfm`

[W-2] NIST Random Bit Generation, `https://csrc.nist.gov/Projects/Random-Bit-Generation`

[W-3] NIST Block Cipher Techniques, `https://csrc.nist.gov/Projects/block-cipher-techniques`

[W-4] NIST Elliptic Curve Cryptography, `https://csrc.nist.gov/Projects/elliptic-curve-cryptography`

[W-5] NIST Digital Signatures, `https://csrc.nist.gov/Projects/digital-signatures`

[W-6] NIST Key Establishment, `https://csrc.nist.gov/Projects/Key-Management/key-establishment`

[W-7] NIST Hash Functions, `https://csrc.nist.gov/Projects/Hash-Functions`

[W-8] NIST Message Authentication Codes, `https://csrc.nist.gov/Projects/Message-Authentication-Codes`

[W-9] Cryptographic Key Length Recommendation, `https://www.keylength.com/en/4/`

[W-10] OpenSSL vulnerabilities, `www.openssl.org/news/vulnerabilities.html`

[W-11] OpenSSL heartbleed, `https://heartbleed.com/`

[W-12] ROCA, `https://crocs.fi.muni.cz/public/papers/rsa_ccs17`, `https://github.com/crocs-muni/roca`

[W-13] NIST Post Quantum Cryptography, `https://csrc.nist.gov/Projects/Post-Quantum-Cryptography`

[W-14] NIST Stateful Hash-Based Signature, `https://csrc.nist.gov/news/2019/stateful-hbs-request-for-public-comments`

[W-15] PQCRYPTO, "Post-Quantum Cryptography for Long-Term Security – Initial recommendations of long-term secure post-quantum systems," `https://pqcrypto.eu.org/docs/initial-recommendations.pdf`

[W-16] Hash-Based Signature, `https://cryptoservices.github.io/quantum/2015/12/04/one-time-signatures.html`, `https://cryptoservices.github.io/quantum/2015/12/07/few-times-signatures.html`, `https://cryptoservices.github.io/quantum/2015/12/07/many-times-signatures.html`, `https://cryptoservices.github.io/quantum/2015/12/08/XMSS-and-SPHINCS.html`

[W-17] Quantum Safe Cryptography, `https://wizardforcel.gitbooks.io/practical-cryptography-for-developers-book/quantum-safe-cryptography.html`

[W-18] Quantum-Safe Cryptographic Algorithms, `https://github.com/open-quantum-safe/liboqs`

[W-19] Quantum-Safe Key Exchange and Authentication Algorithms Using liboqs, `https://github.com/open-quantum-safe/openssl`

[W-20] hash-sigs (RFC-8554), `https://github.com/cisco/hash-sigs`

[W-21] xmss-reference (RFC-8391), `https://github.com/XMSS/xmss-reference`

[W-22] EDKII Crypto Extension Package, `https://github.com/jyao1/CryptoEx`

[W-23] Microsoft Quantum Development Kit, `https://docs.microsoft.com/en-us/quantum/`

[W-24] ProjectQ, `https://github.com/ProjectQ-Framework/ProjectQ`

[W-25] Qiskit, `https://github.com/Qiskit`

CHAPTER 20

Programming Language

In this last chapter of the development part, we will discuss language selection for firmware development. Since there are lots of textbooks introducing the languages themselves, we will not discuss the details of the languages. Instead, we will focus on the security aspects of different languages which may be used in the firmware development.

The main categories of languages are machine language, assembly language, and high-level language. Today probably no one uses the first-generation machine language which has the binary format 0 and 1 to present the machine code. Let's start from the assembly language.

Assembly Language

Assembly language is the second-generation programming language. It is low-level language because it uses a symbol to replace the binary 0 and 1 to represent the machine code. Assembly language is hard to write, debug, review, and maintain. Some common issues in the assembly language are listed here:

1) Non-volatile register access: The non-volatile registers should be preserved in the function call. For example, the RBX is a non-volatile register according to the calling convention. It should be saved in the entry of the function and used and restored upon exit from the function, or it should never be used in the function. If the RBX is used in the function without being saved and restored, the contract between caller and callee is broken.

2) Wrong stack offset: The function uses the stack for the local variable storage and the function parameter. Usually, these data can be accessed with an offset to the stack, such as [RBP – 0x20] or [RSP + 0x38]. RBP is the stack base register. RSP is the stack pointer register. Usually, RBP should be used because it will not be

© Jiewen Yao and Vincent Zimmer 2020
J. Yao and V. Zimmer, *Building Secure Firmware*, https://doi.org/10.1007/978-1-4842-6106-4_20

changed once it is set in the entry of the function. It is dangerous to use RSP and offset because RSP is impacted by the stack PUSH and POP instruction. The data may be accessed correctly with [RSP + 0x38]. But after PUSH, the same data should be accessed with [RSP + 0x40].

3) Register misuse: The instruction set only provides a limited number of registers. With assembly language, the programmer must be very clear on which register is used for what purpose. Sometimes an instruction shall use the register RDX, but the code uses another register RAX. It is typical copy-paste error. The programmer copies a chunk of code from somewhere else but forgets to update all places.

4) Loop counter off by one: An instruction set includes a loop counter register, such as RCX in the IA instruction set. The LOOP instruction will cause RCX decrement. Similar to for loop in the C language, the wrong counter may cause off-by-one error (OBOE) and result in the buffer overflow.

5) Confusing syntax: The assembly language does not have standard. Different assembly syntax may have different ways to translate to the machine code. Take IA instruction as an example. The GNU assembly (GSA) uses the AT&T syntax. The Microsoft assembly (MASM) uses the Intel syntax. The biggest problem is that the source and destination order is different between those two syntaxes. If you want to put the value in RCX register to RAX register, you can write "MOV RAX, RCX" in Intel syntax or "MOVQ %RCX, %RAX" in AT&T syntax. We have seen many cases that a developer uses the wrong order because they are only familiar with one of the syntaxes and copy some code and then translate to another syntax.

These assembly language issues cannot be detected by the assembler because the assembler just follows the instruction to translate to the machine code without knowing the real purpose. In general, the use of the assembly language should be limited to some special areas:

1) Startup code: This is the first instruction when the CPU powers on. The startup code should set up the environment for the high-level language as soon as possible, such as a stack for the C language.

2) Mode switch: An instruction set may define different CPU execution modes, such as 16-bit real mode, 32-bit protected mode, and 64-bit long mode. Switching between different modes needs some special handling, such as setting up a control register or mode-specific register and switching to a different segment. The high-level language usually does not provide such support.

3) Exception handler: If the system runs into a soft exception or hardware interrupt, the CPU switches to the exception handler. The entry of the exception handler is usually written with assembly language because a high-level language does not handle the CPU context save and restore.

4) Set jump and long jump: Those are two standard C functions. setjump() remembers the current position and longjump() jumps to this position later. Because the current position includes the CPU context, those two functions are implemented in assembly languages.

5) Special instructions: Taking the IA instruction set as an example, it includes special register access such as control register (CR), model-specific register (MSR), streaming SIMD extension (SSE), advanced vector extension (AVX), and so on and a special instruction such as serialize load operations (LFENCE), flash cache line (CFLUSH), performance-improved spin-wait loops (PAUSE), and non-temporal store of data into memory (MOVNTI).

It is recommended to provide a library in the high-level language for the abstraction of those actions. As such, the other code should also call the library to do the work. The assembly language is still useful in these limited areas, but the usage should only be limited in those areas. The rest should belong to the high-level language.

C Language

The C language is probably the most popular and successful language since it was born with the Unix operating system. It is a high-level language, but it can also do the low-level work such as modifying memory content or memory mapped I/O registers in a special address. It is the most suitable language in the firmware area because the firmware needs to access the hardware-related content such as memory or memory mapped I/O register directly, and the C language is good and powerful in this area. With the C language, the developer can fully control the machine's hardware. We believe it is because of the nature of the C language – C was born to write the Unix operating system.

Now let's take a look at the C language from the security perspective. According to the Microsoft research, memory safety contributes 70% of the security vulnerabilities in C and C++. We also observed similar data in that the buffer overflow and integer overflow caused 50% of security issues in the firmware area. The reason is that the firmware is also one type of software. Firmware also has the similar memory safety issue including the memory access error such as buffer overflow, use-after-free, and uninitialized data error such as wild pointer, null pointer reference, and so on.

In Chapter 14, we discussed the best practices and guidelines for C programming. In Chapter 15, we discussed the C compiler defensive technology. In Chapter 16, we discussed the firmware kernel enhancements. On the one hand, all of the industry has provided the guidance and tools to address those flaws. On the other hand, people are also looking for a better type-safe language that can help to prevent the developer from introducing the flaws in the first place.

Rust

Rust is a new language. If we treat the C language as portable assembly, then Rust is a safe C language. The Rust language is designed to empower the developer to build reliable and efficient software. It offers

1) Performance: Rust is blazingly fast and memory efficient. It does not have a runtime or garbage collector. It can power performance-critical services and run on embedded devices. Runtime performance and runtime memory consumption are extremely important to the firmware because a typical firmware runs in a resource-constrained environment. Even for the Intel

Architecture (IA) system firmware, it needs to run code in the system management mode (SMM) which only has limited system management RAM (SMRAM), such as 1 MB or 8 MB. Similar constraints are observed by embedded devices. Rust embedded offers flexible memory management, where the dynamic memory allocation is optional. You may choose to use a global allocator and dynamic data structures or statically allocate everything. This is required because the firmware code may run on the flash device without DRAM.

2)   Reliability: Rust introduces a rich type system and an ownership model that guarantees memory safety and thread safety, which enables you to eliminate many classes of bugs at compile time. This is probably the most attractive feature. Rust is not the first language to introduce the type safety concept. One big concern of the type-safe language is the performance degradation because of the runtime type check. The performance impact is hard to accept for embedded system or firmware. The advantage of Rust is that many checks have been done at compile time. As such, the final generated binary does not include such checks. With strict rules of syntax, Rust can trace the lifecycle of a data object. As such, no runtime garbage collection is required. This design not only reduces the binary size but also improves the runtime performance.

3)   Productivity: Rust has a friendly compiler with useful error messages. The compiler not only shows what is wrong but also gives suggestions on how to fix the error. It teaches you how to write the Rust language. Rust has provided a unit test framework. You can write a set of unit tests just after the function implementation. Rust also considers the interoperability with other languages with the foreign function interface (FFI). Rust can generate a C language–compatible application binary interface (ABI). You can let Rust call the C language or call Rust from the C language.

Rust Security Solution

Major classes of security issues in firmware development are the memory safety issue and the arithmetic issue. In Chapter 15, we discussed two compiler defensive strategies: to eliminate the vulnerability and to break the exploit. Rust does a great job on eliminating the vulnerability by introducing a strict rule at compile time. Any violation causes the build failure. Also Rust injects the runtime boundary check for the buffer overflow to break the exploit. The generated code calls a panic handler for the runtime violation. Table 20-1 shows the Rust solution to handle the safety issues. The two classic memory safety issues – the spatial safety issue and the temporal safety issue – are resolved separately. Let's take a look at them one by one.

Table 20-1. *Rust Security Solution*

Type	Subtype	Rust Solution
Access error (spatial)	Buffer overflow (Write)	Use Offset/Index for Slice Runtime Boundary Check – [panic_handler].
	Buffer over-read	Use Offset/Index for Slice Runtime Boundary Check – [panic_handler].
Access error (temporal)	Use-after-free(dangling pointer)	Ownership – compile-time check.
	Double free	Ownership – compile-time check.
Uninitialized data	Uninitialized variable	Initialization – compile-time check.
	Wild pointer	Initialization – compile-time check.
	NULL pointer deference	Use Option<T> enum Allocation Check – [alloc_error_handler].

(continued)

Table 20-1. (*continued*)

Type	Subtype	Rust Solution
Arithmetic issue	Integer overflow	DEBUG: Runtime check – [panic_handler].
		RELEASE: Discard overflow data.
		Compiler flag: -C overflow-checks=on/off.
		Function:
		checkedIoverflowingIsaturatingIwrapping_
		addIsubImulIdivIremIshlIshrIpow().
	Type cast	Must be explicit – compile-time check.
		(Dest Size == Source Size) => no-op
		(Dest Size < Source Size) => truncate
		(Dest Size > Source Size) => {
		(source is unsigned) => zero-extend
		(source is signed) => sign-extend
		}

Ownership

The gist of Rust memory safety is to isolate the aliasing and mutation. Aliasing means there can be multiple ways to access the same data. The data is sharable. Mutation means the owner has the right to update the data. The data can be changed. The danger arises from aliasing + mutation.

Let's take a look at a C program in Listing 20-1. How many issues you can find?

Listing 20-1.

```
===========================
char *a1 = "hello world!";
char *b1 = "hello world!";

int main()
{
  char *a2 = strdup (a1);
  char *b2 = a2;
  char *b3 = strchr (a2, 'h');
  char *b4 = strchr (a2, 'w');
```

```
  *a1 = 'k';
  *a2 = 'l';

  *(a1 + 19) = 'm';
  *(a2 + 19) = 'n';

  printf("a1=%s (%p)\n", a1, a1);
  printf("a2=%s (%p)\n", a2, a2);
  printf("b1=%s (%p)\n", b1, b1);
  printf("b2=%s (%p)\n", b2, b2);
  printf("b3=%s (%p)\n", b3, b3);
  printf("b4=%s (%p)\n", b4, b4);

  free (a1);
  free (a2);
  free (b1);
  free (b2);
  free (b3);
  free (b4);
  printf("OK\n");
  return 0;
}
```

============================

The memory layout in this program is shown in Figure 20-1. Both a1 and b1 are in the global data section. They point to a string "hello world!" in the read-only data section. With the optimization on, the a1 and b1 point to the same location. If we turn off the optimization, the a1 and b1 point to different locations. The a2, b2, b3, and b4 are on the stack. a2, b2, and b3 point to a "hello world!" string in the heap, and b4 points to the middle of the "hello world!" Although the program updates the string pointed by a1 and a2, the string pointed by b1, b2, and b3 is also updated. It might be a side effect. Updating a1 may also cause a runtime crash because the read-only section is marked protected unless the program merges the read-only data section into the normal data section at link phase. The string update also has a buffer overflow access for m and n. Last of all, the free is only required for the data in the heap and only required once. b2, b3, and b4 point to same string as a2. As such, only free(a2) is required. See Listing 20-2 for the comment of the program.

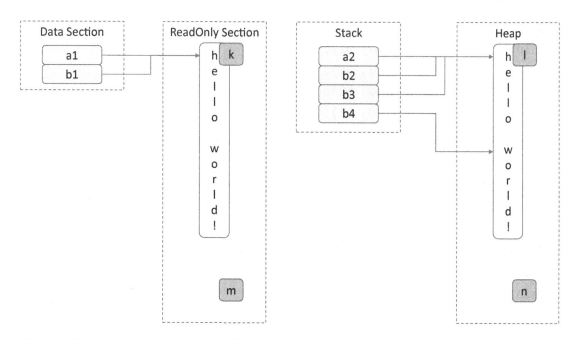

Figure 20-1. *Memory Layout of Listing 20-1*

Listing 20-2.

```
============================
char *a1 = "hello world!";
char *b1 = "hello world!";

int main()
{
  char *a2 = strdup (a1);
  char *b2 = a2;
  char *b3 = strchr (a2, 'h');
  char *b4 = strchr (a2, 'w');

  //*a1 = 'k'; // crash in normal build. Need merge .rdata to .data section.
             // b1 update if optimization on, side effect?
             // b1 not update if optimization off
  *a2 = 'l'; // cause b2, b3 update, side effect?

  //*(a1 + 19) = 'm'; // illegal, but no crash most likely
  //*(a2 + 19) = 'n'; // illegal, crash at free() most likely
```

```c
    printf("a1=%s (%p)\n", a1, a1);
    printf("a2=%s (%p)\n", a2, a2);
    printf("b1=%s (%p)\n", b1, b1);
    printf("b2=%s (%p)\n", b2, b2);
    printf("b3=%s (%p)\n", b3, b3);
    printf("b4=%s (%p)\n", b4, b4);

    //free (a1); // illegal, crash
    free (a2); // legal, required otherwise memory leak
    //free (b1); // illegal, crash
    //free (b2); // maybe legal, only if a2 is not freed.
    //free (b3); // illegal, but works, if a2 is not freed
    //free (b4); // illegal, crash
    printf("OK\n");
    return 0;
}
```

============================

Listing 20-1 can be compiled successfully because the C compiler does not perform any such check. It relies on the developer to do the right thing. With Rust, you cannot write code in such a way. If the data is mutable, it cannot be shared. On the other hand, if the data is shared, it must be mutable. Rust has three basic patterns for programming: ownership, shared borrow, and mutable borrow. Let's look at them one by one.

First, Figure 20-2 shows the concept of ownership. In Listing 20-3, we initialize a string s1, assign s1 to s2, and then assign s1 to s3. It is legal in the C language, but illegal in Rust. The reason is that when s1 is assigned to s2, the ownership of the string "hello world!" is moved from s1 to s2. s1 is no longer valid. As such, when the code wants to assign s1 to s3, the compiler generates an error in Listing 20-4. What if we want to use both s2 and s1? We need to use borrow, also known as reference.

Listing 20-3.

============================

```rust
fn test1() {
    // ownership
    let s1 = String::from ("hello world!");
    let mut s2 = s1;
```

```
    let mut s3 = s1; // error because the ownership is moved to s2
    s2.make_ascii_lowercase();

    println!("s1={}", s1);
    println!("s2={}", s2);
    println!("s3={}", s3);
}
```
===========================

Listing 20-4.

===========================
```
error[E0382]: use of moved value: `s1`
 --> src\main.rs:6:14
  |
4 |     let s1 = String::from ("hello world!");
  |         -- move occurs because `s1` has type `std::string::String`,
             which does not implement the `Copy` trait
5 |     let mut s2 = s1;
  |                    -- value moved here
6 |     let mut s3 = s1; // error because the ownership is moved to s2
  |                    ^^ value used here after move
```
===========================

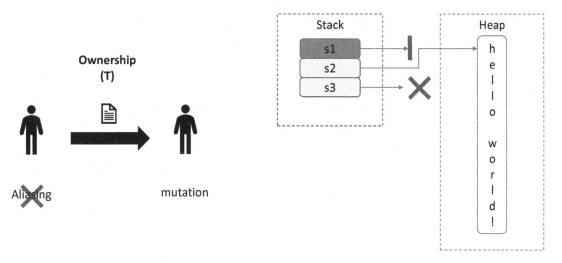

Figure 20-2. *Ownership in Rust*

Second, Figure 20-3 shows the concept of shared borrow. In Listing 20-5, we initialize s1 and assign s1 as a reference to s2 and s3 without any problem. However, if we want to update the string referenced by s2, the compiler generates error in Listing 20-6, because both s2 and s3 are immutable borrow. What if we want to update s2? We need to use mutable borrow.

Listing 20-5.

```
============================
fn test2() {
    // immutable borrow
    let s1 = String::from ("hello world!");
    let s2 = &s1;
    let s3 = &s1;
    s2.make_ascii_lowercase(); // error because s2 is immutable borrow.

    println!("s1={}", s1);
    println!("s2={}", s2);
    println!("s3={}", s3);
}
============================
```

Listing 20-6.

```
============================
error[E0596]: cannot borrow `*s2` as mutable, as it is behind a `&` reference
  --> src\main.rs:18:5
   |
17 |     let s2 = &s1;
   |                  --- help: consider changing this to be a mutable
   |                      reference: `&mut s1`
17 |     let s3 = &s1;
19 |     s2.make_ascii_lowercase(); // error because s2 is immutable
   |                                      borrow.
   |     ^^ `s2` is a `&` reference, so the data it refers to cannot be
   |     borrowed as mutable
============================
```

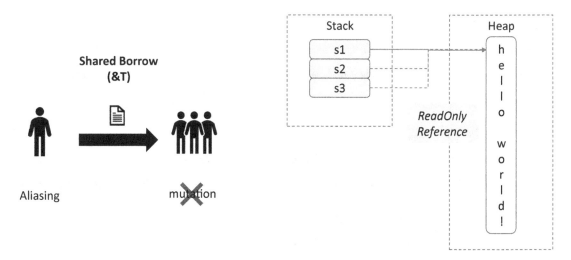

Figure 20-3. *Shared Borrow in Rust*

Third, Figure 20-4 shows the concept of mutable borrow. In Listing 20-7, we initialize s1 and assign s1 as a mutable reference to s2 and s3 because we want to update the s2 later. However, when we assign s1 as a mutable reference to s3, the compiler generates an error in Listing 20-8 because s3 is the second mutable borrow, which is illegal. At most, one mutable borrow is allowed in Rust.

Listing 20-7.

```
===========================
fn test3() {
    // mutable borrow
    let mut s1 = String::from ("hello world!");
    let s2 = &mut s1;
    let s3 = &mut s1; // error because this is second mutable borrow.
    s2.make_ascii_lowercase();

    println!("s1={}", s1);
    println!("s2={}", s2);
    println!("s3={}", s3);
}
===========================
```

Listing 20-8.

```
==============================
error[E0499]: cannot borrow `s1` as mutable more than once at a time
  --> src\main.rs:29:14
   |
29 |     let s2 = &mut s1;
   |                 ------- first mutable borrow occurs here
30 |     let s3 = &mut s1; // error because this is second mutable borrow.
   |                 ^^^^^^^ second mutable borrow occurs here
31 |     s2.make_ascii_lowercase();
   |        -- first borrow later used here
==============================
```

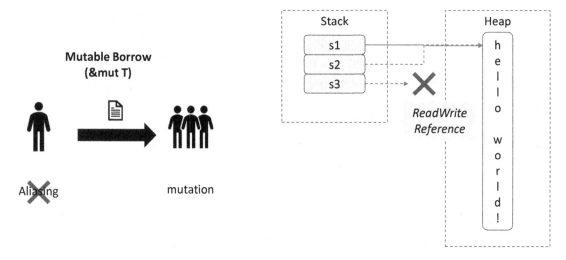

Figure 20-4. *Mutable Borrow in Rust*

You may also find that no free() is called in those functions because free() is not required in the code. free() is injected by the compiler. Listing 20-9 shows the compiler-generated binary for the entry and exit of the test1() function in Listing 20-3. With the strict rule the developer must follow, the Rust compiler can manage the object's lifecycle at build time. As such, the compiler injects __rust_alloc and __rust_dealloc in the code instead of using runtime garbage collection. Many optimizations can also be achieved at build time, and this is one reason that Rust can run fast.

Listing 20-9.

```
============================
  0000000140001140: 55                  push     rbp
  0000000140001141: 56                  push     rsi
  0000000140001142: 48 81 EC A8 00 00   sub      rsp,0A8h
                     00
  0000000140001149: 48 8D AC 24 80 00   lea      rbp,[rsp+80h]
                     00 00
  0000000140001151: 48 C7 45 20 FE FF   mov      qword ptr [rbp+20h],
                                                 0FFFFFFFFFFFFFFFEh
                     FF FF
  0000000140001159: BE 0C 00 00 00      mov      esi,0Ch
  000000014000115E: B9 0C 00 00 00      mov      ecx,0Ch
  0000000140001163: BA 01 00 00 00      mov      edx,1
  0000000140001168: E8 93 08 00 00      call     __rust_alloc
  000000014000116D: 48 85 C0            test     rax,rax
  0000000140001170: 0F 84 D9 00 00 00   je       000000014000124F
  0000000140001176: 48 89 45 F0         mov      qword ptr [rbp-10h],rax
...
  00000001400011C4: 0F 10 45 F0         movups   xmm0,xmmword ptr [rbp-10h]
  00000001400011C8: 0F 29 45 A0         movaps   xmmword ptr [rbp-60h],xmm0
  00000001400011CC: 0F 28 45 A0         movaps   xmm0,xmmword ptr [rbp-60h]
  00000001400011D0: 0F 29 45 D0         movaps   xmmword ptr [rbp-30h],xmm0
...
  0000000140001235: 48 8B 4D D0         mov      rcx,qword ptr [rbp-30h]
  0000000140001239: 41 B8 01 00 00 00   mov      r8d,1
  000000014000123F: E8 CC 07 00 00      call     __rust_dealloc
  0000000140001244: 90                  nop
  0000000140001245: 48 81 C4 A8 00 00   add      rsp,0A8h
                     00
  000000014000124C: 5E                  pop      rsi
  000000014000124D: 5D                  pop      rbp
  000000014000124E: C3                  ret
============================
```

Finally, let's see one more example to show how Rust catches an issue in Listing 20-10. The purpose of str_find_char() is to locate the first occurrence of a character in a string, similar to strchr() in the C language. The s.clear() is followed by the means to truncate this string. Because the result of str_find_char() is a reference to the original string s, this truncation impacts the result. The next println cannot print the expected content. Fortunately, the Rust compiler does a great job to catch this issue and show the error message in Listing 20-11. It notices that there is an immutable reference for s, so the s cannot have a mutable borrow to truncate the content.

Listing 20-10.

```
============================
fn str_find_char(s: &String, c: char) -> Option<&str> {
    let bytes = s.as_bytes();
    let len = s.len();

    for (i, &item) in bytes.iter().enumerate() {
        if item == c as u8 {
            return Some(&s[i..len]);
        }
    }

    None
}

fn test4() {
    let mut s = String::from("hello world");

    let result = str_find_char(&s, 'w');

    s.clear(); // error!

    match result  {
      Some(word) => println!("found: {}", word),
      None => println!("not found"),
    }
}
============================
```

Listing 20-11.

```
===========================
error[E0502]: cannot borrow `s` as mutable because it is also borrowed as
immutable
  --> src\main.rs:71:5
   |
69 |     let result = str_find_char(&s, 'w');
   |                                 -- immutable borrow occurs here
70 |
71 |     s.clear(); // error!
   |     ^^^^^^^^^ mutable borrow occurs here
72 |
73 |     match result  {
   |           ------ immutable borrow later used here
===========================
```

Option<T> Type

In Listing 20-10, there is a data type – Option<&str>. What is that for?

The C language has NULL pointer concept. Dereference of a NULL pointer causes an exception at runtime. Tony Hoare treated the NULL pointer as a "billion-dollar mistake." It was invented in 1965 just because it was easy to implement. Eventually it has led to innumerable errors, vulnerabilities, and system crashes.

Rust uses Option<T> type to resolve the NULL pointer. The definition for Option<T> type is in Listing 20-12.

Listing 20-12.

```
===========================
pub enum Option<T> {
    /// No value
    None,
    /// Some value T
    Some(T)
}
===========================
```

Listing 20-13 is the C program that might have a problem. If a developer forgets to check the NULL pointer in the check_optional() function, a NULL reference might happen in the C version. This will never happen in Rust. Listing 20-14 shows the Rust version. If a data might be NULL, the Option<T> must be used. In order to get data, the program must use Some(T) to get the data from the Option<T> parameter and include None pattern to handle the no-value case. The risk of NULL deference is eliminated.

Listing 20-13.

```
============================
void print_ptr_data (int *optional) {
    if (optional == NULL) { // It might be missing.
        printf ("NULL pointer\n");
    } else {
        printf ("value is %d\n", *optional);
    }
}

void test() {
    int *optional = NULL;
    print_ptr_data (optional);

    optional = malloc (sizeof(int));
    *optional = 5;
    print_ptr_data (optional);
}
============================
```

Listing 20-14.

```
============================
fn print_ptr_data (optional: Option<Box<i32>>) {
    match optional {
        Some(p) => println!("value is {}", p),
        None => println!("Value is None"),
    }
}
```

```
fn test5() {
    let optional = None;
    print_ptr_data (optional);

    let optional = Some(Box::new(5));
    print_ptr_data (optional);
}
============================
```

Boundary Check

In the C language, a buffer overflow is one of the most critical issues. In general, Rust recommends to use the iterator for the buffer access. For example, Listing 20-10 shows that the str_find_char() function uses bytes.iter().enumerate(). However, there are still chances that the developer needs to write the index of the buffer array and may make a mistake. For example, in Listing 20-15, the str_find_char() returns Some(&s[i..len+1]), while it should be Some(&s[i..len]). This skips the build-time check, but it can be caught by the runtime check in Listing 20-16.

Listing 20-15.

```
============================
fn str_find_char(s: &String, c: char) -> Option<&str> {
    let bytes = s.as_bytes();
    let len = s.len();

    for (i, &item) in bytes.iter().enumerate() {
        if item == c as u8 {
            return Some(&s[i..len+1]); // bug
        }
    }

    None
}
============================
```

Listing 20-16.

```
============================
thread 'main' panicked at 'byte index 12 is out of bounds of `hello
world`', src\libcore\str\mod.rs:2017:9
note: Run with `RUST_BACKTRACE=1` environment variable to display a
backtrace.
============================
```

The Rust compiler inserts code to do boundary check for the buffer access at runtime. If there is a violation, the inserted checker will call a predefined function panic_handler(). The default panic_handler() is provided in the standard library. The firmware usually only links the Rust corelib and needs to define its own panic_handler(), such as Listing 20-17.

Listing 20-17.

```
============================
#[panic_handler]
fn panic_handler(_info: &core::panic::PanicInfo) -> ! {
    // Add your own debug information
    loop {}
}
============================
```

Uninitialized Data Check

Rust eliminates the uninitialized data at build time. The compiler does the static analysis to ensure the data used must be initialized in any path, including conditional assignment such as if/else statement. Similar to the C language, there might be false positive, but it is better to eliminate any risk at build time.

Arithmetic Check

In the C language, integer overflow is another big problem. In many cases, it causes a buffer overflow later. Rust makes some improvements on math operations. Take Listing 20-18 as an example. It shows five different ways to get the result from multiplication of two u32 integers.

Listing 20-18.

```
=============================
fn test6(a: u32, b:u32) {

    let c : Option<u32> = a.checked_mul(b);
    match c {
      Some(v) => println!("checked multiple: {}", v),
      None => println!("checked multiple: overflow"),
    }

    let (c, o) : (u32, bool) = a.overflowing_mul(b);
    println!("overflowing multiple: {}, overflow: {}", c, o);

    let c : u32 = a.saturating_mul(b);
    println!("saturating multiple: {}", c);

    let c : u32 = a.wrapping_mul(b);
    println!("wrapping multiple: {}", c);

    let c : u32 = a * b;
    println!("direct multiple: {}", c);
}
fn main() {
    test6(0xFFFFFFFF, 0xFFFFFFFF);
}
=============================
```

Rust provides a set of methods for the primitive:

1) checked_mul(): The result is Option<T>. If no overflow happens, the result is Some<T>. Otherwise, the result is None.

2) overflowing_mul(): The result is a tuple (T, bool). The first element is a wrapped result. The second element is a bool to show if overflow happens or not.

3) saturating_mul(): The result is T type. It is a saturated value.

4) wrapping_mul(): The result is T type. It is a wrapped value.

For the multiplication operator, the Rust compiler treats it as wrapping_mul() in the release build, but injects runtime check code in the debug build. If the violation occurs at runtime, the checker invokes the panic_handler in the debug build. The developer can also use the compiler flag "-C overflow-checks=on/off" to control the runtime overflow check on or off. See Table 20-2.

Table 20-2. *Rust Math Operation – a: u32 * b: u32*

Method	Overflow Result
c : Option<u32> = a.**checked_mul**(b)	c is None.
(c, o) : (u32, bool) = a.**overflowing_mul**(b)	c holds the wrapped value. o indicates if overflow happens.
c : u32 = a.**saturating_mul**(b)	c holds the maximum u32.
c : u32 = a.**wrapping_mul**(b)	c holds the wrapped value.
c = a * b	c holds the wrapped value in release build. Runtime overflow check fails in debug build.

With release build, the result of Listing 20-18 is shown in Listing 20-19. With debug build, the result is shown in Listing 20-20.

Listing 20-19.

```
============================
checked multiple: overflow
overflowing multiple: 1, overflow: true
saturating multiple: 4294967295
wrapping multiple: 1
direct multiple: 1
============================
```

Listing 20-20.

```
============================
checked multiple: overflow
overflowing multiple: 1, overflow: true
saturating multiple: 4294967295
wrapping multiple: 1
```

```
thread 'main' panicked at 'attempt to multiply with overflow', src\main.
rs:90:19
note: Run with `RUST_BACKTRACE=1` environment variable to display a
backtrace.
============================
```

A firmware implementation may have external input, such as a Bitmap (BMP) file, a capsule file, a portable and executable (PE) image, a file system, and so on. If the parser needs to perform some math operation, using checked version methods might be a better idea than direct multiplication. It can guarantee the overflow case is well handled.

Besides math operations, type cast might also lead to the data truncation problem. Rust does the build-time check and requests a data type cast explicitly.

All in all, Rust defines a set of very strict rules on using an object and its reference to eliminate memory safety issues. That is one reason that many developers find it is hard to pass compilation, especially for those who are familiar with the C language and satisfied with the freedom brought from the C language. With the C language, the developer can control everything. That also means the developer needs to ensure the code has no memory safety issue. Rust takes another approach. It makes it very hard to write the code to pass the compilation on the first time. The compiler keeps telling you what is forbidden and that there might be a potential problem. But once the code passes the compilation, the Rust language guarantees there is no memory safety issue.

Unsafe Code

So far, we have discussed lots of security solutions brought from Rust, and these solutions can help reduce the amount of security risks in the firmware development. However, this solution brings some limitations. For example, accessing NULL address actually is legal because the tradition Basic Input/Output System (BIOS) sets up the Interrupt Vector Table there. Sometimes, the firmware code needs to access a fixed region memory mapped I/O, such as Trusted Platform Module (TPM) at physical address 0xFED40000. In order to handle such cases, Rust introduces a keyword – unsafe. If the code is inside of an unsafe block, then the compiler does not perform any security check. This is a contract between the developer and the compiler. Unsafe means that the developer tells the Rust compiler "Please trust me."

According to the Rust language book, we can do the following superpower unsafe actions:

- Dereference a raw pointer

- Call an unsafe function or method.

- Access or modify a mutable global static variable.

- Implement an unsafe trait.

- Access fields of union.

In Listing 20-10 and Listing 20-14, we demonstrated a string and a Box<T> type. These are Rust-defined types. They can be used to point at a data in the heap. However, these types are not available in the C language. In order to interoperate with the C language, Rust has to define a raw pointer to be compatible with the pointer defined in C. Listing 20-21 shows the raw point usage. *mut u32 means a u32 pointer and the content is mutable. Because this code wants to dereference a raw pointer, it must be included in the unsafe block. The Rust language does not provide any guarantee on the memory safety here. At runtime, it might work because the developer may want to write the IVT. Or it might crash because of a mistake.

Listing 20-21.

```
===========================
fn test7() {
  unsafe {
    let p = 0 as *mut u32;
    *p = 4;
  }
}
===========================
```

Calling an external function, such as a C function, is also considered as unsafe because Rust loses control for the external function. Listing 20-22 shows how Rust calls the C abs() function.

Listing 20-22.

```
===========================
extern "C" {
    fn abs(a: i32) -> i32;
}

fn test8(a: i32) -> i32 {
    unsafe {
        abs (a)
    }
}
===========================
```

Global static variables are considered as sharable by many functions. According to the aliasing/mutation rule, it should be immutable. However, there might be a case that we do need to modify the global static variable, such as a global count. Usually a mutable static variable is used for the interoperation with the C language. It is dangerous that Rust requires to use unsafe keyword. Listing 20-23 shows an example.

Listing 20-23.

```
===========================
static mut COUNTER: u32 = 0;
fn increment_counter() {
    unsafe {
        COUNTER += 1;
    }
}
fn test9() {
    increment_counter();
    unsafe {
        println!("COUNTER: {}", COUNTER);
    }
}
===========================
```

Rust supports union type, with the same reason to interoperate with the C language. Union is dangerous because the type of data is undetermined. It violates type safety and may cause problems, such as partial initialization. See Listing 20-24. It outputs garbage at runtime.

Listing 20-24.

```
===========================
#[repr(C)]
union U {
  d8 : u8,
  d32: u32,
}

fn test10() {
  let dataU = U { d8 : 1 };
  unsafe {
    let data32 = dataU.d32;
    println!("get data {}", data32);
  }
}
===========================
```

Current Project

Rust is still a young language. It was designed by Mozilla Graydon Hoare, and the first release is at 2014. Because of its security properties, more and more projects are adopting Rust. For example, c2rust can help you convert the C language to the unsafe Rust language. Then people can do refactoring for the unsafe version and turn it into a safe version. Mozilla uses rust for Firefox. Amazon Firecracker is a Rust-based hypervisor. Baidu released Rust-SGX-SDK for the secure enclave and Rust OP-TEE TrustZone SDK as part of MesaTEE. Facebook uses Rust to develop Libra – a decentralized financial infrastructure. Google Fuchsia uses Rust in some components. The OpenTitan hardware root-of-trust uses the Tock OS, which is written in Rust. OpenSK – a Fast Identity Online 2 (FIDO2) authenticator is written in Rust as a Tock OS application. In 2019, Microsoft announced that they would adopt Rust as a systems programming language. In 2020, Microsoft has introduced open source project Verona, a new research language for safe infrastructure programming, which is inspired by Rust.

Firmware projects are including Rust. A rust hypervisor firmware can boot the cloud hypervisor. oreboot is the downstream fork of coreboot – a coreboot without C. EDK II is also adding support to build Rust module in the full UEFI firmware.

Cryptographic algorithms are also being developed in Rust, such as RustCrypto, MesaLink, rusttls, ring, webpki, and so on. The rusttls project includes a security review and audit report by Cure53, which shows the high quality of the code. Hope they can be the replacement for openSSL or mbed TLS in the future. Currently, the ring/webpki depend upon the OS provided random number generation. In order to use the ring/webpki in the firmware, we need a firmware based random number library. For example, the efi-random crate uses the RDRAND and RDSEED instruction in the UEFI/EDK II environment.

Limitation

Rust brings great enhancements to eliminate memory safety issues in the firmware, but there are still some non–language-specific firmware security issues that need to be taken care of, such as

1) Silicon register lock: We need to use a vulnerability scan tool, such as CHIPSEC.

2) Security policy: We need to perform a policy check to ensure the firmware is configured correctly.

3) Time-of-check/time-of-use (TOC/TOU) issue: We need to carefully perform an architecture review and design review.

4) X86 system management mode (SMM) callout: We need hardware restrictions, such as the SMM_CODE_CHECK feature.

Last but not of least importance, the unsafe code in Rust is always a risk. The Baidu Rust-SGX-SDK project has summarized the rules of Rust unsafe code:

- Unsafe components should be appropriately isolated and modularized, and the size should be small (or minimized).

- Unsafe components should not weaken the safety, especially of public APIs and data structures.

- Unsafe components should be clearly identified and easily upgraded

Writing unsafe code in Rust is same as writing C code. There is no safety guarantee from Rust. Please isolate them, minimize them, and review them carefully.

Others

Other languages are also used in firmware projects. For example, Forth is a language defined in IEEE 1275-1994. It is used for open firmware projects. Some embedded devices use Java Embedded, MicroPython, or the .NET Compact Framework. Those languages require a runtime interpreter. They might be a good candidate as an application language, but they are hard to use as a system language for the firmware development. We also observe that other type safety languages such as Ada or OCaml are used for embedded system, such as the Mirage OS, but they are not widely used.

Summary

In this chapter, we introduced the languages used in firmware development. Because we already introduced a lot on C language in previous chapters, the focus in this chapter is to introduce a new promising language – Rust – including the benefit brought from Rust and its limitation in the firmware security area. This is the last chapter of Part III. In Part IV, we will introduce security testing.

References

Book

[B-1] Peter van der Linden, *Expert C Programming: Deep C Secrets*, Prentice Hall, 1994

[B-2] Jim Blandy, Jason Orendorff, *Programming Rust: Fast, Safe Systems Development*, O'Reilly Media, 2017

[B-3] Brian L. Troutwine, *Hands-On Concurrency with Rust: Confidently build memory-safe, parallel, and efficient software in Rust*, Packt Publishing, 2018

[B-4] Steve Klabnik , Carol Nichols, *The Rust Programming Language* (Covers Rust 2018), No Starch Press, 2019, `https://doc.rust-lang.org/book/`

Conference, Journal, and Paper

[P-1] Nicholas Matsakis, "Rust," Mozilla Research, `http://design.inf.unisi.ch/sites/default/files/seminar-niko-matsiakis-rustoverview.pdf`

[P-2] Tony Hoare, "Null References: The Billion Dollar Mistake," in QCon 2009, available at `www.infoq.com/presentations/Null-References-The-Billion-Dollar-Mistake-Tony-Hoare`

[P-3] Yu Ding, Ran Duan, Long Li, Yueqiang Cheng, Yulong Zhang, Tanghui Chen, Tao Wei, Huibo Wang, "POSTER: Rust SGX SDK: Towards Memory Safety in Intel SGX Enclave," Computer and Communications Security 2017, `https://github.com/apache/incubator-teaclave-sgx-sdk/blob/master/documents/ccsp17.pdf`

[P-4] Florian Gilcher, Robin Randhawa, "The Rust Programming Language: Origin, History and Why it's so important for Arm today," in Linaro Connect 2020, `www.youtube.com/watch?v=yE55ZpQmw9Q`

[P-5] Bryan Cantrill, "The Soul of a New Machine: Rethinking the Computer," Stanford Seminar 2020, `www.youtube.com/watch?v=vvZA9n3e5pc&list=PLoROMvodv4rMW w6rRoeSpkiseTHzWj6vu&index=4&t=0s`

[P-6] Ryan O'Leary, "oreboot," in Open Source Firmware Conference 2019, available at `https://www.youtube.com/watch?v=xJ6zI8MmcUQ`

[P-7] Jiewen Yao, Vincent Zimmer, "Enabling Rust for UEFI Firmware," in UEFI webinar 2020, `https://www.brighttalk.com/webcast/18206/428896`, `https://uefi.org/sites/default/files/resources/Enabling%20RUST%20for%20UEFI%20Firmware_8.19.2020.pdf`

Specification and Guideline

[S-1] IEEE, "IEEE Standard for Boot (Initialization Configuration) Firmware: Core Requirements and Practices," IEEE 1275-1994, available at `www.openbios.org/data/docs/of1275.pdf`

Web

[W-1] Rust, `www.rust-lang.org/`

[W-2] Rust Unsafe code guideline, `https://github.com/rust-lang/unsafe-code-guidelines`

[W-3] c2rust, `https://c2rust.com/`

[W-4x] Amazon Firecracker, `https://github.com/firecracker-microvm/firecracker`

[W-5] Rust SGX SDK, `https://github.com/apache/incubator-teaclave-sgx-sdk`

[W-6] Rust OP-TEE TrustZone SDK, `https://github.com/mesalock-linux/rust-optee-trustzone-sdk`

[W-7] Facebook Libra, `https://github.com/libra/libra`

[W-8] Google fuchsia, `https://fuchsia.googlesource.com/fuchsia/`

[W-9] Tock OS, `https://github.com/tock/tock`

[W-10] OpenTitan, `https://github.com/lowRISC/opentitan`

[W-11] OpenSK, `https://github.com/google/OpenSK`

[W-12] oreboot, `https://github.com/oreboot/oreboot`

[W-13] EDKII rust support, `https://github.com/tianocore/edk2-staging/tree/edkii-rust`, `https://github.com/jyao1/edk2/tree/edkii-rust/RustPkg`, `https://github.com/jyao1/ring/tree/uefi_support`, `https://github.com/jyao1/webpki/tree/uefi_support`, `https://github.com/jyao1/edk2/tree/edkii-rust/RustPkg/External/efi-random`

[W-14] Rust hypervisor firmware, `https://github.com/cloud-hypervisor/rust-hypervisor-firmware`

[W-15] r-efi, UEFI Reference Specification, `https://github.com/r-util/r-efi`

[W-16] Rust wrapper for UEFI, `https://github.com/rust-osdev/uefi-rs`

[W-17] Rust Crypto, `https://github.com/RustCrypto`

[W-18] MesaLink, `https://github.com/mesalock-linux/mesalink`

[W-19] RustTls, `https://github.com/ctz/rustls/`

[W-20] ring – cryptographic operations, `https://github.com/briansmith/ring`

[W-21] webpki, `https://github.com/briansmith/webpki`

[W-22] Microsoft – A proactive approach to more secure code, `https://msrc-blog.microsoft.com/2019/07/16/a-proactive-approach-to-more-secure-code/`

[W-22] Microsoft – why rust for safe systems programming, `https://msrc-blog.microsoft.com/2019/07/22/why-rust-for-safe-systems-programming/`

[W-23] Open Firmware, `www.openfirmware.info/Welcome_to_OpenBIOS`

[W-24] mirage OS, `https://mirage.io/`

[W-25] Cure53, "Security Review and Audit Report RUST TLS," `https://github.com/ctz/rustls/blob/master/audit/TLS-01-report.pdf`

[W-26] Project Verona, `www.microsoft.com/en-us/research/project/project-verona/`, `https://github.com/microsoft/verona`

PART IV

Security Test

Testing is the last step before we deliver the system product to the customer. Different from functional testing, security testing focuses on if the security properties are satisfied. The process may include vulnerability scans for known issues, security assessments on the response of the system, penetration tests to simulate an attack, security reviews for the code and documentation, and security audit for the compliance issues.

CHAPTER 21

Security Unit Test

After we finish all of the code development work, we need to perform security testing. Usually, the developers need to perform security unit testing and then deliver the code to the test team. At this point, the test team needs to perform more thorough system-level security testing. There are many books that introduce software testing techniques. We will not repeat those contents here. Instead, in this chapter, we will focus on the firmware-specific security unit testing from a developer's perspective. In the next chapter, we will focus on the firmware-specific system security testing from a test engineer's perspective.

Security Unit Testing Plan

In Chapter 2, we discussed the whole idea of proactive firmware secure development and described the threat model. The security unit test should focus on the threat model to see if the identified threats are properly mitigated. We also described eight high-risk areas in the firmware and provided guidance for security code review. Table 21-1 shows the security unit test for those areas.

© Jiewen Yao and Vincent Zimmer 2020

J. Yao and V. Zimmer, *Building Secure Firmware*, https://doi.org/10.1007/978-1-4842-6106-4_21

Table 21-1. *Security Unit Test for Eight High-Risk Areas*

Category	Security Unit Test
External input	Identify the external input – SMM communication buffer, UEFI variable, firmware image and capsule image, boot BMP file, PE/COFF image such as an OS bootloader and PCI option ROM, file system, disk image, network packet, and so on.
	Identify the function to handle the external input – boundary function.Identify the function to perform the check for the external input – check function.
	Test the check function with different input.
	Verify the output of the check function.
Race condition	Identify the critical resource – SMM communication buffer, locked silicon registers, and so on.
	Identify the function to handle the critical resource.Create a race condition scenario to access the critical resources.
	Verify the result of the critical resource.
Hardware input	Identify the hardware inputs – read/write silicon register, memory mapped input/output (MMIO) base address register (BAR), USB descriptor, Bluetooth Low Energy (BLE) advertisement data, DMA, cache, and so on.
	Identify the function to handle the hardware input.
	Identify the function to perform the check for the hardware input – check function – or identify the function to prevent the attack, lock function.
	Emulate the hardware input such as MMIO BAR, USB, BLE, and so on; and test the check function.
	Verify the output of the check function.
	Verify the lock function to perform the lock correctly, such as DMA or SMM cache and so on.
Secret handling	Identify the secret/password.
	Identify the function to use the secret.
	Identify the function to clear the secret after use.
	Ensure the secret is cleared in all paths.
	Identify the function to hash or encrypt the secret if the secret needs to be saved.
	Identify the default secret/password handling.
	Verify that the side channel guidelines are followed.

(continued)

Table 21-1. (*continued*)

Category	Security Unit Test
Register lock	Identify the registers to be locked, such as flash lock and SMM lock.
	Identify the function to lock the register.
	Identify the policy to control the lock, such as a policy protocol or variable.
	Ensure the end user cannot control the policy.
	Ensure the lock happens in all boot paths.
	Ensure the lock happens before any third-party code runs.
Secure configuration	Identify the policy to control the security configuration, such as secure boot and measured boot.
	Ensure that the unauthorized end user cannot update the secure configuration.
	Ensure the default configuration is secure.
Replay/rollback	Identify the secure version number (SVN) or lowest supported version number (LSN).
	Identify the storage for the SVN or LSN.
	Ensure the unauthorized end user cannot update the SVN or LSN.Identify the function to perform the version check.
Cryptography	Identify the cryptographic usages in the firmware, such as signature verification or data encryption.
	Identify the cryptographic algorithm used in the firmware.
	Ensure that the cryptographic algorithm follows the latest guidelines from the government and corporations. Do not use any deprecated algorithm.
	Ensure the key length follows the latest guidelines from the government and corporations. Do not use small lengths.
	Identify the key provision function and the key revocation function.
	Identify the key storage.
	Identify the function to protect the key storage for integrity and/or confidentiality. Only authorized users can update the key.
	Verify if the side channel guideline is followed for the confidentiality of the key.
	Ensure the signature verification function can handle cases for a missing key or signature.

Care must be taken for solutions that may involve multiple high-risk areas. Taking SMM-based firmware update as an example, the firmware update image is an external input (#1). The image is put into an SMM communication buffer which may have a potential Time-of-Check/Time-of-Use attack (#2). The flash update function needs to unlock the flash, which leaves open the possibility of a race condition attack (#2). The SMM environment should be protected to prevent a DMA or SMM cache attack (#3). The flash device should be locked during boot to prevent any unauthorized updates (#5). The firmware update function should check the SVN of the firmware to prevent a rollback attack (#7). The new firmware image must be signed with a proper cryptographic algorithm with proper length key (#8).

In order to verify if the developed code follows the general secure coding practices, which we introduced in Chapter 14, static code analysis or dynamic code analysis can be used. In Chapter 16, we introduced the different compiler defensive technologies to eliminate potential vulnerabilities, including Klocwork and Coverity static analysis tools, and we also described the address sanitizer and Undefined Behavior Sanitizer.

Advanced Security Unit Testing

In general, for security unit testing, we may need to write a test function to call the target function with different input in order to assess if the target function works properly, especially to test the target function's ability to handle both external input (#1) and hardware input (#3). One of the biggest problems with this approach is that we don't know if we have created enough input to cover all cases.

Traditionally, equivalence class partitioning (ECP) is a good approach to remove the redundancy by dividing the input data into a reasonable number of partitions. Then we only need to design test cases to cover all partitions. However, although ECP is necessary, it is not sufficient for the security unit testing because the perquisite of ECP is that we are able to define a set of partitions that cover all cases. This is true for simple functions, but in practice, it might be hard to define a complete set of ECP partitions for a complicated data structure, such as a file system, an executable file format, or a network packet. Therefore, we need some other approach.

Fuzzing

Fuzzing, also known as fuzz testing, is an automated testing technique. The fuzzing tool can generate invalid, unexpected, or random data automatically as the input value for a target function invocation. One of the greatest advantages of fuzzing is that it frees the developer from creating equivalent class partitions or test cases. However, fuzzing has a test oracle problem – a test must be able to distinguish expected (normal) from unexpected (buggy) program behavior. The unexpected behavior includes the following items:

1) Crash, hang, or ASSERT is a simple and objective measurement for fuzzing. If those behaviors are observed, then there must be something wrong in the target function.

2) Fuzzing might also trigger some other hard-to-detect problems, such as a buffer out of bound access, use-after-free, or memory leak. In order to catch those failures, fuzzing is usually enabled together with other sanitizers, such as address sanitizer, undefined behavior sanitizer, memory sanitizer, or leak sanitizer.

3) Last but not least, fuzzing may cause the program to return unexpected or wrong results. As such, the developer may need to write assertions for the final result or the final state of the program.

Fuzzing is a testing technique. It is independent of the execution environment. It can be applied to OS applications, OS kernels, or even firmware. Today, most of the fuzzing tools, such as Peach, American Fuzzy Lop (AFL), and LibFuzzer, run in the OS environment. But firmware runs in a special execution environment, and this environment does not provide the same OS-level application program interface (API) or standard C library. This begs the question: How do we run the fuzzing tool to test the firmware code?

Table 21-2 lists different firmware fuzzing mechanisms.

Table 21-2. *Firmware Fuzzing Mechanisms*

Mechanism	Effort	Pros	Cons
1. Run firmware function and fuzzing tool in the firmware environment.	Port the fuzzing tool to run in the firmware.	No need to modify the firmware code.	Big effort to port a fuzzing tool. May have environment limitations, such as memory size, storage size, and CPU processing power.
2. Run firmware function in the firmware environment and fuzz tool in the OS.	a. Create a firmware agent and an OS agent for fuzzing data transmission between firmware and OS via the network.	No need to modify the fuzzing tool. No need to modify the firmware code.	Time-consuming in fuzzing data transmission.
	b. Use a hypervisor for data communication between the firmware function and OS fuzzing tool.	Faster than fuzzing data transmission via network.	Need to enable a hypervisor to run the target firmware.
3. Run the firmware function and fuzzing tool in the OS environment.	a. Port the firmware function to the OS and perform fuzzing of it in the OS.	No need to modify the fuzzing tool. Can fully leverage the instrumented code with the fuzzing compiler. Fastest solution.	Needs effort to create an OS stub for the firmware function.
	b. Analyze the firmware binary and perform fuzzing of the target function.	No porting of the firmware is needed.	Binary analysis is time-consuming. Needs to create a stub function as well.

1) The first option is to port the fuzzing tool from the OS to the firmware environment and run it in the firmware environment. See Figure 21-1. If the fuzzing tool depends upon an OS API, we need to implement a firmware version. Unfortunately, the porting effort is large, based upon our analysis. It also means that continuous porting is required if we need to keep the fuzzing tool up to date. At the same time, we have seen different fuzzing tools created to deal with different scenarios. It is hard to port all of those tools. Even if we can port all of the fuzzing tools, it still might be hard to run the tool because of the limitations of the firmware execution environment, such as ROM size, SRAM size, DRAM size, storage size, and CPU processing power. The fuzzing tool may fail to run or run at a very slow speed.

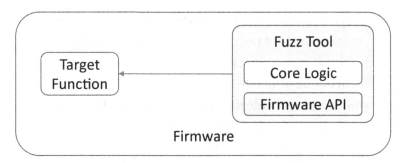

Figure 21-1. *Firmware Fuzzing with Fuzz Tool Running in Firmware*

2) The second option is to create an agent in the firmware and let the firmware agent accept the fuzzing data from the OS. An OS fuzzing agent invokes the fuzzing tool to generate the fuzzing data and transfers the data from the OS to the firmware agent. See Figure 21-2. However, we might run into performance problems because some time is wasted in the communication between the OS and UEFI. Fuzzing usually requires a large amount of data generation and usually needs to run for several days. If the time is wasted in the data communication, then the fuzzing is not efficient.

One possible variant is to enable a hypervisor to run both the target firmware and the OS fuzzing tool on one local machine. It might be faster than communication via the network, but we need to pursue a porting effort in order to let the hypervisor run the firmware.

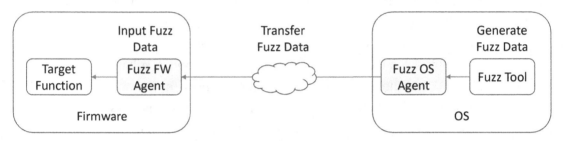

Figure 21-2. *Firmware Fuzzing with Fuzz Agent Communication*

3) The third option is to make the firmware target function run in the OS environment and use the OS fuzzing tool directly. Because the firmware function may rely on the firmware-specific services which might not be available in the OS, we need to create the OS stub function to provide this service. If this can be achieved, we can reuse the OS fuzzing tool directly. See Figure 21-3. The advantage of this approach is that we can fully leverage the capability of an OS fuzzing tool, such as instrumented mode, and the host system resources, including memory size, disk storage. and the host CPU execution power. This is the fastest solution.

One possible variant of this option is that we may fuzz a specific firmware function in a binary in cases where we don't have the source code. Herein, we must carefully analyze the firmware binary and provide all dependent services. The advantage of this approach is that we can fuzz any firmware binary without having the source code, but we lose the benefit of instrumented fuzzing, and it is much slower than with the source code.

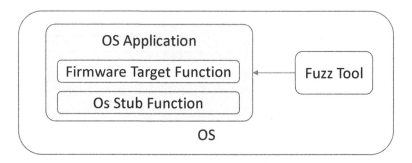

Figure 21-3. *Firmware Fuzzing with Firmware Code Running in OS*

For EDK II UEFI firmware, we introduced the host-based firmware analyzer (HBFA) feature to provide the capability to build a specific EDK II firmware target function as an OS application and run it with a fuzzing tool. Figure 21-4 shows the HBFA-based fuzzing use case design. The firmware function to be tested is built with the OS stub function and the test main function.

Step 1: We run the test application with the OS fuzzing tool.

Step 2: The fuzzing tool generates fuzz data and feeds it to the test main function as an input parameter.

Step 3: The test main function sets up the external input data for the firmware function based upon the fuzzing data.

Step 4: The test main function triggers the firmware function to be tested.

Step 5: The firmware function calls the OS stub function to get the external input. Here the external input can be a communication buffer, a signed firmware capsule image, a PE/COFF executable image, a boot image file, a file system, a network packet, a USB descriptor, a Bluetooth LE advertisement data, and so on. Then the firmware function may call the OS stub to write some output data.

Step 6: The test main function can check the output data based upon the test oracle. At the same time, we can enable the sanitizer for the test application to see if there is any violation at runtime.

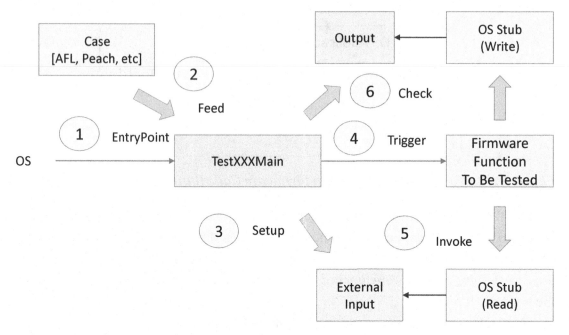

Figure 21-4. *HBFA Fuzz Case Design*

Symbolic Execution

Some fuzzing tools require known good seeds for mutation, and the fuzz data is generated based upon the seeds. Even if the seeds are optional, the good seeds can help improve the efficiency of the fuzzing. There are several ways to get seeds. Seeds can be ascertained via an empty seed, downloading seeds from the Internet, using the existing system configuration as the seeds, and using a tool to generate the seeds. The last one can be achieved by a symbolic execution tool, such as KLEE.

During a normal execution session, the program reads a concrete input value and proceeds with the execution flow, such as assignment, addition, multiplication, and conditional branch until generating a concrete final answer. However, during a symbolic execution, the program reads a symbolic value and proceeds with the execution flow. It can still do assignment, addition, and multiplication, though. When it reaches a conditional branch, the symbolic execution can proceed with both branches by forking down two paths. Each path gets a copy of the program state to continue executing independently in a symbolic fashion with a path constraint. The path constraint here means the concrete value which makes the program choose a specific path in the branch condition. When a path is terminated, the symbolic execution computes a concrete value by solving the accumulated path constraints on the branch condition. After all paths are terminated, the symbolic execution collects all concrete values. Those values can be thought of as test cases to cover all of the possible paths for the given program.

Consider a function in Listing 21-1. The symbolic execution takes "buf" as a symbolic input value and assign "buf[0] * 4" to "a" and "buf[4] * 8" to "c." In the first if branch, it evaluates the "buf[0] * 4 < 0" and forks the two paths: buf[0] < 0 and buf[0] >= 0. In the second if branch, it evaluates the "buf[4] * 8 == 24" and forks two paths: buf[4] == 3 and buf[4] != 3. When the program terminates, the symbolic execution can generate three different cases: (buf[0] < 0), (buf[0] >= 0 && buf[4] == 3), and (buf[0] >= 0 && buf[4] != 3). The final result is useful and important to provide the seed for the fuzzing tool. Without that, it might take a long time to let the fuzzing tool generate a value 3 for buf[4] in order to cover the second path.

Listing 21-1.

```
============================
int test (int *buf)
{
  int a = buf[0] * 4;
  int c = buf[4] * 8;

  if (a < 0) {
    return -1;
  } else {
    if (c == 24) {
      return 4;
    } else {
      return 1;
    }
  }
}

============================
```

Symbolic execution is a way to analyze a program in order to determine what inputs cause each part of a program to execute. After the symbolic execution is finished, it can generate test cases to cover all possible paths for the program. Those test cases can be treated as seeds for the fuzzing tool. Then the fuzzing tool can mutate the fuzzing data based upon those seeds. See Figure 21-5 for the solution to combine the KLEE symbolic execution as the seed generator and the AFL fuzz tool as the fuzzing engine.

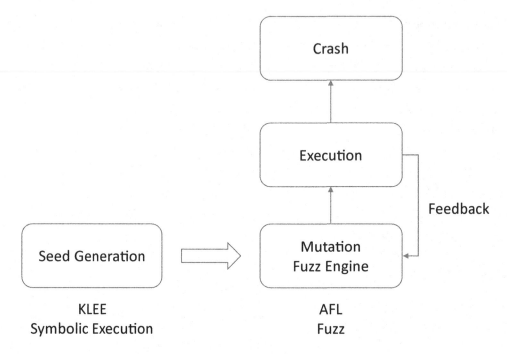

Figure 21-5. *AFL Fuzz + KLEE*

Symbolic execution is a good method to generate the seed. However, it has limitations. Because symbolic execution needs to fork the state based on each branch condition, the number of states to be maintained grows exponentially with the increase in the program size. For a complex program, it may take a long time to generate the final result for all paths. In some cases, it might run into infinite loops or generate an exception.

Formal Verification

Formal verification is a technology to prove the correctness of code in a system with respect to certain specifications or predefined properties by using formal method of mathematics. The approach of the formal verification is model checking, which is a systematically exhaustive exploration of the mathematical model. Symbolic execution is one implementation method that can be used in the formal verification. Spin is an open-source software verification tool, used for the formal verification of multi-threaded software applications. C bounded model checker (CBMC) is a bounded model checker for C and C++ programs which verifies memory safety (which includes array bounds checks and checks for the safe use of pointers), checks for exceptions, checks for various variants of undefined behavior, and user-specified assertions.

A model checking tool is to check if a given model satisfies a set of program properties. Take Listing 21-2 as an example. This program parses the input argc and argv. At the end of the program, it adds one assertion as the property. When we run CBMC for this program, CBMC will report if the assertion can succeed or not. Besides assertions, CBMC also includes build-in instrumentation options, such as bounds check, pointer check, and overflow check etc to catch the potential memory safety issues.

Listing 21-2. =============================

```
#define MAX_NUM 100
void process_arg (void *arg)
{
  // do something
}

int main(int argc, void **argv) {
  int x = argc;
  int i = 0;
  while (i < argc && i < MAX_NUM && i >= 0) {
    process_arg (argv[i]);
    i = i + 1;
    x = x - 1;
  }
  __CPROVER_assert(x >= 0, "postcondition");
}
```

===========================

There are not many software projects passing formal verification, because of the complexity of the software programs. Writing a complete set of program properties is also challenging work. Some operating systems have been verified, such as secure embedded L4 kernel (seL4). Some network stacks are also verified, such as verified HTTPS in project Everest.

Design for Security Test

In order to make the symbolic execution and fuzzing more efficient, we need to consider how we should write a program:

1) We begin by writing small functions and testing the small functions. A small function is easy for code review and testing. For example, in the EDK II UEFI variable driver MdeModulePkg/ Universal/Variable/RuntimeDxe/Variable.c, the UpdateVariable() routine has 600 lines of code and 65 "if" branches. One of the "if" branches misses the "else" branch handling and causes the timestamp field to be filled with a wrong value. This issue had been there for several years. We performed several rounds of code reviews and testing, but no one found this problem. Sixty-five "if" branches in one function is overly complicated.

2) Next, consider combining all input data verifications into one check function and testing the check function itself. Some programs have multiple functions to accept the external input. We refer to those functions as boundary functions. We notice that the boundary function may perform some sanity checks against the external input and subsequently pass control to the business logic function for data processing. See Figure 21-6. A potential risk of this approach is that each boundary function does the check in its own function. If there is one security issue exposed in one boundary function, we have to review all other boundary functions to see if there is a similar issue. Unfortunately, that is time-consuming and people may make mistakes. For example, the first Microsoft ANI bug issue (CVSS 9.3 HIGH, MS05-002) was found in 2005. But after the fix, the same issue (MS07-017) was found in 2007. They shared the same root cause, and it coincidentally happened in two different functions.

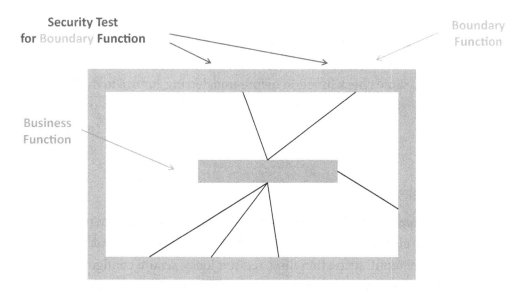

Figure 21-6. *Test for the Security Boundary Function*

In order to reduce the risk, we should consolidate all external input checks into one single check function. All boundary functions can call this check function to perform the data sanity check. We should perform the security review and security test for this check function in order to ensure it is robust enough to handle all of the different cases. If there is an issue in the check function, we just need to fix this check function in one place. The security test can be focused on the check function. See Figure 21-7.

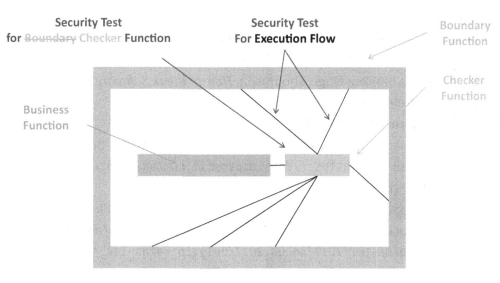

Figure 21-7. *Test for the Security Checker Function*

871

3) Next, let all external boundary functions call the check function and test the execution flow. It is good to define a centralized check function. We need to ensure that all boundary functions invoke the same check function before transferring control to the business logic function by having a security test for the execution flow.

Summary

In this chapter, we introduced the security unit test. The chapter covered the security unit test plan for the eight high-risk areas in the firmware – external input, race conditions, hardware input, secret handling, register locks, secure configuration, replay/rollback, and cryptography. Then we introduced two advanced security unit test methods – fuzzing and symbolic execution – and we provided a suggestion for the check function. In the next chapter, we will introduce the security validation and penetration test methodology for the firmware.

References

Book

[B-1] Brian Chess, Jacob West Secure, *Programming with Static Analysis*, Addison-Wesley Professional, 2007

[B-2] Michael Sutton, Adam Greene, Pedram Amini, *Fuzzing: Brute Force Vulnerability Discovery*, Addison-Wesley Professional, 2007

[B-3] James A. Whittaker, Hugh Thompson, *How to Break Software Security*, Addison-Wesley Professional, 2003

Conference, Journal, and Paper

[P-1] John Neystadt, "Automated Penetration Testing with White-Box Fuzzing," Microsoft, 2008, available at https://docs.microsoft.com/en-us/previous-versions/software-testing/cc162782(v=msdn.10)

[P-2] Yuriy Bulygin, Oleksandr Bazhaniuk, "Discovering vulnerable UEFI BIOS firmware at scale," in 44CON 2017, available at https://github.com/abazhaniuk/Publications/blob/master/2017/44CON_2017/Bulygin_Bazhaniuk_44con.pdf

[P-3] Sugumar Govindarajan, John Loucaides, "The Whole is Greater," in NIST CSRC 2015, `https://csrc.nist.gov/CSRC/media/Presentations/The-Whole-is-Greater/images-media/day1_trusted-computing_200-250.pdf`

[P-4] Brian Richardson, Chris Wu, Jiewen Yao, Vincent J. Zimmer, "Using HBFA to Improve Platform Resiliency," Intel White paper, 2019, `https://software.intel.com/sites/default/files/managed/6a/4c/Intel_UsingHBFAtoImprovePlatformResiliency.pdf`

[P-5] Marek Zmysłowski, "Feeding the Fuzzers with KLEE," in KLEE workshop 2018, available at `https://srg.doc.ic.ac.uk/klee18/talks/Zmyslowski-Feeding-the-Fuzzers-with-KLEE.pdf`

[P-6] Oleksandr Bazhaniuk, John Loucaides, Lee Rosenbaum, Mark R. Tuttle, Vincent Zimmer, "Symbolic execution for BIOS security," in USENIX WOOT 2015, available at `www.markrtuttle.com/data/papers/bazhaniuk-loucaides-rosenbaum-tuttle-zimmer-woot15.pdf`

[P-7] Zhenkun Yang, Yuriy Viktorov, Jin Yang, Jiewen Yao, Vincent Zimmer, "UEFI Firmware Fuzzing with Simics Virtual Platform," in DAC 2020, available at `http://web.cecs.pdx.edu/~zhenkun/pub/uefi-fuzzing-dac20.pdf`

[P-8] Christopher Domas, "God Mode Unlocked Hardware Backdoors in X86 CPUs," in *BlackHat 2018*, available at `http://i.blackhat.com/us-18/Thu-August-9/us-18-Domas-God-Mode-Unlocked-Hardware-Backdoors-In-x86-CPUs.pdf`

[P-9] Byron Cook, Kareem Khazem, Daniel Kroening, Serdar Tasiran, Michael Tautschnig, Mark R. Tuttle, "Model checking boot code from AWS data centers," *Formal Methods in System Design*, 2020, `https://link.springer.com/content/pdf/10.1007/s10703-020-00344-2.pdf`

Web

[W-1] Using HBFA to Improve Platform Resiliency, `https://software.intel.com/en-us/blogs/2019/02/25/using-host-based-analysis-to-improve-firmware-resiliency`

[W-2] HBFA, `https://github.com/tianocore/edk2-staging/tree/HBFA`

[W-3] libfuzzer, `https://llvm.org/docs/LibFuzzer.html`

[W-4] Peach fuzzer, `http://community.peachfuzzer.com/v3/Test.html`

[W-5] AFL fuzzer, `http://lcamtuf.coredump.cx/afl/`

[W-6] KLEE, `https://klee.github.io/`

[W-7] STP, `http://stp.github.io/`

[W-8] Z3, `https://github.com/z3prover/z3`

[W-9] metaSMT, https://www.informatik.uni-bremen.de/agra/eng/metasmt.php

[W-10] mini SAT, http://minisat.se/

[W-11] Verifying Multi-threaded Software with Spin, http://spinroot.com/spin/whatispin.html

[W-12] Bounded Model Checking for Software, https://www.cprover.org/cbmc/

[W-13] Low-Level Bounded Model Checker (LLBMC), http://llbmc.org/

[W-14] Symbiotic, https://github.com/staticafi/symbiotic

[W-15] seL4, https://sel4.systems/

[W-16] Project Everest, www.microsoft.com/en-us/research/project/project-everest-verified-secure-implementations-https-ecosystem/, https://project-everest.github.io/

[W-17] Microsoft Security Bulletin MS05-002, available at https://docs.microsoft.com/en-us/security-updates/securitybulletins/2005/ms05-002

[W-18] Microsoft Security Bulletin MS07-017, available at https://docs.microsoft.com/en-us/security-updates/securitybulletins/2007/ms07-017

CHAPTER 22

Security Validation and Penetration Test

After we have done the development, secure code review, and security unit test, the firmware code is checked in. At this point, the validation team can perform the security validation and penetration activities. The real secure validation work starts much earlier, namely, during the threat modeling phase. At that time, the security validation team needs to be involved in the threat model discussion and prepare both the security validation plan and the penetration test plan.

Security Validation Plan

In Chapter 2, we have discussed proactive secure firmware development, especially the threat model. The security validation plan should focus on the threat model. The validation team or penetration team should treat themselves as the defined adversary and in turn attack the system.

In previous chapters, we introduced the various attacks and mitigations, along with the secure design and implementation. There are eight high-risk areas in the firmware. Those areas will be the first choice of the attacker. Combining this information together, we listed some suggestions for the security validation or penetration test in Table 22-1.

© Jiewen Yao and Vincent Zimmer 2020
J. Yao and V. Zimmer, *Building Secure Firmware*, https://doi.org/10.1007/978-1-4842-6106-4_22

Table 22-1. *Suggestions for the Security Validation and Penetration Test*

Category	Security Validation
External input	Fuzz the external input.
	1) File fuzzing can be used for different file parsers, including the boot logo file, such as Bitmap (BMP) and Joint Photographic Experts Group (JPEG); firmware update capsule file or recovery file, such as UEFI capsule; third-party firmware executable files, such as portable and executable (PE) and executable and linking format (ELF); configuration files, such as Extensible Markup Language (XML) and JavaScript Object Notation (JSON); and so on.
	2) File system fuzzing can be used for the file system and disk partition, including File Allocation Table (FAT), New Technology File System (NTFS), extended file system (EXT2/3/4), Hierarchical File System (HFS), Universal Disc Format (UDF), Compact Disc File System (CDFS), El Torito, Flash File System (FFS), or Firmware File System (FFS).
	3) Protocol fuzzing can be used for the firmware network stack, including Ethernet, WiFi, Bluetooth, Cellular Network (3G, 4G, 5G), Address Resolution Protocol (ARP), Internet Protocol (IP) version 4 and version 6, Internet Protocol Security (IPsec), Transmission Control Protocol (TCP), User Datagram Protocol (UDP), Transport Layer Security (TLS), Dynamic Host Configuration Protocol (DHCP), Preboot Execution Environment (PXE), Domain Name Server (DNS), Hyper Text Transfer Protocol (HTTP), Representational State Transfer (REST), Intelligent Platform Management Interface (IPMI), RedFish, Universal plug and play (UPNP) etc and the device communication protocol, including the Secure Protocol and Data Model (SPDM).
	4) Management mode or trusted world fuzzing can be used for the management mode or trusted world communication buffer and management mode interrupt (MMI) handler, such as X86 system management mode (SMM) or ARM TrustZone, especially the software management mode interrupt for communication.
	5) Data-specific fuzzing can be used, such as UEFI variable data for the UEFI/PI BIOS, PI Boot Script data for S3 resume, Boot Policy Manifest (BPM) for the Platform Root-of-Trust module, the ACPI table for the dynamic root-of-trust (DRTM) module, and so on.
	Side channel attacks.
	1) If the management mode or trusted world includes secrets, check if the management mode handler applies the side channel best practices, such as Spectre.
	2) If the kernel mode includes secrets, check if the kernel handler applies the side channel best practices, such as Spectre and Meltdown.

Race condition	Time-of-check/time-of-use (TOC/TOU) attacks.
	1) A TOC/TOU attack to the management mode or trusted world communication buffer.
	2) A TOC/TOU attack against the data buffer used by the firmware update tool.
	3) A TOC/TOU attack against the firmware image on the flash after it is validated by the Platform Root-of-Trust.
	Multiple processors' race conditions.
	1) Make one processor enter management mode or trusted world to unlock the register and make the other processor take advantage of the unlocked system state, such as flash unlock.
Hardware input	Fuzz the hardware input.
	1) Fuzz a silicon register for the module to access the register, such as memory mapped I/O (MMIO), I/O, PCI configuration space, X86 model-specific register (MSR), and so on.
	2) Fuzz device information, such as a USB descriptor, Bluetooth LE advertisement data, memory DIMM Serial Presence Detect (SPD) data, and so on.
	3) Fuzz a bus communication, such as Serial Peripheral Interface (SPI) bus, Inter-Integrated Circuit (I2C) bus, System Management Bus (SMBus), USB bus, and so on.
	Base address register (BAR) overlap.
	1) Overlap a high-privilege MMIO region, such as Intel Virtualization for Directed I/O configuration or Serial Peripheral Interface (SPI) flash configuration, with a low-privilege MMIO region, such as the traditional PCI express configuration space.
	2) Overlap a critical memory region, such as system management RAM (SMRAM), with a low-privilege MMIO region, such as the traditional PCI express configuration space.

(continued)

Table 22-1. (*continued*)

Category	Security Validation
	DMA attacks.
	1) Try to generate DMA transactions to the system memory in order to inject code.
	2) Try to generate DMA transactions to the system memory to steal secret data.
	Cache attacks.
	1) Perform the cache attack against the management mode code.
	Power surprise removal.
	1) Try to cause a partial update via a surprise power removal while the system is updating a new firmware image.
	2) Try to cause a partial update via a surprise power removal when the system is updating the configuration, such as a UEFI variable.
	3) Try to steal secrets in the OS memory via a power surprise removal to see if the memory content is cleared in the next boot.
	4) Try to steal the secret in the OS from the TCG storage protected region via a power surprise removal to see if the TPer reset is issued on the next boot.
	Chassis intrusion.
	1) Clear CMOS to roll back to the default configuration.
	2) Set the hardware jumper to trigger a special boot mode, such as recovery or manufacturing mode.
	3) Add or replace the hardware device with a malicious one in the platform, such as a PCI card, memory DIMM, and so on.
	4) Update a malicious device firmware on the board, such as PCI device firmware, memory DIMM firmware, and so on.
	Other device attacks.
	1) Flash wear-out attacks for the SPI flash via continual writes of new configuration data.
	2) Row hammer attacks against the DRAM.
	3) Glitch attacks against the DRAM.

Secret handling	User password authentication.
	1) Search for the password in the keyboard buffer.
	2) Search for the password in the management mode communication buffer.
	3) Search for the password in system memory, such as stack, heap, or image global data area.
	4) Search for the password in the system non-volatile storage, such as the UEFI variable store.
	5) The password should be searched in both ASCII format and Unicode format.
	Weak password implementations.
	1) Check if the password is properly hashed in the NV storage, instead of storage as an XOR against a known value.
	2) Check if the non-volatile storage can be updated without authorization.
	3) Check if a salt is used and with sufficient salt length.
	4) Check if the strong password policy is enforced.
	5) Check if there is a password retry limit.
	6) Check if there is an option to forget a password.
	7) Try to clear CMOS and then trigger a recovery manufacturing mode flow in order to see if the password is still required.
	8) Check if there is a default password provisioned or a supervisor password as a backdoor.
	Hard drive passwords.
	1) Try to bypass the HDD password and TCG storage password.
	2) Try to freeze the HDD password or TCG storage SID, especially in a special boot path such as S3 resume, recovery, or manufacturing mode.
	3) Try to steal the HDD password or TCG storage password saved in management mode and/or the non-volatile storage.
	2) Try to steal the password information by comparing the error exit time.

(continued)

879

Table 22-1. (*continued*)

Category	Security Validation
	Network credentials.
	1) Try to steal the deployed WIFI password as a pre-shared key (PSK) or enterprise mode certificate in plain text.
	2) Try to steal the deployed TLS or IPSec private certificate in plain text.
	Device access.
	1) Check if there are any hardcoded access codes for the device, such as EC or battery.
	2) Check if there are any access codes provisioned in the system memory, such as stack, heap, global data region, and so on, or the NV storage such as UEFI variable.
	3) Check if there is any RPMB key provisioned in the system memory or the NV storage.
	4) Check if there is any RPMC key provisioned in the system memory or the NV storage.
	Cryptographic keys.
	1) Check if any symmetric key is left in the memory after processing, such as AES key, HMAC key, and so on.
	2) Check if any asymmetric key is left in the memory after processing, such as RSA private key, the password to protect the private key, and so on.
	3) Check if the keys are cleared in any path, from the provider to the consumer, such as stack, heap, global variable, communication buffer, and so on.
	Side channel attack.
	1) Try to steal the password saved in the management mode RAM.

Register lock	Vulnerability scan.
	1) Run the CHIPSEC scan tool to check if all lockable registers are indeed locked, especially the flash lock and management mode lock.
	2) Run the CHIPSEC scan tool in a special boot mode, such as S3 resume, S4 resume, recovery mode, or even manufacturing mode, to check if the end user can trigger the manufacturing mode restart.
Secure configuration	Break the secure boot policy.
	1) Try to disable secure boot, for example, via UEFI variable.
	2) Try to bypass the secure boot check in each special boot mode, such as S3 resume, S4 resume, recovery mode, or manufacturing mode.
	3) Try to modify the enrolled public certificate without authorization.
	4) Try to delete the enrolled forbidden public certificates without authorization.
	Break the Trusted Computing Group policy.
	1) Try to disable the measured boot feature. For example, disable TPM in the setup option or a UEFI variable.
	2) Try to gain access to the TPM platform hierarchy auth after boot, especially in special boot modes such as S3, S4, recovery, manufacturing mode, and so on.
	3) Try to suspend the system without sending the shutdown command to the TPM in order to see if the TPM device can recover in the S3 resume.
	4) Trigger the TPM S3 resume failure to see if the PCR has not been capped.
	5) Try to disable the TCG memory override (MOR) feature by clearing the MOR variable.
	6) Try to update the TCG physical present flag configuration, especially in special boot modes such as S4 resume, recovery, and manufacturing, for example, if the flag configuration is saved in NV storage.

(continued)

881

Table 22-1. (*continued*)

Category	Security Validation
	Check completeness.
	1) For secure boot, check if the verification happens for all third-party components. Assess the image on the untrusted flash partition, the image on the disk, the image in the PCI card, the image from the network, the image from the recovery media, and so on.
	2) For secure boot, check if the verification happens for all boot modes, especially S3 resume, S4 resume, recovery, manufacturing mode, and so on.
	3) For static root-of-trust for measurement (SRTM), check if all critical code and critical configuration are measured into the TPM. Look for any code that is not measured, such as the Firmware Support Package (FSP); any data not measured, such as an ACPI table or SMBIOS table; and any security policy not measured, such as a public certificate or secure boot enable/ disable.
	4) For the dynamic root-of-trust for measurement (DRTM), check the completeness too. Any DRTM code/data/policy not measured? Does the same measurement happen during S3 resume?
	5) For memory protection, check if all memory that should be protected is indeed protected, especially for the special memory regions, such as above–4 GiB memory, below–1 MiB memory, and untested memory. Is all trusted world memory protected? Is all kernel memory protected?
	6) For system resource protection, check if all resources that should be protected are indeed protected, including memory mapped I/O, I/O, model-specific registers (MSRs), PCI configuration space, Embedded Controller (EC) configuration, System Management Bus (SMBus), Inter-Integrated Circuit (I2C) bus, Serial Peripheral Interface (SPI) bus, and so on.
	Break the recovery process.
	1) Try to delete the golden recovery image.
	2) Try to modify or replace the golden recovery image with a malicious one.

	Trigger manufacturing mode. 1) Try to see if any protections can be disabled in manufacturing mode, including but not limited to secure boot, measured boot, user authentication, UEFI variable protection, and so on. Break other advanced protections. 1) Try to disable DMA protection or downgrade the DMA protection level, for example, via a setup option or a UEFI variable. 2) Try to disable the kernel hardening policy, such as address space layout randomization and data execution protection.
Replay/ rollback	Roll back the firmware code. 1) Try to roll back to an older firmware image with a smaller secure version number (SVN) during the firmware update process. 2) Roll back to an old firmware image with a smaller SVN during SPI flash update to see if it can be detected by the secure boot process. 3) Try to roll back the golden recovery image to a version with a smaller SVN. Roll back the firmware configuration. 1) Try to roll back to some insecure older system configuration data during the configuration data update process. 2) Roll back to some insecure older system configuration via a direct SPI flash update to see if it can be detected. 3) Trigger a special boot mode, such as recovery or manufacturing mode, to see if the configuration is rolled back to an insecure one, such as an older secure boot key. 4) Capture old configuration data and replay this older configuration data at a later time.

(continued)

883

Table 22-1. (*continued*)

Category	Security Validation
Cryptography	Fuzz the input.
	1) Fuzz the digital signature, including malformed signatures and the case of no signature. A certificate fuzzing tool can be used for cryptographic encodings, such as X.509 certificate, Abstract Syntax Notation One (ANS.1), Concise Binary Object Representation (CBOR), and so on.
	2) Fuzz the data structure wrapping the signature, such as PE image before the certificate field, the firmware volume (FV) header before the signed section, and the UEFI capsule header before the Firmware Management Protocol (FMP) capsule auth info.
	3) Fuzz the protocol, such as Transport Layer Security (TLS) and Secure Protocol and Data Model (SPDM).
	Cryptographic algorithm.
	1) Check if a non-cryptographic algorithm is used for the firmware image update and recovery, such as XOR, cyclic redundancy check (CRC), or checksum.
	2) Check if the device firmware update uses cryptographic algorithms for verification, including but not limited to the Baseboard Management Controller (BMC) firmware, Embedded Controller (EC) firmware, management engine (ME) firmware, PCI device firmware, memory DIMM firmware, and so on.
	3) Check if any non-standard cryptographic algorithm or protocol is used, such as a customized Encrypt-and-MAC (E&M), Encrypt-then-MAC (EtM), and MAC-then-Encrypt (MtE), instead of a standard Authenticated Encryption with Associated Data (AEAD).
	4) Check if the key length is large enough.
	5) Check if forward security is considered in the key exchange algorithm.
	6) Check if the random seed is really uniformly random.
	7) Check if the sequence number, counter, nonce value, and initialization vectors are used properly. For example, the sequence number or counter can start with 0. and an initialization vector must be random.
	8) Check if the random number generation function is standard one.

Attack the key.

1) Try to steal the private key in memory or NV storage.

2) Try to steal the symmetric key in memory or NV storage.

3) Try to modify the deployed public certificate or its hash without authorization.

5) Try to delete the deployed revocation key without authorization.

6) Try to steal the key in the special boot mode, such as recovery or manufacturing mode.

Downgrade the protocol version and algorithm.

1) Try to negotiate with the entity to downgrade the protocol to a lower and unknown vulnerable version. An implementation might support a legacy version for compatibility considerations, such as TLS 1.0 and TLS1.1.

2) Try to negotiate with the entity to downgrade the algorithm to a deprecated one. An implementation might support deprecated algorithms for compatibility considerations, such as SHA1.

Cryptography usage.

1) Check if the test key is used in production.

2) Check if there is a way to revoke a certificate.

3) Check if the root key is used to encrypt the data instead of the session key.

4) Check if the public certificate chain is verified according to the trusted root certificate or its hash and the revoked certificate or its hash.

5) Check if the validity period of the certificate is verified.

6) Check if the requested hostname is verified according to the common name of the certificate.

This is necessary but not sufficient. The full security validation plan should be derived based upon the detailed feature-specific security requirements.

Penetration Test Plan

The goal of a penetration test is to gain access to the asset. In older days, the penetration testing focused on attacks against the operating system (OS) from the OS application or network. With the emergence of the hypervisor, people tried to attack the hypervisor from the operating system. Firmware brings a new type of attack surface because it runs even before the hypervisor, and there is a trusted execution environment which can bypass the protections set up by the hypervisor. Figure 22-1 shows the possible attack paths related to the firmware.

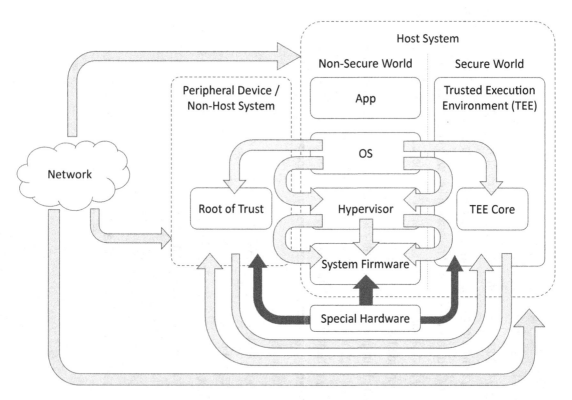

Figure 22-1. *Penetration Attack Path*

1) Network attack

   If the system firmware or the non-host system supports access to the network, then the network attack vector should be considered, such as the BMC Intelligent Platform Management Interface (IPMI) or RedFish remote management or Intel ME Active Management Technology (AMT). If the device firmware has the capability to process network packets, such as ethernet, WiFi, Bluetooth, or cellular networks (3G, 4G, 5G), then a dedicated network protocol attack can be considered.

2) System software attack

   In a host system, the non-secure world operating system may attack the system firmware directly by inputting malicious data to the firmware to process the data, such as OS loader, firmware update capsule image, UEFI configuration variable, and so on.

   The non-secure world operating system may take advantage of the vulnerability of the secure world to attack the trusted execution environment, such as TEE communication and TEE management handler, and implant a shellcode in the TEE. Because of the high privilege of the TEE, the shellcode can consequently be used to attack the hypervisor or the system firmware, such as code injection for the hypervisor or the system firmware image update.

   The host non-secure world can also attack the firmware in the peripheral device or the non-host system, such as a PCI card, baseboard management controller (BMC), or management engine (ME). If the host system trusts the input from the peripheral device or the non-host system, then this input can be used to attack the system firmware. For example, the device can generate the Direct Memory Access (DMA) to the host system in order to inject code or steal a password. A keylogger can be implemented for the input device to record all keystrokes, including bank account information and passwords.

3) Non-host software attack

   The non-host environment is different from the host environment. As such, a shellcode in the non-host system may attack the host TEE to gain more privileges. For example, a malicious PCI card or BMC may attack the system firmware during boot and impact the TEE setup.

4) TEE software attack

   The trusted execution environment (TEE) is an isolated execution environment. Ideally, it should protect itself. In case there is a vulnerability in the TEE, then it may be attacked. For example, a shellcode in the TEE may update the BMC firmware or the system firmware on the SPI flash directly.

5) Hardware attack

   Last but not of least importance, the attacker may bring a special attack device to attack the system, such as a glitch attack, device DMA attack, SPI bus or I2C bus hijack, JTAG debugger, and so on. They can be used to attack system firmware, device firmware, or even the secure world TEE.

Summary

In this chapter, we introduced the security validation and penetration test methodologies. The chapter covered the security validation test plan for the eight high-risk areas in the firmware – external input, race condition, hardware input, secret handling, register lock, secure configuration, replay/rollback, and cryptography. Then we introduced the possible attack paths for the penetration test. In the next chapter, we will introduce the steps for firmware maintenance after the release.

References

Book

[B-1] Alex Matrosov, Eugene Rodionov, Sergey Bratus, *Rootkits and Bootkits: Reversing Modern Malware and Next Generation Threats*, No Starch Press, 2019

[B-2] Darmawan Salihun, *BIOS Disassembly Ninjutsu Uncovered*, A-List Publishing, 2006

[B-3] Bill Blunden, *The Rootkit Arsenal: Escape and Evasion in the Dark Corners of the System, 2nd Ed*, Jones & Bartlett Learning, 2012

[B-4] Greg Hoglund, Jamie Butler, *Rootkits: Subverting the Windows Kernel: Subverting the Windows Kernel*, Addison-Wesley Professional, 2005

[B-5] Kris Kaspersky, *Hacker Disassembling Uncovered, 2nd Ed*, A-List Publishing, 2007

[B-6] Kris Kaspersky, *Hacker Debugging Uncovered*, A-List Publishing, 2005

[B-7] Kris Kaspersky, *Shellcoder's Programming Uncovered*, A-List Publishing, 2005

[B-8] Bruce Dang, Alexandre Gazet, Elias Bachaalany, *Practical Reverse Engineering: x86, x64, ARM, Windows Kernel, Reversing Tools, and Obfuscation*, Wiley, 2014

[B-9] Eldad Eilam, *Reversing: Secrets of Reverse Engineering*, Wiley, 2005

[B-10] Dennis Andriesse, *Practical Binary Analysis: Build Your Own Linux Tools for Binary Instrumentation, Analysis, and Disassembly*, No Starch Press, 2018

[B-11] Michael Sikorski, Andrew Honig, *Practical Malware Analysis: The Hands-On Guide to Dissecting Malicious Software*, No Starch Press, 2012

[B-12] James A. Whittaker, Hugh Thompson, *How to Break Software Security*, Addison-Wesley Professional, 2003

[B-13] Frank van Gilluwe, *The Undocumented PC: A Programmer's Guide to I/O, CPUs, and Fixed Memory Areas, 2nd Ed*, Addison-Wesley Professional, 2001

[B-14] Hans-Peter Messmer, *The Indispensable PC Hardware Book, 4th Ed*, Addison-Wesley Professional, 1996

Conference, Journal, and Paper

[C-1] Yuriy Bulygin, Oleksandr Bazhaniuk, "Discovering vulnerable UEFI BIOS firmware at scale," in 44CON 2017, available at `https://github.com/abazhaniuk/Publications/blob/master/2017/44CON_2017/Bulygin_Bazhaniuk_44con.pdf`

[C-2] Sugumar Govindarajan, John Loucaides, "The Whole is Greater," in NIST CSRC 2015, https://csrc.nist.gov/CSRC/media/Presentations/The-Whole-is-Greater/images-media/day1_trusted-computing_200-250.pdf

Web

[W-1] chipsec, https://github.com/chipsec/chipsec

[W-2] UEFI Firmware Parser, https://github.com/theopolis/uefi-firmware-parser

CHAPTER 23

Maintenance

After the product is shipped, we enter the product maintenance phase. We might subsequently receive a security issue report from either an external or internal customer. Once the issue is identified, we need to fix the issue and prepare a firmware update that can be deployed to all existing products in the field. The time to fix the security issue is important because between the time when the issue is discovered and the time when the issue is fixed, the product is under the risk of being attacked.

Mitigation Strategy and Tactics

Microsoft described the software vulnerability mitigation strategy – make it difficult and costly to find, exploit, and leverage the vulnerabilities – and four tactics (eliminate the vulnerabilities, break the exploitation, contain the damage, and limit the window of time to perform the exploit). These strategies and tactics can be used for firmware vulnerability mitigation as well. Table 23-1 shows the firmware vulnerability mitigation tactics.

© Jiewen Yao and Vincent Zimmer 2020
J. Yao and V. Zimmer, *Building Secure Firmware*, https://doi.org/10.1007/978-1-4842-6106-4_23

Table 23-1. *Firmware Vulnerability Mitigation Tactics*

Tactics	Architecture and Design	Implementation	Maintenance
Eliminate the vulnerability.	Reduce attack surface, such as unnecessary SMI handlers. Adopt secure design principles, such as least privilege. Use the correct cryptographic algorithm.	Enable compiler defensive technologies, such as sanitizer, static analysis, and dynamic analysis. Use a type-safe language, such as Rust. Use vulnerability scan tools.	Enhance vulnerability scan tools.
Break the exploit.	Adopt firmware resiliency – protection, detection, and recovery – such as secure boot. Adopt firmware integrity measurement and attestation, such as measured boot.	Enable compiler defensive technologies, such as stack cookies, address space layout randomization (ASLR), data execution protection (DEP), code integrity guard (CIG), arbitrary code guard (ACG), control flow guard (CFG), and so on. Enable kernel protection technology, such as Supervisor Mode Execute Prevention (SMEP), Supervisor Mode Access Prevention (SMAP), kernel page table isolation (KPTI), and so on.	
Contain the damage.	Adopt container and virtualization (vertical). Adopt isolation and compartmentalization (horizontal).	Enable supervisor mode. Enable hypervisor. Enable trusted execution environment (TEE).	

(*continued*)

Table 23-1. (*continued*)

Tactics	Architecture and Design	Implementation	Maintenance
Reduce the attack windows.	Adopt firmware resiliency – updates. Define firmware update process.	Enable firmware component-level update.	Enable firmware supply chain detection. Enable effective firmware vulnerability detection. UEFI scanner.

Table 23-2. *shows the example in the UEFI/EDK II system firmware*

Tactics	Method	UEFI/EDK II Example
Eliminate the vulnerability.	Reduce attack surface	SMI Handler Profile
	Static analysis/dynamic analysis	Clang static analysis, memory sanitizer, KLEE
	Security test/fuzzing	Host-based firmware analyzer, Peach, AFL
	Vulnerability scan	CHIPSEC
Break the exploit.	Stack guard	MSVC:/GS, GCC:-fstack-protector
	Address space layout randomization	DXE/SMM ASLR
	Data executable prevention	SMM Memory Protection
	Arbitrary code guard	UEFI Core Memory Protection
	Control flow guard	DXE/SMM Control Flow Enforcement Technology (CET)
	Code Integrity Guard	UEFI secure boot

(*continued*)

Table 23-2. (*continued*)

Tactics	Method	UEFI/EDK II Example
Contain the damage,	Sandbox	EBC
	Deprivilege	Ring3-based OPROM, SMI Handler
	Isolation	Ring3-based OPROM, SMI Handler
Reduce the attack windows.	Resiliency	Signed update, secure boot, signed recovery, flash lock
	Measurement and attestation	Measured Boot (SRTM), Secure Launch (DRTM)
	Antivirus	UEFI scanner

Supply Chain for the Firmware Components

In general, supply chain management is a way to manage the lifecycle of products and services. Firmware is one of the most important components in the platform-level supply chain. We need a robust way to trace each firmware image for a given platform and ensure that they are up to date and have not been tampered.

Firmware Component Certificate and Manifest

A firmware component certificate contains assertions about trust made by a component manufacturer. It asserts the component's security properties and configuration as shipped. For example, the TCG platform certificate describes the attributes for the shipping platform. The TCG Endorsement Key Certificate is used to bind an identity to a Trusted Platform Module (TPM) on the platform, and the TCG Attestation Identity Key (AIK) Certificate is used to provide platform authentication based on the attestation capability of the TPM. The TCG Device Identifier Composition Engine (DICE) includes multiple certificates to support the layered certification, including the Initial Device Identifier (IDevID) Certificates issued by the device manufacturer, the Local Device ID (LDevID) Certificates issued by the device owner, the Embedded Certificate Authority (ECA) certificates issued by the CA, and the attestation certificates issued by the ECA or CA. Table 23-3 lists the standards involved in the firmware component certificates.

Table 23-3. *Firmware Component Certificates*

Platform Certificate	Certificate Format	Data Format
TCG Platform Certificate Profile – *TCG Infrastructure working group* TCG Endorsement Key (EK) Credential Profile – *TCG Infrastructure working group* TCG DICE Certificate Profile – *TCG Device Identifier Composite Engine (DICE) working group*	X.509, The Directory: Public Key and Attribute Certificate Frameworks – *ITU X.509* An Internet Attribute Certificate Profile for Authorization – *RFC 5755*	Privacy-Enhanced Mail (PEM) – *RFC 1421, 7468* BASE64 encoding – *RFC 4648* Abstract Syntax Notation One (ASN.1) Distinguished Encoding Rules (DER) – *ITU X.690*

The component certificate should include the reference manifest information. As such, the verifier can get the component information for attestation. For example, the TCG platform certificate includes a PlatformConfigurationURI attribute. From this Uniform Resource Identifier (URI), the verifier can get a reference integrity manifest or measurement (RIM). The format of the reference integrity manifest (RIM) is compliant with the Software Identification (SWID) tag defined in the ISO/IEC 19770-2 specification or Concise Identification (CoSWID) tag defined in the IETF Security Automation and Continuous Monitoring (SACM) working group. The SWID tag is formatted using the Extensible Markup Language (XML), while the CoSWID is formatted using the Concise Binary Object Representation (CBOR). CBOR is a data format whose design goals include the possibility of extremely small code size, relatively small message size, and extensibility without the need for version negotiation. The underlying data model is JSON. The CBOR encoding is much smaller than ASN.1 encoding. As such, it is more suitable for the embedded or Internet of Things (IoT) environment. Besides the CoSWID definition, the IETF Remote Attestation Procedures (RATS) working group added RIM extensions for the CoSWID to meet the needs of the TCG RIM specification.

The firmware update package can also have a manifest. It could be TCG reference integrity manifest (RIM) or the IETF Software Update for Internet of Things (SUIT) manifest based upon CBOR. The SUIT manifest contains not only the firmware update image and its information, but it also contains the command for the recipient to perform. Table 23-4 lists the standards involved in the firmware component manifest.

Table 23-4. *Firmware Component Manifest*

Firmware Component Manifest	Firmware Identification Tag	Data Format
TCG reference integrity manifest (RIM) – *TCG Infrastructure working group* Guidelines for the Creation of Interoperable SWID Tags – *NIST IR 8060*	Software Identification (SWID) Tags – *ISO/IEC 19770-2:2015*	Extensible Markup Language (XML) – *W3C* XML Signature Syntax and Processing – *W3C* XML Schema Definition (XSD) – *W3C*
RIM extension for CoSWID – *IETF Remote Attestation Procedures (RATS) working group* CBOR-based format for SUIT manifest – *IETF Software Update for Internet of Things (SUIT) working group*	Concise Software Identification Tags (CoSWID) – *IETF Security Automation and Continuous Monitoring (SACM) working group*	Concise Binary Object Representation (CBOR) – *RFC 7049* CBOR Object Signing and Encryption (COSE) – *RFC 8152* Concise Data Definition Language (CDDL) – *RFC 8610*

Firmware Attestation Data

At runtime, the Platform Root-of-Trust and chain-of-trust record the evidence for firmware components in the platform and report them to the verifier. Next, the verifier can compare the component data with the reference manifest to see if the system is trusted. Taking the TCG Platform Firmware Profile as an example, the platform static root-of-trust for measurement extends the system firmware hash into the Platform Configuration Registers (PCR) of the Trusted Platform Module (TPM) and records the hash values into the TCG event log. At runtime, the verifier uses the TPM quote process to verify the TPM PCR values signed by the TPM attestation key. Then the verifier can process the hash data in the TCG event log and try to reproduce the hash values in the PCR value. At this point, the verifier can compare the firmware hash value in the TCG event log and the firmware hash value in the platform reference integrity manifest.

Besides the system firmware measurement, the device firmware measurement can be retrieved via the DMTF Secure Protocol and Data Model (SPDM) protocol between the host and the device. The measurement data is signed by the device using its private certificate. The verifier can use the device public certificate to verify the measurement and then compare it with the device firmware hash value in the reference integrity manifest.

If the device implements the TCG Device Identifier Composition Engine (DICE), then the layered DICE certificates can be used. The device identity certificates, such as the Initial Device Identifier (IDevID) Certificates and Local Device ID (LDevID) Certificates, embed a cryptographic identity in the device so that a verifier may be assured that the device is of reputable origin. The device attestation certificates assert that the device's manufacturer has embedded a cryptographic key in a device. It allows a verifier to determine which manufacturer created the device.

The IETF Remote Attestation Procedures (RATS) working group defined the entity attestation token (EAT). The EAT provides a signed (attested) set of claims that describe the state and characteristics of an entity, typically a device like a phone or an IoT device. The EAT token is formatted as a CBOR web token (CWT) or a JSON web token (JWT) signed with the device attestation key.

The IETF Trusted Execution Environment Provisioning (TEEP) working group defined the architecture and the protocol for the Trusted Application Manager (TAM) and TEEP agent. The TAM can manage the Trusted Application (TA) in a device, such as query information, install TA, and delete TA.

Table 23-5 lists the standards involved in the firmware attestation data.

Table 23-5. *Firmware Attestation Data*

Attestation	Attestation Data	Data Format
TCG Platform Firmware Profile (PFP) – *TCG PC Client working group*	TPM Platform Configuration Register (PCR) + TCG event log – *TCG PFP*	Firmware measurement + TPM quote – *TCG TPM*
DMTF Secure Protocol and Data Model (SPDM) – *DMTF Platform Management Components Interconnection (PMCI) working group*	Device Firmware Measurement Block – *DMTF SPDM*	Signed device firmware measurement – *DMTF SPDM*

(*continued*)

Table 23-5. (*continued*)

Attestation	Attestation Data	Data Format
DICE Layering Architecture – *TCG Device Identifier Composite Engine (DICE) working group*	DICE certificate – *TCG Device DICE working group*	(N +1) Layer signed certificate for firmware measurement – *DICE certificate*
Entity attestation token (EAT) – *IETF Remote Attestation Procedures (RATS) working group*	CBOR web token (CWT) – *RFC 8392* JSON web token (JWT) – *RFC 8529*	Entity state and characteristics + signing – *IETF RATS EAT*

Figure 23-1 shows a general firmware attestation flow. A system includes a root-of-trust and other mutable components. At manufacturing time, the system can be provisioned with the identity information and an attestation key. At the same time, a system certificate and a reference manifest are generated to describe the system information. At runtime, the system reports the attestation data, which includes the system identity information and the component hashes and is signed by the attestation key. The verifier collects the attestation data, verifies the signature with the public attestation certification, and finally compares against the component hash. Please be aware that this is a conceptual flow. A real implementation may have slight differences or more complications.

Currently, different industry standard groups are defining the specifications and guidelines to support different aspects of the supply chain in order to support interoperability across components, including the International Organization for Standardization (ISO), Internet Engineering Task Force (IETF), National Institute of Standards and Technology (NIST), Trusted Computing Group (TCG), Distributed Management Task Force (DMTF), and so on. Some of the preceding specifications are still under development. Please always refer to the latest specifications and guidelines when you want to enable the features.

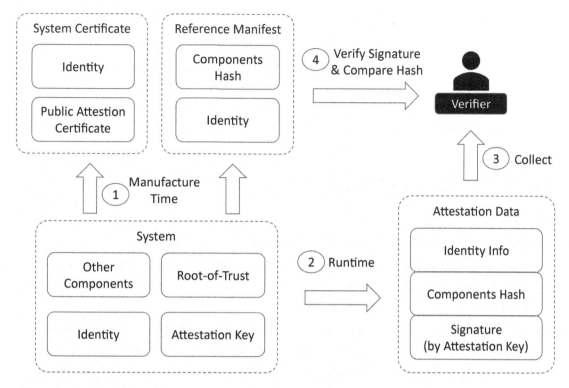

Figure 23-1. *General Firmware Attestation Flow*

Vulnerable Firmware Detection

Once we have received a vulnerability report for a specific version of a firmware release, we need to evaluate the impact scope:

1) Assess how many products have a similar vulnerability. This can be detected via the supply chain management for the firmware component.

2) Assess if other versions of the firmware have the same vulnerability. This can be done by a signature-based scan tool which can collect a signature of a piece of vulnerable code to see if other versions of the firmware have the same piece of code. A detailed code review may be needed to see when this vulnerability was first introduced in the system.

3) Assess if a similar vulnerability exists in another place besides the reported one. This can be done by a vulnerability-based scan tool which can leverage the vulnerability to attack the system. We may use this tool to test different interfaces and different versions of the firmware. Also, a detailed code review for the similar interface is helpful to catch the similar vulnerability.

Antivirus for Firmware

Besides the firmware vulnerability detection in the firmware release, we can use an antivirus component to detect firmware runtime binary status. This can be considered as a complement for the firmware resiliency – detection. For example, Microsoft announced the UEFI scanner, which is a new component of the built-in antivirus solution on Windows 10. It can scan the insides of the firmware and perform the security assessment. The UEFI scanner can detect a known vulnerable component in the firmware or a misconfigured chipset register in the system. The limitation is that the scanner must read the whole firmware. This can be achieved when the firmware is on a Serial Peripheral Interface (SPI) flash. However, if the firmware is on a Non-Volatile Memory Express (NVMe) flash, the scanner cannot read the firmware content. The alternative is to let the scanner check the firmware component measurement to know what the corresponding component is.

Firmware Update

Once we have identified all vulnerable firmware, we need to prepare the firmware update package. In order to reduce the attack windows, the firmware update frequency is a key indicator. If it is too long, then we may give the attacker too much time to attack the known vulnerable system. If it is too short, then we may bring too much burden to the validation team wherein they need to validate the new firmware release again and again.

The firmware update can be done in different ways:

1) We can update the full firmware image, such as the whole SPI flash update including the system BIOS and the management engine (ME), together with the non-host firmware such as the embedded controller (EC) or baseboard management controller (BMC). The benefit is that the system will be in a clean, well-known state.

2) We can enable a component-level firmware update. For example, we can update with system BIOS or the management engine (ME) separately. The "Intel 64 and IA-32 Architecture Software Developer Manuals" also defines a way to update the CPU Microcode independent of the system BIOS. Ideally, the component-level firmware update can accelerate the firmware update process and reduce the validation effort. In practice, we need to do necessary validation for the various possible combinations. There might be a case that two different component versions cannot work with each other, for example.

3) We can enable the firmware configuration update. For example, the UEFI specification defines a way to update the UEFI secure boot key in the UEFI authenticated variable region.

Besides the working image, the system recovery image and the system default configuration data should be updated as well. This is to address the case of the vulnerability also existing in the recovery image or the system default configuration data. For example, if we need to update the forbidden database for the UEFI secure boot key, then the manufacturer's default forbidden database should also be updated. Otherwise, we may expose a rollback attack against the configuration.

Last but not of least importance, in order to track how many firmware updates are deployed, we need to prepare a new reference manifest for the firmware update package. Then the verifier can collect the firmware information and check with the latest platform certificate and reference manifest. If possible, the automated firmware update should be designed to push the latest firmware image to the system if the verifier detects the existence of some vulnerable firmware.

Summary

In this chapter, we introduced the activities for firmware maintenance after the release. We revisited the vulnerability mitigation strategy and tactics, namely, reduce the attack window in the maintenance phase. We went through the supply chain–related industry standards, including the firmware component certificate, such as TCG platform certificate, TPM EK endorsement certificate, and DICE certificate; firmware reference manifest such as TCG RIM using SWID or CoSWID; IETF RIM extension for CoSWID and IETF SUIT manifest; firmware attestation data such as the TCG Platform Firmware Profile; DMTF SPDM device measurement; DICE layered certificate profile; and the IETF EAT token. Finally, we discussed the vulnerable firmware detection techniques and firmware update methods.

References

Book

[B-1] James Ransome and Anmol Misra, *Core Software Security: Security at the Source*, CRC Press, 2014

Conference, Journal, and Paper

[P-1] Matt Miller, "Trends, Challenges, and Strategic Shifts in the Software Vulnerability Mitigation Landscape," in *BlueHat IL 2019*, available at `https://github.com/microsoft/MSRC-Security-Research/blob/master/presentations/2019_02_BlueHatIL/2019_01%20-%20BlueHatIL%20-%20Trends%2C%20challenge%2C%20and%20shifts%20in%20software%20vulnerability%20mitigation.pdf`

Specification and Guideline

[S-1] ISO/IEC 19770-2, "Information Technology – Software Asset Management – Part 2: Software Identification Tag," 2015

[S-2] NIST SP800-193, "Platform Firmware Resiliency Guidelines," 2018, available at `https://csrc.nist.gov/publications/sp800`

[S-3] NIST SP800-155, "BIOS Integrity Measurement Guidelines," 2011, available at `https://csrc.nist.gov/publications/sp800`

[S-4] NISTIR 8060, "Guidelines for the Creation of Interoperable Software Identification (SWID) Tags," 2016, `https://csrc.nist.gov/publications/nistir`

[S-5] TagVault org, "SWID Tag Signing Guidelines," 2017, `https://tagvault.org/swid-tags/guidelines/`

[S-6] TCG, "TCG PC Client Platform Firmware Integrity Measurement," 2019, `https://trustedcomputinggroup.org/wp-content/uploads/TCG_PC_Client-FIM_v1r24_3feb20.pdf`

[S-7] TCG, "TCG PC Client Reference Integrity Manifest Specification," 2020, `https://trustedcomputinggroup.org/wp-content/uploads/TCG_PC_Client_RIM_r0p15_15june2020.pdf`

[S-8] TCG, "TCG Reference Integrity Manifest (RIM) Information Model," 2020, https://trustedcomputinggroup.org/wp-content/uploads/TCG_RIM_Model_v1-r13_2feb20.pdf

[S-9] TCG, "TCG Trusted Attestation Protocol (TAP) Information Model," 2019, https://trustedcomputinggroup.org/resource/tcg-tap-information-model/

[S-10] TCG, "TCG Platform Certificate Profile," 2020, https://trustedcomputinggroup.org/resource/tcg-platform-certificate-profile/

[S-11] TCG, "TCG EK Credential Profile," 2014, https://trustedcomputinggroup.org/resource/tcg-ek-credential-profile-for-tpm-family-2-0/

[S-12] TCG, "Implicit Identity Based Device Attestation," 2018, available at https://trustedcomputinggroup.org/resource/implicit-identity-based-device-attestation/

[S-13] TCG, "Symmetric Identity Based Device Attestation," 2020, available at https://trustedcomputinggroup.org/resource/symmetric-identity-based-device-attestation/

[S-14] TCG, "DICE Layering Architecture," 2020, available at https://trustedcomputinggroup.org/wp-content/uploads/DICE-Layering-Architecture-r19_3june2020.pdf

[S-15] TCG, "DICE Certificate Profiles," 2020, https://trustedcomputinggroup.org/wp-content/uploads/DICE-Certificate-Profiles-r01_3june2020-1.pdf

[S-16] DMTF, "Security Protocol and Data Model Specification," 2020, available at www.dmtf.org/standards/pmci

[S-17] IETF, "RFC 5755 – An Internet Attribute Certificate Profile for Authorization," 2010, https://tools.ietf.org/html/rfc5755

[S-18] IETF, "RFC 7049 – Concise Binary Object Representation (CBOR)," 2013, https://tools.ietf.org/html/rfc7049

[S-19] IETF, "RFC 7519 – JSON Web Token (JWT)," 2015, https://tools.ietf.org/html/rfc7519

[S-20] IETF, "RFC 8152 – CBOR Object Signing and Encryption (COSE)," 2017, https://tools.ietf.org/html/rfc8152

[S-21] IETF, "RFC 8322 – Resource-Oriented Lightweight Information Exchange (ROLIE)," 2018, https://tools.ietf.org/html/rfc8322

[S-22] IETF, "RFC 8392 – CBOR Web Token (CWT)," 2018, https://tools.ietf.org/html/rfc8392

[S-23] IETF, "RFC 8412 – Software Inventory Message and Attributes (SWIMA) for PA-TNC," 2018, `https://tools.ietf.org/html/rfc8412`

[S-24] IETF, "RFC 8610 – Concise Data Definition Language (CDDL): A Notational Convention to Express Concise Binary Object Representation (CBOR) and JSON Data Structures," 2019, `https://tools.ietf.org/html/rfc8610`

[S-25] IETF, "SUIT: A Firmware Update Architecture for Internet of Things," 2019, `https://datatracker.ietf.org/doc/draft-ietf-suit-architecture/`

[S-26] IETF, "SUIT: An Information Model for Firmware Updates in IoT Devices," 2020, `https://datatracker.ietf.org/doc/draft-ietf-suit-information-model/`

[S-27] IETF, "SUIT: A Concise Binary Object Representation (CBOR)-based Serialization Format for the Software Updates for Internet of Things (SUIT) Manifest," 2020, `https://datatracker.ietf.org/doc/draft-ietf-suit-manifest/`

[S-28] IETF, "SACM: Security Automation and Continuous Monitoring (SACM) Architecture," 2019, `https://datatracker.ietf.org/doc/draft-ietf-sacm-arch/`

[S-29] IETF, "SACM: Concise Software Identification Tags," 2019, `https://datatracker.ietf.org/doc/draft-ietf-sacm-coswid/`

[S-30] IETF, "SACM: Definition of the ROLIE Software Descriptor Extension," 2020, `https://datatracker.ietf.org/doc/draft-ietf-sacm-rolie-softwaredescriptor/`

[S-31] IETF, "RATS: Remote Attestation Procedures Architecture," 2020, `https://datatracker.ietf.org/doc/draft-ietf-rats-architecture/`

[S-32] IETF, "RATS: The Entity Attestation Token (EAT)," 2020, `https://datatracker.ietf.org/doc/draft-ietf-rats-eat/`

[S-33] IETF, "RATS: Reference Integrity Measurement Extension for Concise Software Identities," 2020, `https://datatracker.ietf.org/doc/draft-birkholz-rats-coswid-rim/`

[S-34] IETF, "RATS: Reference Interaction Models for Remote Attestation Procedures," 2020, `https://datatracker.ietf.org/doc/draft-birkholz-rats-reference-interaction-model/`

[S-35] IETF, "RATS: Arm's Platform Security Architecture (PSA) Attestation Token," 2020, `https://datatracker.ietf.org/doc/draft-tschofenig-rats-psa-token/`

[S-36] IETF, "TEEP: Trusted Execution Environment Provisioning (TEEP) Architecture," 2020, `https://datatracker.ietf.org/doc/draft-ietf-teep-architecture/`

[S-37] IETF, "TEEP: Trusted Execution Environment Provisioning (TEEP) Protocol," 2020, `https://datatracker.ietf.org/doc/draft-ietf-teep-protocol/`

[S-38] W3C, "XML Signature Syntax and Processing," 2013, www.w3.org/TR/xmldsig-core1/

[S-39] Microsoft, "PE format Authenticode," 2019, https://docs.microsoft.com/en-us/windows/win32/debug/pe-format#appendix-a-calculating-authenticode-pe-image-hash

Web

[W-1] NIST, Software Identification (SWID) Tagging, https://csrc.nist.gov/projects/Software-Identification-SWID, https://github.com/usnistgov/swid-tools

[W-2] CBOR, http://cbor.io/

[W-3] "Rough Guide to IETF 102: Internet of Things," www.internetsociety.org/blog/2018/07/rough-guide-to-ietf-102-internet-of-things/

[W-4] Intel Compute Lifecycle Assurance, www.intel.com/content/www/us/en/security/compute-lifecycle-assurance.html

[W-5] Intel Transparent Supply Chain, www.intel.com/content/www/us/en/products/docs/servers/transparent-supply-chain.html, https://servermarketinglibrary.intel.com/intel-transparent-supply-chain

[W-6] Intel Key Generation Facility, https://intel-epid-sdk.github.io/ecosystem/

[W-7] Microsoft, "UEFI scanner brings Microsoft Defender ATP protection to a new level," www.microsoft.com/security/blog/2020/06/17/uefi-scanner-brings-microsoft-defender-atp-protection-to-a-new-level/

[W-8] Microsoft, "Modern Service Management for Azure v1.1," https://azure.microsoft.com/en-us/resources/msm-for-azure/

Index

A

Access control
- BIOS, 335
- device configuration (*see* Device configuration)
- feature configuration (*see* Feature configuration)
- identification, 336
- object, 335
- PCRs, 335
- security mechanism, 335
- subject/object, 336
- TEE, 335, 347
- TPM, 335
- unauthorized usage, 335

Active Component Root-of-Trust (AC-RoT), 130, 222, 258, 260, 264

Active Management Technology (AMT), 347, 510, 887

Address sanitizer
- definition, 644
- memory tagging, 648–651
- page table-based heap guard, 644–646, 648
- stack guard, 652, 653

Address sanitizer (Asan)
- binary code, 599
- buffer checking environment, 604
- Clang compiler, 602, 603
- dead loop, 600
- MKTME, 607
- Msan, 605
- MTE, 605–607
- /RTCs *vs.* /GS, 598
- uninitialized data reads, 608, 610–613
- 0xCC, 602

Address space layout randomization (ASLR), 5, 512, 579, 625, 713
- data shifting, 635–638, 640
- data shuffling, 641
- definition, 634
- UEFI firmware, 634

Advanced Configuration and Power Interface (ACPI), 25, 206
- global system power states and transitions, 314
- power states, 313
- S3 (suspend to memory), 313
- security challenges, 315

Advanced Encryption Standard (AES), 767

Advanced error reporting (AER), 477

Advanced Host Controller Interface (AHCI), 109

Advanced Programmable Interrupt Controller (APIC), 281, 287

© Jiewen Yao and Vincent Zimmer 2020
J. Yao and V. Zimmer, *Building Secure Firmware*, https://doi.org/10.1007/978-1-4842-6106-4

Advanced secure coding
  fault injection (*see* Fault injection)
  side channel attack (*see* Side channel
    attack)
  speculative execution attack (*see*
    Speculative execution attack)
Advanced Technology Attachment
    (ATA), 26, 360
Advertising data (AD), 270
Amazon Nitro RoT, 136
Amazon Web Services (AWS), 136
AMD secure boot, 137
AMD Secure Encrypted
    Virtualization-Encrypted State
    (SEV-ES), 464–466
AMD Secure Encrypted Virtualization
    (SEV), 461, 462, 464
American Fuzzy Lop (AFL), 55
Android Verified Boot (AVB), 191
Apple File System (APFS), 135
Apple secure enclave processor
    (SEP), 727
Apple T2, 135
Application processor (AP), 71, 298
Application Root-of-Trust (ARoT), 140
Arbitrary code generation (ACG), 578
Arbitrary code guard (ACG), 577, 625, 628,
    661, 702, 713
Arithmetic overflow
  build-time detection and runtime
    error checking, 613
  Data8, 613
  data loss check failure, 615
  UBSan, 616, 617
ARM TrustZone
  architecture, 708
  features, 709

secure normal world interaction,
    710–712
secure world isolation, 710
secure world kernel protection,
    712–716
Assembly language, 825, 827
Assignable Device Interface (ADI), 478
AT Attachment with Packet Interface
    (ATAPI), 360
Attack/mitigation
  authentication/update,
    Non-TEE, 95, 96
  certificate revocation, 98
  data verification, 95
  DMA, 108
  integrity verification, 98
  malformed input
    integer overflow, 100, 101, 103, 104
    scatter/gather list, 100
    UEFI capsule coalesce, 99, 100,
      102, 103
    UEFI capsule layout, 98, 99
  no lock/no authentication, 94
  partial update, 108
  race condition, 107, 108
  rollback, 104, 105
  TOC/TOU, 105–107
  unlock/update separation, 97
Attestation Certificate Authority
    (ACA), 221
Attestation Identity Credential (AIC), 221
Attestation Identity Key (AIK), 894
Attestation key (AK), 205
Authenticated Code Module (ACM), 116,
    123, 125, 232, 234, 276, 497
Authenticated Code RAM
    (ACRAM), 81, 94

Availability protection, UEFI
disk quota management, 406–408
flash wear-out protection, 409–412
FTW, 412–416
variable atomicity, 412
Azure Sphere Security Service (AS3), 223

B

Base address registers (BARs), 695
Baseboard management controller
(BMC), 13, 29, 35, 70, 74, 127, 166,
175, 257, 318, 630, 656, 671
Bell-LaPadula model, 434
Biba integrity model
access control policies, 436
main rules, 436, 437
Binary device object store (BOS), 269
BIOS data area (BDA), 346
BIOS Guard AC module (BGMod), 81
BIOS Guard Platform Data Table
(BGPDT), 81, 83
BIOS Guard Update Package (BGUP), 83
BIOS Guard Update Package Certificate
(BGUPC), 81
BIOS Interface Lock Down (BILD)
register, 749
BIOS Lock Enable (BLE), 746
BIOS password
encryption, 338, 339
enforcement, 339
history, 339, 340
management, 341
recovery boot, 341
retry limit, 340
RMA, 340
S3 resume mode, 341
storage, 337

update enforcement, 339
update mode, 341
verification/update, 340
BIOS Write Enable (BIOSWE), 746
BitLocker, 217, 218
Bitmap (BMP), 51
Block cipher, 774
Bluetooth Low Energy (BLE), 51, 342
Boot access control
biometrics-based authentication, 342
EDKII
user authentication, 343, 344
user authorization, 345
encrypted password storage, 346
multiple-user management, 342
password (see BIOS password)
password memory, 346
SSO, 343
token, 342
traditional password attacks, 345, 346
user enroll enforcement, 342
Boot BIOS Strap (BBS), 170, 178, 749
Boot Device Selection (BDS), 12, 21, 33, 76
Boot firmware secure design practice
configuration, 524
device security, 523
measurement/attestation, 523
protection, 522
S3 script, 523
silicon register lock, 525
TEE, 525
UEFI variables, 524
Boot script implementation
DISPATCH OPCODE, 329
execution engine, 327
metadata, 328
S3 script, 327
Bootstrap processor (BSP), 230, 298

BOS Guard Update Package (BGUP), 81
Bot Guard Key (BG Key), 126
Bot Policy Manifest (BPM), 126
Branch Target Identification (BTI), 594
Branch target injection
    CALL indirect branch, 541
    JMP indirect branch, 540
    memory stack/RSB, 542, 543
    mitigation, 537, 538
    retpoline, 539
    RSB, 539
    UEFI firmware, 537
Branch trace store (BTS), 696
Break the exploit attack
    address sanitizer, 644
    ASLR, 634
    code protection techniques, 628
    control flow guard
        backward-edge, 642, 643
        forward-edge, 643, 644

C

Central processing unit (CPU), 5
Certificate Authority (CA), 187, 784
Certificate Revocation Lists (CRLs), 98
Certificate signing request (CSR), 223
Chain-of-trust (CoT), 20, 68, 70
Chain-of-trust for detection
    (CTD), 68, 115, 163
Chain-of-trust for recovery
    (CTRec)., 68, 163
Chain-of-trust for update (CTU), 68
Checksum or cyclic redundancy check
    (CRC), 52
Cisco Trust Anchor, 136
Clang, GNU CC (GCC), 56
Clang static analyzer (CSA), 598

C language, 828
Clark-Wilson model
    certification/enforcement rules, 439
    concepts, 438
    military security policy, 438
    security properties, 440
    TCG, 440
Cloud service provider (CSP), 460
Component Firmware Manifest (CFM), 92
Code integrity guard (CIG), 577, 578, 625,
    628, 661
Code protection techniques
    ACG, 634
    CID, 628–630, 632
    definition, 628
    DEP, 632, 633
Coherent Accelerator Processor Interface
    (CAPI), 220
Collection Table (CT), 296
Common Name (CN), 375
Common Vulnerability Scoring System
    (CVSS), 41, 57
Compiler defensive methods
    Asan (*see* Address sanitizer (Asan))
    ASLR, 579
    CFG (*see* Control flow guard (CFG))
    code protection, 577, 578
    CSA, 598
    speculative load hardening (*see*
        Speculative load hardening)
    stack overflow attack, 573–576
    static/ dynamic analysis, 571
    technology, 572
Complex Programmable Logic Device
    (CPLD), 94, 132
Component Firmware Manifest (CFM),
    90, 130
Component firmware update (CFU), 86–88

Component Measurement and
    Authentication (CMA), 263
Compound Device Identity (CDI), 207
Computer Express Link (CXL), 263
Concise Identification (CoSWID), 895
Confidentiality, integrity, and availability
    (CIA), 49
Confidentiality protection
    platform key encrypted variable,
        417–421
    user key encrypted variable, 416, 417
Configuration recovery
    data attack, 180
    rollback attack, 180, 181
    selection, 178, 179
    watchdog, 181, 182
Confused deputy attack, 712
Consumption of Speculative Data Barrier
    (CSDB), 596
Contain the damage attack
    system partitioning, 670, 671
    trusted execution
        environment, 669, 670
    user mode/supervisor mode, 654
    VMM, 659
Context Descriptor (CD), 278
Control flow analysis (CFA), 18
Control Flow Enforcement Technology
    (CET), 589
Control flow guard (CFG), 625
    backward-edge, 580
    binary code, 580
    Clang compiler, 586
    Guard CF function table, 583
    hardware based (see
        Hardware-based, CFG)
    injected code, 581
    _my_guard_check_icall() function, 584

MyTrap() function, 587, 588
    PE/COFF dump information, 582
Control flow guard/integrity (CFG/CFI), 5
Control Flow Integrity (CFI), 580
Converged Security and Management
    Engine (CSME), 374, 417
Coprocessor bases TEE
    Apple SEP, 727
    CSME, 724
    Google Titan, 727
    location types, 723, 724
    Microsoft Azure Sphere, Pluton,
        728–732
Core root-of-trust for measurement
    (CRTM), 11
CPU-based TEE
    ARM TrustZone, 707
    X86 SMM, 681
Cyclic redundancy check (CRC), 54, 116

D

Data Encryption Standard (DES), 767
Data execution prevention (DEP), 5, 577,
    578, 625, 628, 632, 661, 702, 713
Data flow analysis (DFA), 18
Datagram TLS (DTLS), 259
Data Object Exchange (DOE), 263
Delivery Mode (DM), 298
Denial of service (DoS), 42, 45
Detection
    secure boot (see Secure boot)
Device access control
    default/static password, 377
    EC access passcode, 376
    S3 resume attack, 378
    smart battery, 377
    TPM2 Hierarchy Auth Value, 375

Device attack prevention
  Bluetooth advertisement attack, 270
  DMA (*see* Direct Memory
      Access (DMA))
  DMA protection (*see* DMA protection)
  identifier data, 268
  interrupt protection (*see* Interrupt
      protection)
  server RAS (*see* Server RAS)
  USB descriptor attack, 269
Device configuration
  physical presence, 350
  secure console, 350
  TCG Physical Presence, 351–353
Device configuration LPP flags variable
      attack, 355
Device Exclusion Vector (DEV), 277
Device firmware, 14
Device Identity Component Engine
      (DICE), 18, 127, 207, 221, 523, 894
  architecture, 208
  CDI, 208
  key protection, 210
  SOC, 207
  TPM key protection, 209
Device interface
  crypto device, 482
  device hot plug, 482
  device input, 481, 482
  emulated hardware, 476
  scalable-IOV, 478, 479
  secure boot, 485–487
  SR-IOV, 477
  synthetic hardware, 476, 477
  trusted boot, 483–485
  virtual I/O device (virtio), 479, 480
  virtual machine bus (vmbus), 480, 481

Differential electromagnetic analysis
      (DEMA), 527, 534
Differential power analysis
      (DPA), 527, 534
Digital Visual Interface (DVI), 347
Direct Memory Access (DMA), 51, 108,
      230, 231, 270
  device source identifier, 273, 274
  features, 271
  hypervisor, 272
  IOMMU address translation, 273–275
  IOMMU translation, 271
  MMU address translation, 271–273
  MMU/IOMMU translation, 271
  MMU translation, 271
Direct Memory Access (DMA)
      attack, 6, 761
discrete TPM (dTPM), 226
Distributed Management Task Force
      (DMTF), 260, 898
DMA protection
  ACPI table bypass, 285
  AMD IO virtualization, 277, 278
  ARM system MMU, 278, 279
  device attack, 283–285
  EDKII IOMMU, 280
    AllocateBuffer/FreeBuffer, 280
    components, 279
    EFI_PCI_IO_PROTOCOL, 280
    IOMMU Hook, 281
    Map/Unmap, 280
    mechanism, 282, 283
    memory solution, 282
    PEI, 281
    UEFI environment, 281
  Intel Virtualization Technology (VT-d),
      275–277

MSI (*see* Message signaled interrupt (MSI))

DMA remapping (DMAR), 238

Driver Execution Environment (DXE), 11, 21, 33, 76, 172

DRTM Configuration Environment (DCE), 227, 234

Dynamically Launched Measured Environment (DLME), 227, 234

Dynamic code analysis, 56

Dynamic launch (DL), 234

Dynamic root-of-trust for measurement (DRTM)

  application processer, 228

  attack/mitigation

    DLME completeness, 240, 241

    hardware configuration, 242

    malicious hardware configuration, DCE, 239, 240

    malicious software input, DCE, 237, 239

    peripheral, 242

    SMM, 241, 242

  DCE, 230, 231

  hot plug, 231, 232

  launch flow, 227, 228

  OEM BIOS, 229

  PCR measurement, 228, 229

  vs. SRTM boot flow, 226, 227

  S3 resume, 229

  SVM architecture, 233, 234

  tboot, 234–236

  TrenchBoot, 236, 237

  TXT, 232, 233

  Windows Defender System Guard Secure Launch, 237

Dynamic Root-of-Trust for measurement (DRTM), 198, 227

E

EDKII UEFI firmware

  adversary identification, 40

  control flow analysis, 37

  data flow analysis, 37, 38

  feature-specific asset, 39

  mitigation

    DISPATCH OPCODE, 43

    implementation, 42

    lockbox, 44

    security objective, S3 Resume, 42

  S3Resume, 38, 39

  S3 resume threat model, 45, 46

  security test strategy, 47, 48

  threat identification, 40, 41

EDKII_VARIABLE_LOCK_PROTOCOL, 330

EFI Byte Code (EBC), 663

EFI_FIRMWARE_MANAGEMENT_ PROTOCOL (FMP), 77

Elliptic curve cryptography (ECC), 793

Elliptic Curve Digital Signature Algorithm (ECDSA), 776

Elliptic curve (ECC), 476

Embedded controller (EC), 13, 29, 70, 81, 94, 224, 376, 671

Embedded Multimedia Card (eMMC), 398

End Of Post (EOP), 556

Endorsement key (EK), 206

Enhanced Privacy ID (EPID), 724

Equivalence class partitioning (ECP), 860

Error Correcting Code (ECC), 303

Exception-level (EL), 142

Executable and linkable format (ELF), 632

Execution-in-place (XIP), 5

Extensible Authentication Protocol (EAP), 259, 372

External page table (EPT), 607

F

Fault injection
  authentication routines, 548
  compiler time, 545
  default path, 547
  hardware, 546
  mitigation, 551
  runtime, 545
  typical enum, 546
  verification stage, 549, 551
Fault-tolerant write (FTW), 412
Feature configuration
  PCD-based attack, 349
  physical presence, 347
  UEFI secure boot, 348
  UEFI variable, 347
Federal Information Processing Standards
    (FIPS), 772
Field Programmable Gate Array
    (FPGA), 93, 94
Firmware
  boot flow/phased handoff, 11–13
  definition, 3
  industry standards, 10
  platform stack, 3–5
  software, difference, 5, 6
  validation approaches, 5
Firmware file system (FFS), 150
Firmware fuzzing mechanisms, 861–866
Firmware Interface Table (FIT), 83, 126
Firmware resiliency
  boot image, UEFI, 451
    public key storage, 451
    signing, 451
    verification, 452

Clark-Wilson model, 444, 449, 450
  configuration recovery (*see*
    Configuration recovery)
  definition, 444
  detection (*see* Detection)
  pattern for verified
    boot, 446
    firmware update, 447
    policy update, 447
    recovery, 448
    runtime communication, 448
  production (*see* Production)
  protection, 443
  recovery (*see* Image recovery)
  signed capsule update, 453
    public key storage, 454
    signing, 453
    verification, 454
  signed recovery, 454
    public key storage, 455
    signing, 455
    verification, 455
  TEE runtime communication
    verification, 455, 456
  UEFI authenticated variable, 452
    public key storage, 452
    signing, 452
    verification, 453
  verification, 445
Firmware support package
    (FSP), 11, 145, 428
firmware Trusted Platform Module
    (fTPM), 226, 709, 724
Firmware volume (FV), 150, 172, 174
First Stage Boot Loader (FSBL), 11

Flash lock
  BIOS register selection, 747, 748
  BIOS write protection, 745–747
  SPI region, 749, 750
Flash wear-out protection, 409–412, 426
Flattened Device Tree (FDT), 148
Flattened Image Tree (FIT), 148
FLUSH+RELOAD attack, 531–533
Function-level reset (FLR), 477
Fuzzing, 55, 56
Fuzz testing, 861

G

General-Purpose Event (GPE), 302
General-purpose input (GPI), 682
General-purpose register (GPR), 464, 694
Generic Interrupt Controller (GIC), 293
GNU assembly (GSA), 826
Google Asylo, 722
Google Binary Block (GBB), 145
Google Cloud Platform (GCP), 134
Google Titan, 134, 135
Guest CR3 (GCR3), 277
Guest domain
  attack guest data
    at rest, 473
    in transition, 474
    in use, 474
  CSP, 460
  hardware root-of-trust, 475
  MKTME, 466, 467
  OVMF, 472
  RAS, 460
  SEV, 461
  SEV-ES, 464
  use cases, 460
GUIDed Partition Table (GPT), 154, 496

H

Handoff Block (HOB), 76
Hard disk drive (HDD), 166, 283, 356
Hardware-based, CFG
  Intel X86 architecture, 589–591
  PAC, 592–594
Hardware Security Module (HSM), 156
Hash-based message authentication code
    (HMAC), 54, 201, 207
Hash-based signature (HBS) schemes, 803
heck_optional() function, 842
High-Definition Multimedia Interface
    (HDMI), 347
High-Precision Event Timer (HPET), 300
High-risk areas
  configuration, 556
  crytography, 558
  external input, 552, 553
  hardware input, 554, 555
  race conditions, 553, 554
  register lock, 556
  replay/rollback, 557
  secret handling, 555
Hostboot Base (HBB), 139
Hostboot Runtime (HBRT), 139
Host Embedded Controller Interface
    (HECI), 671
Host firmware, 9, 10
Host Integrity at Runtime and Startup
    (HIRS), 221
Host ME Region Flash Protection Override
    (HMR FPO), 726
Hot Swap Back Plane (HSBP), 132
HP Sure Start, 174
Human Interface Device (HID), 88, 94, 480
Human Interface Infrastructure (HII), 394
Hypervisor-protected code integrity
    (HVCI), 661

I

Image Execution Information Table
    (IEIT), 387
Image recovery
    ARM trusted-firmware, 177
    attack/mitigation
        hardware configuration, 178
        image downgrade, 178
        recovery image, 177
    BBS, PCH
        layout, 170, 171
    coreboot, 171, 172
    EDKII signed recovery, 172–174
    HP Sure Start, 174, 175
    location, 165, 166
    Project Cerberus, 175, 176
    RTRec selection/recovery
        policy, 163, 164
    selection, 165
    TS, PCH
        flash chip mapping, 166, 167
        layout, 169, 170
        register, 167, 168
        secure boot block, 168, 169
Immutable ROM
    attack/mitigation, 72
    confidentiality, 69
    embedded/IoT area, 71, 72
    golden recovery image, 72
    integrity, 69
    mobile/desktop/server, 70
Incorrect LockBox attribute, 332
Independent Hardware Vendor (IHV), 118
Independent Software Vendor (ISV), 8
Indirect Branch Tracking (IBT), 589, 643
Infrastructure as a Service (IaaS), 473

Initial boot block (IBB), 123, 125,
    126, 215, 229
Initial Device Identifier (IDevID), 897
Insert Random Tag (IRG), 606
Integrated Drive Electronics (IDE), 109
Integration protection, UEFI
    authentication (*see* Variable
        authentication)
Integrity Measurement Architecture
    (IMA), 219
Integrity protection, UEFI
    RPMB, 398, 400
    RPMC, 400–403
    sanity check, 394, 396–398
    TEE, 391
    TPM, 403–405
    variable lock, 392, 393
Intel Converged Security and
    Management Engine (CSME), 724
    fTPM, 724, 725
    secure normal world interaction, 726
    secure world isolation
        debugger attack, 726
        DMA attack, 725
        non-production mode
            prevention, 726
    secure world kernel protection, 726
Intelligent Platform Management
    Interface (IPMI), 30, 887
Intelligent property (IP), 93
Intel SGX
    AMD SEV, 718
    component isolation, 717
    IBM Z, 719
    MKTME, 719
    RISC-V/ARM-M Multizone, 720, 721

RISC-V keystone, 719, 720

secure world isolation, 717

secure world kernel protection, 718

side channel attacks, 717

standards/frameworks/SDKs, 721, 722

Inter-Integrated Circuit (I2C), 88, 127, 280

Internet Engineering Task Force (IETF), 772, 898

Internet of Things (IoT), 71, 207

Internet Protocol Security (IPSec), 373

Inter-process communication (IPC), 655

inter-processor interrupts (IPIs), 288

Interrupt Collection Number (ICID), 296

Interrupt command register (ICR), 288, 297

Interrupt descriptor table (IDT), 286

Interrupt protection

    AMD IO virtualization, 293

    ARM GIC, 296, 297

    ARM GICv2, 293, 294

    ARM GICv3, 294, 295

    ARM GICv3 ITS, 296

    Intel VT-d, 291, 292

    MSI

        alignment Check (#AC) exception injection attack, 299, 300

        SIPI attack, 297, 298

        syscall injection attack, 298, 299

Interrupt remapping table (IRT), 290

Interrupt Request (IRQ), 286

Interrupt Routing Infrastructure (IRI), 294

Interrupt translation entry (ITE), 296

Interrupt Translation Service (ITS), 295

Interrupt Translation Table (ITT), 296

IO memory management unit (IOMMU), 40, 231, 238, 271

    DMA prevention, silicon support, 762, 764

    DRAM, 762

    SRAM, 762

Isolated Memory Region (IMR), 762

IsSignatureFoundInDatabase() function, 518

J

Joint Photographic Experts Group (JPEG), 51

K

Kerckhoffs's principle, 521

Kernel

    attacks

        break the exploit (*see* Break the exploit attack)

        contain the damage (*see* Contain the damage attack)

    defensive technology, 626, 627

Kernel-Based Virtual Machine (KVM), 479, 719

Kernel Data Protection (KDP), 662

Kernel page table isolation (KPTI), 544

Keyboard Video Mouse (KVM), 347

Key exchange key (KEK), 138, 186, 348

Key Manifest Key (KMK), 126

L

Last-in-first-out (LIFO), 539

Launch Control Policy (LCP), 233, 405

Light Emitting Diode (LED), 376

Liverpool Data Research Associates' (LDRA), 598

Local Device ID (LDevID), 894, 897

Locality-Specific Peripheral Interrupt
    (LPI), 295
LockBox, S3
    authorized firmware component, 317
    coprocessor, 331
    implementation, 319
    incorrect LockBox attribute, 332
    integrity, 318
    missing LockBox protection, 332
    missing register lock, 332
    usage, 318
Lowest support version (LSV), 52
Low Pin Count (LPC), 168, 287
Low-Power Subsystem (LPSS), 280

M

Machine check exception (MCE), 759
Machine Owner Key (MOK), 187, 188
Management Component Transport
    Protocol (MCTP), 130, 222, 264
Management engine (ME), 70,
    132, 166, 630
Management Mode (MM), 5, 32
Manufactured SID (MSID), 367
Measured Launch Environment
    (MLE), 232, 234
Measured virtual machine monitor
    (MVMM), 227, 229
Measurement Assessment Authority
    (MAA), 204, 221
Memory controller hub (MCH), 239, 754
Memory management unit (MMU), 270
Memory mapped input/output (MMIO),
    51, 477, 512, 525, 655, 663, 695
Memory-Only Reset (MOR), 370
Memory reference code (MRC), 330

Memory Tagging Extension (MTE), 648
Memory Type Range Registers
    (MTRRs), 688
Merkle Signature Scheme
    (MSS), 801–803
Message authentication code
    (MAC), 93, 259
Message signaled interrupt (MSI), 289,
    290, 477
    APIC, 287–289
    IOMMU, 291
    IRQ, 286
    mitigation, 290
    PCI, 286
    PIC/8259, 287
    remappable format, 290
    X86, 286
Microcontroller (MC), 71
Microcontroller unit (MCU), 223, 721
MicroPython, 852
Microsoft assembly (MASM), 826
Microsoft Azure Sphere, 223, 728
Missing register lock, 332
Model-specific register (MSR), 52
Modern cryptography
    algorithm, 771, 772
    asymmetric, 768, 769
    attacks/mitiation, 790, 791
    Block cipher, 774–776
    digital certificate, 784, 785, 787
    digital signature/signature scheme,
        776–778
    domains, 767
    firmware, 770, 787–789
    hash/message authentication
        code/key deviation, 781–783
    Kerckhoffs principle, 772

key established/forward
    secrecy, 779, 780
    random number/one-time
    pad, 773, 774
Mosca's theorem, 812
Multifactor authentication (MFA), 342
Multi-key Total Memory Encryption
    (MKTME), 466, 607
Multilevel security (MLS) system, 433
Multiprocessing (MP), 6

N

National Bureau of Standards (NBS), 767
National Institute of Standards and
    Technology (NIST), 20, 767, 898
National Security Agency (NSA), 221
Network access control
    Bluetooth, 373
    private certification storage attack, 374
    TCP/IP network stack, 373, 374
    TLS hostname attack, 375
    WIFI, 372, 373
Network interface card (NIC), 127
Next-Generation Secure Computing Base
    (NGSCB), 237
Non-host firmware, 13
Non-host platform (NHP), 231
Non-Secure Processing Environment
    (NSPE), 141
Non-volatile dual in-line memory
    modules (NVDIMMs), 75
Non-Volatile Memory Express (NVMe),
    70, 127, 130, 356, 363, 398
Non-volatile RAM (NVRAM), 191
Non-volatile storage (NVS), 37, 337, 693
NOR flash, 346
Notification destination (NDST), 292
Notification vectors (NVs), 292

O

OEM boot block (OBB), 125, 126
One-time programmable (OTP), 398
One-time programmable read-only
    memory (OTPROM), 138
Online Certificate Status Protocol
    (OCSP), 98
Open Compute Project (OCP), 70, 127
Open Portable TEE (OP-TEE), 722
Open Power Abstraction Layer (OPAL), 25,
    139, 220
OpenPOWER secure boot, 137–140
Open Virtual Machine Firmware (OVMF),
    472, 479
Operating system (OS) loader, 459
    AVB, 191, 192
    Chromium verified boot
        kernel preamble, 189
        keys, 189
        RO firmware, 189
        rootfs verification, 190, 191
        signature verification, 189, 190
    detection, 186
    MOK, Linux
        boot flow, 188
        Grub2, 188
        KEK, 186
        secure boot key, 187
        UEFI secure boot, 186
    protection, 186
    recovery
        automated, 193
        Chromium OS, 194, 195
        UEFI boot option, 193, 194
Operating system vendor (OSV), 11, 118
Original Equipment Manufacturer (OEM),
    8, 11, 31, 118, 204, 221, 707
Out-of-band (OOB), 29, 30, 109, 118, 340

P

panic_handler(), 844

Patform Configuration Data (PCD), 92

Patform Firmware Manifest (PFM), 91

PCI Interrupt Request (PIRQ), 287

Penetration testing, 886

Peripheral Component Interconnect
(PCI), 10, 762

Permanent denial of service (PDoS), 6, 19,
41, 45, 174

Personal Identification Number (PIN), 367

Physical function (PF), 477

Physical memory protection (PMP), 719

Physical Presence SID (PSID), 369

Platform Active Root-of-Trust (PA-RoT),
90, 130, 258

Platform Configuration Database (PCD),
90, 349, 394

Platform Configuration Register
(PCR), 198, 201, 335, 350, 417,
443, 557, 896

Platform Controller Hub (PCH), 745

Platform Diffie-Hellman (PDH), 476

Platform Firmware Manifest
(PFM), 90, 129

Platform Firmware Profile (PFP), 18

Platform Firmware Resiliency (PFR), 70,
131, 132, 134

Platform key (PK), 138, 186

Platform Secure Processor (PSP), 318,
331, 709

Platform security architecture (PSA), 18,
71, 84, 140–145

Platform Security Processor (PSP), 137

Pointer Authentication Code
(PAC), 592, 642

Portable Executable (PE), 118

Posted interrupt descriptor (PID), 291

Posted Interrupt Request (PIR), 292

Power management (PM), 477

Power State Coordination Interface
(PSCI), 713

Power Supply Unit (PSU), 128, 130,
132, 257

Preboot Execution Environment
(PXE), 372

Pre-EFI Initialization (PEI), 21, 33, 77, 172

Pre-shared key (PSK), 261, 372, 416

Pre-UEFI Initialization (PEI), 281

PRIME+PROBE attack, 530

Privileged Access-Never (PAN), 658, 691

Process Address Space ID (PASID), 274

Processor event-based sampling
(PEBS), 696

Processor NOR (PNOR), 139

Production

building block, 67–69

configurable data

attack/mitigation, 110

correctness check, 109

secure by default, 110

user authentication, 109

user confirmation, 109

variable lock, 110

Immutable ROM (*see* Immutable
ROM)

upgradable firmware (*see* Upgradable
firmware)

Product maintenance phase

antivirus, 900

firmware component

attestation data, 896–898

certificate/manifest, 894–896

firmware detection, 899, 900

firmware update, 900, 901

mitigation, 892

UEFI/EDKII system firmware, 893, 894

Programmable interrupt controller
(PIC), 286

Programmable logic controller (PLC), 224

Project Cerberus, 175, 176

Protected High Memory Base and Limit
Register (PHMB/PHML), 281

Protected High Memory Register
(PHMR), 276

Protected Low Memory Base and Limit
Register (PLMB/PLML), 281

Protected Low Memory Register
(PLMR), 276

Protected Memory Register (PMR), 276

PSA root-of-trust (PSA-RoT), 71, 140

Q

Quantum key distribution (QKD), 805

Quantum Random Number Generation
(QRNG), 808

Quantum safe cryptography
algorithms, 810, 811
Mosca's theorem, 812
post-quantum project, 813
QKD, 805, 807, 808
QRNG, 808, 809
quantum safe algorithm, 794, 795,
797–800, 804
security challenges
Grover algorithm, 794
Shor's algorithm, 793

R

Race condition attack, 712

Radio Frequency (RF), 132

Redundant Arrays of Independent Drives
(RAID), 109, 127

Reference integrity manifest (RIM), 895

Reliability, availability, and serviceability
(RAS), 300, 460

Remote Attestation Procedures
(RATS), 897

Replay Protected Memory Block (RPMB),
157, 398

Replay Protected Monotonic Counter
(RPMC), 157, 400

Return merchandise authorization
(RMA), 340

Return-oriented programming (ROP), 580

Return Stack Buffer (RSB), 539

Rich execution environment (REE), 669

Rivest-Shamir-Adleman (RSA), 793

Rollback index location (RIL), 192

Root-of-trust for detection (RTD), 68, 115,
163, 181

Root-of-trust for measurement (RTM),
198, 202

Root-of-Trust for recovery (RTRec), 31

Root-of-trust for report (RTR), 198, 201

Root-of-trust for resiliency (RTRes), 68, 182

Root-of-trust for storage (RTS), 198, 201

Root-of-trust for update (RTU), 68, 80, 84,
85, 104

Root-of-trust (RoT), 59, 68–70, 90, 127, 176

RSB stuffing sequence, 542

_RTC_CheckStackVars() function, 600

Rust
definition, 828
limitation, 851
performance, 828
productivity, 829
project, 850, 851
reliability, 829

Rust (*cont.*)
  security solution, 830, 831
    arithmetic check, 844, 846–850
    boundary check, 843, 844
    Option<T> type, 841, 842
    ownership, 831–838, 840, 841
    uninitialized data check, 844

S

S3 resume
  asset, 315
  implementation, 316
  LockBox (*see* LockBox, S3)
  mitigation, 317
  OS context, 315
  software attack, 315, 316
  suspend to memory, 315
Secondary Program Loader (SPL), 11
Secret-independent code (SIC), 534
Secret-independent data access (SID), 534
Secret-independent runtime (SIR), 534
Secure boot
  additional capabilities, 118
  Amazon Nitro RoT, 136
  AMD, 137
  Apple T2, 135
  Cisco Trust Anchor, 136
  configuration
    detectability, 156
    partial update attack, 157
    rollback attack, 157
  coreboot
    GBB/VBLOCK, 146, 147
    image layout, 145, 146
    keys, 148
    read-only section, 145
    read/write section, 145

verified boot flow, 147
databases, 121
detectability, 115, 116
Google Titan, 134, 135
image verification, 122, 123
Intel boot guard
  components, 124, 125
  flow, 124
  key usage, 125
  manifests, 126
Intel PFR
  boot flow, 133
  diagram, 132, 133
  flash layout, 134
  hardware components, 132
  vs. Intel boot guard *vs.* Intel
    BIOS, 131
key usage, 120
Malformed input
  unsigned data, 150–152
  unsigned storage, 154, 155
  use unverified data, 152–154
non-bypassability, 117
OpenPOWER, 137–140
PE image layout, 118, 119
policy revocation, 117
Project Cerberus
  authentication flow, 129, 130
  components, 128, 129
  key usage, 130
  NIST SP800-193
    requirement, 127, 128
PSA, 140
  ARM SPM, 141, 142
  ARM Trusted-Firmware, 143–145
  bootloaders, 143, 144
  projects, 143
signature database attack, 149

U-Boot, 148, 149

verification flow, 119, 120, 127

version, 117

Secure boot, key usage, 121

Secure boot configuration attack, 149

Secure coding practice

arbitrary buffer access and execution, 499–503

ASSERT, 514–516

avoid arithmetic error, 504–506, 508

bad compiler optimizations, 512, 513

banned functions, 508–510

buffer overrun, 496–498

information leaks, 511

race conditions, 511

Secure design practices

attack surfaces, 520

backdoor, 522

defense in depth, 521

least privilege, 520

old signature verification flow, 517–519

open principle, 521

simple code, 522

trust boundary, 517

Secure device communication

attack/mitigation

malformed input, SPDM, 267

security policy configuration, 267

authentication/measurement, 258

channel, 259, 260

DICE, 260

EDKII device security

authentication, 264

measurement, 264, 265

PCI bus, 265

platform, 266

TCG, 265

MCTP, 264

PCI express authentication, 263

SPDM, 260, 262, 263

USB authentication, 263

Secure Digital Input and Output (SDIO), 280

Secure embedded L4 kernel (seL4), 869

Secure Encrypted Virtualization (SEV), 625, 718

Secure Execution Environment (SEE), 67

Secure kernel (SK), 233, 234

Secure Loader (SL), 233, 234

Secure monitor call (SMC), 84, 520

Secure Partition Manager (SPM), 71, 140, 142, 144

Secure Processing Environment (SPE), 140

Secure Protocol and Data Model (SPDM), 523, 630, 774

Secure unique device identifier (SUDI), 136, 224

Secure version number (SVN), 52, 81, 117, 215

Secure Virtual Machine (SVM), 233, 234

Security

measurement/attestation, 8

resiliency, 7

secure device communication, 8, 9

Security architecture/design

availability, 35

boot trust region, 32

confidentiality, 34

integrity, 35

main trust region, 31

management mode region, 32

mapping, 33

MM recovery trust region, 34

MM trust region, 34

recovery trust region, 31

security test classification, 36

Security Automation and Continuous
    Monitoring (SACM), 895
Security development
    Fallacy/pitfall
        security process, 59, 60
        security technology, 59
    main activities, 17
    people education, 58
    requirements, 17
    security code review, 49–55
    security coding practice, 49
    security incidence response, 57
    security unit test, 49
    test phase
        dynamic code analysis, 56
        fuzzing, 55, 56
        static code analysis, 56
        vulnerability scan, 57
    threat model (*see* Threat model)
Security Identifier (SID), 367
Security Loader Block (SLB), 233
Security model
    Bell-LaPadula model, 434–436
    confidentiality, 433
    integrity (*see* Integrity)
    methodology, 433
Security model (SM), 140
Security penetration plan, 876–882,
    884, 885
    attack path, 886
    hardware attack, 888
    network attack, 887
    system software attack, 887
    TEE software attack, 888
Security Protocol and Data Model
    (SPDM), 260, 262, 263
Security unit test
    design, 870–872

formal verification, 868
    fuzzing, 861, 863–866
    plan, 858, 860
    symbolic execution, 866–868
Security validation plan, 876–882, 884, 885
Security version number (SVN), 104
Self-boot engine (SBE), 11, 138
Serial electrically erasable programmable
    read-only memory (SEEPROM),
    138, 139
Serial Over LAN (SOL), 347
Serial Peripheral Interface (SPI), 20, 69,
    88, 127, 168, 226, 280, 695, 748
Server Base Security Guide (SBSG), 140
Server Platform Service (SPS), 131,
    132, 630
Server RAS
    CPU Hot add, 301–303
    CPU Hot plug attack
        prevention, 306
        SIPI handler, 306
        SMM rebase, 305
    Hot plug mirror memory, 304
    memory threat, 307
    online spare memory, 303, 304
setjump() and longjump(), 643
Set of Roots-of-Trust (RoTs), 198
Shadow stack (SS), 589
Shared Peripheral Interrupt (SPI), 293
Side channel attack
    cache attack, 529
        FLUSH+RELOAD, 531–533
        PRIME+PROBE, 530, 531
    SIC, 534
    SID, 534
    simple analysis, 533, 534
    SIR, 534
    timing attack, 527, 528

worn-out numeric keypad, 526

Side channel attacks, 710

Signed flash address map (SFAM), 81

Simple electromagnetic analysis (SEMA), 527, 533

Simple power analysis (SPA), 527, 533

Single-root IO virtualization (SR-IOV), 292

Single Sign-On (SSO), 343

SkuIds, 429

Small Computer System Interface (SCSI), 363

Smart battery system (SBS), 377

SMI Transfer Monitor (STM), 230, 704

SMM BIOS Write Protect Disable (SMM_BWP), 746

SMM_COMMUNICATE. Communicate(), 325

SMRAM range register (SMRR), 759

Software Development Kit (SDK), 722

Software development lifecycle (SDL), 35

Software-generated interrupt (SGI), 293

Software Guard Extension (SGX), 625, 716

Software Identification (SWID) tag, 895

Software Updates for Internet of Things (SUIT), 74

Solid-state disk (SSD), 166, 356

Speculative execution attack
  bounds check bypass, 535, 536
  branch target injection (*see* Branch target injection)
  meltdown variant 3, 543, 544

Speculative load hardening
  CSDB, 596
  Intel X86 Load Fence (LFENCE), 594, 595

-mspeculative-load-hardening, 596, 597

Square-Reduce-Multiply-Reduce pattern, 533

Stack overflow attack, 573

Stage 2 Translation Table (S2TTB), 278

Startup IPI (SIPI), 298

Startup IPI (SPI), 298

Static code analysis, 56

Static RAM (SRAM), 762

Static root-of-trust for measurement (SRTM)
  attack/mitigation
    completeness, 224
    hijack, 226
    S3 resume, 225
    TPM device, 226
  attestation, 203, 204, 206
  BitLocker, 217, 218
  Cerberus
    architecture, 222
    measurement, 221
    PA-RoT, 222
    RoT commands, 222, 223
  Cisco Trust Anchor, 224
  coreboot, 216, 217
  DICE (*see* Device identity component engine (DICE))
  Grub, 219
  IMA, Linux, 219
  measurement report, 202, 203
  Microsoft Azure Sphere, 223
  OpenPOWER trusted boot, 220
  S3 resume, 206, 207
  supply chain validation, 220, 221
  TPM (*see* Trusted Platform Module (TPM))

Static root-of-trust for measurement (SRTM) (*cont.*)
   UEFI BIOS
      GetEventLog() function, 212
      Intel boot guard, 215, 216
      OS loader, 212
      PCR mapping, 211, 212
      PCR measurement, 211–214
Static Root-of-Trust for Measurement (SRTM), 198, 226
Storage access control
   ATA/ATAPI security commands, 360–363
   auto unlock, S3, 357
   binding, 356
   data leakage, 356
   fast boot impact, 357
   hard disk freeze, 359
   hard drive password, 356
   HDD Freeze Lock/TCG BlockSID, 371
   password update, 359
   retry count, 359
   runtime, S3, 358
   secure console, 359
   TCG storage
      BlockSID, 369
      MSID, 367, 368
      password, 363–366
      PSID, 369, 370
      SID, 367
      TPer reset, 370, 371
   TCG TPer Reset, 372
   user *vs.* master password, 359
   warm reset, 357
Store Allocation Tag (STG), 606
Store Allocation Tag and Pair (STGP), 606
Store Allocation Tag and Zeroing (STZG), 606

Stream Table Entry (STE), 278
str_find_char() function, 840, 843
STRIDE threat model, 19
Structured Query Language (SQL), 50
Supervisor Mode Access Prevention (SMAP), 658, 691
Supervisor Mode Execute Protection (SMEP), 658, 759
System Control Interrupt (SCI), 302, 682
System control processor (SCP), 71, 84, 143
System Management BIOS (SMBIOS), 10
System Management Bus (SMBus), 127
System management interrupt (SMI), 106, 302, 343, 499, 520
System management mode (SMM), 22, 27, 32, 35, 41, 42, 45, 51, 74, 79, 94, 230, 301, 302, 307, 318, 343, 349, 391, 482, 485, 625, 669, 681
   address alias lock, 754, 758
   code access check, 759
   global SMI, 760, 761
   SMRAM access, 751, 752
   SMRAM location, 753, 754
   SMRR, 759
System management RAM (SMRAM), 42, 281, 303, 669, 682, 751
System Memory Management Unit (SMMU), 278
System on a chip (SOC), 5

T

Tag Mask Insert (GMI), 606
TCG Physical Presence (PP)
   ACPI ASL interface, 355
   configuration update, 354
   control, 353

TCG2 PEIM, 355

TPM2.0 and TCG Storage, 351, 352

TCG trusted boot, 197

TEE-Based LockBox

ACPI specification, 320

BIOS phases, 322

boot script, 320, 321

confidentiality rules, 321

DXE phase, 320

DXE/SMM Phase Usage, 325

integrity rules, 321

internal data structure, 324

PEI Phase Usage, 326

PI architecture, 319

preboot configuration, 319

server, 322

SMM_COMMUNICATION
protocol, 324

SmmLockBox driver, 324

SMRAM, 326

TEE-Based LockBox, internal data
structure, 324

Threat model

adversaries, 20

BIOS, 20

boot flow

adversary, 24, 25

mitigation, 25

threat, 24

build tool, 29

EDKII UEFI firmware (see EDKII UEFI
firmware)

flash content, 21

adversary, 22

migration, 23

threat, 21

management mode, 27

adversary, 28

mitigation, 28, 29

threat, 27

non-host runtime service

adversary, 30

mitigation, 31

threat, 30

S3 resume, 25

adversary, 26

mitigation, 27

threat, 26

threat/desired properties, 19

Time-of-check/time-of-use
(TOC/TOU), 5, 23

Time-of-Check/Time-of-Use (TOC/TOU),
95, 105, 117, 482, 698

Top of Low Usable DRAM (TOLUD), 281

Top of Upper Usable DRAM
(TOUUD), 281

Top Swap (TS), 167, 178

Total Memory Encryption (TME), 40

TPM_Shutdown(CLEAR) command, 206

TPM_Startup(STATE) command, 207

Traditional password attacks, 345, 346

Transaction Layer Packet's (TLP), 274

Translation Lookaside Buffer (TLB), 648

Transmission Control Protocol (TCP), 259

Transport Layer Security (TLS), 259,
373, 774

Trust Anchor Module (TAm), 136, 224

Trust Computing Base (TCB), 231

Trusted Base System Architecture
(TBSA), 18, 140

Trusted Board Boot Requirement
(TBBR), 140

Trusted Boot and Firmware Update
(TBFU), 84, 140

Trusted computing base (TCB), 12, 65,
118, 123, 140, 231

Trusted Computing Group (TCG), 23, 51, 197, 265, 350, 363, 440, 898
  vs. Clark-Wilson, 441–443
  MOR
    flow, 243
    policy, 245
    secure, 244
    storage, 244, 245
  physical presence configuration, 246
  storage, 246
Trusted Cryptography Module (TCM), 201, 202
Trusted Executable Technology (TXT), 238
Trusted execution environment (TEE), 79, 94, 106, 318, 335, 347, 349, 373, 485, 520, 525, 625, 669
Trusted Execution Technology (TXT), 232, 233
Trusted Peripheral (TPer), 363
Trusted Platform Control Module (TPCM), 202
Trusted Platform Module (TPM), 109, 191, 198, 257, 335, 417, 441, 443, 523, 894, 896
  device type, 201, 202
  firmware measurement, SRTM, 198, 199
  PCR, 198
  SRTM PCR measurement, 199
  trusted boot *vs.* secure boot, 200, 201
TSEG Memory Base (TSEGMB) register, 753
Type-length-value (TLV), 268

U

__ubsan_handle_add_overflow() function, 617
UEFI PI PCD

DefaultStores, 429
  dynamic, 428
  static, 427
UEFI Security Response Team (USRT), 57
UEFI variables
  availability (*see* Availability protection, UEFI)
  bypass the protection
    authentication disabled, 422
    TOC/TOU attack, 422
    variable lock disabled, 422
  CIA, 383
  confidentiality (*see* Confidentiality protection, UEFI)
  flash wear-out protection, 426
  hardware replay attack, 424, 425
  integration (*see* Integration protection, UEFI)
  malformed input, 421
  partial update attack, 426
  protection mechanisms, 384
  rollback attack, 425, 426
  SetVariable/GetVariable API, 383
  software replay attack, 422, 423
Undefined Behavior Sanitizer (UBSan), 56, 616
Unified Extensible Firmware Interface (UEFI), 10, 23, 118
Unique device secret (UDS), 207, 260
Unique Identifier (UID), 364
Universal Asynchronous Receiver/ Transmitter (UART), 88, 280
Universal Boot Loader (U-Boot), 148, 149
Universal Extensible Firmware Interface (UEFI), 18
Universal Flash Storage (UFS), 398
Universal Serial Bus (USB), 10, 51, 257, 363

Upgratable firmware
    ARM trusted firmware update, 84–86
    attack/mitigation (*see* Attack/
        mitigation)
    authenticated update
        mechanism, 73, 74
    BIOS write protection, 94
    CFU, 86–88
    FPGA bitstream, 93
    integrity protection, 93
    Intel BIOS guard, 82
        data structure, 81
        definition, 81
        flow, 83
        key usage, 82
        verification/update flow, 81
    microcode update, 83
    non-bypass ability, 94
    OOB, 79, 80
    OS runtime update, 79
    principles, 73
    Project Cerberus
        commands, 90
        components, 91, 92
        image layout, 89
        update, 91, 92
    signed UEFI capsule update
        data structure, 78
        disk/RAM, 77
        EDKII BIOS implementation, 75
        flash, 74
        flow, 76, 77
        mechanism, 75
        memory, 76
        process, 75
        security verification, 78
        signature verification, 79
User Datagram Protocol (UDP), 259

User Interface (UI), 335, 337
User/supervisor mode
    ARM privileged execute/access never,
        658
    CPU architectures, 654, 655
    kernel address isolation, 659
    kernel memory protection, 656, 657
    microkernel, 655
    OROM, 656
    user memory execution/access
        prevention, 657

V

Value-Added Reseller (VAR), 204
Variable atomicity, 412
Variable authentication
    formats, 384
    IEIT, 387
    nonce based, 386
    physical user, 389
    ProcessVariable, 391
    ProcessVarWithKek, 390
    ProcessVarWithPk, 390
    secure boot keys, 388
    setup mode *vs.* user mode, 387
    SetVariable() API, 385
    time based, 385
Variable-B based LockBox
    memory configuration data, 331
    MRC, 330
    S3 resume module, 330
Verified boot block (VBLOCK), 145
Video Graphics Array (VGA), 347
Virtual firmware
    guest domain (*see* Guest domain)
    OS, 459
    virtualization architecture, 459

Virtual function (VF), 292

virtual IntID (vIntID), 296

Virtualization-based security (VBS), 661

Virtual machine monitor (VMM), 607,
    625, 659

  control flow integrity, 667, 668

  definition, 659

  HVCI, 661, 662

  KDP, 662

  memory safety, 665, 666

  resource access control, 669

  sandbox, 662–664

  types, 660

  VSB, 660, 661

virtual Processing Element ID
    (vPEID), 296

Virtual Service Provider (VSP), 480

Vital Production Data (VPD), 179

Voltage Regulator (VR), 132

W

WebAssembly (wasm), 664

Windows Update (WU), 87

Winternitz one-time signature (WOTS)
    scheme, 798–800

Wireless-Fidelity (WIFI), 372

X, Y, Z

XE86 SMM

  ACPI, 682

  memory layout, 683, 684

  race condition attack prevention,
      698–701

  secure normal world interaction

    code execution prevention, 691

    communication
        verification, 691, 692

    confused deputy attack prevention,
        692–697

    data access prevention, 691

  secure word isolation

    address alias attack prevention,
        686–688

    cache poisoning attack prevention,
        688, 689

    configuration lockdown, 685

    CPU state protection, 686

    debugger attack
        prevention, 689

    DMA attack prevention, 686

    memory, 684

    non-production mode
        prevention, 690

  secure word kernel

    protection, 701

    load time, 701

    runtime, 702, 703

    STM, 704–707

  secure world enabling enforcement

    hot plug consideration, 690

    side channel attacks, 690

  SMM TEE, 682

Printed in the United States
By Bookmasters